Preventing Mental Illness

Proceedings of a conference
organized by the Department of
Health in collaboration with the
Royal Institute of Public Health and
Hygiene and co-sponsored by the
World Health Organization

Preventing Mental Illness

Mental Health Promotion in Primary Care

Edited by

Rachel Jenkins

*World Health Organization Collaborating Centre,
Institute of Psychiatry, London, UK*

and

T Bedirhan Üstün

World Health Organization, Geneva, Switzerland

JOHN WILEY & SONS

Chichester • New York • Weinheim • Brisbane • Singapore • Toronto

Copyright © 1998 by John Wiley & Sons Ltd,
Baffins Lane, Chichester,
West Sussex PO19 1UD, England

National   01243 779777
International (+44) 1243 779777
e-mail (for orders and customer service enquiries): cs-books@wiley.co.uk.
Visit our Home Page on http://www.wiley.co.uk or http://www.wiley.com

Chapters 9 and 26 copyright © 1998 by Department of Health.
Chapters 2, 8, 15, 16, 24, 27, 33, 40, 41, 42, 44 and 45 copyright © 1998 by the World Health Organization.

Other Wiley Editorial Offices

John Wiley & Sons, Inc., 605 Third Avenue,
New York, NY 10158-0012, USA

WILEY-VCH Verlag GmbH, Pappelallee 3,
D-69469 Weinheim, Germany

Jacaranda Wiley Ltd, 33 Park Road, Milton,
Queensland 4064, Australia

John Wiley & Sons (Asia) Pte Ltd, 2 Clementi Loop #02-01,
Jin Xing Distripark, Singapore 129809

John Wiley & Sons (Canada) Ltd, 22 Worcester Road,
Rexdale, Ontario M9W 1L1, Canada

Library of Congress Cataloging-in-Publication Data

Preventing mental illness : mental health promotion in primary care /
    edited by Rachel Jenkins and T.B. Üstün.
        p.   cm.
    "Proceedings of a conference organised by the Department of Health
in collaboration with the Royal Institute of Public Health and
Hygiene and co-sponsored by the World Health Organization."
    Includes bibliographical references and index.
    ISBN 0-471-97562-1 (cased)
    1. Mental illness—Prevention—Congresses.   2. Mental health
promotion—Congresses.   3. Primary care (Medicine)—Congresses.
I. Jenkins, Rachel.   II. Üstün, T.B.   III Great Britain. Dept. of
Health.   IV. Royal Institute of Public Health and Hygiene (Great
Britain) V. World Health Organization.
RA790.A2P74   1997
362.2'0425—dc21   97–16272
                                                                    CIP

British Library Cataloguing in Publication Data

A catalogue record for this book is available from the British Library

ISBN 0-471-97562-1

Typeset in 10/12pt Baskerville by Mayhew Typesetting, Rhayader, Powys
Printed and bound in Great Britain by Biddles Ltd, Guildford and King's Lynn

This book is printed on acid-free paper responsibly manufactured from sustainable forestation, for which at least two trees are planted for each one used for paper production.

Contents

List of Contributors

Ms Judy Allen *Institute of General Practice, University of Exeter, Barrack Road, Exeter EX2 5DW, UK*

Mrs E Armstrong *General Practice Educational Centre, Institute of Psychiatry, de Crespigny Park, Denmark Hill, London SE5 8AF, UK*

G Berti Ceroni *Department of Psychiatry 'P Ottonello', University of Bologna, Viale Pepoli 5, 40123 Bologna, Italy*

Professor D Berardi *Department of Psychiatry 'P Ottonello', University of Bologna, Viale Pepoli 5, 40123 Bologna, Italy*

Dr J M Bertolote *Mental Disorders Control Unit, Division of Mental Health, World Health Organization, CH-1211 Geneva 27, Switzerland*

Dr Bob Blizard *Academic Department of Psychiatry, Royal Free Hospital School of Medicine, Pond Street, London NW3, UK*

Anna Bosanquet *Senior Lecturer in Health Studies, Roehampton Institute, Whitelands College, West Hill, London SW15 3SN, UK*

Professor N Bosanquet *Department of Primary Health Care and General Practice, Imperial College School of Medicine at St Mary's, Norfolk Place, London W2 1PG, UK*

Mr John Bowis *Formerly Parliamentary Under-Secretary of State for Health, UK, c/o Dr Rachel Jenkins, WHO–UK Office, Institute of Psychiatry, de Crespigny Park, Denmark Hill, London SE5 8AF, UK*

Dr W Eugene Broadhead *Duke University Medical Centre, Durham, NC, USA*

Dr Bela Buda *Semmelweis University of Medicine, Institute of Behavioural Sciences, H-1089 Budapest, Nagyvarad ter 4, Budapest POB 370 H-1445, Hungary*

Dr Hastings E A Carson *The Royal Institute of Public Health and Hygiene, 28, Portland Place, London W1N 4DE, UK*

Maria T Cerqueira *Healthy Lifestyles and Mental Health Program, Division of Health Promotion and Protection, Pan American Health Organization, Washington, DC, USA*

Gloria Coe *Healthy Lifestyles and Mental Health Program, Division of Health Promotion and Protection, Pan American Health Organization, Washington, DC, USA*

Dr Katherine M Conigrave *Centre for Drug and Alcohol Studies, University of Sydney, NSW 2006, Australia*

Professor Roslyn Corney *University of Greenwich, Avery Hill Campus, Southwood Site, Avery Hill Road, Eltham, London SE9 2HB, UK*

Dr Jorge Alberto Costa e Silva *Director, Division of Mental Health, World Health Organization, CH-1211 Geneva 27, Switzerland*

A Cox *Professor of Child Psychiatry, Athens University Medical School, Hellenic Republic Ministry of Health & Welfare, Aghia Sophia Children's Hospital, 115 27 Athens, Greece*

Professor M P Deva *Department of Psychological Medicine, University of Malaya, 59100 Kuala Lumpur, Malaysia*

Th Dragonas *Professor of Child Psychiatry, Athens University Medical School, Hellenic Republic Ministry of Health & Welfare, Aghia Sophia Children's Hospital, 115 27 Athens, Greece*

Professor Leon Eisenberg *Department of Social Medicine, Harvard Medical School, 641, Huntington Avenue, Boston, MA. 02115, USA*

Dr Philip Evans *Institute of General Practice, University of Exeter, Barrack Road, Exeter EX2 5DW, UK*

Dr S Faria *Regional Advisor for Mental Health, World Health Organization Regional Office for Europe, Copenhagen, Denmark*

G Ferrari *Department of Psychiatry 'P Ottonello', University of Bologna, Viale Pepoli 5, 40123 Bologna, Italy*

Professor Sir David Goldberg *Institute of Psychiatry, de Crespigny Park, Denmark Hill, London SE5 9AF, UK*

Dr Michelle Gomel *Division of Mental Health and Prevention of Substance Abuse, World Health Organization, CH-1211 Geneva 27, Switzerland*

Ms Gay Gray *Health Education Unit, School of Education, University of Southampton, Highfield, Southampton SO9 5NH, UK*

Rodrigo Guerrero *Healthy Lifestyles and Mental Health Program, Division of Health Promotion and Protection, Pan American Health Organization, Washington, DC, USA*

Professor C Hosman *Department of Clinical Psychology and Personality, University of Nijmegen, Postbox 9104, 6500 HE Nijmegen, The Netherlands*

Dr Christina Hoven *College of Physicians and Surgeons of Columbia University, Department of Psychiatry, 22 West 168th Street, Box 14, New York, NY 10032, USA*

Dr Rachel Jenkins *Director, UK World Health Organization Mental Health Office, Institute of Psychiatry, de Crespigny Park, Denmark Hill, London SE5 8AF, UK. Formerly Principal Medical Officer, Mental Health Division, Department of Health, UK; now on secondment to WHO.*

Dr David Kessler *Institute of General Practice, University of Exeter, Barrack Road, Exeter EX2 5DW, UK*

G Leggieri *Department of Psychiatry 'P Ottonello', University of Bologna, Viale Pepoli 5, 40123 Bologna, Italy*

Dr Andrew C Leon *Cornell University Medical College, New York, NY, USA*

Dr Itzhak Levav *Regional Adviser in Mental Health, Pan American Health Organization, World Health Organization, 525 23rd Street NW, Washington, DC 20037–2895, USA*

Dr Glyn Lewis *Department of Psychological Medicine, College of Medicine, University of Wales, Heath Park, Cardiff CF4 4XN, UK*

Dr D H O Lloyd *Chairman, Mental Health Task Force, Royal College of General Practitioners, London: Cadwgan Surgery, 11 Bodelwyddan Avenue, Old Colwyn, Clwyd LL29 9LW, UK*

Dr K Lloyd *Head, Department of Mental Health, Wonford House Hospital, Dryden Road, Exeter EX2 5AR, UK*

Dr Kathryn M Magruder *National Institute of Mental Health, Department of Health & Human Services, Room 10c-06, 5600 Fishers Lane, Rockville, MA 20857, USA*

Nada Martinek *Senior Research Assistant, Department of Psychiatry, University of Queensland, Clinical Sciences Building, Royal Brisbane Hospital, Herston, Queensland 4029, Australia*

Mr A McCulloch *Andrew McCulloch Associates, 46 Bincote Road, Enfield EN2 7RB, UK*

Laurie E McQueen *DSM Project Coordinator, American Psychiatric Association, 1400 K Street, Washington, DC 20005, USA*

Dr Doreen Miller *Consultant Occupational Physician, Manor House, Thrupp, Oxford OX5 1LD, UK*

Dr A Mohit *Regional Adviser, Mental Health, World Health Organization, PO Box 1517, Alexandria, Egypt*

Dr Patricia J Mrazek *Prevention Technologies, Bethesda, MD: formerely Institute of Medicine, National Academy of Sciences, 2101 Constitution Avenue, Washington, DC 20418, USA*

Professor M H Mubbashar *Director, World Health Organization Collaborating Centre, Department of Psychiatry, Rawalpindi General Hospital, Rawalpindi, Pakistan*

Professor R Srinivasa Murthy *Department of Psychiatry, National Institute of Mental Health and Neurosciences, Postbag 2900, Bangalore 560 029, India*

Dr Mark Olfson *College of Physicians and Surgeons of Columbia University, Department of Psychiatry, 22 West 168th Street, Box 14, New York, NY 10032, USA*

Dr John Orley   *Mental Health Promotion Unit, Division of Mental Health, World Health Organization, CH-1211 Geneva 27, Switzerland*

Professor D J Pereira Gray OBE   *Department of General Practice, Postgraduate Medical School, University of Exeter, Barrack Road, Exeter EX2 5DW, UK*

A Pezzoli   *Department of Psychiatry 'P Ottonello', University of Bologna, Viale Pepoli 5, 40123 Bologna, Italy*

Luciana Phebo   *Healthy Lifestyles and Mental Health Program, Division of Health Promotion and Protection, Pan American Health Organization, Washington, DC, USA*

Dr H Pincus   *Director, Office of Research, American Psychiatric Association, 1400 K Street, Washington, DC 20005, USA*

Dr Andreas M Pleil   *Worldwide Health Care Economics and Policy Research Department, The Upjohn Company, Kalamazoo, MI, USA*

Professor R Price   *Survey Research Center, Institute for Social Research, University of Michigan, Ann Arbor, Michigan 48106-1248, USA*

Professor Beverley Raphael   *Director, Centre for Mental Health, New South Wales Health Department, Locked Mail Bag 961, North Sydney, NSW 2059, Australia*

Mrs Cathy Reynolds   *69 Langdon Road, Bath BA2 1LT, UK*

S Rubini   *Department of Psychiatry 'P Ottonello', University of Bologna, Viale Pepoli 5, 40123 Bologna, Italy*

Professor N Sartorius   *Department of Psychiatry, Hôpitaux Universitaires de Genève, Bd. St Georges 16–18, 1205 Geneva, Switzerland*

Professor J B Saunders   *Professor of Drug and Alcohol Studies, Department of Psychiatry, University of Queensland, Royal Brisbane Hospital, Herston, Queensland 4029, Australia*

A R Scaramelli   *Department of Psychiatry 'P Ottonello', University of Bologna, Viale Pepoli 5, 40123 Bologna, Italy*

A Scardovi   *Department of Psychiatry 'P Ottonello', University of Bologna, Viale Pepoli 5, 40123 Bologna, Italy*

Dr H Sell   *Regional Advisor on Health and Behaviour, World Health Organization Regional Office for South-East Asia, World Health House, New Delhi 1.10.002, India*

Dr Wolgang Stark   *Munich Self-help Resources Centre, Bayerstrasse 77a, D-80335 München, Germany*

Professor J Tsiantis   *Professor of Child Psychiatry, Athens University Medical School, Hellenic Republic Ministry of Health & Welfare, Aghia Sophia Children's Hospital, 115 27 Athens, Greece*

Dr A Tylee   *General Practice Educational Centre, Institute of Psychiatry, de Crespigny Park, Denmark Hill, London SE5 8AF, UK*

Dr T B Üstün *Acting Chief, Epidemiology, Assessment and Classification, Mental Health Division and Prevention of Substance Abuse, World Health Organization, Avenue Appia, CH-1211 Geneva 27, Switzerland*

Dr A Uznanski *World Health Organization, Regional Office for Africa, Brazzaville, Congo*

M Vittorangeli *Department of Psychiatry 'P Ottonello', University of Bologna, Viale Pepoli 5, 40123 Bologna, Italy*

Dr G Walker *Senior Partner, Oldfield Surgery, 45 Upper Oldfield Park, Bath BA2 3HT, UK*

Ms K Weare *Director, Health Education Unit, University of Southampton, Highfield, Southampton SO9 5NH, UK*

Professor Myrna Weissman *Professor of Epidemiology in Psychiatry, College of Physicians and Surgeons of Columbia University and School of Public Health, Unit 14, 1722 West 168th Street, New York, NY 10032, USA*

Introduction

Mental Health Promotion and Prevention in Primary Care—Introduction

John Bowis
Formerly Parliamentary Under-Secretary of State for Health, UK

I was delighted to open this historic conference and to extend a warm welcome to our speakers and participants from overseas. One thing that I found particularly pleasing was the fact that the event was the result of joint working among several of the most important mental health research and promotion organizations.

It was, for example, the first collaborative conference between the Department of Health and the World Health Organization on mental health. This linkage stemmed from the results of several years of fruitful working together between officials in mental health at the Department and at the World Health Organization, sharing ideas, developments and learning. We were particularly indebted to Dr Norman Sartorius, the previous Director of the Mental Health Division at WHO, to his successor Dr Jorges Coste e Silva and to the members of the WHO team, for their enthusiasm in working closely with us in the field of mental health.

This event was also the first joint conference on mental health between the Department of Health and the Royal Institute of Public Health and Hygiene. This collaboration also stemmed from very productive joint working on the development of a training program in mental health for primary care teams. We were most grateful to the Institute for their enthusiasm and their commitment in taking this forward. The Institute is well known for the excellent quality of its training programs, such as that for care assistants looking after the elderly, but the program for primary care teams was their first venture into mental health. I hope very much that it will be the first of many.

I was delighted that we had as our Chairman for the first morning Professor David Goldberg, Director of a third and equally distinguished organization, the Institute of Psychiatry. The Institute of Psychiatry is a first-rate research organization, ranked by *Science Watch* as the institution whose publications have the greatest impact worldwide (indeed, it was the only European institution to be

Preventing Mental Illness: Mental Health Promotion in Primary Care. Edited by R. Jenkins and T.B. Üstün.
© 1998 John Wiley & Sons Ltd.

included in the Top Ten of their ranking, the other nine institutions all being in the USA). We are therefore justly proud of our Institute. Indeed, the fundamental underpinning of our present knowledge about mental health in primary care stems from work carried out by its General Practice Research Unit, funded by the Department of Health from the 1960s onwards, and led by Professor Michael Shepherd.

MENTAL HEALTH—STRATEGIES AND PROMOTION

The World Bank report of 1993 flagged up just how serious a problem mental illness is in every part of the globe. We were pleased to welcome Professor Eisenberg, Emeritus Professor of Medicine and Science at Harvard University, who talked about the Harvard report on mental health which was launched at the United Nations in May 1995. It called for a United Nations decade of mental health and was, I understand, enthusiastically received by the Secretary General.

In England we have set an overall strategy for health, the 'Health of the Nation' strategy. Mental illness has been identified as one of five key areas for action, and we have set targets for reducing morbidity and reducing mortality, i.e. for secondary (prompt detection and effective management) and tertiary (rehabilitation) prevention. We have not yet done so for primary prevention or for mental health promotion, only because of difficulty of quantifying effective progress in these areas.

The purpose of the conference, therefore, was to draw together experience from all over the world on effective methods of primary prevention and mental health promotion so that we can build on these and use them to develop a coherent preventive strategy.

DEPARTMENT OF HEALTH INITIATIVES

In the meantime, of course, we in the Department of Health and the NHS have not been inactive and have been taking forward a number of important initiatives. Our mental health promotion efforts, for example, include the £1 million public information strategy described by Andrew McCulloch. And the Health Education Authority has been developing a major program of work in this area. Besides concentrating efforts in primary care, we are also developing initiatives to promote the mental health of people in workplaces everywhere. And of course, as Europe's largest employer, it is only right that the NHS should set an example in working to promote the mental health of its own employees.

RESEARCH

Research evaluation of everything we do, whether primary, secondary or tertiary prevention, is crucial if we are to learn which activities are most effective. Within the NHS Research and Development Strategy, the first national programme covered mental health *services*, ensuring that future decisions regarding these services will be underpinned by evidence. Similarly, the Department's strategic *policies* in mental health must be based on sound research if they are to be effective.

I was delighted to announce at the conference a new Mental Health Research Initiative within the Department's Policy Research Program where, for the first time, substantial funds have been ring-fenced for work on mental health. £2.4 million has been set aside for this initiative which, over 5 years, will commission and disseminate the results of a program of policy research. The initiative will run in two phases. The first will be devoted to general adult policy concerns. The second will address the development, implementation and evaluation of policies for mentally disordered offenders, and for the mental health of children and adolescents. After wide consultation and with the help of an expert advisory committee, we have identified seven priority themes where research evidence is most urgently required and which will comprise the first phase of the initiative. These themes are:

- *Inter-agency working:* how best to facilitate work between the many agencies—health, social services, housing and the voluntary sector, to name but a few—which are needed to provide comprehensive needs-led mental health services.
- *The primary/secondary care interface:* how to facilitate cooperation and communication between mental health services in primary and secondary care.
- *Public awareness:* how to reduce the public fear and anxiety which is associated with mental illness and which may stand in the way of effective prevention.
- *Personnel needs:* determining the staffing and training requirements of successful community care.
- *Management of challenging behaviour:* how best to manage in the community challenging behaviour by people with severe mental illness.
- *Carers:* how to reduce the burden shouldered by informal carers of people with severe mental illness.
- *Detection and treatment of 'minor' mental illness:* how to detect and treat effectively the large and important number of people with so-called minor mental illness who present to primary care services.

These themes are all central to the provision of truly effective and appropriate mental health services. We are, of course, already devoting substantial efforts to addressing many of them and the research program will provide valuable learning to help us build on existing work.

£1.2 million was allocated to the first phase of the research initiative. Advertisements inviting researchers to submit outlines of their proposals in these seven areas appeared in the press and were sent to universities and the short-listing and peer-review procedures, culminating in the commissioning of the most outstanding of the applications. The second phase of the initiative was advertised and tendered similarly early in 1996.

The challenge of this Mental Health Research Initiative is not only to ensure high-quality research relevant to the prevention of mental illness, but also to ensure that our future work will be guided by its results. We can have at our disposal the finest and most sophisticated research evidence, but its real worth is only demonstrated when it is put into practice for the direct benefit of service users and the wider public.

CONCLUSION

Finally, I would like to thank the Health Education Authority for having co-funded the conference with us, and also the various private industry sponsors. With their partnership it was possible to stage a truly enjoyable and worthwhile international event.

World Health Organization Perspectives and Prevention of Mental Illness and Mental Health Promotion in Primary Care

Jorge Alberto Costa e Silva
World Health Organization, Geneva, Switzerland

As the Director of the Division of Mental Health and Prevention of Substance Abuse, I have analysed the work of my Division and Organization in depth, in consultation with my colleagues, governmental and non-governmental organizations and experts from different disciplines and countries. In our undertaking to protect and promote mental health we have two great challenges: one is to promote mental health and well-being, and the other is to prevent and treat mental disorders. These are indeed great challenges:

1. It has been shown that mental illnesses are common: one in three people are affected by a mental disorder at some point in their lives.
2. Mental disorders are among the most distressing and incapacitating conditions. For example, according to the World Bank and WHO calculations, the burden of mental disorders alone constitutes 10% of the global burden of diseases.
3. The stigma attached to mental illness represents a prominent barrier and prevents many people from receiving help. People do not disclose their psychological problems to their doctors, which decreases the opportunity for early identification and early intervention.

Yet we have also great opportunities to tackle these problems:

1. Today, mental disorders have been shown to be diagnosable: e.g. the diagnosis of depression can be made with a reliability that is comparable to physical diseases.

Preventing Mental Illness: Mental Health Promotion in Primary Care. Edited by R. Jenkins and T.B. Üstün.
Published 1998 John Wiley & Sons Ltd.

2. Mental disorders are treatable. Treatment efficiency for mental disorders is much better than for physical disorders, e.g. the treatment of hypertension, or bypass surgery.
3. As recognized by 190 member states of the World Health Assembly, a large proportion of these diseases could be prevented, thus reducing human suffering, social distress and economic losses.

It now remains for these advances to be translated into service policies and action programs, and disseminated across the countries of the world. WHO wants to mobilize the international community to find appropriate solutions for dealing with mental health problems. The definition of health which opens WHO's Constitution makes mental well-being one of the central elements of health. This definition states that health is not just the absence of disease and dictates that we should prevent mental illness and promote mental well-being. This broad conception of mental health, including both promotion of mental health and prevention of mental illness, leads to political support for mental health programs.

Let me give you an important example. The WHO is the agency of the United Nations responsible for activities related to international health. In response to the mental health situation worldwide, the WHO's program on Mental Health has gradually built a set of policies, strategies and technologies based on state-of-the-art research. Recently we have begun an international endeavour that would bring a greater awareness of mental health issues and provide practical solutions to these problems. This project is called 'Nations for Mental Health'.

In May 1995, Secretary General of United Nations Mr Boutros Boutros-Ghali, said:

Priorities must change. Mental health must be recognized as a foremost challenge.
. . .

The challenge is to combine concern for mental health issues with humanitarian assistance and protection efforts. Development policies must incorporate a concern for the protection and promotion of mental health.

And he continued:

It is time for mental health problems to be seen by the international community as what they are: a threat to individual well-being, and a threat to peace and development worldwide.

Our objective is to promote the mental health and well-being of all the inhabitants of the planet.

So we have an enormous challenge but we also have considerable support. We should collaborate with other UN agencies and organizations. Our basic strategy in dealing with mental health problems involves working closely with other sectors such as education, justice and interior, welfare, environment, and the media at community level.

We need programs that will have an impact at the regional and country level. Given specific mental health problems in different parts of the world, the extent of our collaboration with WHO Regional Offices has always been our strength. We also have established rewarding collaboration with many centres of excellence worldwide such as WHO Collaborating Centres and several non-governmental organizations.

THE CHALLENGE FOR PREVENTION AND PROMOTION IN MENTAL HEALTH

It is estimated that approximately 500 million people suffer from mental and neurological disorders in the world. It is also estimated that a considerable proportion (nearly half) of those disorders could be avoided by using effective, affordable and simple methods.

Most of the effective prevention of mental health problems and mental health promotion activities fall outside the usual field of responsibility of mental health workers (or outside the health sector altogether). This may be one of the reasons why we tend to underrate the possibilities of prevention and promotion in our field.

This view, however, should not deter us from taking action. We should aim at some role modifications. For protection and promotion of mental health we have to understand that behaviour is a very critical element. Changing behaviour is essential for effective prevention and promotion. Behaviour cannot be seen as matter of individual choice: it is mainly shaped by sociocultural realities (e.g. urbanization and modernization have often been accompanied by increased rates of violence, alcohol and drug use). Once we agree that prevention and promotion activities are needed, we have to focus on where they are made, who makes them, what to prevent and/or promote, how they are made and how effective they are.

Where? Role of Primary Care in Prevention and Promotion

Primary health care is defined by WHO as 'the essential health care that is accessible, practical, scientifically sound and socially acceptable'. It is the basic first contact care, that is comprehensive and continuous. It refers not only to general medical practice, but also to a larger concept involving other sectors in addition to the health sector, such as schools, the workplace and so on.

WHO's recent work on Mental Disorders in General Health Care showed that mental disorders are common among general practice attenders. Nearly 80% of people with mental disorders seek help from primary care facilities.

From these statements, it is natural that we should have prevention and promotion activities rooted in primary care.

Who Is Going to Do It?

The enhancement of primary care workers' capabilities for promotion of mental health and prevention of mental disorders is essential. WHO's work on primary mental health care has also shown that primary care workers could be trained to address the most common mental disorders adequately. In contrast to common beliefs, this approach does not increase the workload; on the contrary, it decreases the burden represented by frequent and recurrent visits by people whose disorders were neither identified nor managed.

The development of detailed guidelines for the assessment and management of mental health problems in primary care is a pressing need. Currently we have developed a very nice model: a short version of the International Classification of Diseases (ICD-10) for use in primary care. The ICD-10 is a very important step to provide state-of-the-art knowledge on diagnosis and management to general practitioners. By management we believe that prevention, promotion, treatment and rehabilitation should go together in a comprehensive package. This package should aim at a unified and consolidated strategy for the comprehensive management of patients. We believe that this conference will help us to refine the guidelines for prevention and promotion and incorporate them into these guidelines. In this way we can reduce the risks for developing mental disorders, prevent undesirable consequences of disorders and, most importantly, fight against the stigma associated with mental health problems.

Speaking of stigma, primary care is important because of the integration of services. In primary care there should be no discrimination between physical and mental disorders. People within the primary care settings can more easily accept that mental disorders are medical illnesses which should be treated in the same way as any other disease.

What to Prevent?

Mental health problems are due to a plethora of causes that are highly diverse in origin and mechanism. Complex health problems do not yield quick and simple solutions. It is impossible to address all forms of mental health problems in primary care. We have to develop a sound strategy to focus our limited resources on specific conditions that are frequent, disabling, controllable and important.

- *Frequent*: the condition is common in primary care.
- *Disabling*: the condition causes a burden to families, communities and society.
- *Controllable*: effective interventions exist that can be carried out in primary care.
- *Important*: public concern on the condition is high.

How to Prevent?

Suicide is among the 10 leading causes of death in developed regions and almost a million people commit suicide every year around the world. In this country the Department of Health has initiated a demonstrative program which proves that suicides could be reduced. The measures include not only the treatment of psychiatric patients such as adequate treatment of depression and substance abuse, but also it extends to other psychosocial measures like gun control, detoxification of domestic gas and car emissions, controlling the availability of toxic substances, and toning down reports of suicides in the press.

Mental retardation cannot easily be treated. However, when it is associated with fetal alcohol syndrome, Down's syndrome, iodine deficiency and phenylketonuria it is known that effective prevention strategies exist. These conditions add up to half of the cases with mental retardation.

The occurrence of *epilepsy* can effectively be reduced if febrile episodes and brain injury could be treated properly. General health measures, such as adequate prenatal care, improvement of the quality of birth attendance and immunization, help. On the other hand, promotion and enforcement of safer driving would also help to almost the same extent.

These are only three examples of measures for preventing mental disorders. This meeting will dwell on many similar topics and directions (such as depression, accidents, violence and many others) and will give us sound advice on how to proceed. In addition, the meeting needs to focus on the second of the greater challenges, of how to promote mental well-being.

WHO's Program on Mental Health is in charge of both the protection and the promotion of mental health. We aim to reduce problems related to mental and neurological disorders, and to facilitate the incorporation of mental health skills, knowledge and understanding in general health care and social development.

This meeting will address these issues in the field of mental health and WHO's Program on Mental Health will make every effort to carry out this plan and contribute to the overall process of promotion and prevention in primary care.

The WHO constitution states that mental health is one of the basic dimensions of health and it is our responsibility to take care of this holistic approach. WHO as a whole—and the Program on Mental Health, in particular—are definitely guided by this principle and we shall do everything to prevent mental illness and promote mental health.

3

Prevention of Mental Illness

Sir David Goldberg
Institute of Psychiatry, London, UK

PRIMARY PREVENTION

By and large, preventive interventions are mainly *sociopolitical*: reducing unemployment, improving schooling and housing, wearing seat-belts to avoid head injury. Politicians and educators are the key players here, although lesser roles are played by members of housing departments and housing associations, as well as by members of voluntary organizations. Our job is to remind them of the evidence for the importance of these key variables.

Some, however, are a matter of *health education*: e.g. low-salt diets, weight reduction in the early control of hypertension to avoid arteriosclerotic dementia, advice to the general public about safe drinking limits, advice to parents about how to avoid trisomy 21—here psychiatrists may play a small part, but once more, the running will be made by others.

Our dilemma is well illustrated by the harm done to children by physical and sexual abuse. Here most of our efforts are tertiary prevention, carried out (more or less effectively) by social workers, when we should be adopting interventions which involve primary and secondary prevention. One of the problems is that the most effective intervention would probably be by teaching parenting in secondary schools: however, educational innovation has not been encouraged until recently, and teachers would possibly be reluctant to teach things which would bring them into conflict with parents.

Another controversial issue is avoiding the damage done to children by divorce: psychiatrists are too used to being non-judgemental, and so they provide poor leadership here. Unfortunately, much effective primary prevention *does* involve being judgemental. Getting obstetricians to take antiseptic precautions, pasteurizing milk and fluoridation of drinking water were all matters of hot controversy once.

In primary care, probably the best primary prevention can be done with high-risk groups, such as the bereaved, children who have experienced parental neglect or abuse, mothers who have had a previous episode of puerperal depression and

Preventing Mental Illness: Mental Health Promotion in Primary Care. Edited by R. Jenkins and T.B. Üstün.
© 1998 John Wiley & Sons Ltd.

those who drink harmful levels of alcohol. In all these examples, health education and support by members of the primary care team can be crucial in preventing episodes of ill-health.

In this book we include chapters on these topics, which are of great interest to public health physicians, psychologists and health educators as well as psychiatrists, including action that can be taken in schools, at home and at workplaces—Drs Üstün and Jenkins have left very little to chance.

SECONDARY PREVENTION

Much work on early treatment is currently being done in two ways: enabling staff in primary care settings to carry out treatments themselves; and providing self-treatment packages in primary care settings. In this area exciting work is being carried out. Self-treatment is an important new modality: for example, in the Institute of Psychiatry, Isaac Marks carried out early work with a self-treatment book for phobias, Janet Treasure has self-treatment manuals for bulimia, and Simon Wessely has evaluated a self-treatment booklet for chronic fatigue states. It appears that disorders are more amenable to interventions if they are caught before they become established, by which time they will have been reinforced by various secondary gains.

These arguments apply to eating disorders, to fatigue states, and of course to the many patients who are presenting to their GPs with somatized forms of psychological illness. For every patient in a specialized clinic with anorexia or chronic somatization, there are literally dozens of patients in primary care with lesser symptoms, or with illnesses at an earlier stage.

Many people who would be unwilling to ask for psychiatric care, as well as many others whose illnesses are in an early stage, can benefit from this approach. My own work is directed at improving the treatment offered by health professionals in primary care settings: psychiatrists have an important role to play in this work, although they are by no means the only major players.

TERTIARY PREVENTION

As care moves into the community, the part played by non-professionals becomes crucial. Good community care is not merely a matter for health and social services: we must enable users' groups, housing associations and voluntary organizations to collaborate with us to provide care.

Home-based rehabilitation has been an eye-opener for me in the past few years, and has alerted me to how little I really knew about my patients' personal lives in the community until it was a matter of planning rehabilitation programs in their own living environment.

We are going to read chapters from all over the world, given by many different professionals. Most readers of this book are probably already pretty enthusiastic about prevention—or they would not be reading this collection of chapters. Their success will be measured by the extent to which we are able to infect others with enthusiasm.

General Aspects

4

Theoretical Frameworks for Mental Health Risk Reduction in Primary Care

Richard H Price

Institute for Social Research and Department of Psychology, University of Michigan, Ann Arbor, USA

Reducing the costly public health burden of mental health problems and disability in primary care settings will require useful theoretical frameworks, promising preventive strategies and rigorous prevention trials. Prevention trials will be needed both initially to evaluate promising approaches to risk reduction and later to estimate their actual impact in clinical and community settings.

This chapter begins by describing conceptual frameworks to guide efforts to reduce risk of mental health problems in primary care settings. Initial preventive trials are needed to evaluate the efficacy of risk reduction strategies. Conceptual frameworks are described for conducting efficacy trials for evaluating research reported in the scientific literature and assessing the quality of outcome evidence. Promising targets for risk reduction are also briefly discussed.

A final but crucial step before implementing risk reduction strategies for mental health problems in primary care settings involves conducting full-scale effectiveness trials. A conceptual framework for effectiveness trials is offered that takes into account not only the demonstrated potency of the risk reduction strategy, but also the organizational readiness of the host organization. Both are critical in assessing the net impact of the risk reduction strategy on the incidence, side effects, and cost–benefit impact of prevention efforts.

CONCEPTUAL MAPS FOR RISK REDUCTION

Primary, Secondary and Tertiary Prevention of Mental Disorders

There is considerable controversy in the field about the merits of various conceptual approaches to prevention. Perhaps the best known and earliest framework

Preventing Mental Illness: Mental Health Promotion in Primary Care. Edited by R. Jenkins and T.B. Üstün.
© 1998 John Wiley & Sons Ltd.

for explicating prevention goals (Caplan 1964) distinguished between three general approaches: (1) *primary prevention*, aimed at reducing the incidence of new cases of disorder; (2) *secondary prevention*, aimed at reducing prevalence of disorder by early intervention, once early clinical signs of disorder have been detected; and (3) *tertiary prevention*, which is not prevention in the usual sense, but instead involves attempts to reduce handicaps associated with chronic disorder. Since some disorders are episodic and the actual time of onset is often difficult to establish, there remains definitional ambiguity in distinguishing between early treatment and prevention efforts in this framework.

Promotion of Mental Health

While prevention concepts have been focused primarily on reducing the likelihood of the development of disorder, *mental health promotion* efforts have been largely concerned with activities that enhance the general coping skills and mental health of non-clinical populations. Mental health promotion efforts have sometimes been advocated because they are believed to reduce vulnerability to disorder. In other cases, promotion has been advocated as an end in itself, quite apart from its potential to prevent disorder (Dinges and Duong-Tran 1993).

Reducing Risk for Mental Disorder

More recently, the Institute of Medicine report (Mrazek & Haggerty 1994) advocates a *risk reduction* approach to prevention and suggests use of an earlier typology proposed by Gordon (1987) (Table 4.1). In this approach, *universal* preventive interventions are targeted to the general public or to a whole population group that has not been identified on the basis of individual risk for mental disorders. *Selective* preventive interventions are targeted to individuals or subgroups of the population whose risk for developing mental disorders is significantly higher than average. Finally, in the IOM approach, *indicated* preventive interventions are targeted to high-risk individuals who are identified as having had prodromal and detectable signs or symptoms, but who do not yet meet diagnostic criteria for mental disorder. These populations with subclinical signs of disorder are presumed to benefit from more intensive interventions that may not be warranted for other groups in the population at lower risk for disorder.

Benefits and Risks

Gordon's (1987) original classification included the idea that universal, selected, and indicated preventive interventions are distinguished partly on the basis of the relative risks and benefits associated with intervention. Gordon argued that

TABLE 4.1   Universal, selected and indicated preventive interventions

Universal interventions
- Targeted to whole populations or the general public
- Effects are widely beneficial with no marked negative side effects
- Example: high-quality prenatal care

Selected interventions
- Targeted to subgroups of the population whose risk is significantly above average
- Anticipated benefits outweigh increased costs, effort and risk
- Example: nurse visiting program for young, poor, first pregnancy mothers

Indicated interventions
- Targeted at high-risk individuals who display minimal but detectable symptoms
- Expected costs and risks are high, but anticipated benefits outweigh costs
- Example: screening and early referral for treatment of symptoms of depression or early dementia

universal interventions were justified for entire populations when evidence suggested that they would be universally beneficial and have very low risks or unintended costs. In the physical health arena, fluoridation and smallpox vaccination are examples of universal preventive interventions where benefits are nearly universal and risks are very low. High-quality prenatal care is another example. On the other hand, a radical pharmacological intervention might be justified as an indicated intervention for people displaying hypercholesteremia. Treatment for patients showing early signs of depression is one mental health example, and parenting training for pregnant low-income mothers is another. In the middle of the distribution, selective interventions might include goggles for persons working at metal-turning lathes. This approach has the advantage of setting aside the question of clinical threshold, and also focuses more explicitly on the preventive intervention and its possible benefits and costs.

Another important contribution of the IOM report (Mrazek & Haggerty 1994) is that it adopts the more modest goal of *risk reduction* in place of the somewhat more ambitious goal of prevention. In doing so, it follows the general orientation used in the prevention of physical illness. In risk reduction for cardiovascular disease, for example, encouraging smoking reduction, exercise and so on represent risk reduction strategies. There is a great deal to recommend this new approach to classifying preventive interventions.

Risk Reduction in the Larger Context of Mental Health Services

The general intervention spectrum for mental disorder shown in Figure 4.1, and also prominently featured in the IOM Report, places universal, selective and indicated interventions in the larger context of other intervention strategies for

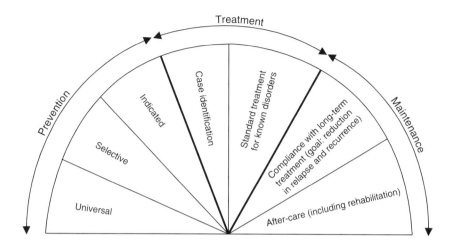

FIGURE 4.1 The mental health intervention spectrum for mental disorders. From Mrazek & Haggerty 1994, by permission of the National Academy Press

mental health problems. Here, for example, maintenance activities include aftercare and compliance with long-term treatment regimes, while treatment includes activities such as standard therapies for known disorders and case identification for later referral and treatment. This framework helps to emphasize the distinctive role of risk reduction in addition to carefinding, treatment and rehabilitation efforts.

THE ESSENTIAL FIRST STEP: PRELIMINARY EVIDENCE FOR RISK REDUCTION THROUGH EFFICACY TRIALS

The Path from Unproven Programs to Demonstrated Effectiveness

The conceptual framework just described represents an *endpoint* for classifying already proven risk reduction strategies for mental health primary care settings. While there are viable candidates for risk reduction strategies in primary care settings, we do not have a full array of proven interventions. Promising interventions must go through a cycle of: (1) basic research to test the efficacy of the interventions for risk reduction (Price 1994; Lorion, Price & Eaton 1989; Mrazek & Haggerty 1994); followed by (2) a series of trials in actual clinical settings to demonstrate the net effectiveness of such interventions when they are actually implemented on a large scale (Price & Lorion 1989).

Some very promising risk reduction strategies, potentially adaptable to primary care settings, have already passed preliminary tests of efficacy and are described below. At least some preliminary trials have also been conducted in actual clinical settings. These interventions may be ready for broader application in the field. On the other hand, for every such potential intervention program or strategy, there are countless programs or intervention strategies that have not yet been examined in rigorous efficacy and effectiveness trials (Price et al 1989). It would be premature to argue that they are ready to be translated into clinical practice guidelines that claim that the risk of mental health problems will be reduced if the guidelines are followed.

So the challenge that faces the field is threefold. First, those few strategies that have been tested in randomized trials, replicated and tested in clinical settings, can begin to be considered for wide-scale implementation. This is a major organizational and institutional challenge, and one of those addressed by many of the papers in the conference.

Second, a great many promising interventions with little research evidence for effectiveness need to be subjected to *efficacy trials* to determine their impact under ideal conditions. Major clinical, financial and scientific resources need to be devoted to this task. Selection of such interventions for efficacy trials needs to be done using available epidemiological research on malleable risk factors. Well-developed theoretical frameworks must support and motivate the interventions themselves. In addition, preliminary evidence about the acceptability, cost and potential potency of the intervention also should be marshalled at this second stage of efficacy trials.

The third challenge, of course, is in testing the survivors of preliminary efficacy trials in actual clinical settings. This stage of research, typically called *effectiveness research*, is critically important (Gramlich 1981; Price & Lorion 1989). Effectiveness research brings to bear questions frequently ignored in implementing programs in clinical practice. These are questions about the organizational, institutional and professional constraints to effective program implementation that abound in primary care settings. They will be described in more detail below.

CHOOSING 'WINNERS' IN EFFICACY TRIALS

Preventive Intervention Research Cycle

The strategy and the criteria for selecting 'winners' from the results of such trials deserves some mention here. Figure 4.2 describes the preventive intervention research cycle as depicted by the Institute of Medicine. The cycle prescribes a series of steps that move from: (1) problem identification; through (2) a focus on risk and protective factors; to (3) strategies for modifying malleable risk factors; through (4) studies to test such interventions under ideal conditions; followed later by (5) large-scale effectiveness trials to assess the applicability and impact in wide-

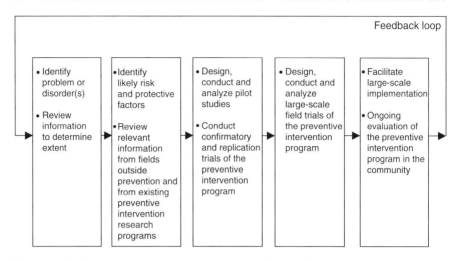

FIGURE 4.2 Preventive intervention research cycle, as depicted by the Institute of Medicine. From Mrazek & Haggerty 1994, by permission

ranging clinical settings. Procedural frameworks of this sort can be of genuine value in planning and implementing efficacy trials (Price & Smith 1985).

Framework for Evaluating the Quality of Preventive Trials

This general framework and others like it are a useful guide to the process of doing research on the efficacy of preventive interventions. But by itself, this framework only provides the most general set of criteria for understanding which programs might be considered good candidates to move on tests of clinical effectiveness. However, another useful framework, shown in Table 4.2, has been developed that provides a more detailed checklist for evaluating the designs and the evidence forthcoming from efficacy trials. It is worthwhile to consider cataloging existing preventive interventions according to these six sets of factors including: (1) description of the risk and protective factors addressed; (2) descriptive information about the targeted population group; (3) detailed information about the intervention program itself; (4) the research methodologies used; (5) the actual evidence concerning implementation of the intervention; and finally (6) evidence concerning outcomes and impact. Similar criteria have been developed by Hosman et al (1988) and Price et al (1988, 1989).

Range of Evidence for Efficacy

The evidence often used to support the implementation of preventive trials varies enormously from anecdotal evidence to the results of large-scale replicated

TABLE 4.2 A framework for examining preventive interventions. This format might be used as a worksheet in determining the methodological rigor of a specific program

Description of the risk and protective factors addressed	Description of the targeted population group	Description of the intervention program	Description of the research methodologies	Description of the evidence concerning implementation	Description of the evidence concerning outcomes
Documentation	Universal, selective or indicated	Goals and content	Methods of recruitment	Exposure of target group to intervention	Changes in status of risk and/or protective factors
Relationship to developmental task	Evidence that group is at risk for disorder or problem	Protocols	Sample size	Fidelity of delivery in accordance with design	Evidence of reduction of new cases
Causal status		Personnel delivering the intervention	Randomization		
Status in malleability		Site	Baseline measures		Evidence of delay of onset
	Sociodemographic				
Correlation with incidence and prevalence		Institutional or cultural content	Statistical analysis		Side effects
		Ethical considerations	Attrition of subjects		Benefit–cost and cost-effectiveness analyses
		Equipment or instrumentation			
		Method of delivery and techniques			
		Duration and extent			
		Multiple components			

TABLE 4.3 Quality of evidence available from prevention programs

Grade I	Evidence obtained from multiple randomized controlled trials (confirmatory and replication trials and large-scale field trials)
Grade II	Evidence obtained from multiple randomized controlled trials (confirmatory and replication trials but no large-scale field trial)
Grade III	Evidence obtained from at least one properly randomized controlled trial
Grade IV	Evidence obtained from well-designed controlled trials without randomization
Grade V	Evidence obtained from well-designed cohort or case control studies, preferably more than one
Grade VI	Evidence obtained from multiple time series studies with or without the intervention. Dramatic results in uncontrolled experiments (such as the results of the introduction of penicillin in the 1940s) could constitute this type of evidence
Grade VII	Evidence suggested by respected authorities, based on clinical experience, descriptive studies, prior service delivery programs or reports by expert committees

randomized preventive trials. Table 4.3 illustrates the range of evidence and provides us with some tentative norms and standards for the range of acceptable evidence about a preventive intervention that would make it a candidate for large-scale implementation. To date very few risk reduction strategies have yielded research evidence at the highest level depicted in Table 4.3. Nevertheless, there are a number of promising targets for risk reduction, several of which are described below.

PROMISING TARGETS FOR RISK REDUCTION IN PRIMARY CARE SETTINGS

There is considerable room for exploration of opportunities to reduce vulnerability to mental disorder in primary care settings. Four classes of opportunities that have not yet been fully explored are (1) systematic attempts to help people cope with health crises and trauma; (2) screening and referral of primary care patients who show signs of mental disorder; (3) reduction of the risk of co-morbid disorders among patients already displaying a mental disorder; and (4) prenatal and perinatal programs with impact on mental health.

Reducing Mental Health Risks Associated with Trauma and Crisis

A great many life-threatening or disabling illnesses bring people to primary care settings. The crises that result can all produce acute psychological trauma.

Enlightened medical practice recognizes these traumatic circumstances and provides supportive services to help patients and their families cope more effectively. In a number of cases, medical practices can be modified in ways that reduce their trauma-producing potential. For example, Tadmor (1988) has reported preventive intervention for a caesarean birth population that increases perceived personal control. She also describes the use of this intervention strategy for a variety of other high-risk populations, including mothers of premature infants (Tadmor & Brandes 1986), mothers who encounter neonatal death (Tadmor 1986), medical staff dealing with terminally ill patients (Tadmor & Hofman 1985), and children undergoing elective surgery and their parents (Tadmor et al in press). Tadmor's model to enhance perceived personal control in the face of traumatic crisis and stress was pioneered by Gerald Caplan (1964), an early advocate of preventive intervention to deal with life crises.

An important approach to risk reduction in primary care settings is to conduct an *audit of current medical care practices* to identify treatment policies and practices that may produce adverse mental health effects. The history of medical practice gives us some hint of where we might look. For example, hospital policies in the USA at one time prohibited parents from staying in the hospital with young children overnight, with predictable effects on children's mental health. Similarly, in the past, preparation of children for surgery did not always include supportive interventions aimed at preparing children to cope with the frightening circumstances of anesthesia, operating rooms and post-surgery discomfort. Now it is widely recognized that preoperative programs for children are effective, not only in reducing psychological trauma but also in speeding recovery from surgery.

Screening and Referral for Early Signs and Vulnerability to Psychological Disorder

A second major opportunity for risk reduction of mental health problems in primary care involves identifying those who are particularly vulnerable to mental health problems (Brown 1990). For example, Munoz et al (1987) has reported a program that identifies poor ethnic minority clients at risk for depression. The program provides them with cognitive restructuring skills that reduce the risk of subsequent symptoms of depression. A randomized trial (Munoz et al 1987) has shown promising results. Beardslee and MacMillan (1993) have shown that early detection and treatment of depression in young mothers has the potential of reducing the risk of depression in the children.

Screening strategies do not necessarily guarantee that cost-beneficial risk reduction will result. The actual value of a screening test depends on the base rate for the disorder in the population under consideration and the sensitivity and specificity of the test. Poor screening tests can be expensive, inefficient and ineffective. Furthermore, even among those accurately screened and referred for treatment, some significant portion will develop a mental disorder in any case. Even if a particular disorder is successfully delayed or even prevented, this does not necessarily mean that the person will not develop a second disorder. Screening strategies must be evaluated for their usefulness and cost-effectiveness in routine practice, or for more selective use depending on accuracy, cost and likelihood of successful intervention. Without (1) a set of guidelines for screening accuracy and (2) effective treatments or preventive interventions, uncritical use of screening strategies may be an expensive and ineffective tactic for reducing risks of mental disorders.

Reduction of Co-morbidity Risk in Identified Cases of Mental Disorder

Kessler & Price (1993) have called for the consideration of a new class of preventive interventions explicitly designed to prevent co-morbidity. They argue that epidemiologic data show that successful interventions of this kind could be valuable since up to half of lifetime psychiatric disorders, and an even larger proportion of chronic and seriously impairing disorders, occur to people with a prior history of some other disorder. The recent epidemiological catchment area (ECA) study found that half of all lifetime psychiatric disorders in the USA occur to people with a prior history of some other psychiatric disorder (Robins et al 1991). More recently, Kessler et al (1994) completed the National Co-morbidity Study (NCS) and showed that more than 80% of all current severe psychiatric disorders in the USA occur among the 13% of the population who have a lifetime history of three or more disorders. This suggests that preventing co-morbidity, that is *preventing the onset of a second disorder*, would reduce a substantial proportion of all lifetime psychiatric disorders. Regier et al (1990) have shown that some psychiatric disorders are likely to form co-morbid clusters, and that one disorder in most such clusters typically occurs at an earlier age than another. People with the primary disorder may be amenable to interventions aimed at preventing development of secondary disorders.

Kessler & Price (1993) mention several advantages of conducting preventive trials in populations at risk for co-morbid disorders. First, identifying people at risk for secondary disorders who already meet criteria for a primary disorder should be accomplished with higher reliability. This should increase the efficiency and power of preventive trials. Second, already developed treatment technologies, including pharmacological and behavioral interventions, can become a part of the available technology for preventive interventions for co-morbid disorders. Third, preventing secondary disorders may eliminate the exacerbation of primary disorders, which often accompanies the onset of secondary disorders. Finally, treatments that have the effect of preventing secondary disorders may increase the social warrant for prevention strategies in general.

Prenatal and Perinatal Programs and Other Health Interventions

There are a number of effective preventive interventions applicable early in life that have a demonstrated impact on health, mental health, child neglect and other critical outcomes. These programs are of considerable importance because they could be incorporated into standard primary care practice, and are likely to have both physical and mental health impacts. Such programs include the prenatal and early infancy projects developed by Olds (1988). This program aims at improving maternal diet and parenting skills, reduced smoking during pregnancy, and actually produces higher-birthweight babies, fewer preterm deliveries and less child abuse. A second example involves a hospital-based intervention developed by Field (1986). The intervention involves tactile and kinesthetic stimulation for preterm low-birthweight babies and produces better physical and mental development of infants. These programs have the interesting feature of being directed at health outcomes for infants, but upon examination in preventive trials also demonstrate impacts on mental health outcomes.

IN PURSUIT OF PREVENTION PROGRAM EFFECTIVENESS IN THE PRIMARY CARE SETTING

Special Challenges of Primary Care Settings

Primary care medical settings may have advantages for the implementation of risk reduction strategies for mental health, but also may have critical organizational and institutional drawbacks (Goldberg & Tantam 1990). There are a number of reasons for this.

First, primary care physicians are typically not orientated toward mental health problems. The skill base of most physicians does not include mental health counseling or special ability to detect mental health problems in patients. This means that opportunities for risk reduction or early intervention may be missed.

Second, most primary care physicians and family practitioners already feel burdened with increasing demands for productivity and efficiency that erode their ability to provide quality care. The 'pressures of production' in medical settings, including time and economic pressures, may push risk reduction activities lower in the physician's priority list.

Third, organizational and economic factors, including arrangements that allow medical settings to externalize the cost of mental health problems, may also be powerful inhibitory forces. For example, in settings where the health organization is not directly responsible for maintaining the overall health and mental health of a population, the costs of mental health problems are often passed on to other agencies through referral. Selectively attending to medical problems that do generate revenue for the organization may also squeeze out mental health services that generate less revenue. Such economic incentives do not bode well for mental disorder risk reduction strategies in primary care settings.

Fourth, in some cases, primary care physicians may not see mental health problems as 'real illness', and regard mental health risk reduction services as ancillary. This may lead them to delegate these mental health responsibilities to other personnel. Delegation may be at times appropriate and even desirable. However, since physicians frequently lead medical teams, an implicit message may be that these responsibilities are less critical or central to the mission of medical care.

A number of these interrelated problems are described by Gersons (1990) and Price (1992). They suggest that even when well-documented and effective risk reduction strategies are available, their effective implementation must take into account a wide array of organizational, economic and institutional factors that are frequently overlooked.

Implementation: Art or Sciences?

While we know a good deal about how to conduct a randomized trial to test the efficacy of a preventive intervention, we are much less sophisticated about strategies for maximizing the ultimate impact of preventive interventions in primary care settings. Indeed, when demonstrably effective preventive programs are well implemented in clinical settings, the success is usually attributed to the 'art' of effective medical administration. But what it takes to maximize the effectiveness of prevention programs is neither arcane nor mysterious. Figure 4.3 presents a framework intended to specify a number of variables in the effectiveness equation.

A FRAMEWORK FOR PREVENTIVE EFFECTIVENESS

Net Effectiveness

Figure 4.3 specifies a number of factors that are critical in maximizing the effectiveness in clinical or field settings. The framework asserts that the goal is to maximize *net effectiveness*, where net effectiveness is defined by a multi-dimensional set of outcomes including: (1) reduction of the incidence of mental health problems; (2) minimum negative side effects; (3) maximum positive multiplier effects; and (4) favorable benefit–cost outcomes.

Strength and Integrity

Figure 4.3 argues that a major but not exclusive determinant of preventive effectiveness is the *strength and integrity* (Yeaton & Sechrest 1981) of the preventive

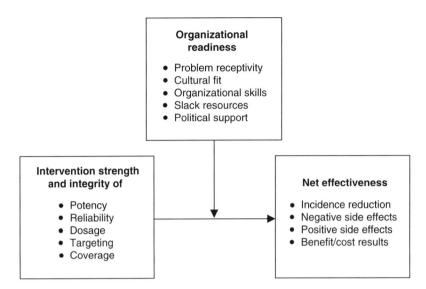

FIGURE 4.3   Maximizing effectiveness in implementation of preventive programs

intervention. Information about the strength and integrity of a particular preventive intervention can only come from carefully conducted efficacy trials of the kind described earlier. In this framework, the strength and integrity of a particular preventive intervention depends on its potency, reliability of delivery, intervention dosage, accurate targeting to vulnerable populations, and its coverage of that population.

Organizational Readiness

However, no matter how great the strength and integrity of a preventive intervention, its net effectiveness critically depends on the *organizational readiness* (Price & Lorion 1989) of the host organization in which it is implemented. It is this set of factors that is most frequently ignored in large-scale implementation. Factors contributing to organizational readiness are knowable, measurable, and have critical impacts on the net effectiveness of preventive programs.

Organizational readiness consists of a number of key factors including: (1) staff and leadership awareness and receptivity to the particular prevention problem; (2) the degree to which there is a cultural fit between the intervention and the organizational culture of the clinical setting; (3) the organizational skills and capabilities of the personnel learned in previous practice; (4) the availability of slack resources, including staff, funds, space and administrative support; and finally (5) the degree to which influential groups or organizations outside the host organization provide legitimacy, advocacy and political support for implementation.

Figure 4.3 suggests that organizational readiness moderates the relationship between intervention strength and its net effectiveness. That is, the model argues that *organizations low in readiness will greatly weaken the preventive impact of even very strong interventions*. On the other hand, organizations high in organizational readiness will maximize the net effectiveness of preventive interventions that have demonstrated high levels of strength and integrity in previous efficacy trials.

A Guide to Research and Effective Practice

Figure 4.3 is intended both to guide the design and implementation of effectiveness trials and to suggest hypotheses concerning variables that are critical in ensuring the effectiveness of prevention programs. As an action guide, the model is intended as a diagnostic framework that can be used in evaluating both host organizations and preventive interventions that are candidates for implementation. The framework provides a starting set of planning guidelines for implementation as well as a set of hypotheses about the role of these variables in the ultimate effectiveness of a preventive intervention.

CONCLUSION

Risk reduction strategies in primary care are still largely uncharted territory. The conceptual frameworks described here should be regarded as preliminary maps in relatively uncharted but promising territory. The challenges before us are both scientific and organizational. The scientific challenges will require that we call on our knowledge of epidemiology, field trial methodology and creative hypotheses about the mechanisms that elicit and maintain mental health problems, as well as those that reduce the risk of disorder.

The organizational challenges must remain clearly in focus as well. The organization, economics and politics of health care raise a second set of questions about organizational readiness for risk reduction of mental health problems. These organizational, economic and political challenges are no less formidable. In a truly integrated system of health care they should also be objects of our scientific study. They must be incorporated into our theoretical models of health care systems, where risk reduction plays a central role in the pursuit of well-being.

REFERENCES

Beardslee W & MacMillan H (1993) Preventive intervention with the children of depressed parents: a case study. *Psychoanal Study Child* **48**, 249–76.
Brown G (1990) Some public health aspects of depression. In D Goldberg & D Tantam (eds) *The Public Health Impact of Mental Disorder*, pp 59–72. New York: Hogrefe & Huber.
Caplan G (1964) *Principles of Preventive Psychiatry*. New York: Basic Books.

Dinges NG & Duong-Tran Q (1993) Stressful life events and co-occurring depression, abuse and suicidality among American Indian and Native adolescents. Special Issue: The comorbidity depression, anxiety, and substance abuse among Indians and Alaska natives. *Culture Med Psychiat* **16**(4), 487–502.

Field TM, Schanberg SM, Scafidi F, Bauer CR, Vega-Lahr N, Garcia R, Nystrom J & Kuhn CM (1986) Tactile/kinesthetic stimulation effects on preterm neonates. *Pediatrics* **77**(5), 654–8.

Gersons B (1990) The competitive relationship between mental health services and family practices: future implications. In D Goldberg & D Tantam (eds) *The Public Mental Health Impact of Mental Disorder*, pp 214–20. New York: Hogrefe & Huber.

Goldberg D & Tantam D (eds) (1990) *The Public Health Impact of Mental Disorder*. New York: Hogrefe & Huber.

Gordon RS (1987) An operational classification of disease prevention. In JA Steinberg & MM Silverman (eds) *Preventing Mental Disorders: A Research Perspective*, pp 20–26. Rockville, MD: NIMH.

Gramlich EM (1981) *Benefit–Cost Analysis of Government Programs*. Englewood Cliffs, NJ: Prentice Hall.

Hosman CMH, Price RH & Bosma MWM (1988) Evaluatie van preventieve interventies. In C Hosman, H van Doorm & H Verburg (eds) *Preventie Inzicht* (Dutch), pp 299–308. Amsterdam: Swets & Zeitlinger.

Kessler RC, McGonagle KA, Zhao S, Nelson CB, Hughes M, Eshleman S, Wittchen HU & Kendler KS (1994) Lifetime and 12-month prevalence of DSM-III-R psychiatric disorders among persons aged 15–54 in the United States: results from the national comorbidity survey. *Arch Gen Psychiat* **51**, 8–91.

Kessler RC & Price RD (1993) Primary prevention of secondary disorders: a proposal and agenda. *Am J Comm Psychol* **21**(5), 607–34.

Lorion RP, Price RD & Eaton WW (1989) The prevention of child and adolescent disorders: from theory to research. In D Shaffer, I Philips & NB Enzer (eds) *Prevention of Mental Disorders, Alcohol and Drug Use in Children and Adolescents*. Prevention Monograph #2 (DHHS Publ. No. ADM 89-1646). Rockville, MD: Office of Substance Abuse Prevention and American Academy of Child and Adolescent Psychiatry.

Mrazek PJ & Haggerty RJ (eds) (1994) *Reducing Risks for Mental Disorders: Frontiers for Preventive Intervention Research*. Washington, DC: National Academy Press.

Munoz RF, Ying Y, Armas R, Chan F & Gurza R (1987) The San Francisco depression prevention research project: a randomized trial with medical outpatients. In RF Munoz (ed) *Depression Prevention: Research Directions*, pp 199–215. Washington, DC: Hemisphere.

Olds DL (1988) The prenatal/early infancy project. In RH Price, EL Cowen, RP Lorion & J Ramos-McKay (eds) *Fourteen Ounces of Prevention: A Casebook for Practitioners*, pp 9–23. Washington, DC: American Psychological Association.

Price RH (1994) In prevention research, nothing is as practical as a good theory. In J Rispens, PP Goudena & JHA Groenendaal (eds) *Van kindmodel naar modelkind*, pp 33–41. Groningen, The Netherlands: Stichting Kinderstudies.

Price RH (1992) Public mental health on the other side of the Atlantic (review of *The Public Health Impact of Mental Disorder*). *Contemporary Psychol* **37**(4), 329–30.

Price RH, Cowen EL, Lorion RP & Ramos-McKay J (1989) The search for effective prevention programs: what we learned along the way. *Am J Orthopsychiat* **59**(1), 49–58.

Price RH, Cowen, EL, Lorion RP & Ramos-McKay J (1988) Introduction. In RH Price, E Cowen, RP Lorion & J Ramos-McKay (eds) *Fourteen Ounces of Prevention: a Casebook for Practitioners*. Washington, DC: American Psychological Association.

Price RH & Lorion RP (1989) Prevention programming as organizational reinvention: from research to implementation. In D Shaffer, I Phillips & NB Enzer (eds) (MM Silverman & V Anthony, Assoc. eds) *Prevention of Mental Disorders, Alcohol and Drug Use in Children and*

Adolescents, pp 97–123. Prevention Monograph #1 (DHHS Publ. No. ADM 89-1646). Rockville, MD: Office of Substance Abuse Prevention and American Academy of Child and Adolescent Psychiatry.

Price RH & Smith SS (1985) *A Guide to Evaluating Prevention Programs in Mental Health* (DHHS Publ No ADM 85-1365). Washington, DC: US Government Printing Office.

Regier DA, Farmer ME, Rae DS, Locke BZ, Keith BJ, Judd LL & Goodwin FK (1990) Comorbidity of mental health disorders with alcohol and other drug abuse. *J Am Med Assoc* **264**, 2511–18.

Robins LN, Locke BZ & Regier DA (1991) An overview of psychiatric disorders in America. In LN Robins & DA Regier (eds) *Psychiatric Disorders in America*, pp 328–66. New York: Free Press.

Tadmor CS (1986) A crisis intervention model for a population of mothers who encounter neonatal death. *J Primary Prevention* **7**(1), 17–26.

Tadmor CS (1988) The perceived personal control preventive intervention for a caesarean birth population. In RH Price, EL Cowen, RP Lorion & J Ramos-McKay (eds) *Fourteen Ounces of Prevention: A Casebook for Practitioners*, pp 141–52. Washington, DC: American Psychological Association.

Tadmor CS, Bar-Maor JA, Birkhan J, Shoshany G & Hofman JE (in press) Pediatric surgery: a preventive intervention approach to enhance mastery of stress. *J Prevent Psychiat* **3**(4).

Tadmor CS & Brandes JM (1986) Premature birth: a crisis intervention approach. *J Primary Prevent* **6**(4), 244–55.

Tadmor CS & Hofman JE (1985) Measuring locus of control in a hospital setting. *Psychol Rep* **56**(2), 525–6.

Yeaton WH & Sechrest L (1981) Critical dimensions in the choice and maintenance of successful treatments: strength, integrity and effectiveness. *J Consult Clin Psychol* **49**, 156–7.

5

Selective and Indicated Preventive Interventions

Patricia J Mrazek

Prevention Technologies, Bethesda, MD, USA
Formerly, Institute of Medicine of the National Academy of Sciences, Washington, DC, USA

In January 1994 the Institute of Medicine (IOM) of the National Academy of Sciences in Washington, DC issued a report entitled *Reducing Risks for Mental Disorders: Frontiers for Preventive Intervention Research* (IOM, 1994a). Even though the Institute of Medicine has been in existence for 20 years, and the Academy for almost 100, this was the first report on prevention research and mental disorders. This intensive 2-year study was the result of a mandate from the US Congress. An interdisciplinary committee of 16 members reviewed the field of prevention research. Somewhat remarkably, and quite independently, similar reviews were conducted at approximately the same time in Australia and the UK. In September 1992 the National Health and Medical Research Council in Australia issued a report entitled *Scope for Prevention in Mental Health*, and in March 1993 the Royal College of Psychiatry in the UK released a report entitled *Prevention in Psychiatry*. Only a few months ago, Harvard University's new report, entitled *World Mental Health: Problems and Priorities in Low-income Countries* (Desjarlais et al 1995), which contains a section on prevention, was endorsed by the United Nations.

This interest in and scrutiny of prevention research and its potential for decreasing mental illnesses should not go unnoticed. This is not an aberrant or fringe movement in only one country. Rather, it is a result of a recognition that the magnitude of mental illness throughout the world requires an approach that includes more than treatment. Prevention efforts have been around for a long time, but the landscape is no longer the same. In the 1920s and then again in the 1960s, prevention activities received considerable attention. For the most part these activities failed, largely because too much was promised by prevention advocates, given the inadequacy of the state of the science. Now, however, research methodologies have improved, and the research base has grown significantly. The time is now ripe for the cautious development of prevention research and service programs for some, but not yet all, mental disorders.

Preventing Mental Illness: Mental Health Promotion in Primary Care. Edited by R. Jenkins and T.B. Üstün.
© 1998 John Wiley & Sons Ltd.

Historically, there have been three main obstacles in the development of prevention research and preventive clinical services for mental disorders: first, the lack of a reasonable and uniform definition of prevention; second, the lack of a theoretical framework that could logically be applied across disorders; and third, the lack of evidence that prevention could produce positive outcomes. These three problems will be reviewed within the basic premise that selective and indicated preventive interventions for some mental disorders are not only possible but will become a major focus of attention as we move into the next century.

Increasingly, health professionals and the public are recognizing that physical and mental health are intricately linked and that medical care must alter its categorical provision of services and finally recognize the 'seamless whole of health'. In 1994 the Institute of Medicine's Committee on the Future of Primary Care issued a provisional definition of primary care that applies this principle:

> Primary care is the provision of integrated, accessible health care services by clinicians who are accountable for addressing a large majority of personal health care needs, developing a sustained partnership with patients, and practicing in the context of family and community (IOM 1994b, p 1).

Personal health care needs are defined as including 'physical, mental, emotional and social concerns that involve the functioning of an individual' (IOM 1994b, p 17).

DEFINING PREVENTION

Prevention literally means 'to keep something from happening'. What that something is has long been a source of contention in the health and mental health fields. The classical public health definition of disease prevention, which was proposed by the Commission on Chronic Illness in 1957, proposed three categories of prevention: primary, secondary and tertiary. This is the system of classification that is most familiar to mental health researchers and clinicians. The goals of the three categories demarcate the distinctions between them. Primary prevention seeks to decrease the number of new cases of a disorder; secondary prevention seeks to lower the rate of established cases of the disorder in the population; tertiary prevention seeks to decrease the amount of disability associated with an existing disorder. In clinical practice, and even in research, these distinctions among categories are not as clear-cut as they might appear.

When this classical system of disease prevention was proposed, there was an implied understanding of mechanisms linking the cause of a disease with the occurrence of a disease; e.g. an infectious agent led to an illness, so elimination of the agent led to successful primary prevention. Public health measures using this approach have been highly successful, and massive epidemics of illnesses such as cholera, polio and diphtheria have been prevented.

Nevertheless, primary care physicians and general practitioners have spent most of their practice hours diagnosing illnesses that already exist, providing treatment and trying to lessen the chances of relapse and disability associated with particular

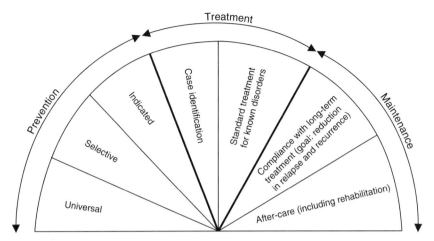

FIGURE 5.1 The mental health intervention spectrum for mental disorders. From Mrazek & Haggerty 1994, by permission of the National Academy Press

diseases. In other words, the focus has been on diagnosis, treatment and maintenance—all of which are referred to as secondary and tertiary prevention.

It is not difficult to see how so much in medicine has come to be called *'prevention'*. It is all too easy to leave off the words primary, secondary and tertiary when describing an intervention. The same overuse of the term 'prevention' has also been true for research. The IOM made a critical examination of the prevention portfolio at the former federal agency called the Alcohol, Drug Abuse and Mental Health Administration. Everything from basic research to community support programs for the rehabilitation of the seriously mentally ill had been included in the definition of prevention research.

After considerable deliberation over a year and a half, the IOM Committee recommended that the term *'prevention'* be reserved only for those interventions that occur before the initial onset of a mental disorder. In place of the old public classification system, the Committee proposed a mental health intervention spectrum for mental disorders that recognizes the importance of prevention, treatment and maintenance and presents them as distinct entities while recognizing that in clinical practice the boundaries may not be so clear-cut (Figure 5.1).

In this classification system, prevention is further subtyped into three categories: universal, selective and indicated. This subtyping is based on a system proposed by Gordon in 1983. Gordon was interested in the primary prevention of physical diseases. He had come to understand that less and less of medicine was based on a straightforward single causal agent model. Many modern diseases were a result of a complex interplay between risk factors. He proposed that preventive interventions be targeted to population groups for whom they were thought to be optimal. This system was based on a risk–benefit point of view, that is, the risk to the individual of getting a disease must be weighed against the cost, risk and discomfort of the preventive intervention. The IOM Committee found this approach compelling, but believed that some important modifications were necessary before it could be applied to mental disorders.

In the IOM mental health intervention spectrum (Figure 5.1), universal preventive interventions are targeted to the general public or a whole population group that has not been identified on the basis of individual risk. The intervention is desirable for everyone in that group. 'General public' implies everyone. A whole population group could, for example, be defined as all pregnant women, or all preschool children, or all the elderly. Universal interventions have advantages because large groups of people can be reached. However, there are two main drawbacks to universal preventive interventions. First, although the cost per individual may be low, the program overall could be quite expensive because of the large size of the target group. Second, unless the intervention is involuntary, the groups at highest risk may not make use of the intervention. This is certainly the case for prenatal programs in the USA. Although prenatal care is available for almost all pregnant women, the poorest women in our inner cities and rural areas are underutilizers. Unless the prenatal programs are targeted more specifically to the needs of these women, the universal intervention never reaches them.

The more targeted preventive interventions in the mental health intervention spectrum have been labeled as selective and indicated. The mental health spectrum moves from universal, focusing on large population groups, to selective, focusing on high-risk groups or individual members of such groups, to indicated, focusing on high-risk individuals. As the target population group becomes more specified, there is an increased likelihood that primary care clinicians will be involved in the delivery of the interventions.

Selective preventive interventions for mental disorders are targeted to individuals or a subgroup of the population whose risk of developing mental disorders is significantly higher than average. The risk may be imminent or it may be a lifetime risk. Risk groups may be identified on the basis of biological, psychological or social risk factors that are known to be associated with the onset of a mental disorder. Such risk groups could include all low-birthweight children born at a particular hospital. Such children are at increased risk for a wide range of developmental and emotional problems. Chronically ill patients, such as cancer patients, are another group at risk. Selective interventions are most appropriate if the interventions do not exceed a moderate level of cost and if negative effects are minimal or non-existent.

Indicated preventive interventions for mental disorders are targeted to high-risk individuals who are identified as having minimal but detectable signs or symptoms foreshadowing mental disorder, or biological markers indicating predisposition for mental disorder, but who do not meet diagnostic levels at the current time. This IOM definition is very different from that used by Gordon. He meant it to apply to only asymptomatic patients. However, in application to mental health problems, it seemed reasonable to the IOM Committee to use a broader definition. Many high-risk individuals demonstrate early signs or symptoms of disorder for a considerable time before a full-blown disorder occurs. They are ripe for a preventive intervention that can decrease the symptoms and prevent the onset of a diagnosable disorder. This is an especially important group of high-risk individuals because often they demonstrate as much or more problematic functioning as those with full-blown disorders. Primary care clinicians are highly likely to see such individuals in their practices and may be providing services that they refer to as 'early intervention'. These indicated preventive interventions may be reasonable even if the costs are high and even if the intervention entails some degree of risk.

There are considerable ethical and cultural issues to be addressed when considering selective and indicated preventive interventions. Labeling a group or an individual as being at high risk is even more controversial in regard to mental disorders than it is with physical disorders. Therefore, it is critical to base the interventions on well-validated and specific risk factors and to work with the local community in developing prevention programs.

SELECTING AND USING A THEORETICAL FRAMEWORK

The vast development of risk research over the last decade has provided the base for a new type of prevention research, grounded in empirical evidence rather than merely in good intentions. The concept of risk has changed from a simplistic notion of a static condition or state to a broader phenomenon that may be related to a developmental phase and may be modifiable. Ongoing research is helping to identify what risk factors predispose an individual for general as well as specific mental disorders and what factors may protect against the occurrence of onset of such illnesses. Risk factor research has tended to focus on either biological or psychosocial factors. Biological factors vary by disorder but may include genetic vulnerability, biological markers, co-occurring medical illnesses, history of head injury, birth complications and low birthweight. Psychosocial risk factors may be common to several disorders and include such items as disturbed family environment, maladaptive personality traits, parental mental illness, and traumatic life events such as child maltreatment, death of a spouse, or being the victim of a violent crime or natural disaster. Only recently has attention been focused on the need for research that illuminates the interaction of potentially modifiable biological and psychosocial risk factors.

Risk research is helping to identify which risk factors may play a causal role in a disorder and which ones may merely be correlated with that disorder. Risk factors that are not causal may still be useful in identifying the target population. The preventive intervention should aim to reduce or modify those risk factors that are thought to be the most causal and/or the most modifiable. Focusing on a 'weak link' to reduce risk while strengthening a protective factor may provide the best avenue for positive outcome.

Using the conceptualization of selective and indicated preventive interventions helps one target the focus population, e.g. all children of mothers with major depressive disorder or all recent widows who are reporting mild difficulties with sleeping. As useful as this definitional and targeting framework is, it does not help us clarify what the content of the intervention itself should be.

Risk factor research, on the other hand, can provide the focus for the intervention. Most preventive interventions are psychosocial in nature, even when the main risk factor is thought to be biological. The rationale for this is that modification of the environment can help to ameliorate the effects of a biological condition, such as prematurity and low birthweight. Eventually we may find that the expression of a genetic vulnerability for a particular mental disorder can be modulated by psychosocial interventions so that full-blown illness does not appear.

Selective and indicated preventive interventions often include techniques to:

- Improve parenting and family functioning.
- Enhance child development, including social competence.
- Enhance academic achievement and school behavior.
- Increase skills to resist social influences regarding early substance use.
- Promote social norms against drug use.
- Enhance marital relationships.
- Improve coping skills following divorce or job loss or death of a spouse.
- Enhance the personal development of new mothers.
- Provide social support to caregivers of chronically ill family members.

EVALUATING OUTCOMES

There is considerable evidence that risk factors associated with the initial onset of some mental disorders can be significantly reduced. The IOM reported on 39 such preventive intervention research programs that met rigorous criteria, including a randomized control protocol. It is noteworthy that 29 of these 39 programs were selective or indicated in type. Of the 10 universal programs, five were drug abuse prevention programs targeted to adolescents. Universal preventive interventions require substantial resources because of their scale and are therefore less likely to be undertaken.

Unfortunately, none of these 39 programs documented an actual reduction in the incidence of first onset of mental disorder. Rather, the positive outcomes were related to the reduction of risk factors and the enhancement of protective factors. This does not mean that mental disorders were not prevented, for indeed they might have been. The lack of evidence of a decrease in the incidence of first onset of disorder is related primarily to two factors. First, most research programs are too limited in their length of follow-up; usually this is because of problems in securing long-term research funding. Second, the documentation of mental disorder onset has not been a priority for many researchers. This may be because most prevention researchers, at least in the USA, are psychologists, often community psychologists. An avoidance of a 'medical model' has led to documentation regarding risks, protections, levels of functioning, and sometimes even symptoms, but rarely has it included systematic assessment and diagnosis.

The 39 preventive intervention research programs had demonstrated efficacy, meaning that they all did what they were designed to do within the confines of a research protocol. Of course, the actual interventions usually took place within community settings, such as homes or schools. What none of these programs have yet demonstrated is *effectiveness*. We do not yet know how well they will work when they are put out into the communities without the research protocols in place.

Another critical piece of missing information, especially for those who value the integration of health and mental health in practical ways, was that none of these programs were developed for use in primary care settings. There may be some programs that have been specifically designed for such settings, but we at the IOM were unaware of them. Just because a program is efficacious when developed for delivery in one setting does not necessarily mean that it will be efficacious when delivered elsewhere. Such programs would need to be tested in primary care. Other prevention programs may develop in those settings and eventually be transferred elsewhere in the community. And finally, there may be some treatment interventions that can be adapted for use as indicated preventive interventions in primary care settings.

The IOM Committee recommended that preventive intervention research efforts concentrate primarily on three areas: research on sequential preventive interventions aimed at multiple risks in infancy, early childhood, and elementary school age to prevent onset of multiple behavioral problems and mental disorders; research aimed at major depressive disorders across the life span; and research aimed at alcohol abuse, especially in children and young adolescents. Primary care is a logical setting for these three initiatives.

PROGRAM EXAMPLES

Two program examples highlight the complexity of prevention research and the encouraging outcomes that have been achieved. The first program is the Prenatal/ Early Infancy Project conducted in Elmira, New York, by Dr David Olds (IOM 1994a; Olds et al 1994, 1990, 1988, 1986). This was a selective preventive intervention, targeting a group of women who were pregnant for the first time and had one or more of the following high-risk characteristics that would predispose their infant to health and development problems: young age (less than 19 years), single-parent status, and low socioeconomic status. The study consisted of four different intervention groups who received different degrees of intensity of intervention: group I received screening and referral; group II received free transportation to well child care clinics; group III received a home visit from a nurse for an average of nine visits during pregnancy; and group IV, the full-dose intervention, received nurse home visitation for nine visits during pregnancy and continued visitation until the child was 2 years of age. Outcomes include benefits to both physical and emotional well-being for the child as well as the mother. Mothers who were home-visited during pregnancy reduced the number of cigarettes they smoked, improved their diets, experienced greater informal support, and made better use of community services than did women in the comparison group. There were also fewer preterm deliveries among nurse-visited women who smoked compared with those among their counterparts in the comparison group. After delivery, nurse-visited women at the highest sociodemographic risk had 80% fewer state-verified cases of child maltreatment while the program was in operation. At ages 3 and 4, children born to women who had been visited by the nurses during pregnancy and who were moderate to heavy smokers during pregnancy had higher IQs than counterparts whose mothers had been assigned to the comparison groups. Among the mothers without a high school diploma when registered for the study, 59% of those nurse-visited, compared to 27% of those in comparison groups, had either graduated or enrolled in an education program by 6 months post-partum. Nurse-visited mothers worked 82% longer than their counterparts over the 2 years, and spent considerably less time on public assistance. Nurse-visited poor, unmarried women had one-third fewer subsequent pregnancies than poor unmarried women in the comparison group.

This program is one of the stars of prevention research. It is currently being replicated with another ethnic population in another part of the country, and the first attempt to transfer the program into service settings has now begun in the State of Colorado. It is noteworthy that this is one of the few preventive intervention research programs that has documented effects across two generations.

The second example is of an indicated preventive intervention research program developed by Dr Gregory Clarke and colleagues (1995). The program was not one of the 39 programs in the IOM report, although it was mentioned as a very promising program in development (IOM 1994a). Clarke's work is a hallmark in the continuing progress in prevention research. For the first time there is evidence of prevention of the onset of mental disorder.

Clarke attempted to prevent unipolar depressive disorder in an at-risk sample of high school adolescents. First, all ninth and tenth graders in three high schools ($n = 1652$) were screened for depressive symptoms using a standard screening instrument. Of the 471 students who received high scores, 222 agreed to participate in a structured diagnostic interview. Forty-six of the 222 met criteria for current major depression and/or dysthymia and were referred for treatment. Of the remaining 172 students with high depressive symptomology, 150 agreed to participate in the prevention study and be randomly assigned to a usual care control condition or to a cognitive group intervention. The group intervention consisted of 15 after-school sessions led by specially trained school psychologists and counselors. The sessions focused on helping the students reduce negative cognitions and develop new and more effective coping mechanisms. Follow-up interviews were conducted at 12 months post-intervention. The intervention students had significantly fewer cases of major depression and/or dysthymia than the students in the control group. Total incidence rates were 25.7% for the control group and 14.5% for the intervention group. Although no cost-offset estimates were made in this study, the authors speculate that this relatively low-cost group intervention has the potential of saving costs related to treatment, including psychiatric hospitalization, if full-blown depressive disorders had occurred.

Obviously, there is room for improvement in the potency of the intervention, because 14.5% of the students who received the intervention still had onset of depression. Also, the positive effects for the group that avoided depression may fade, i.e. the onset of depression may be postponed rather than prevented ultimately. Clarke's work, however, is a significant breakthrough in prevention research. Approximately 12–31% of all adolescents have a significant degree of depressive symptomology. Clarke's earlier attempt to provide a universal preventive intervention to an untargeted group of adolescents was not successful. His current work shows us that the intervention is most useful to those at highest risk, and therefore, indicated preventive interventions are warranted.

CONCLUSION

Despite the excitement generated by selective and indicated preventive intervention research programs such as the ones conducted by Olds and Clarke, there are many barriers yet to overcome. As the next step, consideration must be given to how to test such interventions in primary care settings. As the evidence increases regarding the efficacy and effectiveness of prevention programs, decisions will need to be made regarding how best to incorporate them into primary care settings on a routine basis.

REFERENCES

Clarke GN, Hawkins W, Murphy M, Sheeber LB, Lewinsohn PM & Seeley JR (1995) Targeted prevention of unipolar depressive disorder in an at-risk sample of high school adolescents: a randomized trial of a group cognitive intervention. *J Am Acad Child Adolesc Psychiat* **34**(3), 312–21.

Desjarlais R, Eisenberg L, Good B & Kleinman A (1995) *World Mental Health: Problems and Priorities in Low-income Countries*. New York: Oxford University Press.

Gordon R (1983) An operational classification of disease prevention. *Publ Health Rep* **98**, 107–9.

Institute of Medicine (1994a) P Mrazek & R Haggerty (eds) *Reducing Risks for Mental Disorders: Frontiers for Preventive Intervention Research*. Washington, DC: National Academy Press.

Institute of Medicine (1994b) M Donaldson, K Yordy & N Vanselow (eds) *Defining Primary Care: An Interim Report*. Washington, DC: National Academy Press.

National Health & Medical Research Council (1992) B Raphael (ed) *Scope for Prevention in Mental Health*. Canberra: Australian Government Publishing Service.

Olds DL & Kitzman H (1990) Can home visitation improve the health of women and children at environmental risk? *Pediatrics* **86**, 108–16.

Olds DL, Henderson CR & Tatelbaum R (1994) Prevention of intellectual impairment in children of women who smoke cigarettes during pregnancy. *Pediatrics* **93**, 228–33.

Olds DL, Henderson CR, Tatelbaum R et al (1988) Improving the life-course development of socially disadvantaged mothers: a randomized trial of nurse home visitation. *Am J Publ Health* **78**, 1436–44.

Olds DL, Henderson C, Tatelbaum R et al (1986) Preventing child abuse and neglect: a randomized trial of nurse home visitation. *Pediatrics* **78**, 65–78.

Royal College of Psychiatrists (1993) *Prevention in Psychiatry*, Council Report CR 21. London: Royal College of Psychiatrists.

6

Classification of Preventive Interventions

Clemens MH Hosman

Department of Clinical Psychology & Personality, University of Nijmegen, and Department of Health Education, University of Maastricht, The Netherlands

INTRODUCTION

The possible strategies and methods for promoting mental health and preventing mental disorders show a large diversity, as demonstrated by many examples in this book. Mental health promotion and prevention of mental disorders are many-faceted. On the one hand, this large diversity has many advantages. It shows that this field (and this is also my personal experience) has a large creative potential. For those who like challenges and like to work innovatively in the sometimes conflictual interaction between science and practice and between completely different disciplines, this field offers an optimal working area. It shows that after more than 100 years of development, mental health promotion and prevention of mental disorders has evolved into a scientific specialty. The plurality of our work means that we have a large toolbox at our disposal, full of different tools that we could use to fix all kinds of mental health problems. To date mental health promotion and prevention have much to offer.

On the other hand, this plurality is not beyond question. For example, do we know precisely what is in the toolbox of prevention? For several decades new preventive and health-promoting methods and programs have been offered on the market. What do we know about their use, their suitability for solving different kinds of problems? What do we know about their quality and effectiveness? It would be very helpful if we had available a kind of catalogue of all the available tools, their uses and qualities.

This chapter discusses the need and the opportunities for developing a classification of preventive interventions.

Preventing Mental Illness: Mental Health Promotion in Primary Care. Edited by R. Jenkins and T.B. Üstün.
© 1998 John Wiley & Sons Ltd.

CLASSIFICATION SYSTEMS

Classification is a familiar phenomenon in health care, although so far restricted to classification of *diseases* and *disabilities*. The ICD-10, developed by the World Health Organization (WHO 1993), and the CSM-IV, developed by the American Psychiatric Association (APA 1994), are internationally the best-known and most widely used systems to date. In addition to the ICD-10, the WHO developed the ICIDH, an International Classification of Impairments, Disabilities and Handicaps (WHO 1993). The ICIDH classifies the consequences of diseases.

Several decades ago, the WHO became aware that making progress in the field of health care and health research is strongly contingent on international agreement about definitions of diseases and diagnostic criteria. When experts from different countries, research groups, disciplines or schools are using different concepts to describe diseases, it is very hard to collaborate efficiently and compare scientific findings. Such a confusion of tongues is a serious obstacle to progress. The WHO has invested a lot in stimulating international agreement on their classification of diseases, with striking success. In the development of an internationally accepted classification of mental and behavioural disorders, Professor Norman Sartorius has played a crucial role for many years.

The development of these classification systems has demanded a lot of investment over 30 years. To date, this investment has generally been considered extremely worthwhile. The availability of these classification systems and the growing uniformity in diagnosing diseases have given a strong impetus to epidemiological research on the prevalence of mental disorders and the role of risk factors. It has stimulated the development of internationally accepted diagnostic instruments and effective treatments. These benefits are most visible in *curative* care, but not only there. In developing *preventive* measures, we are strongly dependent on the availability of such classification systems and diagnostic measures. At least it has enabled us to define *what* we need to prevent and to measure the effects of preventive interventions in reducing mental or behavioural disorders.

CLASSIFICATION OF CARE

During recent years the question of whether we need, in addition to a classification of diseases, a classification of care, and as part of it, a classification of preventive care, has repeatedly been raised. In the 1970s and 1980s the Regional Office of the WHO for Europe organized a number of studies on the development of mental health services in Europe. These studies have pointed to the need to develop a classification system of mental health services and their activities. Such a system should be able to describe systematically changes and progress in the availability of mental health services in the European countries.

The need for monitoring the availability and quality of health services has been increased by the adoption of the Targets for Health for All by the European

Committee of the WHO in 1984 (WHO 1985). Targets 26–31 are aimed at improving health services, especially in primary health care, with secondary and tertiary services in a supporting role. Target 27 calls for a distribution of primary, secondary and tertiary care resources according to needs in the population. Target 28 stresses that primary health care should provide a wide range of health-promotive and preventive services in addition to curative and rehabilitative services. Also, several other targets call for investment in the systematic development of prevention of mental disorders and the promotion of (mental) health (targets 12, 15 and 16). Also, the quality of care should be assessed and assured (target 31).

In 1987 the European Office invited the WHO Collaborative Centre for Research and Training in Mental Health of the University of Groningen to start an international project on a classification of mental health care. The centre focused their project on the development of an international classification of curative care and rehabilitative activities. The International Classification of Mental Health Care (ICMHC) developed by them after several international consultations and pilots offers a standardized description of modules of available care (de Jong, Giel & Ten Horn 1990). In addition to curative and rehabilitative activities, the classification system was planned to cover preventive interventions as well.

The WHO Regional Office for Europe invited the Research Group on Prevention and Psychopathology of the University of Nijmegen to advise them about the opportunities for a classification system for preventive interventions and to prepare a first proposal for such a system as part of the ICMHC. The consultation report (Hosman 1989) described several complications in applying the framework of the ICMHC consistently to preventive activities. The four main problems were: the existing lack of clarity about the definition of 'prevention' and 'preventive activities'; the different ways that prevention was often organized compared with curative care and rehabilitation; the focus on non-patient groups and social systems as one of the available strategies; and the lack of well-defined aims of the classification system. The consultation report recommended several solutions and offered first drafts for monitoring tools. In 1993 these forms were improved and a definition list was added, and in 1994 a first international consultation on these forms was organized.

Every classification should serve a certain purpose and should do that optimally. The development of any classification system, irrespective of its subject and field of application, should be based on a painstaking analysis of the needs and uses of such a system in the potential user groups. Accordingly, I will address the following questions:

1. Is there a need for an international classification of interventions to prevent mental disorders and promote mental health? Who would be the user groups and what would be their interests?

2. What should be classified and for what purposes? What kind of a system is needed?
3. Is the development of such a classification system feasible?

FEATURES OF CLASSIFICATION SYSTEMS

A classification system could be considered as a system of concepts, that describes very precisely a set of related phenomena and the relevant differentiations within this set, in such a way that the system supports its user in getting an overview of the complete set of phenomena, and is able to differentiate between types of subsets of phenomena. For the users, the classification system should serve optimally well-defined applications. In professional communities like the health system, public administration or the academic community, such classifications should at least have relevance for diagnostic purposes or for decision making on actions to be taken.

As mentioned, the DSM and ICD are already widely accepted classification systems in mental health care. As such, they have an illustrative function in describing features and uses of classification systems. According to the introductory chapters to both systems (WHO, 1993; APA, 1994), a classification of diseases should possess:

- Mutually exclusive categories.
- Reliable and valid descriptions of categories.
- Broad professional support and consensus.
- Neutrality between different theoretical approaches.

According to their purposes, the classification system should:

- Offer an overview of existing disorders.
- Facilitate communication between professionals.
- Be relevant for clinical practice (diagnosis, decision making).
- Promote research on mental disorders.

In addition, the DSM shows that from different perspectives different kinds of classification are possible. For this reason, the DSM is a multiaxial system.

WHY WOULD AN INTERNATIONAL CLASSIFICATION SYSTEM FOR PREVENTION BE NEEDED?

The rationale for the development of an international classification of preventive interventions is plural, independent of the perspective of the potential user. The main arguments in favour of such an investment are:

- Current confusion about the meanings of concepts in prevention.
- Shortage of adequate concepts.
- Need for state-of-the-art descriptions.
- Growing international market for exchanging programs.
- Need for quality control and quality enhancement.
- Facilitating research.
- Public acknowledgement.

Confusion about Meaning of Concepts

First of all, there is a serious problem concerning the meanings of concepts in prevention. During my 25 years' work in this field, the confusion about the meanings of the terms we use has been a recurring problem. The repeated discussions with colleagues or involved outsiders takes a lot of time.

In addition, our field continuously extends its sphere of action. This means involving more and more parties in the community, parties with diverse backgrounds and conceptual frameworks. The more parties are involved, the greater the risk of a confusion of tongues. In our experience, this is not only a problem with involved outsiders (e.g. financiers, policy makers, managers, community leaders, police, school personnel), but with colleagues as well, given the large diversity of professional approaches and disciplines in our field.

Let me give some examples. What some consider to be 'prevention' is classed as 'therapy' by others. Even so, the distinction between prevention and health promotion is far from clear. Frequently the concept of prevention is used strictly to refer to interventions directed as preventing diseases, while health promotion refers to a more positive approach which empowers people to improve their competence and living conditions, irrespective of disease prevention. However, in prevention these positive approaches are frequently applied with the aim of reducing disorders, and the concept of primary prevention is frequently used to refer to interventions aimed at influencing so-called non-specific or common risk factors, like a lack of self-esteem, social competence, problem-solving skills and social support. Common risk factors could play a risk-increasing role in the development of a diversity of disorders and as such, 'non-specific' preventive interventions directed at community groups at risk could offer a powerful strategy for reducing the risk of mental disorders. In this case, non-specific preventive interventions and mental health promotion are overlapping areas. In decreasing mental and behavioural disorders in society, the choice between a disease-specific approach, a non-specific preventive approach or a combination of both is partly a matter of comparing different strategies towards a common goal on a cost–benefit dimension. Others, such as public authorities, sometimes use health promotion as an overarching concept, including prevention (Department of Health, 1994).

Another familiar conceptual problem is the differentiation between primary and secondary prevention. Many authors define secondary prevention as directed at detection of the early symptoms of a developing disease. The symptoms represent signs that the system is starting to fail in coping with a mental, social or physical problem. Some, however, define secondary prevention as all those interventions aimed at influencing risk factors in groups at risk (Hurrelman 1987, p 230). Yet again many others do not consider the presence of a risk factor as a sign of developing disease, but as a condition that increases the risk of developing a disease. In their view, a risk group approach is considered a cost-effective strategy for primary prevention.

These are just some examples of the many confusions and differences of opinion. Other examples could be given of confusion about the meaning of terms like 'risk factors', 'prevention program' and 'implementation', or about labels referring to certain preventive methods and strategies (e.g. health education, consultation, network development, social action). With the increase of international collaboration and the broadening of involved disciplines and types of preventive and health-promoting strategies, we may expect that the need for clearly defined and commonly accepted concepts will also increase.

One could react with: 'Leave it! This turns out to be an endless academic discussion!' Yet, the situation looks really different when, for example, several financing bodies are involved who, for budgetary reasons, ask us to make a clear-cut distinction between disease prevention and mental health promotion. The same goes for negotiations between managers of primary health care, public health services and community mental health centres about agreeing on differentiation of tasks between organizations or between teams within organizations. These situations call for clear-cut definitions of concepts.

Shortage of Adequate Concepts

Agreement on concepts is not the only barrier to progress in the field, there is also a shortage of concepts. We have been confronted with this problem in running overview studies and meta-analyses on the effectiveness of prevention programs. With the current prevention concepts it is frequently difficult to describe precisely and in a standardized way what the differences between prevention programs are (Bosma & Hosman 1990; Hosman & Veltman 1994). This is not only our observation as researchers. In past years my research group had in-depth individual interviews and group interviews with prevention workers and health educators in community mental health centres and public health services. Our aim was to understand the way practitioners are developing new prevention programs and how they deal with the problem of effectiveness. One of our observations was that prevention workers have large problems describing exactly the goals of their interventions and making explicit the many choices they have to make in building up an effective preventive strategy. Even professionals working in the field for 15 years admit that they lack a conceptual framework that describes clearly the range of possible intervention strategies. As long as such a system is missing, we can not expect practitioners to be in a position to make rational choices on optimal strategies. Making rational choices should be considered one of the preconditions of effectiveness.

This problem is even more urgent given the international trend towards multi-component programs. Integral health-promoting school programs are a well-known example. Many experts in our field, including myself, believe that multi-component programs are in most cases more effective than single component programmes. There is a growing consensus that individual interventions, e.g. distributing written information, offering a course, giving individual counselling or the creation of a support system, are not enough individually to produce the intended, ultimate preventive effects. It is therefore extremely important to make deliberate choices about the best combination of interventions. Especially in primary care, where different disciplines each offer their own contributions to mental health promotion and prevention of mental disorders, it is important from the perspective of effectiveness that these contributions are very well attuned to each other. Besides calling for the availability of a decision model on the selection of interventions, this calls for a well-circumscribed classification of available preventive strategies and interventions. From this perspective, program makers, practitioners and researchers are particularly in need of a classification of types of intervention.

Monitoring the State of the Art

Another argument in favour of a classification system is the need for a description of the state of the art in mental health promotion and prevention. This calls for reliable monitoring instruments. This need is comparable with the original intentions for the DSM and ICD to have a tool for collecting statistical information about the state of psychiatric morbidity in a country or health district.

When setting targets for the implementation of mental health promotion and prevention of disorders, e.g. in the 'Health for All' strategy of the WHO and in national health policies, we need tools to describe the state of the art and the progress made. Policy makers, public authorities and professional organizations are especially in need of such a classification system.

Consider, for example, global targets formulated in the Health of the Nation's key area handbook on mental illness, published in the UK (Department of Health, 1994). The chapter on mental health promotion starts with a global target like 'All National Health Service managers to develop good practice to improve mental health in the National Health Service'. Suppose that in 5 or 8 years from now the Ministry of Health wants to assess how much progress has been made. A valid answer cannot be given without a clear-cut operational definition of what is meant by 'good practice to improve mental health'. To assess services and activities against this criterion, we need a classification of types of mental health promotion, a monitoring tool to assess their presence, and standards for what is considered 'good practice'.

Growing Market for Exchanging Programs

The next argument is the growing national and international market for exchanging programs. The last 10–15 years have witnessed a boom in the development of new programs in the field of health promotion and prevention. In The Netherlands during the last 10 years, several hundred programs have been developed by prevention workers, health educators and caregivers. The more countries and the more districts become active in this field, the more new programs will be developed and offered on the market.

On the one hand you could say 'the more, the better', but this also creates a serious problem. Given the limited budget and manpower for prevention, one does not need much imagination to realize that we are using scarce resources in a very inefficient way. We have experience both in our own countries and internationally, that again and again professionals are independently developing the same kinds of programs, unaware of similar programs already being developed elsewhere.

A further observation is that the most effective programs in our field are those with a long history of scientific work, repeated trials and evaluation (Price et al 1988; Bosma and Hosman 1990). We have to accept that development of an effective prevention program requires a lot of investment over a long period, sometimes 10 years or more.

To increase the effectiveness of preventive interventions and the efficient use of resources, the exchange of programs with proven effectiveness should be promoted strongly between health districts, both nationally and internationally. In Europe a start has been made with the nationwide and worldwide sharing of programs, and in coming years these transfers will be intensified. Several organizations, like the WHO in Copenhagen and Geneva, support such international exchanges on a regular basis. In The Netherlands we are currently implementing several programs originally developed and tested in the USA, UK and Norway.* In Finland a successful training program for the unemployed will be implemented, originally developed by Price and his co-workers at the Michigan Prevention Research Centre. This program has proved to be effective in decreasing episodes of depression in groups at high risk (Price, van Ryn & Vinokur 1992). To stimulate this exchange, some national clearing-houses have created a computer system that offers information on who is running what kind of prevention programs.

---

* Examples are: Prevention of Bullying Program (Olweus, Norway); Coping with Depression Course (Lewinsohn, USA); PREP: Partner Relationship Enhancement Program (Markham, USA).

If we agree that exchange of available programs is urgently needed, we also need instruments for a standardized description of programs and interventions available on the growing national and international market. Suppose one wished to start in one's own primary care practice a program to prevent child abuse. Probably one would like information on two levels: first, answers to questions about what kind of programs are available, what their aims and target groups are, and which intervention methods and strategies have been used? Which of the available programs fits best into the local situation? These are all questions about the content of programs. Secondly, one would like information on quality: do programs meet minimal professional standards? Are interventions based on scientific knowledge about risk factors? These questions concern the quality of the program. Valid comparison of both content and quality of programs requires a kind of standardized international classification.

Quality Control and Quality Enhancement

This brings us to the next argument: quality control and quality enhancement. Classification of preventive interventions along a quality dimension has become more and more important. The recent increase in effect studies in our field is just one sign. Several parties are showing interest in classification of prevention along quality lines.

In both the UK and The Netherlands the professional organizations of health educators and prevention workers are now in the process of defining quality standards of practice. It is in their interests as professional groups to guarantee the quality of work delivered by their members. This fits in with similar developments among general practitioners and psychotherapists.

Different tools are used to improve the quality of preventive interventions, e.g. the implementation of protocols, audit schemes to assess the quality of preventive services, and certification of prevention programs. The idea of certification is that preventive programs could be accredited by a professional organization if an assessment confirms that the program meets certain quality standards. In the future this could be a tool to help practitioners in primary care, financing bodies or interest groups to discriminate easily between programs available on the market with different levels of quality. Health assurance companies in our country are now starting to ask for such classifications before deciding upon financing implementation.

Facilitating Research

Another reason why a classification is needed is for prevention research. For example, some years ago we did a study on the effectiveness of mental health promotion and prevention. The Netherlands government asked us to summarize what was known about the success of interventions to influence determinants of mental health. A main obstacle from the beginning was the difficulty of tracing all the relevant research, looking for publications in all kinds of computerized databases. We found that the terminology used to store and retrieve the literature in our field is poorly developed and shows a tremendous lack of uniformity. As a result, the risk of missing relevant studies is large.

Another serious problem is the difficulty of comparing studies and their results. Such comparisons become very important if we heed answers to questions about which of several preventive strategies yields the best perspective on effectiveness or which of several programs is the most cost-effective, or why two interventions with the same aims differ in effectiveness. Such knowledge is extremely important in developing a theory on effective prevention. To do this we need to describe interventions in a more or less standardized way, otherwise we cannot compare them.

To date this is even more urgent, given the growth in international research networks. An example is the European Network on Prevention of Depression, established by the European WHO Task Force on Mental Health Promotion and Prevention. Under the direction of Professor Greg Wilkinson and Dr Chris Dorwick of the University of Liverpool, six European countries, the UK, Ireland, The Netherlands, Norway, Finland and Spain, have started to collaborate on a Europe-wide epidemiological study and on the implementation of a small selection of programs to prevent depression. A comparative evaluation study will start on the effects of the different programs in each country, supported by a European Committee grant. Comparison of results, both between countries and between different programs, calls for a standardized and elaborate framework for describing the implemented programs and their organizational infrastructure.

I am convinced that the development of a classification system of health-promoting and preventive interventions will give a tremendous boost to discussions among experts in our field on what exactly we have to offer, and on the mechanisms crucial to the creation of preventive effects. In addition, the classification system will lead to a more efficient use of our resources for research.

Public Acknowledgement of Mental Health Promotion and Prevention

Classification could also help us to increase public knowledge about mental health promotion and prevention of mental disorders. I think it is common experience for many years that our specialty does not have a strong position within the health care system and suffers from low status. As a result, our resources are small and our position remains marginal. This is what Professor Larry Green, one of the most prominent experts in health education, once described as the 'Health education circle of poverty'. Poorly defined targets and a poorly developed conceptual system will lead to poorly designed interventions and poorly designed evaluation research, which lowers the potential for demonstrating preventive effects, which in turn keeps our status and much-needed financial resources low.

There are several possibilities for breaking through this vicious circle. Improving the research base of our field and describing sound empirical evidence for successful prevention in mental health is one strategy, and an important one. Several significant general overviews are currently available (Price et al 1988; Bosma & Hosman 1990; Hosman & Veltman 1994, Hosman 1995). The recent report of the Institute of Medicine, *Reducing Risks for Mental Disorders*, gives a particularly impressive and realistic overview of what has been achieved so far (Mrazek & Haggerty 1994). In addition, several recent overviews have been published on the effectiveness of mental health promotion and prevention in specific problem areas and settings, such as early childhood intervention and juvenile delinquency (Zigler, Tausig & Black 1992), prevention of child abuse and neglect (Olsen & Widom 1993), mental health promotion in schools (Bosma & Hosman 1991), depression (Muñoz 1993), suicide (Jenkins et al 1994), relapse prevention (Wilson 1992), material enrichment and families in transition (Guerney 1988; Bond & Wagner 1988), the chronically ill and self-help (Mainzer et al 1994).

Another strategy to improve knowledge about our field is to be clearer about what we have to offer in terms of interventions. My experience has been that many outsiders consider our field vague, elusive and scattered. It is hard for them to form an idea of what tools we use to promote mental health and reduce the risk of mental disorders. When those outsiders control the health system or the financial resources, or when we need their support in implementing prevention programs in schools or work places, their views on the vagueness and woolliness of our field works to our disadvantage. Classification of our interventions is one strategy for clarifying what our products are and what their quality is, and for improving our image.

Problems in getting financial support are exacerbated by struggles between potential financiers about who is in charge of delivering the budget for what preventive interventions. Disagreement about who should pay for what could seriously delay the development and implementation of preventive programs. Experience in The Netherlands suggests that if we could develop a classification of preventive interventions, we would have a much better basis for negotiating whose task it is to implement certain interventions and who is in charge of supplying the budget.

Given these considerations, I conclude that the time is ripe for the development of a classification system. In the field of mental health promotion and prevention of mental disorders there is a great need for a framework of clear concepts, an overview of what we have to offer, and a need for monitoring tools to describe the state of the art and the progress made. Secondly, outlining the arguments shows that many different parties are involved with different interests and needs related to a classification system, such as primary health care professionals, mental health professionals, prevention and health education specialists, policy and public authorities, financiers, community interest groups and researchers.

DIMENSIONS IN CLASSIFICATION OF PREVENTIVE INTERVENTIONS

Given the diversity of needs in respect to classification, the next questions are: *what* needs to be classified and from which perspective? What *kind* of classification system is needed? Is there a need for more than one classification system?

Taking into account the diversity of needs for standardized information, a differentiation should first be made between three levels of measurements:

1. *Interventions* or *programs*.
2. *Organizations* or *organizational units*, offering preventive interventions or mental health promotion.
3. *Geographical areas* (districts or countries), and their activity level in the field of mental health promotion and prevention of mental disorders.

At all these levels mental health promotion and prevention could be described from two different perspectives:

1. A *descriptive* perspective (content). What is the content of a program? What kind of preventive interventions and in what degree?
2. A *qualitative* perspective, classifying interventions, organizations or areas into quality categories, based on assessment of the presence of selected quality criteria.

An open question is still the way the description of available 'resources' should be covered in this framework, and if it needs a place in a classification system at all. The concept of 'resources' refers to the availability of manpower, budgets, training facilities, health policies, and research support. Resources are an important precondition for the availability of preventive services and their quality. For health care managers and public authorities the provision of resources is a powerful instrument for improving both the volume and quality of preventive services; for practitioners the availability of resources is a matter of continuous concern. From this perspective, a standardized assessment of available resources in organizations and areas is of great importance. An option would be to include 'resources' in the descriptive dimension and the quality dimension. However, the mix would decrease the clarity of the framework. For the present, resources will be given their own place. This results in a provisional framework for standardized description and classification consisting of nine potential fields, and we may conclude that the classification system should be multiaxial.

	Programme	Organization	Area
Description			
Quality			
Resources			

FIGURE 6.1 Conceptual framework for a classification system of preventive interventions and mental health promotion

PROGRESS MADE

Progress in making such a classification and developing internationally accepted classification systems will be a difficult and lengthy enterprise. The proposed framework is just a first step towards a classification system. So far, we have defined a need for standardized information in each of the nine fields, describing them or allowing comparisons to be made between different programs, organizations or areas. Based on some preliminary work and the reaction of a small international group of advisors, we have started to formulate items for the four blocks in the upper left of Figure 6.1. Examples of items are given in Figure 6.2. A start has also been made in defining all the relevant concepts and developing indicators or monitoring tools.

Preliminary exercises have already raised many questions and problems, such as:

- How should we differentiate exactly between prevention and curative care?
- Is it desirable to develop one classification system for both mental health promotion and prevention of mental disorders, or should we restrict ourselves to preventive interventions directed at specific disorders, as in the DSM-IV?
- Is it possible to include mental health promoting interventions that are not formulated in terms of specific, transferable programs, but consist of all kinds of activities to support and empower communities in coping with mental health problems among their population?
- Preventive interventions and mental health promotion activities are offered by a large variety of organizations in society, and the type of organization responsible differs from country to country. Should a classification system offer the possibility of covering them all, or should it restrict itself to the interventions and programs offered by health care services?

On the other hand, we see in our field several promising steps supporting the development of classification systems and international agreement.

The WHO in Geneva has developed guidelines for primary prevention, summarizing a large range of possible interventions to prevent a selection of mental, neurological and psychosocial disorders. These guidelines are based on

	Programme	Organization
Description	Targets Target groups Intervention strategy • Selected risk factors • System level • Timing • Methods • Dosage and duration	Disciplines Invested hours/budget Programmes • Type • Amount • Diversity Policy plan Position on organization Interagency collaboration
Quality	Stage of development Preconditions for effectiveness, e.g. • Clear goals • Multi-method • Multi-system • Long-term • Repeated evaluation Proven effects Cost/benefit Side effects	Trained personnel Monitoring quality Needs assessment in community Evaluation research Ethical standards Client participation Resources development

FIGURE 6.2   Examples of items in four classification fields

agreement between international groups of experts. The WHO Collaboration Centre for Health Education and Health Promotion in Utrecht (The Netherlands) has developed a tool to describe systematically health education and prevention programs and their level of effectiveness (conditions). This instrument has also been tested by a large group of experts in Europe (Veen, 1995). In addition, our Nijmegen Research Group on Prevention and Psychopathology made an overview of studies (Hosman & Veltman 1995). A list of quality standards for health education and prevention programs has been developed by both the British and Dutch Societies for Health Education and Health Promotion. Finally, significant contributions are included in the report *Reducing Risks on Mental Disorders* of the American Institute of Medicine described in Chapters 4 and 5 of this book by Rick Price and Patricia Mrazek. Especially relevant are the medical health intervention spectrum, the framework for examining preventive interventions, and their classification scheme to describe the quality of evidence available from prevention programs. Given this progress, I consider the development of an international classification system as a feasible objective, irrespective of the many large problems that have to be solved during the developmental process.

CONCLUSIONS

The development of international classification systems for a standard description of diseases taught us that the development of such systems requires long-term international investment, but also that such an investment produces many benefits. The same will be true for the development of an international classification system to describe preventive interventions. We can expect that many international discussions are needed and that many drafts and versions will succeed each other. In this chapter I have stressed the need for the development of such a classification system from different perspectives, such as the need to improve our conceptual framework, national and international exchange of programs, quality control, facilitation of research and public acknowledgement of mental health promotion and prevention of mental disorders. I have presented some first thoughts about the framework needed for such a classification system. An international core group of experts should be created who are willing to invest in the development of this classification system, consisting of experts from different backgrounds and theoretical schools. Drafts should be tested in multi-site field trials. Finally, I would like to stress that such an endeavour should not be made solely by experts in the field of mental health. In the field of health education and health promotion outside mental health, many of the same questions have been raised and expertise is developed over the years that could be very supportive to our field of mental health promotion and prevention of mental disorders.

REFERENCES

APA (American Psychiatric Association) (1994) *Diagnostic and Statistical Manual of Mental Disorders, 4th edn, DSM-IV.* Washington: American Psychiatric Association.
Bond LA & Wagner BM (eds) (1988) *Families in Transition: Primary Prevention Programs that Work.* Newbury Park, CA: Sage.
Bosma MWM & Hosman CMH (1990) *Preventie op waarde geschat* (Effectiveness of Prevention). Nijmegen: Bêta.
Bosma MWM & Hosman CMH (1991) Programmes for competence enhancement. In MWM Bosma (ed) *Mental Health Promotion and Prevention in Schools.* Utrecht: Dutch Centre for Health Education and Health Promotion.
Department of Health (1994) *The Health of the Nation. Key Area Handbook, Mental Illness.* London: HMSO.
Guerney BG (1988) Family relationship enhancement: a skill training approach. In LA Bond & BM Wagner (eds) *Families in Transition: Primary Prevention Programs that Work.* Newbury Park, CA: Sage.

Hosman CMH (1995) Effectiveness and effect management in mental health promotion and prevention. In D Trent & C Reed (eds) *Mental Health Promotion*. Aldershot: Avebury.

Hosman CMH (1989) *The International Classification of Preventive Activities in Mental Health Care. A WHO Consultative Report*. Nijmegen: Department of Clinical Psychology and Personality, University of Nijmegen.

Hosman CMH & Veltman JE (1994) *Prevention in Mental Health: A Review of the Effectiveness of Health Education and Health Promotion*. Utrecht: Dutch Centre for Health Education and Health Promotion/International Union for Health Promotion and Education.

Hosman CMH & Veltman JE (1995) *Programmaontwikkeling en effectmanagement* (Programme Development and Effect Management). Nijmegen: Research Group on Prevention and Psychopathology, University of Nijmegen.

Hurrelman K (1987) The limits and potential of social intervention in adolescents. In K Hurrelman, F Kaufman & F Lösel (eds) *Social Intervention*. Berlin: Walter de Gruyter.

Jenkins R, Griffiths S, Wylie T, Houston K, Morgan G, Tylee A (eds) (1994) *The Prevention of Suicide*. London: HMSO.

de Jong A, Giel R & Ten Horn GHMM (1990) *The WHO International Classification of Mental Health Care*. Groningen: University of Groningen/WHO.

Mainzer DEH, Hosman CMH, van Lankveld WGJM & Cuijpers WJMJ (1994) *Waarde en effectiviteit van lotgenotencontact bij somatisch chronisch zieken* (Value and Effectiveness of Mutual Support Between the Chronically Somatic Patients). Zoetermeer: Nationale Commissie Chronisch Zieken.

Muñoz RF (1993) The prevention of depression: current research and practice. *Appl Prev Psychol* 2, 21–33.

Mrazek, P & Haggerty R (eds) (1994) *Reducing Risks for Mental Disorders: Frontiers for Preventive Intervention Research*. Washington DC: National Academy Press.

Olsen JL & Widom CS (1993) Prevention of child abuse and neglect. *Appl Prev Psychol* 2, 217–29.

Price RH, Cowen EL, Lorion RP & Ramos-McKay J (eds) (1988) *Fourteen Ounces of Prevention: a Casebook for Practitioners*. Washington: American Psychological Association.

Price RH, van Ryn M & Vinokur AD (1992) Impact of a preventive job search intervention on the likelihood of depression among the unemployed. *J Health Soc Behav* 33, 158–67.

Veen, CA (1995) *Evaluation of the IUHPE-Project—the Effectiveness of Health Promotion and Health Education*. Utrecht: International Union for Health Promotion and Education.

Wilson PH (1992) *Principles and Practice of Relapse Prevention*. New York: Guilford.

WHO (World Health Organization). *The IDC-10 Classification of Mental and Behavioral Disorders. Clinical Descriptions and Guidelines*. Geneva: WHO.

WHO (World Health Organization). *Targets for Health for All*. Copenhagen: WHO.

WHO (World Health Organization (1993). *International Classification of Impairments, Disabilities and Handicaps*, 2nd edn. Geneva: WHO.

Zigler E, Taussig C & Black K (1992) Early childhood intervention: a promising preventative for juvenile delinquency. *Am Psychol* 47, 997–1006.

7

Universal Strategies for the Prevention of Mental Illness and the Promotion of Mental Health

Norman Sartorius

Department of Psychiatry, University of Geneva, Switzerland

THE DISTINCTION BETWEEN PREVENTION AND PROMOTION

Health can be defined as a state of balance which individuals establish within themselves and with their environment. Defined in this sense, health can be pursued or measured even if impairment or disease are present. This definition is less demanding than the definition included in the World Health Organization's constitution ('Health is not merely the absence of disease but a state of physical, social and mental well-being'). A state of balance as defined above may be easier to establish in the absence of disease: the presence of an impairment or disease, however, is not an absolute barrier to being in a state of good health.

Activities which can improve health include the prevention of disease, impairment and disability, the treatment of diseases and the promotion of health. Promotion of health should not be equated with the prevention of disease or with its treatment: it is an operation by which we change the place which health has on the scale of values of individuals, families or societies. Once we have lifted that value, it is likely that people will want to do something to improve their health because it is precious for them.

It is perfectly possible to think of a situation in which an illness is completely prevented while health has a low place on people's scale of values: this could be done by force without people wanting it to be done. Conversely, it is possible to imagine a situation in which people who value their health highly cannot (e.g. for political reasons) do much to prevent the occurrence of disease. The distinction between prevention and promotion is important because it is clear that the methods of health promotion are different from those which we use to prevent or treat

Preventing Mental Illness: Mental Health Promotion in Primary Care. Edited by R. Jenkins and T.B. Üstün.
© 1998 John Wiley & Sons Ltd.

mental illness, and from methods which are used to rehabilitate people who have been disabled by mental illness.

The English language conveniently has three terms which could be used to describe abnormalities affecting health—the terms 'disease', 'illness' and 'sickness'. *Disease* usually refers to the medical substrate, the tissue damage; *illness* to the feeling of being ill; and *sickness* to the societal recognition that a morbid process, a disease, produces a need for protection by society, gives a right to be excused from work or invokes other privileges usually covered by the word 'sickness benefit'. Measures which we undertake to prevent disease will, to a certain extent, differ from those undertaken to deal with illness and those necessary to prevent sickness, although there is an overlap between them. To prevent disease we have to think primarily of dealing with the cause of the disease or with the factors that affect its occurrence. To prevent illness we have to think of ways which will allow us to change the way in which people think about their health and about themselves, about their functioning and about their place in society; tools which can help us in this respect are, for example, those of education. Through education—in a broad sense—we have now managed to convince people that being bald is not worth feeling ill about and that being obese is: until recently in many cultures obesity meant prosperity and baldness old age and weakness. Tools for the prevention of sickness should also be sought in education (and in the culture in which the individual lives), although for sickness legal and administrative measures are of great importance.*

Many preventive measures deal equally with the prevention of illness, disease and sickness; examples of differences that exist between the three aspects of health given above serve only to remind us of the need to define goals of prevention more precisely.

TYPES OF PREVENTION

Another set of distinctions which have to be made are those between primary, secondary, tertiary and quartic prevention. These terms find their correlates in the stages of the process of disablement, as depicted in Figure 7.1.

'*Impairment*' refers to the damage of tissues or derangement of elementary physiological processes subsequent to and due to the presence of a disease; '*disability*', in the proposals made by the World Health Organization, refers to the poor performance in social roles due to the presence of an impairment; and

---

* The discussion about the definition of blindness, for example in the United States of America, was heavily influenced by economic considerations: the decision to take vision of 6/20 or less rather than 7/20 as the limit for blindness was made in cognizance of the fact that by defining that blindness as 6/20 meant that considerably fewer people would receive a full blindness pension than would have been the case had 7/20 been taken as a limit; a decision of a committee meant that several million people suddenly left the category of total blindness although their eyesight did not change.

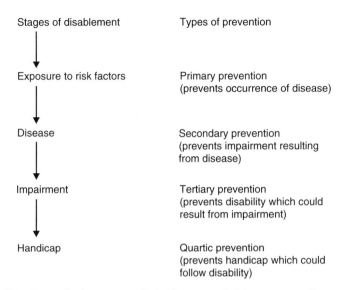

Stages of disablement　　　　Types of prevention

Exposure to risk factors　　　Primary prevention
　　　　　　　　　　　　　　　(prevents occurrence of disease)

Disease　　　　　　　　　　　Secondary prevention
　　　　　　　　　　　　　　　(prevents impairment resulting
　　　　　　　　　　　　　　　from disease)

Impairment　　　　　　　　　Tertiary prevention
　　　　　　　　　　　　　　　(prevents disability which could
　　　　　　　　　　　　　　　result from impairment)

Handicap　　　　　　　　　　Quartic prevention
　　　　　　　　　　　　　　　(prevents handicap which could
　　　　　　　　　　　　　　　follow disability)

FIGURE 7.1　Stages in the process of disablement and different types of prevention

'*handicap*' is used to describe the disadvantage which an individual experiences because of his/her disability (e.g. loss of job).

Primary and quartic prevention have relatively little to do with the individual: the measures which are effective are usually directed at the population, e.g. through legal or educational interventions. Measures of secondary prevention are usually medical and measures of tertiary prevention are a mixture of social and medical engineering. The latter area has experienced spectacular progress with respect to some form of impairment, due to the equally spectacular development of technology of communication and of surgical interventions. Progress in the areas of primary and quartic prevention has been much less pronounced and for some types of impairment could at best be described as having been sporadic.

STRUCTURES IN WHICH HEALTH ACTION OCCURS

The three major actors in the field of prevention and treatment of disease and the promotion of health are governments, the people and the health professions. The professionals, the government and the community are in touch with one another all the time and in their contact assume fairly clearly defined roles. The governments set the limits of the professionals' field of action, often against considerable resistance by the professionals; the professionals, on the other hand, use their knowledge to channel actions of the government into scientifically justifiable activities. In their relationship with the community, the professionals set desirable models of behaviour and act as agents of their own doctrine. Here again, the relationship is reciprocal—the community also has its own doctrines of health and conveys those doctrines to the professionals, either by stating their views or by action (e.g. by rejecting health measures which are in disharmony with the prevailing cultural norms in the community). The relationship between the community and governments is also reciprocal—governments have power and bring their instructions to the community; the community, however, in most countries eventually imposes its views on the government; at the same time the government and the community also act as transmitters of needs to one another. If it happens, and this is rare, that somebody who proposes reforms succeeds in influencing how these roles are played, reforms can succeed: in most other circumstances progress is slower, much more difficult to foretell and much less certain.

AREAS OF PRIORITY ACTION

The three areas of action which could help most to prevent mental illness and promote mental health are legislation, education and action within health services.

Legislation

There are three goals for legislative action that we should consider as being of priority. The first of these is to give mental health the status of a human right in legislation. A revolutionary resolution was recently passed by the United Nations (UN Resolution 119): it declares (a) that mentally ill people have rights and that they should be protected from abuse; and (b) that the treatment of a mental illness is a human right. There is no other group of illnesses which is recognized as being so severe that providing treatment for it must become part of the process of ensuring rights of individuals. The Resolution has not yet become sufficiently widely known and its translation into laws is slow. The first goal for our work in the field of legislation should therefore be to speed up this translation and to think of ways in which we can monitor the application of relevant legal prescriptions.

The second goal for legislative action is to make countries recognize legally that mental illness is a serious illness (and not capricious behaviour) and that therefore health care provisions must help those who suffer from them. In many countries neither mental health nor mental illness are yet given specific attention; prejudice that prevails against mental illness is reflected in laws and administrative provisions.

The third area in which legislative action is necessary is that of the rehabilitation of the mentally ill and impaired. The rehabilitation of those with physical impairments has over the past few decades made spectacular progress: the rehabilitation of the mentally disabled is not an area of priority and progress has been much slower. Legislation could help greatly to facilitate rehabilitation of the mentally ill and make the prevention of handicap possible.

Education

There are numerous activities in the educational sector which could be listed as being of particular importance for the prevention of mental disorders and the promotion of mental health. Three types deserve priority for the simple reason that they are likely to have a high positive yield and yet do not at present receive attention. The first of these is the development of school mental health programs. A vast majority of the world's citizens will spend some time in schools where they could be told facts about mental health and its protection and educated in how they could prevent the occurrence of mental illness in themselves and in their families. Instead of overloading their time with facts about kings and wars, children could be taught about ways of spending leisure time, ways of understanding themselves and others, being tolerant, and living with the disabled or with an impairment.

The second set of educational activities which should have priority is to add knowledge and skills about the prevention of mental disorders to the curricula of training for all health personnel.

The third area of action should be the education of those in other sectors—e.g. social welfare, labour—about possibilities of primary prevention of mental disorders within their area of activity. A prerequisite for success in this field will be the translation of our knowledge into easily understandable and relevant guidelines—a task in which mental health workers usually have little experience and interest.

Action within the Health Service

In this area, I would select three priorities. The first is perhaps the most important: it is to deal with 'burn-out' in health personnel. Burn-out is a disease that has struck health services like an epidemic. Health staff, worldwide, lose their taste for their jobs, become apathetic and dissatisfied, and perform poorly. They are moving out of primary health care, complaining that the recognition of their effort is non-existent, that their sources of gratification are minimal, and that their ideals are betrayed. Performing medicine is experienced as a dehumanized task costing more but giving little satisfaction to the patient, staff and communities. The numbers of health care personnel are vast and the prevention of 'burn-out' would be well worth the investment, not only to render the lives of many more enjoyable and productive but also to avoid burn-out's nefarious effects on the performance of preventive and health-promoting activities.

The second task in the area of health care is the redistribution of funds between treatment tasks, prevention and promotion. Since the Second World War most European countries have significantly reduced funds given for prevention. Having reached 15% or more of health budgets 50 years ago, preventive activities in most European countries today receive a very small part of health budgets. Organization of curative services and provision of care for sick and disabled people are noble tasks, but they must not oust prevention.

The third task in the area of health care should be a managerial change: we should adopt the attitude of democratic centralism in preventive measures. In a number of countries now decentralization has led to a situation in which it is almost impossible to introduce a measure without endless negotiation among the decentralized units about what should or should not be done. The *autonomias* of Spain, the *Länder* in Germany or the *Cantons* of Switzerland will not easily accept preventive tasks suggested by the centre: it may take years to introduce a measure (even a very effective one) in the whole country. Legislative and administrative procedures should be put in place to ensure that useful measures can be introduced everywhere and rapidly for the good of the population.

While it makes sense to argue for central steering of the introduction of preventive measures through the health sector, the flexibility of a decentralized model needs to be given to the agents of welfare. Welfare agencies equipped with capacity and authority can do much to prevent mental disorders: acting in a decentralized framework its agents could concentrate on the direct and concrete support of the family and help in the empowerment of the impaired.

Creating New Alliances

But few of the above suggestions can lead to success if mental health programs do not create new alliances. These should be forged with sectors which have traditionally declined to collaborate with the health sector, convincing them that it is in the interests of all to change this attitude. Labour, planning, the interior are ministries and sectors with money, power and an impatience to achieve; ways in which alliances between mental health programs and those sectors can be established must vary from country to country: no model will universally apply.

A second set of alliances should be established with professional non-governmental organizations. Non-governmental organizations (e.g. the professional associations) are already playing a major role in service organization in many countries: enticing them to become active in the field of prevention may be difficult but should be possible.

A third set of alliances should be established with those countries which are currently in a similar developmental stage. These can help by sharing information and experience, by exerting external pressure stemming from successful examples, and by providing the feeling that one is not alone—a feeling that is of such importance when programs are initiated.

If we manage to implement the above—or even only a part of the above—we will not only be able to confirm the WHO estimate that some 50% of mental disorders are preventable, but may be also able to convince those who matter that the mind and mental function are precious and that no effort should be spared to protect the mind and prevent mental disease that can otherwise have terrible consequences for individuals and societies.

Application of Health Care and Prevention in Primary Care

8

The Primary Care Setting—
Relevance, Advantages, Challenges

T Bedirhan Üstün

Division of Mental Health, World Health Organization, Switzerland

The primary care setting has great relevance for implementing mental health services and prevention and promotion activities. Primary care is comprehensive and continuous: patients are seen from birth to death through regular visits. Primary care physicians bear responsibility for the totality of health care. Preventing illness and promoting health requires a broader perspective and integration of various approaches. Specialist services, which deal with one area in more depth, are disease-orientated, inevitably leading to fragmentation. Primary care services, however, by definition have to be integrative and to co-ordinate different services including protection, promotion, prevention, curative services and rehabilitation. Primary care workers are closer to the milieu of their patients and therefore better positioned to appreciate the social and environmental aspects of illness. The primary care setting is, therefore, the ideal place to begin prevention and promotion activities.

Promotion of mental health and prevention of mental illness in primary care, however, are unfortunately neglected in many parts of the world. The aim of this chapter is to provide an overview indicating the relevance, advantages and challenges of the primary care setting for prevention and promotion in the field of mental health.

DEFINITION OF MENTAL HEALTH: WHAT ARE WE PROMOTING?

While we all speak of 'mental health', there is no common basic definition agreed upon by everybody as to what mental health is and what it is not. The main thrust of the WHO's definition may be used:

Preventing Mental Illness: Mental Health Promotion in Primary Care. Edited by R. Jenkins and T.B. Üstün.
Published 1998 John Wiley & Sons Ltd.

Mental health is not simply the absence of mental disorders and the absence of mental disablement (i.e. impairments, disabilities and handicaps) but it is also the mental and social well-being of the individual.

In this definition of mental health we need to operationalize the concept of *mental well-being*. First, it implies *the capacity to live, function and enjoy*. This is similar to the definition of mental health by Freud as 'leben und arbeiten', that is, to live and to work (Erikson 1950). A second dimension is *the optimum development of mental abilities*: this dimension covers the developmental aspects of brain and personality functions such as memory, learning, judgement and so on. Without proper development of these functions people may not be able to exercise a mentally healthy life. A third dimension covers the *subjective feeling of well-being* (which is often referred to as 'quality of life'), which also entails personal satisfaction with one's self. Another dimension of mental well-being is *the interaction and equilibrium between the individual and the environment*. While a person may qualify for all of the above—i.e. full capacity to function, full development of his/her potential, and feeling content with his/her person—he/she may be hindered or restricted by his/her environment in exercising his/her abilities.

This attempt to define mental health has a comprehensive approach and bio-psychosocial implications. It has important consequences concerning mental health promotion, such as broadening the base of mental health initiatives and implementing programs in primary care settings. Such an approach will enable the extension of prevention and promotion programs in schools, workplaces or in the community. This definition is concerned with 'positive' mental health, quite unlike the euphemism that mental health stands for mental disease control activities (cf. Orley, Chapter 44, this volume). Positive mental health is not confined to mental disorders. It encompasses a great variety of life skills, such as parenthood preparation, child-rearing guidance, positive behaviour development or sex education.

PREVENTION OF MENTAL ILLNESS: IS IT POSSIBLE?

Prevention activities for mental illness benefit from the paradigms of general medicine, which has long recognized the importance of prevention and applied these successfully when dealing with cancer, respiratory diseases or heart diseases, for example. For these disorders we have identified risk factors, such as smoking, diet, lack of exercise, and several intervention programs have been developed. In the field of mental health we are trying to replicate the same model. The ideological approach to prevention in mental health is also changing. For instance, two centuries ago alcohol was seen as conducive to social as well as personal health and it was regularly used in rituals of conviviality. By the end of the nineteenth century, prevention of drinking activities began. Today the same approach is valid for tobacco. Prevention strategies for mental and substance use disorders, such as depression, anxiety or alcohol use disorders, are being developed to reduce the incidence and risks, using various methods for health promotion, early identification and early intervention with risk groups. These strategies have been shown to be more effective than dealing with the consequent disorders once they have been developed.

PRIMARY CARE: IS IT A PHILOSOPHY OR A PRACTICE?

'Primary care' or 'primary health care' are used interchangeably. Primary health care (PHC) reflects both a 'level of care' and an 'approach', as defined in Alma-Ata by the Member States of the World Health Organization as the basic mechanism to attain health for all (WHO 1978). As a level of care, PHC is the first and basic level of health care and is usually understood as the point of entry into the medical services. As an approach or philosophy it reflects universally accessible health services, that are comprehensive, intersectoral, integrated and built on appropriate technology and community participation.

PRIMARY CARE: IS IT MEDICAL OR HEALTH CARE?

While we may need a differentiation between the terms indicating the philosophy and the practice, it is more important to avoid the basic misequation of health with medicine. Indeed, there is a fundamental difference between medical care and health care. Health is a larger concept than medicine and covers a greater universe, encompassing not only medicine but also other social, cultural and environmental factors. This conceptualization is important because primary care has to be integrated and comprehensive: thus prevention of illness and promotion of health could and should be made an integral part of primary care.

THE PRIMARY CARE SETTING: MEETING THE NEED FOR MENTAL DISORDERS?

The primary care setting is, in fact, the place where mental health services are most needed. Figure 8.1 shows the relative frequency of patients with definite mental disorders in different health care settings from various epidemiological studies all over the world (Üstün et al 1995). For every 100 patients in the community, half decide to seek care and attend primary care. In primary care settings, nearly half are recognized. The proportion either referred to or who go directly to specialist outpatient services consists of only 5% of those in the community. The number

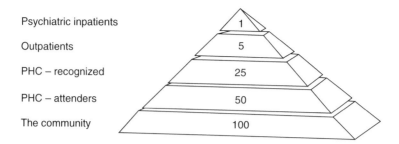

Psychiatric inpatients	1
Outpatients	5
PHC – recognized	25
PHC – attenders	50
The community	100

FIGURE 8.1 Relative frequency of patients with mental disorders in different health care settings

Mental health (13%)
Both (9%)
(78%) Primary care

FIGURE 8.2 Proportions of mental health patients treated in primary care and mental health care facilities: pooled data from 19 countries

admitted to hospital is only 1% of those with a mental disorder. These figures indicate that if only specialist psychiatric services are considered, we are dealing with the tip of the iceberg, whereas if we consider primary care, we are really dealing with the major bulk of the problems.

These figures may change from country to country, since what constitutes primary care services can vary. The WHO study on pathways to care (Gater et al 1991) in Ujung Pandang, for example, shows that only 18% of people go to primary care physicians for their mental health problems, whereas a large proportion of people with mental health problems go to native or religious healers, some of them eventually being referred to psychiatric services. This suggests that efforts in mental health in developing countries should perhaps concentrate on targets other than primary care physicians. However, in Manchester the main proportion, 95%, goes first to a general practitioner and then to a specialist. Pooling the data from 19 countries in which the study was conducted (Figure 8.2) shows that 78% of patients with mental health problems first contacted primary care facilities and were treated there. Only 13% of them went directly to mental health facilities, and 9% were being treated by both primary care and specialist services.

PRIMARY MENTAL HEALTH CARE SERVICES: HOW TO CHOOSE WHAT TO DELIVER?

The comprehensive approach to primary health care appears to be useful for the broad conception and implementation of health care applications. However, it would be unrealistic to load primary care practice with too many responsibilities. Primary care facilities do deliver a wide range of health services and the choice of what should be included in primary care service delivery is certainly a difficult problem. While a comprehensive coverage of health is necessary, activities should be well chosen to include focused interventions that are feasible and effective. For any health care intervention to be incorporated in primary care practice it must present as a real-life problem which is frequent and manageable in primary care settings, using acceptable and effective interventions. What is required in primary care are scientifically sound applications which have been shown to be effective and practical. Implementation of this strategy requires concerned efforts to translate scientific knowledge into action programs, thus requiring complex planning and programming.

Four criteria on which to base prevention and promotion activities in primary care will be reviewed, as well as the evidence of their feasibility and effectiveness:

1. *Frequency*: how common is the condition?
2. *Severity*: what are the consequences for the individual, his family and his community?
3. *Availability of interventions*: are there effective interventions available? Are they acceptable?
4. *Public concern*: how much concern do people and policy makers show about these conditions and interventions?

Frequency

The WHO collaborative study on psychological problems in general health care (Üstün & Sartorius 1995) has shown that 24% of attending patients have a current well-defined mental disorder; 9% show sub-threshold disorders, i.e. clinically significant disorders falling short of the diagnostic criteria of standard classifications; 31% had two or more mental symptoms, e.g. sleep disorders, appetite fatigue. Overall, 64% of patients show a psychological problem that requires attention for differential diagnosis or planning of care.

Severity

People with mental disorders have a significant disability in terms of their daily functioning. Mental disorders are associated with significant disability (Ormel et al 1994) and cause significant problems for patients, their families and their communities. For example, disability caused by depression is comparable to hypertension, diabetes, arthritis or back pain, in terms of dysfunctional days in the last month or subjective disability score. Part of the World Bank (1995) report looked at the global burden of disease—the impact of disability when added to mortality in terms of life-years lost worldwide. The report shows that mental disorders constitute 9.5% of the total global burden of disease as identified in DALYs (disability-adjusted life-years). In this type of estimation, mental disorders rank third after respiratory disease and cardiovascular disease, surpassing cancer (all malignancies combined) and HIV. In terms of the global burden that mental disorders present, this report carries an eye-opening message for the policy makers when setting their priorities.

Interventions

The criteria for evaluating intervention must address whether the intervention is available, feasible, acceptable in a primary care setting and effective. Effective treatments exist to defeat depression, panic disorder and many other mental problems. The success of these treatments is equal to, and sometimes better than, success in the treatment of hypertension or coronary heart disease (NAMHC 1993). Regarding prevention, the interventions are also likely to be successful, although systematic data on their effectiveness is difficult to gather. For example, the prevention of mental retardation by pre- or postnatal care, immunization, family planning, epilepsy control, nutrition, early childhood stimulation, accident prevention, family support, teaching parenthood skills and early recognition of motor and sensory deficits, mental retardation or at least its consequences can be reduced. There is general expert consensus that these preventions are available and acceptable (WHO 1988).

Public Concern

People are genuinely concerned about their mental health. 'Stress' is recognized and admitted and many seek better ways to cope with the stress of daily life. Although there is a considerable stigma attached to mental illness, the association between stress and mental illness must really be brought into awareness. There is room for improvement in the opinions, attitudes and behaviours of the public as well as in those of primary care personnel. Simply spreading the concept that 'mental disorders are medical illnesses and treatment is possible' will help.

PRIMARY CARE: RELEVANCE VS. CHALLENGES

The primary care setting provides comprehensive care with a whole-person perspective that continues from birth to death through regular contacts. Less stigma is attached to mental disorders because in primary care mental disorders can be considered on equal terms to other disorders. Collaborative links between many specialists (e.g. psychiatrists going into primary care facilities, or GPs going into mental health facilities) and other sectors (e.g. schoolteachers, social workers in work places) can be established. Primary care physicians can really be 'networked' within the community and good chains created. The primary care setting is the route to prevention and promotion activities.

There are also some challenges. First, only a few strategies for implementing prevention and promotion activities have been formulated. Although there are many ideas and proposals, they remain largely unstructured. There are few tests of efficacy of the proposed interventions and unfortunately no evidence is available on the effectiveness of these interventions in real life.

Second, the greatest challenge is the real prevention and promotion which go beyond the health sector: there is education, housing, urban development, justice, security, defence, transportation, religious establishments: all these have an impact on mental health promotion and prevention of mental disorders.

The third challenge concerns the costs, for these are yet unknown. Policy makers cannot be convinced if we do not know how much money we should invest into prevention and promotion activities and what benefits are expected. However, the cost of illness in terms of health economics has been well researched. The example of alcohol is telling: last year alcohol cost the American taxpayer $479 without him/her even purchasing any! (Rice 1993). This does not include the emotional burden, family hardship or social consequences—it is based only on most work time global productivity, higher health care and extra loss to taxation. It would of course be wise to spend this money on prevention and promotion related to alcohol abuse.

Fourth, primary care physicians or primary care workers do not generally have a mental health orientation. The unfortunate pitfall of equating mental health with psychiatry leads to the neglect of social and mental components of health and results in a lack of basic knowledge and skills in evaluation and intervention.

The fifth challenge is in terms of the service organization. If one considers the structural incentives in primary care for mental health interventions, there is little appreciation of mental health services in primary care and there are no revenues for these services (i.e. insurance or reimbursement paying for mental health service rendered). It is therefore difficult to appreciate, in terms of time and organization, how much can be added onto the busy schedule of physicians and primary care workers.

Sixth, since these services are not yet structured, the quality of these services and their delivery, the measurement of their effectiveness, and consumer satisfaction with the delivery of these services still remain unknown variables.

PRIMARY CARE: CHALLENGES VS. OPPORTUNITIES

Prevention and promotion activities are not only needed, but also wanted and promising. We believe that we can turn available knowledge into application programs, that we should expand primary care into the media, into schools, into the workplace. We can really use the primary care system better than other health care settings because it can more easily accommodate variations in the health services and be expanded into the community in the form of user groups or self-help groups.

What can be done in terms of primary mental health care regarding promotion and prevention activities? First comes health education: e.g. preparation for parenthood, marriage counselling, sex education and positive behaviour development. For specific prevention activities, there are a wide range of activities proved to be effective such as:

- Immunization.
- Use of specific nutrients (e.g. iodine addition to salt).
- Protection from accidents.
- Smoking cessation.
- Care for children of the seriously ill.

These activities might protect people from developing mental illness, or prevent relapses.

Early identification and interventions could be based mainly on case-finding activities, such as for alcohol, drugs, depression in high-risk groups such as the elderly, the bereaved, socially isolated people, people who are disabled (e.g. with physical disabilities, visual or hearing impairments) or chronically ill. These early identification programs could be used to prevent consequences such as suicide, marital breakdown, occupational problems, accidents and adverse effects in child-rearing. Regarding relapse prevention, data are available showing that relapses in alcohol abuse, depression and anxiety can be prevented by occupational interventions. These activities should find their place in primary care, possibly in the form of practical guidelines (see Üstün, Chapter 16, this volume).

Primary care can and should be extended into the community. With additional team members, life skills education in developing countries could be developed which would then induce support groups for self-help groups or run awareness programs such as the DART (Depression Awareness Recognition and Treatment) Programme (Regier et al 1988) or the Defeat Depression Campaign.

Programs on maternal and child-bearing practices have a significant impact on mental health. Early detection of pregnancy may help avoid the harmful effects of drugs, X-rays and tobacco on mothers and prepare both mothers and fathers for parenthood. Infant–parent relationships can be improved with early childhood stimulation programs and promotion of breast feeding.

PRIMARY CARE—PREVENTION AND PROMOTION: WHO IS GOING TO DO IT, AND HOW?

The primary care team should be extended beyond general practitioners to include other physicians, social workers, nurses, midwives, counsellors, occupational therapists and perhaps other professionals. How can this be done? First, by formulating plans, building up a knowledge base and infrastructure; second, by targeting a problem with defined objectives and indicators; third, by selecting interventions focusing on the identified problem and structuring them; fourth, by training the team for the implementation of these programs and seeing how they are implemented in the field which involves a feedback process; fifth, by evaluating the outcome, process and impact—what are the outcomes in comparison to the standards set earlier, and what is the impact on the program of unforeseen and foreseen results.

There are many possible targets for primary care, such as developmental problems, school problems, teenage pregnancy, safe sex, family planning, marital conflict, couple relationship or intimacy problems, child rearing, drug and alcohol abuse, violence, minority status and occupational problems. We really have to look into these in terms of their cultural relevance, scientific evidence about prevention or promotion and the political support that we can get for implementing possible programs. We have to evaluate different aspects, including the personal, psychological, social and cultural–environmental factors, e.g. personal vulnerability, minority status, family structure, poverty—not only in terms of low income but also of social deprivation.

Training in these topics is a considerable issue. Education programs for early identification and intervention and high-risk group identification can be set up, but educational programmes must also focus on increasing the team skills as well as the psychosocial sensitivity of physicians and on implementing programs for monitoring an evaluation system.

Such a system may take a long time to establish but small changes can begin to be implemented now. Workers in primary care can at least be taught the following approaches:

- Learn to listen. It has been shown that patients are more satisfied and respect their doctors if they listen without interrupting for the first 5 minutes.
- When there is an identifiable mental disorder such as depression or anxiety disorder we have established guidelines for their treatment and prevention of relapse (see Chapter 16, this volume).
- Talk about positive health, encouraging healthy behaviour such as hobbies, exercising and so forth, and be a good role model yourself, practising what you are preaching, not smoking and not eating too much.
- Encourage health responsibility. Health is a basic responsibility of the individual and the meaning of the word 'doctor' in Latin is 'teacher'. As doctors we

ought to 'teach' our patients about health and encourage their responsibility about their own health. In this way we can achieve our aim 'health for all and all for health'.

In conclusion, we are in a position to see the way more clearly to developing prevention and promotion programs in primary care. It is difficult, but possible. It is challenging, but the opportunities are there.

REFERENCES

Erikson EH (1950) *Childhood and Society*. New York: Norton.

Gater R et al (1991) The pathways to psychiatric care: a cross-cultural study. *Psychol Med* **21**(3), 761–4.

NAMHC (National Advisory Mental Health Council) (1993) *Report to the US Senate Committee on Appropriations*. Washington, DC: US Government.

Ormel J, von Korff M, Üstün TB, Pini S, Korten A & Oldehinkel T (1994) Common mental disorders and disability across cultures. *JAMA* **272**, 1741–8.

Regier D et al (1988) The NIMH depression awareness, recognition and treatment program: structure, aims and scientific basis. *Am J Psychiat* **145**, 11.

Rice D (1993) The economic cost of alcohol abuse and alcohol dependence, 1990. Advertisement included in *Alcohol Health Res World* **17**(1).

Üstün TB, Goldberg D, Cooper J, Simon GE & Sartorius N (1995) A new classification for mental disorders, with management guidelines for use in primary care: the ICD-10 PHC, Chapter 5. *Br J Gen Pract* **45**(393), April.

Üstün TB & Sartorius N (eds) (1995) *Mental Illness in General Health Care: An International Study*. Chichester: Wiley.

WHO (World Health Organization) (1978) *Primary Health Care: Report of the International Conference on Primary Health Care 1978*. Health for All Series no. 1. Geneva: WHO.

WHO (World Health Organization (1988) *Prevention of Mental, Neurological and Psychological Disorders*. (WHO/MNH/EVA/88.1). Geneva: WHO.

World Bank (1993) *World Development Report 1993. Investing in Health*. World Development Indicators. New York: Oxford University Press.

9

Policy Framework and Research in England, 1990–1995

Rachel Jenkins*

Institute of Psychiatry, London, UK

This chapter sets out the broad policy framework of England's objectives for mental health, our 'Health of the Nation' strategy, our policy for people with severe mental illness, and the importance of paying attention to the primary care of mental disorders. Primary care presents an excellent opportunity for mental health promotion and primary prevention which it is vital not to miss, and the chapter describes some of the activities in this area in England.

The World Bank (1993) report has drawn attention to the huge public health burden of mental illness, the very high prevalence of morbidity round the world, the social disability, the co-morbidity with other illnesses, the major use of services, and the mortality.

In 1993 the Department of Health (DoH) published an overall broad framework of objectives for mental health in the Public Information Strategy (Department of Health 1993) (see Box 9.1). These are wider than, and intended to incorporate, the three 'Health of the Nation' targets for mental illness (see below).

THE HEALTH OF THE NATION

In 1992, England published its response to WHO's strategy *Health for All by the Year 2000* (Department of Health 1992) and set targets in five key areas. Mental illness was chosen as one of the five key areas, and this has succeeded in bringing mental illness high up the agenda in England. The second target is measured by using pre-existing routine data. Work was directly commissioned to measure the first and third targets.

The targets are set around reducing morbidity and mortality (see Box 9.2). It would also be useful to have a primary prevention target but our present state of

---

* This chapter was written when the author was Principal Medical Officer, Mental Health Division, Department of Health, England, for the period 1988–1996, and does not necessarily apply to the period 1997 onwards.

Preventing Mental Illness: Mental Health Promotion in Primary Care. Edited by R. Jenkins and T.B. Üstün.
Published 1998 John Wiley & Sons Ltd.

Box 9.1   Department of Health objectives for mental health*

Incidence and prevalence
To reduce the incidence and prevalence of specific mental and behavioural disorders (henceforth 'mental disorders') in the general population

Mortality
To reduce the mortality associated with specific mental disorders (viz. deaths from physical illness, e.g. cardiovascular disease, malignancy, respiratory diseases, deaths from suicide and violence)

Associated problems
To reduce the extent and severity of problems associated with specific mental disorders, including problems with mental health, personal functioning, social circumstances, interpersonal relationships and physical health, and problems of family and informal carers

Appropriate care services
To ensure that appropriate care services are provided to address the problems associated with specific mental disorders, whether these be problems of mental health, personal functioning, social circumstances, interpersonal relationships, physical health or of family and informal carers

Attitudes
To reverse people's negative perceptions of mental disorders. This is necessary to counter the fear, ignorance and stigma which surround mental disorders, to create a more positive social climate in which it is acceptable to seek help without fear of labelling or feelings of failure, and to improve the quality of life of people with mental health problems, their families and friends

Research
To underpin the above objectives and to continue research into the causes, consequences and care of specific mental disorders

_____

* Compiled from Department of Health (1993).

Box 9.2   The Health of the Nation mental illness key area targets*

- To improve significantly the health and social functioning of mentally ill people
- To reduce the overall suicide rate by at least 15% by the year 2000 (from 11.0 per 100 000 in 1990 to no more than 9.4)
- To reduce the suicide rate of severely mentally ill people by at least 33% by the year 2000 (from the lifetime estimate of 15% in 1990 to no more than 10%)

_____

* Compiled from Department of Health (1992).

Box 9.3   The mental health public information strategy—booklets produced by the Department of Health

- *Mental Illness: What Does It Mean?* (1993)
- *Mental Illness: Sometimes I Think I Can't Go On Any More* (1993)
- *Mental Illness: What You Can Do About It* (1994)
- *Mental Illness: A Guide to Mental Health in the Workplace* (1993)
- *Mental Illness: Mental Health and Older People* (1994)
- *Mental Illness: Can Children and Young People have Mental Health Problems?* (1994)
- *Down on the Farm? Coping with Depression in Rural Areas: A Farmer's Guide* (1995)
- *Mental Health: Towards a Better Understanding* (1995)

---

knowledge is such that this would be difficult to measure on a routine basis. However, I hope that this will be possible in the not too distant future.

Health of the Nation activity is not only meant to apply to our National Health Service but to all organizations, settings and people in the whole country. Schools, workplaces, cities and rural areas are equally important places where health promotion, prevention, treatment and rehabilitation and prevention of mortality can go on, as well as in hospitals. We are working to build up alliances between different agencies involved. Everyone has a role to play in the Health of the Nation and clearly the government has to play its part, as well as regions and local areas.

We have set a broad tripartite framework to try and achieve these targets, firstly to improve information and understanding about mental health, secondly to build up our local comprehensive services, and thirdly to develop good practice.

IMPROVING INFORMATION AND UNDERSTANDING

Public Information Strategy

There are several aspects of information and understanding. The government is funding a public information strategy to influence public attitudes to mental health services. This aims to increase understanding, reduce stigma and help users to understand both their rights and responsibilities. In addition to publishing specific mental health booklets (see Box 9.3), the Department is continuing to fund the work of the Health Education Authority which is undertaking mental health promotion work focused on World Mental Health Day.

National Psychiatric Morbidity Survey

It is essential to have a sound epidemiological and research base in order to ensure that services meet the needs of the population and it was for that reason that we conducted a national psychiatric morbidity survey.

TABLE 9.1 Prevalence of psychiatric disorders per 1000 population in adults aged 16–64, UK 1993

Broad diagnostic group	Women	Men	All adults
Any neurotic disorder	195 (7)	127 (5)	160 (5)
Functional psychosis	5 (1)	4 (1)	4 (1)
Alcohol dependence	22 (2)	77 (5)	49 (3)
Drug dependence	15 (2)	29 (3)	22 (2)

Data from Meltzer et al (1995a).

TABLE 9.2 Prevalence of neurotic (non-psychotic) disorders per 1000 population in adults aged 16–64, UK 1993

Non-psychotic disorders	Women	Men	All adults
Mixed anxiety and depression	99 (5)	54 (4)	77 (3)
Generalized anxiety	34 (3)	28 (2)	31 (2)
Depression	25 (2)	17 (5)	21 (1)
Phobias	14 (2)	7 (1)	11 (1)
Obsessive-compulsive disorder	15 (2)	9 (2)	12 (1)
Panic	9 (1)	8 (2)	8 (1)

Data from Meltzer et al (1995a).

The survey attempted to measure the population prevalence of illness, to assess the associated risk factors and how far needs are currently being met. We hope that the data will help underpin our prevention strategies for the future (see Tables 9.1–9.5 for a sample of the data available).

The surveys have covered the age group 16–64 in the first instance because we will have to use slightly different methodologies for children and older people. The planning is currently under way for our survey of 4–16 year olds. The surveys included national probability samples of households, institutions and the homeless in England, Scotland and Wales.

The survey is the first of its kind in the UK and will give a national reference source of data for researchers, policy makers, purchasers and planners. We very much want to make sure that policies are firmly rooted in the epidemiology. We will use the surveys as a baseline for our first Health of the Nation target, to help inform our local purchasers of the health and social care needs they need to buy provision for, to supply a core methodology for more intensive local surveys, and to inform the centre of national needs.

These are the first surveys in the world that have used simultaneous probability samples of household, institutional and homeless populations, combining prevalence data with data on risk factors and social disability and drug and alcohol problems. It was also the first national survey of the homeless in the world.

TABLE 9.3 Percentage of people with CIS-R scores over threshold (12) by marital status and sex

Marital status	Men (%)	Women (%)
Married	11	13
Cohabiting	11	17
Single	10	14
Widowed	20	21
Divorced	17	25
Separated	11	14

Data from Meltzer et al (1995a).

TABLE 9.4 Percentage of people with CIS-R scores over threshold (12) by family unit types

Family unit type	Men (%)	Women (%)
Couple, no child	10	14
Couple and children	11	18
Lone parent and children	20	28
One parent only	16	23
Adult with parents	7	12
Adult with one parent	13	17

Data from Meltzer et al (1995a).

TABLE 9.5 Percentage of people with CIS-R scores over threshold (12) by employment status

Employment status	Men (%)	Women (%)
Working full-time	8	16
Working part-time	10	16
Unemployment	18	37
Economically inactive	18	21

Data from Meltzer et al (1995a).

Health of the Nation Outcome Scales

Our first Health of the Nation target is to improve health and social functioning in people with mental illness. We have long been able to measure that in a research context using instruments such as the Present State Examination (Wing et al 1990) or the Clinical Interview Schedule (Goldberg et al 1970), but these are relatively lengthy research instruments and what we needed was something routine, small and simple that could be used by clinicians within the clinical setting. So we commissioned John Wing at the Royal College of Psychiatrists' Research Unit to develop a brief scale that could be used as a routine part of our clinical reviews.

BOX 9.4   Health of the Nation outcome scale

Behavioural items
- Overactive, aggressive, disruptive, agitated
- Non-accidental self-injury
- Problem drinking or drug taking

Physical items
- Cognitive problems
- Physical illness and/or disability

Psychological items
- Hallucinations and delusions
- Depressed mood
- Other psychological symptoms

Social items
- Relationship
- Activities of daily living
- Living conditions
- Occupation and activities

The field trials have just been completed and we hope to introduce the instrument as part of a core minimum data set gradually between 1996 and 1998 across the country.

Box 9.4 illustrates the items in this scale. They are all items a clinician needs to assess for a major review of the patient. You cannot assess a patient properly without knowing about each of these items. There is a glossary that goes with the scale to give simple instructions on scoring and any member of the multi-disciplinary team can use the scale.

The functions of the Health of the Nation outcome scale are to monitor our first target in Health of the Nation, to help give us some standardized measures of case load severity for managing clinical caseloads, to give indications of variations in health outcome between different geographical locations and feed information in for case-mix classification.

DEVELOPING LOCAL COMPREHENSIVE SERVICES

Inputs

A locally based service should include community mental health teams, emergency out-of-hours services, short-term hospital provision, acute beds, new long-stay provision, 24-hour nursed beds, and the less supported move on accommodation and day-care services (see Box 9.5).

BOX 9.5   The service inputs for a local adult comprehensive mental health service*

	Acute/emergency care	*Rehabilitation/continuing care*
Home-based	Intensive home support Emergency duty teams Sector teams	Domiciliary services Key workers Care management
Day care	Day hospitals	Drop-in centres Support groups Employment schemes Day care
Residential support	Crisis accommodation Acute units Local secure units	Ordinary housing Unstaffed group homes Adult placement schemes Residential care homes Mental nursing homes 24 hour NHS accommodation Medium secure units High secure units

* Compiled from Department of Health (1994).

Processes

The processes in a local comprehensive service are described in Box 9.6. Mental health information systems are important to manage a service, the care program approach and supervision registers.

The care program approach (CPA) was introduced here in April 1991 in order to ensure that everybody in contact with secondary care services should have a systematic assessment of his/her health and social care needs—an individually tailored care program which is as simple or as sophisticated as necessary and which is agreed with the multidisciplinary team, social services, GPs, users and carers.

A key worker should be nominated to keep close contact with the patient and there should be regular reviews of progress. Supervision registers are a method of prioritizing those people on the CPA who are in greatest need, by virtue of the risk to themselves or others.

Outcomes

Outcomes for health and social functioning will be measured by the Health of the Nation outcome scales mentioned earlier.

> **Box 9.6** The service processes in a local adult comprehensive mental health service
>
> • Mental health information system
> • Care program approach
> • Supervision registers
> • Assertive outreach
> • Carer and community education
> • Primary care liaison
> • Physical and dental care
> • User advocacy and community alliances

IMPLICATIONS FOR MENTAL HEALTH POLICY

So to summarize, our policy for severe mental illness is that people should be cared for locally, by comprehensive health and social services, so that we can improve health and social functioning and reduce mortality, including suicide.

Policy on severe mental illness will only be effective if we also have effective policy on the minor and moderate illnesses in primary care and, at the other end of the extreme, effective policy on mentally disordered offenders. In other words, policy must take account of the whole spectrum of epidemiology, otherwise it will fail, and it must be developed into a public health framework of primary, secondary and tertiary prevention and prevention of mortality.

The Health of the Nation strategy is helping us set up a coherent policy framework of inputs, processes and outcomes for the range of psychiatric morbidity.

POLICY CONSIDERATIONS FOR MENTAL HEALTH PROMOTION AND PREVENTION

When a country is choosing objectives for prevention, some of the issues that need to be considered include the social cost or public health burden of the topic; how far there is knowledge about the aetiology of the conditions; what the evidence is in terms of public attitudes and political acceptance, the balance between risk and gain and the availability of resources.

Taking depression as an example, the data on social cost may be compiled from data on suicide; prevalence rates of depression; the contribution of depression to sickness absence, labour turnover and reduced productivity; cognitive and physical damage to children from having depressed parents; the costs of marital problems; the effect on physical health and the contribution to high-risk behaviour such as reckless driving and violent crimes; substance abuse and suicide attempts. Our knowledge about the aetiology of depression includes evidence on the genetic risks, predisposing factors, precipitating factors and protective factors.

If one concentrates on high-risk groups, the prevention pay-off or return is probably greater if one concentrates on high-risk *situations*, since these are more likely to be closely followed by illness in the short term, than if one concentrates on high-risk *populations* who may not develop the illness in any case for many years. Furthermore, in general there are more practical opportunities for prevention in the domain of precipitation, rather than predisposing factors. It is also easier to identify those in high-risk situations for the purposes of the preventive interventions rather than those in high-risk populations. Thus, there has been general optimism about microlevel prevention at the individual and family level, but until recently we have avoided thinking about macrolevel prevention because of the difficulty of influencing factors such as unemployment, social discrimination and poverty. But Catalano & Dooley (1980) argue that macrolevel proactive primary prevention should be much more carefully considered.

EXAMPLES OF MENTAL HEALTH PROMOTION AND PREVENTION IN ENGLAND

An example of educational strategies in England aimed at the whole population, i.e. a universal strategy, is the Public Information Strategy mentioned earlier which has been designed to reduce the stigma attached to mental illness and encourage the public to seek early help. This campaign is being evaluated annually by the Public Attitudes Survey. The 'Defeat Depression' campaign, carried out jointly between the Royal College of General Practitioners and the Royal College of Psychiatrists, has aimed to increase knowledge of health care professionals in prevention and treatment of depression, but also to enhance public awareness of the nature of depression, and is therefore an example of a strategy aimed at both professionals and the general population. Other educational strategies aimed at professionals include that of England's Senior GP Fellow in Mental Health Education (see Chapter 22) who, together with the national network of regional fellows, has been working to improve the prevention of depression in primary care; and the development of a multidisciplinary training program in depression for primary care teams by the Royal Institute of Public Health and Hygiene.

Some examples of selective strategies in England aimed at the occupational setting include the Health of the Nation initiative on 'Health at Work in the NHS', which seeks to promote the mental and physical health of the National Health Service workforce, and various activities to promote mental health in the general workplace.

Some examples of indicated strategies in the primary care setting in England include health visitors giving support to isolated young mothers and pre-school children and district nurse support to people with physical and sensory disabilities. We are funding some research projects examining the prevalence of mental health problems in the NHS workplace and their prevention. The Department of Health has funded a 3-year fellowship, job-shared by Dr Ruth Chambers and Dr Richard Maxwell of the Royal College of General Practitioners, to look at the causes of stress in GPs at the moment and ways in which we can help to tackle it. The Department has also funded a 3-year fellowship on occupational mental health, occupied by Dr Doreen Miller of the Faculty of Occupational Health, Royal College of Physicians, to take a national lead in educating occupational doctors about mental health.

For a few years now we have pulled a group together with DoH, Department of Employment, Health and Safety Executive, Confederation of British Industry, TUC, ACAS (advisory conciliation service), the Health Education Authority and the Institute of Personnel Development. We all meet every month or two, to coordinate all our activities on promoting mental health in the workplace. We have done a series of joint conferences and also produced guidelines for employers on introducing mental health policies to the workplace in the same way that they have long had policies of physical health, alcohol and drug abuse (Jenkins & Coney 1992; Jenkins & Worman 1993; Department of Health 1995). We have also put on some publicity stands at different conferences to promote this to a variety of audiences including captains of industry, directors of personnel and the agricultural world.

We are encouraging employers to value the mental health of their workforce in the same ways they value its physical health, to have workplace health policies which pay attention to mental as well as physical health, to promote understanding about mental health problems and reduce the stigma, to reduce stresses in the workplace (primary prevention), to improve prompt detection of management who are depressed and anxious at work (secondary prevention), and to improve rehabilitation back to work (tertiary prevention).

The Primary Care Setting

The huge period prevalence in community populations of mental health problems is now well documented (Goldberg & Huxley 1992) and our own survey showed point prevalence of 14% (Meltzer et al, OPCS Reports 1–8: 1995a, b, c; 1996a, b, c, d). We know the prevalence in GP attenders is very high, about 1 in 3 (Goldberg & Huxley 1992; Üstün & Sartorius 1995). Every 10 years in this country there is a survey of GP consultations (which are recorded as illness diagnosed by the GP), i.e. conspicuous morbidity rather than total (conspicuous and hidden) morbidity. If you look at conspicuous morbidity alone, mental disorder is the second most common reason for consultation, and Professor Pereira Gray has found in his own practice that depression is the most common chronic condition (Pereira Gray 1995).

That helps to underpin why it is so important to think about prevention today: first, of course to improve the welfare of the patients themselves; second, we want to reduce the burden on the primary care teams themselves; third, we want to reduce the burden on secondary care staff so we do not neglect people with severe mental illness; fourth, it helps to reduce the cost to the NHS and reduce the cost to the economy as a whole.

Taking the first reason, the burden to patient and family, there is the personal distress and suffering, the impaired social functioning, the chronicity and the impact on family members and the workplace. At least half of these conditions are chronic and recurrent. Professor Rutter's work has shown that if both parents are depressed the children can suffer cognitive damage. Depression can lead to marital breakdowns and to sickness absence and labour turnover.

Turning to the second reason, the burden to primary care staff is very great; they may often feel very overwhelmed by mental health problems. This can lead sometimes to the use of pejorative terminology to describe people with mental health problems, for example so-called 'heart-sink patients'. We do know that people with depression and anxiety often have increased rates of repeat consultations, often over very many years (Lloyd, Jenkins & Mann 1995).

The burden to secondary care staff is rather less obvious, but if you track patients with mental health problems they have increased rates of consultation to medical and surgical outpatients over many years and increased rates of hospital admission. This has not really been properly costed yet, but it looks as if it is a voluminous cost.

Croft-Jeffreys and Wilkinson (1985) looked at the costs in primary care. There is no doubt that personal contact is very important, although very labour-intensive, and it has been argued that we need to use a combination of different methods if we are to really have effective change.

The Prevention of Mental Disorders in Primary Care

In England we have tried to combine several top-down and bottom-up approaches in an effort to maximize the personal contact with primary care teams, but at the same time we have tried to avoid diverting our specialists from the severely mentally ill. We have not wanted to see specialists go in to one or two primary care teams and do a wonderful job looking after a few people with depression and anxiety, but leaving most primary care teams with no help at all, and meanwhile neglecting some of their work on people with severe mental illness. We have tried to find other solutions which can give *equitable* support to *all* primary care teams.

I have already mentioned our Senior GP Fellow, André Tylee, educating GPs about mental health problems. We have also set up a Senior Nurse Facilitator, Liz Armstrong, to take a national lead in educating nurse facilitators in general practice about mental health. She and André work very much in partnership to do this, and she has identified a network of regional nurse facilitators who can partner André's regional fellows.

We have also set up some developmental projects which are just coming to an end and the evaluations will shortly be with us. One project evaluated the attachment of a GP facilitator to six general practices in Kensington, Chelsea and Westminster, which sounds a very grand area but is in fact one of our most deprived boroughs in the country, with high proportions of homeless and immi-grant populations. Her brief was to improve the primary care of mental health. In another study we attached a practice nurse to a general practice in Bath to try to create a model general practice in its handling of mental health, thinking not only about tertiary and secondary prevention but about mental health promotion and primary prevention as well, by working with the practices to develop good practice protocols for the assessment, diagnosis, management and criteria for referral to secondary care for depression, anxiety, schizophrenia, dementia and alcohol and drug abuse. The GP facilitator and practice nurse also identified the variety of voluntary and self-help organizations available for the practices to refer patients to, compiled a directory of names, addresses, criteria for referral, and dealt with issues of clinical accountability. We have also funded a team in Exeter to audit the management of depression in primary care. These projects are described in more detail in Chapter 20.

The first two studies, (a) Kensington, Chelsea and Westminster and (b) Bath, have had very similar methods of evaluation and we have looked at how the interventions have changed, the GPs' identification index (how good they are at detecting anxiety and depression), their attitudes and knowledge about mental health, the patient outcomes and the costs of consultations, referrals and admission. These will be published in due course.

Before concluding, I would like to refer to suicide prevention. Suicide preven-tion is clearly an integral part of any national approach to mental health pro-motion and prevention and England's strategy has been described elsewhere (Kingdon & Jenkins 1995; Jenkins et al 1994). A national suicide prevention strategy needs to operate on a broad front of not just early identification and treatment of those at risk of suicide but also reducing access to the means of suicide, targeting our high-risk groups, auditing suicide and educating the media (see Box 9.7), and this is the general approach adopted not only in England but also in other countries such as Finland, Sweden, Norway, etc.

In England, we are aiming for a coordinated and comprehensive approach to mental health promotion and prevention which encompasses macrolevel and microlevel interventions, both education and clinical, and a combination of uni-versal, selective and indicated strategies, which are well integrated with our services for secondary and tertiary prevention and reduction of mortality.

We have attempted to obtain commitment to the process by a combination of national, regional and local processes such as the overall national Health of the Nation strategy, many regional and local conferences, and some Department of Health stands at non-health conferences, such as those of the Confederation of British Industry and the Royal Agricultural Show.

We have been working to fill in our knowledge gaps about prevention by the UK Psychiatric Morbidity survey and other research reviews and projects, and by the developing work on measuring health and social outcomes.

A variety of policy levers are available, such as the contracting process, the use of service and clinical guidelines, the dissemination of research, and IT support.

Box 9.7 Components of England's suicide prevention strategy

- Improved detection and management of depression and suicidal risk in:
    Primary care services
    General hospital services
    Mental health services

- Targeting high-risk groups:
    Specific occupational groups (e.g. doctors, dentists, farmers, vets, nurses)
    People with severe mental illness
    Specific sociodemographic groups

- Attitude changes:
    Public information strategy
    Health of the Nation strategy
    Working with media to discourage irresponsible reporting of suicide

- Reducing access to means of suicide

- Audit and research:
    National confidential inquiry into suicides
    Local audit
    Research studies

REFERENCES

Catalano R & Dooley D (1980) Economic change in primary prevention. In RH Price, RJ Ketterer, BC Bader & J Monahan (eds) *Prevention in Mental Health—Research, Policy and Practice*, pp 21–40. London: Sage.

Croft-Jeffreys C & Wilkinson G (1989) Estimated costs of neurotic disorder in UK general practice 1985. *Psychol Med* **9**, 337–53.

Department of Health (1995) *The Health of the Nation: ABC of Mental Health in the Workplace—A Resource pack for Employers*. London: Department of Health.

Department of Health (1994) *The Mental Illness Key Area Handbook*, 2nd edn. London: HMSO.

Department of Health (1992) *The Health of the Nation—A Strategy for Health in England*. London: HMSO.

Department of Health (1993) *Public Health Information Strategy—Improving Information on Mental Health*, pp 3–4. London: Department of Health.

Goldberg DP, Cooper B, Eastwood MR, Keward HB & Shepherd M (1970) A standardized psychiatric interview for use in community surveys. *Br J Prevent Soc Med* **24**, 18–23.

Goldberg DP & Huxley P (1992) *Common Mental Disorders—A Biosocial Model*. London: Routledge and Kegan Paul.

Jenkins R & Coney N (1992) *Promoting Mental Health at Work*. London: HMSO.

Jenkins R, Griffiths S, Hawton K, Morgan G, Tylee A & Wylie I (eds) (1994) Prevention of Suicide. London: HMSO.

Jenkins R & Worman D (1993) *Promoting Mental Health Policies in the Workplace*. London: HMSO.

Kingdon D & Jenkins R (1995) Suicide prevention. In *Emergency Mental Health Services in the Community*, pp. 96–115. Cambridge: Cambridge University Press.

Lloyd K, Jenkins R & Mann AH (1996) The long-term outcome of patients with neurotic illness in general practice. *Br Med J* **313**, 26–8.

Meltzer H, Gill B, Petticrew M & Hinks K (1995a) The prevalence of psychiatric morbidity among adults living in private households. OPCS Surveys of Psychiatric Morbidity in Great Britain: Report 1. London: HMSO.

Meltzer H, Gill B, Petticrew M & Hinds K (1995b) Physical complaints, service use and treatment of adults with psychiatric disorders. OPCS Surveys of Psychiatric Morbidity in Great Britain: Report 2. London: HMSO.

Meltzer H, Gill B, Petticrew M & Hinds K (1995c) Economic activity and social functioning of adults with psychiatric disorders. OPCS Surveys of Psychiatric Morbidity in Great Britain: Report 3. London: HMSO.

Meltzer H, Gill B, Petticrew M & Hinds K (1996a) The prevalence of psychiatric morbidity among adults living in institutions. OPCS Surveys of Psychiatric Morbidity in Great Britain: Report 4. London: HMSO.

Meltzer H, Gill B, Petticrew M & Hinds K (1996b) Physical complaints, service use and treatment of residents with psychiatric disorders. OPCS Surveys of Psychiatric Morbidity in Great Britain: Report 5. London: HMSO.

Meltzer H, Gill B, Petticrew M & Hinds K (1996c) The economic activity and social functioning of residents with psychiatric disorders. OPCS Surveys of Psychiatric Morbidity in Great Britain: Report 6. London: HMSO.

Meltzer H, Gill B, Petticrew M & Hinds K (1996d) Psychiatric morbidity among homeless people. OPCS Surveys of Psychiatric Morbidity in Great Britain: Report 7. London: HMSO.

Pereira Gray D (1995) Primary care and the public health: Harben lecture. *Health Hygiene* **16**, 49–62.

Üstün TB and Sartorius N (1995) *Mental Illness—General Health Care—An International Study*. Chichester: Wiley.

Wing JK, Babar T, Brugha T, Bioke J, Cooper JE, Giel R, Jablensky A, Regier D & Sartorius N (1990) SCAN: schedules for clinical assessment in neuropsychiatry. *Arch Gen Psychiat* **47**, 586–93.

World Bank (1993) *World Development Report: Investing in Health*. Oxford: Oxford University Press.

10

Prevention and Promotion in Australia

Beverley Raphael and Nada Martinek*

New South Wales Health Department, Sydney, NSW, and
**Department of Psychiatry, University of Queensland, Brisbane, Australia*

The National Mental Health Policy, which was accepted and brought into place in Australia in 1992, contains a commitment to the importance of prevention and promotion in mental health in Australia. While there have been significant developments in policy implementation, there has to date been little coherent development of prevention and promotion at a national level within this framework.

The policy objectives for prevention and promotion are:

- To develop programs which educate the public on mental disorders, including those initiated through mainstream health promotion activities.
- To develop and evaluate primary, secondary and tertiary preventive programs as an essential component of all care provided for people at risk of mental disorder.
- To encourage further research into the causes of mental disorders and the development and evaluation of primary prevention interventions in response to emerging scientific knowledge (National Mental Health Policy 1992).

The policy objectives for primary care services are:

- To ensure that educational programs for primary health care professionals and others with a primary care role contain, within their curriculum and continuing education programs, adequate coverage of mental health issues.
- To provide support to primary carers by ensuring that they have access to specialist mental health resources, particularly in rural and remote areas (National Mental Health Policy 1992).

The 1994 report of the National Mental Health Policy identified two national initiatives which it does, however, place in the context of its reporting on

Preventing Mental Illness: Mental Health Promotion in Primary Care. Edited by R. Jenkins and T.B. Üstün.
© 1998 John Wiley & Sons Ltd.

prevention and promotion. The first of these is the National Mental Health Community Awareness Program and the second is the National Goals and Targets for Mental Health.

NATIONAL MENTAL HEALTH COMMUNITY AWARENESS PROGRAM

This project commenced with a national survey of attitudes to and knowledge about mental health and illness. The survey of community attitudes (REARK 1993) found that many people equated mental disorder with schizophrenia. It was also found that people believed that mental illness was a 'fundamental flaw' which could not improve and thus that outcomes were inevitably poor. This failed to recognize that the majority of mental disorders were treatable, often with a demonstrated efficacy at least equal to that for many physical conditions. People were to some degree tolerant of people with mental illness, but only when they were at a social distance, i.e. not neighbours. There were also views that mental disorder was associated with losing control, and that people with mental illness could 'go crazy' at any time. There were damaging stereotypes of such people being 'violent; dangerous; unpredictable; unreliable . . .' (REARK 1993, p 5).

The study also found, positively, that 50% of respondents had an interest in learning more about mental disorder, and that in addition to such facts, there was a 'need to educate the public about key early warning signs of mental health problems and to encourage contact with the local doctor when these occur' (REARK 1993, p 11).

On the basis of these findings, a national media program has commenced with 'national advertising supported and complemented by comprehensive public relations and education strategies' (National Mental Health Services 1994, p 137).

The proposed initial aim is to reduce discriminatory attitudes towards people with mental illness in the community and will link to state-based initiatives, as well as those undertaken by state and territory governments, non-government organizations, consumer and community groups and professional bodies. The degree to which resources (Australian $8 million) can achieve these targets remains to be seen, as there has to date been limited saturation of the relevant media. However, tracking (quantitative studies) and other evaluation has commenced. Original research, primarily about 'community attitudes', led to the establishment of a benchmark study in early 1995. Community attitudes were reassessed by tracking in August and November 1995 and a repeat benchmark study was planned for March 1996 (Community Awareness Program Team, National Mental Health Strategy 1995—personal communication).

This type of program has major significance and is probably a critical antecedent to prevention and promotion programs. Sartorius (1995) has identified this as a primary and priority task for mental health for the future.

NATIONAL GOALS AND TARGETS FOR MENTAL HEALTH

In contrast to earlier national programs to promote health for all Australians, where mental health was considered to be 'too hard', or not to have an 'adequate scientific base', the most recent proposals include mental health as one of the four priority areas. The report *Better Health Outcomes for Australians* (1994) proposes the following goals and specific targets for mental health (pp 248–9):

- To reduce the loss of health, well-being and social functioning associated with mental health problems and mental disorders.
- To reduce the rate of suicide among people with mental disorders.

Goals and targets were prioritized in two areas: depression and related disorder; and schizophrenia and other psychoses. The specific targets for depression and related disorders are:

- Reduce the incidence of depression and related disorders following trauma or bereavement by 20% by the year 2000.
- Improve the quality of life of those affected by depression and related disorders by reducing the duration of disabling symptoms by 20%.
- Reduce likelihood of relapse following a first episode of depression and related disorders.

Targets for schizophrenia and other psychoses are:

- Improve the quality of life, independence and subjective well-being of those affected by schizophrenia and other psychoses.
- Reduce the typical duration of disabling symptoms from an episode of schizophrenia and other psychoses by 20%.
- Significantly reduce the likelihood of relapse following a first episode of schizophrenia and other psychoses.

Targets for suicide reduction are:

- Reduce by 15% the expected Australian suicide rates over 10 years.
- Reduce by 25% the suicide rates in people suffering with schizophrenia and other psychoses over 10 years.

It was also proposed that the achievement of these goals and targets would be 'on the basis of strategies developed nationally', through the working group responsible for implementation of the National Mental Health Policy (the Australian Health Ministers' Advisory Council—AHMAC—National Working Group on Mental Health Policy), and at state and territory level. The Australian Institute of Health and Welfare, the national body responsible for monitoring health data and outcomes, will be responsible for monitoring programs towards the achievement of these goals and targets.

It should be noted that these strategies and goals do not encompass positive mental health as an outcome, so the promotion of mental health is secondary to the impact on, or lessening of, incidence and prevalence of mental disorders, as indicated above. The broader components originally proposed as part of this initiative encompassed positive mental health promotion activities geared to community and primary care levels, and placed some emphasis on community structures and health literacy.

The current approach is much more specifically orientated to mental health care systems or disorders. It should be noted, however, that within the spectrum of these proposed goals and targets, the needs of special groups—for instance, indigenous people, people of non-English-speaking backgrounds (e.g. migrants and refugees) are taken into account. Other frameworks are also suggested, with a need for youth and the elderly to be considered, gender issues and multiple disability and disadvantaged. The aim is to have 'a blend of a population-based approach to prevention and more specific targeting of at-risk groups' (p 252). And it is agreed that there is 'a strong case for a "youth focus"' (p 255).

It must be noted, too, that in the identification of agencies that should be involved in implementing the strategies proposed, general practitioners, Aboriginal and Torres Strait Islander Community Controlled Health Services, and non-government organizations, as well as other agencies acting at a primary care level, are identified as key players. Community development models are also suggested.

Throughout this proposal, accepted by state and federal governments, there is a *strong reliance on primary care*, and many strategies rely on general practitioners. Some of these are exemplified below:

- Studies of the pathways to care and help-seeking, addressing cultural and other barriers to access to primary care and suggestions to overcome such barriers, were due to be reported in a series of publications by the end of 1995.
- Progress towards a standardized system of data collection in primary care, which includes mental health data and studies of depression and related disorders in primary care.
- Development of specific programs for general practitioners in the recognition, effective treatment and relapse prevention of new cases of depression and related disorders; consultation–liaison and related models are suggested with, as a key result, the incorporation of training in these areas into post-graduate and continuing medical education for general practitioners (National Mental Health Services 1994). This could also cover the development and distribution of appropriate *guidelines for best practice in primary care* for the clinical management of depression in primary care.
- Enhance the ability of primary health service providers in the recognition of the early manifestations of schizophrenia and related psychoses.

- Improved recognition of and response to risk factors or disorders such as depression with regard to high-risk situations for suicide with, as a key result, the increased attendance at primary health care services for treatment of depression and related disorders. This would also involve provision of incentives for general practitioners for continuing education on the management of psychiatric problems presenting in primary care.

With regard to such aims, the 1994 National Mental Health Services Report supports the *potential role of general practitioners as primary care providers in mental health*, and identifies a number of initiatives. These include the development of a *Joint Consultative Council on Mental Health* between the professional organizations of psychiatrists and general practitioners to examine their future roles in mental health; the prioritizing of mental health as an area in the funding of projects and programs through divisions of general practice; and work to develop a mental health strategy for *Divisions of General Practice*. While the majority of these proposals and programs have been directed towards the care of those already suffering a mental disorder, it is suggested that they will also deal with health promotion and early intervention strategies in this area.

These frameworks for both early intervention and care are particularly apposite with respect to the mental health needs of rural and remote communities under a *Rural Health Support Education and Training Program*. This has provided priorities and funding for mental health initiatives in rural areas and in developing services, including telemedicine, for the mental health needs of remote centres.

These strategies and initiatives show a commitment to a primary care focus in mental health, although it must be stated that the way in which such proposals will be operationalized, resourced, coordinated, implemented and evaluated at a national level remains to be established. In particular, the achievement of prevention and promotion is even less clear.

The Goals and Targets for Mental Health highlighted the need for the *development of baseline data for prevalence of major disorders and indicators such as suicide*. These were seen to need to encompass longitudinal aspects (i.e. components which could be serially repeated for monitoring purposes), to be culturally sensitive, and to provide for studies in special contexts (e.g. primary care) and outcome and quality of life measures. To this end, it was proposed that there be a *research network of Australian mental health epidemiologists* operational by end of 1995. Also planned was a *national mental health survey*, conducted in 1996. While this would cover major disorders and age groups, there must be concern from a prevention point of view that it was proposed that it would not include significant risk factors in the domains to be surveyed, except a history of family violence in the adult population, although it was proposed that it would do so for children and young people (up to age 18).

While these initiatives provide a framework which can contribute to prevention and promotion in mental health, they do not as yet provide any specific proposals to take these issues forward.

OTHER NATIONAL INITIATIVES

Within Australia there is also a national organization addressing health issues. The National Health and Medical Research Council (NHMRC) operates with both health advisory and research arms. Under its auspices, a major report was published—*Scope for Prevention in Mental Health* (Raphael 1992). Specific proposals for prevention and promotion in mental health have also been taken forward with current initiatives examining the role of *childhood sexual abuse* and *opportunities for prevention in mental health*, related to this area. This comes within the Health Advancement Standing Committee spectrum, and this group is also examining healthy schools and workplaces and will include mental health considerations in these contexts. Health promotion has been identified as an area that needs further development. Within the Quality of Care and Health Outcomes Committee structure, adolescent depression was determined to be a key area. A working party has developed guidelines for the assessment, prevention, diagnosis and treatment of *adolescent depression.*

The NHMRC has also provided some research funds for projects dealing with prevention in mental health, over the years. However, it is difficult to gather a reliable picture of the extent of funding in the area of preventive psychiatry. In examining trends in NHMRC spending in preventive psychiatry, it can be seen, for example, that in 1989, of the approximately $716 000 spent on preventive medical research, only 9.7% was apparently spent on work in preventive psychiatry. It is also noted that by 1992 there was a remarkable increase in expenditure on mental health research, bringing the budget for this year to $10 million, and on increasing the number of grants made in the general mental health area. But despite this increase in funding, a mismatch remains between the amount of money spent on research in mental health and the cost of providing psychiatric care in the community (Raphael 1992).

Another national initiative was the *Report of the National Inquiry into the Human Rights of People with Mental Illness* (HREOC 1993). This report emphasized the importance of prevention and promotion and also targeted the needs of children and young people, the children of mentally ill parents, homeless people, Aboriginal and Torres Strait Island people and other groups. Its specific recommendations for prevention and promotion were as follows:

- Nationwide campaign to educate the general community and specific groups such as young people at school about mental illness.
- Prevention programs for young people must address youth suicide, depression, conduct disorder and other disruptive behaviour, the needs of young homeless people, those involved with our 'juvenile justice system', and other groups with special needs.
- Education, support and respite must be provided for those who care for people with schizophrenia, dementia or other serious illness (HREOC 1993).

Other national contributions are sporadic and not coordinated. These are as follows:

- *National Mental Health Week.* Currently held in October of each year, this is an opportunity for education, public awareness and a variety of programs, many of which have mental health promotion components which may enhance knowledge and encourage early care seeking.
- *National programs in intersectoral or related areas* that may contribute to positive mental health outcomes. These include violence prevention; suicide prevention; child abuse prevention and others. Unfortunately, mental health outcomes are rarely directly identified and evaluated. Research support, e.g. the *RADGAC Mental Health Research Program*, has specified 'prevention and promotion' as a target area demanding attention in mental health.
- *Healthy Families, Healthy Nation.* This review (Sanders 1995) suggests strategies for promoting family mental health in Australia and was supported by the National Mental Health Policy. The review suggests that the National Mental Health Policy should be changed to reflect: the central importance of healthy family relationships as a fundamental goal in mental health; that priority should be given to services for families, with emphasis on training primary care workers; demonstrated projects in family intervention; that primary care settings should be used more extensively for the development of specialist family intervention services to improve access and enhance effectiveness; specific strategies for indigenous families, those from ethnic minorities, and those who are disadvantaged; recommendations concerning training of mental health professionals in the field of family mental health; recommendations for research priorities; and recommendations for Aboriginal and Torres Strait Island families.
- *Mental Health Promotion within a National Framework.* This report of a national workshop was held under the auspices of the Victorian Health Promotion Foundation and is noted below. It makes recommendations to take mental health promotion forward at a national level.
- *National Aboriginal Mental Health Strategy.* This report places heavy emphasis on primary care through Aboriginal community-controlled primary health care services as a focus for an holistic approach to mental health, with a strong focus on mental health promotion and prevention for children and young people ('Our Children, Our Future') as well as direct prevention and promotion— targeting violence as the first priority (Swan & Raphael 1995).

Despite these approaches, there has not really been significant coherent development nationally in this sphere. It is really not surprising, in view of Australian political contexts, that there have been initiatives at state levels which are exciting and relevant. But despite proposals, there has been no coordinated national linkage of these towards the proposed targets or for the development of prevention and mental health promotion. This is the more so because mental health has traditionally been a state and territory responsibility in Australia and it is only with the National Mental Health Policy that there has been a coordinated approach.

STATE-BASED MENTAL HEALTH PROMOTION AND PREVENTION

While it is acknowledged that at a state level commitment is sporadic, there are indicators that it may be increasing (National Mental Health Services 1994, p 138). However, it should be noted that in the responses of different Australian states to the survey for this paper, some states had specific, detailed and important initiatives in this sphere. In some instances these were drawn alongside state health goals, while in others they had been areas of strength, evolving over years. In such instances there was strong support from state health promotion foundations, particularly in Victoria (VicHealth) and also to a lesser but significant degree in Western Australia (Healthway). More recently, South Australia has also pursued the development of prevention and promotion for mental health (Foundation, SA), with a particular focus on youth. University departments of psychiatry (and psychology, in some instances) have been actively involved in this field, often over many years (e.g. University of Queensland), as have some research institutes.

It is useful to view these multiple levels and contributions in the context of the types of prevention issues they address; the scientific base on which they operate; the age groups or other groups that they target; the degree to which they are simply proposed or planned or implemented in direct programs. Evaluation of these such programs, however, needs further development in many instances.

EDUCATION, COMMUNITY AWARENESS—UNIVERSAL AND OTHER BROADLY-BASED INTERVENTIONS

Mental Health Associations in each state are actively involved in programs of community education about mental illness. Other non-government organizations are also influential in this area, with organizations such ARAFMI (Association for the Relatives and Friends of the Mentally Ill) running educational programs in a range of settings such as schools and involving people with mental illness in these. This approach is reported to have been helpful to young people in terms of coming forward with their own problems, perhaps at an earlier stage. There is a need for more formal evaluation, and if such benefits are further substantiated, the broadening of such programs.

Educational initiatives may include a wide range of formal and informal approaches. They are often supported and promoted by government and frequently link to consumer, non-government and community organizations. They may formally reflect national agendas, be linked to or funded through these, or simply be locally and state-based arising from local interests, enthusiasms or need.

Consumer and non-government agencies that are prominent include the Australian National Association for Mental Health (ANAMH) and state mental health associations, e.g. the Australian Psychiatric Disability Coalition, ARAFMI and many other groups. It should be noted, however, that the involvement of such groups frequently focuses on the illness, disability and treatment, i.e. on tertiary prevention and not mental health promotion and prevention at primary or secondary (early intervention) levels. An initiative through mental health groups is a depression awareness and treatment program in the DART model which derives support from the Australian National Association for Mental Health (Chapman 1994). This is heavily orientated to primary care providers. Another primary care-focused project where consumers, government and industry worked *together* to develop consumer educational outreach regarding medicines is an Australian pharmaceutical health promotion strategy (Mant 1994).

Non-mental health agencies and non-government organizations play an important part, however, in prevention and promotion activities relevant to mental health. For instance PaNDA (Post- and Antenatal Depression Association) is very committed to public education and education of midwives, general practitioners, obstetricians and well-baby clinics to the prevention, early detection and rapid and effective management of postnatal depression.

Other associations which may contribute to mental health outcomes include the bereavement self-help associations (e.g. Sudden Infant Death Association; Compassionate Friends; Solace; Still-birth and Neonatal Death Association). These provide education, support and counselling in many instances and may contribute to lessening risk of post-bereavement morbidity. Sexual assault counselling and support programs and domestic violence programs, be they based on non-government or government organizations, may potentially assist mental health outcomes. For the most part, however, here too there may be a failure to explore mental health outcomes formally and evaluate the effectiveness of processes in achieving promotion or prevention in this field—the more so because this is often not identified as the raison d'être of such groups, and even to them mental disorders may be stigmatized.

Commitment to mental health promotion, primary, secondary and tertiary prevention at a state level is also variable, and while in many instances it is 'written in', actual programs may be lagging.

HEALTH PROMOTION FOUNDATIONS AND THEIR ROLE

VicHealth

An example of the excellent leadership demonstrated by health promotion foundations is provided by the work of VicHealth—the Victorian Health Promotion Foundation. This leadership was against the trend of such groups which tended to focus on alcohol/tobacco/physical health. Galbally, the Chief Executive Officer of this group, identified mental health as a priority area, chaired a workshop in this area (1988) and has demonstrated national leadership since this time. The programs have focused on research to establish a sound foundation through funding of significant academic programs. In addition, community-based interventions have been developed, directed towards mental health promotion.

The commitment to mental health research and programs from 1988 to the present is ongoing and very substantial, amounting to tens of millions of dollars. Studies with prevention and promotion programs arising from them cover a large number of areas.

EPPIC: the Early Psychosis Prevention Intervention Centre

This centre provides a specialized program but one that interacts with primary care through education to detect indicators and promote early intervention and treatment through its community arm. This is an integrated and comprehensive psychiatric program aimed at addressing the needs of older adolescents and young adults. The aims of this centre and its related programs are: early identification and treatment of the primary symptoms of psychiatric illness; reduction of secondary mental illness such as post-traumatic stress syndromes arising from the impact of psychotic decompensation and treatment; reduction of relapse frequency and severity; reduced disruption of psychosocial functioning; lessened impact on psychosocial development in the critical period when most disability tends to occur; and reduction of the burden on carers with promotion of well-being in family members.

There is a key focus on assisting the individual and family to maximize recovery. This program is soundly based on extensive research and evaluation of outcomes, has shown itself to be effective in prevention goals and is a preventive approach to management. It has a number of components, including the early psychosis assessment team, the inpatient unit, outpatient and day programs.

This program operates in interaction with primary care services, e.g. for young people through schools and youth programs, as well as health care settings and including general practice. It is actively involved in training. Program extension covers the State of Victoria and there have been training and best practice program evolution in other states. Further intended directions include selective and indicated interventions, e.g. further identification and study of the prodrome of psychosis and development of preventive interventions orientated to this; preventive interventions with children of high-risk groups, e.g. children of psychotic parents; examination of help-seeking and pathway to care, including those through primary care settings.

The program will also form the central pillar of the Centre and Program for Young People's Mental Health, which has been developed in association with the work funded by VicHealth. This will deal with adolescent depression and health risk behaviours, as well as other negative mental health outcomes for young people.

The evaluation of this program has been systematic and has set a model for other developments. The basis of the program has been reviewed (McGorry & Singh 1995). It has led to lower levels of neuroleptics being necessary (about one-third), a shorter hospital stay, positive consumer satisfaction, better quality of life and social role functions, and no cases of post-traumatic stress disorder (McGorry 1993; Edwards et al 1994). In addition, recent reports suggest cost benefits as well (McGorry & Singh 1995). There have been significant research publications and educational material as a product of this program.

This is a model initiative of prevention and early intervention in mental health which has attracted national and international attention. It has significant inter-action with primary care and potential impact there, despite having a specialized mental health focus.

Galbally (1995; personal communication) outlined the current status and aims of mental health promotion, including the areas identified above, at a nationally convened planning forum. Proposals were developed for a draft report (Galbally 1994) which defined mental health promotion, reviewing its importance; outlined the requirements of such a national program; described proposed elements; and suggested focal areas and directions for future development.

State Health and Community Services Department programs for prevention and promotion in mental health in Victoria in many instances complement the above. They include: young people's programs such as the Victorian Adolescent Cohort; a youth suicide prevention project; local mental health education and prevention programs for high-risk young homeless people; the CHAMP project, which is developing a proactive approach to the children of seriously mentally ill parents; an options project promoting mental health and human rights in 19 Government schools, focusing on reducing bullying and promoting healthy relationships; education sources on CD-ROM and other media on various aspects of adolescent health; and a school kit on schizophrenia. In addition, there is a positive parenting strategy developing materials relating to promotion of health, psychosocial development and early intervention with families at risk, under the auspices of the Primary Care Division.

ACADEMIC STUDIES IN MENTAL HEALTH PROMOTION AND PREVENTION

The study described above (EPPIC), the Western Australian Child Health Survey and many of the others reported, have a strong academic base, but are also linked to State Health Department and Health Promotion Foundations for aims relating to implementation. In other states, e.g. Queensland, the focus for prevention and promotion has been chiefly at the level of research programs in university departments, either establishing the basis for preventive intervention, or testing its effectiveness.

CONCLUSIONS AND RECOMMENDATIONS

There is a substantial general interest in and support for mental health promotion and for prevention in the mental health field. This is characterized by enthusiasm, multiple approaches and some areas of emphasis: suicide prevention; children; young people and families; women; and so forth. The majority of these programs are implemented at community and/or primary care levels, or have the potential to be so. Recent refocusing on prevention in the mental health field has led to a number of reviews from the levels of WHO to UK, USA, Canadian, Scandinavian and Australian syntheses (Sartorius et al 1993; Paykel et al 1993; OSAP 1989; Mrazek & Haggerty 1994; Leighton & Murphy 1987; Raphael 1992). Many of these describe studies of programs with a primary care focus, although this more often relates to screening and early intervention for instance in general practice, with a lesser emphasis on mental health promotion or primary care (Tippett 1994). A *Handbook of Preventive Psychiatry* has also been produced (Raphael & Burrows 1995).

What is significant about this next wave of Mental Health Promotion and Prevention, 25–30 years after Caplan (1964) is that there is now, in many instances, a systematic scientific base, epidemiological studies identifying baseline levels of morbidity and risk factors, and evaluations of preventive interventions. A coordinated approach is generally lacking.

However, there is still much to suggest, as was highlighted by Eisenberg in other contexts, e.g. HIV/AIDS (Eisenberg 1995), that interventions, promotion and prevention programs rarely deal with those broad social influences such as poverty and inequity that contribute so pervasively to adverse mental health outcomes (Freedman 1995). Neither are they shaped for access by, or taken up by, the disadvantaged, cultural minorities and so forth, or other groups who might be at greatest risk and in greatest need. Nowhere is this more obvious than, for instance, with indigenous populations where falling health status reflects a failure to address issues of mental health and well-being in ways that are holistic and culturally appropriate. Prevention belongs to the middle class who change their lifestyle for such outcomes, but may already be less at risk. However, some programs are shaped to the needs of those who are socially disadvantaged, of different culture or minority status and have utilized locally developed formats relevant to and in collaboration with those groups who are potentially affected. This methodology, so relevant in HIV/AIDS, must also be taken to the mental health field.

It is essential that there is a more coordinated approach to achieve identified goals and measurable outcomes. In this context it would be appropriate to adopt a framework for implementation, such as that proposed in Australia's National Mental Health Goals and Targets (Better Health Outcomes for Australians, 1994, pp 273–4). Of the prevention-orientated strategies it says:

> The implementation and monitoring of these strategies requires an effective coordinating structure to facilitate this national process. The opportunity exists to build on progress already made in a number of centres to formalize a collaborative network of preventive psychiatry centres.
>
> Such collaboration would facilitate mental health promotional and community education strategies, support and resource the development of early intervention programs and address the detection of hidden psychiatric morbidity. These centres could facilitate, in each state, the coordination of strategies such as depression awareness campaigns, support the evaluation of strategies, national goals and targets

and play a key role in the development of educational programs for primary care and mental health professionals. They should also facilitate intersectoral linkages and involvement of consumers, carers and local community groups in mental health promotion and service delivery (pp 273–4).

The Second National Mental Health Strategy will take these issues forward.

POSTSCRIPT

Since the material in this chapter was first presented, many of the suggested initiatives have occurred. Most importantly, an agreed and coordinated approach to mental health promotion and prevention has been established. This commenced with National Mental Health Policy initiatives including a workshop on Prevention, Promotion and Early Intervention; the funding of early intervention programs for depression and anxiety in schools; a best practice early intervention network; and a report *Mental Health Promotion Australia*. A National Survey of Mental Health and wellbeing in adults, children and young people will provide data on prevalence, need and risk, and add a further basis for preventive initiatives. A National Consultancy between psychiatrists and general practitioners has also supported the need for an approach focused on primary care. The National Standards for Mental Health Services have also been produced. These set in place requirements for the provision of prevention and promotion indicated in the central standard.

> The Mental Health Services has policy, resources and plans that support mental health promotion, prevention of mental disorders and mental health problems, early detection and intervention.

Most importantly, however, the National Mental Health Strategy has been extended for an additional period of the years from 1998 to 2003 with prevention, promotion and early intervention one of the three key areas to be addressed throughout this period. This will be further supported by National Public Health Partnership commitment to address mental health prevention and promotion in a public health framework, and by the identification of depression and related disorders as a National Health Priority Area also to be targeted in this way. Key indicators, programs and initiatives will be supported by research, education and evaluation to systematically enhance mental health outcomes. Primary care will be not only one of the chief settings, but also a key partner and stakeholder to take forward this coordinated priority framework for mental health.

REFERENCES

Better Health Outcomes for Australians (1994) *National Goals, Targets and Strategies for Better Health Outcomes Into the Next Century*. Canberra: Commonwealth Department of Human Services and Health, AGPS.

Caplan G (1964) *Principles of Preventive Psychiatry*. New York: Basic Books.

Chapman M (1994) Depression campaign to target GPs and public. *Australian Doctor*, 20 May, p 18.

Edwards J, Francey SH, McGorry RD, Jackson HJ (1994) Early psychosis prevention and intervention: evolution of a comprehensive community-based specialized service. *Behaviour Change* **11**(4), 223–33.

Eisenberg L (1995) Social policy and the reality of prevention. In B Raphael & G Burrows (eds) *Handbook of Preventive Psychiatry.* Amsterdam: Elsevier.

Freedman AM (1995) Promoting mental health. In B Raphael & G Burrows (eds) *Handbook of Preventive Psychiatry.* Amsterdam: Elsevier.

Galbally R (1994) Draft: Towards a Mental Health Promotion Strategy. Victorian Health Promotion Foundation.

HREOC (Human Rights and Equal Opportunity Commission) (1993) *Human Rights and Mental Illness.* Canberra: AGPS.

Leighton AH & Murphy JM (1987) Primary prevention of psychiatric disorders. *Acta Psychiat Scand* (Suppl) **337**(76), 7–13.

Mant A (1994) Editorial. Pharmaceutical health promotion: a new concept in therapeutics. *Soc Sci Med* **39**(3), 305–6.

McGorry P (1993) Early psychosis prevention and intervention centre. *Australas Psychiat* **1**, 32–4.

McGorry P, Mihalopoulos C, Henry L, Dakis J et al (1995) Spurious precision: procedural validity of diagnostic assessment in psychotic disorders. *Am J Psychiat* **152**(2), 220–23.

McGorry P & Singh B (1995) Schizophrenia: risk and possibility. In B Raphael & G Burrows (eds) *Handbook of Preventive Psychiatry.* Amsterdam: Elsevier.

Mrazek PJ & Haggerty RJ (eds) (1994) *Reducing Risks for Mental Disorders: Frontiers for Preventive Intervention Research.* Washington, DC: Institute of Medicine National Academy Press.

National Mental Health Policy (1992) Australian Health Ministers' Conference 1992. Canberra: AGPS.

National Mental Health Services (1995) *Second Annual Report: Changes in Australia's Mental Health Services in Year Two of the National Mental Health Strategy (1994)* Canberra: Australian Government Publishing Service.

National Mental Health Strategy Community Awareness Program (1995) Community awareness program team (personal communication).

OSAP (1989) *Prevention of Mental Disorders, Alcohol and other Drug Use in Children and Adolescents.* Washington, DC: US Department of Health and Human Services.

Paykel ES, Caldicott F, Cox J, Day K, Jenkins R et al (1993) *Prevention in Psychiatry.* Report of the Special Committee on the place of prevention in psychiatry. London: Royal College of Psychiatrists.

Raphael B (1992) *Scope for Prevention in Mental Health.* NHMRC, Canberra: Australian Government Publishing Service.

Raphael B & Burrows G (eds) (1995) *Handbook of Preventive Psychiatry.* Amsterdam: Elsevier.

REARK (1993) *Community Attitudes to Mental Illness.* A report on qualitative research. Canberra: Department of Health, Housing, Local Government and Community Services.

Sanders M (1995) *Healthy Families, Healthy Nation: Strategies for Promoting Family Mental Health in Australia.* Brisbane: Australian Academic Press.

Sartorius N, De Girolamo G, Andrews G, Allen German G, Eisenberg L (1993) *Treatment of Mental Disorders.* New York: World Health Organization, American Psychiatric Press, Inc.

Sartorius N (1995) Preface. In B Raphael & G Burrows (eds) *Handbook of Preventive Psychiatry.* Amsterdam: Elsevier.

Swan P & Raphael B (1995) '*Ways Forward': National Aboriginal and Torres Strait Islander Mental Health Policy.* Report prepared for Office for Aboriginal and Torres Strait Islander Health Services, Commonwealth Department of Human Services and Health.

Tippett VC (1994) Targeting opportunities for change: mental health promotion in primary care. *Behav Change* **11**, 153–66.

11

Policy and Research in Developing Countries

MP Deva

Department of Psychological Medicine, University of Malaya,
Kuala Lumpur, Malaysia

The Third World or the developing countries of the world are by no means uniformly underdeveloped or uniformly poor in an economic sense. In the past half-century, the rapid economic and industrial development in East and Southeast Asia has made the term 'Third World' take on a different meaning, while famine, political strife and wars have in no small way undermined the once well-off countries of Africa and Asia to much lower levels of existence.

The rate at which the health care systems of many developing countries have likewise risen or fallen is often determined not only by economic factors. Thus, policies governing the promotion of health and prevention in primary care vary considerably from one region to the other among these countries.

Primary care has several meanings, depending on the different settings in which it is applied. In the developed nations of the world, the term usually applies to the care provided by general practitioners in non-specialist settings. In developing countries, where the doctor:patient ratio may be 1:16 000 in Nepal to 1:2857 in Vietnam (Asiaweek 1995), reliance on a variety of allied professionals and traditional healers as deliverers of primary medical care for the population is often the norm in rural areas. In the socialist countries such as China, Vietnam or Laos, a variety of trained medical assistants also provide primary health care for large portions of the population. In Malaysia, with 8000 doctors for its 19 million people in large areas of the sparsely populated state of Sarawak, primary care is delivered by nurses and even traditional healers. Projects are under way to train traditional midwives in basic medical and health care while rural hospitals are manned by trained male nurses.

Thus primary care in developing countries is a bewildering variety of systems usually contingent on availability of resources and manpower.

Preventing Mental Illness: Mental Health Promotion in Primary Care. Edited by R. Jenkins and T.B. Üstün.
© 1998 John Wiley & Sons Ltd.

POLICY AND RESEARCH PRIORITIES IN DEVELOPING COUNTRIES

The delivery of primary care in developing countries usually involves care at the most basic level and all available resources are geared to this. The high morbidity and mortality in rural areas is a source of concern. Most of the policy in primary care is geared towards this end: i.e. preventing mortality in countries where infant mortality is high (e.g. 88/1000 live births in Nepal) and calorie intake may be less than 2500 calories/day. Life expectancy is often less than 60 and is as low as 49 in Bhutan. Policy related to primary health care is often aimed at correcting these gross defects in the health of the population and improving the survival and sustenance of the population at risk.

Research is also geared towards reducing infant mortality and improving calorie intake and life expectancy. Primary prevention, therefore, is largely one that prevents mortality and morbidity.

It is only in the past few decades that the emotional health of the population has started to become important in developing countries as well as the developmental health of children, adolescents and adults.

HEALTH PROMOTION PREVENTION PROGRAMS IN THE DEVELOPING COUNTRIES

Despite limited resources and expertise, many developing countries are putting into practice a variety of programs in health promotion and prevention in the field of mental health and general health. Not all of them have reached the stage of fruition and evaluation. These programs may be considered from the point of view of the countries' primary and secondary prevention.

PRIMARY PREVENTION

Developing countries facing enormous economic problems and poverty eradication find it difficult to concentrate on primary prevention in the area of mental health. Perhaps the single most important positive factor in primary prevention is the relatively intact family structure that allows parenting and family life to provide a protective environment for the growing child. Child care is still largely provided by natural parents with considerable support from the extended family where village life or custom allow. Increasingly, urbanization and industrialization are encroaching on this practice, as income, housing and distances separating families put traditional child care practice under strain. To this end, some countries such as Malaysia are taking bold steps to set up workplace creches for working mothers. The rapid rise in the cost of living and the education freely available to them has put many women in a dilemma over their roles as mothers and home-makers while fulfilling their aspirations as working women. This dilemma has no easy solutions and contributes in no small way to the stress and tension among women in developing countries. Some countries are experimenting with part-time work for women and home industries.

The pace of urbanization has also contributed to a tendency to break out of traditional practices in courtship and marriage, with greater recourse to temporary relationships with their attendant disappointments, which can result in attempts at suicide and sometimes substance abuse.

Rapid expansion of growth centres in industry and increasing the time spent on commuting to and from work also contribute to problems. To prevent fragmentation of family life and traditional values, some countries are taking industry to the home or the neighbourhood. Most developing countries encourage breastfeeding and maternal child bonding through provision of at least 6 weeks' maternity leave. In Malaysia, the decentralization of many electrical, electronic and food-based industries to rural and semi-urban areas, along with free transport for workers from villages, have helped reduce the rural urban drift with its attendant mental and social problems.

In the high-density urban areas of some newly industrialized countries such as Singapore, the government actually encourages families of several generations to own high-rise apartments next to each other to encourage, support and maintain family ties.

Another inherent mental health protection system is the traditional policy of encouraging fostering and adoption of orphans by relatives, rather than sending them into care. Relatives are often quite willing to take care of orphans rather than allow the law to decide on their future. Only abject poverty, as seen in some large developing countries, prevents such adoptions.

The schools in many developing countries do not enjoy their own health or psychology services and use the general health care system meant for the public. As such, there are practically no separate systems in schools to help children in most developing countries.

SECONDARY PREVENTION AND PROMOTION OF MENTAL HEALTH

The early detection of emotional problems of children and adults in developing countries has only recently started to make itself felt. For many decades the severe shortage of mental health professionals has contributed to this deficiency in prevention and mental health promotion. The change has really come about because of increasing awareness of problems among children in school, e.g. delinquency, substance abuse and child abuse. Many mental health programs were limited to poorly run mental hospitals with budgets that were totally inadequate.

The biggest change that has occurred in the past two decades is the training of mental health professionals in developing countries. Whereas in the 1960s the training of psychiatrists and allied professionals was largely confined to developed countries, the last 20 years have seen a rapid growth in indigenous training programmes such as those in India, Pakistan, Sri Lanka, Malaysia, Thailand, Indonesia, The Philippines, Kenya, Nigeria and elsewhere. The foreign-trained psychiatrists of old often did not return for economic reasons. Thus today there are hundreds of psychiatrists of Bangladeshi origin in the UK, and Sri Lankan psychiatrists in the USA and UK, but less than 100 in their home countries. The same is true of Pakistan, India, The Philippines or the African countries.

The start of indigenous training programs has in many ways reduced this trend and contributed to a psychiatrist population of 1:2–300 000, rather than 1 million as was the case in the 1960s. The training of allied professionals such as nurses, occupational therapists, social workers and psychologists has also grown in many developing countries.

These large numbers of new psychiatrists have begun contributing to the early detection and management of emotional problems. They have also contributed to the more humane care of mentally ill people and improved their quality of life through secondary prevention. The psychiatric hospitals or institutions of the 1940s and 1950s have in some cases lost their position as the mainstay of psychiatric care while new short-stay non-custodial units have begun treating patients in larger numbers. In Malaysia the four mental hospitals with over 4500 beds today treat fewer patients than do the 20 short-stay units with less than 1000 beds. The custodial and prohibiting attitude in psychiatric care that contributed to many cases of institutional neurosis, not to mention abuse of power, is unfortunately not on its way out.

The decline of the stigma of mental illness so closely linked with institutional psychiatry is today less pervasive and likely to contribute to a more positive image of psychiatry. The growth of liaison psychiatric services in general hospitals and the growth of professional bodies of psychiatrists has also contributed to this trend. In 1960 there were no psychiatric associations in South-east Asia. Today there are five associations and a federation of these associations at regional level founded 14 years ago.

TEACHING OF PSYCHIATRY

Prevention and promotion of mental health in primary care settings cannot be done successfully without a wider awareness of mental health issues in society at large. The mere training of psychiatrists, no matter how many, will not bring about expected changes in promotion of mental health or prevent diseases, if psychiatrists practising in clinical settings are wholly concerned with treating ill patients. The undeniable fact that the vast majority with emotional problems and psychiatric diseases never reach the clinic of a psychiatrist calls for strategies other than ones based on mental hospital teaching.

One of the major problems in the promotion of mental health and prevention of psychiatric problems is still the strong belief in a variety of supernatural causes of mental illnesses—that everything from bedwetting to depression and psychosis is caused by evil spirits or retribution for wrong-doing. While the belief system is by no means unique to the developing world, added problems or poor education, frequent illnesses and high mortality reinforce such beliefs. The answer lies in a wide public education by psychiatrists and mental health workers and through better training of medical students, nurses, health care workers and the community. Even in developed economies, programs such as the Defeat Depression campaign have an important role in improving the wider prevention and promotion of mental health.

In developing countries the biggest handicap in this effort to spread awareness seems to be the sheer lack of trained mental health professionals who can act as agents of change. The psychiatrist population ratio in three countries bears this out. Malaysia and Australia have populations of about 18 million people, but while Australia has about 2000 psychiatrists, Malaysia has only 95. India, with a population of 800 million, has the same number of psychiatrists as Australia. Any effort at spreading psychiatric awareness is going to be severely handicapped by such obvious problems in developing countries.

The answer to these huge problems lies not only in efforts to train more psychiatrists locally but also to spread a simple and easily understood version of psychiatry that can be taught to medical students, general practitioners and all health care workers. While this teaching may not be important for developed countries with good psychiatrist:population ratios, in the developing world it can be crucial.

A country like Malaysia, which has 95 psychiatrists, also has over 8000 medical doctors, most of whom have little or no understanding of basic mental health, let alone classification or diagnostic skills or knowledge of how to treat even the simplest of psychiatric disorders. Trained in an era when psychiatry was taught through 5–10 lectures or demonstrations and exposed the students to bewildering terms and concepts and alarmed them with severe psychoses, they never got to see the psychosomatic, neurotic or depressive illnesses that present in primary care without ever reaching the psychiatrist. On graduation, many such doctors could not detect, let alone treat, common psychiatric problems in primary care.

A User-friendly Teaching of Psychiatry for Primary Care

After many years of teaching psychiatry as was traditionally taught to medical students the world over, in 1992 the Department of Psychological Medicine of the University of Malaya embarked on programmes to make psychiatry training more orientated to primary care settings than to psychiatric wards.

First, a simplified classification was formulated which divided psychiatric disorders into anxiety disorders, depressive disorders, psychotic disorders, personality-related disorders and child psychiatric disorders. This was closely linked to treatments available to the primary care doctors, viz. anxiolytics, antidepressants, antipsychotics and counselling. Simple definitions were made of each of these conditions, which students could easily understand and remember.

Students were taught in both psychiatric wards and primary care settings, where they would be more likely to work on graduation. Although seminar and theoretical teaching is carried out for all students in the 8-week psychiatric clerkship, a proportion are posted to medical, surgical, paediatric, gynaecological and primary care wards or clinics to clerk and discuss psychiatric cases for presentation to lecturers. In this way the medical student sees psychiatric problems in non-psychiatric wards.

The other students see patients in psychiatric wards, then half-way through the 8-week posting, the students are switched over to do the clerkship the other group has already done.

The students, after 3 years of this training system, are more aware of the emotional problems in all patients and not merely severely ill patients who from necessity fill the psychiatric wards.

The students are also taught basic interview techniques with non-psychiatric patients, using video equipment to familiarize themselves with understanding the patient rather than eliciting symptoms: patients' non-verbal cues, feelings and emotional state and responses are emphasized in teaching interview techniques. Real patients are preferred to role play in teaching these techniques.

No teaching is complete without evaluation and students are expected to pass two tests during the 8 weeks, and a proportion actually have psychiatric long cases in their final year examination.

GROWTH OF MENTAL HEALTH MOVEMENTS IN PREVENTION AND PROMOTION

Despite the many handicaps that the developing countries face in terms of resources and trained manpower in mental health, a surprising number of developments to promote mental health and help in prevention have been evident in the past two decades. In Malaysia the first mental health association with these aims was started in 1969, and today there are about a dozen of these throughout the country. Similar associations are found in India, Sri Lanka, Thailand, Indonesia and The Philippines.

These community associations sometimes help run day programmes for mentally ill people but most of their efforts are geared towards the promotion of mental health through public talks, exhibitions and discussions in the media. They regularly take an active part in drug and alcohol prevention campaigns, are a focal point for supporting the families of mentally ill people and play a vital role in advocacy for the mentally ill.

There are other organizations involved in mental health promotion, telephone counselling services and those devoted to the mental health of children and women.

MENTAL HEALTH POLICIES IN DEVELOPING COUNTRIES

As life-saving appears a far greater priority for most health ministries in developing countries, mental health policies take a back seat in health care plans. However, several countries stand out in their efforts to emphasize mental health promotion and prevention. About 10 years ago Indonesia implemented a mental health policy which involved setting up mental health committees in each of the 27 provinces, with the governors as chairmen. These committees discuss both psychiatric and mental health issues, such as those affecting work, children, women and substance abuse and their members include educationalists, health officials, social agencies, psychiatrists and police personnel. The primary health care service or PUSKESMAS has access to psychiatrists for treating mentally ill people at a primary care level.

In India, although public health policy as an instrument of social change was given importance after Independence in 1947, mental health policy has been slow to develop (Reddy 1992). In 1982 the Central Council of Health of India adopted the National Mental Health Programme (Directional General Health Sciences 1982). Among its objectives are:

1. To ensure the availability and accessibility of minimum mental health care for all in the foreseeable future, particularly the most vulnerable underprivileged sector of the population.
2. To encourage the application of mental health knowledge in general health care and in social development.
3. To promote community participation in mental health service development and stimulate efforts towards self-help in the community.

However, Reddy feels that planners should be involved in efforts to implement the National Mental Health Policy because professionals, even with training, are not able to put into practice what they have learnt if planners at state and district levels have not been sensitized to the importance of mental health. In Thailand the Institute of Mental Health, instituted by the government of Thailand's division of mental health, promotes preventive efforts in the area of mental health through regular columns and cartoons in newspapers, posters and brochures as well as television programs.

CONCLUSION

The promotion of mental health and prevention of mental illness in developing countries as active policies have only recently gained importance as life-saving aspects of health and cure of mental illnesses has been a priority for the limited resources available.

Despite extremely small numbers of professionals in many developing countries, active improvements in teaching and the initiation of community-based mental health programs have begun to have an impact on health. More needs to be done but there are encouraging signs that the future for mental health is a bright one.

REFERENCES

Reddy NGN (1992) Mental health planning and policy development at national level. In S Murthy & B Burns (eds) *Proceedings of the Indo-US Symposium on Community Mental Health*, pp 17–37 (NIMHANS Publication No 29). Bangalore: National Institute of Mental Health and Neuroscience.

Directional General Health Sciences (1982) *National Mental Health Programme for India*. New Delhi: Government of India publication.

Asiaweek 22 March (1995) The bottom line—vital statistics of countries.

12

Application of Interventions in Developing Countries

R Srinivasa Murthy
National Institute of Mental Health and Neuroscience, Bangalore, India

Preventing mental illnesses and promotion of mental health in developing countries has a different implication in view of the extremely limited number of mental health professionals as well as mental health infrastructure. On average, most developing countries have less than 1% of the number of mental health professionals available to care for comparable populations in Western countries. In addition, due to the greater emphasis on mental illness and institutional care, mental health is of low priority in health planning and funding.

However, there are advantages in terms of all the patients living in the community. There is limited need for deinstitutionalization. It is also fortunate that the community mental health movements in Western countries give credibility to the emerging mental health programs in developing countries, which are essentially community-based. In order of priority organization of essential mental health services to prevent chronicity is the most important. This has to be carried out by integrating mental health with primary health care. The possibility for preventing mental disorders by linking with public health measures like antenatal care, immunization and school mental health is also an avenue in developing countries, most of which have a strong family and community life, along with deep-rooted religious and cultural beliefs and practices. Promotion of mental health can be achieved by strengthening positive practices and de-emphasizing negative practices. In view of the emerging social changes, a large part of promotion and prevention activities would occur through large-scale measures of social policy making and intersectoral developments. These developments also require the support of international organizations.

This chapter examines this wide area and also highlights positive developments in different countries utilizing the above approaches. Most of the developments are of recent origin and it is hoped that in the coming decades these efforts will reach a critical mass to make a significant change in the areas of prevention of mental disorders and promotion of mental health.

Preventing Mental Illness: Mental Health Promotion in Primary Care. Edited by R. Jenkins and T.B. Üstün.

ADVANCES IN MENTAL HEALTH IN DEVELOPING COUNTRIES

Developments in the twentieth century have dramatically changed concepts of mental health care as a result of new knowledge. There has been a shift from mental illness to mental health. This change is important to understand in terms of both the factors and the direction of change.

During the last two decades, especially following the WHO (1975) Expert Committee Recommendations and the results of the WHO study on strategies for extending mental health care (1975–1981) (Sartorius & Harding 1983) there have been a number of initiatives at national, regional and local levels. These have been in the form of formulation of national programs of mental health (WHO 1991), pilot programs for integration of mental health in primary health care, such as in India (Wig, Murthy & Harding 1981; Murthy 1992; Murthy & Wig 1993), Uganda (Edgell 1970), Tanzania (Schulsinger & Jablensky 1991), China (Phillips, Pearson & Wang 1994), Colombia (Climent et al 1978), Sri Lanka (Mendis 1990) and Nigeria (Asuni 1990) and other developing countries of South East Asia (Community Mental Health News 1989; Murthy 1983).

The urgent need for the organization of mental health care has been expressed by leaders from Africa (German 1975; Giel 1975; Lambo 1966; Swift 1976), Asia (Carstairs 1973; Lin 1983), from WHO (1975, 1984, 1990, 1992), Biegel (1983) and in more recent times by the Harvard Medical School (1995).

In the last two decades, significant progress has occurred in developing countries. This has ranged from formulation of national policies to development of programs of care and integration of community care involving families, volunteers and other community resources.

The most striking aspect of the mental health care in developing countries is the choice of community mental health care as the primary approach to provide care to the general population. In almost all the developing countries, there are very limited institutional facilities for the care of the mentally ill. There are also only a small number of mental health professionals to provide services. For example, in the countries of South East Asia (viz. India, Pakistan, Bangladesh, Sri Lanka, Nepal and Myanmar) there was only one psychiatric bed per 30 000 population in contrast to 2–13 beds per 1000 population in Europe (Sartorius 1990). The number of mental health professionals was also very limited, often amounting to only a handful. Even in 1995, only minor improvements had occurred in manpower development. The major increase has occurred in the number of psychiatrists (e.g. India had 500 psychiatrists in 1972 and in 1995 there were about 3000) but without a consequent increase in trained clinical psychologists, psychiatric social workers, psychiatric nurses and rehabilitation personnel (Wig & Murthy 1994).

The information from developing countries of importance for mental health care is:

1. Information about the prevalence and pattern of mental disorders in rural and urban populations, school children and populations exposed to special stresses like war, disasters and migration have shown that mental disorders are of public health importance (Murthy 1922a, b).
2. In developing countries, there have been extremely limited mental health facilities and manpower (less than 1% of that in Western countries). As a result, much of the care has occurred in non-institutional settings, mainly in the family and community (NMHP 1982; WHO 1991).
3. The organization of the national level mental health care program in India (and other developing countries) is of recent origin. The National Program of Mental Health was launched in 1982 in India (WHO 1991).
4. The attitudes of the community continue to be supportive and most families prefer to care for ill family members. This is a specific advantage for mental health planning (Whyte 1991; Shankar 1994; Pai & Kapur 1983; Pai et al 1983).
5. Research studies into schizophrenia and acute psychoses from different parts of India and Africa (Murthy & Wig 1993; Wig, Murthy & Harding 1981) have identified the importance of: (a) early identification; (b) regular treatment; and (c) good outcomes with social recovery for the majority of the ill persons. Similarly, studies of elderly persons with emotional problems have shown the importance of family integration and care of physical problems to limit the occurrence and progress of emotional problems.
6. A number of studies have demonstrated the value of rehabilitation measures for the care of chronically ill persons. The value of family education, work therapy, group interaction, social skills training, vocational training and sheltered workshops have been especially well demonstrated (Asuni 1990; Mendis 1990; Pai & Kapur 1981, 1982; Edgell 1970; Lambo 1966).

MENTAL HEALTH CARE INITIATIVES AT PRIMARY HEALTH CARE IN DEVELOPING COUNTRIES

Need

Non-availability of mental health services and negative community perceptions about mental hospitals result in most mentally ill persons seeking help in primary care facilities. These patients are important, as they are most often not diagnosed appropriately, are treated with non-specific drugs and are unnecessarily investigated; Harding et al's (1980) study in four developing countries, as part of a WHO study, found an overall frequency of 13.9%. In this study, using a two-stage screening procedure, 1624 were screened. It was also found that the great majority of cases were suffering from neurotic illness. For the majority the presenting symptom was physical. Ormel et al (1994) have reported that there is high disability among the mentally ill attending primary care facilities. There was a dose response relationship between severity of mental illness and disability.

Interventions

A major development is interventions developed at primary health care level. The stimulus for the many national level initiatives was the WHO collaborative project, part of a WHO multi-centre international collaborative project entitled *Strategies for Extending Mental Health Care* (1975–1981) and involving seven developing countries—Brazil, Colombia, Egypt, India, The Philippines, Senegal and Sudan (Sartorius & Harding 1983; Murthy & Wig 1983; Wig, Murthy & Harding 1981).

The focus for the project was the evaluation of an intervention approach of integrating mental health care with general health services.

A number of other developing countries in Asia, Africa and South America have been experimenting with this approach. In Colombia, ancillary nurses have been found to be able to provide care for the non-psychotic problems. In Tanzania, a national program has been launched with this approach. In recent years, pilot programs have been started in Bangladesh, Egypt, Nepal, Pakistan (Mubbasher et al 1986) and Indonesia, involving population groups of 30 000–417 000 (Murthy 1983). Regular training of primary care personnel has been organized in Bangladesh, Bhutan, India, the Maldives, Nepal, Pakistan, Egypt, Yemen, Iran, Somalia, Afghanistan, Iraq, Sudan and in a number of countries of Africa. In Sri Lanka, a program for children at risk to promote mental health has been completed. In India, alternative community care facilities like hostels, half-way homes, day care centres, crisis intervention centres, community level detoxification camps, self-help groups for families, and the use of traditional systems like yoga and meditation have developed (Wig & Murthy 1994). Initial reports suggest that the approach is not only relevant but also effective in reaching sections of the population not reached by institutional facilities. An interesting observation is that there are variations in the type of personnel involved in mental health care, the degree of responsibility given for use of drugs and the mechanism of support and supervision by the professionals, in the different countries (Wig 1993).

A significant development is the availability of training manuals for different categories of health personnel ranging from doctors to village level workers (WHO 1991).

Evaluation of primary care initiatives have been not adequate. Three things are significant. First, in most countries pilot programs have not become national programs. Second, the impact has mostly been assessed in terms of the members identified, change in diagnostic accuracy and changes in knowledge and attitude. Only isolated studies have studied the course, outcome and impact on disability and social functioning (Murthy 1983, 1992a, b). Third, cost–benefit and cost-effectiveness studies are lacking. These are areas for future work.

In addition to primary health care personnel in the formal health sector, there have been a number of preventive activities in other sectors. These have been a result of the limited primary health care infrastructure in developing countries.

The most important of these initiatives involve school children and lay volunteers to prevent mental handicap and suicide and provide rehabilitation (Wig & Murthy 1994; Mubbashar et al 1986).

In India, reflecting these developments (by both government and NGOs) a number of innovating approaches to treatment and rehabilitation of the mentally ill have been initiated in the 1980s, outside the mental hospitals and institutions. The most important are:

1. Integration of mental health care with general health care. This aims to provide care within easy access of ill individuals, to enable early and regular treatment; currently, models for integration at district level have been developed (e.g. Bellary District Mental Health Program: Wig, Murthy & Harding 1981; Murthy 1992a, b).
2. The School Mental Health Program, involving schoolteachers and students, for promotion of mental health as well as care of ill persons.
3. Promotion of child mental health through the involvement of the Anganwadis (ICDS program) and other pre-school child care personnel.
4. Crisis intervention for suicide prevention and crisis help, utilizing the services of volunteers for the community.
5. Half-way homes for mentally ill individuals for social skills training, vocational training and preparation for community living.
6. Education of family members of persons with schizophrenia about coping skills, understanding of the illness, crisis support and reducing family stress and burden.
7. Education and involvement of the general public through the activities of the non-governmental organizations (e.g. treatment of drug dependence).
8. Medical materials for public education in the form of books in local languages, pamphlets, videos and movies.
9. Sheltered workshops for mentally ill and mentally retarded individuals.
10. Training for non-professionals to work with the different categories of mentally ill individuals (Murthy & Burns 1992).

The scope for intervention is illustrated by a project on high-risk infants (Naik & Plumber 1994), in which infants with (a) hypoxic ischaemic encephalopathy; (b) low birthweight; (c) hyperbilirubinaemia; (d) convulsions; (e) meningitis; and (f) birth trauma were identified soon after birth for home care.

Lay home visitors were trained in infant care, nutrition, child development and teaching of developmental skills. Portage program was used for intervention and monitoring the development of children over 3 years. During weekly visits, home visitors worked with the mothers to promote child development. At the end of 3 years, 74% had normal development. It was also found that health visitors and mothers could care for the infants with regular support. The economic benefits of preventing developmental delays far outweigh the cost of intervention.

Application of Available Knowledge

The initial experiences of the developing countries is positive. A number of guidelines can be identified for interventions (WHO 1986; Sartorius et al 1993). Public health-related measures include: (a) prenatal and perinatal care; (b) programs for child nutrition; (c) immunization; (d) family planning; (e) training of primary health care personnel; (f) early identification of disabilities and their effects; (g) treatment of hypertension; (h) home stimulation programs for 'at-risk' children; (i) education about the harmful effects of dependence-producing drugs; (j) early and regular treatment of epilepsy; (k) early recognition of psychotic conditions such as schizophrenia and depression; and (l) promotion of positive attitudes towards mentally ill persons and mental health.

Another excellent initiative is the parental training initiative in Iran. In Istahan groups of parents were brought together for weekly seminars on child mental health. The results were striking in increasing the competence of mothers.

POLICIES INFLUENCING PREVENTION AND PROMOTION OF MENTAL HEALTH

The role of governments in developing countries is much greater than in developed countries for community initiatives. Policies can define the way society views illness, specific needs and provision of services. Some of the other areas in which government actions can promote mental health are:

1. Formulation of appropriate alcohol-related policies, since alcohol is the source of many physical and mental health problems affecting individuals, families and the community.
2. Policy formulation relating to working mothers and provision of services, e.g. creches for children of working mothers, parental leave, etc.
3. Housing policies, especially in urban areas.
4. Appropriate legislation relating to mental health. By measures that least stigmatize the recipients of care, there will be a greater possibility of the public having positive attitudes to mental health. Similarly, the way mental health issues are reflected in civil and criminal laws can influence community attitudes and responses.
5. Laws relating to family life can significantly contribute to the promotion of mental health. The Family Court Act (1984) of India is a positive measure as its goal is 'reconciliation'.

6. Development of services. The easy availability of care and universal coverage of basic mental health services reduces the impact of illness on the individual, family and community. The progress in this area is illustrative of how governmental action can bring about major changes at community level.

7. Support to NGOs. The most important need for promotion of mental health is community action, which has to be based on local norms and local resources. This type of 'self-help' can occur chiefly through NGOs, the government sharing these efforts by its policies and programs relating to NGOs.

8. Developmental programs. There is growing awareness of the role of governmental actions that impact on mental health. Some of these are: housing projects that worsen mental health due to inappropriate design; industrial development projects that destroy local culture and lead to family disruption; widespread use of pesticides, which can lead to brain damage; and provision of appropriate disaster care.

9. Social support to the elderly. Provision of welfare measures such as pensions, family support and medical care to the elderly that optimizes their functioning and family and social integration can promote mental health of the elderly.

The above examples are illustrative and not comprehensive and identify areas of governmental action that can contribute to the prevention and promotion of mental health.

Involving People

A number of initiatives are possible with the involvement of the general public. Important areas are: (a) better day-care facilities for children; (b) formation of self-help groups; (c) volunteers for suicide prevention; (d) parenting skills, especially for parents in urban areas and nuclear families; (e) preventing accidents; and (f) enhancing the prestige and practice of cultural practices with good mental health value, like grief-related rituals and multiple parenting of children.

Training of Non-specialist Personnel

For application of the available knowledge in the area of mental health among all categories of personnel in an appropriate manner, it is important that mental health information should not be restricted to professionals only. Already there have been excellent efforts to develop manuals (WHO 1991) and there is a need to promote this activity. The general approach should be to: (a) identify priority information relevant to a group of individuals; (b) develop training materials using visual aids; (c) provide training in small homogeneous groups, using an interactive, experience-sharing approach; (d) provide follow-up support periodically; and (e) evaluate the impact of intervention. The overall approach should be to enable the individual to recognize mental health as important and take actions at his/her own level (Murthy & Wig 1983).

Role of Professionals

It has to be recognized that for the integration of mental health with primary health care there is a need for the role of the professional to be different. To be more specific, the role is different from the hospital-orientated one.

The psychiatrist, for example (and other professionals such as clinical psychologists, psychiatric social workers and psychiatric nurses) will have to devote a significant portion of their time to supervision rather than direct patient care. Furthermore, because their work is carried out in a field setting rather than in the protected environment of a hospital or clinic, they often have to accept different levels of care appropriate to the field situations in which they are working. This calls for simplification of mental health work. Finally, they also need to acquire new skills and the capacity to coordinate, which are not normally seen as being within the purview of a psychiatrist's abilities in more traditional settings. At an individual level, it is not uncommon for supervising psychiatrists to feel overwhelmed by and inadequate for a multipurpose role in the community. Needless to say, with a sense of openness and willingness to learn from people, the experience can be very satisfying and comparable to the satisfaction from clinical responsibility in a hospital.

To support planned mental health programs in the community, training of psychiatrists should include supervised experience in the above areas. This has been one of the important recommendations of the WHO Expert Committee on Mental Health:

> Specialized mental health workers should devote only a part of their working hours to the clinical care of the patients; the greater part of their time should be spent in training and supervising non-specialized health workers who will provide basic health care in the community. This will entail significant changes in the role and training of the mental health professionals (Recommendation 10, WHO 1975).

At a practical level there is an urgent need to have field practice areas attached to psychiatric training centres.

There are other sensitive issues of which cognizance needs to be taken. The new approach will give no results if the different professionals set up artificial rigid boundaries between the different mental health personnel, or do not devote enough time in terms of research, etc., to enhancing know-how in this area of work. One will also come face-to-face with issues like allowing for limited use of drugs by para-professionals and non-professionals, as has happened in the areas of maternal and child welfare, tuberculosis, family welfare, leprosy and malaria.

To summarize the issues in this area, it can be said that the need is to accept this approach as the 'real alternative' rather than as a second-rate method. This can result in a new generation of mental health professionals growing up with these ideas, wide discussion, sharing of ideas and critical appraisal of the pilot schemes and inclusion of skills in this area during the training period.

ROLE OF NON-GOVERNMENTAL ORGANIZATIONS (NGOs)

In the developing countries, the availability of primary health care is not adequate. This is especially true in rural areas, where NGOs have an important role to play in initiating small-scale, culturally acceptable initiatives. NGOs are also more open to innovations high in commitment and sensitive to local practices, and both national and international agencies need to support their activities and view them not as competitors but as partners. Specific areas where NGO initiatives have been most effective are: (a) suicide prevention; (b) detoxification camps; (c) day-care centres; (d) half-way homes; (e) parental self-help groups; (f) public education; (g) legal action to improve mental hospitals; (h) rights of mentally handicapped individuals; (i) policy development for mental health through political lobbying; (j) disaster mental health care; and (k) geriatric services at community level.

Research

One of the most important aspects of the integration of mental health care with primary health care is research on a continuous basis. The aspects of evaluative research and related areas reviewed in the earlier sections point to its value. The efforts and focus should be to consider this alternative in depth and define the boundaries of care, as well as placing community care on a sound foundation from a professional, administrative and organizational point of view. As integration progresses there will be shifts in priorities and changing roles of professionals and para-professionals, and all of these should be the result not of *ad hoc* individualized decisions but the outcome of systematic study.

ROLE OF INTERNATIONAL ORGANIZATIONS

Promotion of mental health is an emerging agenda. In developing countries there is often neglect of this area relative to other areas of health such as communicable diseases, nutrition and family planning. International organizations like WHO, UNICEF, ILO and ODA have specific roles in policy and program development in developing countries illustrated by the positive experiences in the eradication of smallpox and polio during the 1970s. Some of the ways in which they can contribute towards the promotion of mental health are discussed below.

Policy and Program Development

The efforts of organizations such as WHO can facilitate the development of national level policies and programs, a positive example in mental health being the initiative of the Division of Mental Health, WHO Geneva, from the 1970s. The publication of the document 'Organization of mental health services in developing countries' (WHO 1975) was largely instrumental in developing mental health programs in a number of developing countries. This initiative has become the focal point for a number of initiatives in the area of mental health (Wig 1989; WHO 1991; WHO 1990).

Sharing of Know-how

This is an important contribution from international organizations. The area of promotion of mental health depends on psychosocial factors in terms of both causes and interventions. It is often considered that promotion of mental health is not cost-effective in developing countries, but by avoiding the pitfalls and negative experiences of developed countries developing countries can appropriately utilize limited resources. An illustration is in the area of disaster care, where the accepted focus now is not provision of external professionals but use of local community resources. Another emerging area for sharing of information is AIDS-related mental health issues. The free sharing of 'know-how' could accelerate the development of promotional activities in the broad area of mental health.

Support for National Efforts

The area of mental health promotion is strongly rooted in cultural, social and political aspects. Owing to paucity of funds, initial experiments are likely to be small-scale in terms of aims, population covered, range of activities, etc. Examples of such efforts are the promotion of child mental health in school programs in Pakistan and Iran, and crisis intervention activities in India. These initial efforts often receive national recognition when international organizations study them and share them with other countries. Another aspect of this need is the importance of evaluation by an outside group. In both these roles international organizations can play an important role.

Intersectoral Cooperation

Promotion of mental health involves actions by a number of sectors, at many levels and over long periods of time. It is often noted that the activities of different sectors are not coordinated owing to problems of territoriality, lack of awareness of ongoing work and other personal factors. The availability of a neutral setting, as with an international seminar or conference, or an external consultant, can bring together different groups to coordinate the work so that it can lead to larger programs. International organizations can play the role of 'mediator', breaking barriers and building bridges within and across national initiatives.

Funding

The initial funding support for innovative efforts can prove valuable when the existing system is unable to provide funds and considers the need as unimportant, as in the case of mental health promotion. In India and other developing countries, a number of effective initiatives have depended on such initial funding supports. However, it is important that funding is kept to a realistic level in terms of manpower support and materials, to avoid the problems of large-scale replication and extension at a later stage.

CONCLUSION

The integration of mental health into primary health care can be viewed from two different angles. First, it can be seen as a way of providing an identified level of basic mental health care by simple approaches to limited population groups. Such a need is not only present in developing countries with limited mental health professionals but in developed countries for the care of the rural population and isolated population units.

The second way of viewing this integration in developing countries is to consider it as the primary method of mental health care, avoiding some of the problems of high institutional and professional group emphasis. German (1975) has described this situation aptly as follows:

> The major advantage for the psychiatrist in a developing country is the very paucity of previous provision for the mentally sick. Thus, he does not have to expend his energies in frustrating attempts to dismantle an inert and cumbersome administrative infrastructure; nor does he have to concern himself with finding a method of absorbing large numbers of solidly built, prison-like mental hospitals into a more efficient and humane psychiatric programme. There is little need for him to struggle with large armies of personnel in various categories, each . . . unwilling to change from the security of well-defined roles to meet the challenge of the present and future. [He has] at least a fairly clean canvas on which to develop [his] themes.

Wig (1989) has reviewed development in developing countries and concluded as follows:

> So far psychiatry has played only a marginal role in the health programs in developing countries. However, psychiatry has the potential of becoming a major force in these countries provided it overcomes the limitations and changes on the following lines: (i) psychiatry must change its scope from a clinical specialty to a comprehensive mental health movement which is content not only with the treatment of mental illness but equally involved in the prevention of mental illness and promotion of mental health; (ii) psychiatry must develop programs of psychiatric care which are relevant for the needs of the majority of the population; and (iii) psychiatry must keep its theoretical base wide to include both the biological and psychosocial sciences.

It is fortunate that the needs of mentally ill persons in developing countries is receiving special attention by national and international agencies. This can be a window of opportunity for new programs and new initiatives (World Development Report 1993; Commission on Health Research and Development 1990; Harvard Medical School 1995).

In summary, with the shift in focus of the goals of the developing countries in the health, welfare, education, social and developmental sectors, the *promotion* of mental health will become important. Promotion has to be rooted at the level of individual actions and the strengthening of the family. Support from national and international organizations is important. In these efforts, the individuals, families, communities and national and international organizations should be partners working towards a common goal.

REFERENCES

Asuni T (1990) Report on the care, treatment and rehabilitation of people with mental illness. *Psychosoc Rehabil J* **13**, 35–44.

Biegel A (1983) Community mental health care in developing countries. *Am J Psychiat* **140**, 1491–2.

Carstairs GM (1973) Psychiatric problems in developing countries. *Br J Psychiat* **123**, 271–7.

Climent C et al (1978) Development of an alternative, efficient low-cost mental health delivery system in Cali, Colombia. 1: The auxiliary nurse. *Soc Psychiat* **13**, 29–35.

Commission on Health Research for Development (1990) Health Research—Essential Link to Equity in Development. Oxford: Oxford University Press.

Community Mental Health News (1989) Mental health care in developing countries. *Comm Ment Health News* **13** and **14**, 1–16.

Edgell H (1970) Medical assistant and psychiatric care. *Psychopathol Africa* **6**, 83.

German A (1975) Trends in psychiatry in Black Africa. In S Arieti & G Chrzanowski (eds) *New Dimensions in Psychiatry—A World View*. New York: Wiley.

Giel R (1975) Notes on psychiatric needs in a developing country. *Afr J Psychiat* **1**, 25–9.

Harding TW et al (1980) Mental disorders in primary health care. *Psychol Med* **10**, 231–41.

Harvard Medical School (1995) *World Mental Health: Problems and Priorities in Low-income Countries. Executive Summary*. Oxford: Oxford University Press.

Lambo TA (1966) The village of Aro. In M King (ed) *Medical Care in Developing Countries.* Oxford: Oxford University Press.

Lin TY (1983) Mental health in the third world. *J Nerv Ment Dis* **171**, 71–8.

Mendis N (1990) A model for the care of people with psychosocial disabilities in Sri Lanka. *Psychosoc Rehabil J* **13**, 45–52.

Mubbashar MH, Malik SJ, Zar JR & Wig NN (1986) Community-based rural mental health care programme—report of an experiment in Pakistan. *EMR Health Serv J*, 14–20.

Murthy R (1983) Treatment and rehabilitation of the severely mentally ill in developing countries. Experience of countries of South-East Asia. *Int J Ment Health* **12**(3), 16–29.

Murthy R (1992a) Mental health. In *State of India's Health*, pp 400–414. New Delhi: Voluntary Health Association of India.

Murthy R (1992b) Integration of mental health with primary health care—Indian experience. In RS Murthy & B Burns (eds) *Community Mental Health*, pp 111–42. Bangalore: National Institute of Mental Health and Neuroscience.

Murthy R & Wig NN (1983) A training approach to enhancing mental health manpower in a developing country. *Am J Psychiat* **140**, 1486–90.

Murthy R & Wig NN (1993) Evaluation of the progress in mental health in India since Independence. In P Mane & KY Gandevia (eds) *Mental Health in India—Issues and Concerns*, pp 1–21. Bombay: TISS.

Murthy R & Burns B (eds) (1992) *Community Mental Health Proceedings of Indo–US Symposium.* Bangalore: National Institute of Mental Health and Neuroscience.

NMHP (National Mental Health Programme) for India (1982) Director General of Health Services, Ministry of Health and Family Welfare, New Delhi.

Naik & Plumber G (1994) High-risk infants. *Health for the Millions* **20**(4), 19–21.

Ormel J, Vonkortb M, Üstün BT et al (1994) Common mental disorders and disability across cultures. *JAMA* **272**, 1741–8.

Pai S & Kapur RL (1983) Evaluation of home care treatment for schizophrenic patients. *Acta Psychiat Scand* **67**, 18–88.

Pai S, Kapur RL & Roberts EJ (1983) Follow-up study of schizophrenic patients initially treated with home care. *Br J Psychiat* **143**, 447–50.

Pai S & Kapur RL (1981) The burden on the family of a psychiatric patient. Development of an interview schedule. *Br J Psychiat* **138**, 332–5.

Philips MR, Pearson V & Wang R (1994) Psychiatric rehabilitation in China. *Br J Psychiat* **165**, suppl 24.

Sartorius N & Harding T (1983) The WHO collaborative study on strategies for extending mental health care. I: The genesis of the study. *Am J Psychiat* **140**, 1470–79.

Sartorius N, Girolomo G, Andrews G, German A & Eisenberg L (1993) Treatment of Mental Disorders—A Review of Effectiveness. Washington, DC: American Psychiatric Press.

Sartorius N (1990) Mental health care in continental Europe: medley or mosaic? In IM Marks & RA Scott (eds) *Mental Health Care Delivery: Innovations, Impediments and Implementation*, pp 154–5. New York: Sage.

Schulsinger F & Jablensky A (eds) (1991) The national mental health programme in the United Republic of Tanzania. *Acta Psychiat Scand* (suppl), 364.

Shankar R (1994) Interventions with families of people with schizophrenia in India. In AB Hatfield (ed) *Family Interventions in Mental Illness. New Directions for Mental Health Services*, no. 62, pp 79–88. New York: Cambridge University Press.

Swift CR (1976) Mental health programming in a developing country: any relevance elsewhere? *Am J Orthopsychiat* **42**, 517.

Whyte SR (1991) Family experiences with mental health problems in Tanzania. *Acta Psychiat Scand* **83** (suppl 364), 77–111.

Wig NN (1989) The future of mental health in developing countries. *Comm Ment Health News* **14**, 1–4.

Wig NN, Murthy R & Harding TW (1981) A model for rural psychiatric services—Raipur Rani experience. *Indian J Psychiat* **23**, 275–90.

Wig NN & Murthy R (1994) From mental illness to mental health. *Health for the Millions* **20**(4), 2–4.

World Bank (1993) World Development Report. Investing in Health. New York: World Bank.

WHO (World Health Organization) (1990) The *Introduction of a Mental Health Component into Primary Health Care*. Geneva: WHO.

WHO (World Health Organization) (1991) A new era in mental health. In *EMRO—Partner in Health in the Eastern Mediterranean, 1949–1989*, pp 296–303. Alexandria: WHO–EMRO.

WHO (World Health Organization) (1992) *Evaluation of Methods for the Treatment of Mental Disorders*. Technical Report Series 812. Geneva: WHO.

WHO (World Health Organization) (1975) *Organization of Mental Health Services in Developing Countries*. Technical Report Series 564. Geneva: WHO.

WHO (World Health Organization) (1984) *Mental Health Care in Developing Countries. A Critical Appraisal of Research Findings*. Technical Report Series 698. Geneva: WHO.

WHO (World Health Organization) (1986) *Prevention of Mental, Neurological and Psychological Disorders*. WHO/MNH/EVA/88. Geneva: WHO.

13

Economic Perspectives

Nick Bosanquet and Anna Bosanquet*

*Imperial College School of Medicine and * Roehampton Institute, London, UK*

Family doctors within the UK are involved in an increasing amount of care for patients with mental health problems, especially those suffering from depression and anxiety. In 1994 British GPs wrote 11.8 million prescriptions for anti-depressants at a cost of £117 million (DOH 1995). Twenty per cent of their consultation time is with patients with psychiatric symptoms and of these about half receive some explicit treatment in drug therapy or counselling. At least 30% of practices now offer counselling (Sibbald et al 1993), yet many seem doubtful about whether all this activity achieves results for patients. This chapter sets out how economics could define choices and assist professionals to develop services which are more cost-effective.

Epidemiological research demonstrates the extent and type of psychiatric problems with which patients present in the primary care setting. Most mental health problems are treated there, with only a small fraction of patients being referred to specialists such as psychiatrists, psychologists or psychotherapists. Depression and anxiety are the commonest of the mental disorders.

In order to set the priorities for developing new programs and policies it is important to estimate costs of different health problems and to compare the cost-effectiveness of their treatment and prevention. Against a background of demographic changes in populations and increasing expectations and demands on health services worldwide, health economists have developed techniques in order to assist choices and decisions on effectiveness and efficiency. Concern about cost-effectiveness in health care does not equal a search for a lowest-cost solution. Both costs and effectiveness must be considered. Economic appraisal is a method of assisting the decision-making process by collecting information about the costs, benefits or effectiveness of alternative claims on resources.

Research into economic aspects of prevention of mental illness and mental health promotion in primary care is a very recent phenomenon. Psychiatry, like geriatrics, has been regarded for a long time as a 'Cinderella', not only of health services but also of health economics. This was especially true of primary care psychiatry. Emphasis in economic evaluation until recently has been on the

Preventing Mental Illness: Mental Health Promotion in Primary Care. Edited by R. Jenkins and T.B. Üstün.
© 1998 John Wiley & Sons Ltd.

curative, as opposed to a preventive or health promotion approach and therefore on the cost and outcomes of specific treatments. The outcomes of mental health problems are particularly difficult to assess and quantify. This is the main challenge for the future: but past research has already shown the size of the burden of disease, e.g. a 1985 estimate put the cost to society of neurotic disorder treated in UK general practice at £373 million (Wilkinson 1989).

COST OF MENTAL ILL-HEALTH

Non-psychotic mental illness causes substantial costs to the NHS in terms of treatment costs: to individuals in terms of reduced quality of life and social functioning: and to society in terms of lost production. Treatment costs are mainly borne in primary care. They cover consultation costs, both for depression/anxiety and for psychosomatic illness, prescribing and the cost of counselling. Over the past 5 years there have been significant increases in expenditure on prescribing and on counselling. Neurotic disorders also generate some referrals to secondary care.

Direct treatment costs are significant. The fourth National Morbidity Survey reported for 1991–1992 that the number of consultations for neurotic, personality or other non-psychotic mental disorder 'was exceeded only by that for acute respiratory infection' (OPCS 1994).

Indirect costs of lost production are of three types: (a) primary productive losses—work lost because a person is too ill to work; (b) discounted future earnings of those whose illness caused them to retire or die prematurely; (c) secondary productive losses, the result of people leaving the workforce to care for an ill person or suffering a reduction in their productivity because a co-worker is unwell.

Mental health problems may also cause absence from work even when people are still employed. Jenkins (1985) found in a study of employed individuals that minor psychiatric morbidity was a major determinant of the level of all types of sickness absence, both certified and uncertified. She found that over 32% of employees with sickness absence were psychiatric cases and that these people missed an average of 8.5 days per year. The absence rate of non-cases was 2.65, implying a rate of sickness absence directly attributable to minor psychiatric morbidity of 5.8 days. This implies that the actual number of days of lost production is about 93 million, and the value of production lost around £2.9 billion. This would increase still further if we could quantify the reduced productivity of those with neurotic disorder who continue working, and of those working beside them.

Depression and anxiety often present to family doctors in terms of consultations for physical illness. Shepherd et al (1966) found that the average number of physical illnesses recorded among psychiatric patients in general practice was 50% higher than that for non-psychiatric patients. Some of these may be instances of hidden psychiatric morbidity or somatic symptoms, but there is evidence that psychiatric illness is genuinely associated with a raised level of physical morbidity.

Goldberg & Huxley (1980) found in primary care settings in Manchester that 57% of psychiatric cases in primary care involved somatization, complaints of physical symptoms which are in fact of psychological origin; 24% have unrelated physical and mental disorder; and 3% have physical illness with secondary mental disorder. It could well be argued that probably two in three of outpatient referrals for these patients could be avoided given better education and support of primary care teams in identification and treatment of neurotic distress.

POLICY IMPLICATIONS: EVALUATING THE COST-EFFECTIVENESS OF MENTAL HEALTH PROMOTION

Successful programs in this area have the potential for reducing both direct treatment costs and indirect costs in lost production. The greatest effects of neurotic disorder, and consequently the greatest opportunities for therapeutic progress, lie in the area of lost production and impaired economic functioning of sufferers (and their families), rather than from reducing direct cost.

The real cost of psychiatric disorder is higher than might appear from current treatment levels. The findings of all studies estimating costs of psychiatric morbidity are based on those patients who were actually diagnosed as suffering from neurotic disorder by their GP. But doctors vary in their reported rates of mental illness, diagnosing between 4% and 65% of the practice population. Goldberg & Huxley (1980) estimated that approximately 40% of patients with psychiatric morbidity seen by GPs did not receive a psychiatric diagnosis. There is a challenge of identifying patients who could benefit from the services and targeting of help to ensure that they get it.

New interventions and increased activity in primary care have important cost implications. The role of the economist is to assist in the development of new programs through search for evidence on cost-effectiveness. There is scope for new kinds of partnership in program development.

Innovative methods of treatment should be systematically evaluated at a local level before being introduced more widely. There is an increased emphasis on cost-effectiveness of treatments in addition to the traditional issues of clinical efficiency and safety. This concern is desirable and ethical in any health care system that has a fixed budget. Inefficient use of resources prevents patients deriving the maximum possible benefits from those resources.

Cost-effectiveness analysis (CEA) is most relevant to development of programs in this area. The cost-effectiveness of a mental health promotion activity in primary care should ideally be evaluated from a social perspective, i.e. it should consider costs of a program and assess its possible benefits on a number of levels: the NHS, the local authority, voluntary organizations, informal carers, patients themselves, their families and co-workers.

Evaluation of cost-effectiveness of mental health promotion activities in primary care should consist of the following elements:

1. Identification and measurement of costs.
2. Identification and measurement of benefits.
3. Estimation of effectiveness of a program by balancing the costs against the benefits.

Identification and Measurement of Costs

Costs can be direct, indirect or intangible.

- *Direct costs* are resources required to produce a service. They include costs to the NHS or health authority such as the cost of doctors, nurses, counsellors and other therapists, drugs and other treatments and hospitalization. Costs incurred by patients and their relatives include paying for private consultations with specialists outside the NHS, over-the-counter drugs, cost of prescriptions and, possibly, inflated insurance premiums. These costs can be fixed or variable, increasing in volume of activity.
- *Indirect costs* do not stem from transactions for goods or services. They include detrimental effects on quality of life, as well as production-related costs of mortality and morbidity—to the society and to the individual. Costs of lost production consist of primary and secondary losses: decreased productivity (paid as well as non-paid work such as parenting), discontinued earnings, or becoming 'unemployable' in the future even when recovered, due to a loss of competitiveness in the market economy and stigma attached to the mental illness.
- *Intangible costs* are those of pain, suffering and grief. These are difficult to measure and often omitted in clinical economic research.

Social scientists have developed a number of quality-of-life scales which can be used in economic evaluation. Financial information can be obtained from the practices direct, from the annual reports, information on prescribing (PACT data) or a regional authority. Estimation of the wider costs to the NHS will come from factual information about hospitalization and outpatient contracts.

Identification and Measurement of Benefits

Benefits should be also considered from a broad societal perspective. These will include effects of interventions on patients themselves and their families in terms of positive effects on the health status and quality of life of individuals, reduction of symptoms and better productivity at home and in paid employment. There should be some benefits to the operation of the general practice and possible benefits to the NHS.

A variety of instruments, including quality-of-life measures and clinical assessment, are employed to measure the outcomes for patients. The societal benefits can be assessed by looking at empirical data on the level of change on such measures as the use of health care resources; patients' productivity; unemployment or days off sick; marital breakdown, etc. before and after the introduction of a program.

Estimation of Cost-effectiveness

A program of treatment can be classified as effective, efficient or cost-effective. An effective program is one that provides good outcomes. An efficient program is one that gives the best outcomes at the lowest cost. The cost-effectiveness of a program should be assessed by the estimation of the cost incurred by its implementation and running in view of benefits for individuals, health services and society which result from that program. There are many possible combinations of costs and benefits: a new program which is run in addition to usual management will incur some extra costs, but the resulting benefits may justify this extra spending; or a new program may replace another one—here the costs can be either equal, lower or higher than the costs of the original programs, but there should also be a gain in benefits.

We would like to exemplify this societal approach to economic evaluation by a description of the design of an evaluation of three separate projects aimed at increasing GPs' skills in diagnosing and treating depression and anxiety in primary care.

ECONOMIC EVALUATION OF THE MENTAL HEALTH INTERVENTION IN PRIMARY CARE USING COST-EFFECTIVENESS ANALYSIS

The Department of Health has recently funded three innovatory projects aimed at increasing GPs' skills in diagnosis and management of depression and anxiety and other psychosocial problems (Armstrong 1995). The health economists were presented with a task of assessing whether the amount of money spent on the projects themselves and on the more forthcoming and active mode of management by GPs can be justified by better outcomes for patients. What was the economic effect of interventions on general practices concerned? Is it feasible to argue that local initiatives like these could have an effect on the operation of the NHS and society as a whole?

Rationale for Economic Analysis

The reasoning behind the economic evaluation was as follows (see also Figure 13.1): Through the intervention (educational activities, audit, etc.) GPs would be able to recognize patients with mental health or social problems more easily than before, and more patients with such problems will be treated. This would lead to an increase in the time GPs spent with these patients and an increase in the use of resources such as psychotropic drugs or referrals to specialist agencies. Therefore, there would be an increase in short-term costs.

However, this increase in activity would be accompanied by the increase in the effectiveness of treatment: more acute referrals, better prescribing of psychiatric drugs and more effective use of time during consultations. Doctors would be aware of many management options available, some of which would not involve extra costs, e.g. advising patients to contact appropriate voluntary agencies and self-help groups.

In addition, there would be savings in the cost of management of psychosomatic symptoms. Doctors would develop skills in differentiating those patients in whom physical symptoms are influenced by underlying psychosocial problems. Time and resources spent at attempts to diagnose and treat these symptoms, such as laboratory tests, specialist referrals and drugs to control the symptoms, would be replaced by psychosocial interventions. This would lead to savings in the longer term.

As GPs improve their ability to diagnose and treat psychiatric symptoms and psychosocial problems they would be able to achieve better results for patients who would experience fewer symptoms and improved social functioning. Because patients would be diagnosed earlier and treated in a more energetic way, the symptoms would be experienced by patients for a shorter duration of time, and psychiatric morbidity would decrease among patients consulting. This would lead to benefits to society in terms of the individuals functioning better in their daily lives, savings for health services in terms of decrease in ineffective use by patients with psychosomatic problems, and benefits for the general practice in terms of released time and resources (through increased effectiveness of psychiatric treatment) which could be directed at other needy groups of patients.

Ethical Issues

With an increased ability to detect mild psychiatric problems and a decrease in the threshold for treatment, there could be concern about issues of medicalization of 'problems with living'. This becomes particularly important in terms of the effect that any form of psychiatric diagnosis or treatment has on patients' insurance premiums and future employment prospects, as well as patients' self-esteem (Cribb & Dines 1993). During the process of research we have come across some patients for whom these ethical concerns may apply.

Some patients who consult for physical symptoms may find it objectionable to be questioned about their social and personal circumstances. The doctor–patient relationship may seem to be based on a very patronizing—instead of a partnership—model of interaction.

In any case, medical treatment is only one among many factors affecting outcomes. There are other—social and economic—factors strongly affecting people's

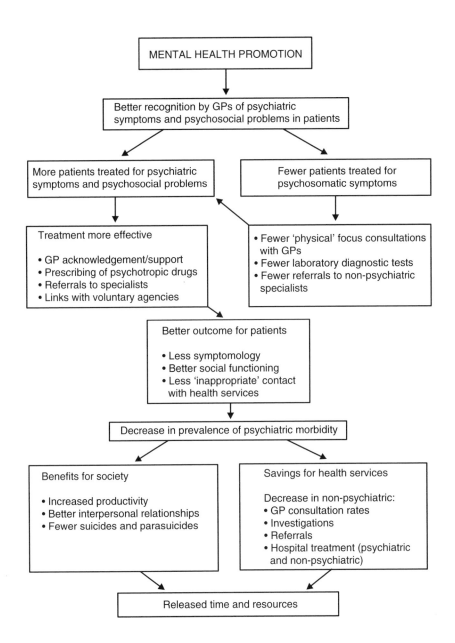

FIGURE 13.1 Economic evaluation: rationale

well-being. GPs and psychiatrists—who are a powerful professional group in society—are well placed to be able to influence these factors. Lader (1978) provided a criticism of a strictly medical approach to mental health problems:

> In cost-effective terms tranquillizers are cheap. It is cheaper to tranquillize distraught housewives living in isolation in tower blocks with nowhere for the children to go play, than to demolish these blocks and to rebuild on a human scale or even to provide playgroups. The drug industry, the government, the pharmacists, the tax payer and the doctor all have vested interests in 'medicalizing' socially determined stress responses.

Mental health promotion programs can help in resolving some of these problems. Patients can be encouraged to seek other than medical forms of support through links with voluntary agencies and self-help groups. Referrals to counsellors and psychologists could have positive results in empowering people to take control over their own lives.

CONCLUSIONS

Family doctors are treating many different groups of patients: patients with depression and anxiety are one of the largest groups. They also often generate frustration for doctors and the primary care team. The new challenge is that of turning treatment activity into targeted effective programs.

The challenge in primary care is how to develop programs that can deliver these benefits. Some of the key elements in these programs are:

- Early identification of patients with depression and anxiety, so as to allow early treatment and reduce wasted time and money chasing down somatic blind alleys. Within the UK there have been programs using nurse facilitators to help family doctors and primary care teams to improve identification.
- Effective management of drug therapy, both to improve initial choice of drug and to help with motivation to follow the treatment programs.
- Development of counselling: brief intervention psychotherapy has much to offer here.

Economics stresses that resources for such programs are bound to be limited. One challenge will be in the initial investment—how to fund the management and professional time to design the program at the local level. There will then be a continuing challenge in maintaining momentum and standards. The program will need local audit as well as wider evaluation: and there will be much to learn as experience is gained. The benefits are substantial—but not easy to achieve in practice. Some of the development work has already been done, however, and there is the potential for moving from activity to targeted, effective programs.

REFERENCES

Armstrong E (1995) *Mental Health issues in Primary Care. A Practical Guide.* London: Macmillan.

Cribb A & Dines A (1993) Ethical issues in health promotion. Mental health promotion: early detection of depression in primary care. In A Cribb & A Dines (eds) *Health Promotion—Concepts and Practice*, chapter 4. Oxford: Blackwell Scientific Publications.

DOH (Department of Health) (1995) *Statistical Bulletin* 15 July.

Goldberg D & Huxley P (1980) *Mental Illness in the Community: the Pathway to Psychiatric Care.* London: Tavistock.

Jenkins R (1985) Minor psychiatric morbidity in employed young men and women, and its contribution to sickness absence. *Br J Indust Med* **42**, 147–54.

Lader M (1978) Benzodiazepines—the opium of the masses. *Neuroscience* **3**, 159–65.

OPCS (1994) *Morbidity Statistics from General Practice: 4th National Survey.* London: HMSO.

Shepherd M, Cooper B, Brown AC & Kalton GW (1966) *Psychiatric Illness in General Practice.* London: Oxford University Press.

Sibbald S, Addington-Hall J, Brenneman D & Freeling P (1993) Counsellors in English and Welsh general practices: their nature and distribution. *British Medical Journal* **306**, 29–33.

Wilkinson D (1989) Estimated costs of neurotic disorder in UK general practice. *Psychol Med* **9**, 337–53.

14

Public Health Importance

Leon Eisenberg
Harvard Medical School, Boston, MA, USA

In the five decades since World War II, there has been an unprecedented reduction in infant mortality and increase in life expectancy in low-income countries. In a single generation, the average life expectancy at birth in India, Egypt and Zaire has jumped from 40 to 66 years, during an interval in which infant mortality fell from 1 to 4 live births to 1 in 10. Specific disease prevention and health promotion measures have been major players in this drama. Smallpox, which as recently as 30 years ago killed millions each year in Asia and Africa, has been completely eradicated for almost two decades (Breman & Arita 1980). UNICEF estimates that immunization programs prevent about 3 million child deaths each year. Currently, about 80% of infants under 1 year in the developing world are receiving measles, polio and DPT vaccinations (Grant 1995). The childhood immunization campaign in the Americas has succeeded so well that the Pan-American Health Organization has been able to announce that indigenous transmission of wild poliovirus had been interrupted in the Western Hemisphere since 1991 (Centers for Disease Control and Prevention 1994).

In sharp contrast, mental health has remained stagnant or has deteriorated. An increase in the incidence and prevalence of schizophrenia, dementia, depression and other chronic illnesses has accompanied the increase in life-span. Mort Kramer (1989) projected that there will be a 45% increase in cases of schizophrenia in low-income societies between 1985 and 2000 as the inevitable consequences of the corresponding growth in the 15–45 year-old age cohort, the years at which the disorder becomes manifest. By the year 2025, three-quarters of all elderly persons with dementia—about 80 million—will live in low-income societies. Mental retardation and epilepsy rates continue to be 3–5 times higher in low-income societies because of preventable complications of pregnancy and childbirth, nutritional deficiencies, untreated central nervous system infections, avoidable parasite infestations and brain trauma. In some Asian and African countries, the great majority of patients with epilepsy—a condition for which there is cost-effective drug therapy—do not receive anticonvulsants.

Preventing Mental Illness: Mental Health Promotion in Primary Care. Edited by R. Jenkins and T.B. Üstün.
© 1998 John Wiley & Sons Ltd.

Poor countries must contend with a greater burden of problems—from disasters, to low-intensity conflicts, to dislocated populations—problems exacerbated by the lack of economic and political means to provide food, housing and health care. Faced with a choice between reducing deficits and investing resources to address this illness burden, poor and rich nations alike have opted to reduce deficits. Yet there are cost-effective treatments for certain disorders (e.g. depression, epilepsy, schizophrenia) and others that can be prevented (e.g. certain forms of mental retardation). In the closing days of this century, it is simply unacceptable that in so many countries the chronically mentally ill are abandoned in conditions of filth and brutality, without treatment and without rehabilitation. It should not be tolerable that tens of millions of patients with depressive disorder suffer mental anguish, lost opportunities, family stress and premature death because their disorder is not recognized and not treated appropriately, despite the effectiveness of available methods. It is insufferable that women are regularly beaten by alcoholic spouses and have no recourse. It is a crime against humanity that 7 and 8 year-old girls are sold into sexual slavery as part of a globally commercialized system of sexual abuse that fosters criminality and spreads sexually transmitted diseases.

To examine mental health problems in a comprehensive fashion, Arthur Kleinman, Chair of the Department of Social Medicine at Harvard Medical School, initiated a 2-year study by faculty members in our Department. The product, published by Oxford University Press under the title *World Mental Health: Problems and Priorities in Low Income Countries* (Desjarlais et al 1995) was made public in May 1995 at a press conference at the United Nations. In endorsing the report, the Secretary General, Boutros Boutros-Ghali, had this to say:

> Poverty, social upheaval, and conflict—especially if accompanied by cruel and degrading treatment—can cause severe mental harm. People lacking mental health and well-being are unable to realize their potential. They are unlikely to contribute to their own or to their society's development . . . Mental health must be recognized as our foremost challenge.
>
> Compartmentalization must be overcome. Medical and social issues which are often viewed separately may need to be dealt with as a whole. We must never lose sight of the impact on the mental health of the individual. But when the sources of harm lie in social or political events, those causes must be addressed on a larger scale. The challenge is to combine concern for mental health issues with humanitarian assistance and protection efforts. Development policies must incorporate a concern for the protection and promotion of mental health.

Until now, the priority assigned to mental illness on the international public health policy agenda has been, by any criterion, vanishingly small. In relation to the staggering toll of disability resulting from mental and behavioral pathology, so low a priority is simply perverse. Why does mental illness fare so badly?

In most societies, mental disorders are stigmatized. Its victims are hidden from public view or excluded from the family altogether. The mentally ill have lacked an organized political constituency. The difficulty is not limited to wrong-headed public attitudes. All too many physicians regard mental disorders as not being 'real' because they lack pathognomonic laboratory test results. Paradoxically, the very same physicians may consider mental illness incurable; prevention is dismissed as a farce. The facts belie these biases, but it is not easy to get time for mental disorders proportionate to their clinical relevance into the medical curriculum.

There is a further reason. Health statistics began with mortality data when numerical methods were first introduced into public health. In the seventeenth century, William Petty's invention of political arithmetic, 'the art of reasoning by figures upon things related to government', was embodied in John Graunt's *Natural and Political Observations . . . upon the Bills of Mortality*. Graunt was able to demonstrate the regularity of certain social and vital phenomena, e.g. the variation in mortality by season of year, the excess of urban over rural deaths, etc. (Rosen 1958). Two centuries later, the pioneers of social epidemiology made their case with mortality data. In inaugurating his journal, *The Medical Reform*, in 1847, Rudolph Virchow wrote that 'medical statistics will be our standard of measurement; we will weigh life for life and see where the dead lie thicker, among the workers or among the privileged' (Rosen 1947). With death a constant companion of the poor and life expectancy low, mortality was the salient statistic. It captures far less of the truth in an era of chronic degenerative disease.

Mortality data grossly underestimate the disease burden resulting from mental and behavioral disorders. In part, this stems from the way death is assigned a medical cause: e.g. a death from a liver destroyed by uncontrolled drinking is listed as a death from cirrhosis; or a death in an automobile collision resulting from vehicular suicide or reckless driving or driving while drunk is classified under trauma rather than depression or personality disorder or alcoholism. Further, mental and behavioral disorders exact their toll in morbidity rather than mortality.

It was, therefore, a major step forward when the World Bank (1993), in cooperation with the World Health Organization, developed a new index to measure total disease burden, disability-adjusted life years (DALYs). This statistic summates the morbidity and the mortality resulting from identifiable diseases into a single numerical measure. The full impact of mortality is taken into account by factoring in the age at which death occurs; that is, the number of years of potential life lost by that death is calculated by subtracting the age at which it occurred from the expectation of life remaining at that age. To give the same weight to premature death in poor and rich countries, the figure for life expectancy chosen is the one for low-mortality countries. Moreover, the calculus recognizes that years of life do not have the same value to individuals throughout the life-span; that is, most persons value a year in young adulthood as worth several times more than a year in late life. To measure disability resulting from disease, each surviving year is discounted against the severity of the disability and the expected duration of the disability. The disadvantage from a given handicap is assigned a position on a scale from 0 for complete health to 1 for death by expert consensus; for example, blindness is rated at a severity of 0.6 whereas disease of the female reproductive tract is assigned a severity of 0.22. Thus, DALYs take into account the age at which a specific disease is acquired, the potential years of life lost, the relative value of those years, and the years compromised by persisting handicap.

The DALY is imperfect. There are inherent limitations to any single measure, given the uncertainty of the database from which it must draw and the assumptions that go into its calculation. In many low-income countries, population denominators and mortality data, let alone morbidity data, are unverifiable. Metrics for determining the 'value' to an 'average' citizen of a year of life at age 20 vs. a year at age 65, or for estimating the relative severities of the disability resulting from blindness vs. paraplegia, remain problematic. Despite these cautions, the DALY provides a far better measure of the impact of diseases with a high ratio of morbidity to mortality, in contrast to the ratio for the infectious diseases of traditional importance for public health.

By this measure, the World Bank estimates that mental health problems account for 8.1% of the global disease burden (GDB). Among young adults (15–44 years of age) in low-income societies, neuropsychiatric disorders account for 12% of the GBD. When intentional self-inflicted injuries are added in, the GBD for women rises to 15.1% and for men to 16.1%. Of mental health-attributable GBD, the largest single component stems from depressive disorders. Next in order come self-inflicted injury, dementia and alcohol dependence. Epilepsy, psychoses, drug dependence and post-traumatic stress disorders, in that order, are the other major contributors to disease burden for mental illness.

Why is depression so prominent on this measure? Its prevalence, if US data are representative, is 10 times that for schizophrenia (Robins & Regier 1992). Because suicide is a far greater risk in depression than in schizophrenia, depression has a much greater impact on years of life lost. In 1990 in the USA, the cost of depressive illnesses (about $44 billion) was equal to that of cardiovascular disease (Rice, Kelman & Miller 1992). Depressed patients suffer as much disability and distress as patients with chronic medical disorders such as hypertension, diabetes, coronary artery disease and arthritis (Wells et al 1989). Although treatment is more effective for depression than for many chronic medical disorders, relapse is common; care over the long term is essential (Kupfer et al 1992). Because many patients experience depression as a disabling set of physical symptoms, patients with depression are common in primary care practice. All too often, the cause of their symptoms is not recognized by generalists; treatment for depression is either not provided or is prescribed in homeopathic doses (Eisenberg 1992a).

A 14-country WHO study screened more than 25 000 patients in primary care. The prevalence of psychological problems was high (24% on average), with depression, anxiety, and alcoholism being the most common disorders. Despite the high prevalence of mental distress, only 1 in 5 patients listed psychological problems as the reason for seeking help (Üstün & Sartorius 1995). Rates for depression have been increasing in the USA, Western Europe, Puerto Rico, Lebanon and Taiwan in recent decades; depression is now seen at younger ages and in greater frequency (Cross-National Collaborating Group 1992); comparable data for developing countries are not available.

If these figures portray the proportion of global disease burden resulting from diagnosable psychiatric disorders, they fail to capture the impact of maladaptive behavior on health. The ways in which individuals behave are important determinants of whether they stay well or become ill; and if they become ill, whether and how fast they recover. Sexually transmitted diseases (STDs) provide an apt illustration. Unprotected sexual acts place individuals at risk; disease outcomes for those who acquire treatable infections depend upon the availability of treatment, the decision to seek it out, and the extent of compliance. At the same time, the likelihoods for each individual decision from risk-taking through care-seeking to treatment follow-up are all constrained by the social context. The sexual mores, the epidemiology of infection, and the ease of access to treatment are functions of culture, social structure and economics of the community in which individual decisions are made.

To provide a measure of behavioral effects on health, my colleagues and I reconfigured the World Bank data to cluster the global burden from diseases which include a major behavioral component in their pathogenesis. They account in aggregate for more than one-third of total GBD! Yet, this total is far from complete; it does not include the death and disability attributable to smoking, which increases rates of heart disease, cancer, stroke and respiratory disease. In emphasizing a behavioral link, we do not imply that the behavior *per se* is pathological or that psychiatric intervention is appropriate. Commonplace as they may be, these behaviors have serious health consequences. Changing commonplace behaviors will require the skills of behavioral scientists, media experts, legislators and more.

To continue with the example of STDs, it is true that an effective vaccine against HIV would confer protection faster than education can change sexual behavior. But there is no vaccine; if one is developed, it will be 5 years or more in coming; in the interim, the epidemic cannot be contained without behavior change. The behavioral link in diarrheal disorders lies in patterns of water use, waste disposal and personal hygiene. Yes, social action to supply pure water and municipal sewage management would eliminate risk far more effectively than campaigns to teach individuals to boil water, use latrines and wash hands. However, a billion people in low-income countries are without access to safe water; twice that number lack sanitation (World Bank 1992, p 47); and there is no international commitment to invest the resources to supply water and sanitation. The one recourse for those at risk is education. Can it work? Ahmed et al (1993) have shown that educational interventions by village workers can influence cleanliness, diarrheal morbidity and child growth in rural Bangladesh; this, however, cannot protect the population during periodic severe floods. West and co-workers (1995) have demonstrated that a face-washing campaign in rural Tanzania modified child behavior in two out of three villages and by so doing significantly reduced the risk of trachoma.

A powerful index of the impact of socially determined individual behaviors on sheer survival is provided by the enormous difference between the 1.05:1.0

female:male population ratio in Western Europe and North America and the 0.94:1 female:male ratio in India, China, North Africa and South-west Asia. Professor Amartya Sen (1990) has calculated that 100 million women are missing, a figure derived from extrapolating the 1.05 ratio to the populations where it is 0.94. The female biological advantage in longevity clearly evident in the North has been overridden by the combined effects of sex preference in abortion and infanticide; making less food, education, and medical care available to girls and women; women's inability to control their own reproductive functions; their lack of economic independence; and their subjugation to violence.

No justification is needed for our decision to include motor vehicle collisions, war, homicide and violence under the rubric 'behavior-related', but how does tuberculosis qualify? Tuberculosis, which kills and debilitates more adults than any other single infectious agent, is a *social* disease; the world over, tuberculosis rates vary inversely with socio-economic status, both between nations and within nations (Feacham et al 1992; World Bank 1993). Although there are methods to prevent (Colditz et al 1995) and treat (Advisory Council for the Elimination of Tuberculosis 1993) the disease, risk of infection as well as access to prevention and treatment are functions of class status. The poor are not only more likely to be exposed to the bacillus because of crowded living conditions and high prevalence rates in the slums, but malnutrition makes them more vulnerable to clinical disease and more resistant to treatment; food is necessary before drugs are effective (Farmer et al 1991). The impact of national economic decisions is evident from what happened to tuberculosis control in China over the last decade. The People's Republic of China had made substantial progress against the disease in the 1960s and 1970s by providing antibiotics at a purely nominal charge. Policy changed in 1981; as part of the new market economy, health institutions were required to recoup their operating costs from sales of drugs and services. The big jump in treatment costs for patients led to a marked decline in registration for treatment. Untreated patients spread infection in their communities; tens of millions of new cases and hundreds of thousands of avoidable deaths resulted (World Bank 1993). The human costs of economic restructuring are rarely reckoned in the accounting provided by fiscal experts; this may be why the International Monetary Fund is known in many developing countries as the 'Infant Mortality Fund'.

If the data I have presented highlight the 'public health importance of health promotion and disease prevention' in mental and behavioral health, that does not establish effectiveness or feasibility. Are health promotion and disease prevention possible? The answer (Eisenberg 1981, 1988, 1992b) is an emphatic 'Yes!'.

Let me now cite briefly examples of secondary prevention, primary prevention and health promotion.

The fact that the primary prevention of the schizophrenias or the depressive disorders is not possible at present has led many to overlook the remarkable reductions in human suffering and health care costs by treatments which shorten illness episodes, diminish recurrence rates, and rehabilitate the chronically ill; treatment effectiveness has been reviewed recently by a WHO Expert Study Group

(Sartorius et al 1993) and the findings are impressive. Moreover, treating the first disease in a causal series prevents its sequelae; e.g. treating hypertension avoids stroke. Detection and treatment of depression prevent suicide; rates among untreated depressed patients are an order of magnitude higher than among the general population. What is the evidence that it works? Rimer et al (1990) have shown in an observational study in administrative regions across Hungary that the suicide rate varies inversely with the rate of treated depression. Even more persuasive is the report by Rutz, Von Knorring & Walinder (1989) of a significant reduction in the rate of suicide on the Swedish island of Gotland a year after an educational program for general practitioners on the island, a program which was shown to have increased the rate at which GPs detected and treated depression.

Turn now to the primary prevention of three specific causes of mental retardation: public health programs to prevent hypothyroidism, neural tube defects and Tay–Sachs disease.

More than 1.5 billion persons the world over are at risk for iodine deficiency disease (IDD). In one year, about 18 million women suffering from silent IDD will become pregnant. Sixty thousand of those pregnancies will end in miscarriage or still-birth; twice as many will result in the birth of children with overt cretinism; a million of the offspring will have deafness, squint, speech impediment or other neuromuscular disorders; and 5 million will have significant impairment of cognitive abilities. Yet, at a cost of approximately 5 US cents per person per year, IDD can be prevented by iodizing all salt produced for human consumption (Grant 1995).

Randomized trials (MRC Vitamin Study Research Group 1991; Czeisel & Dudas 1992) have demonstrated that folic acid supplementation during pregnancy reduces the risk of recurrent neural tube defects (NTDs) in newborns and case controls indicate that it reduces the risk of occurrence (Werler, Shapiro & Mitchell 1993). The rate of NTDs is 6–10 times higher in the People's Republic of China (PRC) than it is in the USA. A reasonable working hypothesis is that folic acid deficiency is widespread in rural China. Currently, the US Centers for Disease Control and Prevention, the PRC Ministry of Health and Beijing University are jointly undertaking a program to provide folic acid supplements to prospective mothers in four Chinese provinces including 12 000 villages (Tyler 1994). Implemented on a population-wide basis, nutritional supplementation with folic acid has the potential to prevent as many debilitating handicaps as mass vaccination programs against poliomyelitis in the PRC.

Voluntary programs to offer families at high risk for congenital defects the option of aborting homozygous defective fetuses permits such families to give birth to healthy children (without, of course, a net effect on carrier rates). A prime example is Tay–Sachs disease. The carrier rate among the Ashkenazi Jewish population in the USA is about 1 in 31, nine times higher than the rate among non-Jews. Voluntary enrollment of Jewish populations in screening programs in the USA and Canada has reduced newly diagnosed cases of Tay–Sachs disease from an average of 60 per year in the 1960s to no more than 3–5 a year in the 1980s (Kaback et al 1993).

There is a sizeable array of other proven primary prevention programs (Eisenberg 1992). A partial list includes: immunizations against infectious agents that can cause brain damage (measles, pertussis, *Haemophilus influenza b*); preconceptional and prenatal care designed to minimize alcohol consumption, cigarette smoking and substance abuse and to encourage an appropriate diet during pregnancy; perinatal care by trained birth attendants with transport services and obstetrical back-up for high-risk deliveries; newborn screening for phenylketonuria and hypothyroidism; pre- and post-natal home visitors to reduce child neglect and abuse; surveillance by growth monitoring for adequate protein–calorie intake during childhood; enriched daycare and Head Start programs for pre-school children to stimulate mental and emotional development; injury prevention counseling (Miller & Galbraith 1995); childproof tops for medication containers and household chemicals to prevent poisoning; lead-free gasoline; mandatory air bags, seat belts, child safety seats and bicycle helmets to minimize head injury; school-based age-appropriate education on health promotion, human sexuality and substance abuse; and universal secondary school education.

I will conclude by citing three health promotion campaigns not ordinarily thought of in terms of mental health but in fact decisive for it. The first is family planning; the second is the defence of women's rights; the third is universal education through secondary school.

The evidence in favor of family planning as health promotion is overwhelming. The more numerous and more closely spaced the pregnancies in the reproductive lives of women, the greater the risks for maternal and infant mortality and the worse the developmental outcomes for the children. In Bolivia, Brazil, Ecuador, Guatemala and Peru, infant mortality rates are twice as high for an interbirth interval of less than 2 years than they are when the interval is 4 years or more (Mackwardt & Ochoa 1993). Unplanned and unwanted teenage pregnancies are associated with high risk for mother and child (Population Council 1989). The larger the number of children in a family (socio-economic status having been controlled for), the lower their educational attainment. Taken together, these findings indicate the primacy of family planning services to delay the age of first pregnancy, to reduce the total number of offspring, and to lengthen interbirth intervals in order to optimize the ability of parents to care for their children. The health risks associated with modern contraception are far less than those associated with pregnancy and childbirth (Brown & Eisenberg 1995). Enabling parents to control family size is essential for the health of mothers and children; thus, every nation should provide sex education in public schools, including information about contraceptive methods and their reliability. Sexually active individuals should have access to condoms and other contraceptives. Safe abortion should be an available option when contraception fails.

Investing in the health, education and well-being of women should be given high priority in any program to improve population mental health. The average number of years of schooling women attain in a given society is more closely correlated with improvement in infant mortality rates than is the Gross National

Product per capita (Caldwell 1986)! Thus, investment in universal education is an investment for the health of men, women and children. Such education empowers women in controlling family income and in making them more receptive to public health programs. Educated mothers are more likely to receive prenatal care, to obtain tetanus toxoid before delivery and to opt for trained birth attendants, thus experiencing less prenatal morbidity and mortality. They marry later, start bearing children later, have fewer children and are less likely to die in childbirth. The magnitude of this effect in low-income countries is such that it can reduce the risk for their children of becoming orphans to less than one-fifth of the rate among those born to uneducated mothers (Hobcraft 1993). In an ethnographic study in Mexico (Levine et al 1991), maternal schooling was found to be a predictor of reductions in fertility and in risks to child survival in both urban as well as rural settings. More schooling led to better contraceptive practice and better use of health services. More educated mothers had a new kind of mother–child relationship:

> . . . One built around reciprocal verbal interaction, one which helps mothers monitor the needs of their preschool children but which also demands so much of their attention that fertility control becomes imperative. Their children grow up better prepared for school, equipped with verbal skills and with a set of new expectations concerning family life, fertility, parent–child relations and health care.

The desirability of universal secondary school education hardly needs defence to a professional readership. But one facet of the relationship between mental health and education has only become evident from epidemiologic studies in recent years. A review of studies in countries as different as the USA, France, Italy, Sweden, Finland, Israel and China reveals an inverse relationship between the amount of schooling received in youth and the prevalence of dementia in old age (Katzman 1993). A clear example of the 'schooling effect' is provided by differences in the prevalence of cognitive impairment in two Australian cities, Canberra and Hobart (Jorm et al 1994). Mean Mini-Mental State Examination scores were higher in community surveys of elders in Canberra than they were in Hobart; however, all the difference disappeared when the higher level of education of the average adult among the Canberra elderly cohort was taken into account. Even more impressively, limited formal education predicted a *decline* in cognitive function in a 3-year follow-up of an elderly community population (Evans et al 1993). It is, of course, a bold extrapolation from these correlational data to contend that more educated individuals have a greater 'brain reserve' which delays the appearance of clinical symptoms despite early pathological changes in the brain. It is, however, not without some support from animal studies; environmental stimulation leads to an increase in synaptic density in several mammalian species (Eisenberg 1995). It is thus possible that the intellectual stimulation provided by prolonging education has similar effects on the human brain. If this argument is correct, the increase in years of schooling, which is gradually taking place in many countries, might be accompanied by a reduction in rates of Alzheimer's disease among coming generations of the elderly.

How far do health promotion and disease prevention apply in the practice of primary care *per se*? It is necessary to distinguish the role of the health worker as a social advocate for disadvantaged persons in the community (Virchow termed the physician 'the natural attorney of the poor') from that of clinician in the face-to-face encounter with individual patients (Eisenberg 1988). Physicians have a moral imperative to use their prestige and power to improve the health of the public. Secondary prevention (early diagnosis and treatment to reduce morbidity and interrupt disease cascades) is clearly part of daily practice but are health promotion and disease prevention possible?

That fact is that clinicians promote health, including mental health, when they enjoin smoking and excess alcohol consumption and recommend appropriate diet, a balance between work and recreation, and giving priority to marital and parental responsibilities. Most physicians underestimate the importance of such counseling because only a minority of patients comply with recommendations. But consider: there is evidence that as many as 1 in 20 or 30 patients who smoke or who drink to excess will change their behavior at the doctor's urging, a paltry rate at first glance. Yet, given that some 40 million Americans smoke, a 3% success rate will mean that 1.2 million individuals will have reduced their risk for cancer, heart disease and lung disease on the basis of a simple, low-cost intervention; if the rate is as high as 5%, then the beneficiaries rise to 2 million. In either case, the result is a major public health triumph! Physicians underestimate their effectiveness because they remember the 19 who continue to smoke and forget the one who stops; they expect efficacy like that produced by antibiotic treatment of infectious diseases. The findings take on new meaning, once a population perspective is adopted (Kessler 1995; Lynch & Bonnie 1994; Surgeon General's Report 1989).

Primary care provides unparalleled opportunities for pre-conceptional counseling. Physicians should use routine clinical encounters with women of childbearing age to inquire about goals for family size and contraceptive knowledge and practice. Similar questions can be put to every postpubertal male patient. The stance that is called for must be proactive, and not one of waiting for the patient to raise the topic. Helping families to have only the children they want and to maximize the likelihood that those children will be born healthy is a major contribution to mental health promotion (Brown & Eisenberg 1995).

These injunctions apply with equal force to detecting abuse of children, women and the elderly. Any sign of trauma should arouse suspicion of abuse and lead to careful questioning. Unless the explanation is clear-cut, the physician should probe further. Potential victims deserve an opportunity to tell their stories in confidence. Battered women are five times more likely to require psychiatric treatment and to attempt suicide than women spared this savagery (Stark & Flitcraft 1991). Physicians able to make use of resources in the community (or to create the necessary resources) to support victims and to deter victimizers can make a major contribution to abuse prevention. They can provide leadership for violence prevention programs in the community; they have an obligation to do so precisely because of what they know and what they confront in daily practice.

REFERENCES

Advisory Council for the Elimination of Tuberculosis (1993) Initial therapy for tuberculosis in the era of multidrug resistance. *Morbid Mortal Weekly Rep* **42**, RR/7.

Ahmed N, Zeitlim M, Beiser A, Super C & Gershoff S (1993) A longitudinal study of the impact of behavioral change intervention on cleanliness, diarrheal morbidity and growth of children in rural Bangladesh. *Soc Sci Med* **37**, 159–71.

Breman JG & Arita I (1980) Confirmation and maintenance of smallpox eradication. *N Engl J Med* **303**, 1263–73.

Brown SS & Eisenberg L (eds) (1995) *The Best Intentions: Unintended Pregnancy and the Well-being of Children and Families*. Washington, DC: National Academy Press.

Caldwell JC (1986) Routes to low mortality in poor countries. *Pop Dev Rev* **12**, 171–220.

Centers for Disease Control and Prevention (1994) Certification of poliomyelitis eradication—the Americas. *Morbid Mortal Weekly Rep* **13**, 720–22.

Colditz GA et al (1995) The efficacy of bacillus calmette–guerin vaccination of newborns and infants in the prevention of tuberculosis: meta-analyses of the published literature. *Pediatrics*, **96**, 29–35.

Cross-national Collaborating Group (1992) The changing rate of major depression. *J Am Med Assoc* **268**, 3098–105.

Czeisel AE & Dudas I (1992) Prevention of the first occurrence of neural tube defects by periconceptional vitamin supplementation. *N Engl J Med* **327**, 1832–5.

Desjarlais R, Eisenberg L, Good B, Kleinman A (1995) *World Mental Health: Problems and Priorities in Low-income Countries*. New York: Oxford University Press.

Eisenberg L (1981) A research framework for evaluating the promotion of mental health and prevention of mental illness. *Publ Health Rep* **96**, 3–19.

Eisenberg L (1988) *Prevention of Mental, Neurological and Psychosocial Disorders* (WHO/MNH/EVA/88.1). Geneva: WHO.

Eisenberg L (1988) The social context of behavioral pediatrics. *J Dev Behav Pediat* **9**, 382–7.

Eisenberg L (1992a) Treating depression and anxiety in primary care. *N Engl J Med* **326**, 1080–84.

Eisenberg L (1992b) Child mental health in the Americas: a public health approach. *Bull Pan Am Health Org* **26**, 230–41.

Eisenberg L (1995) The social construction of the human brain. *Am J Psychiat* **152**, 1563–75.

Evans DA et al (1993) Level of education and change in cognitive function in a community population of older persons. *Ann Epidemiol* **3**, 71–77.

Farmer P, Robin S, Ramilus St L & Kim JY (1991) Tuberculosis, poverty, and 'compliance': lessons from rural Haiti. *Sem Resp Infect* **6**(4), 373–9.

Feachem RG, Kjellstrom T, Murray CJL, Over M & Phillips MA (1992) *The Health of Adults in the Developing World*. New York: Oxford University Press.

Frenk J (1993) The new public health. *Ann Rev Publ Health* **14**, 469–90.

Grant JP (1995) *The State of the World's Children 1995*. New York: Oxford University Press, published for UNICEF.

Hobcroft J (1993) Women's education, child welfare and child survival. *Health Transition Rev* **3**, 159–75.

Jorm AF et al (1994) Does education protect against cognitive impairment? A comparison of the elderly in two Australian cities. *Int J Geriat Psychiat* **9**, 357–63.

Kaback M, Lim-Steele J, Dabholkar D, Brown D, Levy N & Zeiger K (1993) Tay–Sachs disease—carrier screening, prenatal diagnosis and the molecular era: an international perspective (1970–1993) *J Am Med Assoc* **270**, 2307–15.

Katzman R (1993) Education and the prevalence of dementia and Alzheimer's disease. *Neurology* **43**, 13–20.

Kessler DA (1995) Nicotine addiction in young people. *N Engl J Med* **333**, 186–8.

Kramer M (1989) Barriers to prevention. In B Cooper & T Helgason (eds) *Epidemiology and the Prevention of Mental Disorders*, pp 30–55. London: Routledge.

Kupfer DJ, Frank E, Perel JM, Cornes C, Mallinger AG, Thase ME, McEachran AB & Grochocinski VJ (1992) Five-year outcome for maintenance therapies in recurrent depression. *Arch Gen Psychiat* **49**, 769–73.

Levine RA et al (1991) Women's schooling and child care in the demographic transition: a Mexican case study. *Pop Dev Rev* **17**, 459–96.

Lynch BS & Bonnie RJ (eds) (1994) *Growing up Tobacco-free: Preventing Nicotine Addiction in Children and Youth*. Washington, DC: National Academy Press 8.

Mackwardt AM & Ochoa LH (1993) *Population and Health Data for Latin America*. Washington, DC: DHS/Macro International Inc, Pan-American Health Organization.

MRC Vitamin Study Research Group (1991) Prevention of neural tube defects: results of the MRC vitamin study. *Lancet* **338**, 131–7.

Miller TR & Galbraith M (1995) Injury prevention counseling by pediatricians. *Pediatrics* **96**, 1–4.

Population Council (1989) *International Conference on Adolescent Fertility in Latin America and the Caribbean: Overview*. Oaxaca, Mexico: Population Council.

Rice D, Kelman S & Miller LS (1992) Estimates of economic costs of alcohol and drug abuse and mental illness, 1985 and 1988. *Publ Health Rep* **106**, 280–91.

Rimer Z, Barsi J, Veg K & Katona CL (1990) Suicide rates in Hungary correlate negatively with reported rates of depression. *J Affect Dis* **20**, 87–91.

Robins LN & Regier DA (eds) (1992) *Psychiatric Disorders in America: The Epidemiologic Catchment Area Study*. New York: Free Press.

Rosen G (1947) What is social medicine? A genetic analysis of the concept. *Bull Hist Med* **21**, 674–733.

Rosen G (1958) *A History of Public Health*. New York: M.D. Publications.

Rutz W, Von Knorring L & Walinder J (1989) Frequency of suicide on Gotland after systematic post-graduate education of general practitioners. *Acta Psychiat Scand* **80**, 151–4.

Sartorius N, DeGirolamo G, Andrews G, German GA & Eisenberg L (1993) *Treatment of Mental Disorders: A Review of Effectiveness*. Washington, DC: American Psychiatric Press.

Sen A (1990) More than 100 million women are missing. *N Y Rev Books* **37**(26), 61–7, December 20.

Stark E & Flitcraft A (1991) Spouse Abuse. In M Rosenberg & M Fenley (eds) *Violence in America: A Public Health Approach*, pp 123–57. New York: Oxford University Press.

Surgeon General's Report (1989) *Reducing the Health Consequences of Smoking . . . 25 years of Progress*, pp 131, 188. Washington, DC: Government Printing Office.

Tyler PE (1994) Chinese to start vitamin program to eliminate a birth defect. *N Y Times*, 11 January, C3.

United Nations (1986) *The Nairobi Forward-looking Strategies for the Advancement of Women. World Conference to Review and Appraise the Achievements of the United Nations Decade for Women*. New York: United Nations Press.

Üstün TB & Sartorius N (eds) (1995) *Mental Illness in General Health Care*. New York: Wiley.

Wells KB, Stewart A, Hays RD, Burnam MA, Rosels W, Daniels M, Perry S, Greenfield S & Ware J (1989) The functioning and well-being of depressed patients. *J Am Med Assoc* **262**, 914–19.

Werler MM, Shapiro S & Mitchell AA (1993) Periconceptional folic acid exposure and risk of occurrent neural tube defects. *J Am Med Assoc* **269**, 1257–61.

West S, Munoz B, Lynch M, Kayongoya A, Chilangwa Z, Mmbaga BBO & Taylor HR (1995) Impact of face-washing on trachoma in Kongwa, Tanzania. *Lancet* **345**, 155–8.

World Bank (1992) *World Development Report: Development and the Environment.* New York: Oxford University Press.

World Bank (1993) *World Development Report 1993: Investing in Health.* New York: Oxford University Press.

Guidelines as a Tool for Prevention and Health Promotion

15

WHO Guidelines for the Primary Prevention of Mental, Neurological and Psychosocial Disorders

JM Bertolote

World Health Organization, Geneva, Switzerland

Interest in the prevention of mental disorders has followed a cyclical pattern, depending on prevailing concepts about the aetiology of mental disorders, progress achieved in relation to the treatment of those disorders and the overall climate in medicine in general.

The first evident bout of interest can be traced back to the beginning of the twentieth century, when the aetiology of mental disorders was either identified (e.g. neurosyphilis) or proposed (e.g. the psychoanalytic theory of neuroses and other types of mental disorders). Following the golden era of bacteriology, medicine as a whole was living in a highly optimistic period, and the control of diseases seemed within reach.

On the one hand, the biological—or rather bacteriological—model of diseases set the tone for understanding the causation of any disease; the discovery in 1917 of *Treponema pallidum* as the causative agent of general paresis—at that time the great scourge of all neuropsychiatry—came to confirm this belief. On the other hand, the availability of significantly better methods of treatment (e.g. malario-therapy, lobotomy—both of which won their proposers the Nobel prize—and ECT) indicated that the same impressive results could be obtained in relation to prevention effects.

The second peak of interest in the prevention of mental disorders came by the middle of the twentieth century, when medication efficient for the control of depression (tricyclics and MAOIs), anxiety (benzodiazepines), schizophrenia and other psychotic disorders (neuroleptics) was made widely available, together with the popularization of psychoanalytic concepts. The development of antibiotics on

Preventing Mental Illness: Mental Health Promotion in Primary Care. Edited by R. Jenkins and T.B. Üstün.
Published 1998 John Wiley & Sons Ltd.

the one hand and the overall upsurge of social medicine (and social psychiatry) on the other hand set the stage for this renewed interest in the prevention of mental disorders.

Until then, prevention meant actions believed to preclude the appearance of a particular form of disease. The publication and rapid acceptance of Leavell & Clark's (1965) epidemiological approach to community medicine, with its different levels of prevention, despite its importance for public health, created a lot of terminological and conceptual confusion. Since then, interventions—be they of a preventive, curative or rehabilitative nature—gradually started to be designated by Leavell & Clark's terminology; i.e. primary, secondary and tertiary prevention, respectively.

Unfortunately, owing to economy or slovenliness, the qualifiers primary, secondary and tertiary were gradually dropped and any intervention was identified with prevention, without specification. This contributed to a certain degree of disrepute for preventive programs and their proponents.

Despite these fluctuations in both the conceptualization and interest in prevention of mental disorders, a lot has been achieved. The current situation can be described as one in which there is much knowledge—not necessarily properly applied—side-by-side with efforts to identify new approaches to the prevention of disorders not previously thought to be preventable.

The key issue continues to be that of aetiology. Until sufficient light is shed on the causal factors of a given disorder, no scientific method for its prevention can be proposed. It is clear, by now, that the syndromic approach is much less advantageous than that of specific diseases. A good example of this assertion is given by mental retardation.

Taken as a whole, the prevention of mental retardation syndrome is a frustrating enterprise; the best estimates indicate that, on the whole, a reduction of no more than 15% can be obtained with current knowledge and means. However, when we break down this syndrome into specific diseases—e.g. mental retardation due to iodine deficiency of phenylketonuria, or even Down's syndrome—much more rewarding results are obtained, and it is even conceivable to eliminate those specific conditions. This is also true for other neuropsychiatric conditions such as epilepsy, suicide and, perhaps, depression. Contrasting with this, we have conditions such as Alzheimer's disease and schizophrenia, for which no specific aetiological mechanisms have yet been evidenced.

Against this background, in 1986 the 39th World Health Assembly recognized the importance and feasibility of the prevention of mental, neurological and psychosocial disorders and adopted a Resolution (WHA39.25; WHO 1988) on this subject. The present chapter briefly describes the main points of the work conducted by the World Health Organization (WHO) Division of Mental Health related to the implementation of that Resolution.

Given the WHO mandate, guidelines were produced and made available to all member states. With them remains the task of adapting the guidelines to their specific situations and issuing them as local norms and programs.

A PARADIGM FOR PREVENTION

Definitions

Primary prevention is considered here in a strict sense, corresponding to that of 'specific protection' proposed by Leavell & Clark (1962), and refers to methods designed to *avoid the occurrence* of a specific disorder or group of disorders. It should be differentiated not only from treatment and rehabilitation, but also, and more specifically, from health promotion, conceived as 'procedures employed in promoting health not directed at any particular disease or disorder but serving to further general health and well-being (Leavell & Clark 1965).

In discussing primary prevention measures for mental, neurological and psychosocial disorders, a number of caveats should be kept in mind:

1. Primary prevention efforts, especially in a sociocultural context, inevitably have implications for a number of conditions, in addition to the specific target; that is, many of the conditions that predispose to one disorder are also involved with other disorders. We cannot, at the outset, identify exactly who will manifest this or that disorder, if any. Therefore, any recommendations for prevention have to be quoted within the context of a broadly based conceptual model. A particular aspect associated with the prevention of mental, neurological and psychosocial disorders is that specific activities involving simple and inexpensive technology may benefit much beyond the specific target.
2. The many causes of mental, neurological and psychosocial disorders are highly diverse in origin, effect, timing and mechanism. Complex, multivariate, social and health problems yield no simple and quick solution. Therefore, comprehensive but culturally sensitive prevention plans must be tailored to a specific cause and effect.
3. Most preventive activities must reflect an understanding that behaviour is a very critical element in the equation. Changing attitudes and behaviour in individuals and in systems is essential for effective prevention.

Evaluation

Public health actions cannot go on without evaluation. Indicators are particularly useful to evaluate health actions; for the assessment of preventive measures, the following are not only useful but also necessary in order to avoid misunderstandings and unwarranted expectations (WHO 1971):

- *Efficacy:* the benefit or utility to the individual of the service, treatment regimen, drug, preventive or control measure advocated or applied.

- *Effectiveness:* the effect of the activity and the end-results, outcomes or benefits for the population achieved in relation to the stated objectives.
- *Efficiency:* the effects or end-results achieved in relation to the effort expended in terms of money, resources and time.

The extreme example of birth control can provide a helpful illustration of the range and importance of these concepts. In terms of *efficacy*, the best and safest measure for birth control is total abstinence from sexual intercourse. In practice, this may be unacceptable, or extremely difficult, if not impossible, to reach for the majority of the population; therefore, its *effectiveness* is quite low and its *efficiency* negligible, from a public health perspective. Hence, there is a need to find other means of birth control. For each of the other means eventually found, the same indicators—efficacy, effectiveness and efficiency—must be carefully analysed before those means are proposed as a public health measure.

A more specific example is given by the fetal alcohol syndrome (FAS). According to the best available information this syndrome is found in children born to mothers who have indulged in an excess of alcohol consumption during pregnancy, particularly around the time of conception of that particular child. With this clear link between alcohol ingestion and the syndrome, eliminating the alcohol ingestion would be the most efficacious measure to avoid FAS—theoretically 100%. Its effectiveness would be given by the amount of women of child-bearing age willing to stop drinking alcoholic beverages around the time of conception and afterwards. Many—but not all—women would do so once they learnt about their pregnancies, but not necessarily before; moreover, for some women, drinking or getting intoxicated with alcohol is part of a behavioural pattern that may include sexual intercourse, with the risk of a pregnancy. This lowers the high *efficacy* of the measure to a more modest level of *effectiveness* (around 50%). Adding the availability of resources, time and money needed to pass on the appropriate message to all women at risk of giving birth to a child affected by FAS would tell us about the *efficiency* of this measure, estimated at 0.08% of all births (Crocker 1982).

Yet another example is given by the question of the treatment of depressed patients as a means of reducing suicide rates. Unpublished data available to WHO and based on a large series of cases indicate that depression is implicated in approximately 25% of all cases of suicide. Data from other sources also indicate that not more than 50% of people with depression are seen by a doctor; of those seen and properly identified, approximately 70% will accept the treatment proposed. Given a treatment efficiency for depression of about 80%, the *efficiency* of the treatment of depression, including primary health care doctors, for the prevention of suicide—although highly beneficial and eventually life-saving for many people—is in the range of 6.5% of all suicides. Additional information on the costs involved in the training of primary health personnel and the direct costs of the treatment of depression (e.g. drugs, hospitalization) will indicate the appropriateness of such an approach, which could be used alone or in combination with other approaches.

Effectiveness has been proposed as the indicator of choice for the recommendation of preventive measures, with the quality of evidence considered to increase in the following order:

1. Opinion of experts and respected authorities.
2. Multiple time series studies, with and without intervention.
3. Well-designed cohort or case-control controlled analytic studies.
4. Well-designed controlled trials, without randomization.
5. At least one properly randomized, controlled trial.

Public acceptance and compliance (related to effectiveness) and costs (related to efficiency) seem to be the greatest limiting factors to some measures with an otherwise good degree of efficacy, as we shall see below.

Cost–benefit analyses have had a major importance for the assessment of the efficiency of many health activities, including prevention. The reasons why cost–benefit analyses are not more frequently used are twofold:

1. Information on health cost in general is badly needed; specific information on the cost of some preventive activities is indeed extremely rare—guesses are mostly found. This renders efficiency analyses almost impossible. Also, in many instances only very partial costs are provided, which are almost useless;
2. As can be expected, the little information on costs available comes from developed countries. Transposed to developing countries—or even to other developed but with different socioeconomic and health system arrangements—these costs become meaningless.

However, cost–benefit analysis only acquires a meaning when using real costs, in a real epidemiological and socioeconomic situation. Standards are to be set taking both desirable targets and costs into consideration, and health authorities are strongly recommended to carefully analyse the balance between them in order to avoid setting either too high standards—impossible to reach at local resources level—or too low standards—missing any significant impact at the health level of populations.

Finally, cost–benefit analyses are usually done using economic costs only. It is indeed very difficult to calculate or estimate social or emotional costs. Adding ethics and humanitarian dimensions to a cost–benefit analysis may be a task for which no specific technology yet exists. The other side of the dilemma is that ignoring ethics and humanitarian principles to simplify economic analysis is unacceptable.

A Paradigm

Based on the above considerations, the following paradigm underlies the WHO (1993–1994) *Guidelines for the Primary Prevention of Mental, Neurological and Psychosocial Disorders*:

1. Most mental and neurological disorders have multiple and interacting causes, with biological, psychological and sociocultural components.
2. Preventive action should have a wide array of targets.
3. Preventive action should aim at the public health level rather than the individual level.
4. Whenever a difference in prevalence or incidence is found across comparable population groups, there is scope for primary prevention. This difference indicates the least magnitude of the expected results of preventive actions.

As is now known, most of the effective prevention of mental and neurological disorders falls outside the usual field of responsibility of mental health professionals (in fact, in many cases outside the health sector altogether). This may be one of the reasons why many mental health professionals tend to underrate the possibilities of primary prevention in their fields: what they usually can do has low—if any—preventive power, whereas what does have preventive power is usually beyond their professional mandate.

This view, if correct, should not deter mental health workers willing to work in primary prevention from doing so. This calls for innovative approaches which integrate mental health action into other health and social sector activities. It also reminds us that perhaps some role modifications must occur, e.g. the enhancement of mental health workers' capabilities as *advocates* and *advisers* to professionals in other sectors, in relation to some interventions and results specific to their domain. As Eisenberg (1981) has put it:

> What matters is not the mode of action of the agent, the venue in which it is applied, or the academic discipline of the practitioner, but the effectiveness of the measure in preventing diseases manifested by disturbances in mental function.

SELECTION OF PRIORITIES

Given the impossibility of addressing the primary prevention of all forms of mental, neurological and psychosocial disorders, a decision has to be made to select some of their forms. To this end the following criteria (Bertolote 1992) are proposed:

1. *Frequency:* a measure of either incidence or prevalence of a specific condition.
2. *Severity:* measured by mortality rates or by the degree of impairment, disability and handicap brought about to an individual by a specific condition, or the burden it causes to families, communities and society.
3. *Importance:* measured by the degree of concern expressed by the community or by health workers in relation to a given condition, irrespective of its severity.
4. *Controllability:* a general measure of the existence of efficient—hence efficacious and effective—interventions for specific conditions. It is also a measure of the 'preventability' resulting from such intervention.

5. *Cost:* includes costs incurred from physical facilities, equipment, supplies and personnel for the provision of a specific intervention.

With this in mind, an extensive review of the pertinent literature, particularly on the effectiveness and efficiency of primary preventive actions, was conducted. An attempt was made to utilize only the information obtained from sources adhering to internationally accepted scientific standards, and to rank the information according to the quality criteria listed above. When the information was unexpected or at variance with current knowledge, an effort was made to obtain confirmation from other sources, always checking for its quality. In some instances, very little information, or none at all, could be found in relation to developing countries. This was particularly true for epidemiological and aetiological data, which may exist but are not easily available—the so-called 'fugitive literature'. In these cases the available information was included, a due acknowledgement to the fact being made.

As a general rule it was preferred not to include doubtful or non-confirmed statements or findings, concentrating instead on what was reliably found in distinct and independent sources. The following were considered priorities for the production of guidelines:

1. Mental disorders
   - *Mental retardation,* associated with fetal alcohol syndrome, Down's syndrome, iodine deficiency and phenylketonuria.
   - Relapses of *depressive and schizophrenic episodes,* as well as of *harmful use of psychoactive substances.*
2. Neurological disorders:
   - *Epilepsy,* associated with febrile episodes, brain injury and neurocysticercosis.
   - *Brain injury,* associated with cerebrovascular problems and intoxication.
3. Psychosocial disorders:
   - *Suicide.*
   - *Staff burnout syndrome.*

WHO GUIDELINES

A series of fascicles (WHO 1993–1994) on the *Primary Prevention of Mental, Neurological and Psychosocial Disorders* has been issued by WHO Division of Mental Health. The series is available upon request to WHO. Forthcoming issues will deal with the prevention of relapses of depressive and schizophrenic episodes, as well as of harmful use of psychoactive substances, and the prevention of brain injury, associated with cerebrovascular problems and intoxication.

An array of actors and partners are involved in the prevention of mental disorders, and the WHO fascicles have been produced for a wide audience. The main target groups are policy makers, health workers and the general public. Specific needs and both the degree of complexity of the information and the language are different; therefore the same information has been produced in three versions adapted for these groups and printed in pages of different colours:

- *White* pages contain extensive, detailed technical information providing the scientific evidence about the facts and the measures proposed; they are intended for health professionals and the technical and scientific communities.
- *Yellow* pages contain more detailed information at a technical level; they are intended for primary health care workers or workers in other technical sectors, e.g. education or water supply.
- *Green* pages contain brief and to-the-point information; they are intended for those readers with not much time available or interest in scientific literature, e.g. the general public, policy makers, journalists, etc.

Eminently practical, the fascicles have the same format, which includes basic information on clinical and epidemiological aspects of each condition considered, aetiological mechanisms and preventive measures; these are specified in terms of both 'what-to-do' and 'who-does-what', in different sectors. In each section, prevention is proposed both in terms of specific interventions (e.g. salt iodization) and of settings where those interventions can be developed (e.g. what can be done by the Ministry of Industry and Commerce).

The last word is a call for practical action. Enough is known but too little is done. We need practical programs which immediately benefit people and we should concentrate our resources and efforts on this. It is unacceptable that we continue with high incidence rates of conditions with lifelong impact and which could be completely avoided, such as is the case with mental retardation due to iodine deficiency. Money spent in the development of methods of prevention for conditions whose aetiology and causal mechanisms are far from being elucidated should be more conscientiously and adequately used for the prevention of those conditions whose prevention is warranted by current scientific knowledge but is not done on a worldwide basis.

REFERENCES

Bertolote JM (1992) Planificación y administración de acciones en salud mental en la comunidad. In I Levav (ed) *Temas de salud mental en la comunidad* (Serie PALTEX No 19). Washington, DC: OPS.

Crocker AC (1982) Current strategies in prevention of mental retardation. *Pediat Ann* **11**(5), 450–53.

Eisenberg L (1981) A research framework for evaluating the promotion of mental health and prevention of mental illness. *Publ Health Rep* **96**(1), 3–19.

Harris SS et al (1989) Physical activity counselling. *J Am Med Assoc* **261**(24), 3588–9.

Leavell HR & Clark EG (1965) *Preventive Medicine for the Doctor in His Community: An Epidemiological Approach*, 3rd edn. New York: McGraw-Hill.

WHO (1971) *Statistical Indicators for the Planning and Evaluation of Public Health Programmes* (TRS No. 472) Geneva: WHO.

WHO (1988) *Prevention of Mental, Neurological and Psychosocial Disorders* (WHO/MNH/EVA/88.1). Geneva: WHO.

WHO (1993–1994) *Guidelines for the Primary Prevention of Mental, Neurological and Psychosocial Disorders. 1. Principles for Primary Prevention* (WHO/MNH/MND/93.21); *2. Mental Retardation* (WHO/MNH/MND/93.22); *3. Epilepsy* (WHO/MNH/MND/93.34); *4. Suicide* (WHO/MNH/MND/93.24); *5. Staff Burnout* (WHO/MNH/MND/94.21). Geneva: WHO.

16

Guidelines for the Application of Prevention Strategies in a Practical Management Framework

T Bedirhan Üstün

World Health Organization, Geneva, Switzerland

Prevention of common mental disorders in primary care settings is a sound approach, since these disorders are frequently encountered in primary care settings. The knowledge available for prevention strategies should be made available to primary care physicians in a practical format so that it can be applied with ease. The management guidelines incorporated in the primary care version of the ICD-10 classification of mental disorders provide a practical and comprehensive approach to implement prevention strategies in primary care settings.

We now have conclusive evidence from different countries all over the world that mental disorders in primary care settings constitute a major public health problem (Üstün & Sartorius 1995) because they are frequent, disabling and contrary to the beliefs that they are transient or self-limiting most are chronic or recurrent. Although effective treatment or prevention strategies exist for managing these disorders they are not applied to a sufficient degree. There are many reasons for this phenomenon: primary care physicians are busy and many services are demanded from them without setting priorities according to objective measures of effectiveness (i.e. what brings most reduction in terms of burden of disease, patient outcomes and consumer satisfaction). On a global scale, most primary care services are not designed rationally to meet the needs of consumers with mental disorders. We therefore need a sound and comprehensive strategy that will work in various primary care settings, which will allow incorporation of knowledge for prevention of common mental disorders into practice.

Preventing Mental Illness: Mental Health Promotion in Primary Care. Edited by R. Jenkins and T.B. Üstün.
Published 1998 John Wiley & Sons Ltd.

MANAGEMENT GUIDELINES ACCOMPANYING THE PRIMARY CARE VERSION OF THE ICD-10 MENTAL DISORDER CLASSIFICATION

The world of primary care is practical: for any intervention to have its place in primary care practice it has to be realistically applicable, effective and simple. The management strategies in primary care facilities have to be selected carefully to address problems that are common, have important consequences, and can be effectively managed in primary care settings. If primary care practitioners cannot apply the management strategy in their usual practice, they will rightly devote their limited time and resources to more applicable interventions.

Management guidelines accompanying the Primary Care Version of the ICD-10 Mental Disorder Classification (Üstün et al 1995) provide a practical approach for the treatment and prevention of common mental disorders in primary care settings. It contains only the most frequent disorders encountered in primary care settings. It is primary care-friendly in that it provides management guidelines so that these conditions can be treated as they are identified. ICD-10 PC for mental disorders therefore contains only 24 conditions—in contrast to some 450 conditions in the original ICD-10 scheme in Chapter V for mental and behavioural disorders. Each condition is presented as having both diagnostic and management guidelines. The diagnostic guidelines include: (a) presenting complaints; (b) diagnostic features; and (c) differential diagnosis. These are followed by management guidelines which include: (a) essential information for patient and family; (b) specific counselling for patient and family; and (c) medication—when and how to give medication, how much to give, under what conditions and how to explain the medications, their usage and continuation; (d) specialist consultation—when and how to refer to a specialist.

The ICD-10 primary care version also contains *flow-charts* to assist users to make differential diagnosis, a *symptom index* to link presenting symptoms with possible diagnoses and *patient leaflets* that general practitioners can go through with their patients and hand out to them.

INCORPORATION OF PREVENTION GUIDELINES INTO ICD-10 CHAPTER V PC

In summary, this system allows a user-friendly framework to incorporate promotion and prevention information into the package. For example, in the depression card, the information is given to the patient and the family that depression is common and effective treatment is available. The primary care practitioners are instructed to discuss with their patients the concept of depression not being weakness or laziness. Doctors are asked to to assess the risk of suicide and the package contains guidelines on how to assess this risk. The depression card also contains guidelines for relapse prevention. The practitioners are reminded to identify the signs of relapse, plan and suggest to the patient what action is to be taken if signs of relapse occur. Doctors are also warned about the transition of disorders from anxiety to depression and substance abuse to depression, so they are reminded to check whether harmful alcohol and drug use exists.

The approach seems to be simple and brief: hence it is applicable. In the field trials of the ICD-10 Primary Care version the system was found to be easy to use and reliable (Üstün et al, in press). In 19 countries, groups of 12–20 primary care workers were introduced to the system. Their knowledge and attitudes were measured at baseline and a month later. Some 500 GPs had pre-test and post-test measurement. Overall ratings for the ICD-10 PC was found very useful by a majority of participants (> 90%). In comparison of pre- and post-test attitudes, optimism about the treatment of mental disorders in primary care among the participating GPs had indeed increased. The confidence that they could make diagnoses of mental disorders had increased, as had the perceived importance of the causes of mental disorders in primary care.

The ICD-10 Chapter V Primary Care version seems to be a valuable and practical tool for use in busy primary care settings and it seems to be accepted by users. However, it remains to be seen whether the introduction of the system has a favourable impact on patient outcomes, relapse prevention and other factors.

WHO's Division of Mental Health is planning to develop this system further by means of accompanying assessment tools for case-finding (e.g. checklists and questionnaires), reference materials (e.g. an annotated volume which will serve as a basic reference for essential interventions); and computerized applications. The ICD-10 Chapter V Primary Care version will also be accompanied by an 'educational kit' so that the system can be a self-learning package for primary care workers in different parts of the world. These materials will definitely include applicable guidelines for the prevention of mental disorders. In this way we aim to integrate prevention strategies into the daily practice of primary care practitioners.

REFERENCES

Üstün TB, Goldberg D, Cooper J, Simon GE, Sartorius N (1995) New classification for mental disorders, with management guidelines for use in primary care: ICD-10 PC, Chapter 5. *Br J Gen Pract* **45**(393), April.

Üstün TB & Sartorius N (eds) (1995) *Mental Illness in General Health Care: An International Study*, Chapter 6, pp 371–5. Chichester: Wiley.

WHO (1996) *ICD-10 Diagnostic and Management Guidelines for Mental Disorders in Primary Care: ICD-10, Chapter V Primary Care Version*. Hogrefe and Huber.

17

Community Education and Screening Programs

Kathryn M Magruder
National Institute of Mental Health, Rockville, MD, USA

Community education programs have often been employed to promote awareness of diseases and conditions for which prevention and early interventions are effective. When opportunities also exist for people to be screened, seek help, or otherwise take action, the likelihood of having a positive impact on health is improved. These approaches have been used for hypertension and breast cancer, among others. Education campaigns about hypertension and the availability of blood pressure machines in pharmacies mean that most Americans are aware of whether their blood pressure is elevated or not. Similarly, public campaigns about breast cancer and the ready availability of mammography screening have increased the percentage of women in the USA who undergo this kind of screening. In both cases, early intervention and treatment increase the likelihood of beneficial outcomes.

Mental illness has always been treated somewhat differently, not because early intervention is not effective but because of the stigma attached to being mentally ill. In the past 10 years, the National Institute of Mental Health has launched several programs to promote the awareness, recognition and treatment of specific mental illnesses. Depression and panic disorder have been well covered by these programs, and an eating disorder campaign is under development. Independently, several organizations have initiated national screening days for specific mental illnesses—a day on which various facilities agree to screen individuals and, if needed, make referrals to care. The National Depression Screening Day was the first of these programs, followed by a National Anxiety Disorder Screening Day. Although the education and screening campaigns in mental illness developed independently, the fact that they developed so closely in time is probably not accidental and certainly serendipitous. Each is aimed at a slightly different segment of the population of those with the condition, matching the needs of those who are at different stages of readiness to change. This fits nicely in a theory of stages of change (Prochaska, DiClemente & Norcross 1992).

Preventing Mental Illness: Mental Health Promotion in Primary Care. Edited by R. Jenkins and T.B. Üstün.
© 1998 John Wiley & Sons Ltd.

TABLE 17.1 The five stages of change

Precontemplation	Has no intention to change behavior in foreseeable future
Contemplation	Is aware that a problem exists, is seriously thinking about changing it, but there is no commitment to take action
Preparation	Is intending to take action in the next month and has unsuccessfully taken action in past year
Action	Has modified behavior, experiences, or environment to overcome problems; there are overt behavior changes
Maintenance	Is working to prevent relapse and consolidate gains attained during action

From Prochaska, DiClemente & Norcross (1992), by permission.

Most mental illnesses (particularly the anxiety disorders and major depression) are made up of constellations of various somatic and psychological symptoms. Although it is generally clear to trained mental health professionals how to interpret such symptomatology, this is definitely not the case with the lay public, and unfortunately often not with primary care providers. Many who suffer from depression or anxiety are unaware of what they have, owing to their inability to interpret their symptomatology. Thus, education and screening programs serve an important purpose to help those with these conditions consolidate their own thinking about their symptoms, and hopefully take action.

Research has shown that there are five predictable stages that individuals move through as they change from unhealthy to healthy behaviors of lifestyles (Prochaska, DiClemente & Norcross 1992) (see Table 17.1). Individuals start at the precontemplation stage, in which they may not even be aware that they have a problem and certainly have no intention to change behavior in the foreseeable future. The second stage is the contemplation stage, in which individuals are aware that a problem exists and seriously think about changing it, but make no commitment to take action. The third stage is the preparation stage, during which there is intention to take action in the next month and there may have been unsuccessful attempts to take action in the past year. The fourth stage, the action stage, is characterized by true commitment, with individuals overtly modifying their behaviors, experiences or environment to overcome problems. The last stage is the maintenance stage, during which people work to prevent relapse and to consolidate the gains made in the action stage.

Learning more about a problem and oneself in relation to the problem is a process which can facilitate moving forward through the stages of change. Clearly, public education campaigns can play a critical role in providing information about particular problems (such as depression), as well as information about treatable and availability of treatment resources. When an underlying knowledge base is established in a community, then opportunities to take more targeted action towards making changes have the potential for being more powerful.

This paper will describe a community education approach (the Depression Awareness, Recognition and Treatment program; (D/ART) and a community screening program (National Depression Screening Day; NDSD). Taken together, these programs help raise the level of awareness about depression in a community and provide an opportunity for depressed individuals to enter treatment.

DEPRESSION AWARENESS, RECOGNITION AND TREATMENT—D/ART

D/ART was launched in 1988 by the United States National Institute of Mental Health and was described as an early identification and treatment approach to reduce morbidity and duration of depressive disorders. As such, it would be considered a secondary prevention program. The purpose of D/ART is to increase awareness, recognition and treatment of depressive disorders through a national education campaign focused on three major target audiences: the general public, primary care providers and mental health specialists.

The message of D/ART is kept relatively simple: (a) clinical depression is a common illness that usually goes unrecognized, but when identified can be treated; (b) there are effective medications and psychological treatments which are often used in combination, and in serious depression medication is usually required; (c) the large majority of clinical depressions, including the most serious, improve with treatment (usually in a matter of weeks), and continued treatment will prevent recurrence.

There are three program components to D/ART: the public education campaign, the national worksite program, and the professional education program. Most relevant to this chapter is the public education campaign, which provides the substratum for launching other activities. The public education campaign has three objectives: (a) to increase knowledge and awareness of depression; (b) to change attitudes and beliefs regarding depression; and (c) to motivate changes in behavior regarding depression.

NATIONAL DEPRESSION SCREENING DAY—NDSD

National Depression Screening Day began in 1991 as a part of Mental Illness Awareness Week (the first week in October). It is a non-profit project sponsored by the American Psychiatric Association, Harvard Medical School Department of Psychiatry, McLean Hospital, the National Depressive and Manic-depressive Association, and the National Institute of Mental Health. The purpose is to increase recognition of depression in the general population and facilitate access to appropriate health care for those suffering from depression. It was felt that by offering free, anonymous screening, where people had the opportunity to discuss their depressive symptoms with a mental health professional during a screening interview, individuals who were depressed but not in treatment would be encouraged to attend. NDSD was advertised extensively for several weeks before the actual day in popular magazines, newspapers and the press. A toll-free telephone number was given so that anyone interested could call and find out the screening site most convenient to them.

NDSD grew from 435 participating sites in 1992 to over 2000 sites projected for 1995. Registered sites are sent a Depression Screening Procedure Manual as well as informational packets and test materials for distribution on the actual screening day. Since 1992, all 50 United States and the District of Columbia have been represented among the sites. Typically, about half the screening sites are located in general hospitals, one-third in private psychiatric hospitals, one-tenth in public mental health facilities, and the rest in academic centres and college health services.

Those who attended NDSD were administered the Self-rating Depression Test (SDS) (Zung 1965). The SDS is a short 20-item screen which has been used extensively throughout the world. It was scored on the spot and interpreted to the participant by a mental health professional. SDS scores can be divided into four categories: < 50, $50-59$, $60-69$, and ≥ 70. The corresponding clinical global impressions are: no psychopathology, presence of minimal to mild depression, presence of moderate to marked depression, and presence of severe to extreme depression. The SDS has good performance characteristics relative to DSM-III-R criteria for major depressive disorder, and four studies found the following range of sensitivity and specificity: at a cutpoint of 50, sensitivity 83–97%, specificity 63–82%; at a cutpoint of 60, sensitivity 58–76%, specificity 82–93%.

In addition to the SDS, participants provided information on age, gender, level of education, current employment status, marital status and current and/or prior treatment for depression.

After the SDS was scored, each participant was given the opportunity to discuss the results of his/her written screening test with a mental health professional and to receive recommendations for follow-up referrals if appropriate. When referrals were given, a number of options (including low-cost options such as community mental health centers) were provided.

NDSD Results

Respondent participation grew from over 5000 participants in 1992 to 45 811 in 1994. Table 17.2 shows sociodemographic characteristics of the 1992 sample. The profile is nearly identical for 1993 and 1994. Women outnumber men by 2 to 1; about half the respondents are ≤ 44 years old; most are at least college-educated; most are married; and most are employed full- or part-time. Of particular note is the fact that 61% report never having been treated for depression, with 24% having been treated in the past and 15% in current treatment.

Table 17.3 shows the remarkable stability of the depression screening results from 1992 to 1994—despite the ninefold increase in the number of people taking the test. Each year slightly less than one-quarter of those who were screened fell in

TABLE 17.2   Respondents' sociodemographic characteristics ($n = 5367$)

Males (%)	33.9
Age	
18–24	6.6
25–34	19.0
35–44	25.9
45–54	20.0
55–64	14.3
65–74	10.7
≥ 75	3.5
Education	
Grade school	3.9
High school	43.5
College	36.6
Post-college	16.0
Marital status	
Married	53.8
Widowed	6.3
Divorced	18.0
Never married	21.9
Employment status	
Full-time	44.2
Part-time	15.5
Not employed	40.3
Depression treatment history	
No treatment	61.2
Current treatment	14.9
Past treatment	23.9

TABLE 17.3   Percentage of attendees for each year by the SDS index categorized into clinical global impressions

Year	SDS score				
	≤ 49	50–59	60–69	≥ 70	n
1992	23.9	23.3	30.7	22.6	5 367
1993	22.1	23.6	30.4	23.9	33 911
1994	23.6	24.9	29.5	22.0	45 811

the severely depressed range, with about 30% in the moderately depressed range. Less than one-quarter were in the normal range. For 1992, 53.3% were in the depressed range if a cutpoint of 60 is used, and 76.1% if a cutpoint of 50 is used. Because of the similarity of results across years, we report 1992 data in the remaining tables.

TABLE 17.4 Treatment history by SDS category

Variable	SDS category								Analysis		
	≤ 49 (n = 1116)		50–59 (n = 1116)		60–69 (n = 1441)		≥ 70 (n = 1062)				
	(n)	(%)	(n)	(%)	(n)	(%)	(n)	(%)	χ^2	df	p
No treatment	843	75.5	714	64.0	831	57.7	510	48.0	186.99	6	< 0.0001
Current treatment	99	8.9	154	13.8	230	15.9	222	20.9			
Past treatment	179	15.6	248	22.2	380	26.4	330	31.1			

TABLE 17.5 Clinical global equivalents by reasons for not seeking treatment, according to the number of participants providing reasons for not seeking treatment (National Depression Screening Day 1993)

Characteristic	Percentage responding with SDS index scores*			
	≤ 49	50–59	60–69	≥ 70
Reasons for not seeking treatment				
Do not feel depressed	54.7	14.0	5.1	2.0
Did not recognize depression	39.8	50.3	38.5	28.3
Do not want others to know	7.2	18.1	23.2	28.4
Not sure where to go for treatment	10.1	30.4	41.5	47.5
No insurance	6.4	14.2	21.3	31.2
Limited or no insurance coverage	9.1	19.3	22.9	24.1
Treatment too expensive	8.8	23.4	33.0	42.0
Treatment does not work	3.1	7.4	10.0	10.2
Treatment not available	0.8	1.4	2.1	2.4
Number of participants providing reason	4351	5027	6893	5626

Prepared by the Services Research Branch, NIMH July 5 1995

* An index score of less than 49 is equivalent to no depression; between 50 and 59 is equivalent to mild depression; between 60 and 69 is equivalent to moderate depression; of 70 or greater is equivalent to severe depression.

Table 17.4 shows treatment history by depression category. While the likelihood of treatment increases with depression severity, there is still a high percentage (48%) of individuals with severe depression (SDS ≥ 70) who have never been treated, and 58% of those with moderate depression have never been treated.

We also ran an analysis to see how efficient our screening procedure was in terms of identification of those with clinically significant depression (major depression by DSM-III-R criteria). In other words, if all the screen positives received a complete mental health evaluation, what percentage would be classified as having major depression? Table 17.5 shows various levels of population prevalence, the corresponding screening prevalence, and positive and negative predictive values for SDS cutoffs of 50 and 60. From this table, it is clear that with a screening prevalence of 76% at a cutpoint of 50 (as was obtained in the 1992

NDSD), the positive predictive value is 88.7–92.3%. With a screening prevalence of 53% at a cutpoint of 60, the positive predictive value is 92.5–95.5%. Clearly, regardless of which cutpoint is used, about 90% of those who are screened positive would be found to have major depression.

In 1993 we asked respondents their reasons for not seeking treatment (multiple reasons could be checked) (see Table 17.5). The most common reason cited by those in the severely depressed category was, 'Not sure where to go for treatment' (47.5%), followed by 'Treatment too expensive' (42.0%). Few checked that treatment was not available (2.4%) or that treatment does not work (10.2%). Of note is that 28.3% of the severely depressed did not recognize that they had depression and 28.4% did not want others to know. It appears that many respondents were in the paradoxical position of knowing that treatment was available, but not being certain of where to go to get treatment, and feeling that the cost of treatment and lack of insurance coverage were barriers to seeking care.

SUMMARY AND DISCUSSION

We have described two early intervention approaches—the D/ART program and NDSD—which are aimed at moving untreated depressed people in the community into appropriate treatment. Although there are no data from the D/ART program, it is our hypothesis that by raising the level of awareness of depression through community education, people (including those who are depressed) are able to take advantage of opportunities to improve their mental health—e.g. the National Depression Screening Day. Clearly the NDSD attracts individuals who are depressed and currently not in treatment. It is likely that for many of these individuals, this was the first step in the process of seeking help. In terms of the readiness to change model, these individuals are moving from contemplation to preparation.

Obviously of interest is whether individuals identified as depressed through NDSD accepted and followed through with the referrals that were made at the time of screening. Data on this are currently being collected.

It is noteworthy that the US Preventive Health Services Task Force does not recommend routine screening for depression in primary care. It should be pointed out, though, that voluntary screening is a very different thing from routine screening in primary care, where in the latter case, the true prevalence is apt to be 20% or less. This makes the efficiency of the screening procedure much lower, as positive predictive values are considerably lower. Although akin to case-finding in its non-randomness, voluntary screening is slightly different in that it is patient- or client-initiated, whereas case-finding is clinician-initiated. Consideration should be given to the utility of voluntary screening in primary care settings where, based on the findings from NDSD, higher prevalence would be expected, thereby increasing positive predictive values. The link to services could also be much more immediate.

For those who wish even more anonymity than is provided in the NDSD as it is currently organized, telephone screening may be an option. A trial of telephone screening for depression using the SDS showed nearly identical results to those obtained in NDSD (Baer et al 1995).

Voluntary screening for other mental disorders, especially the anxiety disorders, may also be feasible. A national day for screening for anxiety disorders has been held twice, and appears to be successful. Consideration could also be given to screening for multiple disorders.

In summary, NDSD has proven to be an efficient strategy for earlier identification of depressed individuals. Its success points to the need for more emphasis on strategies to encourage unidentified and untreated depressed clients to seek treatment.

REFERENCES

Prochaska JO, DiClemente CC & Norcross JC (1992) In search of how people change: applications to addictive behaviors. _Am Psychol_ **47**, 1102–14.

Zung WWK (1965) A self-rating depression scale. _Arch Gen Psychiat_ **12**, 63–70.

Baer L, Jacobs DG, Cukor P, O'Laughlen J, Coyle JT & Magruder KM (1995) Automated telephone screening survey for depression. _J Am Med Assoc_ **273**, 1943–4.

18

Local Guidelines in Primary Care Health Promotion by Practice Nurses

Elizabeth Armstrong

Institute of Psychiatry, London, UK

The Kensington and Chelsea and Westminster Family Health Services Authority Mental Health Facilitator Project (KCW FHSA Project) was one of two facilitation projects in general practice funded by the UK Department of Health and which started in 1991. The KCW project, a part of which is described in this chapter, was designed to evaluate the role of a facilitator working with general practice teams and attempting to improve the recognition and management of people with depression and anxiety. One of the facilitator's tasks was to find ways of helping GPs and their staff identify and offer support to people at risk of becoming depressed (Jenkins 1992a).

In 1988, Newton (p 217) had suggested that a usable framework for preventive mental health work already existed within the British primary care services. In fact a great deal of preventive activity was already taking place, much of it led by practice nurses. Practice nurses work in GP surgeries and health centres, and are normally employed directly by the GP. They are usually registered general nurses (RGNs) and often have additional qualifications such as family planning certificates. Like most nurses they are hospital-trained and less than one-fifth have community nursing qualifications, such as district nursing or health visiting certificates. Just under half have done a course in practice nursing—probably because, at the time of writing, practice nursing certificates are not recognized by the UK Central Council for Nursing, Midwifery and Health Visiting (UKCC). Relevant to this chapter is the fact that less than 2% of practice nurses have completed a psychiatric nursing course (Atkin et al 1993). That being said, many are highly experienced nurses with considerable expertise in health promotion.

Preventing Mental Illness: Mental Health Promotion in Primary Care. Edited by R. Jenkins and T.B. Üstün.
© 1998 John Wiley & Sons Ltd.

EXISTING ACTIVITIES

Before 1982 most preventive and health promotion activities in primary care were undertaken by health visitors. That year saw the beginnings of the Oxford Heart Attack and Stroke Prevention Project, which used a facilitator to improve the ability of general practice teams to identify the risk factors for cardiovascular disease (Fullard, Fowler & Gray 1987). Since then, facilitators have been in the forefront of developments in health promotion, often training practice nurses in the appropriate skills.

For these historical reasons and encouraged by both the 'Health of the Nation' targets (1992) and a system which rewards some health promotion activities in general practice, most of these activities are orientated towards physical health, and towards the prevention of heart disease and cancers. There is no direct financial benefit to a practice in screening for depression, but there is in cervical cancer screening and in helping people to stop smoking.

In 1991, most health promotion by practice nurses took place in clinic settings, e.g. during well woman clinics which offered cervical cytology and sometimes breast examination, in registration 'health checks' which were offered to all new patients in a practice, and in 3-yearly health checks which were also offered. Practice nurses used a variety of protocols and guidelines, and although most of these were in effect assessments of health risk, few looked at the social and emotional factors which are known to be linked with depression.

PREVENTING MENTAL ILLNESS

Newton (1992) laid down three main principles which she suggested should underpin prevention-orientated services:

- They should target the people at risk.
- They should help people take control over their own lives.
- They should make maximum use of voluntary and community networks.

In addition, she states that such activities should not threaten existing services for people with serious mental illness.

The system which will be described here seems to fulfil all of those criteria. But in order to target those at risk, it is necessary first to identify them. The risk factors for depression are well known. They include bereavement; relationship problems with spouse or partner; other family difficulties, e.g. with children or long-term caring for an ill or disabled relative; work-related problems, such as unemployment, fear of redundancy, sexual or racial harassment or bullying; housing or financial problems; chronic, painful, disabling or life-threatening illness, especially hearing or vision impairment; social isolation; and previous history of depression.

In general practice settings, some of these things will be known about some patients, but by no means all will be written down in patient records. Similarly, they may not be recorded in the practice computer. Manual review of records to identify people at risk would be an almost impossible task in an average practice of 6000–8000 patients. Use of a computer would be easier, but only if it could be assumed that the appropriate information had first been entered, and if the available software could retrieve the information in a usable form. In the KCW study, most of the intervention practices did not have computers.

Further, the purpose of identifying people at risk is to enable some form of support to be offered, but to offer support to every patient with one risk factor clearly represents an unmanageable workload. In any case, the list of risk factors above does not take into account other variables such as coping skills and what Newton (1988) and others have called 'vulnerability'. For example, in the case of bereavement, Parkes (1986) suggested that it was those whose bereavement reaction was either prolonged, delayed or both who were the most likely to develop symptoms of illness. Although support offered by members of the primary care team to the recently bereaved may be preventive, Newton suggests that it is likely to be most effective for those who have few alternative sources of support.

The task, then, was to devise a method of identifying and offering preventive support to people who might be at higher than average risk of developing a depressive illness because of stressful life events or circumstances.

Practice nurses, who were already familiar with the concept of assessing risks to health, and helping people modify their risks, seemed the obvious people to undertake this work, but whatever method was used, it needed to be relatively easy for the nurse to use and not take up too much time, considering the extreme pressures which many in general practice are under, especially in inner cities. It also had to be acceptable to both nurse and patient. In addition, it was important to recognize that practice nurses cannot fill the gaps for people who have inadequate social networks, but they can help people in distress gain access to alternative sources of support and help for their problems (Jenkins 1992b).

The solution was to design an opportunistic 'add-on' assessment which could be used by practice nurses in their regular clinics alongside assessments of physical health. There needed to be a way of recording the information gained, and a means of alerting the GP to the patient's risk status.

THE ASSESSMENT

A *Health Risk Assessment Card* was designed, of a suitable size to fit in the record envelopes used by all the practices in the study (Armstrong 1995). It listed all the risk factors, and across the top was a line of boxes called the risk indicator. The idea was that for patients with four or more risk factors, a corresponding number of boxes would be highlighted. GPs should thus be made quickly aware of higher-risk patients when they consulted. Patients with four or more factors were considered 'high-risk'—although for the reasons stated above, this was an arbitrary decision and it did not take existing coping skills into account. The cut-off point proved reasonably workable in practice, although nurses were advised to allow people with fewer risk factors to ask for help if they wanted it.

To go with the card, a semi-structured interview was compiled, for which detailed guidelines were written. Questions needed to be asked sensitively, since some of the factors involved intimate relationships and areas which, in Britain, are traditionally regarded as private. Indeed, in the initial pilot study of the method, one GP employer said 'You cannot ask my patients personal questions like that'. In fact, the nurse persisted and, far from being offended, patients were positively grateful for being given the opportunity to express their worries and concerns.

It was necessary, too, to help nurses avoid getting themselves into situations they could not deal with; to help them cope if 'the floodgates opened' and to enable them to recognize when professional counselling might be required. It was stressed that the assessment was not intended as a method of counselling, neither was it a way of diagnosing mental illness, although inevitably some of the patients assessed might already be depressed. In the latter situation, nurses were advised to refer to the GP. In practice, there was little evidence that nurses could not cope with distressed people. They recognized the value of listening and most were well aware of their limitations. One nurse said she had been motivated to seek more training in counselling skills.

OFFERING SUPPORT

A number of authors (e.g. Wilkinson 1989; Barbee 1990) have advocated a problem-solving approach to helping distressed people learn to cope with their difficulties. Problem-solving techniques seem to appeal to general-trained nurses who are accustomed to fairly structured procedures. Such methods also provide the means by which nurses who are used to giving advice can be retrained to empower their patients, rather than create more dependency.

The method used was as follows:

- Identify problem(s).
- Agree with patient which to tackle first.
- List possible solutions.
- Agree the most realistic.
- Give information about where to get help.
- Agree action plan.
- Arrange follow-up.

Participating nurses were trained by their local facilitators not to 'prescribe' help, i.e. they were not to tell patients what they should do. Neither were they to make direct referrals to helping agencies. Their role was to provide information about the help which was available locally, and about the ways in which this help may be obtained, to encourage the patient to make contact and report back the results. It was important that they acknowledged to the patient an acceptance of the difficulties they were under, but in a positive way, not in a way which might reinforce the distress. Brown (1992) has suggested that one important component of support-giving is the avoidance, by the helper, of making any negative comments about the person seeking help. Follow-up helps to improve motivation and also provides the nurse with feedback on the effectiveness of the actions taken and agencies used.

To help the nurse in her task, a problem-oriented list of local helping agencies was compiled by the local facilitator. It is the experience of many facilitators that those members of the primary care team who work almost exclusively from within surgery premises, particularly GPs and practice nurses, have very little knowledge of the sources of support that exist within their local community. Health visitors and district nurses are often more familiar with these agencies, but are rarely asked by other members of the team. A concerted effort was therefore made to ensure that local information was accessible to doctors, practice nurses, the practice receptionists, and to patients directly.

Several different methods were used:

- A problem-orientated directory.
- An *aide memoire* card for the desk, listing contact details of frequently used agencies.
- A problem-solving booklet for patients which was available in the waiting room.

A subsequent project has also designed a wallchart which is displayed in all consulting rooms, at the reception desk and in the waiting area. It is essential that all of these resources are kept up-to-date, a role which a number of health promotion units are taking on.

Most help and support for people who are distressed by their problems, and at risk but not clinically depressed, will be available from local advice agencies, self-help and support groups, counselling organizations and other voluntary groups. National charities and help lines may also be useful. Very few of these people will need referral to mental health services. The system does not, therefore, impinge upon the care of people with serious mental illness, except insofar as it might help to make referrals to community psychiatric nurses, for example, more appropriate.

In practices which employ their own counsellor, a clear system of referral between this professional and other members of the team may be developed. A further source of support within the primary care team, especially for parents and young families, is the health visitor. The health visitor's role in preventing mental illness is frequently overlooked, but their skills in teaching good parenting and in providing emotional as well as practical help for young unsupported mothers are crucial.

CONCLUSION

In the first pilot the system described here proved highly acceptable to nurses and patients. In over 300 patient contacts, only three people declined to answer the questions in the assessment. Nurses commented that the assessment identified health risks which would not be found in any other way. Typical remarks were that it 'Improved holistic care'; 'Mental health has been neglected . . . in our new patient health checks'; 'Identified a deficiency in our care'.

Its main disadvantage is that it might add an average of 10 minutes to a health assessment, although this is highly variable and will depend, amongst other things, on the skill of the nurse, how well she knows the patient, her familiarity with the tool and the time allowed by the practice for each consultation. Most nurses did not find time a problem, but lengthy assessments are not popular with many GPs, particularly those who regard their practice nurses as simply income-generators. However, if quality health care is the aim, there is a limit to how far patient/ professional contact time can be reduced.

There does seem to be scope for developing this assessment method further. A second pilot evaluation is under way in Yorkshire, linking use of the tool to a 4-day training program for practice nurses, run at the local college of health. Feedback so far suggests that nurses are enthusiastic about its potential. Another project has devised a new screening tool which links the assessment to a psychiatric questionnaire. Funds are currently being sought for a validation study.

The main lessons from the first pilot were: that it is possible to assess risks to mental health in general practice attenders; that such an exercise is acceptable to patients; but that much more work is needed before it is clear whether or not the assessment is actually preventive. Further, attempts to help people reduce their risks must make use of the plethora of voluntary and community groups which exist in most areas—but that knowledge of these groups needs to be made more widely accessible to both patients and professionals.

REFERENCES

Armstrong E (1995) _Mental Health Issues in Primary Care_, p 92. London: Macmillan.

Atkin K, Lunt N, Parker G & Hurst M (1993) _Nurses Count. A National Survey of Practice Nurses._ University of York: Social Policy Research Unit.

Barbee AP (1990) Interactive coping: the cheering-up process in close relationships. In S Duck (ed) _Personal Relationships and Social Support._ London: Sage.

Brown G (1992) Life events and social support: possibilities for prevention. In R Jenkins, J Newton & R Young (eds) _The Prevention of Depression and Anxiety: The Role of the Primary Care Team._ London: HMSO.

Fullard E, Fowler G & Gray M (1987) Promoting prevention in primary care: controlled trial of low-technology, low-cost approach. _Br Med J_ **294**, 1080–82.

Health of the Nation (1992) _A Strategy for Health in England._ London: HMSO.

Jenkins R (1992a) Developments in the primary care of mental illness—a forward look. _Int Rev Psychiat_ **4**, 237–42.

Jenkins R (1992b) Depression and anxiety: an overview of preventive strategies. In R Jenkins, J Newton & R Young (eds) *The Prevention of Depression and Anxiety: The Role of the Primary Care Team.* London: HMSO.

Newton J (1988) *Preventing Mental Illness.* London: Routledge.

Newton J (1992) Crisis support: utilizing resources. In R Jenkins, J Newton & R Young (eds) *The Prevention of Depression and Anxiety: The Role of the Primary Care Team.* London: HMSO.

Parkes CM (1986) *Bereavement: Studies of Grief in Adult Life.* Harmondsworth: Penguin.

Wilkinson DG (1989) *Depression: Recognition and Treatment in General Practice.* Oxford: Radcliffe Medical Press.

19

Model Mental Health
Care Practice Project

George Walker
Oldfield Surgery, Bath, UK

THE PROJECT

This paper describes, from the doctors' viewpoint, what happened in the practice as a result of it being the subject of a Department of Health-funded project to develop a model for mental health care of patients within a group general practice.

THE PRACTICE

The practice comprises 10 500 patients in an urban setting whose medical care is provided by seven general medical practitioners (GPs) (four principals, two assistants, and one GP registrar). There is a full complement of practice nurses, health visitors and community (district) nurses. Two counsellors work 9 hours per week (plus supervision).

The practice is first-wave fundholding.

There is no special psychiatric expertise in the practice and the project practice nurse taken on for the project has only general RGN training. There is a parallel between her position and that of a practice asthma or diabetes nurse.

An aim of the project was to make the detection and management of psychiatric problems of our patients within the surgery or on visits to them at home as everyday as the management of patients with bronchitis, diabetes or hypertension.

WHERE TO START?

Because depression, mixed anxiety/depression and anxiety are so common in general practice, to suddenly decide to 'lift the lid' off every affected patient is likely to overwhelm the practitioner. The project showed that the first step in managing

Preventing Mental Illness: Mental Health Promotion in Primary Care. Edited by R. Jenkins and T.B. Üstün.
© 1998 John Wiley & Sons Ltd.

change in working practice for the GP is to introduce efficient methods for dealing with the patients found to need help, within the time and cost constraints, of everyday general practice.

Protocols for the referrals to voluntary agencies as well as to practice counsellors and members of the mental health care team, and protocols for effective pre-scribing of antidepressants, all need to be in place before increased detection is initiated. These patients are often found to be time-consuming to the practice, although eventually there can be a 'trade-off' between the time saved against the time spent on new clinical activities to address the psychiatric state of affected patients. Nevertheless, time is still at a premium and a structured psychiatric interview can be a prolonged affair, partly because the patients themselves need time to assimilate the issues raised.

Initially the practice saw the mental health practice nurse as the person who would solve this problem by accepting referrals of every affected person. The arithmetic of this exercise had not been fully appreciated and the large numbers involved quickly overwhelmed the nurse. Clearly, if the practice was going to make permanent headway in making a wholesale change in its approach to patients with mental health problems it would need to devise some other way of approaching the problem.

One of our ways was to invent a booklet (*Oldfield Stressed State Assessment—OSSA*) for the patient to work through at home. This enabled the practitioner, whether doctor or nurse, to:

1. Terminate the initial interview with the offer of 'home-work' for the patient to carry out.
2. Enable the patient, at leisure at home, to work through the booklet, accepting that he/she might have a mental health problem for which help is available.
3. Split the time involved and structure the follow-up consultation when the patient returned with the booklet for review by the doctor or nurse.
4. Provide a summary and follow-up flow chart similar in style to those used for hypertension, asthma and obstetric care.

ROLE OF THE PRACTICE NURSE

A nurse may be employed in seeing patients but, as described above, is unlikely to be able to cope with the total work-load of the practice population. The option of increasing the number of practice nurses to enable this to occur is expensive and still leaves the GP with time-consuming negotiation with the patient. The option of a practice nurse seeing some patients for follow-up may prove useful, but this was not an option that this project developed as a major way of dealing with patients detected by the doctors, although the practice nurse accepted patients for further assessment who had been detected by nurses.

In the project, the mental health practice nurse was seen as having an important role in providing:

1. A focus for mental health knowledge and innovations within the practice.
2. An information resource for doctors, nurses and patients.
3. A link between the practice and voluntary organizations.
4. A link with the secondary health care services.
5. A communicator and link within the practice in establishing agreement on protocols, etc.
6. A model for the practice nurses, including health visitors.

Members of the practice team looked to the mental health practice nurse for information and help in obtaining assistance for patients with mental health problems, including:

1. Leaflets on services and conditions.
2. Support by discussion of patients and general issues with doctors, nurses and reception staff.
3. Information and advice on referrals, whether to a voluntary agency or to the secondary mental health care team.
4. Organizer of outside lectures.
5. Link with voluntary agencies.

She also broke down the barriers between patients with mental health illness and the nursing and administrative teams, including receptionists.

Where the nurse had more difficulty was in teaching GPs in direct small group work. As time went by this improved, due in part to acquisition of teaching skills by attending courses, e.g. 'Relaxation for Living' and a half-day course on 'Presentation Skills' provided by 'Speech Speech'. It would have been of enormous advantage to the project if the need for teaching and management skills had been recognized and training for these provided at an early stage.

A practice nurse taking on this mental health role in the practice will also need training in the use of tools such as those developed in this project, as well as training in the specific medical aspects of detection, prognosis and treatment options for patients with non-psychotic mental illness.

HOW DID WE MANAGE CHANGE IN THE PRACTICE ATTITUDE?

Changing the Attitude

Although the intention was to change the attitude of doctors, patients, nurses and reception staff towards the mental health problems of their patients, this change of culture did not take place overnight. I have mentioned already how solutions need to be provided before more patients have their mental health problems uncovered, but persuading the nurses as well as doctors that the mental health of their patients would benefit from more detailed attention, such as that already evolved for patients suffering from hypertension or asthma, is likely to need specific action, such as measuring the size of the problem and the ability of individual doctors to detect it.

Evolving changes in the management of patients can also be addressed by education, but we found that using an interview in which clinicians are invited to say how they treat particular problems such as depression was a very effective training utility, which we named 'Practice Audit Method' (PAM).

'PAM' comprised a structured interview, in which the doctor (or nurse) is asked initially about his/her treatment of depression, the types of treatment used and the clinical features which would dictate the choice of treatment. The interviewer then asks about methods of assessing the severity of the condition and finally asks how the clinician detects/diagnoses depression.

'PAM' uses an unexpected order of enquiry, starting with treatment and ending with detection, but this builds on the experience of the project, which found that this was the most effective order in which to lead people through change in this area. Other tools used included the identification index and treatment index to audit doctors' ability to identify and willingness to treat patients with mental distress. Concurrent with audit and the 'PAM' is the provision of information about voluntary services, referral mechanisms and education on assessing severity and recommendations on medical prescribing.

In the project, clinical information was principally provided to the doctors by Dr Rachel Jenkins, Dr André Tylee, Dr Linda Gask and local psychiatrists.

Box 19.1 shows a 'PAM' designed to investigate a different field, that of alcohol over-use.

What Changes Are Still Taking Place?

The principal current changes are the relationship between the GPs and the psychiatrist, who is a member of the local mental health care team, and takes the form of regular meetings to discuss individual cases as well as general principles.

What About the Role of the Community Psychiatric Nurse?

Community psychiatric nurses (CPNs) were attached to the practice during this project as linkworkers, but had little impact on its development. This may well have been because the CPNs did not see practice patients on the premises and also

---

Box 19.1   Questions for Alcohol 'PAM'

Treatment/Management
Do you do any home detox?   Yes/No
If yes, what influences you to decide to do a home detox?

Would you use any drugs for this?   Yes/No
Which drug and what dosage and regime?

When would you make a decision to admit someone to hospital for detox?

Do you ever suggest to patients to try a reducing regime?   Yes/No
What do you say to them?

How often do you review their condition?

Do you get anyone else involved to help in the support?

Identification
When do you choose to question patients about their alcohol intake?

How do you go about doing this (what do you ask)?

Is there anything that 'alerts' you to wonder whether someone may be
    drinking too much, e.g. smell of their breath, or their past history?

---

were unlikely to have practice patients assigned to them. Also, CPNs are not usually trained to deal with patients suffering from non-psychotic mental illness, which is the commonest mental health problem found in general practice.

WHAT IMPACT DID THE PROJECT HAVE ON THE PRACTICE?

The major impact has been that the doctors and nurses feel that mental health care of their patients is a problem which is now 'under control'.

We have taken on board more mental health clinical activity with our patients. There has been no increase in the time spent by doctors on these patients and the impression is that the doctors spend less time. As one receptionist commented: 'The doctors don't seem to have those long interviews with their patients which used to disrupt surgeries'. The doctors in the practice are spending more time counselling their patients with psychiatric problems than they were before the project started.

An early intention of the project was to make managing patients with mental health problems as 'everyday' as managing patients with bronchitis, hypertension

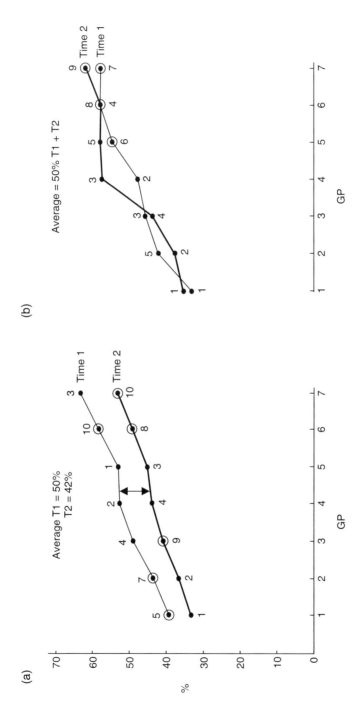

FIGURE 19.1 Percentage of patients' attending surgery with a 'positive' GHQ score. On average, the GPs at the 'model practice' (a) reduced this score from 50% to 42%, whereas the GPs at the Bath 'comparator' practice (b) kept its average at 50% over the 2-year period from Time 1 to Time 2

or arthritis. There has been more psychological activity, there has been more referral to the psychiatric team and there has been more use of antidepressants.

Patients with mental health problems attending their GP in the practice are not only more likely to have a psychiatric intervention as a part of their consultation, but also more likely to have 'surgery' investigations such as thyroid function or haemoglobin estimation. It could be interpreted that patients with mental health problems are being treated more intensively.

Interestingly, patients registered with the two principals with higher psychiatric intervention are less likely to find themselves listed by the hospital for admission for investigation or operative treatment. Our practice has no rise in admissions associated with high General Health Questionnaire (GHQ) scores, unlike comparable practices in Bath and London.

Will this increased mental health activity encourage patients with mental health problems to come more often to see the doctor (or indeed to join the practice)? An interesting result is that there has been a fall by 16% in the number of patients who are GHQ-positive attending the surgery (see Figure 19.1).

What Has Been the Impact on the Nurses?

A nurse said, 'I feel that if a patient tells me he/she is feeling low, it is easier for me to provide help. We (nurses and doctors) talk the same language now'. The nurses at the outset of the project tended, when describing a patient with a psychiatric problem, to focus on *factors* which were distressing the patient, rather than the *degree* of the distress. The concept that measuring the severity of the distress determines the amount of attention which needs to be given to it, is now generally accepted by nurses as well as doctors. Nurses therefore feel better able to obtain help for their patients because they are better able to describe their patients' psychiatric condition to other agencies or to a doctor.

At the start of the project, detection and management of depression and mixed anxiety/depression tended to be based on:

1. A patient's direct statement that he/she felt depressed (the psychologizer).
2. Frequent attention with various physical complaints (the hypochondriac or somatizer).

The main diagnostic question related to sleep. The practice which we developed during the project of asking patients, 'How do you feel in yourself?' and further questions to those who answered 'tired', 'low', 'depressed', 'worried' or similar for more than 2–4 weeks, enabled the assessment of the mental state to be undertaken at a much earlier stage. The ideal would be to ask everyone this question: 'How do you feel in yourself?'—which we nicknamed the 'one-line GHQ'.

What Impact Has the Project Had on the Doctors?

As well as feeling that the problem is under control and there is no extra work involved, it is felt that, 'Working with patients is less stressful. It is better structured; the problem patients no longer seem to be the overwhelming workload and stress creator that they once seemed to be'.

What Impact Has there Been on the Counsellors?

Two counsellors were providing 9 hours per week of counselling at the outset of the project and one of these had been a counsellor in the practice for 15 years. The doctors valued the option to refer to the counsellors, but even before the project were pressing the counsellors to provide very brief assessments. The counsellors had developed, in the meantime:

1. An interest in a psychoanalytical approach to counselling.
2. Increasing opposition to medical management of depression, wanting the patients to retain their depressed state during 'their counselling' so that this could be manipulated by the counsellor.
3. Insistence on continuing with complete confidentiality of the interview between the counsellor and the patients.

The doctors:

1. Valued the facility of referring patients to the counsellors.
2. Wanted the emphasis to move towards very brief assessments.
3. Found the counsellors' opposition towards medical assessment and physical treatment of depression impeded the development of the Mental Health Care Model in the practice team.
4. Found that the extreme confidentiality of the content of the patient/counsellor interview meant that on subsequent occasions the doctors (and nurses) had 'no handle' to open the door with the patient to discuss the psychosocial issues previously uncovered by the counsellor.

So, What Happened?

The counsellors left to work privately in psychoanalytical 'counselling'. During the interval between their departure and the appointment of new counsellors (some 3 months), the practice made increasing use of the 'OSSA', already described, reducing this usage once new counsellors were in place. This suggests that 'OSSAs' may be in some way an alternative to some of the counsellors' work.

A new job description was written for the counsellors and candidates for the new post were asked if they were content to work within the constraints of:

1. Counselling sessions limited to two 1-hour sessions per patient.
2. Concurrent prescription of antidepressants where indicated.
3. Stating to the patient that information, whilst confidential, would be recorded and available to doctors and nurses in the practice (similar to their confidential records about other conditions).

Twenty candidates were interviewed and only five were happy to work within these constraints. Two counsellors were appointed, working the same number of hours as the previous counsellors. Counselling remains an important referral, particularly for patients with relationship and grief problems.

What Impact Did the Project Have on the Practice's Relationship with the Secondary Mental Health Care Team?

The attachment of CPNs or psychiatric social workers were experimented with but provided little impact on everyday practice. The doctors became keen to have an effective liaison with a psychiatrist, and changes were made in the mental health care team which enabled a closer relationship to develop between the practice, the psychiatrist and his team towards the end of the project. This closer relationship continues to develop, with regular meetings at the practice to review patients and their problems.

The psychiatrist is seen as adviser to the practice on the likely benefits to the patients of the medley of psychological, psychosocial or psychiatric interventions offered by the mental health team to which he/she belongs.

What About the Voluntary Services?

Confidence in referral to voluntary services has been enhanced by meetings which the mental health practice nurse arranged. Of particular benefit were:

1. Alcoholics Anonymous (AA).
2. Triumph Over Phobia (TOP).
3. MIND.
4. Employment agency for sufferers from psychiatric conditions (Sulis Trust).
5. CRUSE.

> **BOX 19.2**   The case of Ann
>
> 'Ann', a secretary from a building company, developed polyarthralgia of uncertain origin. Treatment with analgesics gave only temporary benefit and she remained angry and depressed, appearing to blame doctors for their failure to improve her condition. A referral to a rheumatologist led to new treatment initiatives, with only temporary improvements. One year later, disillusioned by the help from specialists, she accepted treatment with antidepressants and over the next 10 weeks, her pains and mobility steadily improved. One year later, off antidepressants, she attended in good health, 'Just to let you know how well I am, but why didn't the rheumatologist know about the help that an antidepressant could give?'

What Was the Impact on the Patients?

Patients often took a long time to accept that their disability had a significant psychiatric aspect. Patients tended to think that their condition must be all physical or all psychological. Patients also felt that the offer of psychiatric help implied blame or some criticism. I'm sure you find that patients with somatic complaints and depression are often reluctant to accept psychiatric investigation and treatment as part of the help that the GP can give. The GP has limited time and the patient limited patience!

As the whole clinical team developed a coherent approach towards mental health issues, other team members were able to support the doctor in facilitating a change in attitude in patients that they shared and enabled the patients to accept help. Where psychiatric treatment was helpful, a frequent comment followed: 'Why did I not have this help before?' It is a common experience that patients with alcoholism may take years before taking up the offer of help. Similarly, patients with depression as part of their physical illness can also need time and repeated approaches before they will accept help.

Sympathetic perseverance by the clinicians can pay off, as in the case of 'Ann' (see Box 19.2).

What Changes Did We Evolve in Working Method?

Doctors found that asking patients, 'How do you feel (in your spirits)?' proved an acceptable screening mechanism. Assessment of severity was by use of the DSM-III-R questions or modified Hamilton questionnaires for both depression and anxiety. All of these proved acceptable to the patients. The modified Hamilton questionnaires were included in the stressed state assessment (OSSA) booklet.

How About Negotiating with the Patient?

Negotiating with the patient proved to be the area which required the most effort. Linda Gask helped with a lecture, 'Changing the Agenda'. There was no one single approach to persuading the depressed patient that the symptoms he/she was presenting would benefit from attention to his/her mental state. This is where the paper-based questionnaire (OSSA) was of particular assistance. By structuring the approach to the patient so as to allow him/her to work through the assessment at home, the patient's understanding was facilitated. *The structure of the questionnaire brought authority to the assessment over and above that of the GP's verbal assessment.*

The doctors found that it was stressful, yet satisfying, to negotiate with patients that they may be depressed. The OSSA removed much of that stress. It was found that:

1. At the initial consultation, patients readily accepted the offer of the 'second opinion' in the form of the OSSA to be completed by themselves at leisure at home.
2. The patients at home organized their ideas about their illnesses and allowed this to happen without consuming vital consultation time.
3. The return visit could perhaps be planned to be a double appointment and the patient and the doctor knew that the main purpose of this visit was to review the mental state by going through the OSSA.
4. The summary included in the OSSA was completed with the patient present, and sometimes a photocopy was given to the patient. This openness:
   (a) Involved the patient.
   (b) Allowed the patient some insight into what was going on in his/her illness.
   (c) Allowed a 'care plan' to be agreed between the doctor and the patient as to where they would go from there, so that consultations could be structured with a flow chart recording progress and treatments.
5. The OSSA was the basis for problem-solving.

What About Referrals?

Referrals were made both within the practice and outside. Within the practice, the main referral continues to be the counsellors. The counsellors are used differently by different doctors, but the main referrals continue to be for relationship problems and grief.

Outside the practice, referrals are mainly to the voluntary sector, including CRUSE, Relate, and Triumph Over Phobia.

Referrals to the mental health care team are principally directed to the consultant psychiatrist, either at regular 6-weekly discussions or by formal written referral to the team.

The practice made very few direct referrals to psychologists and their work continues to be less easily understood than that of other members of the psychiatric team.

WHAT ABOUT OTHER AREAS OF MENTAL HEALTH?

Attention to depression and mixed anxiety/depression in patients aged 18–65 was the first activity of the project. The condition is common and accompanies the other mental health conditions studied in the project. The other conditions are:

- In the elderly:
  (a) Depression.
  (b) Cognitive failure.
- Alcohol over-use.
- Long-term mentally ill.

In the Elderly

Assessment of depression in the elderly proved more difficult than in the adult population. In initial detection in the over-75s, the question 'How do you feel about the future?' replaced the 'How do you feel (in your spirits)?' question used in the adult population. Assessment of severity of depression in the elderly is complicated by more complex social circumstances and physical illnesses than in the younger adult population.

Alcohol Over-use

Alcohol over-use is a more complex area than it was first thought to be. The Health of the Nation health promotion targets have made assessment of alcohol consumption a routine matter for general practitioners.

Long-term Mentally Ill

An aim of the project was to ensure that the practice had a register of patients with long-term mental illness, in particular those with a history of psychosis, and to ensure, by working with the members of the mental health care team, that each patient has a care plan. What became apparent during the study is that care plans are seldom understood by the patient and rarely read by them.

Considerable inroads were made in conjunction with the mental health care team in ensuring that patients had a care plan produced for them, but the usefulness of this to the general practitioner and patient was limited by the format. Further work is continuing in this area.

20

The Exeter Depression Audit Package for the Primary Care of Depression

Keith Lloyd, Judy Allen, Philip Evans, David Kessler, Denis Pereira Gray, Bob Blizard* and Anna Bosanquet**

University of Exeter, *Royal Free Hospital School of Medicine, London, and **Roehampton Institute, London, UK

Epidemiological research over the past 30 years has clearly demonstrated the very high levels of psychiatric morbidity that exist in primary care populations. The most prevalent disorders are depression and anxiety. Indeed, depression is the most common chronic condition in one general practice (Pereira Gray 1995). Only around half of the psychiatric morbidity is recognized by GPs, according to studies in this country and abroad (Goldberg & Huxley 1992; Üstün & Sartorius 1995). Not all the recognized mental illness is adequately managed, but all of it impacts upon the primary care workload. Opinions differ as to the best strategy for optimizing the primary care management of common mental disorders such as depression.

The Exeter Depression Audit Package (EDAP) is one of a series of projects funded by the NHS Executive to evaluate different methods of improving the primary care of mental illness (Lloyd & Jenkins 1995). EDAP is a tool to audit the detection, assessment and management of depression at practice level. The intervention is a practice-based educational session, after which the practice sets its own targets for the second loop of the audit cycle. Additionally the EDAP has been subjected to a research-based evaluation. The model on which the EDAP is based is the Oxford Prevention of Heart Attack and Stroke Project (Fullard, Fowler & Gray 1987). The innovative team behind that project clearly demonstrated that it is possible to devise simple, effective, low-cost audit packages that are acceptable to the primary health care team.

The present team comprises GPs, psychiatrists, a nurse, a medical statistician and a health economist. The team was keen to develop a package that was

Preventing Mental Illness: Mental Health Promotion in Primary Care. Edited by R. Jenkins and T.B. Üstün.
© 1998 John Wiley & Sons Ltd.

acceptable to and owned by the primary health care team (PHCT) and which did not appear as something imposed from secondary care. The project is set in two general practices in the south-west of England, one in Bristol and one in Exeter. Both are demographically similar urban practices with list sizes of about 7500. The Bristol team consists of five GPs, two practice nurses (one of whom is a specialist in health promotion), and an attached community psychiatric nurse. The Exeter practice has four partners, all of whom hold academic appointments in the Institute of General Practice at Exeter University. It is a training practice involved in a wide range of health-promotion activities.

METHODS

The First Loop of the Audit Cycle

Aim one was to develop an audit tool for improving detection and recognition of depression. This part of the EDAP is based on the established method of screening consecutive attenders with a suitable screening instrument (the general practitioner) and comparing GP detection rates with those of an external standard. In this case the comparators were the 12-item General Health Questionnaire (Goldberg & Williams 1988) and the Hospital Anxiety & Depression Scale (Snaith & Zigmond 1988).

Several measures of performance in the recognition of depression were investigated. The identification index is a measure of the clinician's ability to identify appropriately symptomatic patients as cases and ignores his/her ability to identify asymptomatic cases as normals. In other words, it is the number of true positives to the number of expected positives as calculated from the sensitivity of the diagnostician. Some measure of the accuracy of diagnosis is given by the specificity of the GP as screening instrument.

A sample was taken of 50 eligible patients for each GP, who recorded whether a psychiatric disorder was present or not and whether it was depression, anxiety or both. There is nothing new about this. The idea here was to package the methodology so as to make it acceptable to any interested PHCT. Judy Allen, the practice nurse who went into the surgeries, was a major factor in achieving the PHCT's acceptance of the exercise.

Aim two was to see how the general practitioners were performing psychiatric assessments. Data were derived from a random case-note audit, involving 300 notes in each practice. The main audit measure was the proportion of patients with one or more risk factors for depression who had received an adequate mental state assessment. Notes were examined for evidence of a mental state examination, using an instrument developed specifically for this project, to permit an operational measure of the quality of mental state examination performed and recorded by the GP. There is a debate about the issue of care provided as opposed to care recorded. More is done for patients than is ever recorded and one of the real problems for general practice is that it is simply not possible to record even a fraction of the advice and care given. All surveys based on records therefore underestimate work done. However, it was felt that there was no other simple alternative for the purpose of the audit. The real debate is whether the audit changes practice or merely records habits.

The third aim was to look at management of depression among those patients in whom the GP has made a diagnosis of depression. In order to make the audit as unintrusive as possible to the practices, this section also was based on a case-note and computer audit. Details were recorded of all physical, psychological and social interventions. Data were also taken from PACT^{TM} prescribing data. This completed the first run of the audit cycle, the baseline measures.

The Intervention

It is important that the intervention should be generalizable and consideration was given to developing a video and manual. Eventually it was decided that the practices should select their own facilitator or 'expert' to lead a meeting with the partners. In both practices the facilitator was a member of the project team. The intervention took the form of an educational meeting with Postgraduate Education Association approval. It involved feedback of the baseline results, educational materials about depression in primary care and a commitment on the part of the partners to develop practice protocols and targets for assessment detection and management. The most important factor was that the practices set their own targets for what they felt was achievable. Six months later the measures were repeated to complete the audit cycle.

Evaluation

In audit terms the study would be complete. However, the team also wished to evaluate the health gain and resource implications of implementing this package. The research component of the study has several elements. First, a simple computer record-based risk assessment for high primary care consultation and high psychological distress was developed. This is intended to be a viable alternative to self-rating or interview-based assessments. It can be derived from existing practice data with minimal disruption to surgery life and gets around the resistance that many people have to questionnaires.

Second, a variety of quality of life measures to assess change over time and attitudes to depression are being employed. Patients' self-reported use of psychiatric services during follow-up and all primary care contacts are recorded. These will permit us to provide costings for the implementation of the package. Patient outcome in terms of symptom resolution is also being studied.

TABLE 20.1 Recognition of moderate to severe depression (Hospital Anxiety and Depression Scale > 11) before and after the intervention expressed as mean sensitivity

Practice	Time 1		Practice target set (%)	Time 2	
	n	Sensitivity (%)		n	Sensitivity (%)
		(%)			(%)
Exeter	200	62.5	70	197	79.5
Bristol	250	52.7	60	249	65.3

RESULTS

Improvements have been demonstrated in detection, assessment and management of depression. In terms of detecting depression, both practices showed an improvement against the Hospital Anxiety and Depression Scale with a cut-off of 11 (indicative of moderate to severe depression). This threshold was chosen by the practices because it had face validity for the GPs as being a level of depressive symptomatology to which they were able to relate as a meaningful caseness threshold[1] (Table 20.1). In line with the literature, the doctors were recognizing 50–60% of the moderate to severe depression at baseline. As shown in Table 20.1, they were able to agree targets for improvement and both practices exceeded their self-imposed targets after the intervention. Both showed an improvement in sensitivity. This was not, however, because they started diagnosing as depressed everyone who came through the door; there was little change in specificity in either practice, which is ideal in terms of the efficient diagnosis of depression. Both practices had a specificity of over 75% at time 1 and time 2.

The second area of the audit was assessment. The assumption underlying this section of the study was that logically, when a GP uncovers risk factors for depression, he/she should enquire further to see if there is a mental health problem present. Of those with risk factors, only 26% had a recorded mental state assessment in Exeter and only 14.5% in Bristol at time 1. The proportion of depressed subjects receiving an adequate mental state assessment increased from 54% at time 1 to 95% at time 2. Suicidal risk assessment showed a similar improvement among depressed patients from 20% to 78%. Recording of alcohol consumption has increased from 36% to 59%.

Initial analyses show improvements in management. Prescribing of antidepressants has increased from 78% to 86% among patients with detected major depression and the mean dose of tricyclic antidepressants has increased from 65 mg to 85 mg. Offering a non-drug intervention has increased from 28% to 35%. At the time of writing the economic analyses are still under way.

---

[1] Meaningful caseness threshold: the score on a validated questionnaire above which an individual is considered to have the disease of interest or be very likely to have it.

DISCUSSION

This limited pilot study suggests that it is possible to achieve ownership by two PHCTs of effectiveness data and research and in the process improve their detection and recognition of depression. Neither practice felt that their workload was increased unacceptably by this exercise. All the GPs felt more empowered to manage depression effectively.

It is important to intervene where depression is present for a number of reasons. Although most disorders encountered by general practitioners are non-psychotic in nature—mostly depression and anxiety—these disorders are still responsible for considerable personal distress and suffering and impaired social functioning, and around half are chronic and recurrent, lasting for longer than 12 months (Mann, Jenkins & Belsey 1981). The pejorative term 'worried well' is entirely inappropriate to describe this group of patients who are certainly not well, and are responsible for a massive public health burden. Disability is proportional to mental health status (from cross-sectional data) and co-varies with it over time (Üstün & Sartorius 1995).

People with undiagnosed and untreated/poorly treated depression and anxiety tend to have increased rates of repeat consultations in primary care, often over many years, making a major contribution to those called 'fat-folder' and 'heart-sink' patients. A recent prospective study (Lloyd, Jenkins & Mann 1996) for 11 years of 100 people with depression and anxiety in general practice showed that 58% were cases 11 years later, the 11-year standardized mortality ratio was 173, 48% had a relapsing or chronic psychiatric course and 72% had a relapsing or chronic physical course. The mean number of consultations was 10.8 per year over the 11 years. These data support the view that neurotic illnesses in general practice is associated with high morbidity, raised mortality from all causes and high service use, emphasising both that those patients are not the 'worried well' and that there is a need for early intervention and effective treatment.

Although most of the morbidity in general practice never reaches the attention of secondary care services, around 5% of morbidity seen in general practice is referred to secondary care, and many people seen in psychiatric outpatient clinics have non-psychotic disorders. This referral process of depression and anxiety to secondary psychiatric care results in the distraction of specialist staff and skills from the most severely mentally ill, particularly those with psychotic disorders. This is not to say that staff in secondary care should see only people with psychosis. Rather, they should see only those who derive most benefit from specialist treatment (mainly because their illness is more severe), whatever the diagnosis, if we are to make most appropriate use of limited resources.

Initiatives such as the Defeat Depression Campaign have contributed to an increasing awareness of the extent of depressive illnesses among primary care populations (Paykel & Priest 1992). Strategies for improving the detection of depression will only be acceptable to primary care, and implementable, if they are linked to simple strategies for treatments of proven effectiveness. The present study demonstrates that primary care teams can set their own targets for improving detection, assessment and management of depression.

REFERENCES

Fullard EM, Fowler GH & Gray JAM (1987) Promoting prevention in primary care: a controlled trial of low-technology, low-cost approach. *Br Med J* **194**, 1080–82.

Goldberg D & Huxley P (1992) *Common Mental Disorders. A Biosocial Model.* London: Routledge.

Goldberg D & Williams P (1988) *A User's Guide to the General Health Questionnaire.* Windsor: NFER Nelson.

Lloyd K & Jenkins R (1995) The economics of depression in primary care. Department of Health initiatives. *Br J Psychiat* **166**(s27), 60–62.

Lloyd K, Jenkins R & Mann AH (1996) Long-term outcome of patients with neurotic illness in general practice. *Br Med J* **313**, 26–8.

Mann A, Jenkins R & Belsey E (1981) The twelve-month outcome of patients with neurotic illness in general practice. *Psychol Med* **11**, 535–50.

Paykel ES & Priest RG (1992) Recognition and management of depression in general practice: consensus statement. *Br Med J* **305**, 1198–202.

Pereira Gray D et al (1995) Primary Care and the Public Health: Harben Lecture. *Health Hygiene* **16**, 49–62.

Snaith P & Zigmond AS (1988) Anxiety and depression in general medical settings. *Br Med J* **297**, 1544–6.

Üstün TB & Sartorius N (1995) *Mental Illness in General Health Care: An International Study*, pp 361–76. London: World Health Organization/Wiley.

E

Education of Primary Care Team

21

Education of General Practitioners in the UK

Huw Lloyd
Royal College of General Practitioners, UK

In this chapter the current arrangements for undergraduate training, postgraduate vocational and higher professional education, and the continuing medical education for general practice are reviewed, and some suggestions are put forward about possible alterations and improvements for the future to enhance the abilities of general practitioners (GPs) in the UK in dealing with mental health promotion and disease prevention.

UNDERGRADUATE EDUCATION

At the undergraduate stage, the future GP receives the same training as any other medical student embarking on higher medical training. The style and content of the undergraduate curriculum varies from one medical school to another, but the pressure on medical students to cover a large curriculum during the course of their training means that they have only a fairly limited amount of time to learn about mental health issues and, in particular, mental health issues that relate to the primary health care setting.

At the end of the undergraduate years, when the final medical degree examinations have been sat and passed, all newly qualified doctors enter a year of preregistration house jobs which, whilst providing valuable experience and general training in medicine and surgery in a hospital setting, rarely give the newly qualified doctor any further understanding of the nature of the problems associated with mental health in the community. Following this preregistration year, once the doctor has become fully registered with the General Medical Council, the doctor has to begin to make career decisions and, in particular, if he/she wishes to enter general practice, then vocational training lasting at least 3 years will have to be undertaken.

Preventing Mental Illness: Mental Health Promotion in Primary Care. Edited by R. Jenkins and T.B. Üstün.
© 1998 John Wiley & Sons Ltd.

VOCATIONAL TRAINING

The Royal College of General Practitioners can be justifiably proud of its involvement in the evolution of vocational training for general practice within the UK. The proposal for vocational training was first put forward by the College in 1965 and documented in evidence to the Royal Commission on Medical Education the following year (CGP 1966). Although neither the recommendations of the Royal College of General Practitioners nor those of the Royal Commission on Medical Education (1968) were eventually implemented in full, the basic concept of vocational training was taken up and the statutory arrangements were put in place which involved a minimum period of postregistration experience, of which 2 years would be spent doing a minimum of four hospital jobs and 12 months would be spent as a trainee in general practice.

No particular stipulation is made about which posts in hospital are undertaken, although the posts must have been recognized as appropriate for vocational training. Some doctors will enter specific programs that have been developed for vocational training, where the hospital posts and general practice year are linked within a 3-year cycle but doctors are allowed to select their hospital posts and general practice if they wish.

The content of the vocational training years and the teaching required were initially developed and laid out by the College in 1972 (RCGP 1972). Whilst psychiatry in particular, and mental health issues in general, are not compulsory elements within the vocational training period, the intention has always been that vocationally trained GPs should have a good understanding of mental illness and health promotion. The membership examination for entry into the Royal College of General Practitioners, which is sat by the vast majority of those completing their vocational training period, includes within its syllabus all aspects of mental illness and mental health promotion relevant to general practice.

A Joint Working Party of the RCGP and the Royal College of Psychiatrists produced a report on training of GPs in psychiatry, which was published in 1978 (RCGP/RCPsych 1974). Later it was recognized that a further revision of the content of vocational training in general practice in relation to mental health issues was needed. In view of the fact that looking after people with mental health problems takes up a great deal of a GP's time (Shepherd 1991), and taking into consideration that in any one year only about 5% of people with mental illness obtain specialist care (Shepherd et al 1981), the need for well structured and complete training on mental health issues was apparent. Once again, the Royal College of General Practitioners joined forces with the Royal College of Psychiatrists to make suggestions about the psychiatric component of general practice vocational training. The resulting booklet (RCGP/RCPsych 1993) was one of a series produced by the Royal College of General Practitioners in association with the other specialist organizations, and it describes the appropriate content of training and makes suggestions about the setting in which this training should take place.

During the vocational training period it is intended that the doctor should acquire a wide range of skills and understanding related to mental health issues in a variety of settings:

- Hospital psychiatric posts.
- Other hospital posts.
- General practice.
- Half-day release schemes.

Hospital Psychiatric Posts

According to information from the Joint Committee on Postgraduate Training for General Practice, just over 40% of doctors completing their vocational training period will have spent some time in an approved psychiatric post and this figure is steadily rising. These posts may be in general psychiatry or old-age psychiatry, and sometimes there may be sessions in child and adolescent psychiatry or learning-disability psychiatry. Whilst these posts are usually in a hospital setting, the need for a community bias is appreciated as this is more appropriate for future GPs.

Other Hospital Posts

It is recognized that there are opportunities within our disciplines for learning about mental health problems. For example, there is an opportunity during an obstetrics post to learn about the bonding between a mother and baby, whilst paediatrics is an ideal setting for learning about school refusal, temper tantrums and the impact on children of parental mental illness. In all hospital posts there should be the opportunity to understand the doctor–patient relationship and its therapeutic value, to acquire skills in consultation and particularly in listening, and to recognize clues and to provide explanations. These generic attributes of a good doctor are vital in the field of mental health.

General Practice

Many of the objectives for the psychiatric component of general practice vocational training need a substantial contribution from training in the setting of primary care if they are to be achieved. For example, general practice is an appropriate setting in which to come to understand the psychological causes and consequences of physical illnesses, as well as individual development, in terms of a patient's inter-personal relationships and his/her membership of social and family groups. It is also the appropriate setting in which to be able to recognize deviations from the expected norms of development, such as mental handicap, dyslexia, behaviour disorders and personality disorders. The psychological aspects of physical illnesses and of medical and surgical treatments are also best covered in the general practice setting and these include influenzal depression, the effects on the young child of admitting the mother to hospital, and the psychological effect on patients of surgical operations in general.

The general practice component of vocational training is spent within selected practices where one or more of the principals will have undergone training and assessment to be recognized as suitable to act as a trainer. Part of the assessment of the trainer would involve establishing that the trainer was aware of the appropriate curriculum, which would include all the aspects to do with mental illness and health promotion and how the trainer would propose to cover this curriculum during the 12-month period.

Half-day Release Schemes

Throughout their 3-year vocational training period doctors are encouraged to attend the weekly half-day release scheme organized in the local postgraduate centre by the general practice vocational training course organizer. The content of these half-day sessions is expected to enhance and complement learning in other settings. The material covered is largely decided by the course organizer and will contain topics from all areas of general practice, but invariably will have some elements of mental health topics within the half-day release scheme.

Assessment of Posts

As has already been mentioned, trainers and their practices are assessed by the Regional Advisers in General Practice to ensure that they reach the required standards laid down by the Joint Committee on Postgraduate Training in General Practice. The hospital posts are also assessed and this is usually done during a joint hospital visit conducted by representatives from the Royal College of General Practitioners and the Royal College of Psychiatrists. The assessment looks at the educational value of the post, as it is recognized that these posts are largely educational and that, whereas service commitment is an important element, it should not predominate to exclude the educational activity. During the visit to the hospital the Visitors will interview the senior medical staff and also those in training posts. They will wish to ensure that appropriate educational objectives are achieved, such as:

- Protected time for teaching.
- Study leave readily available.
- Possibility of attendance at the half-day release scheme.

- Clear educational objectives.
- Regular assessments with appropriate feedback to the doctor in training.
- Appropriate supervision and support for clinical activities.

This list, of course, is not complete and fuller guidelines have been produced to help Visitors assess the posts thoroughly.

The Visitors will also wish to ensure that other administrative factors have been covered, such as ensuring that a contract of employment has been signed and that domestic arrangements are appropriate, including residential quarters of a suitable standard and adequate canteen facilities. There will usually be an inspection of the library to ensure that relevant textbooks and journals are available, with suitable help for literature searches, etc.

HIGHER PROFESSIONAL EDUCATION

Higher professional education, lasting 2 or 3 years immediately after the vocational training period, has so far been undertaken by a relatively small number of GPs. The vast majority have, as yet, not taken up the opportunity to extend the broad base of experience that vocational training provides but rather follow the path of continuing medical education throughout their years as a principal in general practice. However, those who have undertaken higher professional education have done so in a variety of areas of clinical practice. Some have gained experience in teaching and training and others will have learned more of the techniques of research in general practice. Some of the programmes that are now on offer lead to diplomas and degrees.

CONTINUING MEDICAL EDUCATION

The continuing medical education of UK GPs has, for many years, been centred around the postgraduate centres of district general hospitals. Currently, participation in continuing medical education is rewarded through the payment of a postgraduate education allowance, which was first introduced as part of the contract of 1990 (Health Departments of Great Britain 1989). This allowance is paid to GPs who complete 5 days of approved continuing medical education material, which may be undertaken in a variety of settings although the postgraduate centre continues to be a common site for much of this activity. However, gradually a wider range of ways of learning is being established and various initiatives are developing the ways in which GPs learn about mental health issues, notably the RCGP Mental Health Fellowships and the Defeat Depression Campaign. The pharmaceutical industry provides a lot of educational material, much of which is non-promotional. Other sources of educational material for the GP come from postgraduate departments, journals and distance learning packages.

There is no particular compulsion for GPs to follow any area of learning and therefore it is possible at present for them to decide on their own educational priorities, which may or may not include those to do with mental illness and mental health promotion. So, although the postgraduate education allowance has encouraged active participation in continuing medical education, some have raised doubts about quality and content (Agnew 1992). There is currently a plethora of educational material from a very wide source of providers and it is perhaps not surprising that GPs do not always make the wisest choice.

Most learning in the continuing medical education context is uniprofessional. It can take the form of lectures, small group work, one-to-one teaching or self-directed learning with textbooks, journals, distance learning packages, etc. However, there are increasing numbers of examples where multidisciplinary learning is taking place in the field of mental health.

POSSIBILITIES FOR THE FUTURE

General Approach

There are examples of good educational practice within the UK at all stages of the education of GPs. One of the challenges for the future will be to promulgate these examples, to ensure that there is a uniformly high standard throughout the country. Certain possibilities are applicable to all stages of a GP's education, such as:

- Multidisciplinary learning.
- The wider use of guidelines.
- The use of audit as an educational tool.
- Information technology.
- The involvement of patients and their carers.

Multidisciplinary Learning

The field of mental health promotion and disease prevention lends itself particularly well to the process of multidisciplinary learning. General practice frequently involves working with other professionals and therefore learning with others enhances the ability to understand the viewpoint and concerns of other professionals.

The Wider Use of Guidelines

Evidence-based guidelines are being used more frequently. They offer an opportunity for national authorities such as the royal colleges or university departments to produce material that can be widely disseminated and then adapted and adopted at local level. Textbooks still have a part to play in the educational process but as research leads at a rapid pace to a better understanding of clinical practice, it is more difficult for textbooks to remain up-to-date. The local implementation of guidelines, which should also be multidisciplinary, increases the sense of ownership by the whole team, whether this be the primary health care team, or the community mental health team or, ideally, when the two teams work in conjunction to implement guidelines. Guidelines can then be seen as an effective means of improving care, at the same time as establishing understanding and cooperation between those involved in their implementation.

The Use of Audit as an Educational Tool

Medical audit, and now more recently clinical audit, has become an integral part of everyday practice. One of the prime aims of audit is to ensure the quality of services provided but, at the same time it is a useful educational tool. Throughout the education of GPs audit should be encouraged as part of gaining a better understanding of current clinical practice. In particular, clinical audit involving other disciplines and professions outside medicine can be a vital component of multidisciplinary teamwork.

Information Technology

Current capabilities and future possibilities in the world of information technology lead to all sorts of opportunities in the field of GP education, ranging from computer-aided distance learning packages for the individual at home to teleconferencing, bringing together groups of interested people from all corners of the earth. It is a challenge for all of us to make appropriate use of this important new technology.

The Involvement of Patients and Their Carers

Patients have traditionally been involved in the education of doctors but usually this is predominantly at the undergraduate level and in the earlier years of a doctor's training. It is less common for patients to be involved in continuing medical education. Their carers are infrequently involved at any level of education. However, there is an increasing realization that there is much to be learned, not only from patients but also from their carers at all stages in a GP's education. Particularly in the field of mental health, a far better understanding of the problems facing patients and their carers can be obtained by involving them directly in educational programs.

CHANGES SPECIFIC TO CAREER STAGES

Undergraduate Education

The General Medical Council recommendations for a more modular approach for the undergraduate curriculum (GMC 1993) has not yet been fully implemented. This will have a substantial impact on the education of UK GPs when it is fully implemented.

The Royal College of General Practitioners produced a policy statement (RCGP 1994) on education and training for general practice. This important document makes a large number of recommendations to improve on the current situation in relation to vocational training, higher professional education and continuing medical education. Amongst the many significant recommendations contained within this statement are the following:

Vocational training
- Increased learning time in the setting of general practice.
- Additional time in general practice to develop skills in working as members in multiprofessional primary care teams.
- The length of the training period to be determined by educational needs.

Higher professional education
- Development of new ideas for high professional education.
- Development of research training fellowships.

Continuing medical education
- Relevant to the needs of doctors and the services that they provide.
- To take account of clinical developments, changes in health service organization and changes in patients' expectations.
- To build upon the opportunities in everyday practice.
- To encourage the development and the evaluation of multiprofessional approaches to continuing medical education.

CONCLUSION

The education of UK GPs has progressed over the last few decades and now arguably represents one of the best systems in the world. However, there are still changes that need to be brought about and evaluated: no educational system can remain static, neither can it be of value without proper assessment.

REFERENCES

Agnew T (1992) Is cheap and cheerful PGEA junk? *General Practitioner* **31 January**, 36.

CGP (College of General Practitioners) (1966) *Evidence of the College to the Royal Commission on Medical Education. Report from General Practice 5*. London: CGP.

GMC (General Medical Council) (1993) *Tomorrow's Doctors. Recommendations on Undergraduate Medical Education*, p 160. London: GMC.

Health Departments of Great Britain (1989) *General Practice in the National Health Services. The 1990 Contract*. London: HMSO.

Royal Commission on Medical Education (1968) *Report* (Todd Report). London: HMSO.

RCGP (Royal College of General Practitioners) (1972) *The Future General Practitioner: Learning and Teaching. Br Med J*; republished 1990, RCGP, London.

RCGP (Royal College of General Practitioners) (1994) *Education and Training for General Practice. Policy Statement 3*. London: RCGP.

RCGP/RCPsych (Royal College of General Practitioners and Royal College of Psychiatrists) (1974) Training general practitioners in psychiatry. In *Some Aims for Training for General Practice*. Occasional Paper 6. London: RCGP.

RCGP/RCPsych (Royal College of General Practitioners and Royal College of Psychiatrists) (1993) *General Practitioner Vocational Training in Psychiatry*. London: RCGP.

Shepherd M, Cooper M, Brown AC et al (1981) *Psychiatric Illness in General Practice*, 2nd edn. London: Oxford University Press.

Shepherd M (1991) Primary care psychiatry: the case for action. *Br J Gen Pract* **41**, 252–5.

22

Education of Primary Care Team: RCGP Senior Mental Health Education Fellowship and the Defeat Depression Campaign

André Tylee

Institute of Psychiatry, London, UK

Epidemiological research over the last 30 years has demonstrated that around one in three general practice attenders have a psychiatric disorder (Goldberg & Huxley 1980). General practitioners (GPs) themselves report mental disorder to be the second most common reason for consultation after respiratory diseases. However, on average only around half of the psychiatric morbidity present in attenders to general practice is recognized and acknowledged (Goldberg & Huxley 1980) and acknowledgement is less likely when physical illness is present (Freeling et al 1985; Tylee, Freeling & Kerry 1993). Of those who are acknowledged, only a minority of patients receive a therapeutic course of treatment (Keller et al 1982; Donoghue & Tylee 1996). People with undiagnosed, untreated or undertreated psychiatric illness may be a burden to primary care staff because they may have higher rates of repeat consultations in primary care. These patients may be falsely labelled as 'worried well' but often have severe mental illness, causing considerable personal distress, impaired social functioning, high sickness absence and high labour turnover (Jenkins et al 1985). In 1985 it was estimated that the cost of neurotic disorder treated in UK general practice was £373 million (Croft-Jeffreys & Wilkinson 1985), simply in terms of consultation and treatment in primary care. The Confederation of British Industry has estimated that the costs of minor psychiatric morbidity to the economy (sickness absence, labour turnover and accidents) is £5 billion. Impaired productivity and industrial relations problems would add to this figure.

An average GP's list of around 2000 patients could contain at any one time at least 300–400 patients with depression and anxiety. Even if that GP has a counsellor in the practice he/she could have only a handful of patients on his/her

Preventing Mental Illness: Mental Health Promotion in Primary Care. Edited by R. Jenkins and T.B. Üstün.
© 1998 John Wiley & Sons Ltd.

caseload at any one time. An attached community psychiatric nurse would be able only to look after a handful of that GP's patients with long-term mental illness. Around one-third of GPs have a 'counsellor' in their practice (Sibbald et al 1993) and this trend has grown rapidly over the last 5 years, despite the lack of rigorous evaluation of efficacy in this area.

As a part of overall Department of Health strategy a series of initiatives combining both top-down and bottom-up approaches has been developed to maximize the potential of the primary care team and avoid diverting specialists from their task of caring for the severely mentally ill. The bottom-up projects have been described by other authors in this volume. The top-down project is for a senior GP fellow to take a continuing national lead in educating GPs about mental health in England.

The RCGP Senior Mental Health Education Fellowship was established in April 1992 (Jenkins 1992). Before describing the activities of the Fellowship it is essential to describe the current situation regarding the provision of mental health education for GPs. Accepting that there is a real need for this, it is also important to consider perceived need. We know that some GPs want training in skills such as psychodynamic counselling, stress management and cognitive therapy (MORI Poll 1992; Branthwaite et al 1988). The MORI Poll only achieved a GP response rate of 48%, so this may have been a self-selected group of GPs and, furthermore, the survey by Branthwaite and colleagues simply asked their respondents to list the topics on which they would like to receive training without giving any indication of priority.

One of the first tasks of my fellowship was to conduct a survey of GPs to obtain more information about in which areas they felt confident and competent, in which areas they felt less confident regarding mental health, and in which areas they wished to receive more training (Turton & Tylee 1996). We obtained a better response rate than the MORI Poll, but confirmed their findings that GPs want to learn about the talking therapies. In the UK there currently is no requirement to undertake continuing medical education in mental health and the categories which are rewarded by a postgraduate education allowance are simply health promotion, clinical and service management. Only around 40% of general practice trainees do a 6-month job in psychiatry, so many GPs will have had a variable degree of exposure to mental health. It is also debatable whether a 6-month job in psychiatry is always relevant to general practice. Personally, I only had undergraduate experience in mental health before going into general practice, and found that I was completely unprepared for the large numbers of patients presenting with emotional distress. Consequently, I joined a Balint group which met weekly to discuss cases in a peer group. I undertook short training courses in stress management techniques and basic cognitive therapy. This personal experience closely mirrors the findings from our survey.

The next issue to address is whether the provision of training is worthwhile in that it actually changes GPs' behaviour and benefits patient outcome. Rutz and colleagues (1995) have demonstrated (albeit with a small number of GPs and patients) that a relatively simple training on the recognition and treatment of depression and suicide can reduce rates of suicide, referral, inpatient admissions, prescribing for tranquillizers and sick certification, and can increase prescribing rates for antidepressants. The reduction in suicide rates has since been shown to have occurred in patients who were depressed (Z Rihmer, personal communication, so this indicates that training on the recognition and treatment of depression may bring about a reduction in suicide. We are awaiting the results of a larger replication study, the Hampshire Depression Project (Professor C. Thompson personal communication) and need to remember that in Gotland after 3 years the effect returned to baseline, suggesting that educational programs need to be continuous (Rutz, Von Knorring & Walinder 1992).

The Defeat Depression Campaign was launched in January 1992 (Priest 1991) for 5 years by the Royal College of Psychiatrists in association with the Royal College of General Practitioners, and was an important initiative designed to increase awareness and improve understanding of depression in the community, so that those suffering from this common and disabling condition will not be afraid to seek and receive appropriate treatment. The public phase began in earnest in March 1994 with Defeat Depression Action Week, which provided an opportunity to highlight key aspects of depression, its nature and its consequences. This led to a Defeat Depression Day in 1995. Amongst the materials available were 'help-is-at-hand leaflets' on: depression; depression in the elderly; sleep problems, anorexia and bulimia; surviving adolescence; anxiety and phobias; bereavement; postnatal depression; and depression in the workplace. Apart from English, factsheets were available in Chinese, Hindi, Gujarati, Bengali and Punjabi. Audio tapes for the public were available on coping with depression and books, *Down with Gloom* and *So Young, So Sad, So Listen* were also available, as was a package for employers.

One aim of the campaign has been to increase professional knowledge and skills and this was achieved by the publication of a consensus statement on the recognition and treatment of depression (Paykel & Priest 1992) and the development of other statements on depression in the elderly, ethnic groups, postnatal women, and children and adolescents. These statements formed the basis of training material for GPs and, in particular, two video packages on depression: *From Recognition to Management* and *Counselling in Depression*. The former package showed how to diagnose depression from a knowledge and skills perspective, and showed that depression can be diagnosed in everyday general practice; the latter demonstrated simple talking treatments that can be done by GPs, e.g. how to undertake simple problem-solving when the problem is soluble; coping strategies when the problem is insoluble; and cognitive–behavioural approaches when the patient's perspective requires examination.

Other materials produced for GPs by the Defeat Depression Campaign included: a book, sent to all members of the Royal College of General Practitioners (RCGP) and Royal College of Psychiatry, *Depression. Recognition and Management in General Practice* (Wright 1993); a booklet with the guidelines described in reader-friendly terms, sponsored by the Department of Health and sent to all GPs in England; and a laminated card which was an *aide memoire* about diagnosis and the treatment of depression and assessment of suicide (Armstrong & Lloyd 1993). These materials were central also to the activities of the RCGP Senior Mental Health Education Fellowship, particularly as I was a member of the management committee and the scientific advisory committee of the campaign. One of my first activities as RCGP Fellow was to ensure that around 200 video-packages were sent to key teachers in the existing continuing medical education (CME) network via an entirely new cascade structure that I found it necessary to establish in England.

Some of the initial contacts with district GP tutors in the English CME network led me to realize that too much of a 'top-down' approach would not be successful, as the potential recipients would be either disinterested or hostile. Consequently, with the help of the 14 Regional Advisers in general practice in England, I began the process of establishing the appointment of a new breed of Regional Mental Health Education Fellows in Primary Care, whose job is mainly to assess the training needs of each region's GPs, GP trainees, GP tutors (who provide training for GPs) and course organizers (who teach the GP trainees). This was necessary to ensure that perceived needs are aligned with real needs, so that a 'bottom-up' learner-centred approach is adopted, which ensures better attendance whilst real needs are tackled as well. During the first 18 months, 11 of the 14 Regional Advisers appointed a Regional Mental Health Education Fellow from their own regional budgets (see Figure 22.1) and I arranged bimonthly meetings residentially with the regional fellows to discuss perceived needs and to develop strategies for developing and providing knowledge and skills-based training in mental health through the existing CME structure. In addition, the Regional Fellows were identifying and collaborating with key non-CME teachers, such as local psychiatrists who teach GPs and the national network of nurse facilitators. Overall, we aimed to raise the profile of mental health within the CME structure, as it had had a relatively low priority with as many as two-thirds of district tutors (constituting as little as 2% of total CME in one region). We also aimed to foster mental health audit, and I later received additional Department of Health funding to develop a national mental health audit resource for primary care teams that included the best models of mental health audit available (Figure 22.2).

During 1993–5, I and the regional fellows developed several core competencies that included a strong understanding of perceived training needs of the tutors themselves, so, for example, we developed training in interactive skills for district tutors, who had often had little training in this area. We learnt how to convert key mental health consensus statements and guidelines into training materials accompanied by clear guidance for district tutors on how to use it. Another activity was to help develop distance learning material on depression and anxiety for primary care teams with the Royal Institute of Public Health & Hygiene (RIPHH), and this was piloted and launched in 1995. This material was developed from a successful course in recognizing and managing depression and anxiety, developed at the RIPHH by a team of which I was a member and which we had piloted with three practices. This involved up to 6 months of preparatory work by the whole team (in my own practice, which was the first pilot practice, it included four GP principals,

Kelvin Ford............... Trent
Anthony Hazzard....... N.Thames(E)
Barry Lewis................ North West
David Fish.................. West Midlands
Malcolm McCoubrie... Yorkshire
Simon Prince............. Anglia
Frank Smith............... S.Thames(W)
Susan Summers........ N.Thames(W)
Andrea Tree.............. North West
Ingrid Wallace........... Oxford
Niki Wright................. South and West

FIGURE 22.1   National Health Service Regions from 1 April 1994

Critical success factors	Core competencies
Strong links/endorsement from key agencies	Understanding of perceived needs
Ready access to appropriate funding	Conversion of empirical evidence into
Continued belief/support from sponsoring	practical approaches
bodies in mental health education	Strong utilization of media opportunities
Maintaining integrity and independence of the	Delivery of skill-based educational packages
unit	

Strategy
1. The development and provision of knowledge/skills-based educational packages in mental health through the CME structure
2. Identification and collaboration with non-CME teachers
3. Raising the profile of mental health issues
4. Fostering mental health audit

Issues	Opportunities
Resistance/apathy towards MHE by providers, recipients and sponsors	Mental health now top of priority and planning guidance
Previous low priority afforded to mental health	Collaboration with other key initiatives in MHE
	Higher media/public awareness and research interest in mental health
	Commissioning agencies/fundholders are at an early stage in priority setting to persuade CAS/fundholders to attach priority to MH resource allocation
	Capitalizing on existing marketing skills resource within industry

FIGURE 22.2 RCGP Unit for mental health education in primary care: strategic objective—'to improve GP detection and management of mental illness'

a GP trainee, three practice nurses, the counselling psychologist, the clinical psychologist, the health visitor, the community nurse, a community psychiatric nurse from the mental health team, and our practice manager and computer manager). The preparatory work involved auditing our care of patients with depression and anxiety and a group discussion about a suicidal patient. The whole team was helped by two facilitators (a GP and a nurse teacher) to develop criteria and protocols for managing depression and anxiety on a 2-day residential course and then to complete the audit cycle by 1 month later. My practice identified clear training gaps for individual members of the team and arranged further training for them. We developed protocols for the management of depression and anxiety for use in the practice and set up regular team meetings to monitor progress. We later had regular critical incident reporting at these meetings (which expanded to include representatives from Social Services and Housing) whenever someone attempted suicidal or killed him/herself.

With the Regional Fellows, we developed a 1-day experiential workshop on suicide (jointly with the training section of the Samaritans), a package on alcohol misuse, a package on schizophrenia, and a package on how to measure detection rates or identification index. Problem-based interviewing was taught to us by Dr Linda Gask, who demonstrated its effectiveness in GPs and GP trainees (Gask 1989, 1988). This involved watching video-taped consultations in peer groups to identify how consultation skills and problem-solving could be improved. The Regional Fellows became able to provide problem-based interviewing for groups of GPs, GP trainees or teachers.

We also received media training as a group, because of the increasing interest in the media on mental health issues. We made full use of the opportunities that existed to collaborate with other training initiatives in mental health education, particularly those undertaken by the pharmaceutical companies. It was estimated that there might be as many as 1000 drug company representatives talking to GPs about mental health issues (particularly depression) at any one time, and it was important to ensure that their messages were appropriate and complementary. In the UK there was a considerable climate of change, with purchasers and commissioning agencies increasingly wanting to understand about mental health service provision. It was crucial that purchasing by GP fundholders and other commissioning bodies was appropriate and congruent with national priorities, and training material needed to reflect this. A major continuing issue was that it is always necessary to overcome widespread resistance and apathy to mental health issues amongst providers, funders and even the public, who often have other issues as priority areas (e.g. heart disease, cancer, HIV, etc.). It helped enormously that mental health became the top priority in the Priority and Planning Guidance in the Department of Health in addition to its high priority as part of the 'Health of the Nation' initiative.

As a group we had strong links with key mental health related agencies, which included many of the user and carer groups, and needed to incorporate user involvement in multidisciplinary training. The whole project was evaluated at several levels to take account of the action research nature of the project and its national nature as is the Defeat Depression Campaign.

FUTURE PROSPECTS

Further funding has been obtained to continue the work of the original fellowship until the year 2000. A new RCGP Unit for Mental Health Education in Primary Care has been established (under the directorship of Dr Tylee) in the Section of Epidemiology and General Practice at the Institute of Psychiatry. The main strategic objective is to improve GP detection and management of mental illness by the development and provision of learner friendly skills and knowledge-based training for whole practice teams. This is currently under way through a national 'Teach the Teachers' course for pairs of trainers (one GP and one nurse) at the Royal College of General Practitioners. These pairs of trainers assess the mental health learning needs of whole practice teams and then use a variety of teaching methods to meet those needs.

The Defeat Depression Campaign finished in January 1997 and is currently being evaluated. The Depression Alliance are continuing the public awareness campaign with the support of many voluntary organizations.

CONCLUSION

If mental health is to retain a high priority in GP training, the RCGP Unit for Mental Health Education needs to continue developing and providing key knowledge and skills-based training in mental health. Considerable effort has so far been put into establishing a new national cascade structure that can work within the existing CME structure, whilst developing links with other non-CME teachers. The Unit continues to raise the profile of mental health issues in primary care and fosters mental health audit. It is hoped that the regional fellowship posts will become more integrated into mainstream regional training, that they will continue to be funded, and that regions without Fellows will recognize their worth in the future. Similar projects currently being established in other countries may benefit from the unit's experience. Although CME structures may differ, many of the barriers and resistances will be similar largely because of the subject area.

The Department of Health has a key role in encouraging an increased uptake of mental health CME by encouraging provision centrally, regionally and at district level, and they also need to consider raising demand by GPs by providing better incentives to undertake such training.

REFERENCES

Armstrong E & Lloyd K (1993) Defeat Depression Campaign Management Committee.

Branthwaite A, Ross A, Henshaw A & Charmian D (1988) Continuing Education for General Practitioners. RCGP Occasional Paper 38, May. London: Royal College of General Practitioners.

Croft-Jeffreys C & Wilkinson G (1989) Estimated costs of neurotic disorder in UK general practice 1985. *Psychol Med* **19**, 549–58.

Donoghue JM & Tylee AT (1996) The treatment of depression: prescribing patterns of antidepressants in primary care in the United Kingdom. *Br J Psychiat* **168**, 164–8.

Freeling P, Rao BM, Paykel ES, Sireling LI & Burton RH (1985) Unrecognized depression in general practice. *Br Med J* **290**, 1880–83.

Gask L, McGrath G, Goldberg DP & Millar T (1987) Improving the psychiatric skills of established general practitioners: evaluation of group teaching. *Med Ed* **21**, 362–8.

Gask K, Goldberg D, Lesser AL & Millar T (1988) Improving the psychiatric skills of the general practice trainee: an evaluation of a group training course. *Med Ed* **22**, 132–8.

Goldberg DP & Huxley P (1980) *Mental Illness in the Community. The Pathway to Psychiatric Care.* London: Tavistock.

Jenkins R (1992) Developments in the primary care of mental illness—a forward look. *Int Rev Psychiat* **4**, 237–44.

Jenkins R, Smeeton N, Marinker M & Shepherd M (1985) A study of the classification of mental ill health in general practice. *Psychol Med* **15**, 403–9.

Keller MB et al (1982) Treatment received by depressed patients. *J Am Med Assoc* **248**, 1848–55.

MORI Poll (1992) *Defeat Depression Campaign*, London.

Paykel ES & Priest RG (1992) Recognition and management of depression in general practice: consensus statement. *Br Med J* **305**, 1198–202.

Priest RG (1991) A new initiative on depression (editorial). *Br J Gen Pract* **41**, 487.

Rutz W, Walinder J, Eberhard G, Holmberg G, von Knorring A-L, von Knorring L et al (1989) An educational programme on depressive disorders for general practitioners on Gotland: background and evaluation. *Acta Psychiat Scand* **79**, 19–26.

Rutz W, von Knorring L, Pihlgren H, Rihmer Z & Walinder J (1995) An educational project on depression and its consequences: is the frequency of major depression among Swedish men underrated, resulting in high suicidality? *Primary Care Psychiat* **1**, 59–63.

Rutz W, von Knorring L & Walinder J (1992) Long-term effects of an educational program for general practitioners given by the Swedish Committee for the Prevention and Treatment of Depression. *Acta Psychiat Scand* **85**, 83–8.

Sibbald B, Addington-Hall J, Brenneman D & Freeling P (1993) Counsellors in English and Welsh general practices: their nature and distribution. *Br Med J* **306**, 29–33.

Turton P, Tylee A & Kerry S (1995) Mental health training needs in general practice. *Primary Care Psychiatry*, **1**, 197–9.

Tylee AT, Freeling P & Kerry S (1993) Why do general practitioners recognize major depression in one woman patient yet miss it in another? *Br J Gen Pract* **43**, 327–30.

Wright A (1933) *Depression. Recognition and Management in General Practice*. Durham: Royal College of General Practitioners.

23

US Primary Care Training and the Role of the DSM-IV Primary Care Version (DSM-IV–PC)*

Harold Alan Pincus and Laurie E McQueen

American Psychiatric Association, Washington, DC, USA

The high prevalence of mental and addictive disorders is well established, as is the fact that these conditions often go undiagnosed and untreated. Most care is rendered in the primary care sector, where there exists great potential for prevention, detection, treatment and referral of these patients.[1] Unfortunately, a series of barriers related to physician preparation and attitudes, patient attitudes and behaviors, and the constraints of health care systems, inhibit the capacity of the primary care sector to play an optimal role in this area.[2]

This chapter will first provide a brief definition of what is meant by 'primary care' in the USA and will describe the structure of training in the relevant specialties. Specific expectations for primary care training in mental health care and prevention will be provided, as well as the training recommendations of leading organizations and a typology of models for providing primary care training in mental health and prevention. Available information on outcomes of primary care training models will be reviewed.

Finally, the barriers to primary care training in mental health will be examined and potential strategies for overcoming these barriers will be presented. The role of a taxonomic and curriculum tool such as the *Diagnostic and Statistical Manual of Mental Disorders, 4th edn, Primary Care Version* (DSM-IV–PC)—developed with primary care physicians to accommodate their needs and interests—will be discussed.

---

* Portions of this chapter are reproduced by permission of Rapid Science Publishers Ltd from Pincus HA & McQueen LE (1996) US primary care training in mental health and the role of the DSM-IV primary care version (DSM-IV–PC). *Primary Care Psychiat* **2**, 139–54.

Preventing Mental Illness: Mental Health Promotion in Primary Care. Edited by R. Jenkins and T.B. Üstün.

DEFINITIONS

While the 1994 definition proposed by the Institute of Medicine[3] establishes a useful, nuanced conceptualization for primary care, most definitions include concepts of first contact, comprehensiveness, continuity and coordination.[4] For practical purposes, the major influence on the development of primary care training programs has been the definition used by the federal government, which has been concretely applied through the development of formalized primary care programs supported by federal funding for family practice, general internal medicine and general pediatrics programs. Recently, in health care reform discussions in the USA, the importance of primary care was strongly emphasized and the need to increase the proportion of physicians providing it was an important component of many federal health care reform proposals.[5] The majority of these proposals tended to include internal medicine, family practice, pediatrics, obstetrics and gynecology in their definitions.[6] While there has been some dispute over obstetrics/gynecology as a primary care specialty, both in regard to the structure and the intent of the training, it has also been recognized that many women in the USA routinely see obstetricians/gynecologists as their only source of medical care. In addition, while not considered a primary care specialty, emergency medicine programs have grown significantly in the USA, with emergency departments representing an important source of 'regular' care for both emergent and non-emergent needs. In this chapter we focus on internal medicine, family practice, pediatrics and obstetrics/gynecology.

The basic structures for training in each of these specialties are described in Table 23.1. While each has established a minimum of 3 years' formal training (obstetrics/gynecology has 4), they vary with regard to the focus on outpatient care and the degree of structured curricular requirements, as established in the American Medical Association's essentials for residency training.[7,8,9,10] Importantly, both internal medicine and pediatrics have evolved training programs that focus specifically on preparing individuals for 'generalist' training. Federal support for these general/primary care internal medicine and general/ambulatory pediatrics programs emphasize teaching in outpatient settings and the ongoing, continuous and comprehensive care of patients. This support has enabled expanded teaching and curricular time for the various elements associated with primary care, including mental health training. It is also important to note that, within pediatrics, there has also evolved a 'sub-specialty' of developmental/behavioral pediatrics that focuses on psychosocial and behavioral issues in children. While not recognized as a formal sub-specialty, there is a society as well as a journal devoted to this sub-specialty.

EXPECTATIONS FOR PSYCHIATRIC TRAINING

There is considerable variation in the expectations for the inclusion of psychiatric topics in the curriculum of the various primary care specialties, as demonstrated in

TABLE 23.1 Basic structures for training in four specialties

	Basic expectations		Overall curriculum specification
	Duration (years)	Locus	
Family practice	3	Longitudinal continuity of patient care across settings Family practice center primary setting	++++
Internal medicine	3	20 Months inpatient 25% Ambulatory	++
Pediatrics	3	6 Months ambulatory ½-Day continuity clinic	+++
Obstetrics/gynecology	4/3	Not specified but experience in ambulatory setting essential	+

Table 23.2. There is also variation across the different mandates placed on the training programs by the residency accreditation[7,8,9,10] and individual certification processes.[11,12,13,14] In addition, for some specialties, specific reports providing recommendations for training have been made by major organizations, e.g. Society of General Internal Medicine (SGIM),[15] American Academy of Family Physicians (AAFP).[16] Family medicine has the most extensive and differentiated set of expectations in all of these areas. For example, the AAFP recommends that curricula should include knowledge of mental disorders and therapeutic skills, and training should include experience in assessment, psychotherapy and psychophar-macology.[16] Obstetrics and gynecology has the least. Traditional 'straight' internal medicine programs have not set high expectations for residency accreditation and individual certification,[8,12] but some organizations have recommended more detailed and intensive expectations for general internal medicine programs (e.g. SGIM[15]).

EXPECTATIONS FOR PREVENTION

Beginning in the 1970s, the USA federal government established prevention efforts as a major priority in policy and programs. One approach has been the establish-ment of specific prevention goals for the country, and a task force was established to evaluate prevention efforts to be potentially implemented as part of primary care.[17] Included in the systematic evaluation of data supporting the use of various preventive interventions were a number related to mental health care, specifically those in the following areas (for children/adolescents and adults/other adults): depression and suicide; alcohol and other drug abuse; tobacco; violent behavior

TABLE 23.2 Expectations for inclusion of psychiatric topics in primary care training

	Rating	Accreditation: examples	Rating	Certification
			Expectations—mental health	
Family practice	++++	Didactic program to include: • Recognition, diagnosis, management of mental disorders, alcohol/substance use • Elements of psychotherapy, psychopharmacotherapy, counseling • Psychiatrists and family physicians as teachers	+ ½	American Board of Family Practice • 7% Of board exam on psychiatry or behavioral sciences

Internal medicine	+	• Sufficient experience in psychiatry and neurology to diagnose and manage care or refer to psychiatrists or manage jointly	½	American Board of Internal Medicine
				• Board examination primary content area:
				  4% Psychiatry
				  6% Prevention
				  2% Substance abuse

Pediatrics	++	Training program should include: • Behavioral–developmental pediatrics • Special attention to anticipatory guidance, developmental/behavioral issues, including emotional handicaps • Adolescent medicine should include chemical dependency	+	American Board of Pediatrics • 5% Of board exam relates to mental health and prevention issues
Obstetrics/gynecology	+	Training program should include: • Obstetrics—genetic amniocentesis and patient counseling • Gynecology—clinical skills in family planning; psychosomatic and psychosexual counseling	+	American Board of Obstetrics and Gynecology • Board exam includes category on medical, surgical and psychiatric disorders in women • 2–5 Questions pertain to mental illness • Primary preventive medicine including substance abuse and crisis intervention

and firearms; and other areas with important behavioral components (e.g. sexually transmitted diseases (STD)/HIV prevention).

Interestingly, the task force did not find sufficient evidence to recommend routine screening for depression or anxiety in primary care, but nonetheless did suggest that primary care providers should be alert to signs and symptoms of depression/suicide risk and inquire about the patient's mental state. As an accompaniment to this project, the Department of Health and Human Services also published an associated guide for clinicians[18] which included the specific recommendations from both the task force and major professional organizations with regard to prevention expectations.

MODELS OF TRAINING

In an attempt to lay the groundwork for the evaluation of primary care residency training programs,[19,20,21] six distinct conceptual models were identified to describe the ways in which psychiatric training was incorporated. This taxonomy was developed on the basis of literature reviews, analysis of federal grant applications, and visits to several dozen programs.

Three specific variables are central to the formulation of the taxonomy: content (what is taught); form (how it is taught); and administrative organization (who controls and establishes content and form). The characteristics of program/models depicted in Figure 23.1 are summarized below.

Consultation Model (Figure 23.2)

Teaching of behavioral/psychiatric content occurs almost exclusively around informal psychiatric consultation requests for specific patients and there is rarely specification of curriculum or formal evaluation of students. Inasmuch as the content is case-derived, it focuses on problems that exist in a given patient population and setting (e.g. acute pharmacologic management of psychiatric disturbances on medical wards, diagnosis of delirium). The amount of teaching time received per resident averages about 3 hours each year. Both the administration and teaching are delegated, in a *de facto* manner, to the psychiatric service that provides clinical consultation. Most traditional internal medicine programs, obstetrics and gynecology programs, and many traditional pediatrics programs apply this model.

Liaison Model (Figure 23.3)

Some ongoing educational efforts are offered in addition to requested consultations, e.g. a psychiatric consultant may be present on ward rounds or regular

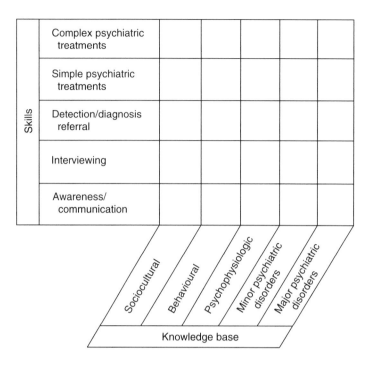

FIGURE 23.1 A model of domains of knowledge and skills

patient care liaison conferences may be held. Increased involvement of primary care faculty in teaching behavioral/psychiatric content may stem from the longitudinal 'presence' of psychiatric faculty (e.g. through 'ombudsman's rounds' or establishment of Balint groups). Although content remains case-determined, the extended relationship allows for emphasis of other areas and the opportunity to track topics presented (e.g. 'We've talked enough about low back pain, let's talk about depression') to ensure that 'core' problems are covered. Psychological reactions to medical illness and the importance of psychosocial history data are stressed. Administration and teaching for the program are generally delegated to psychiatry, although primary care must allocate some teaching time for residents and occasionally may fund some portion of the psychiatrists' time. Some internal medicine, pediatrics and occasionally obstetrics/gynecology programs apply this model.

Bridge Model (Figure 23.4)

This model is characterized by a more formal, pedagogic structure, more total teaching time and a greater variety of teaching methods (e.g. videotaped interview

Consultation

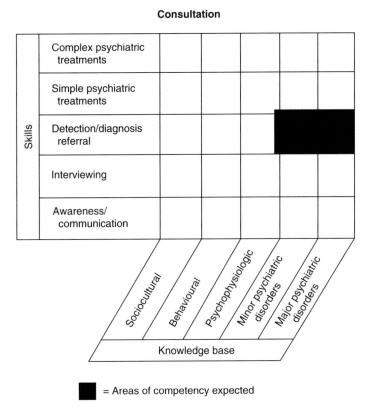

■ = Areas of competency expected

FIGURE 23.2 Consultation model of training

conferences) devoted to psychiatric issues. Administratively, the primary care program purchases teaching from the department of psychiatry but retains administrative involvement. Increased intensity and breadth of the training experience allow for greater emphasis in such areas as interviewing skills and behavior and life-style issues. Some primary care internal medicine and primary care pediatric programs apply this model, as do some family practice programs.

Hybrid Model (Figure 23.5)

The primary care department acts as a 'broker' to obtain different mental health teaching components from sources both within the department (i.e. primary care physicians and staff social workers) and outside (i.e. the department of psychiatry staff). A substantial amount of mental health teaching time is allotted and structured with diverse educational modalities and a wide range of problems and skills are addressed, with an emphasis on issues most relevant to ambulatory care:

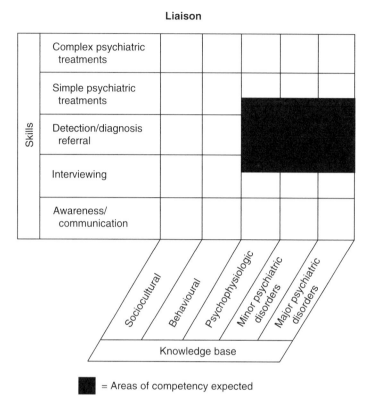

Liaison

FIGURE 23.3 Liaison model of training

interviewing, life stress issues and compliance. A strong psychiatric focus on the diagnosis of common mental disorders prevails in the portion of the program taught by psychiatry. A hybrid model is applied in general internal medicine, general pediatrics, and many family practice programs.

Autonomous Model (Figure 23.6)

The primary care department assumes responsibility for administrative control and implementation and there is little or no contact with an external department of psychiatry. Typically, the primary care department employs an in-house staff of non-medical behavioral scientists to play an important role in teaching the mental health component. Although content is variable, relatively little emphasis is placed on diagnosis and treatment of psychiatric disorders and curricula usually reflect the particular interest of the behavioral scientists directly involved in the program. It may range from an emphasis on learning and providing formalized teaching in

Bridge

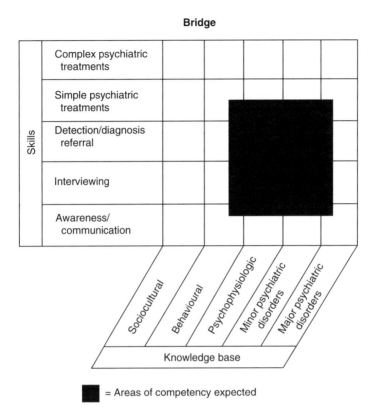

FIGURE 23.4 Bridge model of training

family therapy to a focus on interviewing and sensitivity training. This type of program is most common in family medicine.

Postgraduate Specialization (Figure 23.7)

This model is a full-time and intensive block rotation within a specialty mental health setting that allows a primary care trainee (usually post-residency) to function as a mental health specialist in training. Content can be extremely variable, ranging from a 2-year program in psychological aspects of medical problems in various settings to an emphasis on developing proficiency in specialized areas such as marriage and family counseling and substance misuse. Other examples include programs that provide 'double-boarded' training (Figure 23.8), e.g. in medicine and psychiatry, or 'triple-boarded' programs in pediatrics, psychiatry and child psychiatry. This is a relatively uncommon type of model and is generally not applied as part of formal basic residency training.

Hybrid

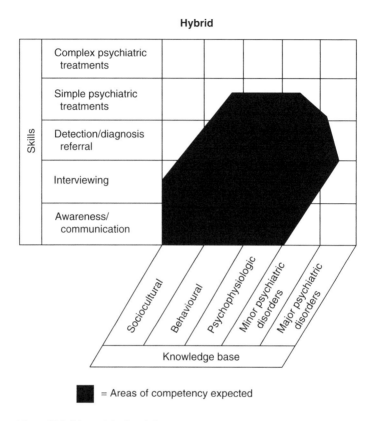

= Areas of competency expected

FIGURE 23.5   Hybrid model of training

Content and Form Differences

The content of primary care programs is depicted in Figure 23.1 as a grid (initially conceptualized by Burns et al[22] and later elaborated by Strain et al[23]), encompassing non-hierarchical domains of mental health knowledge and skills for providers. Figures 23.2–23.8 describe the variations of content emphasized in the various models. Consultation and liaison programs emphasize a limited range of skills and problem areas which are expanded upon in the bridge and hybrid programs. Autonomous programs generally exclude attention to mental illness *per se*. The double-boarded program at a few sites obviously stresses a full range of issues, while the Engel fellowship program at Rochester excludes attention to complex psychiatric problems, not seeking to make internists into 'mini-psychiatrists'.

From a national survey of residency programs in family, traditional and primary care internal medicine, Strain et al[24] codified the teaching methods into three

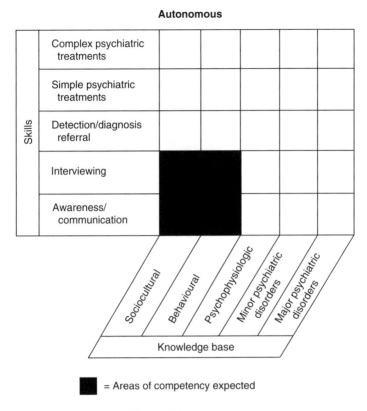

FIGURE 23.6 Autonomous model of training

categories: psychiatric consultation, formal curriculum and informal curriculum. For example, internal medicine employs psychiatric consultation for over 68% of their mental health training in contrast to 30% and 22.5% for family practice and primary care, respectively (Figure 23.9). Internal medicine rarely uses block rotation but relies upon the inpatient setting for 80% of their mental health training. Since the modal internal medicine resident requests three to four psychiatric consultations per year and spends on the average less than 15 minutes with the consultant per case, the accumulated teaching, through its primary vehicle—the psychiatric consultation—results in only 3–4 hours of instruction over the course of internal medicine residency for those residents inclined to initiate a consultation. Some never do. Furthermore, there is no assurance that they will encounter the appropriate range of psychiatric issues.

These six models, each with distinct strengths and limitations, offer useful starting points for discussion. The selection of a particular model by a primary care department depends on numerous considerations related to the ecology of the given setting (i.e. funding availability, specialty requirements, patient populations,

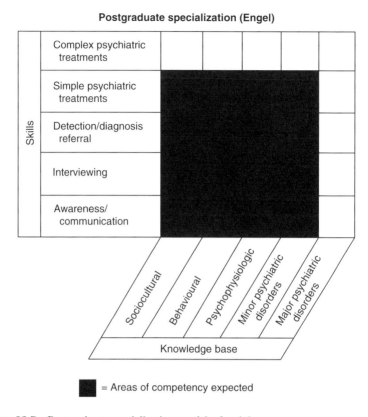

Postgraduate specialization (Engel)

■ = Areas of competency expected

FIGURE 23.7 Postgraduate specialization model of training

and the personal philosophy of the director) and the application of these models has important implications. Some family medicine programs, for example, while maintaining a strong focus on communication skills, may fail to provide equivalent attention to the careful assessment and management of psychiatric disorders. These programs (e.g. the autonomous model) often isolate themselves from departments of psychiatry by hiring less expensive non-medical behavioral scientists to teach mental health content. Federal grant support has allowed other programs (e.g. the hybrid model) to arrange for the department of psychiatry to augment and diversify the mental health component.

Internal medicine training, which requires little content in mental health, is dominated almost exclusively by the case method of teaching, with a focus on clinical pathophysiology and therapeutics and little time available for considering psychosocial issues. Furthermore, to the extent that health care reimbursement policies reward procedural-oriented practice, indebted residents and under-funded departments have few incentives to focus training on time-consuming psychological management techniques. Internal medicine programs that lack outside support

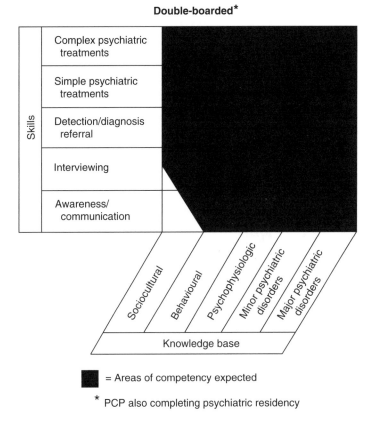

FIGURE 23.8 Double-boarded model of training

typically use the consultation model, despite its limitations as a teaching vehicle. These limitations include: no assurance that a range of problems will be encountered; an emphasis on service over teaching; and the likelihood of limited or even no time devoted to psychosocial issues. Psychiatric consultation-liaison programs have sometimes allowed more structured training of residents, largely through liaison or bridge models. For some programs in primary care internal medicine, federal grants have afforded development of a hybrid model using blocks of psychiatric, didactic and clinical training time to augment other psychosocial components.

OUTCOMES

While several reviews[22,25,26,27] have documented a large number of reports or programs for primary care physicians on psychiatric topics, very few have

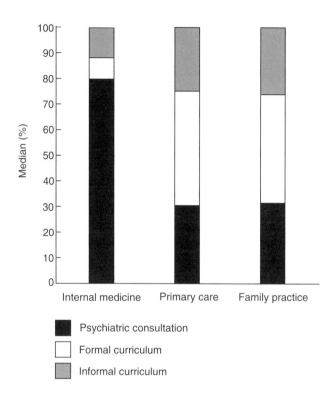

FIGURE 23.9 Mental health teaching during residency training program

reported on the outcomes of psychiatric education for primary care physicians. Cohen-Cole reviewed nine such evaluation studies in 1980[26] and more recently reviewed 13 additional studies reported between 1980 and 1989.[28] He concluded that the studies, in general, support the efficacy of mental health training for primary care physicians (e.g. 11 showed positive change, although two suggested little or no change). Those that were more methodologically advanced (e.g. applied control groups) tended to show positive change. In addition, he found that those studies that maintain specific training objectives and then establish outcome measures directly related to the educational interventions demonstrate the most efficacy. The negative studies appear to teach non-specific psychiatric knowledge and skills and typically measured only one outcome (e.g. diagnostic accuracy). In general, the studies were more likely to indicate changes in attitudes and knowledge and were less likely to measure skills or to find that the routine behavior of trainees was altered by the teaching intervention. Few studies evaluated patient outcomes.

BARRIERS

There are a number of barriers to establishing effective training programs in psychiatric and preventive issues in primary care, including:

- *Stigma.* The patients are wary of bringing up emotional, alcohol, or other drug problems, believing they are not legitimate topics to discuss with a general physician, and many deny that they have a problem. Physicians may share these perspectives and avoid opening up a 'Pandora's box' or risking a patient's negative reaction to the suggestion that he/she visit a psychiatrist or other mental health specialist. Such attitudes result in reluctance by program directors to devote substantial curricular time to mental disorders, and residents are often averse to requesting such training.
- *Skepticism.* Many in primary care, particularly those in traditional programs, are skeptical about diagnostic and treatment approaches in mental health, and are unfamiliar with, or directly question, the data base underlying psychiatric approaches. With regard to preventive screening and interventions, important scientific assessment bodies (e.g. the US Public Health Service Prevention Task Force[17,18]) have questioned the evidence base supporting the use of certain interventions as noted above.
- *Time constraints.* There is an enormous array of topics to be included in a primary care curriculum. Given the accreditation requirements for various rotations as well as the demands of patient care, there is little flexibility to expand the time devoted to psychiatric issues.
- *Clinical/reimbursement constraints.* An important barrier to improved primary care training is third party reimbursement systems in the USA that tend to reward procedures, rather than time spent talking with patients assessing mental health and substance abuse problems.[29] Given how busy primary care physicians are, there is little incentive to explore these problems, since such exploration is not actively reimbursed. Rost et al[30] have indicated that many primary care physicians purposely fail to code mental conditions that are recognized because of concerns about inadequate reimbursement. Many US insurance companies limit payments for care of mental illness by various mechanisms and there is an increasing trend in the USA for the 'carve out' of mental health programs from primary care, resulting in even more potential barriers and fewer incentives.
- *Specialty isolationism.* As budgets decrease and financial pressures increase within medical schools, primary care and psychiatry have become more isolated from each other, with a 'hunker down' effect resulting in reduced awareness of the clinical and educational needs of the other. In particular, as funding availability for psychiatric liaison programs has decreased, there is less likelihood that primary care programs will connect to psychiatric faculty in tune with their needs. As a result, specialty psychiatric developments (e.g. DSM-III and -IV)

and advances in more specialized psychotherapeutic and psychopharmacologic interventions have not been well communicated and translated for primary care use.

STRATEGIES

Despite the limitations of the current system and the significant current barriers, there are a number of strategies that can be used to improve primary care training in mental health and prevention, provided that certain principles are applied in developing them.

- *Understand the primary care perspective.* It is essential to get to know the pressures on primary care practitioners, residents and residency program directors to get a better sense of the incentives and disincentives that drive curriculum and practitioner behavior.
- *Enhance scientific credibility of diagnostic, preventive and treatment approaches.* Some primary care practitioners question the scientific basis of many practices of mental health professions. It is important to specify and emphasize the empirical basis for these efforts, presenting comparative data, e.g. on the relative reliability of diagnostic assessment in psychiatry as compared to X-ray interpretation, fundoscopic examination, heart sound oscultation, etc. This could provide useful background information to aid acceptance of mental health teaching.
- *Develop 'digestible' curriculum tools.* It is important not to be too ambitious, given the extensive time and curriculum pressures in primary care training programs. Smaller, more specific and concrete 'how-to' approaches, specially tailored to primary care needs, are essential.
- *Initiate truly collaborative efforts.* Primary care physicians and residents, like anyone else, do not like being talked down to. Family medicine, in particular, has emphasized that their preferred teachers are family practitioners, teaching *family practice* rather than specialty practice. It is essential to involve primary care educators from the very beginning in the development of teaching tools and curricula. In many cases, they will be the teachers actually providing the material.
- *Incorporate relevant educational and clinical outcome measures.* As medicine in general has faced increased demands for accountability, the testing of educational efforts and the measurement of clinical outcomes increasingly become staples in residency training and a fact among physicians in practice. This provides an opportunity for maintaining the same type of accountability with regard to expectations for training and practice in mental health and prevention. To paraphrase from *Field of Dreams*, 'If you test for it, they will come'.

DIAGNOSTIC AND STATISTICAL MANUAL OF MENTAL DISORDERS, 4TH EDN, PRIMARY CARE VERSION (DSM-IV–PC)

One important example of a curriculum tool for educating primary care physicians about mental health issues is the DSM-IV–PC,[31] which was explicitly developed applying the strategies noted above.

DSM-IV–PC Development

In July 1989 and January 1990, two meetings sponsored by the National Institute of Mental Health brought together those responsible for the development of the *Diagnostic and Statistical Manual of Mental Disorders*, 4th edn (DSM-IV), and leading experts from the primary care disciplines. Participants identified a number of reasons why the DSM-III and DSM-III-R, DSM-IV's predecessors, are not used widely in training or practice by primary care physicians.

They regarded the DSM system, which includes detailed and complex information and diagnostic roles regarding a number of disorders rarely diagnosed in the primary care setting, as cumbersome for those primarily interested in a limited number of conditions. The DSM-IV may not contain information valuable to the primary care physician (e.g. the typical presentation of mental disorders in primary care; a rubric for differentiating among disorders with similar symptom presentations; and explanations of terms or criteria which may not be familiar to the primary care physician), so a system based on presenting symptoms and emphasizing recognition and differential diagnosis should be more useful. Participants agreed that a DSM created for primary care practitioners would be appropriate.

Work on the DSM-IV–PC began in 1990. Primary care organizations participated to ensure that the primary care version would be tailored to their needs. Representatives included those from internal medicine (Society of General Internal Medicine, American College of Physicians), family practice (American Academy of Family Practice, Association of Departments of Family Medicine, American Board of Family Practice, Society of Teachers of Family Medicine), obstetrics/gynecology (American College of Obstetricians and Gynecologists), pediatrics (American Academy of Pediatrics) and psychiatry (American Psychiatric Association). The American Medical Association was also represented.

The development of the manual was guided by the following principles:

- *Clinical utility.* The manual must be user-friendly, succinct (given restricted consultation time) and designed to reflect how a physician manages the primary care visit.
- *Educational utility.* The manual should provide a rubric for differential diagnosis and informative 'clinical pointers'.

- *Research utility.* Appropriate cross-reference to research criteria sets in the DSM-IV Appendix B should be provided for presentations seen commonly in the primary care setting.
- *Compatibility.* To insure correct medical record-keeping and to facilitate communication, the manual must be compatible with DSM-IV.

The Process of Development

Sub-workgroups were formed to focus on major diagnostic classes; mood/anxiety disorders, somatoform disorders (including disorders of sleep, sex, eating and pain), psychosocial/environmental problems, substance use disorders and childhood disorders. Disorders less frequently diagnosed in the primary care setting were reviewed by all sub-workgroups and the DSM-IV–PC succinctly describes disorders usually first diagnosed in infancy, childhood or adolescence.

Each sub-workgroup sorted the DSM-IV disorders into three groups: those rarely diagnosed in primary care (e.g. paraphilias) and thus easily summarized; those adequately described in the DSM-IV already (e.g. sleep disorders); and those for which an expanded description would be helpful (e.g. mood disorders, psychosocial problems). This determination was based upon the overall prevalence of the disorder, prevalence of the disorder in primary care settings, salience of the condition (e.g. importance of its identification by primary care physicians), evidence of frequently missed or misdiagnosed disorders in primary care, and educational significance.

The DSM-IV diagnostic definitions were then reworded for clarity in the primary care setting. In some cases, this involved eliminating or simplifying subtypes, providing explicit examples of criteria, or explaining technical terms and, in other cases, adding information beyond the set criteria (e.g. differential diagnosis pointers). The work groups then grouped the conditions under various symptom clusters, and those symptom clusters common in primary care organized the conditions algorithmically.

Using the Manual

The manual is partitioned into four sections (see Table 23.3). Section 1, consisting of nine algorithms, describes the disorders and conditions most frequently encountered in primary care. The second section includes psychosocial problems that attract clinical attention but are not considered to be mental disorders, e.g. relational (family) problems. Section 3 describes disorders which are rarely first identified in primary care, e.g. dissociative disorders, and clusters them by common symptomatology rather than algorithmically. The final section describes, similarly by cluster, disorders usually first diagnosed in infancy, childhood or adolescence.

TABLE 23.3 Contents of DSM-IV–PC

Chapter 1	Using the DSM-IV–PC
Chapter 2	DSM-IV–PC classification coding guide
Chapter 3	Quick reference to the diagnostic algorithms
Chapter 4	Algorithms for common primary care presentations
4.1	Depressed mood algorithm
4.2	Anxiety algorithm
4.3	Unexplained physical symptoms algorithm
4.4	Cognitive disturbance algorithm
4.5	Problematic substance use algorithm
4.6	Sleep disturbance algorithm
4.7	Sexual dysfunction algorithm
4.8	Weight change/abnormal eating algorithm
4.9	Psychotic symptoms algorithm
Chapter 5	Psychosocial problems
5.1	Psychological and behavioral factors that affect health care
5.2	Relation (family) problems
5.3	problems related to abuse or neglect
5.4	Problems related to personal roles
5.5	Social problems
5.6	Problems listed in other sections
Chapter 6	Other mental disorders
6.1	Manic symptoms
6.2	Impulse-control symptoms
6.3	Deviant sexual arousal
6.4	Dissociative symptoms
6.5	Abnormal movements/vocalizations
6.6	Dysfunctional personality traits
Chapter 7	Disorders usually first diagnosed in infancy, childhood or adolescence
7.1	Common childhood/adolescence presentations classified in other chapters
7.2	Disorders/conditions associated with sub-average intellectual functioning
7.3	Disorders associated with academic skills
7.4	Disorders/conditions associated with motor skills/coordination problems
7.5	Disorders associated with impulsive/hyperactive or inattentive behavior
7.6	Disorders/conditions associated with negativistic/antisocial behavior
7.7	Disorders/conditions associated with feeding, eating or elimination problems
7.8	Disorders/conditions associated with communication problems
7.9	Disorders/conditions associated with impairment in social interaction
7.10	Disorders/conditions associated with issues of gender identity
Appendices	DSM-IV multiaxial system

As with other diagnostic systems designed for primary care physicians, the clinician is guided to the appropriate algorithm(s) by an index of presenting symptoms. Within each algorithm a series of steps, or 'rule out' or 'consider' statements, guide the clinician. Each algorithm is organized according to what is most relevant for that group of disorders. The order of the algorithm may be based on prevalence (e.g. disorders encountered more frequently are listed first); salience (e.g. disorders considered more important to clinical care or most important to recognize are listed first); or severity (e.g. the most impairing disorders are listed first). Although the organizational principles differ somewhat across algorithms, consistency was maintained in part by making the first step of each (to consider if the presenting symptoms may be better accounted for by a general medical condition, substance use, or other mental disorders not included in the grouping) essentially identical.

Within each step, additional clinical information is provided, which may include the following: specifier/subtype information; differential diagnostic pointers; definitions of terms used in the criteria sets; specific examples of the criteria; and onset and course information. Each algorithm is prefaced by introductory text discussing epidemiology, primary care presentation, differential diagnosis and common associated conditions, and organization of the algorithm.

An Example—Depressed Mood Algorithm

To illustrate the manual's approach, the *depressed mood algorithm* (Table 23.4) guides the clinician through the 'presenting symptoms' of sadness/depressed mood, decreased energy, insomnia, and unexplained general medical complaints. Somatic complaints are included because the primary complaint of a large number of persons with a depressive disorder is a somatic complaint. When the presenting symptom occurs in more than one algorithm, the clinician is also referred to those.

The 'steps' guide the clinician through the disorders included in the grouping. The first step in this and every algorithm is to consider whether the presenting symptoms might be better accounted for by a general medical condition, substance use, or other mental disorders not included in the algorithm, and clinicians are reminded that symptoms may be caused by a general medical condition (e.g. hypothyroidism causing depressive symptoms), substance use (e.g. alcohol dependence causing depressive symptoms) or another mental disorder not listed within the algorithm (e.g. a primary sleep disorder causing insomnia; depressive symptoms associated with schizophrenia). The remaining steps guide the clinician in differential diagnosis through the depressive disorder.

Because it is so important to recognize, and is so often undetected, the consideration of *major depressive disorder* is the second step. Two notes remind the clinician that sub-threshold symptoms may be related to *major depression in partial remission*, or *bipolar disorder* (if there is a history of a manic or hypomanic episode). Step 3 directs the clinician to the consideration of *dysthymia* if depressive symptoms have persisted for a 2-year period. A summary of the more complex DSM-IV criteria set for *dysthymia* is provided in the definition box. In step 4, the clinician is reminded to consider the presence of bereavement as a possible cause for the depressive symptoms and is provided with differential pointers to help distinguish 'normal bereavement' from the potentially more serious *major depressive disorder*. Adjustment disorder is the next step, because it is not diagnosed if the symptoms are accounted for by one of the preceding disorders in the algorithm. The residual

TABLE 23.4   Depressed mood algorithm

Presenting symptoms might include:	
	Decreased energy
	Insomnia
	Weight loss
	Unexplained general medical complaint (e.g. chronic pain, gastrointestinal distress, dizziness)
Step 1	Consider the role of *a general medical condition or substance use* and whether the depressed mood is better accounted for by *another mental disorder*:
	(A) 293.83 *Mood disorder due to a general medical condition*
	(B) 291.8 *Alcohol-induced mood disorder*
	292.89 *Other substance-induced (including medication) mood disorder*
	(C) *Other mental disorders*
Step 2	If depressed mood or loss of interest or pleasure *persists over a 2-week period*, consider:
	296.20* *Major depressive disorder, single episode*
	296.30* *Major depressive disorder, recurrent*
	Note: If individual has *ever* had a major depressive episode (but current symptoms do not meet full criteria), consider *296.×5 Major depressive disorder, in partial remission*
	Note: If criteria for a major depressive episode are met, and there is a history of elevated, expansive or euphoric mood, consider *296. Bipolar I disorder* or *296.89 Bipolar II disorder*
Step 3	If depressed mood has been present for *most of the past 2 years* (in adults; or 1 year in children), consider:
	300.4 *Dysthymic disorder*
Step 4	If depressed mood is associated with *the death of a loved one and persists for less than 2 months*, consider:
	V62.82 *Bereavement*
Step 5	If depressed mood occurs *in response to an identifiable psychosocial stressor* and does not meet criteria for any of the preceding disorders, consider:
	309.0 *Adjustment disorder, with depressed mood*
	309.28 *Adjustment disorder, with mixed anxiety and depressed mood*
Step 6	If the depressed mood is clinically significant but the *criteria are not met for any of the previously described disorders*, consider:
	311 *Depressive disorder not otherwise specified*
Step 7	If the clinician has determined that a disorder is not present but wishes to note the presence of *symptoms*, consider:
	780.9 *Sadness*
	780.7 *Decreased energy*
	780.52 *Insomnia*

* More specific codes to denote severity and subtypes are available.

not otherwise specified (NOS) category is next to last for clinicians who feel that a disorder is present but does not meet the specific criteria for the preceding disorders in the algorithm. The additional text provides brief definitions of NOS categories (e.g. minor depression) noted in the DSM-IV Appendix B ('Criteria sets and axes provided for further study'), with the reader being referred to the DSM-IV Appendix for further information. The algorithm's final step identifies symptom codes that can be used if the clinician has determined that a disorder is not present, but wishes to note the presence of symptoms.

Other Features of the Manual

In addition to the four sections previously mentioned, explanatory sections describing the 'Use of the manual' and 'Steps common to all algorithms' are provided. Included in the front is a brief distillation of the manual consisting of pictorial summaries of the nine algorithms and a classification guide. An Appendix includes aspects of the DSM-IV multiaxial system, e.g. 'The psychosocial/environmental checklist' (Axis IV), to remind clinicians to consider the potential effect of the individual's environment on his/her care, and the 'Global Assessment of Function Scale' (Axis IV) provides a measure of overall social and occupational functioning. The 'Symptom index' is also included in the Appendix.

Conceptual Issues

Two conceptual issues central to the development of the manual were compatibility and inclusiveness. While it was important to ensure that the manual be as relevant to primary care policies as possible, compatibility with the DSM-IV (and ICD-9-CM) was also necessary (although compatibility does not mean that the systems needed to be identical, e.g. a complex set of DSM-IV criteria was often summarized and simplified in the DSM-IV–PC, but was still consistent in terms of the categorization of cases). Because there had been complaints that the DSM-III-R was overwhelming, one of the primary goals of the project was to provide a succinct manual, while still providing enough information to assist the physician in recognizing a disorder. This was achieved by providing a different level of detail for presentation of different sets of conditions; disorders more commonly seen in primary care are more extensively discussed.

Primary care clinicians expressed concern about the extent to which individuals manifest psychiatric symptoms falling below the threshold for a specific DSM-IV disorder. Because these presentations may involve impairment in functioning and may represent an increased risk for the development of a mental disorder, primary care physicians were especially concerned that such presentations be discussed in the DSM-IV–PC. For these situations, a NOS category was used which provides a brief description of common sub-threshold syndromes (e.g. minor depressive disorder). For those interested in research criteria, a cross-reference citation to the appendix of the DSM-IV is provided.

The DSM-IV process required an extensive empirical review, and changes were made only when they were supported by significant empirical evidence. The DSM-IV–PC was built on that evidence but, because there is much less research on diagnosis and assessment of mental and addictive disorders in primary care, the DSM-IV–PC relied more on extrapolation of specialty setting data and clinical consensus. The process has additionally resulted in the elucidation of a research agenda for primary care.

Development of the DSM-IV–PC is only a first step in the promotion of educational, clinical and research collaboration among psychiatrists and primary care physicians. As such, the manual should be a useful tool for improving communication, collaboration and educational linkage with primary care clinicians. The involvement of the major primary care associations has provided a foundation for outreach to the primary care field. Post-publication efforts are focused on the promotion of more extensive training in mental and addictive disorders in primary care programs, and research on these disorders within the primary care setting. It is also hoped that the manual will provide a standard training instrument for use in primary care residency education. Ultimately, however, it will be up to individual psychiatrists and primary care providers in their respective practices and within their respective institutions to make that next step.

REFERENCES

1. Regier DA, Narrow WE, Rae DS et al (1993) The *de facto* US mental and addictive disorders service system. *Arch Gen Psychiat* **50**, 85–94.
2. Kamerow DB, Pincus HA & Macdonald DI (1986) Alcohol abuse, other drug abuse, and mental disorders in medical practice. *JAMA* **255**, 2054–7.
3. Committee on the Future of Primary Care, Institute of Medicine (1994) *Defining Primary Care: An Interim Report.* Washington, DC: National Academy Press.
4. US Department of Health and Human Services (1992) *Improving Access to Health Care Through Physician Workforce Reform: Directions for the 21st Century.* Council on Graduate Medical Education, Third Report. Washington, DC: Health Resource and Services Administration, October.
5. Kindig D (1994) Counting generalist physicians. *JAMA* **271**, 1505–7.
6. Rivo ML, Saultz JW, Wartman SA et al (1994) Defining the generalist physician's training. *JAMA* **271**, 1499–1504.
7. American Medical Association (1992) *Essentials of Residency Training, Family Practice.* Accreditation Council on Graduate Medical Education: June. Chicago: American Medical Association.
8. American Medical Association (1994) *Essentials of Residency Training, Internal Medicine.* Accreditation Council on Graduate Medical Education: July. Chicago: American Medical Association.
9. American Medical Association (1991) *Essentials of Residency Training, Obstetrics/Gynecology.* Accreditation Council on Graduate Medical Education: July. Chicago: American Medical Association.

10. American Medical Association (1990) *Essentials of Residency Training, Pediatrics.* Accreditation Council on Graduate Medical Education: January. Chicago: American Medical Association.
11. Blacker M (1995) American Board of Family Practice; personal communication, May.
12. Day S (1995) American Board of Internal Medicine; personal communication, May.
13. Oliver TK (1995) American Board of Pediatrics; personal communication, May.
14. Gant NF (1995) American Board of Obstetrics and Gynecology; personal communication, May.
15. Cole SA, Sullivan M, Kathol R & Warshaw C (1995) A model curriculum for mental disorders and behavioral problems in primary care. *Gen Hosp Psych* **17**, 13–18.
16. American Academy of Family Physicians (1994) *Recommended Core Curriculum Guidelines for Family Practice Residents—Human Behavior and Mental Health.* Kansas City, MO: American Association of Family Physicians.
17. US Preventive Services Task Force (1989) *Guide to Clinical Preventive Services.* Baltimore, MD: Williams & Wilkins.
18. Public Health Service, US Department of Health and Human Services (1994) *Clinician's Handbook of Preventive Services: Put Prevention into Practice.* Washington, DC: Government Printing Office.
19. Pincus HA, Strain JJ, Houpt JL et al (1983) Models of mental health training in primary care. *JAMA* **249**, 3065–8.
20. Strain JJ, Pincus HA, Houpt JL et al (1985) Models of mental health training for primary care physicians. *Psychosom Med* **47**, 95–110.
21. Strain JJ, George LK, Pincus HA et al (1987) Models of mental health training for primary care physicians: a validation study. *Psychosom Med* **49**, 88–98.
22. Burns BJ, Scott JE, Burke JD & Kessler LG (1983) Mental health training of primary care residents: a review of recent literature (1974–1981). *Gen Hosp Psych* **5**, 157–69.
23. Strain JJ, Pincus HA, Gise LH & Houpt JL (1986) The role of psychiatry in the training of primary care physicians. *Gen Hosp Psych* **8**, 372–85.
24. Strain JJ, Pincus HA, Gise LH & Houpt J (1986) Mental health education in three primary care specialties. *J Med Ed* **61**, 958–66.
25. McKegney FP & Beckhardt RB (1982) Evaluative research in consultation–liaison psychiatry: review of the literature 1970–1981. *Gen Hosp Psych* **4**, 197–218.
26. Cohen-Cole SA (1980) Training outcome in liaison psychiatry: literature review and methodological proposals. *Gen Hosp Psych* **2**, 282–8.
27. Strain JJ, Bender-Laitman L, Gise LH et al (1983) Mental health training programs in primary care: a bibliography. *J Psych Educ* 208–31.
28. Cohen-Cole S, Howell EF, Barrett JE et al (1991) Consultation-liaison research: four selected topics. In FK Jedd, GD Burrows & DO Lipsitts (eds) *Handbook of Studies on General Hospital Psychiatry.* Amsterdam: Elsevier.
29. Pincus HA (1990) Assessing the effects of physicians' payment on treatment of mental disorders in primary care. *Gen Hosp Psych* **12**, 23–9.
30. Rost K et al (1994) Deliberate misdiagnosis of major depression. *Arch Fam Med* **3**, 333–7.
31. American Psychiatric Association (1995) *Diagnostic and Statistical Manual of Mental Disorders, 4th edn—Primary Care Version.* Washington, DC: American Psychiatric Association.

Training Packages in Developing Countries

Ahmad Mohit

World Health Organization, Alexandria, Egypt

It is now accepted that almost no country or community can afford to provide highly specialized services to all who need mental health care, not only because it is expensive, but also because it is inefficient compared with other measures, e.g. integrating mental health services into the general health care system, or employing different forms of community care. Furthermore, it has been demonstrated in numerous studies that considerable psychiatric morbidity exists in inpatient, outpatient and casualty department populations, much of which goes unrecognized.[1,2,3] In addition, although direct referrals to psychiatrists are not uncommon in developing countries,[4] psychiatric patients are often first seen by a non-mental health professional or non-professionals in the community. These factors are all important in developing countries, where there is shortage of specialists and facilities.

Following the declaration of Alma-Ata in 1978,[5] which set the goal of 'Health for all by the year 2000' by using the primary health care (PHC) strategy, integration of mental health into PHC became the most important avenue for provision of mental health services in many developing countries. The main assumption of this strategy was the belief that many general health workers are potentially capable of providing mental health services at a certain level of complexity. The task is to identify corresponding levels of complexity and expertise, and proper training (see below) to different levels, by utilizing appropriate technology and evaluation mechanisms.

Other training requirements in a comprehensive national mental health program[6] are not aimed at people who would be directly involved in service delivery, and include different groups in the community whose attitudes and knowledge affect mental health in one way or another. These training packages are discussed below.

Preventing Mental Illness: Mental Health Promotion in Primary Care. Edited by R. Jenkins and T.B. Üstün.
Published 1998 John Wiley & Sons Ltd.

TRAINING METHODS RELEVANT FOR PRIMARY CARE[8]

Lectures are still among the most economical and useful methods of training. A lecture given by a trainer to PHC workers of various levels differs from one given to medical or other students. A lengthy lecture on the details of disease conditions will be forgotten by busy PHC doctors or health workers. These lectures should be prepared carefully, keeping in view the needs of trainees, and linked to the tasks in their daily work. The lecturers may start by asking a few general questions to assess trainees' existing knowledge. The lectures should not exceed 40 minutes and should make use of appropriate teaching aids such as slides and transparencies.

Case Demonstration

This method is among the most common and useful ways of training GPs. As far as possible, patients who are commonly seen by primary care physicians should be selected.

Learning to perform a mental status examination/interview is perhaps the most important skill a GP or health worker can acquire during a training course. This simply comprises how to listen and how to talk to the patient in day-to-day practice. Interview training can be given with a patient in the group or by role-playing. Whenever possible joint sessions, TV or other audiovisual facilities can be used. *Audiotapes* can usefully be employed to demonstrate samples of patients' conversations, generally or with the doctor. And *publications* are still an important medium for transferring knowledge, information and messages.

TRAINING OF POTENTIAL CARE PROVIDERS

Concept of Levels

Sociocultural and economic considerations, as well as the structure of the health system and development scheme of each country, should be taken into consideration in defining levels of trainees. Without this definition it would not be possible to discuss proper training material.

Goldberg & Huxley[10] provide a model of five levels and four filters. Although they use this model to introduce a framework for collecting survey data, their concept of levels can be used to identify training requirements for different groups involved in the provision of mental health services. Identification of levels for training purposes in any given community should be carried out according to specific conditions. For instance, in a country where most basic health services are provided by health workers, the first level of expertise above that of community at large is the 'multipurpose health worker'; in countries or communities where either no comprehensive health system exists or it is not practically functioning, the first level may be teachers, religious leaders, traditional healers or traditional birth attendants.

In the countries of the Eastern Mediterranean Region of WHO, three patterns of health care are predominant:

- Systems which rely on PHC GPs as first-level health providers, e.g. Egypt and the United Arab Emirates.
- Systems which have one level below GPs, e.g. Iran, Pakistan and Syria.
- Systems which may officially belong to either of these groups but in practice rely on powerful non-health-system groups like traditional healers, e.g. the Sudan.

Accordingly, the different levels playing a role in the delivery of mental health services and for whom separate training packages should be prepared, are as follows:

- Those who are not officially linked to the health system but in practice perform the duties of first-level health providers, e.g. teachers and traditional healers.
- Non-medical multipurpose health workers.
- Nurses, psychologists or social workers assigned to a part of the mental health delivery system.
- GPs working in the PHC system.
- Psychiatrists or specially trained GPs, replacing psychiatrists in the health system.*
- Psychiatrists working in hospitals or other specialized centers.

General Objectives of Training

The mental health training package for any of these levels is quite different from formal training material and may have the following objectives:

- It should be relevant to the daily work of the target group and more skill-orientated than knowledge-orientated.
- It should affect the attitude of the trainees, making them aware of the importance of psychosocial factors in health and disease.
- It should increase the awareness of trainees and enhance their management skills without indulging in unnecessary complexities and technical jargon.
- It should have an impact on existing services by decreasing unnecessary referrals, tests or hospitalization.
- It should be compatible with the level of trainees.

---

* An example is a 1-year course in Egypt, after which graduates are given a mental health certificate and perform the duties of a psychiatrist in the health system.

TRAINING IN THE COMMUNITY

Training in the community should also be planned for different levels. The *community at large* needs awareness and attitudinal training. This is basically mass media work, which should be continuous, structured, flexible and respectful of many cultural factors and sensitivities. Achieving attitudinal changes in the community is a very slow process and is influenced by many interacting cultural, religious, traditional, historical and even mythological beliefs and value systems, comprehensive knowledge of which is necessary when planning such campaigns. This knowledge cannot be gained by only using familiar, quantitative research methods, and should be collected in each country with assistance from sociologists, anthropologists, ethnographers and even writers, poets, historians and artists, who have first-hand knowledge and a deep intellectual and emotional appreciation of their own culture. Mental health education of the public needs serious attention. In many countries it is limited to lectures by psychiatrists or psychologists on national radio and television services, the impact of which is questionable and has never been fully studied.

Non-governmental community leaders such as religious authorities, opinion makers and media personalities, sports people, artists, community elders, women's leaders, village chiefs and the like need specific training, and their attitudinal change may be very helpful in influencing the community at large. Training of each of these groups should be specifically designed based on a thorough knowledge of their present attitudes, sensitivities and interests.

Schools and education systems are among the most important resources for mental health promotion, preventive activities, case finding, etc. Mental health training for teachers, students, school health workers, administrators and members of parent–teacher associations needs clear objectives. Training packages may be included in curricula and manuals. In the countries of the Eastern Mediterranean Region of WHO, special efforts are being made to enhance school mental health and a special consultation meeting on the subject was held in 1993.[11] Relevant training packages, e.g. manuals for teachers and school health workers, have been prepared in Bahrain, Egypt, Iran, Pakistan and Tunisia. Two manuals for teachers and school health physicians are also in the final stages of production by WHO's regional office in Alexandria.

Non-health-sector administrators and decision-makers, high-level government officers, members of Parliament, the judiciary and police and authorities dealing with planning and budgets are among influential groups who can make or break programs. Each of these groups represent special concerns and interests and need convincing by simple evidence about the relative importance of mental health, in a form familiar to them and preferably by using their own jargon. This should help them to persuade other decision makers to change their attitudes and priorities too.

Health administrators and officials in ministries of health do not always have a positive attitude towards mental health. Among the various reasons for this is the traditional image mental health professionals have projected of mental health as a never-ending chain of theories and jargon which cannot be broken down into everyday administrative issues, budget figures, percentages, manuals, etc. Training or briefing material for health administrators should be provided taking account of such attitudes. It should contain enough data in non-technical language to persuade them that mental health services and programs can help them to solve some of their other pressing problems.[12] Such data may include statistics related to the prevalence of mental illness in general outpatient or inpatient services or the number of misdiagnosed cases who go through expensive examinations, laboratory tests and even surgical procedures. They should also be briefed with convincing evidence about the impact of mental health programs. Such briefings should be concise, precise and without any unnecessary ambiguity.

SOME PRACTICAL POINTS

Shortage of manpower in many developing countries makes health supervisors and provincial administrators reluctant or even unable to release technical and field personnel for training courses. In such circumstances, flexible training packages combining different health disciplines or the inclusion of mental health training in other packages is needed, and on-the-job supervision may also be considered.

The initial phase of training is usually training of the trainers. It is important that trainers understand the differences between this and formal training at university level. Even experienced academics often fail to appreciate this point.

The amount of information provided for each level of trainees should be linked to the duties each is expected to perform. This is particularly true for multipurpose workers. Psychiatrists working in a PHC-linked system also need training in referrals, back-referrals, supervision and evaluation, and basic research.

EVALUATION[7–14]

Direct measures of evaluation include trainee evaluation of a course or package and pre- and post-training knowledge and attitude tests. About 1 month after the completion of each course, trainees can be surveyed by postal questionnaire or similar means to ascertain the impact of training on their practice. In addition, it is possible to use health service statistics to monitor the impact of newly trained personnel on existing services; health administrators would find such data invaluable because they are always looking for research evidence showing that training has achieved the objectives set for it and has had an impact on services.

CONCLUSION

Training packages are among the main requirements for integration of mental health into the primary health care system. Different technologies may be employed for the development of a training package according to the level of trainees and availability of resources. The philosophy and objectives for developing and using these packages are quite different from formal undergraduate or postgraduate training. They are intended to provide skills for performing certain tasks at a certain level of the mental health delivery system, and/or necessary information to the community at large or to those who have some influence over decisions related to mental health.

Training should be seen as an integral part of the whole process of implementing mental health programs and as dynamically related to, and interacting with, all other aspects. Training requirements and details of the contents of each training level need further elaboration, and should be adjusted to the needs and cultural realities of each country.

REFERENCES

1. R Mayou & E Hawton (1986) Psychiatric disorder in the general hospital. *Br J Psychiat* **149**, 172–90.
2. Dhedphale M et al (1983) The frequency of psychiatric disorders among patients attending semi-urban and rural general out patient clinics in Kenya. *Br J Psychiat* **142**, 379–83.
3. Sartorius N, Davidian H, Ernberg G, Fenton FR, Fuzi CO, Gastpan M, Gnlbinnt W, Jublenksy A, Kielholz P, Behman H, El Naraghi N, Shimizn M, Shinfukn N & Takahashi R (1983) *Depressive Disorders in Different Cultures.* Geneva: WHO.
4. Gater R, de Almeida e Sousa R, Caravies J, Chandrasekar C, Dhadphale M, Goldberg D, Al Kalhiri A, de Llano, G, Mubbashar M, Silhan K, Thong KD, Torres F & Sartorius N (1991) The pathways to psychiatric care: a cross-cultural study. *Psychol Med.*
5. World Health Organization and United Nation's Children's Fund (1978) *Primary Health Care: Report of the International Conference on Primary Care,* Alma-Ata, 6–12 September.
6. National Mental Health Programmes of, for example, Afghanistan, Bahrain, Egypt, Iran, Jordan, Morocco. Unpublished documents, present at EMRO.
7. WHO/EMRO (1987) Report of Intercountry Workshop on Training in Mental Health in Primary Health Care (EM/MENT/114-e), Islamabad, Pakistan, March.
8. Wig NN (1988) Mental health training for health personnel. *Teaching and Learning Newsletter for Health Personnel Educators,* Editorial.
9. Examples of some manuals in EMR Countries:
   - Dr Bura Asefi. *Mental Health (Psychiatry) For All* (Teb-i-Ravani Dar Khidmat-e Hameh—in the Dari Language, Afghanistan). A free translation from RS Murthey, *Mental Health for All,* Bangalore, India.
   - Dr T Basshir & Dr AN Qutri. *Manual for Primary Mental Health Care* (Dalil el Raayah E Sehyiah El Nafsyia El Awalia—in Arabic, Egypt).
   - Dr J Bolhari & Mrs Ansar. *Mental Health for Health Workers* (Behdasht-i-Ravaan Baraay e Behvarzan—in the Farsi language, Iran).
   - Mubbashar M. *Manual of Mental Health for Multi-purpose Health Workers* (Rahnemai tarbyiat Barai Kasirelmaghaed-Karkonan Sehat, Zehni Sehat—in the Urdu language, Pakistan).
10. Goldberg D & Huxley P (1993) *Common Mental Disorders. A Bio-social Model.* London: Routledge.

11. WHO/EMRO (1993) Report on the Consultation on School Mental Health, Islamabad, Pakistan, 14–17 November. (EM/MNH/138.E/L). Islamabad: WHO.

12. Mohit A (1987) Why mental health? (Cheraa Behdnasht e Ravaani?). *Iranian Bulletin of Continuing Medical Education*, FAA 1990 (in Farsi, based on a briefing presented to a national conference in Kermen, Iran, 1987) which decided to include mental health as the 19th element of PHC in 1987.

13. Shahmohamadi Davoud (1992) Comprehensive report on integration of mental health into primary health care system (in the Farsi language, limited circulation). Ministry of Health and Medical Education, Iran.

14. Wig NN (1988) Mental health training for health personnel. *Editorial Teaching and Learning News* **3**(2). WHO/EMRO Newsletter for Health Personnel Editorials.

25

The Collaborative Project, Bologna—Psychiatry and Primary Care

**D Berardi, G Berti Ceroni, G Leggieri,
A Pezzoli, S Rubini, AR Scaramelli,
A Scardovi, M Vittorangeli & G Ferrari**
University of Bologna, Italy

Most people in the general population who suffer from psychological disorder refer to their general practitioner (GP); almost one-quarter of the patients who visit a GP are affected by a well-defined psychiatric disorder and a similar proportion present psychological problems, as the WHO International Study has shown (Üstün & Sartorius 1995). These psychiatric disorders can be severe and represent one of the most important causes of disability in general practice. However, clinical features, co-morbidity and outcome of psychiatric disorders in general practice are not sufficiently studied and GPs deal with these conditions without well-defined diagnostic criteria and management guidelines. Studies on the epidemiology of psychiatric disorders in primary care and the implementation of effective cooperation between general practice and psychiatric services seem to be among the most important needs in the field of public health in Italy, as in other countries.

Psychiatric facilities in the public sector in Italy are organized on a community basis, after the '180' law of 1978, as is general practice. The administrative unit of the Italian National Health System is the local health unit (LHU), which is designed to answer all health problems, including primary care, in a given territory. However, primary care cannot properly be considered a LHU service, because GPs are private doctors engaged by the LHU on a patient allowance scheme; in this case, the LHU has a coordinating role and sees to reimbursement. The Local Mental Health Service (LMHS) is mainly based on outpatient facilities, is one of the first-level services of the LHU and is mainly fee-free. People are allowed to attend LMHSs directly without the need for referral by GPs. Although LMHS and

Preventing Mental Illness: Mental Health Promotion in Primary Care. Edited by R. Jenkins and T.B. Üstün.
© 1998 John Wiley & Sons Ltd.

general practice are both first-level community facilities, their cooperation is usually limited to the practice of referral, without more specific programs.

In Bologna, several aspects of psychiatric disorders in primary care have been studied: the prevalence and course of psychiatric disorders (Berti Ceroni et al 1992); social predictors of their outcome (Berti Ceroni, Gherardi & Rucci in press); the burden placed upon doctors by the psychological problems of their patients; and the pharmacological treatment of depression (Fioritti et al 1993). In 1992, a group was set up to continue and widen these research studies, composed of the Italian Medical Association (Bologna section), the Italian Society of General Practice, the Institute of Psychiatry of the Bologna University and some of the LMHSs of the Bologna area. The first step was a series of conferences involving 12 psychiatrists and 12 GPs, which focused on identifying problems and needs in the field. Two main conclusions emerged from these meetings: (a) that cooperation based exclusively on the traditional 'referral' system was an inadequate strategy for GPs' real needs; (b) that GPs do not usually receive satisfactory academic training in the recognition, management and treatment of patients with psychiatric problems. As a result of close ongoing collaboration, a specific project called 'The Collaborative Project: Bologna—Psychiatry and Primary Care' was set up. The project consisted of:

1. An epidemiological study to gain current information in the field where the intervention programs were to be developed.
2. A training program designed to improve GPs' communication skills.
3. Effective consultation and liaison in psychiatry.

THE EPIDEMIOLOGICAL STUDY

In Italy, there have been a few epidemiological studies on psychiatric disorders in general practice (Bellantuono et al 1987; Berti Ceroni et al 1992), including the Verona contribution to the WHO Collaborative Study (Piccinelli et al 1995). In these researches a relatively low prevalence of mental disorders was found compared with other European countries.

Out study was conducted in the Bologna municipality and three surrounding sites. Bologna, with a population of some 417 000 inhabitants, is the seventh largest city in Italy and is located in the north-east, covering an area of 141 km^2; San Lazzaro is a suburban area (44 km^2) close to Bologna, with a population of 30 000 inhabitants; San Giovanni in Persiceto is a rural area (115 km^2) 21 km from Bologna, with 23 000 inhabitants; and Imola is a small town (205 km^2) 33 km from Bologna, with roughly 63 000 inhabitants. The Bologna area is one of the wealthiest in Italy and its health services are considered among the best in the country.

Thirty GP clinics were involved, serving a total of some 45 000 patients.* The two-stage epidemiological study followed the same methodology and used the same main instruments as the WHO Collaborative Study; some instruments concerning the severity of psychiatric disorders, nature and severity of physical disease and disability were different; 1647 patients were screened. The most significant results (Berardi et al 1995) concerned the prevalence** of ICD-10 psychiatric disorders in primary care, which was as low as in Verona in the WHO study (12.4%). Both Bologna and Verona are located in north-eastern Italy, where health and social services are among the country's best developed. In our opinion, this could in part explain the low prevalence of psychiatric disorders in primary care in the two towns.

Beyond the ICD-10 cases, 18% of the 1647 screened patients were found to have a sub-threshold condition. One important difference between ICD-10 cases and sub-thresholds, besides the severity of illness, was the initial motivation to consult a physician: pain in sub-threshold and psychological problems in ICD-10 cases. There were no differences between them in respect of health characteristics (including self-perception of health status) or disability.

TRAINING PROGRAMS

A program has been set up to implement and evaluate the efficacy of a specific training course for established GPs, focusing on the recognition and management of psychological problems in primary care (Scardovi et al 1995). Above all, we were interested in seeing whether the Goldberg and Gask training methodology (Goldberg et al 1980; Gask et al 1987, 1988) would be feasible in an Italian context. We worked using video-feedback in a group setting of 11 established GPs, with two psychiatrists as trainers. Videotaped clinical interviews of patients selected by the GPs from their practices were discussed. Three main clinical problems emerged: (a) patients with well-defined psychiatric disorders; (b) patients with somatization of psychological distress; and (c) patients psychologically distressed by intrinsic problems.

Training efficacy was tested following the same evaluation program used by Gask et al (1987, 1988) and the results, after 12 training meetings, were almost the

---

* In urban and suburban areas, GPs shared most of the facilities with other colleagues, while in the rural area and the small town, a larger number of clinics were run by a single GP. The GPs were recruited for participation in the study by the Italian Medical Association (Bologna section), on the criteria that they were well-established physicians, active participants in learning and research programs, and had at least 10 years' experience and 1000 patients.
** This study has shown that 35% of the patients interviewed had an ICD-10 disorder, 45% a sub-threshold disorder and 20% fewer than two symptoms. The estimated prevalence of ICD-10 psychiatric disorders in the overall sample (1647 patients) is 12.4%. The most common diagnoses were generalized anxiety disorder, current depression, neurasthenia and pain disorder. The prevalence of psychological problems was nearly twice as high in females as in males (15.7% vs. 8.2%), this ratio being quite stable across diagnoses but not across age, the 25–44 age group being the most unbalanced.

same as theirs.* The GPs were very satisfied with the experience and all asked for further training, which was considered a good opportunity to select some future trainers from among them. The university clinic psychiatrists were sufficiently satisfied to introduce parts of the training in their regular psychiatry teaching programs targeted at students and residents.

After this first training experience, two major programs were planned: (a) nationwide training held in collaboration with the Italian Society of General Practice and the participation of 26 GPs from every Italian region; and (b) a study in the Bologna area to compare the outcomes of patients treated by trained GPs and by a control group.

CONSULTATION LIAISON PSYCHIATRY

A cooperative programme between GPs and LMHSs has been set up in Bologna, as an alternative to referral (Berti Ceroni et al 1993). The programme consists of case discussion groups between GPs and LMHS psychiatrists, a telephone consultation service and other facilities.

Fifteen GPs, randomly chosen from the 30 participating in the Bologna project, together with four psychiatrists, worked in small groups, meeting every 2 weeks over a 6-month period. Biopsychosocial characteristics of cases identified during the epidemiological study were fully examined and treatment and management strategies were discussed.** In the follow-up carried out 1 year later, the outcomes of the trained GPs' patients were compared with those of the control group patients. Analysis of the data is currently in progress.

An ongoing telephone consultation service was set up to provide GPs with advice in real time during consultations. Experienced psychiatrists from the LMHSs deliver this service; follow-up telephone consultations are usually held with the same psychiatrist to ensure continuity. A specific form has been prepared to record notes made during the telephone consultation.

CONCLUSION

Psychological problems in general practice represent an important public health problem in Italy, as in other countries. New informational and educational

---

* We have evaluated the pre- and post-training correlation between GPs' and patients' ratings of psychological problems (using a six-point rating scale and patients' score on GHQ 12) in a group of seven established GPs. Spearman rho was calculated for each GP before and after the training. The average pre-training Spearman rho was 0.40, and post-training was 0.57. In the Gask study of 1988 the corresponding values, obtained working with a trainee group, were 0.41 and 0.59 respectively.

** Three main characteristics emerged regarding the doctors' approach towards their patients' psychological problems: a) considering physical and emotional problems as alternative rather than complementary; b) having difficulty evaluating the relationships between patients' life events and their clinical disorders; c) collusion at times with patients who avoid speaking about the emotional components of their problems.

materials and programs have been developed to improve the psychiatric skills of GPs, including the British 'Defeat Depression' program, the 'Depression Awareness Recognition and Treatment' (DART) program, the American PRIME-MD (Spitzer et al 1994) and the WHO program (Üstün et al 1995).

In Italy, both LMHSs and general practice are first-level services which *de facto* share the burden of managing many health and social problems in the community. However, their cooperation has been poorly organized. There is now a growing need for effective cooperation from LMHSs and GP associations. The collaborative project 'Bologna—Psychiatry and Prime Care' is aimed at effective integration between these two agencies through the implementation of:

1. Local targeted epidemiological studies.
2. National training programs in communication skills.
3. Regional cooperation programs between LMHSs and GP associations.
4. Educational and informational campaigns, like WHO 'Flip-Cards' (Üstün, personal communication) and the Defeat Depression Campaign.

A training course in communication skills is, in our experience, particularly useful as a first step in collaboration between GPs and psychiatrists because of its potential to increase GPs' confidence regarding psychological problems and to facilitate communication between them and psychiatrists in order to acquire a common language. Effective cooperation programs in the country between LMHSs and GP associations must have a common frame of general purposes, main instruments and evaluation measures, while recognizing and respecting local needs and experiences.

REFERENCES

Bellantuono C, Fiorio R, Williams P & Cortina P (1987) Psychiatric screening in general practice in Italy: a validity study of the GHQ. *Soc Psychiat Psychiat Epidemiol* **22**, 113–17.

Berardi D, Berti Ceroni G, Rucci P, Galgano S & De Marco P (1995) I disturbi psichici nella medicina di base: lo studio epidemiologico di Bologna. Report at the Second National Congress of the Italian Society of Psychiatric Epidemiology (SIEP): La Ricerca Epidemiologica e la Pratica Psichiatrica, Bologna, October 12–14.

Berti Ceroni F, Gherardi S & Rucci P (in press) DSM-III mental disorder in general medical sector: predictors of outcome. *Int J Soc Psychiat.*

Berti Ceroni G, Berti Ceroni F, Bivi R, Corsino MA, De Marco P, Gallo E, Giovannini G, Gherardi S, Pezzoli A, Rucci P & Neri C (1992) DSM-III mental disorders in general medical sector. Follow-up and incidence study over a two-year period. *Soc Psychiat Psychiat Epidemiol* **27**, 234–41.

Berti Ceroni G, Berardi D, Berti Ceroni F, Bivi R, Corsino MA, De Marco P, Ferrari G, Gherardi S, Leggieri G, Neri C, Pezzoli A, Rucci P & Vittorangeli M (1993) General medicine and psychiatry: from epidemiological research to experimental collaboration. Report at the VIth Congress of the International Federation of Psychiatric Epidemiology: Epidemiology in Psychiatry and Mental Health. Lisbon, April 14–17.

Fioritti A, Berardi D, Cervino G, Aiello P & Ferrari G (1993) General practitioners' psychotropic drug prescription in Bologna. *Ital J Psychiat Behav Sci* **3**, 45–50.

Gask L, McGrath G, Goldberg D & Millar T (1987) Improving the psychiatric skills of established general practitioners: evaluation of group teaching. *Med Ed* **21**, 362–8.

Gask L, Goldberg DP, Lesser AL & Millar T (1988) Improving the psychiatric skills of the general practice trainee: an evaluation of a group training course. *Med Ed* **22**, 132–8.

Goldberg DP, Smith C, Steele JJ & Spivey L (1980) Training family doctors to recognise psychiatric illness with increased accuracy. *Lancet* **ii**, 521–3.

Piccinnelli M, Pini S, Bonizzato P, Paltrinieri E, Saltini A, Scantamburlo L, Bellantuono C & Tansella M (1995) Results from Verona Centre. In TB Üstün & N Sartorius (eds) *Mental Illness in General Health Care. An International Study*. Chichester: Wiley.

Scardovi A, Scaramelli AR, Carta G, Sciulli S, Gherardi S, Berti Ceroni F & Ferrari G (1995) Il Programma di Training in Tecniche di Comunicazione Medica. Report at the Second National Congress of the Italian Society of Psychiatric Epidemiology (SIEP): La Ricerca Epidemiologica e la Pratica Psichiatrica, Bologna, October 12–14.

Spitzer RL, Williams JBW, Kroenke K, Linzer M, Verloin deGruy III F, Hahn SR, Brody D & Johnson JG (1994) Utility of a new procedure for diagnosing mental disorders in primary care. The PRIME-MD 1000 study. *JAMA* **272**(22), 1749–56.

Üstün TB & Sartorius N (eds) (1995) *Mental Illness in General Health Care. An International Study*. Chichester: Wiley.

Üstün TB, Cooper JE, Goldberg DP, Simon GE & Sartorius N (1995) A new classification for mental disorders with management guidelines for use in primary care: the ICD-10–PHC. *Br J Gen Pract* (in press).

Education of the Community

26

Public Education in England

A McCulloch

Andrew McCulloch Associates, Enfield, UK
Formerly Assistant Secretary, Department of Health, UK

This chapter explains what we in the Department of Health in England have done to foster public education on mental health issues. I am sure there are lessons which can be learned from both our successes and our failures.

HISTORICAL CONTEXT

Our strategy for mental health promotion in England centres on the Government's health gain strategy set out in the 'Health of the Nation' initiative. This was launched in 1992, and mental health is one of its five 'key areas'. The strategy includes targets for reducing the rate of suicide and for improving the health and social functioning of mentally ill people.

We realized when we launched 'Health of the Nation' that our objectives in the area of mental illness could not be achieved unless the general public was better informed about mental illness. For a long time fear and anxiety have surrounded this subject. Within living memory of a large proportion of our population, mental illness was not a concept which English society really accepted or confronted. Mentally ill people were fundamentally 'different', regarded with fear, suspicion and ridicule. Fears and misunderstandings around issues of inheritance, morality and abnormal behaviour prevailed. I am sure such fears related and still do relate not only to the perceived threat posed by mentally ill people but also to inner fears about madness and loss of control. I am also sure that with improved treatments and the shift away from institutionalized care, which was evident from the late 1950s, there was some change in public attitudes (although evidence is purely anecdotal). However, there is still a long way to go.

THE IMPORTANCE OF PUBLIC ATTITUDES

The launch of 'Health of the Nation' gave a new impetus and focus to efforts to educate the English public about mental illness. The targets it set sharpened our

Preventing Mental Illness: Mental Health Promotion in Primary Care. Edited by R. Jenkins and T.B. Üstün.
Published 1998 John Wiley & Sons Ltd.

understanding and concern about the impact of public attitudes. A lack of proper public awareness and understanding has at least two important effects. It makes life in the community more difficult for people with mental illness if they are regarded with fear and suspicion by their neighbours. It can affect not only their quality of life, but also their prognosis. And if people are not educated to acknowledge that they or members of their families can become mentally ill, and they are able neither to recognize the symptoms nor to admit their significance, then they will find it difficult to seek help. This results in a huge amount of unnecessary misery and probably in preventable suicides and other negative outcomes.

Hence the aim of our modest attempts to start some public information work is to educate the public in their attitudes both to mentally ill people and mental illness itself, their perceptions of others with mental illness and their level of consciousness about their own mental health.

PUBLIC INFORMATION BOOKLETS

The Department of Health launched its first Mental Illness Public Information program in 1993. It was funded to the tune of well over £1 million over 3 years, which may not sound much in comparison with the amounts spent, for example, on discouraging smoking, but did represent a significant new departure.

At the core of our strategy has been our series of mental illness public information booklets (see Box 26.1). These are short, simply written guides aimed at the educated lay reader, as well as service users and carers, the first of which, *Mental Illness; What Does It Mean?*, was launched in the spring of 1993. Others addressed particular aspects of mental illness: suicide, young people, elderly people, mental health in the workplace, and most recently a booklet explaining to people what they themselves can do about mental illness. A specially packed version of the suicide booklet was issued for farmers, who are a high-risk occupational group, and a new booklet about ethnic minority mental health is in preparation.

The booklets, particularly that on suicide, are very relevant to our 'Health of the Nation' targets, and there has been no shortage of takers for them: in 1994 alone we distributed over 2 million copies.

HEALTH EDUCATION AUTHORITY (HEA)

I am pleased to say that the Department is not working alone in its efforts to educate the public about mental illness and mental health. As well as the excellent work done by a number of professional and voluntary sector organizations (and I should like in particular to mention the trail-blazing work of the Mental Health Media Council), the Health Education Authority is now explicitly including mental health promotion as one of its areas of work. Among other things, the HEA co-ordinated central activity in England for World Mental Health Day on 10 October

---

Box 26.1   Mental illness public information booklets

Mental Illness: What Does It Mean?
Mental Illness: Sometimes I Think I Can't Go On Any More
Mental Illness: Can Children and Young People Have Mental Health Problems?
Mental Illness: Mental Health and Older People
Mental Illness: A Guide to Mental Health in the Workplace
Mental Illness: What You Can Do About It

1995. This work had a particular focus on the mental health of young people, which is in line with the theme adopted for the 'Health of the Nation' strategy as a whole.

THE MEDIA

We would be deceiving ourselves if we thought that even the combined efforts of the Department of Health, the HEA and the professional and voluntary sectors could be as powerful in shaping people's perception of mental illness as the popular media. Both the press and television are key sources of information for the vast majority of the population, they reach the widest possible audience and I have to say that in recent years the portrayal of mentally ill people by the popular press in this country had done no-one any favours, least of all mentally ill people themselves. Some newspapers unfortunately see that there is money to be made from prejudice and fear. This has led them to concentrate almost exclusively on negative images of mental illness. They have created, in the complete absence of any scientific evidence, the spectre of an alleged epidemic of violence by mentally ill people.

The large numbers of mentally ill people living safely in their own homes in the community do not make good news stories. The very small numbers of severely mentally ill people who commit acts of violence, and occasionally homicide, almost invariably make the front pages. This is the distorted image of mental illness with which many people in this country are faced on a day-to-day basis.

But the role of the media is not all bad. The quality press, as one would expect, adopt a more responsible and balanced approach. One of the most important and positive media initiatives on mental illness was broadcast in the spring of 1995, when the British Broadcasting Corporation (BBC) ran *States of Mind*, a Social Action Season on Mental Health. As well as radio programs, there was a whole series of TV programs and documentaries promoting a balanced and mature debate on mental illness in England today. In support of this initiative, the Department sponsored the production of *Contact*, a guide to sources of help and information about mental illness, and the BBC distributed on request a resource pack, comprising the best available information literature from a variety of sources.

Box 26.2	Mental illness public information booklets: key evaluation results
Concept	Initiative warmly welcomed
	Target audience perhaps too broad—should focus more on users and carers
Content	Clear, informative and accessible
	Some respondents felt the booklets should be less 'informing' and more 'advising'
Presentation	Cover designs too 'sunny' for the subject
	Bold 'Mental Illness' logo was seen as off-putting
	Typeface not very clear
	Presentation unlikely to attract a 'voluntary' readership
Future work	Should be focused on improving the presentation and appeal of current publications

EVALUATION

How, then, do we know whether our public information work is having the desired effect? As far as the booklets are concerned, the HEA recently carried out an evaluation study on our behalf. They questioned service users, professionals, voluntary workers and the general public to find out what they thought of our publications. The results were encouraging (see Box 26.2). The initiative itself was universally welcomed. Not one person had questioned the worth of spending money to educate people about mental illness, and the information in the booklets themselves was felt to be clear, comprehensive and relevant. Of course, the evaluation identified some room for improvement. Some people felt that the booklets could be more sharply focused—that they should be aimed at users and carers rather than trying to capture everyone. Others had difficulty with the presentation. The designs of the booklets were seen as too 'sunny' for the topic, although paradoxically people were also put off by the bold Mental Illness logo; the latter finding in itself might be an indication that there is still a lot of educating to do. In terms of future work, people felt that we should concentrate on making presentational improvements to the existing booklets to try to encourage more people to read them.

PUBLIC ATTITUDES

Reactions to our booklets can only be a proxy indicator for what we are really trying to achieve—a change in public attitudes to mental illness. The most important tool for measuring this is our annual 'Attitudes to Mental Illness' survey, which was carried out in 1993, 1994 and 1995 asking the same questions of a

---

Box 26.3 Mental illness public attitude surveys. A. Benevolent attitudes*

We need to adopt a far more tolerant attitude toward people with mental illness in our society

Level of agreement: 1993, 92%; 1994, 93%; 1995, 91%

We have a responsibility to provide the best possible care for people with mental illness

Level of agreement: 1993, 94%; 1994, 95%; 1995, 94%

---

* Based on a sample of 2000 adults (aged over 16) selected to be representative of the adult population in Great Britain.

Box 26.4 Mental illness public attitude surveys. B. Understanding of the nature of mental illness

Virtually anyone can become mentally ill

Level of agreement: 1993, 92%; 1994, 91%; 1995, 89%*

One of the main causes of mental illness is a lack of self-discipline and willpower

Level of agreement: 1993, 16%; 1994, 15%; 1995, 13%

---

* Significant at a 95% confidence level.

---

representative sample of 2000 people. The initial 1993 survey gave us a baseline of public attitudes and the subsequent two gave us a sense of the way in which public opinion is or is not shifting.

The results make fascinating reading. Our starting point is the level of public sympathy towards mentally ill people. This is really as high as one could hope, and gives us a fair base on which to build (see Box 26.3). The level of public sympathy seems fairly stable, unlike some of the other figures. Two questions are designed to gauge people's appreciation of the causes and nature of mental illness. However, it is difficult to discern a clear trend. People seem to be increasingly willing to accept that mental illness is not just a function of a weak character, but at the same time marginally fewer seem willing to admit that anyone, and by implication they themselves, can become mentally ill (see Box 26.4). This may be due in part to people's perceptions of what 'mental illness' means. There is some evidence that the term is equated with what we would term *severe* mental illness, and in particular with schizophrenia. Perhaps if we had asked these people whether virtually anyone could become severely depressed, making the link for them, we would have got a rather different answer.

Box 26.5   Mental illness public attitude surveys. C. Giving responsibility to mentally ill people

Anyone with a history of mental health problems should be excluded from public office

Level of agreement: 1993, 30%; 1994, 30%; 1995, 31%

People with mental illness should not be given any responsibility

Level of agreement: 1993, 18%; 1994, 18%; 1995, 19%

Box 26.6   Mental illness public attitude surveys. D. Fear of mentally ill people

People with mental illness are far less of a danger than most people suppose

Level of agreement: 1993, 65%; 1994, 63%; 1995, 63%*

It is frightening to think of people with mental health problems living in residential neighbourhoods

Level of agreement: 1993, 14%; 1994, 16%; 1995, 19%*

_____

* Significant at a 95% confidence level.

As we move onto more specific questions, we can see that people remain reluctant to allow mentally ill people real responsibility, and attitudes here seem relatively static (see Box 26.5). Our own findings were echoed in a recent commercial survey which showed that while only 5% of people thought that mentally ill people should be allowed to become airline pilots, 47% were quite happy for them to become actors and 61% would approve of a mentally ill person sweeping our streets. One area which is of particular concern, and which may well have something to do with the high media profile of rare violent incidents, is the increasing level of fear which people seem to experience in relation to mentally ill people. Fewer people than in 1993 now agree that mentally ill people are less of a risk than is commonly supposed and, more alarmingly, the number who think it is frightening to think of mentally ill people living in residential neighbourhoods has gone up by more than one-third in 2 years (see Box 26.6). It also seems that people's attitudes towards mental illness in their own communities are taking a turn for the worse. This may well be linked with changing perceptions about the potential of mentally ill people to be violent (see Box 26.7).

In conclusion, our survey work seems to show that while levels of sympathy for mentally ill people remain high and understanding of the causes and nature of mental illness seems to be improving, we still need to tackle the increasing levels of

---

Box 26.7   Mental illness public attitude surveys. E. 'Not in my back yard'?

Locating mental health facilities in a residential area downgrades the neighbourhood

Level of agreement: 1993, 19%; 1994, 22%; 1995, 24%*

I would not want to live next door to someone who had been mentally ill

Level of agreement: 1993, 9%; 1994, 8%; 1995, 11%*

No-one has a right to exclude people with mental illness from their neighbourhood

Level of agreement: 1993, 78%; 1994, 76%; 1995, 69%*

---

* Significant at a 95% confidence level.

---

fear and mistrust which many people experience. In particular, we face a challenge in convincing the public that mentally ill people can and should live safely, not just in the community, but in *their* community.

NEXT STEPS AND CONCLUSION

So what, then, are the next steps? We will be revisiting our public information literature in the light of evaluation work, but there is also a need to develop avenues for communicating mental health promotion messages to groups who are perhaps less receptive to the written word. For example, we have been conducting pilot work to explore the possibility of using commercial radio to reach young men and women with suicide prevention messages. Also, we need to work to tackle public fear and suspicion of mental illness.

It is increasingly evident that our public information work must be a long-term commitment. It is also evident that if it is to succeed we must use the full range of means and resources at our disposal. This means working with the HEA, the professions and the voluntary sector. These relationships are already well established. But in the longer term it also means working more closely with the mass media, harnessing its power to convey constructive messages about mental illness rather than destructive ones. The BBC's Social Action Season was an excellent start, but this is an area which will require more work in the future if we are to achieve our aim of a public who are perhaps not so much 'educated' as on a wider level *aware* of the reality of mental illness in our society.

ACKNOWLEDGEMENTS

The author would like to acknowledge the work of the Health Education Authority in evaluating the information booklets and of Taylor Nelson AGTS plc: Research Surveys of Great Britain, who carried out the attitude surveys.

27

Public Education in Africa

A Uznanski

World Health Organization, Brazzaville, Congo

Prevention of mental illness and promotion of mental health are noble aims which will improve global health and quality of life in general. On the other hand, most principles for prevention and promotion are 'general' and 'global'. It is imperative that this global/general approach is brought down to earth and that concrete implementation projects are carried out—and there is nowhere on earth more challenging than the African region for this task. In this chapter I will review the current situation in Africa regarding mental health services, WHO Regional Office activities and the achievement of mental health programs in Africa. In the second part recommendations are outlined for further action in the health sector, health-related sectors of governments and other organizations.

THE CURRENT SITUATION OF MENTAL HEALTH PROBLEMS IN AFRICA

Mental health problems in the African region are characterized by:

1. High prevalence of mental and neurological disorders which affect all age-groups. Their social significance is increased by the fact that they are particularly frequent in children.
2. High prevalence of psychosocial problems, often related to the stress of migration, resettlement and urbanization. Alcohol and drug abuse in particular are recognized in a number of African countries as a problem of rapidly growing importance.
3. Increasing number of people with chronic disability due to mental disorders, e.g. schizophrenia and epilepsy, often having severe secondary social effects on the family.

The psychological aspects of health are still neglected in most African countries because the knowledge necessary for application in this area is still lacking. The

Preventing Mental Illness: Mental Health Promotion in Primary Care. Edited by R. Jenkins and T.B. Üstün.
Published 1998 John Wiley & Sons Ltd.

awareness of the authorities that this is an area of priority in training and service provision is still very inadequate.

In contrast to the magnitude of mental health problems, the mental health infrastructure in the African region, regarding both services and research, is still very weak. Although centres of excellence in mental health research, e.g. university departments, exist in some countries, there are far too few in the region as a whole.

Mental Health Services

Mental Health Services in many African countries were, for many years, low priority. The characteristics of mental health services in Africa are as follows:

1. The mental health facilities in many countries are asylums which are seriously over-crowded; in some instances there is a need to rely on prisons and other custodial institutions.
2. There is a lack of sufficient health personnel, e.g. psychiatrists, nurses, social workers, psychologists and auxiliaries.
3. Lack of mental health components in existing training programs for general health workers and a lack of suitable teaching materials.
4. Lack of interest in, and a negative attitude to, mental health among general health personnel as well as health planners and administrators.
5. Over-centralization, over-specialization and lack of mental health facilities in the rural areas.
6. The undetermined nature and role of traditional and faith-healing facilities.
7. Inappropriate mental health laws in many African countries.

These and other shortcomings exist in the face of increasing demands by an ever-increasing population. However, it needs to be stressed that the general situation is slowly improving.

Response of the African Regional Office of WHO

The situation has been giving the WHO Regional Office some concern and efforts have been mounted to improve mental health services in African countries. Resolution AFR/RC38/R1, adopted by the Regional Committee (1988), laid out some principles on 'Prevention and Treatment of Mental, Neurological and Psychosocial Disorders'. This resolution called on member countries to develop comprehensive mental health programs, which would be community-based, and the establishment of national coordinating bodies.

AFRO is collecting information and appropriate documents on mental health issues and informing countries and is organizing and supporting seminars and workshops on mental health, stressing the role of promotion of mental health, prevention of illnesses, and community-based treatment and rehabilitation of the mentally ill.

It was reported in 1993 that 21 countries had established national mental health programs; a National Mental Health Coordinating Group had been established in 9 countries; the mental health program had been integrated with the primary health care services in 14 countries, and 14 countries had some training activities, while 12 had specific training for the primary health care personnel. Undergraduate curricula had been revised in 14 countries to include a mental health component; 12 countries had revised postgraduate programs, while 19 had revised the curriculum for nursing and social workers' training. There has therefore been appreciable initial momentum in the attempt by African countries to develop community-based primary mental health care. Some countries have progressed, but the overall indication is that a lot more has to be done for the concept to take root.

Recommended Further Actions

The recommendations for preventive action are presented under three headings relating at the operational level to the health sector, health-related sectors of other Ministries and the NGOs, and finally at the strategic (central) level of the national government.

1. Improvement of mental health workers' skills.   Success in carrying out preventive and therapeutic measures in the health sector by the operational health team depends greatly on their psychosocial skills (sensitivity, empathy and ability to communicate) as well as on their knowledge of the community, its system of government, culture and resources. Therefore, training in generic psychosocial skills is no less essential to the education of these workers than is the customary technical training. In addition, without such skills in clinical practice, diagnostic errors multiply, the patient's adherence to treatment recommendations declines, and the health facility will fail to achieve its goals. Among specific measures which can be undertaken by the health sector, the following groups stand out as being particularly timely and promising.
2. Individual health care
   - *Prenatal and perinatal care.* In view of the need to protect the fetus and the newborn child and to provide optimum conditions for development, and in view of the high mortality and morbidity associated with prematurity and low birthweight, high priority should be given to: (a) education about nutrition to all pregnant women in order to prevent cognitive failure in their children; (b) providing pregnant women with information about the importance of immunization and the schedules for immunization for their infants which they should follow.

- *Immunization of children* against measles, poliomyelitis, tetanus and diphtheria would prevent brain damage caused by these diseases.

3. Measures to prevent abuse and dependence on psychoactive substances
   - Health workers should routinely *ask about smoking* and counsel patients against this practice. This simple intervention is as effective as more elaborate measures. Though only 3–5% of patients will respond by stopping smoking, this measure has a large public pay-off in view of the prevalence of smoking in the population. Moreover, repeated efforts to quit have cumulatively higher rates of success: thus, low initial response should not discourage subsequent attempts.
   - Health workers can be trained, using an appropriate short set of questions, to *identify alcohol and drug abuse* early in its genesis, using manuals and guidelines produced and tested by WHO in a number of countries. Brief counselling can help a significant number of patients (although not all) to alter their behaviour before dependence and irreversible damage is produced. Using these same manuals, health workers can also play a key role in mobilizing community action to combat alcohol and drug abuse.

4. Minimizing chronic disability
   - Education of health workers to *recognize sensory and motor handicaps* in children, in the use of prosthetic devices to minimize these handicaps, and about the importance of drawing attention of educational authorities to the existence and frequency of such handicaps, is feasible and can prevent both cognitive under-achievement and social maladjustment.
   - Health workers can and should be trained to *manage febrile convulsions*, to *recognize epilepsy* and to *control seizures* by low-cost anticonvulsant drugs, which would help to minimize damage to the central nervous system from prolonged seizures, reduce accidental injuries (such as burns in epileptics), and reduce the psychosocial invalidism and isolation which results when treatment is not provided.
   - Health workers should be trained to *recognize schizophrenia* and manage it using low-dose antipsychotic drugs, and should provide educational counselling and support to family members to minimize chronicity and avoid the social breakdown syndrome which, if unmanaged, leads to severe social disability.

5. Family health care
   - *Family planning.* In view of the strong evidence that child development is adversely affected when mothers have too many children at too short intervals, and when they are under 15 years of age, education on family planning and access to effective means of contraception are essential elements of maternal and child care.
   - *Prevention of iatrogenic damage.* Health workers can be trained to enquire routinely about psychosocial problems in the course of evaluating new patients. This will enable them to recognize symptoms which are the expression of psychological distress and to avoid overuse of psychotropic

(and other) drugs and the iatrogenic disorders which result from such practices.

6. Community health care
   - *Crisis intervention in primary health care.* In the event of acute loss (e.g. death of a spouse, which increases morbidity and mortality among survivors), evidence in the traditional culture of most African societies during the mourning period shows that group and individual counselling of the bereaved will diminish risk. These measures can be incorporated into health services by short courses of training.

7. Action in health-related sectors
   - *Enriched day-care programs for children.* Retarded mental development and behaviour disorders among children growing up in families unable to provide appropriate stimulation can be minimized by early psychosocial stimulation of infants and by day-care programs of good quality, particularly if such programs involve parents as participants.
   - *Teaching of parenting skills.* A variety of risks to mental health and psychosocial development can result from the lack of parenting skills and parents' insufficient knowledge of children's needs. Urbanization may result in a growing number of young parents without such skills. Therefore, education for parenthood may well have to become a responsibility for public education.
   - *Health education.* Instruction about premarital counselling, family life, sexuality, child development, nutrition, accident prevention and substance abuse are among the subjects most frequently recommended for inclusion in school curricula. A particularly promising area of work is the new strategy to prevent substance abuse in early adolescence by equipping youngsters through group work with the behavioural skills to resist the ubiquitous solicitations to use cigarettes, drugs and alcohol. This approach, which uses the young people themselves as educators of their peers, has proved successful in delaying (and sometimes eliminating) the start of alcohol consumption.
   - *The role of the teacher.* With appropriate training, teachers can play an important role in identifying children: (a) with sensory or motor handicaps; and (b) with mental health problems that have not been detected by the health sector. Collaboration between teacher, parent and health worker is central to the identification and rehabilitation of children with chronic handicaps and in the avoidance of social isolation and other untoward consequences in such cases.
   - *Self-help groups.* These groups, organized by lay citizens, are effective in: (a) reducing the chronicity of certain disorders (e.g. Alcoholics Anonymous); (b) enabling the handicapped to improve their functional ability (e.g. societies organized to help patients with epilepsy); (c) educating the community about the nature of such disorders; (d) playing an advocacy role and facilitating changes in legislation, better resource allocation and

satisfaction of other needs of groups of people with specific disorders. Furthermore, community self-organization for local development has been shown to reduce the psychopathology associated with alienation and helplessness.

- *Role of the media.* Radio, television, newspapers and drama have the potential to play a major role in public health education for the better (e.g. by explaining why sanitation is essential for health) or for the worse (by advertising cigarettes or making smoking look glamorous because heroes and heroines in TV dramas smoke).

- *Cultural and religious forces.* Cultural factors are among the principal determinants of human behaviour. Knowledge of cultural and religious forces can be used by health workers in their efforts to reduce health damaging modes of life. There have already been encouraging experiences in which local religious groups have played a key role in providing a focus for community action on alcohol and drug abuse in some African countries.

- *Collaboration with non-governmental organizations.* Alliance with non-governmental organizations (e.g. local, national and international organizations concerned with mental health, epilepsy and alcoholism) can help to educate the public and supply care to the victims of disease.

8. Action at government level

- An effective prevention program will be possible only if there is a commitment to such a program by the national government and additional resources are provided for this purpose. Such commitment must find its expression in a policy for the prevention and control of mental, neurological and psychosocial disorders, a policy which will be an identifiable part of a comprehensive national health program based on primary health care.

- The implementation of the policy directives will require intersectoral cooperation and the formulation of medium-term program plans developed on a realistic basis. These tasks should be entrusted to a coordinating group on mental health, comprising a broad range of persons—professional psychiatrists, administrators, religious officials, police, teachers, jurists, etc.

- Continuing education of health workers is best organized in provincial health institutions.

- It will also be important to introduce appropriate training about measures for preventing mental, neurological and psychosocial disorders into the curricula of workers in non-health sectors. Mental, neurological and psychosocial disorders constitute an enormous public health burden. Review of the evidence demonstrates that the implementation of a comprehensive program of prevention based on methods currently available could produce a substantial reduction in the suffering and destruction of human potential and the economic loss which they produce. Such a program would attack both the biological and social causes which underlie these disorders. For success, it requires a national commitment and coordinated actions in many social sectors. The establishment of a national mental health coordinating group is particularly useful in this respect.

BIBLIOGRAPHY

1. *World Health Organization Magazine* **August/September**, 1986.
2. Olatawura MO (1986) *Mental Health in the African Region—Present Situation in the Context of Primary Health Care.* Brazzaville: WHO/AFRO.
3. WHO/AFRO (1979) *Mental Health.* Technical Report Series No. 7. Brazzaville: WHO, Regional Office for Africa (AFRO).
4. WHO/AFRO (1974) *The Place of Mental Health in the Development of Public Health Services.* Technical Papers No. 8. Brazzaville: Regional Office for Africa (AFRO).
5. WHO Expert Committee on Mental Health (1975) *Organization of Mental Health Services in Developing Countries.* Technical Report Series No. 564. Geneva: WHO.
6. WHO (1979) *Report of the International Conference on Primary Health Care*, Alma-Ata, USSR, 6–12 September. Geneva: WHO.
7. Newell KW (ed) (1975) *Health By the People.* Geneva: WHO.
8. Djukanovic V & Mach EP (eds) (1975) *Alternative Approaches to Meeting Basic Health Needs in Developing Countries.* Geneva: WHO.
9. Sartorius N (1978) WHO's new mental health programme. *WHO Chron* **32**, 60–62.
10. Leighton AH, Lambo TA, Hughes CC et al (1963) *Psychiatric Disorders Among the Yoruba.* Ithaca, NY: Cornell University Press.
11. Baasher TA & Cederblad M (1968) A child psychiatric study on Sudanese Arab children. *Acta Psychiat Scand* (suppl) **200**.
12. Bash KW & Bash-Liechti J (1969) Studies on the epidemiology of neuropsychiatric disorders among the rural population of the province of Khuzestan, Iran. *Soc Psychiat* **4**, 137–43.
13. Giel R & van Luijk JN (1969) Psychiatric morbidity in a small Ethiopian town. *Dr J Psychiat* **155**, 149–62.
14. WHO (1974) *International Pilot Study of Schizophrenia, Vol 1.* Offset Publication 2, Geneva: WHO.
15. WHO/AFRO (1986) *Problems of Mental Health in the African Region.* Report of a Round Table, Brazzaville, 9–11 July. Brazzaville: WHO.
16. WHO (1984) *Report of a WHO Study Group: Mental Health Care in Developing Countries: A Critical Appraisal of Research Findings.* Technical Report Series No 698. Geneva: WHO.
17. WHO/AFRO (1986) Eight General Programme of Work Documents (AFR/RC36/10). Brazzaville: WHO.
18. WHO/AFRO (1988) *Prevention of Mental, Neurological and Psychosocial Disorders* (Doc. AFR/RC38/4). Brazzaville: WHO.
19. WHO/HQ (1987) *Care for the Mentally Ill* (Doc. WHO/MNH/PO4(87.10)). Geneva: WHO.
20. WHO/HQ (1990) *The Introduction of Mental Health Component into Primary Health Care.* Geneva: WHO.
21. WHO/AFRO (1986) *Accelerating the Achievement of HFA/2000 through Activities at the Local Level* (Doc. RPM9/WP/03 Rev. 3) Brazzaville: WHO.
22. WHO (1981) *Social Dimensions of Mental Health.* Geneva: WHO.
23. Monekosso GL (1989) *The Bamako Initiative: Some Guiding Principles.* Brazzaville: WHO/AFRO.

24. Research Component of Programme 10 Protection and Promotion of Mental Health Report to the AFRO/ACME. Brazzaville: WHO.

25. Monekosso CL (1991) *Meeting the Challenge of African Health Crisis in the Decade of Nineties.* Brazzaville: WHO/AFRO.

26. WHO/AFRO (1990) *Community Mental Health Care Based on the District Health System Approach in Africa.* Brazzaville: WHO/AFRO.

27. Monekosso CL (1989) *Accelerating the Achievement of Health for All Africans: The Three-phase Health Development Scenario.* Brazzaville: WHO/AFRO.

28. WHO/AFRO (1987) *The Role of the District Level in Accelerating Health for All Africans* (Doc. AFR/RC37/TD/1). Brazzaville: WHO/AFRO.

29. WHO/AFRO (1990) *Recommendations for the Development of a Comprehensive National Mental Health Programme* (Doc. No. 0132K). Brazzaville: WHO/AFRO.

28

The Role of the Practice Nurse in Identifying and Managing Depression and Liaising with Voluntary Groups

Cathy Reynolds

Group Practice, Bath, UK

The practice nurse may be well placed to pick up depression presenting in the nurse clinic for various reasons:

- Patients often see nurses as having more time to talk and listen than GPs—and sometimes as more understanding.
- Patients often find themselves in quite exposed situations (e.g. when coming for smear tests) and this can prompt them to communicate.
- A nurse may sense that a patient has something on his/her mind and, while taking care to handle things delicately, can take the opportunity to discuss deep-seated problems.

Practice nurses are not counsellors, but they can use communication skills to listen to patients' problems and decide how to manage the consultation.

LISTENING SKILLS

If nothing else is done, allowing patients to talk may help, because this gives them a chance to 'off-load' and to feel that they have been heard without critical judgement being passed. There is a whole gamut of communication skills that can be used, and the key is to practise them in order to establish which ones might work, e.g.:

- Asking 'open' questions ('How did you feel about that?' rather than 'Did you feel so-and-so about that?').

Preventing Mental Illness: Mental Health Promotion in Primary Care. Edited by R. Jenkins and T.B. Üstün.
© 1998 John Wiley & Sons Ltd.

- Allowing a pause after a question, to make space for a response.
- Maintaining eye contact while listening (putting the notes and the computer to one side).
- Leaning forwards in the chair (while being careful not to invade the patient's space).
- Reflective listening (e.g. 'I didn't sleep last night'—'Oh, so you didn't sleep last night; how long has this been a problem?').
- Watching for non-verbal clues (e.g. monotone voice, downturned face, changes in personal hygiene or grooming, slowness or restlessness).

It is also important to know when to stop the patient and either structure the consultation, decide on a course of action, or retrace a particular issue. If, when the patient leaves the room, the nurse feels 'depressed', there is a good chance that the patient was pretty miserable and has left feeling somewhat better after off-loading his/her depression onto someone else. The nurse has done a good job!

IDENTIFICATION

Not all practice nurses are naturally organized or, if they are, they may not know what skills to use and when, which can leave the consultation a bit 'messy'. The following tools can be used to identify a patient's condition and manage the discussion, and if the nurse uses some—preferably all—of these, the patient stands a better chance of being assessed properly and hence of improving more quickly.

- DSM-IV—This uses a checklist of symptoms of depression which, when the symptoms are added up and a time specified, gives an idea of how depressed the patient is.
- BECU Depression-Inventory, Hospital Anxiety Scale, etc.
- Rating scales can give a score for the patient's depression (i.e. mildly, moderately or severely depressed).
- An estimate of how the patient's symptoms affect the activities of daily living may be important, because different patients have different levels of coping skills.
- And finally, there is no substitute for clinical judgement or 'gut feeling'.

CONSULTING COLLEAGUES

It is a good idea for the nurse to check with colleagues about what has been done, not least because this will help them in turn to off-load. It may also happen that a colleague notices something the nurse has missed, which helps piece the jigsaw together.

Nurses might consider asking about all the symptoms of the DSM-IV when a patient comes in for a full blood count and is tired or communicates 'unhappiness'. Other patients who might be at risk and should be considered are those with a chronic or painful illness, such as asthma, diabetes or arthritis, and elderly people who are isolated and lonely.

It is very important, however, for practice nurses to discuss with the rest of the primary health care team—and in particular the GPs—what groups of patients are going to be identified. There must be agreement about this, or the team may feel unable to cope or to offer effective and satisfactory treatments for the patients. Protocols can be the ideal means for a team to share ideas and consider how to move forward. Where possible the protocols should involve all members of the team, and include identification, management strategies, who will do what, when and for how long, and when it should be reviewed.

MANAGEMENT STRATEGIES

Possible management strategies which can be adopted for depressed patients include the following:

- *Counselling*—where it is important to know what the practice or local counsellor can and cannot do; e.g. some may be very good at bereavement counselling, among other things, but no good on children or relationships.
- *Family therapy*—which usually has to be a special referral.
- *Cognitive therapy*—which can be used by a practice nurse because it involves looking forwards with the patient (which is not harmful to the individual) rather than at the past. Depressed patients often think in a characteristically negative way, and cognitive therapy helps to build self-esteem and turn negative thoughts into positive ones by the use of diaries, problem-solving, goal-setting, etc.
- *Alternative therapies*—exercise (which can have a positive effect by releasing endorphins, producing a 'feel-good' factor and helping release adrenalin and stress), acupuncture, yoga, massage, etc., all have their place, and if the patient has made an informed choice about using one of these, then this too helps restore self-confidence because he/she has done something for him/herself.

Other strategies are antidepressant drugs and contacts with voluntary groups, both discussed below.

VOLUNTARY GROUPS

Increasingly nowadays, various socioeconomic factors result in family members moving away from one another. One unfortunate consequence is that people may not have family or friends nearby to confide in and thus need to rely more and more on voluntary groups for this—who themselves are often working within very minimal budgets. Their advantage is that they can give individuals the chance to 'off-load' as a group, which lets them know that they are not alone and allows them to share their feelings with others who have had similar experiences. They can also help people to build up their social lives again, particularly when social skills have been lost, e.g. because of isolation while caring for a loved one at home.

Two useful voluntary groups are:

- *The Samaritans*—whose advantage is their provision of 24-hour 'drop-in' care. Clients can get to know the care-workers and to trust them. Samaritans can also provide a stand-alone service for people to 'off-load', not only in a crisis but when they are lonely or need counselling. They often act as 'baby-sitter' until the client chooses to speak with the primary health care team.
- *Triumph Over Phobia*—this is a self-help group originally developed by Professor Isaac Marks from the Institute of Psychiatry in London. The advantage of the group is that it attracts everyday people—often businessmen and women—and this helps reduce any stigma. The group helps people with phobias, e.g. those of flying, spiders, open spaces, etc., and with obsessive behaviour, e.g. continual hand-washing. Any of these can disrupt family and working lives, and the group, through very simple measures and support of members, can help overcome the problems.

It is very important for the primary health care team to know what help is available nearby. Not only does this empower patients by providing them with the information they need to make choices about the help they would like to try, but it gives the team's members a basis for feeling that they are doing something positive to help, even if the patient chooses to use the information at a later date.

A useful source of information is the Winchester Help for Health Trust, which has a database from which print-outs can be produced of help available in a particular area.

ANTIDEPRESSANTS

When antidepressants have been prescribed, practice nurses can play a role in aiding compliance, e.g:

- By explaining that antidepressants may be used as adjuncts to other therapies and as a means of setting them on the right track, they can encourage patients to feel positive about starting another therapy once their mood has lifted.
- It is important for patients to know that antidepressants are not addictive, and that they cannot get 'hooked'. They should be told that they are different in this respect from sedatives and tranquillizers.

- It may be helpful to ask patients if they know why the drugs have been prescribed, how long they take to work, and how long the course of treatment is expected to last.
- If a patient does not agree with the diagnosis this can obviously affect compliance, and giving a physical diagnosis may help (e.g. explaining the biochemical effects which depression has on sleep patterns, etc.).
- It is important to explain that the tablets take about 4 weeks to work, and that they may need to be taken for 6 months to prevent a relapse.
- Finally, constant follow-up and monitoring is important if the patient is to 'stick with' their tablets. It is not uncommon for drugs to be given up because of side effects, and it should be explained that these will hopefully wear off as the benefits become apparent, and that after 2 months the patient should feel much better. This is a good time to encourage continued compliance, because stopping the tablets at this stage may induce a relapse.
- The mood of patients should also be assessed again at this point, because once they feel better they may find the insight and energy needed to end their lives.

29

Empowerment and Self-help Initiatives—Enhancing the Quality of Psychosocial Care

Wolfgang Stark

Self-help Resources Centre, Munich, Germany

The concept of empowerment is to enable individuals to take control of their own lives and their situations in a social environment. The ability of a person to control his/her own life (Illich 1982; Hoff & Hohner 1983; Kieffer 1989; Gronemeyer 1988) is an important premise for emotional and psychosocial well-being. This concept of empowerment is reversing and reinterpreting traditional goals and concepts of social and health care: the focus is no longer on deficits of people or settings which are to be cured or prevented. A social policy of empowerment (Rappaport 1981) focuses on processes which enhance the participation of the individual in planning and implementing his/her needs for health care.

It is not easy to define empowerment, for we are used to the semantics of needs, weaknesses and deficits. The absence of empowerment is quite comprehensible for us: powerlessness, learned helplessness, alienation, loss of sense of control over one's life. 'Empowerment' therefore requires a radical change in our comprehension of psychosocial and health issues. Focusing on the strength of (re)gaining control over one's life, empowerment:

(1) Refers both to the phenomenological development of a certain state of mind (e.g. feeling powerful, competent, worthy of esteem, etc.) and to the modification of structural conditions in order to reallocate power (e.g. modifying the society's opportunity structure)—in other words, empowerment refers both to the subjective experience and the objective reality; and (2) is both a process and a goal (Swift & Levin 1987).

From a community study on the empowerment process of poor citizens, Kieffer (1980, p 18) derived the following dimensions of empowerment:

Preventing Mental Illness: Mental Health Promotion in Primary Care. Edited by R. Jenkins and T.B. Üstün.
© 1998 John Wiley & Sons Ltd.

1. Development of a more positive and potent sense of self (self-concept).
2. Construction of knowledge and capacity for more critical comprehension of the web of social and political relations which comprises one's experienced environment.
3. Cultivation of resources and strategies, or more functional competence, for efficacious and protective attainment of personal and collective socio-political goals.

Empowerment does not aim at any specific outcome or at normative goals. The process for a single elderly person resisting placement in a nursing home may look very different to that for a young single mother struggling through life, for people in a mutual aid group on chronic diseases, or a group of citizens trying to protect their homes from a new housing development plan. Empowerment processes are not run or controlled by professionals, they occur in everyday life among all kinds of people, groups and structures; although there are situations and conditions which either foster or hinder the process.

Empowerment means to develop a sensitivity for strengths in people and settings. The work with self-help groups is an extraordinarily valuable and helpful setting for learning more about empowerment on different levels.

SELF-HELP GROUPS—AN APPROPRIATE AREA FOR LEARNING MORE ABOUT EMPOWERMENT AND ENHANCING THE QUALITY OF PSYCHOSOCIAL CARE

Various questions have been asked about self-help and mutual aid groups, why people gather in such groups and what kinds of benefits they receive through their activity. Professionals, politicians and social scientists have initiated numerous studies to assess the potential of this new social movement and to find out how to handle mutual aid groups from a professional point of view. One of the major background interests can be stated within the following questions: Is this kind of non-professional action going to be in competition with our professional services? Is it really for the good of the people if they just get together and try to solve sometimes severe social and psychological problems without professional expertise? How can we use the innovative resources of mutual aid groups to enhance the compliance of our clients toward our professional services?

These questions indicate that there has been considerable confusion among professionals about the emergence of a self-help movement. This has led to divergent reactions on both sides:

- Some professionals and institutions ignore mutual aid as a serious alternative or supplement to professional services (this is true for many traditionally orientated psychotherapists).

- Others—especially medical doctors—try to co-opt mutual aid groups as a new kind of prescription for difficult clients (you realize this whenever people call and say, 'My doctor asked me to join a self-help group').

The mutual aid group's side shows similar divergencies, i.e. groups which:

- Remain distinct from the professional system and try to establish service systems on their own (i.e. most of the 'Anonymous' groups).
- Still have a strong orientation toward professional services. They tend to be dominated by professionals and are often serving as another (low-cost) deficit-orientated approach indirectly sold by professionals.
- Challenge the professional system trying to shape traditional services according to their needs.

Despite the fact that mutual aid and/or self-help represents a patchwork of different groups with a variety of interests and orientations, the movement has started to change things in the sociopolitical area. The self-help movement has lost its innocence—it means more than pure mutual help of individuals sharing certain problems or illnesses. Mutual aid groups and other forms of self-organization are viewed as a considerable sociopolitical force by professionals and politicians, and this fact is put to good account by the groups in their efforts to avoid being tossed around by the traditional sociopolitical forces.

The power and energy of self-organization in mutual aid groups is based upon what Frank Riessman called the 'self-help ethos'. Its most important dimensions are:

- A non-competitive, cooperative orientation.
- Being helped through helping (the helper-therapy principle).
- A shared, often circulating leadership.
- Offering help *not* as a scarce commodity to be bought and sold.
- A critical stance toward professionalism, which means an emphasis on the 'prosumer'—i.e. the consumer as a producer of help and services.
- The recognition that the group is the key—that de-isolation is critical.
- An accent on empowerment—the control over one's own life (see Riessman 1986, p 59).

The topics of self-help initiatives (SHI) represent more than the private issues of their members. SHIs raise new social issues which are or have been neglected by traditional institutions or by social policy.

Many examples, like the women's movement or mutual aid groups of the disabled or the chronically ill have shown this in the past. SHIs view social and health problems in a more holistic way—they realize, for instance, the psychosocial aspects and consequences of medical diseases. They emphasize the necessity to control one's own life, especially in times of major crises, instead of using specialized passive care provided by traditional professional services.

A recent study we conducted in Munich showed (Engelhardt et al 1985) that SHIs:

- Serve as an early detector for current and new psychosocial problems.
- Build comprehensible social networks for their members where they feel safe and appreciated.
- Are activating their members to foster and enhance their individual abilities.
- Use traditional professional knowledge, but overcome their weaknesses by developing new creative ideas for social support.
- Develop problem-orientated forms of cooperation with professionals and corresponding networking and organizational structures.

Furthermore, a study of cost–benefit effects of SHIs showed that the SHI in Munich alone provided social support worth more than 35 million DM per year (more than £15 million).

Counselling is also a growing part of the work of self-help initiatives. As a part of the Munich Public Health Research Network we are conducting a study into the different approaches of self-help initiatives and professional services when they provide counselling. The reason for this study was because the Munich Self-help Resources Centre realized that self-help initiatives—especially in the health area— are increasingly used by the general public as counselling agencies for particular problems. That means that people are increasingly relying on self-help initiatives instead of professionals to solve their problems.

SHIs serve also as an innovative power for professional services. Numerous examples show that SHIs are not only adopted as a new resource for the clients of professional services, they also inform the latter about the topics they have to deal with in the future; they add to the quality of psychosocial care by developing new forms of social support.

In addition, SHIs are increasing the opportunities to participate in public policy decision-making and are fostering citizen participation. SHIs have shown in the last 10 years that they have the potential to add valuable resources and knowledge to a variety of advisory boards on social and health issues, public hearings and other events. Thereby they are able to shape local and state politics. At the same time SHIs promote citizen participation within neighbourhoods, organize cooperative planning of social services and provide a basic opportunity structure for their members and others so that 'ordinary' people can make a difference without having to be dependent on large institutions or policy-makers.

This kind of 'new populism', which creates processes of empowerment, provides new opportunities and risks. On the one hand, there is a chance that SHIs contribute to a much more direct and sharing democracy than we currently have. They can provide a fertile ground for actively shaping public opinion on certain, often marginalized, topics. They are also creating a political atmosphere of tolerance and empowerment.

On the other hand, SHIs—because of their amateur status—can easily be coopted by major social forces and large welfare or health institutions. Therefore, an appropriate infrastructure and an advocacy mentorship is necessary to foster empowerment within these groups.

What we have learned from our broader work within the Munich Self-Help Resource Centre is that it is necessary to work on three different levels in order to enhance and maintain empowerment processes (Stark 1996): sociopolitical impact; group-enhancing and neighbourhood projects; and detecting and promoting individual strengths. Each level linked with each other is necessary to initiate empowerment processes and social change. The combination of the three creates unique resources and enhances the strengths on each level. It also helps to prevent the weaknesses and restrictions connected with specific types of action or research, be it political work, grass-roots activism, conducting a scientific study, or just providing professional services.

Empowerment in this sense is a very fragile yet durable process. It requires specific types of support, providing space for reflection and discovery. There is also a need for a structure of everyday life which allows us to shape situations, physical environment or social institutions. If we want everybody to be an active and reflective member of his/her community (and once again this seems to be one of the important preventors of health and mental health problems) there have to be various kinds of resources to rely on—financial, interactive or emotional. We still know very little about the processes and conditions which foster or hinder community participation and empowerment.

EMPOWERMENT AND THE PROFESSIONAL'S ROLE

If we talk about the role of professionals, perhaps the first and most important task for professionals, if they want to adopt an empowerment perspective in their work, is learn to ask questions rather than give answers. It is necessary to distinguish the kinds of questions relevant to psychosocial phenomena—questions which either enhance the empowerment process of people, settings and structure, or which tend to pacify. These different types of questions can be called 'needs-questions' and 'resources-questions': The 'needs-question' tends to fit into our socialization towards a society of needs and quick fulfillment. 'What are the needs of a person or a situation?' is, at the same time, a pacifying question. It implies that if one is successful in satisfying needs, the process has already come to an end. The corresponding action for the person in need is 'waiting'—which most often means passivity.

If you ask for resources inherent in a person or a situation, you are asking for things you could use in the future. If you ask for situations that cause scarcity, and the lack of resources makes life hard for the people or prevents the enhancement of their potential, you are not only asking for 'what is', but also for the causes and the background. And, most important, you start a process without controlling the outcome, you tackle the curiosity of the people. Here, the corresponding action type is 'searching'. You are starting a process which is expanding, because searching cannot be restricted to one individual, you have to be in contact with people and settings.

We have to develop a sensitivity for strengths in people and settings. In order to enhance and expand these strengths in the sense of initiating empowerment, connections are necessary between people, groups, institutions and the social environment. There have to be possibilities to shape these connections and linkages, for this will change and enhance both people and settings.

There are thus three ways to support empowerment processes professionally:

1. To provide and to foster opportunities of linking people and groups in order to start a process of sharing experiences and organizing and shaping people's own lives and their social environment.
2. To emphasize especially intermediary lines between the different levels of empowerment. To initiate exchange between these levels and make it possible to influence one another is one of the most important parts of fostering empowerment processes. To establish linkages between these different levels also means enhancing community participation.
3. To re-analyse our own profession and find out where we are encouraging empowerment processes on different levels; and, even more important, where we are stopping those processes from happening by professional routines, language and the traditional helper–helpee relationship.

Perhaps the most important part is to identify our own resources as professionals and enhance them in a transactional way with our clients. Therefore, we have to redirect ourselves from a client orientation towards a consumer orientation (where the consumer shares equal rights with the provider) and even towards a prosumer orientation (where we have to learn that in many cases consumers are better off providing their own services).

In sum, professional community psychology work on empowerment often means a very indirect way of working with people. It is working with people, but with people in context.

Mankind until now has spent an incredible amount of time and energy controlling and exploiting our natural resources. Maybe now, at the turn of the century, the time has come to develop and foster primarily human resources. Human resources and power will be productive under conditions of freedom and promotion. This requires the courage to initiate processes which are not totally predictable or even evaluable. Perhaps this constitutes the future role for professionals in the human services: to be infectious for empowerment and sometimes even cause epidemics.

REFERENCES

Engelhardt HD, Simeth A & Stark W (1995) *Was Selbsthilfe leistet.* Freiburg: Lambertus.

Gronemeyer M (1988) *Die Macht der Bedürfnisse. Reflexionen über ein Phantom.* Reinbek: Rowohlt.

Hohner HU & Hoff EH (1983) Prävention und Therapie. Zur Modifikation von objektiver Kontrolle und Kontrollbewußtsein. *Psychosozial* **20**.

Illich I (1982) *Vom Recht auf Gemeinheit.* Reinbek: Rowohlt.

Kieffer C (1980) Empowerment: an alternative approach to prevention. Ann Arbor: University of Michigan, unpublished paper.

Kieffer C (1984) Citizen empowerment: a developmental perspective. *Prevent Hum Serv* **3**, 9–27.

Rappaport J (1981) In praise of paradox: a social policy of empowerment over prevention. *Am J Comm Psychol* **9**, 1–25.

Riessman F (1986) The new populism and the empowerment ethos. In HC Boyte & F Riessman (eds) *The New Populism: The Politics of Empowerment.* Philadelphia: Temple University Press.

Stark W (1996) *Empowerment. Neue Handlungsmöglichkeit für die psychosoziale Praxis.* Freiburg: Lambertus.

Swift G & Levin G (1987) Empowerment: an emerging mental health technology. *J Prim Prevent* **8**, 71–8.

Early Identification:
Case-finding/Screening
Instruments in Primary Care

30

A Diagnostic Aid for Detecting Multiple Mental Disorders—The Symptom-driven Diagnostic System for Primary Care (SDDS–PC®)*

Myrna M Weissman,[1] W Eugene Broadhead,[2] Mark Olfson,[1] Andrew C Leon,[3] Christina Hoven[1] and Andreas M Pleil[4]

[1] *College of Physicians and Surgeons of Columbia University and New York State Psychiatric Institute;* [2] *Broadhead Family Practice, Yancyville, NC, and Duke University Medical Center, Durham, NC;* [3] *Cornell University Medical College, New York;* [4] *The Upjohn Company, Kalamazoo, MI, USA*

A high rate of undiagnosed mental disorders in primary care has been well documented for nearly three decades (Shepherd, Cooper & Brown 1966; Regier, Goldberg & Taube 1978; Regier et al 1993; Goldberg et al 1980; van Hermert et al 1993; Olfson & Klerman 1992; Barrett et al 1988). Failure to recognize mental illness has been shown to lead to undertreatment, greater impairment, and a longer duration of illness (Ormel et al 1990). The few efforts to change the diagnostic practice of primary care physicians, either through providing information from a patient screen completed prior to the physician visit or through physician education, have provided equivocal results (Higgins 1994; Rand, Badger & Goggins 1988; Goldberg et al 1980). The effects of improved physician recognition on decreasing patients' health care use have also been equivocal, probably because there are many steps between recognition and patient outcome. These steps include accurate diagnosis, proper treatment, patient compliance, and timely follow-up with adjustment in treatment as needed.

Efforts to improve detection of mental disorders have concentrated on developing patient screens, which usually include a list of psychiatric symptoms

---

* Portions of this material appeared in Weissman et al 1995; Broadhead et al 1995; and Olfson et al 1995. Permission has been granted to reproduce this material. Copyright 1995, American Medical Association.

Preventing Mental Illness: Mental Health Promotion in Primary Care. Edited by R. Jenkins and T.B. Üstün. Published 1998 John Wiley & Sons Ltd.

TABLE 30.1 The SDDS–PC®: a diagnostic aid for multiple mental disorders in primary care

Screening questionnaire screens patients according to six subscales	Select appropriate diagnostic modules	Six possible diagnostic modules conduct selected interview(s) from:	Confirm diagnosis	Longitudinal tracking form use to follow changing patient symptom profile
	→	1. Major depression		
		2. Panic disorder	→	
		3. Alcohol abuse/ dependence		
		4. Generalized anxiety disorder		
		5. Obsessive- compulsive disorder		
		6. Suicidal ideation		

From Olfson et al 1995, by permission. Copyright © American Medical Association.

independent of specific diagnoses (Goldberg et al 1980; Borgquist et al 1993; von Korff et al 1987), or which screen for one diagnosis—depression or alcoholism (Selzer 1971; Babor et al 1992). The former approach is limited because symptoms are not directly related to a treatable disorder; the latter is also limited because patients may have more than one treatable psychiatric disorder (Kessler et al 1994). Moreover, screens are not widely used in primary care (Nelson & Berwick 1989). Because most primary care visits are 15 minutes long or less, there is a need to develop rapid assessment methods that can be incorporated into routine care (Barrett 1991; Mitchell, Schurman & Cromwell 1988; Anderson & Mattsson 1989).

The diagnostic process for mental disorders, however, does not end with the results of a patient-completed screen. There is a need for a next stage, an interactive process with the patient to follow up the positive screen results, clarify symptoms, confirm the diagnosis and decide what action to take.

The Symptom-Driven Diagnostic System for Primary Care (SDDS–PC®) (Pharmacia-Upjohn Co, Kalamazoo, Michigan) was developed in an attempt to fill the gaps in methods of detecting and diagnosing mental disorders in primary care. The three sequential components of the SDDS–PC® are the screening questionnaire, the diagnostic module interviews, and the longitudinal tracking form (Table 30.1). They are used together to assist the primary care physician in making an appropriate diagnosis and evaluating ongoing treatment. The system adapts structured diagnostic interviewing to primary care. These methods are commonly used in psychiatric research and have more recently been used in clinical psychiatric settings (Klerman 1990).

The patient self-administered screening instrument was developed and tested for six diagnoses seen in primary care—major depression (MDD), generalized anxiety disorder (GAD), panic disorder, obsessive-compulsive disorder (OCD), and alcohol and drug abuse and dependence—as well as for detection of suicidal ideation or attempts (see Broadhead et al 1995 for a complete description of the screen results). Next, brief structured diagnostic interviews were developed with patients who screened positive for these disorders. The purpose of the first-stage screen is to separate out normal from potentially abnormal cases, rather than to establish a diagnosis (comparable to a mammography). The purpose of the diagnostic modules is to follow up the potentially abnormal cases to clarify the symptoms, make a diagnosis, and determine the next steps (if any) to management (comparable to a biopsy). Finally, a longitudinal tracking form was developed to follow patients' symptoms and impairment over subsequent visits.

Although structured diagnostic interviewing methods have a long history in psychiatry (Klerman 1990), with the exception of a recently reported project by Spitzer and colleagues (Spitzer et al 1994), to our knowledge this is the first time that these methods have been adapted for primary care. This chapter begins by reviewing the initial testing of the screen and physician-administered diagnostic interviews portion (the diagnostic modules) in two separate studies. Then new developments in the SDDS–PC® system are described. These developments include a computerized nurse, rather than the physician-administered interview which was tested in a third study, and a computer-assisted telephone interview (CATI), currently under testing. Both were developed to meet the constraints on physicians' time in primary care.

THE SDDS–PC® SCREENING QUESTIONNAIRE

The SDDS–PC® screening questionnaire originally consisted of 62 items and was later reduced to 54 items in the second study, with 16 core items used in scoring. The screening questionnaire is self-administered by the patient in the waiting room prior to the medical visit. Results are entered into a personal computer by a health care worker and automatically scored. The computer administration speeds processing of the clinical information, but limits the utility of the system to practices with access to a personal computer. In addition to the screening symptoms, three impairment questions are completed by the patient, which address the patient's overall state of mental health, work impairment and social functioning.

Six types of mental disorders commonly seen in primary care—major depression, panic disorder, alcohol and drug abuse and dependence, generalized anxiety disorder (GAD), and obsessive-compulsive disorder (OCD), along with suicidal ideation—are simultaneously screened.

The screening component of the SDDS–PC® has been investigated through three separate studies. The first, a preliminary validation study, screened 937 primary care patients in a Rhode Island family practice (Broadhead et al 1995). Of these, 388 patients received a diagnostic interview, the SCID-P (Structured Clinical Interview for the DSM-III-R, version P; Williams et al 1992; Spitzer et al 1992), administered by a mental health professional who was blind to the SDDS–PC® results. Table 30.2 shows the sensitivity (the proportion of all patients with a

TABLE 30.2 Scale operating characteristics for the SDDS–PC® screen preliminary validation study

Scale	Sensitivity (%)	Specificity (%)	PPV (%)	NPV (%)
Major depression ($n = 61$)	90	77	40	98
Panic disorder ($n = 27$)	78	80	21	80
Alcohol abuse/dependence ($n = 12$)	62	98	54	99
Generalized anxiety disorder ($n = 12$)	90	54	5	99
Obsessive-compulsive disorder ($n = 8$)	65	73	5	99
Suicidal ideation ($n = 70$)	43	91	51	88

Operating characteristics data from Broadhead et al 1995. © 1995, American Medical Association.

PPV = positive predictive value; NPV = negative predictive value; n = number of patients with this SCID-P diagnosis.

TABLE 30.3 Patient impairment and SDDS–PC® screen status—preliminary validation study

Impairment measure	SDDS–PC® screen positive (%)	SDDS–PC® screen negative (%)
Fair or poor emotional health	39***	4
Missed work or school due to emotional problems (past month)	16**	4
Not getting along with partner	13*	5
Endorsed one or more of above	48***	12

From Broadhead et al 1995, with permission. © 1995, American Medical Association.

Ns vary due to absence of a partner and non-response from 119 to 137 SDDS–PC® screen negative cases and 204–247 for SDDS–PC® screen positive cases. *$p < 0.05$, **$p < 0.0005$, ***$p < 0.0001$.

disorder who are correctly identified by the screen), specificity (the proportion of all patients without a disorder who are correctly identified by the screen), positive predictive value (PPV) (the proportion of all patients who screen positive that have the disorder), and the negative predictive value (the proportion of all patients who screen negative that do not have the disorder) for each of the six scales. The low PPVs and GAD and OCD may limit the general utility of these screens in unselected primary care samples.

In the first study, patients also received a standard screen for depression: the eight-item Medical Outcomes Study (MOS) brief depression screener (Burnam et al 1988). The results of the study indicate that the operating characteristics of the four-item SDDS–PC® depression screen (sensitivity = 90, specificity = 77, PPV = 40, NPV = 98) are comparable with the eight-item MOS screener (sensitivity = 79, specificity = 90, PPV = 51, NPV = 97) at the recommended cutscore. These findings lend criterion-related validity to the SDDS–PC® depression screen. Table 30.3 shows that as compared with patients who screened negative, those who

TABLE 30.4 Scale operating characteristics for the SDDS–PC® screen cross-validation study

Scale	Sensitivity (%)	Specificity (%)	PPV (%)	NPV (%)
Major depression (n = 47)	67	83	43	93
Panic disorder (n = 16)	65	84	20	98
Alcohol abuse/dependence (n = 10)	38	99	60	97
Generalized anxiety disorder (n = 14)	85	60	11	99
Obsessive-compulsive disorder (n = 10)	24	81	5	96
Suicidal ideation (n = 34)	63	92	48	95

Data from Broadhead et al 1995.

PPV = positive predictive value; NPV = negative predictive value; n = number of patients with this SCID-P diagnosis. Any disorder excludes suicidal ideation.

screened positive for at least one SDDS–PC® disorder had a significantly greater likelihood of reporting occupational impairment, marital distress and fair or poor overall emotional health.

The second study, a cross-validation, involved 775 primary care patients in Rhode Island and South Carolina family practices, 257 of whom received the SCID-P. Independent replication in this sample shows attenuated but acceptable operating characteristics for most of the scales (Table 30.4). Because screen items were selected for optimal operating characteristics in the first study, some decrease in screen performance was to be expected during the cross-validation study.

A third screen validation study (to be described), using DSM-IV criteria and involving 1001 primary care patients, has been recently completed at Kaiser Permanente in Oakland, California.

The SDDS–PC® Diagnostic Modules

The diagnostic process does not end with the results of a patient-completed screen. Physicians must then establish an interactive communication with their patients to clarify the implications of the symptoms reported on the SDDS–PC® screen. To help facilitate this process, brief structured diagnostic interviews, termed diagnostic modules, were developed for use with patients screening positive on the SDDS–PC® screening questionnaire scales.

The diagnostic modules were developed to be administered by a primary care physician, but clinical experience has shown that other health care professionals can administer the modules as well. The modules used in this study are based on the American Psychiatric Association Diagnostic and Statistical Manual, third edition, revised (DSM-III-R) criteria (American Psychiatric Association 1987). Each interview is completed in less than 5 minutes, and includes questions to determine the presence and duration of symptoms as well as the algorithms for DSM-III-R

TABLE 30.5 Scale operating characteristics for the SDDS–PC® diagnostic interview modules

Scale	Sensitivity (%)	Specificity (%)	PPV (%)	NPV (%)
Major depression ($n = 47$)	57	86	80	72
Panic disorder ($n = 62$)	39	88	46	84
Alcohol abuse/dependence ($n = 8$)	–	100	–	88
Generalized anxiety disorder ($n = 97$)	38	81	15	94
Obsessive-compulsive disorder ($n = 51$)	0	96	0	92
Suicidal ideation ($n = 72$)	79	73	59	88

Data from Weissman et al 1995.

PPV = positive predictive value; NPV = negative predictive value; n = number of patients who completed the SCID-P and diagnostic interview module for that diagnosis. Calculations were not completed in empty cells because of the limited sample size.

criteria. Each module also provides relevant information about related subsyndromal conditions and common general medical disorders that may mimic the mental disorder in question.

Based on the clinical data gathered during the module interview, the physician makes a clinical judgement as to the diagnosis. While it is possible to accept the diagnosis based solely on the criteria evaluation, the physician has wide latitude in accepting or rejecting criteria-based diagnoses. It is recommended that clinical judgement, medical considerations, and knowledge of the individual patient be factored into the diagnostic process, with the module serving as an aid in developing a final diagnosis.

The diagnostic modules were pilot-tested concurrently in the sample used for the SDDS–PC® screen cross-validation study (Weissman et al 1995; Olfson et al 1995). Of the 775 patients completing the screen, 246 received at least one physician-administered diagnostic module and 158 received at least one diagnostic module and the independent SCID-P interview.

Most of the diagnostic modules exhibited acceptable agreement with the results of the structured diagnostic interview (Table 30.5). However, the operating characteristics varied across specific diagnoses. The low prevalence of GAD in the study sample may have limited the PPV for this scale. Similarly, the sensitivities and PPVs for alcohol abuse and dependence and OCD were incalculable or unacceptable, perhaps due in part to the low sample prevalence.

One possible source of disagreement between the SDDS–PC® module diagnoses and the SCID-P diagnoses is that in interpreting module data, physicians may have incorporated considerations of non-psychiatric causes of the patient's psychiatric symptoms. On the other hand, some physicians may have failed to rule out medical sources of the patient's psychiatric symptoms which were subsequently uncovered on the SCID-P interview.

Following the second study, a survey of the participating physicians was conducted to evaluate their experience with the modules. The diagnostic modules were reported to be useful by 15 of the 16 participating primary care physicians. Thirteen of the physicians stated that the modules helped them to become aware of at least one previously unrecognized psychiatric problem in their practice. Four of the physicians thought that the interviews were too time-consuming.

Physician diagnoses of a mental disorder were highly correlated with patient impairment ratings. As compared to patients who did not receive a module diagnosis, patients who received a module diagnosis missed work or school more frequently during the past month because of an emotional problem (40% vs. 15%); were not getting along well with their partner (27% vs. 13%); and rated themselves as in fair or poor emotional health (47% vs. 24%). The association between independent patient impairment ratings and module-derived mental disorder diagnoses supports the criterion validity of the diagnostic modules.

The identification of mental disorders with diagnostic modules was also strongly associated with mental health care intervention reported by the physicians on a physician action form at the time of the index medical visit. More than three-quarters (82%) of the patients who received a module diagnosis ($n = 76$) received some mental health intervention from their primary care physician. In contrast, only about one-third (36%) of the module-negative patients ($n = 146$) received such an intervention. The mental health interventions provided by primary care physicians to module-positive patients were usually verbal interventions, such as listening to problems (65%), giving advice (53%), or counseling the patient (40%), but sometimes included the prescription of a psychotropic medication (33%), or referral to a mental health professional (21%).

The SDDS–PC® Longitudinal Tracking Form

A longitudinal patient tracking system has been developed and is being pilot-tested. The longitudinal tracking form charts the symptoms of patients who meet diagnostic criteria, as well as those patients with subsyndromal conditions who fail to meet full diagnostic criteria but nonetheless warrant clinical monitoring.

The tracking form is a computer-generated one-page symptom and impairment summary which is placed in the patient chart prior to each successive medical visit. It provides the physician with a current description of the patient's symptoms, an historical overview of how the symptom pattern has changed over time, and a clinical global improvement scale. Such information may prove valuable in the ongoing process of reassessment and treatment readjustment which characterizes high quality clinical care.

Study 3: Nurse Administered Diagnostic Interviews

Further development and testing of the SDDS–PC® screen and diagnostic modules has been recently completed on a sample 1001 patients, ages 18–70 years, at Kaiser

Permanente, Oakland, California, a large prepaid group practice (Leon et al 1996; Weissman et al, submitted; Hoven et al, in preparation; Olfson, Weissman & Broadhead 1995). For this study, the modules were modified to accommodate the time concern expressed by some of the physicians in the second study. The wording, layout, and presentation of the diagnostic modules was made more efficient. Module questions were further updated according to the DSM-IV (American Psychiatric Association 1994). In this study, the modules were administered by registered nurses and then computer scored. The information was given to physicians on a one-page summary form listing positive symptoms and computer-generated provisional diagnosis based on the interview data. The physicians then used this information and the responses to each question to make the final diagnosis.

A brief description of the protocol design follows. Each patient completed the screening form. A nurse administered structured diagnostic interviews. An assessment was conducted by the patient's primary care physician. Finally, a structured diagnostic interview was administered over the telephone by a mental health professional.

The SDDS–PC® screening form achieved acceptable operating characteristics with respect to the nurse-administered structured diagnostic interview for each of the six disorders (sensitivity, 50.0–88.5; specificity, 82.1–99.6; positive predictive value, 14.7–60.0; and negative predictive value, 94.5–99.4) (Leon et al, submitted). These findings compare favourably with several commonly used medical screening tests.

The nurse-administered diagnostic interviews also demonstrated acceptable agreement with the physician diagnoses and with the structured telephone interview diagnoses. Patients who scored positive on the SDDS–PC® reported significantly poorer emotional health and were significantly more likely to report occupational impairment and marital distress than patients who scored negative. Many of the patients diagnosed by the physicians with the aid of the SDDS–PC® reported never having been previously told by a physician that they had an emotional problem or an addictive disorder. This third study provides additional evidence to support the diagnostic accuracy and clinical utility of the DSM-IV SDDS–PC® in primary care practice. Research is currently being planned to examine the effects of the DSM-IV SDDS–PC®, including its longitudinal tracking form on critical patient outcomes, and to study the administration of the SDDS–PC® via computerized automated telephone interviewing.

Computer-assisted Telephone Interview (CATI)

SDDS–PC® is currently available in three formats: pen/paper patient self-report for batch entry; computer-based clinical interview; and computer-assisted telephone interview (CATI). The pen/paper and computer-based direct entry systems require a certain level of resource commitment in personnel and technology that not all health care providers may have. A CATI application was developed to provide access to the SDDS–PC® system to those providers who lack either sufficient computer capability or staff to assist patients in filling out forms, or who have unique requirements that make other applications impractical.

The CATI system allows on-site or off-site (including in the patient's home) screening and diagnostic interviewing to occur using a touch-tone telephone. The results are stored on a centrally located computer. Based on screening responses, diagnostic interviews are administered and all results are sent via facsimile directly to the physician.

This approach to using SDDS–PC® in a primary care environment overcomes the prevalent limitations inherent to a computer-based system. However, there are additional considerations regarding a CATI application's usefulness in clinical practice. An initial usability study recently completed (Barr & Pleil 1995) indicated that both practitioners and patients found the CATI to be an acceptable approach to diagnostic screening for mental health problems. However, further studies are needed to evaluate the CATI in different environments and under different conditions.

CONCLUSION

Growing pressure in the USA and elsewhere to contain health care expenditures and limit access to subspecialty care has focused attention on the provision of mental health services by primary care physicians. The expanding clinical roles of primary care physicians underscore the importance of developing brief and sensitive tests to identify, diagnose and monitor mental disorders in primary care. The SDDS–PC® is an accessible procedure to diagnose and monitor multiple mental disorders in routine primary care practice.

Criterion-based systems such as the SDDS–PC® have the potential to focus clinical care more sharply on specific mental disorders and thereby improve patient care. As a result, the SDDS–PC® may increase the efficiency with which mental health care is provided in primary care practice. Experimental research is needed to measure the extent to which criterion-based systems such as the SDDS–PC® influence the pattern of health care delivery, the amount of health care expenditure and, most importantly, the quality of clinical outcomes.

ACKNOWLEDGEMENTS

Gerald L Klerman MD was the initial Principal Investigator of this project until his death in 1992. W Eugene Broadhead MD, PhD was Principal Investigator 1992–1994, succeeded by Roger G Kathol MD in 1995. The Upjohn Company, Kalamazoo, MI, sponsored and supported the development of the SDDS–PC® through its Pharmacosurveillance Unit, Mr James A Coleman, Director, and Andreas Pleil PhD, Senior Health Care Economist. Allen

Frances MD (Duke University), Helena Kraemer PhD (Stanford University), Michael Liebowitz MD (Columbia University; John Rush MD (University of Texas, Dallas) provided advice.

Advisory Council

Macaran Baird MD, SUNY Health Science Center; Dave Baron DO, American Osteopathic Association; Donald R Bennett MD, American Medical Association; Susan Blumenthal MD, Assistant Surgeon General; Jorge A Costa e Silva, World Health Organization; Leah Dickstein MD, University of Louisville School of Medicine; Mary Jane England MD, Washington Business Group on Health; Shervert H Frazier, MD, McLean Hospital; Roman H Hendrickson MD, American Academy of Family Physicians; Norman B Kahn MD, American Academy of Family Physicians; Kathryn Magruder PhD, National Institute of Health; Harold A Pincus MD, American Psychiatric Association; Darrell A Regier MD, MPH, National Institute of Mental Health; Rene Rodriguez MD, National Confederation of Hispanic American Medical Association; Richard Rupper MD, American Society of Internal Medicine; Normal Sartorius MD, World Health Organization; William Van Stone MD, Department of Veterans Affairs; Elinor Walker, Agency for Health Care Policy and Research; and Paul Young MD, American Board of Family Practice. Their presence on the Advisory Council in no way signifies an endorsement by these individuals or organization.

Trademark

The SDDS–PC® is a trademark of the Pharmacia-Upjohn Company.

REFERENCES

American Psychiatric Association (1987) *Diagnostic and Statistical Manual of Mental Disorders*, 3rd edn, revised. Washington, DC: American Psychiatric Association Press.
American Psychiatric Association (1994) *Diagnostic and Statistical Manual of Mental Disorders*, 4th edn. Washington, DC: American Psychiatric Association Press.
Andersson SO & Mattsson B (1989) Length of consultations in clinical practice in Sweden: views of doctors and patients. *Family Practice* **6**, 130–34.
Babor T, De la Fuente RJ, Saunder J & Grant M (1992) The alcohol use disorders identification test: guidelines for use in primary care. Geneva: AUDIT, World Health Organization.
Barr CE & Pleil AM (1995) Usability testing of a computerized telephone interview system to screen for mental and emotional disorders in primary care. In workshop, *The Need for an Interface between Behavioural and Medical Informatics*, 8th World Congress on Medical Informatics, Vancouver, BC, Canada.
Barrett J (1991) Treatment practices in primary care: setting directions for health outcome research. *Journal of Family Practice* **33**, 19–21.
Barrett JE, Barrett JA, Oxman TE & Gerber PD (1988) The prevalence of psychiatric disorders in a primary care practice. *Arch Gen Psychiat* **45**, 1100–106.
Borgquist L, Hansson L, Nettelbladt P, Nordstrom G & Lindelow G (1993) Perceived health

and high consumers of care: a study of mental health problems in a Swedish primary health care district. *Psychol Med* **23**, 763–70.

Broadhead WE, Leon AC, Weissman MM, Barrett JE, Blacklow RS, Gilbert TT, Keller MB, Olfson M & Higgins ES (1995) Development and validation of the SDDS–PC® screen for multiple mental disorders in primary care. *Arch Family Med* **4**, 211–19.

Burnam MA, Wells KB, Leake B & Landsverk J (1988) Development of a brief screening instrument for detecting depressive disorders. *Med Care* **26**, 775–89.

Goldberg DP, Steele JJ, Smith C & Spivey L (1980) Training family doctors to recognize psychiatric illness with increased accuracy. *Lancet* **2**, 521–3.

Higgins ES (1994) A review of unrecognized mental illness in primary care. *Arch Family Med* **3**, 908–17.

Hoven CW, Chiang P-H, Weissman MM, Moore R, Olfson M, Broadhead WE, Leon AC, Blacklow RF, Sheehan DZ, Farber L, Conolly P & Fireman BH (in preparation) A computerized system for use in primary care to screen, identify and track mental disorders.

Kessler LG, McGonagle KM, Zhao S, Nelson CB, Hughes M, Eshleman S, Wittchen H & Kendler KS (1994) Lifetime and 12-month prevalence of DSM-III-R psychiatric disorders in the United States: results from the National Comorbidity Survey. *Arch Gen Psychiat* **51**, 8–20.

Klerman GL (1990) Paradigm shifts in USA psychiatric epidemiology since World War II. *Soc Psychiat Psychiat Epidemiol* **25**, 27–32.

Leon AC, Olfson M, Weissman MM, Portera L, Fireman BH, Blacklow RS & Broadhead WE (1996) Brief screens for mental disorders in primary care. *J Gen Intern Med* **11**, 426–30.

Mitchell JB, Schurman R & Cromwell J (1988) The changing nature of physicians' office visits. *Health Serv Res* **23**, 575–91.

Nelson EC & Berwick DM (1989) The measurement of health status in clinical practice. *Med Care* **27**, 577–90.

Olfson M, Leon AC, Broadhead WE, Weissman MM, Barrett JE, Blacklow RS, Gilbert TT & Higgins ES (1995) The SDDS–PC®: a diagnostic aid for multiple mental disorders in primary care. *Psychopharmacol Bull* **31**, 415–20.

Olfson M & Klerman GL (1992) The treatment of depression: prescribing practices of primary care physicians and psychiatrists. *J Family Pract* **35**, 627–35.

Olfson M, Weissman MM, Broadhead WE (1995) The SDDS–PC®: a novel diagnostic procedure for mental disorders in primary care. *Primary Psychiat* **4**, 16–18.

Ormel J, Lieter MWJ, van den Brink W & Van de Willige G (1990) Recognition, management and outcome of psychological disorders in primary care: a naturalistic follow-up study. *Psychol Med* **20**, 909–23.

Rand EH, Badger LW & Goggins DR (1988) Toward a resolution of contradictions. Utility of feedback from the GHQ. *Gen Hosp Psychiat* **10**(S), 189–96.

Regier DA, Goldberg ID & Taube CA (1978) The de facto US mental health services system: a public health perspective. *Arch Gen Psychiat* **35**, 685–93.

Regier DA, Narrow WE, Rae DS, Manderscheid RW, Locke BZ & Goodwin FK (1993) The *de facto* US mental and addictive disorders service system: epidemiologic catchment area prospective 1-year prevalence rates of disorders and services. *Arch Gen Psychiat* **50**, 85–94.

Selzer ML (1971) The Michigan Alcoholism Screening Test: the quest for a new diagnostic instrument. *Am J Psychiat* **127**, 89–94.

Shepherd M, Cooper B & Brown AGK (1966) *Psychiatric Illness in General Practice.* Oxford: Oxford University Press.

Spitzer RL, Williams JBW, Gibbon M & First M (1992) The Structured Clinical Interview for DSM-III-R (SCID). I. History, rationale, and description. *Arch Gen Psychiat* **49**, 624–9.

Spitzer RL, Williams JBW, Kroenke K, Linzer M, DeGruy FV, Hahn SR, Brody D &

Johnson JG (1994) Utility of a new procedure for diagnosing mental disorders in primary care: the PRIME-MD 1000 Study. *J Am Med Assoc* **272**, 1749–56.

van Hermert AM, Hengeveld MW, Bolk JH, Rooijmans HG & Vanderbroucke JP (1993) Psychiatric disorders in relation to medical illness among patients of a general medical outpatient clinic. *Psychol Med* **23**, 167–73.

von Korff M, Shapiro S, Burke JD, Teitlebaum M, Skinner EA, German P, Turner RW, Klein L & Burns B (1987) Anxiety and depression in a primary care clinic: comparison of diagnostic interview schedule, general health questionnaire, and practitioner assessments. *Arch Gen Psychiat* **44**, 152–6.

Weissman MM, Broadhead WE, Olfson M, Sheehan DV, Hoven C, Conolly P, Fireman BH, Farber L, Blacklow RS, Higgins ES & Leon AC (submitted). A diagnostic aid for detecting (DSM-IV) mental disorders in primary care.

Weissman MM, Olfson M, Leon AC, Broadhead WE, Gilbert TT, Higgins ES, Barrett JE, Blacklow RS, Keller MB & Hoven C (1995) Brief diagnostic interviews (SDDS–PC®) for multiple mental disorders in primary care: a pilot study. *Arch Family Med* **4**, 220–27.

Williams JBW, Gibbon M, First MB, Spitzer RL, Davies M, Borus J, Howes MJ, Kane J, Pope HG, Rounsaville B & Wittchen H (1992) The Structured Clinical Interview for DSM-III-R (SCID). II. Multisite test-retest reliability. *Arch Gen Psychiat* **49**, 630–36.

31

Case-finding in Primary Care

Glyn Lewis
University of Wales College of Medicine, Cardiff, UK

A number of studies have demonstrated that a large proportion of people with psychiatric disorder remain undetected and therefore untreated within primary care (e.g. Goldberg & Huxley 1992). Estimates will obviously vary according to a variety of factors but, in the UK at least, it is suggested that about 50% of cases are undiagnosed. These figures are superficially alarming and are often presented in such a way as to suggest that relatively modest improvements in vigilance and knowledge amongst primary care physicians would lead to a major improvement in detection. There are a number of reasons why this is not the case, including the observation that many primary care physicians who are also trained psychiatrists 'miss' a similarly large proportion of cases. One of the most important reasons why detection is difficult is that about 80% of new presentations with a psychiatric disorder do not complain of psychological symptoms to their primary care physician (Kessler et al 1987). This phenomenon is often referred to as somatization and may be a behaviour dictated mostly by current symptomatology (Weich et al 1995). Psychiatrists sometimes find it easy to forget that the physician will have to attend to and deal with this presenting complaint, which may have little to do with any coexisting emotional disorder.

It must also be recognized that psychiatric disorder in the community and in primary care is most accurately viewed as a continuum (Meltzer, Gill & Petticrew 1995). Primary care physicians, unlike specialist psychiatrists, are seeing the whole spectrum of morbidity. Although the more severe disorders, such as major depression, are individually more disabling, data from the Epidemiological Catchment Area program (ECA) suggest that the larger numbers of people with disorder below the DSM-III threshold (American Psychiatric Association 1980) lead in aggregate to more disability than those with major depression (Broadhead et al 1990). Detection of psychiatric disorder in primary care is a difficult task, though potentially of great benefit.

Preventing Mental Illness: Mental Health Promotion in Primary Care. Edited by R. Jenkins and T.B. Üstün.
© 1998 John Wiley & Sons Ltd.

There has been a great deal of work on developing courses to improve interviewing skills amongst primary care physicians and demonstrating that these improve detection rates (Gask 1992). However, these valuable interventions lead to a relatively modest improvement in detection rates. An easier way of improving detection rates would be to use some kind of case-finding test. The General Health Questionnaire (Goldberg 1972), although originally developed for research, seems ideal for this task and its use in clinical practice has been advocated (Goldberg 1986). The validity of the GHQ has been established (Goldberg & Williams 1988) and the 12-item version can be fitted on one side of A4, can be completed by a patient while waiting to see the doctor and can be scored in less than 5 seconds. Despite these considerable advantages the GHQ has hardly been used in clinical practice and it is reasonable to ask why this might be so.

There are probably four reasons. First, the GHQ does not produce information with much clinical relevance. There is no indication of the duration of symptoms, not much guidance on severity and the results are not presented in a clinically useful form. Second, there is often a fear amongst physicians that uncovering psychiatric disorder will raise more problems than it will solve. Many primary care physicians often feel unsure in dealing with cases of psychiatric disorder once they have been detected. Third, empirical evidence has produced contradictory evidence on whether feedback of results from case-finding questionnaires such as the GHQ improve clinical outcome (Goldberg & Huxley 1992; Katon et al 1994). There are suggestions that the effectiveness of feedback from case-finding depends upon the training given to the primary care physician about how to use the information. The fourth reason is that many clinicians do not believe that the 'missed' cases are of clinical importance, and in the main are false positives. As far as one can judge this is not the case, but in general studies are stronger in assessing symptomatology than assessing need for or acceptance of treatment.

One way forward is not to abandon the prospect of case-finding as a routine clinical activity but to increase the amount of information given to the primary care physician. One could, for example, adopt a two-stage procedure in which those scoring above the threshold on the GHQ were then given a more detailed assessment, which could be combined with guidelines on management. In the UK, primary care physicians are increasingly using computers for practice administration, prescription and recording of consultation details. One method of developing case-finding into a more clinically acceptable and effective intervention would be to use self-administered computerized assessments which, in the most technologically advanced form, could be combined with individually tailored clinical guidelines, themselves generated by computer.

With a number of colleagues, I have been involved in developing a computerized assessment for psychiatric disorder, christened PROQSY (PROgrammable Questionnaire SYstem) (Lewis et al 1988) which is based upon the lay-interviewer-administered Revised Clinical Interview Schedule (CIS-R; Lewis et al 1992) as used in the OPCS National Surveys of Psychiatric Morbidity (Meltzer,

TABLE 31.1 Reliability of the CIS-R

Study	Interview	Observer rating	Re-interview design
*Kendell et al (1968)	PSE	0.73	0.41
**Goldberg et al (1970)	CIS	0.71	–
+Wing et al (1977)	PSE	0.52*	0.34 (0.37)
+Cooper et al (1977)	PSE	0.67	0.38
+Sturt et al (1981)	PSE	0.60 (0.43)*	–
+Rodgers & Mann (1986)	PSE	0.71 (0.61)*	–
+Lewis et al (1992) UK Study	CIS-R	–	0.55 (0.72)
+Lewis et al (1992) Chilean Study	CIS-R	0.87 (0.87)	–
+Lewis (1994) Human vs. Computer	CIS-R	–	0.63 (0.70)

The results given are the mean weighted kappas (or other agreement index) across symptoms. The figures in parentheses are the kappas for agreement on 'cases'.

* Audiotapes were used.
** Psychiatric hospital-based studies.
+ Lay interviewers were used.

Gill & Petticrew 1995). The CIS-R generates some of the common neurotic ICD-10 diagnoses. Unlike some of the more ambitious self-report interviews, the CIS-R only asks about neurotic symptomatology and concentrates on obtaining detailed information about the week preceding the interview, on the grounds that this produces the most reliable information. Results from studying the reliability of the CIS-R are encouraging (Table 31.1; Lewis et al 1992) and there does not appear to be any bias between administration by human or computer (Lewis 1994).

There are always concerns about the validity of self-report assessments of psychiatric disorder. Assessing the validity of psychiatric assessments is difficult and carries a tendency for circular argument. An earlier version of the computerized CIS-R was compared with the Clinical Interview Schedule (Goldberg et al 1970) administered by clinicians and the level of agreement was comparable to that found when two clinicians are compared (Lewis et al 1988). In addition, the CIS-R total score was compared with clinical judgements on severity, which again indicated close agreement (Lewis et al 1992). The CIS-R was developed for research purposes. However, the probable advantages in reliability of using a highly standardized assessment such as the CIS-R could also be of value in clinical work, especially when trying to apply the results of clinical trials to one's own patients (see below).

Using self-administered computerized assessments could have a number of advantages. They can provide more information, including some diagnostic information for the physician. In addition, such assessments provide a standardized and more reliable assessment than is possible within the clinical confines of primary care and therefore may be more useful as a basis upon which to build clinical guidelines. The difficulty of making a reliable assessment of psychiatric disorder within primary care is legendary (Jenkins, Smeeton & Shepherd 1988). Without providing a standardized assessment it would appear to be very difficult to provide guidelines of very much value.

One important advantage of using a standardized assessment within primary care is to provide a way of bridging the gap between research and clinical practice. We are currently carrying out a clinical trial which will try, amongst other things, to estimate the severity of depression above which tricyclics are effective (Lewis 1995). The computerized CIS-R is being used in this trial, so in the future it should be possible to link the results of this randomized trial with a standardized assessment, potentially available in the primary care physician's clinic. In this way guidance about severity or other clinical characteristics from clinical trials could be used within primary care.

Despite the potential advantages of computerized assessments it is important that any novel interventions are evaluated in order to establish their cost-effectiveness (Pelosi & Lewis 1989; Advisory Group on Health Technology Assessment 1992). We have completed a randomized trial that was designed to examine the cost-effectiveness of providing feedback from a computerized assessment and compared this with providing feedback from the GHQ and 'usual care'. The results suggested a modest clinical improvement in those given feedback from the computerized CIS-R but this was definitely not apparent at 6 months (Lewis et al 1995). There did not appear to be any difference in consulting or prescription rates in the three groups, so any improvement in outcome occurred without increasing the workload of the primary care physician. The results did not show any disadvantage from using computerized assessments and the signs of improved clinical outcome were encouraging enough for us to plan a new study to evaluate computerized clinical guidelines.

The study described below will start shortly and is funded by the National Health Service Research and Development strategy, primary secondary care interface initiative. The other applicants are Scott Weich, Deborah Sharp and Keith Lloyd. The intervention we propose to evaluate is case-finding using the GHQ combined with clinical guidelines, based upon the results of the computerized CIS-R. This will be compared with usual clinical practice, including the use of locally agreed guidelines. It is worth commenting about the choice of both the control and intervention groups. The control group has access to the guidelines as this is now regarded as best current practice, even though there is no real evidence for the effectiveness of guidelines for psychiatric disorder within primary care. Guidelines are being increasingly disseminated within primary care, and it would seem unrealistic to prevent the clinicians from having access to them. It would also be impracticable in view of the active dissemination of guidelines and allowing access to guidelines will permit randomization on an individual basis. In fact, evidence from other parts of medicine suggests that guidelines alone are far less effective than guidelines which are individually tailored to the specific patient (Grimshaw & Russell 1993), so this design will allow a test of this observation with psychiatric disorder.

The intervention in the trial is both case-finding and the provision of patient-specific guidelines to the general practitioner. The GHQ will be used and those scoring above the threshold would then complete the computerized CIS-R. We plan to develop the computer program so that guidelines would be specifically tailored to the individual patient who is consulting, e.g. by providing suggestions that suicide risk should be specifically assessed, or recommending sedating anti-depressants if the subject had difficulty in sleeping. The program would produce a report on one side of A4 that could be given to the GP and used in conjunction with his/her usual clinical assessment in order to guide management. Follow-up will be for 6 months and the GHQ will be used to measure clinical outcome. Service use will also be monitored in order to establish the economic costs involved. We plan to recruit about 630 subjects to each group and this should provide sufficient statistical power (80%) to detect the difference between 40% and 30% recovery.

CONCLUSIONS

Case-finding has potential for dramatically improving the outcome of psychiatric disorders within primary care. Although the more severe disorders are more likely to be detected, there is a large pool of untreated psychiatric disorder within primary care and presumably a corresponding unmet need. However, there are probably some very good reasons why primary care physicians have chosen not to adopt widespread case-finding in primary care. At present there is not good empirical evidence for the clinical effectiveness of this approach and there are some unanswered questions about the right strategy to adopt. As always it is important to ensure that suggested interventions are properly evaluated.

A promising avenue for developing case-finding further is to provide primary care physicians with more advice on how to manage patients with psychiatric disorder using clinical practice guidelines. One method of doing this inexpensively may be to use computerized assessments and computer-generated guidelines. It is important to emphasize that such computerised aids cannot replace the clinical experience and acumen of the primary care physician. Managing psychiatric disorder and the interplay between physical and emotional disorder within primary care is a subtle and challenging skill. Technological tricks, such as case-finding and computerized assessments, can only be a small contribution towards the challenge of improving the treatment for these common conditions.

REFERENCES

Advisory Group on Health Technology Assessment (1992) *Assessing the Effects of Health Technologies*. London: Department of Health.

American Psychiatric Association (1980) *Diagnostic and Statistical Manual*, 3rd edn. Washington, DC: American Psychiatric Association.

Broadhead WE, Blazer D, George L & Tse C (1990) Depression, disability days and days lost from work. *J Am Med Assoc* **264**, 2524–8.

Cooper JE, Copeland JRM, Brown GW, Harris T & Gourlay AJ (1977) Further studies on interviewer training and inter-rater reliability of the Present State Examination (PSE). *Psychol Med* **7**, 517–23.

Gask L (1992) Training general practitioners to detect and manage emotional disorders. *Int Rev J Psychiat* **4**, 293–300.

Goldberg D (1986) Use of the General Health Questionnaire in clinical work. *Br Med J* **293**, 1188–9.

Goldberg D & Huxley P (1992) *Common Mental Disorders: A Biopsychosocial Approach*. London: Routledge.

Goldberg DP (1972) *The Detection of Psychiatric Illness by Questionnaire*. Maudsley Monograph 21. Oxford: Oxford University Press.

Goldberg DP & Williams P (1988) *The User's Guide to the General Health Questionnaire*. Windsor: NFER-NELSON.

Goldberg DP, Cooper B, Eastwood MR, Kedward HB & Shepherd M (1970) A standardised psychiatric interview for use in community surveys. *Br J Prevent Soc Med* **24**, 18–23.

Grimshaw JM & Russell IT (1993) Effect of guidelines on medical practice: a systematic review of rigorous evaluation. *Lancet* **342**, 1317–22.

Jenkins R, Smeeton N & Shepherd M (1988) *Classification of Mental Disorders in Primary Care Settings*. Psychological Medicine Monograph, Supplement 12. Cambridge: Cambridge University Press.

Katon W, von Korff M, Lin E, Walker E, Simon G, Robinson P, Bush T & Irvin S (1994) Methodologic issues in randomized trials of liaison psychiatry in primary care. *Psychosom Med* **56**, 97–103.

Kendell RE, Everitt B, Cooper JE, Sartorius N & David ME (1968) The reliability of the 'Present State Examination'. *Soc Psychiat* **3**, 123–9.

Kessler LG, Burns BJ, Shapiro S, Tischler GL, George LK, Hough RL, Bodison D & Miller RH (1987) Psychiatric diagnoses of medical service users: evidence from the epidemiologic catchment area program. *Am J Publ Health* **77**, 18–24.

Lewis G (1994) Assessing psychiatric disorder with a human interviewer or a computer. *J Epidemiol Comm Health* **48**, 207–10.

Lewis G (1995) Severity of depression and dosage of antidepressants in primary care. *Primary Care Psychiat* (suppl 1).

Lewis G, Pelosi AJ, Araya R & Dunn G (1992) Measuring psychiatric disorder in the community: a standardized assessment for use by lay interviewers. *Psychol Med* **22**, 465–86.

Lewis G, Pelosi AJ, Glover E, Wilkinson G, Stansfeld SA, Williams P & Shepherd M (1988) The development of a computerized assessment for minor psychiatric disorder. *Psychol Med* **18**, 737–45.

Lewis G, Sharp D, Bartholomew J & Pelosi AJ (1996) Computerized assessment of common mental disorders in primary care: effect on clinical outcome. *Family Practice* **13**, 120–26.

Meltzer H, Gill B & Petticrew M (1995) *OPCS Surveys of Psychiatric Morbidity in Great Britain. Report No 1. The Prevalence of Psychiatric Morbidity among Adults Aged 16–64 Living in Private Households in Great Britain*. London: HMSO.

Pelosi AJ & Lewis G (1989) The computer will see you now. *Br Med J* **299**, 138–9.

Rodgers B & Mann SA (1986) The reliability and validity of PSE assessments by lay interviewers: a national population survey. *Psychol Med* **16**, 689–700.

Sturt E, Bebbington P, Hurry J & Tennant C (1981) The present state examination used by interviewers from a survey agency: report from the MRC Camberwell Community Survey. *Psychol Med* **11**, 185–92.

Weich S, Lewis G, Mann AH & Donmall R (1995) The somatic presentation of psychiatric morbidity in general practice. *Br J Gen Pract* **45**, 143–7.

Wing JK, Nixon JM, Mann SA & Leff JP (1977) Reliability of the PSE (9th edn) used in a population study. *Psychol Med* **7**, 505–16.

Specific Areas for Prevention and Mental Health Promotion through Primary Care

32

Mental Health Promotion in Schools

J Sampaio Faria, Katherine Weare*
and Gay Gray*

World Health Organization, Copenhagen, Denmark and
*Health Education Unit, University of Southampton, UK

As stated in the WHO Report on the Prevention of Mental, Psychosocial and Neurological Disorders in the European Region (1988), there is a growing proportion of the population exposed to psychosocial situations that are known to be associated with increased risk and vulnerability to disease. Such adverse situations include prolonged unemployment, high cultural and geographical mobility, weakening and disruption of family and social networks, lack of social support and social isolation. In fact, high prevalence figures for milder forms of depression, anxiety and psychosomatic disorders have been observed among the population as a whole and in patients seen by the general health services, especially Primary Health Care Services. The consumption of psychoactive pharmaceuticals such as anxiolytics and hypnotics is high and continues to increase in some European countries.

On the other hand, there is an increasing emergence, especially among young people, of certain patterns of health-damaging behaviour which will tend to result in increases in the prevalence and incidence of mental and neurological disorders. These particularly include abuse of psychoactive substances, violent behaviour and increasing rates of suicide and attempted suicide in many member states.

Along with the opportunities for the *prevention* of mental health related problems arising from exposure to these social and psychosocial factors, intervention is also needed which is orientated towards mental health *promotion*. This serves to strengthen the potentialities of individuals, groups, communities and society at large so that people can cope in a health-orientated way with these stressful demands.

The Mental Health Programme of WHO for the European Region is addressing this need for mental health promotion by developing and stimulating international collaborative initiatives. These aim at:

- Preventing severe psychological vulnerabilities through promotion of an appropriate psychosocial development for children during their first years of life (0–5 years old).

Preventing Mental Illness: Mental Health Promotion in Primary Care. Edited by R. Jenkins and T.B. Üstün.
© 1998 John Wiley & Sons Ltd.

- Reinforcing the communities' potentialities for assisting specific groups of the population who are exposed to very stressful conditions.
- Strengthening coping skills in young people.

For the promotion of an appropriate psychosocial development for children, a multicentre project on the 'psychosocial development of children through the primary health care services' was launched in 1991. This project involves 8 countries and its main aim is to convey to pregnant women and parents of 0–5 year-old children, who contact the primary health care facilities, relevant information on the basic psychosocial developmental needs of their children. A training package has been developed and tested. An evaluation of the effectiveness of the interventions is at present being carried out. Since 1994 this project has been co-funded by the Commission of the European Union.

On the issue of reinforcing the communities' potentialities for stress management, a meeting on 'Approaches to stress management in the community setting' was held in Prague on 24–26 June 1992. In this meeting the minimum set of community structures and programs for comprehensive stress management was identified and the stages to be followed for action described in detail.

For the strengthening of coping skills and psychosocial competence in young people, particular attention is given to settings such as the family and the school, in their potentialities for mental health promotion.

The potentialities of the *family* have been reviewed in a symposium on 'Health Promotion by the Family—the Role of the Family in Enhancing Health Behaviour'. This was organized in collaboration with the WHO Collaborating Centre for Health, Psychosocial and Psychobiological Factors, Belgium, in 1992. More recently, the special needs of the family for supporting the mental health of young people in societies in transition were identified in a meeting held in October 1994 in Romania and organized in collaboration with UNICEF and the Romanian Institute for Child and Family.

Regarding the *school*, ongoing programs for enhancing coping skills in young people through the school setting were reviewed in the first meeting of the WHO European Task Force on Mental Health Promotion and Prevention, held in August 1991 in collaboration with the WHO Collaborating Centre for Health Education and Promotion, Utrecht, The Netherlands. A book on mental health promotion and prevention in schools was published on the meeting's discussions.

PROMOTION OF MENTAL AND EMOTIONAL HEALTH IN THE EUROPEAN NETWORK OF HEALTH-PROMOTING SCHOOLS

In 1993, it was decided to integrate a mental health promotion component in the project: the European Network of Health-promoting Schools (ENHPS). This project is a joint and cooperative activity between the WHO, the Commission for the European Communities and the Council of Europe. Each country is asked to nominate 10–15 schools that it will support in becoming more health-promoting. The project began in 1992, with seven countries joining the network. By July 1995, 34 countries were involved, with 500 core schools. In addition more than 1600 schools were linked to the network through national and sub-national arrangements.

The project takes a 'whole school' approach, which sees the curriculum and teaching programs as just one of the building blocks which go to making the 'health-promoting' school; equally important are the school environment, the ethos of the school and its links with the outside community, including parents. A key insight of the project is the recognition that for a school to be health-promoting, it is important to consider the health of all who work there: teaching and support staff, as well as young people.

Those countries who first joined the network, particularly in Eastern and Central Europe, identified mental and emotional health as essential priorities in their task of developing the health-promoting school. There was also a strong request for training in this area. In collaboration with the Health Education Unit at the University of Southampton, and with financial support from Johnson and Johnson Philanthropy Committee, a project was set up to pilot training courses in Eastern and Central Europe and to develop a training manual which could be used by countries in the network. The aim of the training courses and the manual is to help participants take practical steps to improve the mental and emotional health of all who work in their schools.

The Development of the Project through Partnership

The project is seen very much as a partnership, involving close consultation with the National Coordinator in each country, as well as with teachers and others who work with young people. It was considered essential to find out 'where people are coming from', concerning their perceptions of what affects mental and emotional health, rather than making assumptions about their needs. This applied not only to staff but also to young people.

Research

The first step was to develop and pilot research techniques that teachers could use to find out young people's perceptions. The Health Education Unit at the University of Southampton is particularly well-known for its innovative work using projective techniques. These involve asking students to respond spontaneously, with writing or drawing, to an open-ended invitation. This can be completed in a whole range of ways and has no 'right' answer.

Specific techniques used in this project included speech bubbles and a 'draw and write' technique. The speech bubbles contained an unfinished sentence to complete, such as 'What I would most like to change about myself or my life is . . .'. In the 'draw and write' technique, children were asked to imagine and draw someone their age who is feeling good about him/herself and to write and draw all around that person what is making them feel good. Then they were asked to repeat the process, drawing and writing about someone who is not feeling good about him/herself.

These research techniques were piloted initially in three British schools and analysis of British students' replies provided a trigger for discussion in other countries. The statements written by young people were used in some of the workshop activities.

Active Learning Methods in Education and Training

The main thrust of modern educational research and theory has been to demonstrate the importance of involving people in their own learning. Health promotion has been at the forefront in developing strategies and techniques to make participative or active learning a reality. Within the ENHPS, the emphasis is on participatory methods of teaching and learning at all levels, in schools and on training courses that support the initiative. Especially when promoting mental health, we need to help people to recognize that their opinions and feelings are valid, so that they develop a sense of their own worth. A key feature of this particular project is therefore the range of active and participatory methods it offers, which are important in health education generally and for promoting mental health and emotional well-being in particular.

Workshop 1: Clarifying Ideas and Starting Points

An initial workshop of 2–3 days' duration was piloted in three Eastern European countries. Through the workshop, it was intended to consult teachers and others, and pilot the content, methods and pacing of the training and the manual.

The workshop's objectives were to help participants to:

- Clarify what they mean by mental and emotional health.
- Explore ways of finding out what affects students' and staff's mental and emotional health.
- Identify and practise some of the basic skills involved in communicating effectively and building relationships.
- Identify ways in which schools can promote mental and emotional health and enhance self-esteem.
- Experience a variety of active learning methods.

The first workshop encouraged participants to use a range of research techniques back in their schools. As well as the 'projective techniques', these included conventional techniques such as questionnaires to use with colleagues. In several countries teachers sent the results via their National Coordinator to the project team, who found these invaluable in determining the content of future work.

Visits to Schools

The project team also visited a small number of schools involved in the network on their first visit to countries where the workshops were run. The purpose was to gain some basic understanding of the context from which participants came, and the constraints and opportunities with which they worked.

Workshop 2: Managing Stress and Change

The sheer amount and accelerating nature of the social, economic and cultural change that many countries in Eastern Europe have experienced in a very short time has meant that two issues emerged strongly as the project progressed. These were the issues of managing and preventing stress and managing change. Moreover, participants on the workshops emphasized the importance of staff having a chance to promote their own mental and emotional health before being able to help others.

The second workshop was therefore designed with this in mind and focused on the causes of stress for staff in schools, and strategies which might help to prevent and manage this stress, not only through developing personal coping strategies, such as assertiveness and relaxation techniques, but also through changes in systems and structures in schools, such as establishing clearer goals and better systems of communication.

Progress to Date

To date the workshops have been run in Estonia, Poland, Slovenia, the Czech and Slovak Republics and Hungary. Participants have been mainly teachers from both primary and secondary schools, but also school psychologists, the central support team of the network and staff from universities and teacher training colleges. Evaluation of the training has been extremely positive, with the great majority commenting that they had learnt new methods which would be of use to them in their teaching, and how to create a good atmosphere and raise self-esteem.

A training manual has been developed as a result and has been distributed to every National Coordinator in the network right across Western as well as Eastern and Central Europe. Besides the countries involved in the workshops, other countries are now translating the manual. These include Russia, Spain, Greece, Lithuania and Latvia.

The Next Stage

Many participants who have attended the workshops to date, although they now have an experience of working in a participatory way, appear to need more support before they are equipped to run similar workshops with their colleagues. The next phase of the project is to identify a team of people in each country who can act as trainers for this type of work. They will then be invited to participate in workshops to gain a greater understanding of group dynamics, of the theories behind active and participatory learning and to develop their skills in planning, running and evaluating training courses. As a result, it is hoped that there will be a pool of competent trainers in Eastern and Central Europe who can disseminate further both this work and other active learning projects.

33

School Mental Health Program in Pakistan

Malik H Mubbashar

World Health Organization Collaborating Centre for Mental Health and Institute of Psychiatry, Rawalpindi Medical College, Pakistan

Mental health care is the most neglected area of general health consideration in Pakistan. A report of the sub-group of the National Program for Mental Health Care in Pakistan (1988) cited various studies to conclude that there were about 1 million severely and 10 million mildly mentally ill persons in the country. A large area of Pakistan is iodine-deficient. If psychosomatic disorders were included, about 15–20 million people would be in need of attention. According to one estimate, there is about one psychiatrist per million of the population in Pakistan.

Recently there has been WHO interest in involving schools in mental health programs (El Din et al 1991; Hendren, Birril Wiesen & Orley 1993). Sponsored by WHO, a community-based school mental health program was instituted in some schools near Rawalpindi, Pakistan. The objective of the program was to make the schoolchildren—and through them the community—understand mental health problems and the available treatments for mental disorders (Mubbashar et al 1989). This chapter attempts to describe the program and evaluate its impact on the schoolchildren and the community.

The need to develop models of mental health care relevant to the needs of developing countries has been recognized for many years. In order to address this, the WHO Collaborating Centre, Rawalpindi, initiated a demonstration project in the Gujar Khan Tehsil of Rawalpindi Division. Subsequently this program has been expanded to include four other Tehsils: Fateh Jang, Murree, Kahuta and Taxila (Figures 33.1, 33.2 and 33.3).

In rural and urban Pakistan, the approximate number of children of school age is 42 million, out of a total population of 122 million. It is thought that only 50% of children enrol for primary education and that half of these drop out.

The objectives of the program can be described in four phases (see Box 33.1). These service developments are now being evaluated.

Preventing Mental Illness: Mental Health Promotion in Primary Care. Edited by R. Jenkins and T.B. Üstün.
Published 1998 John Wiley & Sons Ltd.

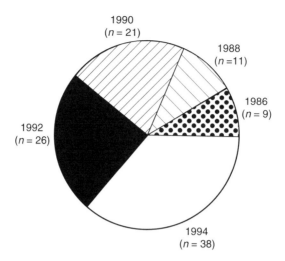

FIGURE 33.1 Training of education administrators: district education officers and their staff members. Series 1, WHO collaborating centre for mental health

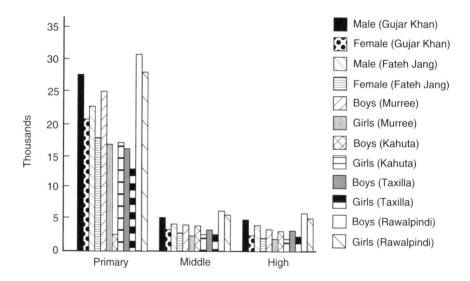

FIGURE 33.2 Number of students in the schools

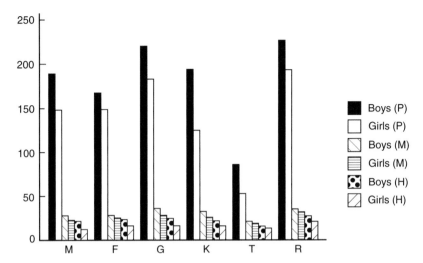

FIGURE 33.3   Number of schools in Rawalpindi division. (P) = primary; (M) = middle; (H) = high. M = Murree; (F) = Fateh Jang; (G) = Gujar Khan; (K) = Kahuta; (T) = Taxilla; (R) = Rawalpindi

---

BOX 33.1   Four phases of development of the community mental health program

Phase I
Collection of demographic data about the project area
Assessment of knowledge, attitude and practices related to mental illness
Need and demand appraisals
Sensitization of community members regarding mental health needs
Sensitization of administrators regarding mental health services provision

Phase II
Development of teaching and training material for primary care physicians, multipurpose
  health workers, female health visitors and traditional birth attendants
Education and training of primary care personnel in a decentralized manner

Phase III
Stimulation of community efforts using innovative methods, e.g. addressing religious
  congregations, setting up of community mental health committees
Development of referral channels using colour-coded cards
Generation of data about identification, holding, referral and cure of cases using
  indigenously developed information systems, for different types of health professionals

Phase IV
Evaluation of impact of community-based rural mental health program. During this the
  realization that schools can play a powerful role in stimulating community efforts for
  mental health care provision led to the development of a School Mental Health
  Program at Gujar Khan, which has been extended to the whole of the Rawalpindi
  Division covering the largest possible population

SCHOOL MENTAL HEALTH PROGRAM

The literacy rate in Pakistan is roughly 27% and in rural areas is even lower; female literacy may be as low as 7%. Therefore, teachers and schoolchildren constitute most of the literate population and the latter read and write letters for their elders, fill in official forms and read newspapers for them. Thus they become eminent in the community and induce some parents to send their children to school. They are rightly called 'the eyes and ears of the community' (Mubbashar et al 1986).

The objectives of school mental health programs are:

- To develop greater awareness of mental health among schoolchildren, schoolteachers and the community.
- To provide essential knowledge about mental health principles to schoolteachers to enable them to impart such knowledge to schoolchildren, recognize common mental health problems in schoolchildren and increase community awareness of mental health needs and services.

These objectives are being met through a four-phase series of activities: familiarization, training, reinforcement and evaluation (see Box 33.2).

Familiarization Phase

Before the program began, the district school authorities were contacted, the aims and objectives of the program were explained, and their cooperation was sought. This phase involved collection of background information on existing educational facilities. In addition, teams visited various schools in the area to assess current mental health knowledge among school heads, teachers and students and their willingness to support and own the program. During this phase, weekly medical camps were organized at various schools providing counselling about various medical and psychiatric illnesses. The aim of this exercise was to gain confidence and establish rapport with the school authorities for the acceptance and success of the program.

Teachers' knowledge of mental health and illnesses was also assessed. It was noted that the majority had very limited knowledge of mental health and many shared the rural community's views about the cause of mental illness being the influence of evil spirits, etc. Socioeconomic stress and unhappy environments were also considered potent causes of mental ill health.

Training of Teachers

In the second phase, training was organized for the heads and other teachers, in collaboration with the district education authorities. Before the actual training of

---

BOX 33.2 Four phases of the school mental health program

Familiarization
Sensitization of educational administrators to the application of mental health principles
  to education
Collection of data about knowledge of and attitudes to mental health among schoolteachers and students

Training of teachers
Male and female teachers trained with the aim of providing knowledge and counselling
  skills

Reinforcement
Visits to schools by community support team
Organization of parent–teacher associations
Organization of speech and essay competitions about mental health
Development of slogans carrying primary, secondary and tertiary prevention messages

Evaluation
Effects of program assessed using the following parameters:
  Number of students scoring better grades
  Number of absentees and drop-outs
  Number of case referrals to health centres for general and mental illness

---

teachers, it was decided to first provide school heads with orientation about mental health and the aims of the program. The headmasters and headmistresses of various schools of the Tehsil were invited in batches of 15–20 to attend the Tehsil's education offices weekly for a minimum of 4 weeks; the staff of the Department of Psychiatry put forward the aims and objectives of the program, the importance of mental health in schools, and its effect on the psychosocial profile of the community.

Training for the teachers was more elaborate and comprehensive because their direct interaction with students meant they were the ones on whom the success of the program depended. The training was carried out in their respective schools by teams consisting of a psychiatrist, psychologists and social workers, helped by specially prepared manuals, slides, case demonstrations and special mental health slogans.

The training was mainly directed towards changing attitudes towards mental health. In addition it was intended to provide knowledge of common mental illnesses and the basic aims of psychological counselling when appropriate. The lectures covered the following topics:

- Brain and behaviour.
- Psychological and emotional development in the child.
- Learning disabilities among children.
- Sensory deficit among children.

- Mental retardation.
- Common psychological problems among schoolchildren.
- Promotion of healthy lifestyles at an early age.

Duration of Training

The training was in two parts, the first consisting of 2-hour sessions held weekly for 8–12 weeks, and the second a refresher course focusing on the doubts and difficulties encountered by teachers, such as:

- The additional time needed for the mental health program, which might hinder other educational activities (better health will mean better education in the long run).
- The concern that the mental health program would be expensive (it will be done mainly by teachers themselves and existing health staff).
- Additional burden of paperwork (paperwork should be reduced and we should concentrate on essentials).
- Possible objections from parents (experience has shown that parents are appreciative).

Reinforcement Phase

This phase involved visits to schools, promulgation of the program through slogans and competitions, and the organization of parent–teacher associations. After initiating the training of schoolteachers and heads, the teams from the Department of Psychiatry began visiting various schools in the area with the objective of supporting attitudinal changes resulting from the teacher training and enhancing its effect on the overall educational atmosphere of the schools. To strengthen the impact of the program, the following slogans were selected to convey a mental health message, and teachers were encouraged to concentrate on them for 5 minutes every day in class:

- Smoking is injurious to health.
- Mental illnesses are not due to possession by evil spirits but are like any other bodily disease and are treatable.
- People are different and some have disabilities; do not laugh at others' disabilities but help them.

Numerous posters carrying these slogans were designed by the schoolchildren themselves and are now displayed in most classes and staff-rooms. From their own resources the teachers organize the production of rubber stamps carrying these catchy phrases. The children's exercise and report books (which are seen by their parents) are stamped with the slogans, which were selected after considering many factors. The primary aim was to emphasize fundamental messages about prevention and treatment of mental illness and the promotion of mental health.

Essay and speech competitions were held and parent–teacher associations were also established in this regard. A week-long managerial training workshop of senior education officers of the Rawalpindi Division was organized at the Department of Psychiatry.

Evaluation Phase

In the fourth and final phase, an attempt was made to evaluate the program. Although it is still being expanded and consolidated, its impact was felt both in improved educational activities in the schools and in changed attitudes in the community. The results of studies carried out in this phase are being published and further studies are in progress to evaluate the school mental health program.

CONCLUSION

Mentally ill people have always been objects of curiosity in rural areas. Stigmatization, although modified by religious teachings, is always present. Curious young minds, being very receptive, absorb a substantial amount of the information presented to them. Interestingly, the schoolchildren absorbed more information challenging traditional beliefs about mentally ill people. Factual knowledge, e.g. about depression, psychosis, and mental retardation, improved as a result of the program. The program has highlighted the following points:

- Schoolchildren and teachers are a potential resource for mental health promotion, prevention and identification of illness.
- They can also be used to educate their families and the community at large.
- The school mental health program in developing countries can be initiated and maintained with existing resources without incurring much additional expenditure.

On the whole it can be concluded that the program was successful in achieving its objective of developing awareness of mental health among teachers, students and the community.

REFERENCES

El Din AS, Wigg NN, Billington DR & Sadek A (1991) A multi-sectoral approach to school mental health in Alexandria, Egypt. *East Mediterr Reg Health Serv J* **11**, 24–30.

Government of Pakistan (1987) *Report of the Sub-group of the National Program for Mental Health Care in Pakistan.* Islamabad: Planning Commission, Government of Pakistan.

Hendren R, Birril Wiesen R & Orley J (1993) *Mental Health Programmes in Schools.* Geneva: Division of Mental Health, WHO.

Mubbashar MH, Malik SJ, Zar JR & Wigg NN (1986) Community-based mental health care programme. Report of an experiment in Pakistan. *East Mediterr Reg Health Serv J* **1**, 14–20.

34

Immigrants—Experiences in Hungary

Bela Buda
Semmelweis University of Medicine, Budapest, Hungary

The mental health of immigrants is a much studied and well known subject in psychiatry. There is a standard set of knowledge concerning it. At the turn of our century psychiatrists had already noted that the morbidity rate of immigrants was higher than that of a comparable host population with regard to psychiatric diseases. The higher rate of schizophrenia was explained by the higher probability of drift and mobility of those who carry the risk of disease (either by constitution and heredity or by vulnerability due to personality factors), while the high rate of depression and neuroses was attributed to the stresses of accommodation and acculturation.

It was pointed out that paranoid reactions are more common among older immigrants, while younger ones are more prone to alcoholism and drug abuse. Family life among immigrants was found to be more stressful because of the higher frequency of marital tensions and intergenerational conflicts, often resulting in the early departure of adolescent children. The bigger the difference between the culture and degree of civilization of the host country and that of the country of origin of immigrants, the greater have been found to be the stresses of acculturation. This rule is influenced by the presence of an extended family, kinship system or native community, since these interpersonal structures can act as natural support networks and can mitigate stresses and enhance coping, but usually at the price of delaying acculturation and adaptation to the new social environment.

In recent decades immigrants who reach the host country as refugees or expatriates have been observed to suffer from post-traumatic stress disorder (PTSD), psychosomatic symptoms and depression. Unfortunately, tortured and psychically traumatized persons are nowadays more frequently found among immigrants in many countries.

Immigrants might need special mental health care facilities where difficulties of language and cultural patterns of behaviour can be taken into consideration. Protection and care of multiproblem immigrant families are needed; for example, prevention services for youth have to deal with special risks and conflicts, e.g.

Preventing Mental Illness: Mental Health Promotion in Primary Care. Edited by R. Jenkins and T.B. Üstün.
© 1998 John Wiley & Sons Ltd.

substance abuse, violence, suicide, disorders of communication and relating, problems connected with gender role and identity, etc. Immigrants usually come from underdeveloped countries where they are not socialized to cooperate with mental health services and are often reluctant to accept the sick role because of psychological problems. They tend to react with somatizations, functional disturbances and anxiety. Therefore, general practitioners and primary care health workers have a better chance to help them than psychiatrists. Health carers, social workers and voluntary helpers also have greater advantages in assisting immigrants when they belong to the same ethnic group and speak the native language.

This is roughly the essence of the present psychiatric view of mental health problems of immigrants. There is a proliferation of publications and studies in this field because the number of immigrants is increasing in the industrial countries and parts of, for example, the UK and Belgium, and in Scandinavian countries there are more than 100 different, small or larger ethnic and cultural groups of immigrants, often living within a city or a district and having a wide variety of mental health problems.

By comparison, Hungary's immigrant population is much smaller and the mental health issues connected with it are much simpler. Nevertheless, some experiences and observations of immigrants might be of interest.

After World War II, Hungary came under Communist rule and was a relatively closed country until the 1980s. There was only one influx of immigrants, when, at the end of the 1940s, tens of thousands of Communist Greek soldiers and refugees settled in Hungary and other middle-European Socialist countries after the end of the Greek civil war. This population lived in separate communities and its adaptation to the Hungarian way of life began only in the 1960s, when the dream of a restoration of the Communist regime in Greece had to be abandoned and Greek children began to attend Hungarian schools. In the 1960s and 1970s most of these people left Hungary, mainly for Greece, and now there are only around 2000 Greeks in Hungary, completely integrated into the country. Greek immigrants were known in psychiatric circles in Hungary as violent patients, with many somatization complaints and hysterical symptoms.

Besides the Greeks, the only immigrants were individuals, mainly spouses of Hungarians coming from the Soviet Union or East Germany. Although many foreigners have been living in Hungary since 1990, some with long-term work permits and some who are illegal immigrants (especially from mainland China and Taiwan), their psychiatric situation and mental health status are not sufficiently understood.

The typical immigrant in Hungary is an ethnic Hungarian who left a neighbouring country, mainly Romania or Yugoslavia, or the Subcarpathian regions of the Soviet Union (now Ukraine) or Czechoslovakia (now Slovakia). After World War I the Trianon Treaty had transferred around two-thirds of the original territory of Hungary to the neighbouring countries, some of which had been created as new states by this treaty. In subsequent decades millions of ethnic Hungarians were expelled from these countries and repatriated to Hungary, a small country of around 10 million inhabitants but millions remained in their original places of residence and became citizens of the new states. Often ethnic Hungarians, especially where they were living in large numbers in homogenous communities, were subjected to discrimination, harassment and forced assimilation. In some countries Hungarians were denied Hungarian-language schools and were expected to use only the host country's language for official affairs. This issue was suppressed during the first decades of Communist rule, but from the 1970s, an era of slow liberalization, it became known, partly because by then Hungarians living on opposite sides of the borders were allowed to visit one another.

There were three waves of immigration of Hungarians from neighbouring countries. The first, in 1970–1985, consisted of several thousand families who were legal immigrants. These people had to wait for years for travel permits, during which time they suffered much discrimination and were treated as enemies or traitors. They were allowed to carry only personal belongings with them. Many had psychiatric problems, anxieties, paranoid reactions, depressions and difficulties of adaptation. Children adapted quickly and well since school systems were similar in these countries, but adults had to overcome traumas, to mourn losses and to cope with problems of identity. Although they have not had to master a new language, they had to become accustomed to new cultural and social standards (Hungary having been in a more advanced state of liberalization with higher living standards, but at the same time more impersonal and competitive). Authorities in Hungary were not too helpful towards these immigrants, but they encountered much solidarity in the Hungarian populations.

From the middle of the 1980s, and especially before 1989, the Ceausescu regime in Romania became more dictatorial and discriminated even more against Hungarians, but also against the Romanian population. Refugees began to cross the Romanian border illegally in large numbers asking for asylum and/or for travel permits to Western European countries. While formerly such cases had been deported back to the country of origin, in the atmosphere of increasing democratization and liberalization under Gorbachov's rule, public opinion supported the claims of these refugees and they were given the opportunity to settle down in Hungary. Roughly in the same way as East Germans in West Germany, citizenship was granted immediately to the Hungarians and settlement was offered to Romanians who returned to Romania after the revolution in 1989 or who left for Germany or Austria. Tens of thousands of people became immigrants in Hungary during these years. Sympathy and support were great, the immigrants acquired jobs and accommodation, so adaptation was made easier. Skilled workers and poor people adapted without difficulties, while intellectuals often had many psychological problems and became only slowly integrated into their new communities, where they had much to learn since the working conditions and standards of physicians, engineers, teachers, etc. were rather different in the two countries and there was a higher degree of individualization in Hungary. Difficulties of communication and relationships, stresses connected with work, frustrated aspirations, etc. contributed to the development of neurotic symptoms among them.

A particular psychological problem was a mixture of guilt, grief, alienation and depression. People felt themselves to be traitors who had abandoned their region, town or village, and thereby their friends, but who did not want to change their values and habits and did not feel at home in their new environment. Many vacillated for some time between wishing to return and wishing to leave for Western countries.

This population motivated some psychiatrists and mental health workers to develop services to diagnose and treat psychiatric problems related to refugee and immigrant status, because those professionals who met immigrants as patients began to sense subtle differences and hidden interconnections between life histories, life events and symptoms. Small study groups were formed. Some professionals initiated Balint groups as supervision tools for working with immigrants and they began to collect information about transcultural issues, social psychiatry, ethno-psychiatry, etc.—knowledge thought to be helpful in dealing with problems of immigrants. First, the psychodynamic perspective was adopted, later the concept of family therapy and still later the cognitive–behavioural view (when groups of immigrants were given communication and assertivity training, relaxation training, etc.). In this work, the author's experience extended to several hundred immigrants, partly among his own clients and patients, partly as referred in supervision and special teaching seminars.

Psychiatric problems were also, as ever, common problems of human existence, but for these people, they were specially coloured and transformed by the impact of a political system and way of life which had created infantilization, alienation, mutual suspicion and fear, double-talk, challenges to identity, guilt and conflicts around group loyalty, ethical dilemmas, and problems of self-esteem and self-image. After emigration these issues had to be elaborated and solved but there were strong inhibitions about communicating them and support systems which would have assisted the processes of elaboration were usually missing. Symptomatic reactions were caused by these problems as well as by manifest conflicts and frustrations such as illness, marital and family tensions, etc. Psychotherapy was needed to overcome these inhibitions; family therapy was especially helpful in bringing the relevant processes of communication into play. Many immigrants rejected psychiatric treatment but responded well to approaches from general practitioners, doctors at the workplace, community nurses, district paediatricians treating their children, and social workers or psychologists at child guidance or family support centres. In the late 1980s church organizations and voluntary groups were allowed to give assistance to these immigrants and many of them asked our study groups and interested professionals for support and supervision; this helped them gain more insight into the problems of immigrant existence in Hungary. It became obvious that a network of services and contact persons could help immigrants to work effectively through their specific situations, in respect of both elaborating the past and adapting to the present and future. Depression, suicidal crises, anxiety states, etc. were in many instances resistant to proper drug treatment and psychological support when the immigrants' existential problems were not also taken into consideration. Efforts to organize self-help and mutual aid groups, awareness-raising groups or local political structures were successful only in the 1990s, when the political transition in Romania and Hungary slowly neutralized the ingrained fear and alienation in these people (who would have faced severe punishment in Romania for such activities). This population still bears the scars of its pre-immigration period and cannot yet be regarded as fully integrated, therefore as a risk group it needs programs of mental health prevention and promotion.

From 1990 to about 1993, thousands of ethnic Hungarians living in Serbia, Vojvodina, Croatia, Kraina and Bosnia fled to Hungary and settled, mainly in the southern part of the country—probably nurturing hopes of return to their villages and towns and therefore wanting to remain close to the border of their country of origin. These persons were usually traumatized and often had symptoms of PTSD, depression and hopelessness. They get a lot of support from the neighbouring Hungarian population and from the region's professionals. While immigrants from Romania settled in great numbers in Budapest and its suburbs, the efforts made to improve their mental health status and to deal with their specific psychodynamic and family dynamic problems are outside the author's area of knowledge, although it is clear that these immigrants suffer a lot and are at risk from many symptoms and functional complaints.

The third wave of immigrants came in the 1990s as 'economic migrants', fleeing economic hardships of Romania, Ukraine or Serbia. Mainly unskilled workers, alone or with a spouse, leaving children behind, and not wanting to settle down, they constitute a mixed group. They are mainly young people. Many of them visit their homeland frequently and are engaged in smuggling and other kinds of illegal activities; they can be found frequently among participants in the black markets and the black labour force. They are not liked by the Hungarian population and therefore often become isolated. Their illegal businesses, however, in many cases constitute a sort of interpersonal network which provides them with human support. Many of them are prone to substance abuse and are diagnosed by psychiatrists as having personality disorders. They have had low levels of adaptation and integration in their own lands and therefore adaptation in Hungary *per se* is not too difficult for them. People coming from different countries vary in their characteristics and forms of deviant behaviour. Immigrant Hungarians from Serbia are frequently active in smuggling and organized criminality; those from Romania in illegal work; while Ukrainians perform services for Ukrainian and Russian mafias, sometimes operating through Hungary in other Eastern or Western European countries. Psychiatric services do not often encounter these immigrants; they can be reached only by primary medical and social care. Since they are not interested in legalizing their status in Hungary, they are often in conflict with police or the local administration. Voluntary workers, family support services and counselling offices provide them with some help, mainly in the form of crisis intervention. Services for homeless people and welfare agencies encounter them in greater numbers. Psychologically, they show a great deal of mistrust, manipulative behaviour and unstable patterns of relating to others; on the other hand, they are adaptable to and tolerant of economic difficulties. Many are beggars, young children being also used for begging and they have a high representation among prostitutes in Hungary. They are populations at risk. Since their number is unknown, the organization of special services for them is difficult. In some regions of the country and in Budapest there are attempts to give training to general practitioners, other primary health workers, and activists in social and voluntary services, to enable them to understand and help these immigrants more effectively.

Overall, ethnic Hungarian immigrants in different stages of assimilation and integration are estimated to number 200 000–300 000 people. The interesting feature of their case is that despite the same language, a largely shared cultural tradition and many similarities in social structure between the countries concerned, they have a lot of mental health problems concerning immigration and changing lifestyles and environments. The lessons learned from Hungarian immigrants are similar to those described in the psychiatric literature concerning the people of the former East Germany. Totalitarian systems and the social organization of life in them have a great impact and they elicit special conflicts and dilemmas which produce characteristic coping mechanisms. Communist regimes penetrated such basic human structures as family, kinship, local community, work groups, etc. and their obsession with control generated fear, mistrust and regression, and encouraged passivity, drifting, lack of self-confidence and initiative. Emigration is a manifestation of maladaptation and conflict in these countries, and psychological and interpersonal problems brought to the host country carry the risk of mental health impairment and make adaptation more difficult, generating new stresses.

Immigrants of different periods in Hungary will probably have different types of mental health problems, e.g. psychiatric disorders among those who get older in Hungary and are separated from their children, or children and young adults who grow up and are educated in Hungary. It is obvious that mental health services must pay special attention to immigrants and there is a need for mental health promotion programs for them. The best way to reach them is to use the primary health services. Networking among those engaged in these services can help voluntary support organizations, special counselling and care units (where professionals and activists who have been immigrants themselves can do an excellent job) and humanitarian groups. As they become more integrated into Hungarian society, immigrants manifest problems generated by the Hungarian way of life which plague the host population—alcoholism and problem drinking, depression, overwork, marital conflicts and a high rate of divorce, etc. This suggests that the whole population needs more support from improved mental health services and through more developed forms of mental health prevention and promotion.

35

Workplaces

Doreen Miller

Private Practice, Thrupp, Oxford, UK

Mental health problems can affect employees in any business, large or small. There are 25 million people in work in the UK, and nearly three in every ten employees will have a mental health problem each year. Understanding how poor mental health can affect not only individuals' well-being but their performance at work is important for employers if they are to maintain their workforce in an optimum state of mental health. Mental health problems are one of the top three causes of time off work in the UK, contributing to 119.9 million days lost every year at a cost to industry of £3.7 billion. However, there is an additional unknown cost to employers relating to those employees who are at work but underperforming, 'the sickness presence group'.

THE EMPLOYER

Employers are increasingly motivated to address the health of their workforce due to the constant and unremitting rate of change that is affecting all businesses. This also takes its toll on employees, some of whom fail to cope with the changes and need support and help to avoid underperformance and absence from work. In addition, the global marketplace is forcing organizations to increase their efficiency and employers are motivated to look at ways of enhancing the performance of employees to avoid unnecessary losses associated with health and safety.

Employers' Legal Position

Employers have a duty under the Health and Safety at Work Act 1974 to ensure as far as reasonably practicable that their workplaces are safe and healthy for employees. Under the Management of Health and Safety Regulations 1993, employers are obligated to assess the nature and scale of risks to health in their workplace, including mental health, and base their control measures on it.

Preventing Mental Illness: Mental Health Promotion in Primary Care. Edited by R. Jenkins and T.B. Üstün.
© 1998 John Wiley & Sons Ltd.

Managers now have the responsibility for health risk assessment in the work-place, and for the management of performance of individuals: knowledge of mental health is obviously an important agenda item for managers. Employers have a legal duty to take reasonable care to ensure that employees' mental health is not placed at risk through excessive and sustained levels of stress arising from the way work is organized. Mental health problems at work which may lead to ill-health and absence need to be addressed in a similar manner to ill-health caused by physical factors in the workplace.

Employers' liability insurance annual premiums, which in some industries are increasing by up to 150% per annum, are causing employers to review what action they should take to prevent/minimize health risks in the workplace, including mental health.

THE EMPLOYEE

Employees are unlikely to have access to, and be able to take advantage of, any mental health promotion activities that their general practitioners provide unless they are ill and have need to visit the surgery. People at work spend half their waking hours in the workplace, and there is a real opportunity for employers to provide health education on mental health at work to raise awareness and enable employees to make more informed decisions about their own mental health.

WHAT IS A MENTAL HEALTH PROBLEM?

Everyone may feel low, anxious or confused at times. However, when feelings are strong, are more than a passing phase, or interfere with daily life, a mental health problem may have developed that requires help.

Anxiety and depression are the most common mental health problems. They are readily amenable to a range of treatments, which may include medication. Most people make a full recovery, often without interruption to their working lives. Serious forms of mental ill-health, such as schizophrenia and manic depression, are much rarer. Specialist treatment is needed, but people can often continue full and productive working lives.

Life today places demands and pressures on us all. No longer does employment offer 'jobs for life' and living with uncertainty is becoming the norm for most people. We all need some demands on us to remain motivated, healthy and perform at our best. However, when the pressures exceed our coping capacity, or last too long, we may fail to cope and become stressed. Prolonged stress may lead to physical and mental health problems.

WHAT CAN EMPLOYERS DO?

Employers can include mental health within their health and safety policy to demonstrate the company's commitment to a healthy workforce and to emphasize the value placed on not only physical but also mental health. To be effective, this policy should be drawn up with the involvement of management, employees and unions to ensure their commitment. The policy could address the following:

1. Recognize that there are many factors to consider in looking at the causes of mental health problems of employees, including stress at work and out of work.
2. List current factors which may be adding to stress in the organization.
3. State the organization's commitment to a course of action, which might include:
    * Educating employees to understand mental ill-health and the effect it may have on work performance.
    * Action to identify and address workplace stress, and to help employees manage pressures to avoid stress.
    * Provision of confidential and appropriate advisory and counselling services to help the individual with problems.
    * Management and facilitation of an early return to work of those who have been absent with mental health problems, taking professional advice on rehabilitation to avoid losing skilled employees.
    * Employment of appropriate occupational health professionals or provision of a contracted out occupational health service based on the organizational needs.

Factors in the Workplace Contributing to Poor Mental Health

There are many factors in the workplace that contribute to poor mental health that can be easily modified and prevent such problems. For example:

Organizational function and culture:
* Poor problem-solving environment.
* Poor communication.
* Non-supportive culture.
Role in the organization:
* Role ambiguity.
* Role conflict.
* High responsibility for people.
Career development:
* Career uncertainty.

- Career plateau.
- Poor pay.
- Fear of redundancy.

Decision latitude/control:

- Lack of decision making.
- Lack of control over work.

Interpersonal relationships at work:

- Social or physical isolation.
- Poor relationships with superiors.
- Interpersonal conflict or violence.
- Lack of social support.

Home/work interface:

- Conflicting demands of work and home.
- Low social or practical support at home.
- Dual career problems.

Task design:

- Ill-defined work.
- Uncertainty of work.
- Lack of variety or short work cycles.
- Continual exposure to people, clients or customers.

Workload:

- Work overload or underload.
- Lack of control over pace of work.
- Time pressures—tight deadlines.

Work schedule:

- Shift work.
- Long unsociable work hours.

RECOGNIZING MENTAL HEALTH PROBLEMS

Occupational health services can identify mental health problems through an occupational health audit. Through the audit process, by addressing the organization, the people, the work process and the environment, health symptoms can be identified which are associated with both the organization and the individual's performance at work and personal health. In so doing employers can prevent costly underperformance of employees associated with mental ill-health by recognizing the early signs of mental ill-health before clinical symptoms and signs lead the employee to visit his general practitioner. These may be recognized through *organizational symptoms*:

- Labour turnover.
- Absence.
- Quality problems with products.

- Late deliveries of products.
- Low morale of workforce.

These may recognized *at work* through *individual work performance symptoms*:

- Poor quality of work.
- Poor time-keeping.
- Poor decisions/lack of decision-making.
- Withdrawal from social contact.
- Unusual absences.
- Poor interpersonal relationships.
- Unusual changes in behaviour, drinking habits, smoking.

These may be also recognized through *individual health symptoms*:

- Headaches, backache, insomnia, constant tiredness.
- Feeling low or guilty, loss of confidence or sense of humour, tearfulness or tension.

If these symptoms last for more than 2 weeks, help may be needed. Most mental health problems abate completely after a couple of months. However, the earlier they are recognized and treated, the faster they will be resolved, and the workplace can provide this opportunity.

It is worthwhile for organizations to adopt a positive approach to mental health in the workplace, to take action at an early stage and prevent costly absence and disability of employees from mental ill-health. Good health of employees is good for business too.

WHAT CAN OCCUPATIONAL HEALTH SERVICES DO?

Occupational health services aim to promote the optimum state of mental, physical and social well-being of people at work and, in so doing, contribute to increasing the efficiency of the business.

Where organizations have access to an occupational health service, the mental health needs of employees and the organization can be managed effectively by the service working in partnership with employers and employees. The first step is to undertake an occupational health audit to identify the needs of the organization and the employees. In this way the following issues can be addressed:

1. Understanding the culture of the organization and the business goals.
2. Identifying the mental health needs of the employees and the organization through job and employee surveys and relevant health screening.

3. Advising management on job design to minimize risks associated with mental health, e.g. work overload, lack of control of job.
4. Providing training to improve life and managerial skills of employees, and to enhance their ability to manage pressures.
5. Providing clinical services to address individual problems with access to psychiatrists, chartered psychologists and other therapists as required.

These will now be discussed in turn:

1. *Understanding the culture of the organization and the business goals.* Understanding the culture is important because health behaviour may reflect some negative aspects of the culture, leading to stress, ill-health absence and ultimately labour turnover. It is of equal importance to have a clear idea of the business goals of the organization and the likely changes that are about to occur. In so doing, early recognition by the occupational health service of potential health problems, such as stress, anxiety and depression of employees resulting from the proposed action, may avert costly problems.

2. *Identifying mental health needs of employees and the organization.* These should be based on the recognition of the *mental health risks* in the workplace which may arise from organizational or individual sources, as already described, e.g. change in the organizational structure and systems, which may result in redundancies, psycho-social risks such as work overload, lack of control in the job, customer aggression, working in isolation; physical risks like noise and heat; chemical and ergonomic risks. Line managers have a responsibility to identify health risks in the workplace and good communications with them will assist in identifying problems early. The use of screening tools such as the Occupational Stress Indicator can be valuable in identifying the organizational aspects of mental health risks, before any action is taken.

It is important to identify where policies and procedures need to be introduced to demonstrate the organization's positive approach to mental health and to remove or minimize the risks, e.g:

- Occupational health policy to include mental health.
- Policies and procedures for sickness absence, smoking, alcohol, recruitment and ill-health retirement.
- Review of private health insurance mental health claims experience, where available, to identify trends which suggest that the mental health of employees is being affected. Thus action can be taken to prevent not only costly claims but underproductivity of employees, which may lead to labour turnover.

3. *Job design.* Review of the job description, the health risks of a job, and the health symptoms associated with those performing the job, often provides valuable information on which one can base recommendations for change to improve the job design. Occupational physicians working with psychologists

using the occupational stress indicator may be able to quantify problems of job design and make recommendations for change to avoid health symptoms in the future.

4. *Training.* The occupational health service can play an important part in the *selection process*, by identifying the health risks profile of jobs for management before assessing the fitness of employees for the job. *Specific training for all jobs* is essential and is a continual process which needs to be constantly reviewed, often through the appraisal programme. *Life skills training* is important to enable employees to make more informed decisions about their mental and physical well-being, e.g. time management, assertiveness training, handling conflict, and understanding of the dynamics of relationships. This training can be addressed through exhibitions and workshops. *Management skills training* is vital in the world of work today, with fewer people undertaking more work to provide added value for organizations. The important management skills which should be considered as a series of training courses are:

- *Two-way communication*: the ability to communicate regularly with the team and to *listen* to their communication is vital, particularly at a time of great change, as in industry today. In this way, the team members feel involved in the process of change and that they are contributing to the progress of the team/organization. At the same time, better decisions will be made with this wider communication as long as the decision-making ability of the team leader is satisfactory.
- *Decision making*: good communications are of no value unless they go hand in hand with effective decision making.
- *Team work*: leadership and the ability to delegate to team members is vital if the team is to be effective.
- *Provision of fair criticism and appraisal*: training to acquire effective skills in this area is essential for any manager.
- *Time management, assertiveness and negotiation skills training* are an important aspect of management training.

Training employees to improve their ability to *manage pressures* and prevent stress that results in clinical problems is vital, particularly at this time of great and continuing change within organizations. This not only enables individuals to identify stress symptoms in themselves and take ownership of the problem, but also enables managers to recognize problems in team members more readily and to take appropriate action. There is a plethora of stress management training available today, but the individual will gain little benefit if the organizational factors contributing to the stress are not recognized and addressed as well.

5. *Clinical services.* When symptoms of mental ill-health present in the workplace, the occupational health physician is in a key position to address the work-related aspects of the problem and to liaise with the employee's general practitioner. In some instances, referral to a psychiatrist or psychologist may be

required, and early rehabilitation back to work can be managed by the occupational health department in discussion with the employee, management, the general practitioner and specialist adviser.

Increasingly, fitness activities, back care clinics and osteopath and chiropractor services are complementary activities now associated with an occupational health service. In providing these services, often on a fee-paying basis, employers can promote good physical and mental health and prevent ill-health. Studies are now under way to quantify the benefits to the individual and the organization.

LIAISON WITH THE PRIMARY CARE TEAM

Occupational health services work closely with those in the primary care team in sharing the work- and home-related aspects of employees' health problems. In many organizations, general practitioners are invited to visit the organization to see where their patients work. This liaison serves to prevent unnecessary misunderstandings and often assists the rehabilitation back to work—e.g. following depression—where medication and the job responsibilities need to be reviewed. In this way, effective communication between general practitioner, occupational health professionals and the employee is created and time away from work is likely to be minimized. Similar liaison between other members of the primary care team and the occupational health team are likely and this partnership is worth fostering.

'HEALTH OF THE NATION' STRATEGIC PLAN

This plan aims to improve the health of all in England by addressing coronary heart disease, accidents, cancers, mental health and sexual health/AIDS, with similar programmes in Ireland, Wales and Scotland. Activities are now emerging to address the targets for mental health to improve the mental health of those at work, and for those in the community.

OPPORTUNITIES FOR THE FUTURE

An occupational health audit is an integral part of managing any quality organization, and brings mental health issues into the main business agenda. Through the health plan resulting from the audit, the services required are listed in priority order and guidance is given on how they can be introduced and implemented through in-house or contracted-out occupational health services. Regular audit provides the opportunity to monitor the targets set, measure the health symptoms and review progress at a later date. Financial and outcome measures can be addressed through this process.

Where occupational health services do not exist, caution is needed to avoid buying 'health products' such as stress management training in isolation. An audit to provide an assessment of needs resulting in a strategic plan to address the mental health needs of the organization and the employees must still be carried out. In this way the costs and benefits that may arise from services to promote good mental health can be identified and the action taken justified.

There is an opportunity for occupational health services and primary care teams to develop a joint strategy to market an agenda for mental health promotion topics in both the workplace and the community, at the same time. The Health Education Authority could complement this activity by providing new training material on a regular basis.

Members of a family would then obtain mental health messages from both the workplace and the community, providing an opportunity for more informed debate in the home on aspects of mental health.

The promotion of mental health in the workplace has started with raising the awareness of the effects of stress on work and health. Now there is an opportunity to broaden the agenda on mental health and continue the education process, recording the costs of taking no action, through measurement of health indices in the workplace, and the health benefits and savings that can be made if the appropriate action is taken. Good health is good for business too.

BIBLIOGRAPHY

Department of Health (1994) *ABC of Mental Health in the Workplace*. London: Department of Health.

Cooper CL & Williams S (1994) *Creating Health Work Organizations*. Chichester: Wiley.

Jenkins R & Coney N (1992) Prevention of Mental Ill Health at Work. London: HMSO.

Jenkins R & Warman D (1993) *Promoting Mental Health Policies in the Work Place*. London: HMSO.

36

Bereavements and Trauma

Beverley Raphael & Nada Martinek*

New South Wales Health Department, Sydney, NSW,
*and *Department of Psychiatry, University of Queensland, Brisbane, Australia*

Interest in adverse life circumstances as possible precipitants, or as having some other aetiological role in the development of pathology, is longstanding. Freud's (1917) conceptualization of the differences between mourning and melancholia provided a psychoanalytic view. He also and separately described the traumatic neuroses. Deutsch (1937) in her paper *The Absence of Grief* suggested that this would inevitably lead to pathology and Lindemann (1944) gave his first systematic presentation in his classic paper, *The Symptomatology and Management of Acute Grief.* Lindemann was the first to suggest that by correcting abnormalities in the grieving process to 'normal' grieving, positive outcomes would be achieved. However, this descriptive paper provided nothing in the way of systematic data to support such a claim.

There have been difficulties in defining the normal processes that may follow the loss of a loved one and the relationship between deviations of the grief process, other risk factors, and adverse health outcomes associated with bereavement. These factors must be identified, but it is also now recognized that the reactive processes following the loss of a loved one (grief and bereavement) differ from those following an encounter with death (traumatic stress), be this through personal life threat or the deaths of others (Figure 36.1). This latter constitutes in effect a traumatic stressor (e.g. criterion A, DSM-IV) and it is likely to lead to traumatic stress reactive processes. It is also possible that both processes may occur together in those instances which constitute traumatic bereavements (Raphael 1977; Rynearson 1984; Dyregrov & Mattheisen 1987). Interventions may need to be specific to grief reactions, post-traumatic stress reactions or both, when they occur together, and prevention may have to incorporate these understandings. The differing phenomenology and outcomes of bereavement and trauma have been reviewed elsewhere (Raphael 1995).

Preventing Mental Illness: Mental Health Promotion in Primary Care. Edited by R. Jenkins and T.B. Üstün.
© 1998 John Wiley & Sons Ltd.

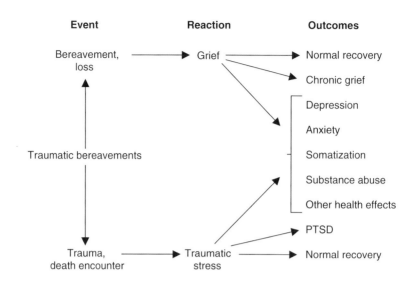

FIGURE 36.1   Reactions to different kinds of bereavement

THE BASIS FOR PREVENTION: MORBIDITY AND MORTALITY OUTCOMES

Recent reviews (Stroebe & Stroebe 1993) conclude that there is evidence that the bereaved are at heightened risk of mortality; that men are more vulnerable; that the highest risk is in weeks to months following the loss; that younger bereaved, especially men, are at higher risk as they may be socially isolated; and excess risks are chiefly in the areas of heart disease, suicides, accidents and cirrhosis of the liver. Psychiatric morbidity studies highlight the relationship of bereavement to depression: there are many symptoms of grief that are similar to depression, although these can in fact be clearly separated (Raphael 1977; Byrne & Raphael 1994). However, there is increased vulnerability to depressive episodes such as major depression (Jacobs 1993; Zisook, Shuchter & Summers 1995). Early major depressive syndromes meeting such criteria may persist, becoming chronic or recurrent with general impact on health and adaptation. Furthermore, Zisook, Shuchter & Summers (1995) report that early major depression 2–7 months after the loss, and a past history of such depression, are likely to predict depression 2 years later. Anxiety disorders are also frequent. Jacobs et al (1990) found both higher than expected levels of panic and generalized anxiety disorder in the first year post-bereavement, as well as agoraphobia and social phobia.

Post-traumatic morbidity may evolve in the form of post-traumatic stress disorder and depression or anxiety syndromes. Substance use disorder also frequently complicates the picture and co-morbidity levels are high. While there are fewer prospective studies following a traumatic incident, as has occurred for bereavements, those studies that exist, for instance after disasters (Shore, Tatum & Vollmer 1986a, b), or sexual assault (Foa et al 1991) indicate high levels of morbidity such as post-traumatic stress disorder, such rates being as high as 47% at one year after sexual assault and 20–50% after a disaster.

There have been studies of traumatic bereavements (e.g. Lundin 1984), indicating high levels of pathological outcomes, and descriptive studies such as those of Rynearson (1984) after homicide bereavements support this. Such trauma was identified as a risk factor for bereavement outcomes even prior to DSM-III diagnosis being available, with the recognition of the adverse effects of such traumatic bereavement on outcomes (Raphael & Maddison 1976).

Unanswered in these studies is the definition of *normal grief*; by what criteria grief may be determined to be pathological; and whether this may or may not have significance for outcomes. Recent studies (Middleton et al 1993; Middleton 1995) have attempted to address these issues systematically by seeking the opinions of experts and determining what were coherent concepts of pathology. The most strongly supported concepts were delayed grief, chronic grief and anticipatory grief. Absent grief was also supported but concepts of inhibited, distorted and unresolved grief tended to merge with other entities. Systematic assessment of a normal population over time established some validity for these areas with *chronic grief* occurring in about 9% of instances and there being some support for delayed grief (Middleton 1995; Byrne & Raphael 1994). Whether *chronic grief* in itself constitutes a pathological diagnosis could be argued, although it may well fit criteria for disorder and is frequently associated with both distress and impaired function. In many ways it is to bereavement what post-traumatic stress disorder is to traumatic stress, and thus could perhaps also be an appropriate focus for preventive programs.

Bereavement and trauma also lead to periods of distress and vulnerability when they occur in childhood and may be associated with risk of pathology at that time; may impact on development; or constitute risk factors creating vulnerability in adult life, either generally or in response to subsequent precipitants (e.g. Brown & Harris 1978). These factors have been reviewed in the case of bereavement (Black & Young 1995) where, while results are variable, there appears support for the view that death of a parent, before age 5, especially the mother, may be associated with subsequent vulnerability to depression for women in adult life, the more so if there is a pathway of adolescent pregnancy, non-supportive marital relationship and subsequent loss. Recent studies of women's mental health (Romans et al 1993; Mullen et al 1993) have identified patterns similar to this with childhood sexual abuse, which has strong correlations with the development of depression and suicidal behaviours in adult life. Effective interventions in childhood for both these circumstances may potentially prevent these adverse outcomes. It should be noted in the context of childhood that Pynoos & Nader (1990) have been able to demonstrate the separate phenomenology associated with grief reactions, trauma reactions and effects of separation, and that separate psychopathology syndromes (depression, post-traumatic stress disorder and anxiety syndromes) are the more likely patterns of outcome in each case.

Thus, preventive programs aimed at dealing with bereavement and trauma must address the separate phenomenology and outcomes of each. In addition, preventive programs should address both antecedent factors contributing to risk, preventing unnecessary impact of these events, and identifying those at highest risk within the population so that interventions may be focused. Thus, there are likely to be universal, selected and indicated interventions for preventive programs for bereavement and trauma.

RISK FACTORS ASSOCIATED WITH ADVERSE OUTCOMES

In each instance risk is associated with certain biographical or demographic factors (e.g. age, stage of development, gender), individual factors (coping styles, past experience, appraisal, personality), type and mode of death or trauma (including its anticipated or unanticipated nature, the degree of shock or horror, and nature of threat) and circumstances following the loss or trauma (social support as it is perceived, the recovery environment). These have been summarized for bereavement by Sanders (1993) and for traumatic stress by Green (1993).

Biographical/Demographical

There is increased risk for the bereaved of younger age for health problems, more intense grief, depression, anxiety and increased alcohol use (reviewed by Sanders 1993). Females are likely to show more intense grief reactions and in some instances poorer health outcomes, particularly in terms of psychiatric morbidity, although overall there is clear evidence that mortality is higher in men (Stroebe & Stroebe 1993; Jacobs 1993). There has been inadequate investigation of gender/age interactions. There have been no systematic reports comparing race, ethnic background or other such variables, although it has been inferred that different relationship patterns and cultural practices may influence outcome. Female gender and younger age are prominent risks (Jacobs 1993).

With regard to traumatic stress, it is likely also that younger age and female gender correlate with increased psychological vulnerability, although interaction with the severity or intensity of the stressor is clearly important (Davidson & Foa 1993). This might also be said to apply in bereavement where some bereavements have greater intensity, such as the loss of a spouse or a child.

Race, ethnic background and culture have been inadequately researched, although veteran studies showed higher rates of current post-traumatic stress disorder (PTSD) in black veterans and higher still in Hispanic male veterans (Kulka et al 1990). Poverty and reduced material circumstances are likely to add to negative outcomes in both these instances, as is likely in any circumstances of adversity and mental health outcomes.

Individual Factors

These include personality, relationship or attachment in the case of bereavement, coping styles, and past experience including experience of illness and health.

Personality Factors Relevant to Bereavement and Trauma Outcomes

These include: apprehensiveness, anxiousness and low emotional stability (Vachon et al 1982); low self-esteem and a sense of personal competency (Lund, Caserta & Dimond 1993); 'neurotic' styles (Stroebe & Stroebe 1987) (see Table 36.1). Sanders (1980), in a systematic controlled study, suggested that those with personality styles reflecting feelings of inadequacy, inferiority and insecurity were more likely to be 'disturbed' following bereavement, while those with emotionality, tension and sensitivity were more likely to become 'depressed'; a 'denial' pattern was more likely to be associated with psychosomatic outcomes; and those with adaptive coping strategies were more likely to show a normal grief reaction. Neuroticism is also a personality trait likely to add to risk and reflecting many of these variables (Middleton 1995). With respect to previous relationships, the bereaved were more likely to have highly ambivalent and/or particularly dependent relationships with the person they had lost (Raphael 1977; Saunders 1979; Parkes & Weiss 1983).

Past experience, including *previous losses* and bereavements, might well contribute, particularly those in childhood (e.g. Brown & Harris 1978). The issue of childhood losses and their longer-term consequences has been reviewed by Jacobs (1993), showing that these may constitute a risk factor for depression or anxiety disorders in adult life, but only to a minor degree. However, the implication of these contributions in the face of a subsequent loss in adulthood has not been dealt with, except in Brown & Harris's model. It is likely that past experience of inadequate parenting might also contribute, for instance through impact on patterns of relationships, but this has not been adequately assessed in bereaved populations, neither has experience of child abuse, a now established risk factor generically, especially childhood sexual abuse. *Past history of poor physical and mental health* may also contribute risk and vulnerability in the bereaved (Zisook & Shuchter 1991; Jacobs 1993, pp 158–9), although better systematic studies are also required in this context.

With respect to *traumatic stress* and *personality* factors, those that have been demonstrated to be relevant include neuroticism and introversion (McFarlane 1989; Breslau, Davis & Andreski 1991). There has been some suggestion that active problem-focused coping may be more effective, but this has not been examined broadly and systematically.

TABLE 36.1 Risk factors for morbidity (i)

	Bereavement	Trauma
Sociodemographic factors	Female Younger Lower SES	Female Younger Lower SES
	? Culture/race	? Culture/race
Individual factors	Past loss? Personal past psychiatric problems Anxiousness Low self-worth Neuroticism Attachments	Past trauma, e.g. CSA Past psychiatric problems Neuroticism Lack of hope Negative coping styles Attachments

Previous relationships may have some effect on the outcome of trauma, with respect to the support they may lend afterwards, the sources of stress that may relate to them, and the power of attachment behaviours as survival mechanisms (Henderson & Bostock 1977). However, this aspect has not been considered systematically, except in terms of social support.

Past experience in childhood is well established as a risk factor for post-traumatic stress disorder and is reviewed by Davidson & Foa (1993). They conclude from various studies that past history of child abuse, sexual assault before 16, separation or divorce of parents before the patient was aged 10, family poverty in childhood and poor education, are all risk factors contributing to the likelihood of poorer mental health outcomes.

Past history of psychiatric disorder in self or family also contributed to risk, including especially childhood conduct or behaviour disorder, or behaviour problems, personal or family history of psychiatric disorder, or substance abuse (Davidson & Foa 1993).

This constellation of variables is relevant, and is likely (see Table 36.1) to interact with event characteristics.

Nature of the Event

There is clear evidence for both bereavement and trauma, that the intensity of the experience may be the significant factor. Furthermore, it is in this area where the overlap of bereavement and trauma is most significant (see Table 36.2).

The *particular relationship* lost in bereavement is associated with various intensities of grief, with death of a child, then spouse, then of parent of adult child being associated with highest intensities to lower intensities (Middleton 1995). With the loss of still-born, neonate death or sudden infant death syndrome (SIDS), the latter is associated with the greatest level of problems (Vance et al 1991). Circumstances of the death may be associated with greater risk, for instance where the death is

TABLE 36.2 Risk factors for morbidity (ii)

	Bereavement	Trauma
Event character	Nature of loss, e.g. child	Life threat
		Encounter with death
	Sudden/untimely	Intensity
	Unexpected	Accident
	Ambivalent—Dependent	Sudden/shock
	Stigma, e.g. AIDS, suicide	Stigma, e.g. rape
Post-event circumstances	Intensity of early reaction	Intensity and duration of early reaction
		Arousal/dissociation
	Cultural rituals	Cultural rituals?
	Funeral/mourning	'Macho'
	Making meaning	Making meaning
	Recognition	Meaning, recognition
	Concurrent crises	'Concurrent' adverse life events
	Perceived social support	Perceived social support

sudden, unexpected, unanticipated and untimely (Raphael 1977). However, in some instances this relates to the 'traumatic' circumstances of the death, e.g. suicide, violence, murder, and so the complementary variables may be co-existent traumatic stress effects (Raphael & Maddison 1976). Studies of the reaction of children to death of a parent indicate that this is likely to have very significant effects, but studies of severity and risk factors are not readily available. Stigmatized bereavements such as the following AIDS deaths, and suicide, etc., may have additional problems associated with such effects.

For the instance of *traumatic stress* effects there is ample evidence that the perceived intensity of the stressor—or traumatic experience—be it combat or other, is likely to powerfully influence outcome and may, at high levels of intensity, override any other vulnerability or protective factors (Davidson & Foa 1993). For instance, intensity of life threat as indicated by wounding has been found to increase risk of PTSD in both combat veterans and rape victims. Intensity of exposure to combat, proximity of exposure to life threat and degree of exposure to the gruesome and mutilating deaths of others, have all been found to correlate with a greater risk of adverse outcomes (Davidson & Foa 1993). It should be noted, however, that McFarlane's studies suggest that risk may be greatest for acute PTSD (McFarlane 1989) as well as chronic recurrent traumatic stress disorder. The finding that other risk factors become less important with severity of exposure is also supported by Shore, Tatum & Vollmer's studies (1986a, b) of the Mt St Helen's eruption in the USA. Green (1993) identified eight generic dimensions of trauma: threat to life and limb; severe physical harm or injury; receipt of intentional injury or harm; exposure to the grotesque; violent/sudden loss of a loved one; witnessing or hearing of violence to a loved one; learning of exposure to a noxious agent; causing death or severe harm to another. These factors are encompassed in the above and can be differentiated from bereavement (i.e. if this is not complicated by trauma).

Circumstances in the Period Following the Death or Trauma

This may be classed, as it has been in the field of trauma studies, as the 'recovery environment'. There are a number of relevant factors here: the immediate and early reaction and its intensity and duration; the 'meaning' made of the event by the individual and others; concurrent adversity or stressors; and social support.

There is evidence for *bereavement* that *intensity* of early reaction may predict later difficulties, with those with highest intensity being most at risk (Vachon et al 1982; Zisook & Shuchter 1991). The capacity to view the body, undertake the prescribed cultural rituals of funeral and grieving, and find '*meaning*' in the death is frequently described in clinical studies, but lacks an adequate systematic research base (Raphael 1983). The experience of *concurrent* crises, including adverse life events and multiple bereavements, is well established as a contributing risk to adverse outcome (Raphael 1977; Parkes 1975). *Social support* is one of the most regularly identified factors associated with outcome, and perception of social support for facilitating the grieving process is a critical issue (Maddison & Walker 1967; Raphael 1977; Vachon & Stylianos 1988). A recent review (Stylianos & Vachon 1993) indicates the multiple and complex aspects of social support, its different sources, qualitative and quantitative aspects and the structure of the social network. Different sorts of support may be relevant at different phases of recovery, and 'supports' may also add stress. Personality of the individual may influence the nature of the social supports available, and unwritten rules surrounding the death, and prescriptions for behaviour following it, may influence the form, nature, expectations and percep- tions of the effects of social support. Emotional support may be vital, but practical support may also contribute. These different elements have not always been well differentiated in the research; perceived inadequacy or unhelpfulness does, how- ever, appear to be clearly established as a risk factor for adverse outcome.

With respect to *traumatic stress*, similar factors can be delineated. For instance, *intensity* and duration of initial reaction is likely to predict increased risk for PTSD, as evidenced by Weisaeth's (1993) studies and the review of Davidson & Foa (1993). High or increasing levels of *arousal persisting* in early weeks are likely to be particularly problematic. There is less evidence that here, as in bereavement, the absence of early response (either traumatic stress or grief) is associated with adverse outcomes, despite long-term belief that this is the case (e.g. Singh & Raphael 1981). Again, the *meaning* made of the event is seen as significant clinically, but is less well validated in research studies, although there is much to indicate the significance of this for the individual and in interaction with others, particularly within the culture or a subculture (Wilson 1989). The presence of *concurrent stressors* in the form of adverse life events, either before or after the trauma, have been correlated with heightened risk (McFarlane 1989).

Social support factors in traumatic situations from disasters (Murphy 1988) to combat (Solomon & Benbenishty 1986), perceptions and availability of social support and the degree of emotional support, may all contribute to outcome by means of the ways in which they facilitate emotional 'working through' of the experience, the practical assistance they may give, including advice, the opportunities for social interaction and integration, and the role models for recovery or non-recovery. Here too they may involve families, partners, others with the same experience, friends, neighbours, workmates, or support and self-help groups. The role for prevention and favourable recovery needs to be developed further as a base for prevention.

Thus, there are a number of factors identifying high-risk bereavement and trauma situations—there is potential overlap and interaction. They fit well with the theoretical concepts of trauma and integration of the recovery from it (e.g. Green, Grace & Gleser (1985) but fewer models exist to inform similar empirical findings in bereavement.

BEREAVEMENT AND PREVENTION

Prevention may operate in ways that prepare and strengthen the individual before an experience, either generally or where it is anticipated; in the response to or management of the episode; and as general or focused intervention programs afterwards.

The nature of human attachments, and the inevitability of death, mean that bereavement cannot be prevented, and in one sense grief is a tribute to the deceased. It is certainly possible, however, to prepare people for bereavements, and in ways that may alleviate potential negative impact.

Universal Interventions

While there has been *extensive public education* in many countries concerning bereavement, its consequences and the needs and care of the bereaved, there is no data on whether or not this has made any difference to the health outcomes experienced by bereaved people. This is a pity. Starting with the popularization of death and dying through the work of Elizabeth Kubler-Ross, through to the establishment of death education foundations, to the provision of bereavement courses in many different centres, there is a significant social movement to provide information for and care to bereaved people as an identified group of 'victims'. Much of this is framed in terms of prevention, as well as compassionate response. In a way it is not dissimilar to the social movements identifying the needs of the traumatized, which will be discussed subsequently. What is unclear is whether benefits have accrued for bereaved people as a consequence; for the purposes of this chapter, as to whether or not they have prevented morbidity and enhanced mental health outcomes.

Alteration of cultural prescriptions, and the social or health care structures associated with them, should also come into this context. One example of this is the pattern in Western society of making it easier for a bereaved person to see the dead body of the deceased and make his/her peace with the deceased. This was most obvious with still-birth, where in many countries it was 'prohibited' for the mother to see her dead baby, with the view it would only 'make her worse' or 'upset her'. Social movements supporting parents at this time changed these prescriptions so that parents could see, hold, spend time with, attach to and properly relinquish their dead infant (still-birth and neonatal death support programs). Photographs of the dead baby, dressing the baby and allowing other children to hold it are now common practice and perceived as helpful. The capacity to attach to the baby has been found to be associated with positive outcomes. Thus, there can be the assumption of prevention benefit although there are no controlled trials.

In *multicultural* societies there is increasing recognition of the provision for differing cultural practices surrounding death, dying and bereavement (Rosenblatt 1993; Selby 1994). This should provide for better outcomes for bereaved people in such settings, but no cross-culturally-based studies to determine this are available.

Thus, in terms of *universal interventions* there is much to suggest potential benefits, including greater knowledge and awareness, recognition of appropriate patterns of care, and when and how to get help. It is likely, but by no means established, that these have preventive benefits.

Selective Interventions for the Bereaved Likely to Be at Risk

There have been a number of trials or programs for bereaved people who are likely to be vulnerable, but not identified as specific high risk groups. This latter may be seen as those at high risk, defined as such and targeted with more focused programs, usually in the borderland between primary and secondary prevention or early intervention. The former could be considered selective interventions, the latter indicated.

Studies of those with *anticipated death*, for instance terminal illness, have shown that children whose parents are dying were less anxious, had fewer symptoms and better school and social functioning with counselling interactions than children in a non-treated control group, but there was no follow-up after the death (Zisook, Shuchter & Summers 1995).

Hospice care provides the framework for preparation for death, education to deal with it, involvement in care, resolution of unfinished business, communication, and a holistic approach to self-care for the bereaved.

Zisook's group report that in their own attempts to set up a controlled study of supportive/educational group intervention for the families of the terminally ill, the pilot study was so overwhelmingly received that this approach was incorporated as standard service (Zisook, Shuchter & Summers 1995). The National Hospice Study on care-givers' post-bereavement status gives equivocal support, in that it showed that hospital-based hospice care-givers had lower distress, greater satisfaction with patient care and less burden than cases of home-based hospice care (Greer & Mor 1986). However, after the death, home family carers, despite being more distressed, were more socially integrated and within 3 months there were no differences in utilization. Other descriptive studies provide support for such programs around anticipated deaths (Moseley et al 1988).

Some studies of *self-help, mutual support programs* have demonstrated benefits of interventions in preventive outcomes. Silverman's classic studies (1972, 1986) of the widow-to-widow interventions showed positive outcomes and generated the growth of other organizations for different bereavements: CRUSE for widows and widowers in the UK; Compassionate Friends for parents who have lost a child; Parents of Murdered Children; Military Widows; Still-birth and Neonatal Death Support; SIDS, and many others. Few of these groups have been evaluated, neither have there been many controlled trials of the interventions they offer, in terms of preventive outcome. While most trials that have been carried out are equivocal in their results (Barrett 1978), Liebermann & Videka-Sherman (1986) reported significant positive results, with widows and widowers who participated actually reporting less depression and anxiety and greater well-being and self-esteem than those who did not, although unfortunately assignment to different groups was not random.

Vachon's study is another testing *widow-to-widow individual intervention* for widows (*not* deemed to be at higher risk) and is seen as the most important contribution in this field (Vachon et al 1980). The majority of deaths were anticipated. The intervention commenced 1 month after bereavement and involved a wide range of activities, including supportive counselling. It was determined that the 'pathway of adaptation' had been facilitated by the intervention and, as has consistently been found with the preventive programs for the bereaved, was most effective with those who were at higher risk in terms of higher initial distress (although this did *not* form a basis for intervention). The high-distress women who had not received this intervention had high levels of overall psychiatric disturbance 24 months after the death. Those receiving intervention were shifted to a pattern or process similar to that of the low-risk groups. Thus, this ended up operating in the way an indicated intervention may have done. Of particular interest were the findings that intra-personal adaptations were significant and facilitated by intervention through the first 6 months, whereas at 12 months there were more social and interpersonal adaptive processes.

A study testing *counselling interventions* was carried out by Polak et al (1975), which explored effectiveness of counselling for persons following sudden deaths who were contacted 1–6 hours after the death and followed up at 6 months. Interventions of 2–6 sessions in the first 10 weeks aimed to increase the effectiveness of the family in coping with the deaths, which appeared to be traumatic for the most part. Follow-up (6 and 18 months) for both bereaved groups showed symptoms of impairment compared to non-bereaved, which is not surprising in view of the high levels of trauma. However, the non-intervention group did show a greater increase in psychiatric rating compared to the intervention, suggesting some possible benefits. Gerber et al's (1975) evaluation of intervention for the elderly showed positive benefits and was not a controlled trial.

Most other reports of *broad interventions*, for instance with groups, show that they were perceived positively. Most are without formal outcome evaluation, except for Lieberman & Yalom's (1992) study of brief group therapy for the spousally bereaved, which showed marked improvements, and similarly Summers et al's (1992) therapy for AIDS bereavements. These tend to merge more into the treatment studies, however.

Thus, there are some positive findings for these selective interventions for bereaved where, particularly following spousal bereavement, these tend to be most effective for those at higher risk, and where significant prevention has been achieved with the use of skilled volunteers, especially those who have been through the same bereavement.

Indicated Interventions for those Defined at Higher Risk

Both Raphael and Parkes showed the effectiveness in preventive terms for high-risk bereaved individuals of a focused intervention program. Raphael (1977) conducted a controlled trial with *widows thought to be at risk* from earlier studies, in terms of perceived lack of support, 'traumatic' circumstances of the death, 'pathological' ambivalence or dependence in the relationship with the spouse, or concurrent crises. Widows were allocated randomly if they met a predefined set of operational criteria including those factors. Interventions took place 3–12 weeks after the death and averaged 6–8 sessions. They aimed to support the grieving process, and to deal with the particular risk issues. There was significant benefit from intervention for high-risk widows, whose outcomes differed significantly in terms of decreased risk of adverse psychosocial effects. Benefits were most pronounced for those at risk in terms of perceived non-support, where effects appeared chiefly in health care utilization. Where intervention had dealt with a pre-existing ambivalent relationship with the husband, effects were found in lessening the severity of depressive symptomatology.

Parkes also used a *high-risk methodology* and a validated assessment of risk factors, which included: a clinging, angry and self-reproachful relationship with the deceased before death; perceived lack of support from family; young age; low socio-economic status; and nurses' rating of bereaved's likely coping ability (Parkes 1979). Interventions to those randomly allocated were provided by volunteers with training for this and who were supported by psychiatrists and social workers. Twenty months later there were positive benefits from intervention in terms of lower levels of adverse changes in health; physical and mental morbidity here too was shifted to the level of the low-risk group. It should be noted that Parkes (1980) also found that increased training was associated with better outcomes (up to 2 years).

These findings support Parkes's (1980) conclusion that bereavement counselling works. They merge into studies that examine *counselling for those already suffering adaptive difficulties*. For instance, Kleber & Brom's (1987) study of intervention for pathological bereavements deals with these chiefly in terms of their traumatic elements. They found that trauma desensitization, trauma psychotherapy and hypnotherapy were all effective, chiefly, however, in terms of effects on symptoms of stress response syndromes, compared to the wait list control. However, this is clearly treatment of disorder in traumatized bereaved people, seen an average of 23 months after the loss, and showing pretest levels of psychiatric symptomatology. Similarly, Marmar et al (1988) showed that bereaved widows suffering adjustment disorders, PTSD and major depression benefited from brief dynamic psychotherapy and mutual self-help groups, with some advantages for the psychotherapy.

Other treatments for bereaved people with pathology include behavioural treatments, such as guided mourning (Mawson et al 1981) and cognitive-behavioural treatments (Walls & Meyer 1985), although the latter demonstrated little benefit. Religious psychotherapy has also been used for depressed bereaved individuals and found to be effective (Azhar & Varma 1995).

There are numerous other reports of interventions, but these are usually descriptive, rarely controlled, and not provided in prevention formats. They include psychotherapy, behaviour therapy, groups, self-help programs and medication for those suffering depression (Jacobs 1993).

Other Bereavements

Of particular concern was the high distress and possibility of morbid outcome for parents following the death of a child, which, as noted above, is the loss associated with the highest levels of bereavement distress. Forrest, Standish & Baum (1982) found that mothers whose babies died within 7 days of birth showed better social and emotional adjustment at 6 months with support and counselling than those who did not receive it. However, there were no differences at 14 months, showing, as have some other studies, that time was a significant factor, and that intervention may simply have helped resolution earlier. This was not a delineated high-risk group with this sample, however.

A more recent study (Murray 1995, personal communication) shows significant benefits. Murray, on the basis of previous research from her group and others on risk factors for parents following the death of an infant, developed a resource package on dealing with the loss, including aspects for the self and family, as well as information for those providing support. A prototype of this intervention was tested with bereaved families randomly allocated to intervention or usual care. The experimental families were interviewed at 1–2 months after the death and

Box 36.1   Controlled trial of resource
package intervention—still-births, neonatal
and SIDS (Murray 1995)

- Prevention outcomes, 6–15 months
- Reduced depression/anxiety
- Better social and mental function
- Reduced physical symptoms
- Better for those at high risk

allocated to counsellors. Although risk was determined in terms of factors as above, they were not used for intervention or conveyed to counsellors. Independent evaluation was conducted 6–15 months following the loss, and showed beneficial outcomes in terms of depression/anxiety, physical symptoms, sense of isolation and desolation, and cohesion and satisfaction with the marital relationship. While those at low risk also benefited, those at higher risk showed greatest benefit, significant in terms of prevention outcomes. The intervention was of variable time as mutually decided by family and counsellor and the intervention was delivered via the resource package (see Box 36.1).

The broad multifaceted approach in this study offers significant benefits for universal, selective and indicated interventions. Knowles (1994) has provided a further valuable example of the implementation of support for this type of bereavement in the work of the West Australian Rural Pregnancy Loss Team. This program suggests very positive benefits and deals with those in situations where access to all other services and supports would be low.

Bereaved Children and Young People

While there have recently been more studies delineating risk following bereavement for children, there has been limited preventive interventions despite the potential for morbidity at the time, impact on development and subsequent psychiatric vulnerability (Figure 36.2).

Black & Young (1995) reviewed the current status of understanding and preventive programs for bereaved children. Risk factors include age, cognitive understanding, development and emotional maturity, past experiences and family circumstances, nature of the death and associated trauma, child's inclusion in social rituals, surviving parent's grief, continuity of parental care, and subsequent family function and structure. There have been descriptions of pre-bereavement preparation and preventive intervention with some enhanced outcomes; support programs for parents; explanation and support for child, etc. However, there has been only one trial—Black and Urbanowitz's (1987) finding of brief family therapy intervention—which produced better outcomes for prevention. Another trial is in

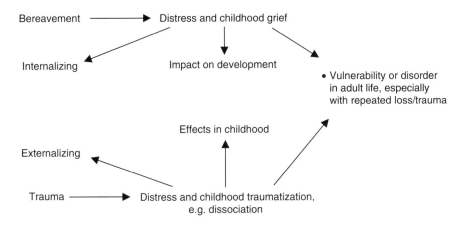

FIGURE 36.2 Bereavement and trauma in childhood and possibilities for prevention. *(see Pynoos & Nader 1990)

progress with this group. Sadly, there are few studies with adolescents and no trials of preventive intervention were identified.

Other Losses

Whether the bereavement model of preventive intervention can be applied to other situations of loss has not been established. Successful prevention has been demonstrated with divorce (Bloom et al 1982), although there is little to suggest that this utilized a bereavement approach. Parkes (1993) suggested that other psychosocial transitions, for instance loss of a limb, might be considered in this way, but there are no trials of preventive intervention in such contexts.

Evaluation of Preventive Bereavement Programs

It is somewhat surprising that, despite such significant evidence of demonstrated benefits, there have been few systematic preventive intervention programs for high-risk bereavements, or evaluation of the counselling programs that so often apply. Bereavement counsellors are attached to primary care practices and some hospices. In short, they operate alongside or as informal carers in the community, or through self-help group programs.

Box 36.2   Some Australian programs of interest

- *Rural Pregnancy Loss Team*
  Perinatal loss. Flying team; seminars, public meetings and interviews across rural Western Australia, covering some 250 000 km^2 (Knowles 1994)
- *Narrative therapy for aboriginal families*
  For loss and trauma (Howsen, personal communication 1994); also holistic counselling
- *Post-disaster intervention for the bereaved*
  Evaluation; some benefits (Singh & Raphael 1981)

Evaluation of a disaster response for high-risk bereaved individuals was carried out after a rail disaster in Australia and demonstrates some limited effects in terms of being helpful for those who perceived it positively, needed social support and had some skilled intervention (Singh & Raphael 1981). Studies evaluating hospice programs were noted above.

Some other developments of interest in Australia (see Box 36.2) include the Rural Pregnancy Loss Team noted above and the evolution of narrative therapy for culturally appropriate counselling with indigenous people for loss and trauma.

There is clearly a need to build on current findings, and to develop and implement prevention programs in areas where they are likely to be of benefit. The difficulties and resistances to such prevention should be noted (Eisenberg 1995). Policies favouring early intervention and prevention could have one focus in this area, as recent national goals and target initiatives in Australia suggest. Such programs for bereavement could contribute to prevention of depression and related disorders. However, even though such policy proposals exist, their operationalization would be another matter (Better Health Outcomes for Australians 1994).

TRAUMA AND PREVENTION

The opportunities for prevention with respect to traumatic incidents have been less well investigated empirically. Here too, however, there is a need to consider whole-system interventions, including those that may prevent traumatic incidents or minimize their impact; as well as those directed towards traumatized populations who may be further defined by level of risk for PTSD or other morbid outcomes. Wilson (1995) has provided a very valuable overview of the opportunities in this field. The attractiveness of this field is clear: it is the only area of psychiatric morbidity where diagnosis is clearly defined in terms of the aetiology, and where clear evidence exists of the role of the external stressor in the development of disorder. Nowhere, either, do attempts at prevention confront so clearly our inability to change human behaviour, with increasing levels of violence, damaging effects of current wars and terrorism, and significant levels of post-trauma morbidity, now systematically measured. As Wilson states:

> Many of the conditions that cause post-traumatic stress disorder and co-morbid states . . . are embedded in the historical and cultural forces that may lead to violence, destruction, chaos, genocide, torture and forms of brutality and inhumanity.

Universal Interventions

Community-wide programs could range from those aimed at preventing traumatic incidents, e.g. violence or war, to those of education and structural change to lessen impact. There are national programs, and other strategies, goals and targets aimed at lessening violence. These matters are beyond the scope of this chapter and are dealt with elsewhere.

Public education about trauma and its effects has been carried out in some instances, both with the broader community and with organizations. In some instances this has been in response to a disaster or similar event. While inherently there appear to be advantages to such an approach, this has not as yet been established. A component of such education is awareness of self-response and capacity to care for others. One example of such an approach is a pocket card for broad use in primary care or emergency response settings (see Box 36.3). Some programs of this type at a primary care level have been evaluated (Meldrum 1995), but their effects for prevention not assessed. Furthermore, there must be concern if normal trauma reactions are identified as pathological in such circumstances, especially where litigation or secondary gain are involved.

Altering cultural prescriptions about trauma through information or other change could constitute an important element of prevention. This is particularly relevant in those organizations such as the military, police or emergency services where there have been very strong prescriptions that any reaction to trauma is a sign of personality inadequacy, where it may be seen as interfering with career progression, or where the only sanctioned forms of coping may be through heavy alcohol or drug use. There has recently been recognition by such services, which are often dominated by men and male gender values, that some form of counselling or debriefing is appropriate. While these interventions are sanctioned, longer-term pathology tends to be condemned and is still seen to reflect some failure of the individual.

The culture which recognizes both the suffering and achievements of the individual is relatively rare, and those that recognize suffering may provide undue reinforcement of victim status. Social movements of victim groups, ranging from crime victims' associations through to veterans' groups, have been powerful in building new cultural prescriptions. These may provide significant emergency support and longer-term models of identification and social networks. Lobbying is

---

BOX 36.3 Public education—a pocket card for management of normal trauma reactions (Meldrum & Raphael 1994)

Traumatic events such as the one you have witnessed or been involved in may cause you to experience some reactions

Reactions may be physical, emotional or cognitive (thinking)

Anger is a common reaction and may cause you or those close to you some concern. Or you may have a lack of feeling and withdraw from those close to you

Usually these reactions settle after a short period. If they do not it is important for you to seek advice from your medical practitioner or a mental health professional (psychiatrist, psychologist or social worker)

Memories of the event can occur as dreams when sleeping or as intrusive thoughts during waking moments. These reactions are part of the normal recovery process. If these intrusive thoughts continue for more than one month it is important that you seek help from a medical or mental health professional

Always take care of yourself, particularly after exposure to a traumatic event—maintain a healthy diet, have adequate sleep, be careful when driving. If you feel you are not 'back to normal' within a few weeks, it is very important that you seek help from your own medical practitioner or a mental health professional

---

also a major function on behalf of victim needs, and these groups have been valuable in identifying needs for services, mental health, social welfare, legal and other. But for the most part there has been no estimation or evaluation of preventive or other benefits.

Combat effects leading to psychiatric morbidity have been clearly defined for a substantial period of time. Yet despite specific recommendations, there is no evidence that prevention goals have been achieved. Indeed, the first report of preventive psychiatry suggesting an epidemiological approach made specific recommendations concerning combat-related population disorders (Appel & Beebe 1946). These reports identified the role of danger, the duration of time in combat and the means of reducing manpower loss from combat-induced psychiatric disorders. Their recommendations included limiting combat tours of duty with the 'promise of an honourable release from combat duty at a definite time'; rewards for achievement, i.e. special privileges for the special types of soldiers, those who were combat soldiers, with acknowledgement of their specialist role; tactical orientation, e.g. better briefing of combat troops about the purposes of a particular operation; strategic orientation, i.e. why they are fighting and the necessity for it. Other aspects dealt with more evaluation systems, replacement systems, training, command. These findings were said to be so compelling that they resulted in changes even in the latter part of World War II, with some benefit. The degree to which findings were tested and incorporated subsequently is not clear. This was the first proper initiative in terms of an environmental approach to prevention in mental health, was public health in orientation and was testable. As the authors state, it provided a model.

BOX 36.4   Selective interventions for traumatized populations

Debriefing and CISD
- Popular, widely used (Mitchell and others)
- Perceived as helpful to a major degree (evaluation) (Robinson & Mitchell 1993)
- No controlled trials—some negatives
- Studies with follow-up (4 areas). No effect to prevent PTSD (Raphael et al 1995; Deahl et al 1994)
- Individualized counselling often preferred

Community Disaster Interventions
- Generic—evaluation lacking
- Children after bushfires workbook preliminary results, prevention benefits (Storm 1995)

The possibility that psychiatry can contribute to mental health of the population by recommending environmental changes involving policy and procedure in industry, education and elsewhere bears further study (Appel & Beebe 1946, p 1475).

Selective Interventions for Traumatized Populations

These interventions have been developed in a number of formats (see Box 36.4). The most widely utilized of these is debriefing. This has been built for the most part on the model put forward by Mitchell (1983, 1988) of critical incident stress debriefing (CISD). This is extensively used following a wide range of community trauma situations such as severe accidents, incidents and disasters. Despite a number of positive evaluations in terms of levels of perceived helpfulness (Robinson & Mitchell 1993) there are to date no systematic studies indicating it is effective in preventing PTSD or other post-trauma morbidity. Studies to date after transport disasters, earthquakes, military body handling and other circumstances all failed to find a positive effect (Raphael, Meldrum & McFarlane 1995). Indeed, there is even some cause for concern that debriefing as currently used may lead to greater risk of delayed or negative outcomes. Many express positive feelings about the opportunity to share their experiences with others who have been through the same experience, but a significant number see the timing as inappropriate, the format as unsuitable, or feel the need for an individualized counselling approach. The extremely positive views about the likely benefits of debriefing have meant that there has been little in the way of randomized controlled trials to date, but much in available data indicates cause for concern.

Wilson (1995) has suggested that interventions aiming to modify, by strengthening, seven dimensions that have been found in various studies to relate to vulnerability could provide a direction for interventions. These include: loss of control (a sense of efficacy and determination); self-disclosure of the trauma story to sympathetic others; a sense of group identity and a sense of the self as a survivor (rather than a victim); the perception of personal and social resources to aid coping; altruistic or pro-social behaviour; the capacity to find meaning in the traumatic experience and life afterwards; connection; bonding and social inter-action with a significant community. These general approaches are likely to be helpful, but have not been tested for preventive outcomes.

Indicated Interventions Following High Risk with Traumatized Populations

This merges with early interventions for those in the early months following trauma for, as Davidson & Foa (1993) indicate, it is likely that PTSD is established with chronicity within the first 3 months.

Circumstances of *sexual assault or rape* are clearly identified as leading to high rates of PTSD symptomatology which, although decreasing over time, is still associated with high levels of residual morbidity (Davidson & Foa 1993). This also applies to those victimized criminally in other ways. Interventions of counselling or cognitive behavioural therapy have been shown to be effective in reducing PTSD outcomes and thus have potential preventive benefit (Foa et al 1991).

Childhood sexual abuse is another circumstance with profound traumatizing effects. It is only very recently that there has been an attempt to evaluate the beneficial or other effects of a short-term therapy, also in the cognitive–behavioural mode, for this group (Deblinger, McLeer & Henry 1990).

Both these circumstances should be dealt with compassionately, in ways which do not lead to secondary traumatization, and also supported and evaluated further for optimal prevention outcomes.

Another area where effective prevention of PTSD has been demonstrated is with that PTSD which occurs *in association with psychotic decompensation* and its treatment (McGorry 1995). Changing structures and support has been effective in reducing the co-morbidity from 40% of admissions to nil—a startling achievement (McGorry & Singh 1995). This indicates, however, that it may be possible to prevent other identified post-traumatic morbidity associated with medical conditions or pro-cedures, using structural changes, support and education, and perhaps counselling.

Combat stress reactions represent an acute early decompensation in the face of stress. They have been extensively reviewed by Solomon (1993) in her studies of the Israeli Army. Active interventions for this population follow the military psychiatry model of proximity, immediacy and exposure. Interventions have been successful in returning troops to combat. However, these same soldiers are more vulnerable to levels of PTSD subsequently than those who have not had a combat stress reaction, so that prevention benefits cannot be demonstrated.

Other acute interventions for those decompensating are usually built on such models, or that of psychological first aid. Often they are behavioural programs.

Prevention outcomes have not been established. Clearly, further research is needed in this regard.

There have also been studies of traumatized populations who have decompensated with PTSD or related morbidity. These include the studies of PTSD bereavements, noted above, and more recently studies following accidents (Brom Kleber & Hofman 1993). None, however, have provided evidence of effective early intervention or prevention of specific PTSD.

Studies of the *treatment* of established PTSD have been lacking and are usually directed towards veteran populations with chronic disorder. There are few controlled trials, although there is some demonstration of the benefits of medication to deal with arousal or other elements of disorder; self-help groups, holistic therapies, cultural rituals such as the Smoke Lodge and specific inpatient programs have all been tried, while few have had systematic study until recently, for instance through national centres for PTSD.

It is very attractive to consider prevention in the context of trauma, but there is much to suggest that approaches to date have either been simplistic, inappropriately timed, fail to meet individual needs or to deal with the damage to trust that is central for many traumatized people, particularly with trauma resulting from the action of others. There is an urgent need to develop and test scientifically and theoretically valid preventive interventions for traumatized populations.

It is also critical that where *traumatic bereavements* occur, the high risk associated with them (Raphael 1983) is recognized, and that prevention addresses both stressor components, perhaps the trauma first (e.g. Lindy et al 1983). This group needs more focused and probably extended interventions.

CONCLUSIONS

While there is good evidence for the value of preventive interventions with the bereaved, and models for implementation of programs in primary care and other settings, few systematic national policies or programs exist to enhance mental health outcomes for those who are at high risk following bereavement.

With trauma populations there is less to support a hopeful approach, although hope itself is central to outcome. Structural changes and altered cultural prescriptions could potentially be helpful, as could workplace health and safety initiatives for trauma and mental health (Turner, Meldrum & Raphael 1995). While simple approaches have been attractive, they have failed to achieve preventive benefits and there is an urgent need for randomized controlled trials.

Clearly, as many of these interventions rely on counselling or interpersonal interaction and empathy for the telling of the trauma story, the giving of testimony or the sharing of grief, there will be many implications of trauma for the care-providers, be they primary or specialized health workers. Curricula are necessary on this account to develop appropriate skills and knowledge. In addition, such populations run the risk of themselves being traumatized by the nature of their work (Raphael, Meldrum & Donald 1993) and need work-place structures, supervision, recognition and release to prevent the development of burn-out or other stress-related consequences.

Action at primary care levels within the community and through general practitioners, community nurses and others, can be both compassionate and effective. It needs to be matched with other public health interventions to optimize the potential which currently exists for prevention in mental health, in relation to these environmental influences.

REFERENCES

Appel JW & Beebe GW (1946) Preventive psychiatry: an epidemiologic approach. *J Am Med Assoc* **131**, 1469–75.

Azhar MZ & Varma SL (1995) Religious psychotherapy as management of bereavement. *Acta Psychiat Scand* **91**, 233–5.

Barrett CJ (1978) Effectiveness of widows' groups in facilitating change. *J Consult Clin Psychol* **46**, 20–31.

Better Health Outcomes for Australians (1994) *National Goals, Targets and Strategies for Better Health Outcomes into the Next Century*. Canberra: Commonwealth Department of Human Services and Health, AGPS.

Black D & Young B (1995) Bereaved children and preventive intervention. In B Raphael & G Burrows (eds) *Handbook of Preventive Psychiatry*. Amsterdam: Elsevier.

Black D & Urbanowicz MA (1987) Family intervention with bereaved children. *J Child Psychol Psychiat* **28**, 467–76.

Bloom BL, Hodges WF & Caldwell RA (1982) Preventive intervention programme for the newly separated: initial evaluation. *Am J Comm Psychol* **10**, 251–64.

Byrne GJA & Raphael B (1994) A longitudinal study of bereavement phenomena in recently widowed elderly men. *Psychol Med* **24**, 411–21.

Breslau N, Davis GC, Andreski P (1991) Traumatic events and post-traumatic stress disorder in an urban population of young adults. *Arch Gen Psychiat* **48**, 216–22.

Brom D, Kleber RJ & Hofman M (1993) Victims of traffic accidents: incidence and prevention of post-traumatic stress disorder. *J Clin Psychol* **49**(2), 131–40.

Brown GW & Harris T (1978) *Social Origins of Depression*. London: Tavistock.

Davidson JT & Foa EB (eds) (1993) *Post-traumatic Stress Disorder, DSM-IV and Beyond*. Washington, DC: American Psychiatric Press.

Deahl MP, Gillham AB, Thomas J et al (1994) Psychological sequelae following the Gulf War. Factors associated with subsequent morbidity and the effectiveness of psychological debriefing. *Br J Psychiat* **165**, 60–65.

Deutsch H (1937) Absence of grief. *Psycho-Anal Quart* **6**, 12–22.

Deblinger E, McLeer SV & Henry D (1990) Cognitive behavioural treatment for sexually abused children suffering post-traumatic stress: preliminary findings. *J Am Acad Child Adolesc Psychiat* **29**(5), 747–52.

Dyregov A & Mattheisen SB (1987) Stillbirth, neonatal death and sudden infant death syndrome (SIDS): Parental reactions. *Scand J Psychol* **28**, 104–14.

Eisenberg L (1995) Social policy and the reality of prevention. In B Raphael and G Burrows (eds) *Handbook of Preventive Psychiatry*. Amsterdam: Elsevier.

Freud S (1917) *Mourning and Melancholia*. In Sigmund Freud Collected Papers, vol 4. New York: Basic Books.

Foa EB, Rothbaum BO, Riggs DS & Murdock TB (1991) Treatment of post-traumatic stress disorder in rape victims: a comparison between cognitive–behavioural procedures and counselling. *J Consult Clin Psychol* **59**(5), 715–23.

Forrest GC, Standish E & Baum JD (1982) Support after perinatal death: a study of support and counselling after perinatal bereavement. *Br Med J* **285**, 1475–9.

Gerber I, Weiner A, Battin D & Arkin A (1975) Brief therapy to the aged bereaved. In B Schoenberg & I Gerber (eds) *Bereavement: Its Psychosocial Aspects*, pp 310–13. New York: Columbia University Press.

Green BL, Grace MC & Gleser GL (1985) Identifying survivors at risk: long-term impairment following the Beverly Hills Supper Club fire. *J Consult Clin Psychol* **53**, 672–8.

Green BL (1993) Identifying survivors at risk: trauma and stressors across events: In JP Wilson & B Raphael (eds) *International Handbook of Traumatic Stress Syndromes*, pp 135–44. New York: Plenum.

Greer DS & Mor V (1986) An overview of national hospice study findings. *J Chron Dis* **39**, 5–7.

Henderson S & Bostock T (1977) Coping behaviour after shipwreck. *Br J Psychiat* **131**, 15–20.

Jacobs SC (1993) *Pathologic Grief: Maladaptation to Loss*. Washington, DC: American Psychiatric Press.

Kleber RJ & Brom D (1987) Psychotherapy and pathological grief: controlled outcome study. *Israeli J Psychiat Rel Sci* **24**, 99–109.

Knowles S (1994) A passage through grief: the Western Australian rural pregnancy loss team. *Br Med J* **309**, 1705–8.

Kulka RA, Schlenger WE, Fairbank JA et al (1990) *Trauma and the Vietnam War Generation*. New York: Brunner Mazel.

Lieberman MA & Yalom I (1992) Brief group psychotherapy for the spousally bereaved: a controlled study. *Int J Group Psychother* **42**, 117–32.

Lieberman MA & Videka-Sherman L (1986) The impact of self-help groups on the mental health of widows and widowers. *Am J Orthopsychiat* **56**, 435–49.

Lindemann E (1944) Symptomatology and management of acute grief. *Am J Psychiat* **101**, 141–8.

Lindy JD, Green BL, Grace M & Tichener J (1983) Psychotherapy with survivors of the Beverly Hills Supper Club fire. *Am J Psychother* **37**, 593–610.

Lund DA, Caserta MS & Dimond MF (1993) The course of bereavement in later life. In MS Stroebe, W Stroebe & RO Hanson (eds) *Handbook of Bereavement: Theory, Research and Intervention*. Cambridge: Cambridge University Press.

Lundin T (1984) Morbidity following sudden and unexpected bereavement. *Br J Psychiat* **144**, 84–8.

Maddison D & Walker WL (1967) Factors affecting the outcome of conjugal bereavement. *Int J Psychiat* **113**, 1057–67.

Marmar CR, Horowitz MJ, Weiss DS, Wilner NR & Kaltreider NB (1988) A controlled trial of brief psychotherapy and mutual-help group treatment of conjugal bereavement. *Am J Psychiat* **145**, 203–9.

Mawson D, Marks IM, Ramm L & Stern RS (1981) Guided mourning for morbid grief: a controlled study. *Br J Psychiat* **138**, 185–93.

McGorry P & Singh B (1995) Schizophrenia: risk and possibility. In B Raphael & G Burrows (eds) *Handbook of Preventive Psychiatry*. Amsterdam: Elsevier.

McGorry P (1995) Personal communication.

McFarlane AC (1989) The aetiology of post-traumatic morbidity: predisposing, precipitating and perpetuating factors. *Br J Psychiat* **154**, 221–8.

Meldrum L & Raphael B (1994) *Trauma Information Card*. Monel Print Department of Psychiatry, University of Queensland.

Meldrum L (1996) How Healthy Is Your Workplace in Time of Trauma? Training Program presented at Cunningham Centre, Toowoomba Base Hospital, 30 June.

Middleton W (1995) Bereavement Phenomenology and the Process of Resolution. MD Thesis, University of Queensland.

Mitchell J (1983) When disaster strikes. The critical incident stress debriefing process. *J Emerg Med Serv* **8**(1), 36–9.

Mitchell J (1988) Stress: the history, status and future of critical incident stress debriefing. *J Emerg Med Serv* **44** (December), 47–52.

Moseley JR, Logan SJ, Tolle SW & Bentley JH (1988) Developing a bereavement program in a university hospital setting. *Oncology Nurses Forum*, **15**, 151–5.

Mullen PE, Martin JL et al (1993) Childhood sexual abuse and mental health in adult life. *Br J Psychiat* **163**, 721–32.

Murphy SA (1988) Mediating effects of intrapersonal and social support on mental health 1 and 3 years after a natural disaster. *J Traumat Stress* **1**, 155–72.

Murray J (1995) *An Ache In Their Hearts*. Resource Package, Department of Child Health, University of Queensland (personal communication).

Parkes CM (1975) Determinants of outcome following bereavement. *Omega* **6**, 303–23.

Parkes CM (1979) Evaluation of a bereavement service? In A DeVries & J Carmichael (eds) *The Dying Human*, pp 389–402. Ramat Gan, Israel: Turtledove.

Parkes CM (1980) Bereavement counselling: does it work? *Br Med J* **281**, 3–10.

Parkes CM & Weiss RS (1983) *Recovery from Bereavement*. New York: Basic Books.

Parkes CM (1993) Bereavement as a psychosocial transition: processes of adaptation to change. In MS Stroebe, W Stroebe & RO Hanson (eds) *Handbook of Bereavement: Theory, Research and Intervention*. Cambridge: Cambridge University Press.

Polak PR, Egan D, Vandenburgh R & Vail Williams W (1975) Prevention in mental health: a controlled study. *Am J Psychiat* **132**, 146–9.

Pynoos RS & Nader K (1990) Children's exposure to violence and traumatic death. *Psychiat Ann* **20**, 334–44.

Raphael B & Maddison DC (1976) The care of bereaved adults. In OW Hill (ed) *Modern Trends in Psychosomatic Medicine*. London: Butterworth.

Raphael B (1977) Preventive intervention with the recently bereaved. *Arch Gen Psychiat* **12**, 1450–54.

Raphael B (1983) *Anatomy of Bereavement*. New York: Basic Books.

Raphael B (1995) *The Intervention of Trauma and Grief*. Department of Psychiatry, The University of Psychiatry.

Raphael B, Meldrum L & Donald M (1993) Survey of mental health professionals working in the field of trauma. Paper presented at the Australasian Society for Traumatic Stress Studies National Conference, Adelaide, April 22.

Raphael B, Meldrum L & McFarlane AC (1995) Does debriefing after psychological trauma work? *Br Med J* **310**, 1479–80.

Robinson R & Mitchell J (1993) Evaluation of psychological debriefings. *J Traumat Stress*, **6**(3), 367–82.

Romans SE, Walton VA et al (1993) Otago women's health survey 30 month follow-up 11: remission patterns of non-psychotic psychiatric disorder. *Br J Psychiat* **163**, 739–46.

Rosenblatt PC (1993) Grief: the social context of private feelings. In MS Stroebe, W Stroebe & RO Hanson (eds) *Handbook of Bereavement: Theory, Research and Intervention*. Cambridge: Cambridge University Press.

Rynearson EK (1984) Bereavement after homicide: a descriptive study. *Am J Psychiat* **141**, 1452–4.

Sanders CM (1979) The use of the MMPI in assessing bereavement outcome. In CS Newmark (ed) *MMPI: Clinical and Research Trends*, pp 223–47. New York: Praeger.

Sanders CM (1980) A comparison of adult bereavement in the death of a spouse, child and parent. *Omega* **10**, 303–22.

Sanders CM (1993) Risk factors in bereavement outcome. In MS Stroebe, W Stroebe & RO Hanson (eds) *Handbook of Bereavement: Theory, Research and Intervention.* Cambridge: Cambridge University Press.

Selby J (1994) A Cross-cultural–Religious Study of the Aspects of Death and Dying. MD Thesis, University of Queensland.

Shore JH, Tatum E & Vollmer W (1986a) Evaluation of mental effects of disaster: Mount St Helen's eruption. *Am J Publ Health* **76**, 76–83.

Shore JH, Tatum E & Vollmer W (1986b) Psychiatric reactions to disaster: the Mt St Helen's experience. *Am J Psychiat* **143**, 590–95.

Silverman PR (1972) Widowhood and preventive intervention. *Fam Coordinator* **21**, 95–102.

Silverman PR (1986) *Widow-to-Widow.* New York: Springer.

Singh B & Raphael B (1981) Post-disaster morbidity of the bereaved: a possible role for preventive psychiatry. *J Nerv Ment Dis* **169**, 203–12.

Solomon Z & Benbenishty R (1986) The role of proximity, immediacy, and expectancy in frontline of central stress reaction among Israelis in the Lebanon war. *Am J Psychiat* **143**, 613–17.

Solomon Z (1993) Immediate and long-term effects of traumatic combat stress among Israeli veterans of the Lebanon war. In JP Wilson & B Raphael (eds) *International Handbook of Traumatic Stress Syndromes*, pp 321–33. New York: Plenum.

Storm V (1995) Personal communication, Rozelle Hospital, Sydney.

Stroebe W & Stroebe M (1987) *Bereavement and Health.* New York: Cambridge University Press.

Stroebe, MS & Stroebe W (1993) The mortality of bereavement: a review. In MS Stroebe, W Stroebe & RO Hanson (eds) *Handbook of Bereavement: Theory, Research and Intervention.* Cambridge: Cambridge University Press.

Stylianos SK & Vachon MLS (1993) The role of social support in bereavement. In MS Stroebe, W Stroebe & RO Hanson (eds) *Handbook of Bereavement: Theory, Research and Intervention.* Cambridge: Cambridge University Press.

Summers J, Zisook S, Atkinson JH, Brown S, Gutierrez R, Pace P, McCutcheon A & Grant I (1992) *Predicting Grief Resolution in Bereaved Men at High Risk for HIV.* Scientific Proceedings of the 39th Annual Meeting of the Academy of Psychosomatic Medicine, San Diego, California, Oct 29–Nov 1.

Turner J, Meldrum L & Raphael B (1995) Preventive aspects of occupational mental health. In B Raphael & G Burrows (eds) *Handbook of Preventive Psychiatry.* Amsterdam: Elsevier.

Vachon ML, Lyall WA, Rogers J, Freedman-Letofsky K & Freeman SJ (1980) A controlled study of self-help intervention for widows. *Am J Psychiat* **137**, 1380–84.

Vachon M, Sheldon AR, Lance WJ, Lyall WA, Rogers J & Freeman S (1982) Correlates of enduring distress patterns following bereavement: social network, life situation, and personality. *Psychol Med* **12**, 783–8.

Vachon MLS & Stylianos KL (1988) The role of social support in bereavement. *J Soc Issues* **44**, 175–90.

Vance JC, Foster WJ, Najman JM, Embleton G, Thearle MJ & Hodgen FM (1991) Early parental responses to sudden infant death, stillbirth or neo-natal death. *Med J Austral* **155**, 292–7.

Walls N & Meyer AW (1985) Outcome in group treatments for bereavement: experimental results and recommendations for clinical practice. *Int J Ment Health* **13**, 126–47.

Weisaeth L (1993) Torture of a Norwegian ship's crew. Stress reactions, coping and psychiatric after-effects. In JP Wilson & B Raphael (eds) *International Handbook of Traumatic Stress Syndromes*, pp 743–50. New York: Plenum.

Wilson JP (1989) *Trauma, Transforming and Healing.* New York: Brunner Mazel.

Wilson JP (1995) Traumatic events and post-traumatic stress disorder and prevention. In B Raphael & G Burrows (eds) *Handbook of Preventive Psychiatry*. Amsterdam: Elsevier.

Zisook S & Shuchter SR (1991) Depression through the first year after the death of a spouse. *Am J Psychiat* **148**, 1346–52.

Zisook S, Shuchter SR & Summers J (1995) Bereavement risk and preventive intervention. In B Raphael & G Burrows (eds) *Handbook of Preventive Psychiatry*. Amsterdam: Elsevier.

Marital Problems and Their Prevention

Roslyn Corney
University of Greenwich, London, UK

THE PREVALENCE OF MARITAL DISTRESS AND BREAKDOWN

In England and Wales, as in many parts of the world, the rates of divorce are still on the increase. In 1992, a record rate was recorded of 13.7 persons divorcing per thousand married population. This was six times the divorce rate in 1961 and more than double that of 1971 (OPCS 1994). If these rates are maintained, more than four out of ten new marriages will end in legal separation. More than one-fifth of today's divorces occur within 5 years of the wedding and another one-quarter dissolve after 5–9 years of marriage (OPCS 1994).

In 1992, 168 000 children under 16 in England and Wales experienced their parents' divorce, including 57 000 children aged under 5. This was double the rate in 1971. If present trends continue, one in four children born today will see their parents divorce before reaching the age of 16 (Utting 1995). The picture is similar elsewhere in the European Community, although there are variations in rates which can be mostly explained by religious, cultural and social differences. The divorce rate in Canada, the USA and Europe is now close to 50% of the marriage rate and has been climbing steadily in recent decades (Inglehart 1990).

These statistics, however, exclude the breakdown of relationships amongst couples who are cohabiting and have never married. The prevalence of cohabiting has increased in recent years. In the UK, the proportion of unmarried women aged 18–49 who were cohabiting increased from 11% in 1979 to 27% in 1987 (Haskey & Kiernan 1989).

In addition to the high number of couples who divorce there are considerable numbers of couples who are unhappily married and those who live together without marriage seem to have similar levels of relationship disharmony (Greeley 1991). Studies which have looked at the amount of distress in marriages which have not ended in divorce report high levels. Rust and colleagues present data on a

Preventing Mental Illness: Mental Health Promotion in Primary Care. Edited by R. Jenkins and T.B. Üstün.
© 1998 John Wiley & Sons Ltd.

random selection of general practice attenders. They found 10% of marriages on the verge of splitting up and a further 5% were seriously disturbed, showing constellations of problems which might be expected to lead to separation. A further 15% had difficulties which would have warranted intervention (Rust, Golombok & Pickard 1987). In the USA, reports have suggested that approximately 20% of the total population of married couples are 'maritally distressed' (Beach & O'Leary 1986) and it has been estimated that only one-third of those who married in the early 1970s are now still married and consider their marriage very happy (Greeley 1991).

Commentators have hypothesized on the reasons for this increase in divorce and marital dissatisfaction. The fact that divorce is now easier and carries less stigma is of obvious importance. In addition, the large-scale social and psychological changes that have taken place in our society over the last few decades will have had a profound effect on the expectations and behaviour of couples and families (Dominian 1968). This includes the changes in equality between men and women, the increased proportion of women who work, the smaller-sized family and our increased control over conception. As material standards have risen, expectations have increased for fulfilment at the next layer of 'being', namely that of emotional and instinctual fulfilment (Dominian 1968). Contemporary couples place a heavy emphasis on deriving personal and emotional satisfaction from their relationship with their spouse (Phillips 1988). Men and women now expect far more from each other and are less prepared to tolerate lower standards of personal happiness. This can be seen by the courts who have gradually set higher standards for what is considered to be the minimum standard of behaviour acceptable to a man or woman.

IMPLICATIONS OF MARITAL DISTRESS AND BREAKDOWN

Health Status of the Individuals Concerned

Marital distress and breakdown have many damaging implications for the families concerned and for society at large. For the individuals involved there are high personal costs in terms of their physical and mental health, although other factors, such as the poorer living conditions found among the separated and divorced, may also have relevance. Research has shown that the divorced and separated have higher death rates than other categories (Chester 1987). They commit suicide more often (Schneidman & Farberow 1961; Gove 1972); they suffer more fatal car accidents (McMurray 1970); they are hospitalized more often for acute alcoholic psychoses at ages below 45 (Rosenblatt et al 1971) and they die more often from cirrhosis of the liver, cancer of the lung and stomach (Chester 1987). In addition, they are more likely to suffer from tuberculosis and heart conditions (Bloom et al 1978) and from certain infectious diseases (Lynch 1977).

Divorced and separated individuals also have the highest rates of acute and chronic health conditions, particularly those known to be associated with stress, e.g. ulcers, skin complaints, chest and stomach complaints, migraines, etc. (Chester 1987). One study claims that marital disruption is the single most powerful socio-demographic predictor of stress-related illness, with separated individuals having about 30% more acute illnesses and physician visits than married adults (Somers 1979; Jacob 1985; Westhead 1985). The link between marital quality, marital disruption and immune function has been demonstrated in at least one study (Kiecolt-Glaser et al 1987) which found poor marital quality associated with depression and a poor response on three qualitative measures of immune functioning.

Rounsanville et al (1979) found that 50% of individuals requesting treatment for depression were also suffering from marital distress. Other studies have also noted the correlation between marital distress and depression (Paykel et al 1969; Briscoe & Smith 1975; Brown & Harris 1978; Segraves 1980; Jenkins, Mann & Belsey 1981; Birtchnell & Kennard 1983). In a study of women in general practice conducted by the author, over 60% of the women ascertained as depressed considered that they had a major problem in their marital or sexual relationship (Corney 1987).

Studies have repeatedly demonstrated the association between depression and poor marital quality. Brown & Harris (1978) in their study of women in Camberwell, pointed to the protective effect against depression of a good confiding relationship with their partner. They found that women with marital relationships characterized by negative interaction (discord, tension, coldness and indifference) were over three times more likely to become depressed after a severe life event than married women with a better relationship (Brown et al 1986). Of the four vulnerability factors that they identified, a confiding tie with a husband or lover was seen to be the most important, in that this could protect against depression whether or not any one of the other three factors were present.

This finding was replicated by Birtchnell & Kennard (1983), who considered that the quality of marriage exerts a more powerful influence upon mental health than earlier traumas. Shepherd et al's (1966) study of general practice found that marital problems headed the list of complaints of those women who were found to be psychiatrically disturbed. Marital difficulties were also found to be crucial factors in determining the prognosis of minor mental illness in two other studies in general practice (Huxley et al 1979; Jenkins, Mann & Belsey 1981). Birtchnell & Kennard (1983) found the incidence of marital maladjustment to be significantly higher in Chichester female psychiatric patients than in matched local controls. Within the control series, the mental health of women with marital maladjustment was significantly worse than that of women in good marriages. A significant association was demonstrated between pre-morbid marital maladjustment and onset of symptoms of depression before the age of 40, suggesting that it was the poor marital quality which caused the depression. Life events studies also indicate that marital difficulties and separations often precede the onset of mental ill health (Holmes & Rahe 1967; Paykel et al 1969).

Effect on Children's Health and Behaviour

There is also evidence of the negative effects of divorce and disharmony on the health and well-being of the children in the family. Children experiencing parental divorce tend to suffer from depression and psychological disturbance (Duck 1986). They are more harmed when the separation occurs before the age of 5, and boys seem to suffer more than girls. Children's school performance, general health, including a higher rate of enuresis, their personal relationships and levels of delinquency can all be affected (Martin & Fisher 1986; Burges 1994). It is also now apparent that the effects felt by some of these children continue into their adult lives. Children of separated or divorced parents are more likely to leave school at an earlier age, fail to obtain educational qualifications, leave home due to friction, cohabit, marry and have children at an earlier age (Burges 1994). They are also more likely to suffer stomach ulcers, colitis and high blood pressure (Martin & Fisher 1986) as well as depression and mental health problems (Burges 1994).

While parental divorce has been assumed to have deleterious effects on children, it has been considered by many that it is the marital conflict which precedes the separation and the stressful events which follow it that are the real sources of difficulty. Hetherington (1979) considered that if marital separation led to a cessation of hostilities and conflict, this was less damaging for children than remaining in a discordant, unhappy but intact home. The 'acute distress syndrome' (Rutter 1971) which children manifest immediately after divorce is usually time-limited, whereas the effects of family conflict are often more enduring.

The evidence seems to suggest that the process of divorce often involves conflict which is more distressing and damaging to children than the separation itself (Mechanic & Hansell 1989). In a review of the literature, Burges concludes that a number of factors were important in determining how much children are affected by a divorce, including the amount of absence of one of the parents (usually the father), the degree of child poverty resulting from the break-up, and the levels of family conflict (both before and after the divorce or separation). A meta-analysis of the results of 92 British and American studies indicated that all three factors were important, but that the level of conflict was the most important in determining the amount of distress and damage caused to children (Amato & Keith 1991). Marital conflict can also mean that less care and attention is given to the children. The quality of life which the divorced or remarried family make for themselves may become the most important factor in determining whether any disturbed behaviour in the children persists.

Violence is another factor to be considered. Reviews of empirical evidence and relevant theory in the USA (Goode 1971; Steinmetz & Straus 1974) and the Newsomes' descriptive study in Nottingham (Newsome & Newsome 1976) leave no doubt that violence is a common feature of some families' interactions. Violence between spouses and directed towards the children has its consequences. The children who were involved in one study of interparental violence displayed a mixture of behavioural and psychological problems, which included enuresis, truanting from school, aggressive behaviour, bullying siblings, anxiety disorders, insomnia and tics (Levine 1975).

Financial Costs

The financial costs of the consequences which flow from this marital distress are borne by the state and industry as well as by the individuals involved. The ill-health results in increased visits to GPs and casualty departments of hospitals, increased admissions to hospitals and increased drug prescriptions. Other government departments may be involved: the probation service, the police and the Home Office in cases of violence or delinquency; the social services and the local authorities in cases of financial need when families may need supplementary benefit, shelter and/or accommodation; the law courts, legal aid and the Citizens' Advice Bureaux when marriages finally break down. Industry will be affected through days off, loss of concentration resulting in malfunctioning and under-functioning, job losses and job change (Chester 1987).

PREVENTION OF MARITAL DIFFICULTIES AND ASSOCIATED HEALTH PROBLEMS

Prevention in primary care can take place at a number of levels. This chapter will consider the type of interventions that could be targeted for the adult population as a whole, as well as those interventions which would need to be targeted at the groups which are at the highest risk of experiencing either marital difficulties or ill-health resulting from marital difficulties.

The Role of Primary Care

Prevention can take place in a number of settings—schools, youth clubs, the workplace and primary health care. In addition, there are a number of specialized agencies who offer counselling and voluntary agencies who offer support to individuals, couples and families.

General practice, or primary health care, is important as it is often the first place to be approached in times of difficulty. It is also the place routinely visited by parents (particularly women in pregnancy or with young children) and thus an ideal place to screen for difficulties. Although there are specialized agencies for marital problems, couples or individuals tend to visit them only as a last resort (French 1995). Research findings indicate that the family doctor is usually not only the first, but sometimes the only professional to be consulted for marital problems (Keithley 1982; Martin & Fisher 1986; Corney 1987; Alexander 1987). One study of 100 divorced petitioners revealed that just over half had consulted their doctors whereas only one in four had approached other specialized agencies (Murch 1979). Corney, Cooper & Clare (1984) reported that over half of the patients identified as having marital problems had discussed them with their GP and Hunt (1985) found a similar percentage.

The decision to seek help from others for their marital problems does not come easily to most couples. The wife or husband may attend their GP or a workplace health scheme for a physical symptom, or for insomnia or for tiredness. The marital problem may emerge after a discussion around the presenting symptom, disclosure depending in part on the skills of the doctor involved.

Now that most general practices consist of teams of different professionals, other practitioners may also be consulted for symptoms linked to marital distress (Thomas & Corney 1993). Primary care professionals are also in regular contact with individuals at particularly vulnerable periods of their lives and in their marriages. The health visitor is in touch with families with young children. He/she has a statutory obligation to visit all new parents and is therefore in contact with families at a time of often high stress. The midwife will also be in contact with couples during pregnancy. In addition, the majority of family planning clinics and consultations for contraception now take place within primary health care. They provide an opportunity for discussion on preparing for sexual relationships and parenthood, or provide a forum for patients to discuss sexual and marital difficulties.

Preparation for Sexual Relationships and Marriage

The majority of this preparation needs to take place in schools, youth clubs and other venues. General practice or primary health care can also have a role in the education of young women as the provision of contraception is normally undertaken in this setting.

Interventions in general practice or primary health care are perhaps most likely to be effective if they are aimed at those at high risk, e.g. teenage girls asking for contraceptive advice, teenage mothers and young women with a background of family abuse or neglect. Early sexual relationships and premarital pregnancy are associated with the increased likelihood of depression in adulthood. Brown, Harris & Bifulco (1986) found an association between lack of parental care in childhood with early sexual relationships. Together these brought about an increased risk of adult depression in women. In addition, women who were trapped into an unsatisfactory lifestyle by pregnancy were more likely to become depressed. Quinton & Rutter (1983) similarly found an association between lack of care in childhood, premarital pregnancy and later emotional vulnerability and psycho-social difficulty. They also found that the lack of parental care was often repeated in the next generation.

However, research has suggested that the cycle can be broken by positive experiences, either at school or in relationships with peers/partners (Quinton,

Rutter & Liddle 1984). In particular, a supportive marital relationship can markedly reduce the risk of adult depression and subsequent lack of care of the next generation of children.

Brown, Harris, Quinton and Rutter all emphasize the need for preventive interventions aimed at reducing the girls' feelings of helplessness and enhancing their self-esteem. They need to be encouraged to take control of their lives, to plan ahead rather than regard themselves as being victims of fate.

Would it be possible to offer this type of intervention to vulnerable teenage girls considered most at risk of either becoming pregnant or marrying an unsupportive partner? Flaherty et al (1983) were unable to find any evidence that intervention programmes with teenage child-bearers offering intensive family planning education had any success at all in preventing repeat pregnancies, although others had less discouraging experiences (Osofsky et al 1973). Sex education needs to be educational in the broadest sense and to encourage foresight and planning, discouraging feelings of hopelessness and inevitability. It needs to focus on personal changes that will enhance self-esteem and self-efficacy and increase coping skills. Life skills should be an essential part of every school's curriculum and different methods of delivery should be tested and evaluated.

In primary health care, the attachment of counsellors to family planning clinics could also be evaluated. One scheme would be to offer all teenage, young and vulnerable mothers the opportunity to see a counsellor at their first antenatal appointment in the practice. The counsellor could aim to see women either individually or in a discussion group, with the aim of enhancing self-esteem and the feeling of being in control.

Preparation for Parenthood

Marital satisfaction has been shown to decline during the years of child-bearing and child-rearing (Cowan & Cowan 1992). Starting a family is the event which appears to present the greatest single challenge to the personal relationship of a couple, severely testing their adaptability. For couples who are unprepared for change, the birth of a child can seriously disrupt the intimacy of the relationship. The division of labour in the home may become a serious bone of contention and force the couple to adopt more stereotypical roles (Utting 1995).

Studies in the UK and the USA have found that male partners who involve themselves in child care not only strengthen their own identity as parents but also provide their spouses with the evidence that the work of child-rearing is to be valued. Couples who find the transition to parenthood easiest have an awareness of what to expect and have considered the inevitable change in their relationship.

Although health services have been developed to reduce the health risks in childbirth, we have not developed services which address emotional issues, including the psychological impact of parenthood. The midwife, GP and health visitor could all be involved in this process. The inclusion of men in antenatal classes should be encouraged (not least by running the classes at suitable times), and discussions should take place not only on the physical effects of childbirth and the practical aspects of child-rearing but also on the emotional effects, the changing roles and the possible strain on the marriage.

Support for Fathers as well as Mothers

Antenatal classes provide an opportunity for first-time parents to meet others, start friendships and provide support to each other. The National Childbirth Trust, a voluntary agency, provides all of their members with the name of another mother who acts as a postnatal supporter. This type of scheme could also be adopted in general practice and some health visitors do try to match pairs of mothers so that they can support each other both practically and emotionally.

However, the focus of all of these schemes is around mothers and babies rather than fathers. There is very little recognition that fatherhood may also impose strains. Support schemes for men may help reduce the likelihood of marital difficulties arising, or the likelihood that men will opt out of their role as fathers or in taking a more equal part. While it is recognized that it may be very difficult to get men to either take part in such groups or admit to difficulties, different methods of encouraging participation need to be tried and tested. Some research suggests that some men do attend groups run specifically for parents. IKEA (a Swedish furniture chain store) and the Midland Bank have both found that between one-third and one-half of those taking part in parent groups have been men. However, this may be due to the fact that both these schemes are work-based (Burnell 1993).

There needs to be much more consideration in the workplace of the needs of both mothers and fathers. The development of work-based schemes on parenting skills and the emotional consequences of parenthood should be evaluated. However, employers should also consider how to help parents by becoming more flexible in their conditions of employment. Creating more flexibility in working arrangements, hours and leave provision may be cost-effective by reducing the amount of sickness absence or the loss in productivity.

In addition to the development of schemes to develop parental involvement and parenting skills, counselling could be offered to those couples most at risk. Difficulties in parenting can be predicted from the level of stress and distress couples experience in pregnancy (Cowan & Cowan 1992) and it is possible that marital difficulties could also be identified at that stage. Midwives and GPs could screen both in pregnancy and postnatally and refer on to others.

Other Times of Adjustment

Most marriages will also have to undergo other periods of transition and adjustment. In order to reduce the strain on the marriage, there is a need to consider the support given not only to the individual but also to his/her spouse during periods of chronic or acute illness, unemployment, the menopause or when their children are leaving home. Marriages can also be placed under great stress when one of the partners reaches retirement and the couple have to adjust to new roles. Finally, increased disability and becoming a carer may also impose many difficulties on the marital relationship. Primary health care staff and work-based schemes need to be alert to these potentially vulnerable periods and referral to counsellors or the involvement of other non-professionals should be considered as a means of providing support.

Counselling

The therapeutic approach to marital therapy can range from the psychodynamic to the behavioural. Therapists who use the behavioural perspective aim to help couples identify and change specific problem behaviours, replacing detrimental behaviours with more productive ones. They also teach communication and problem-solving skills. In integrative behavioural couple therapy, more cognitive strategies are employed. These are designed to help partners accept marital behaviours that they cannot change—e.g. to reinterpret marital differences as complementary, or be encouraged to see the positive features of certain problem behaviours.

In the UK there are a number of agencies who specialize in offering marital counselling. Relate is the largest and others include the Catholic Marriage Advisory Council and the Jewish Education Marriage Council. There are a number of agencies for those who are considering divorce, including the probation and divorce court welfare service and the conciliation/mediation services affiliated to the National Mediation Council.

In 1994, around 76 000 'cases' visited Relate (French 1995). This agency has 128 centres in England, Wales and Northern Ireland, including 2300 counsellors. It offers marital and relationship counselling, psychosexual therapy, divorce counselling and family mediation. In 1994, 13% of its work was with men only, 36% with women only and 51% with couples. Counselling is available to those individuals or couples who anticipate that they will separate as well as those where either or both are committed to saving the relationship. While the first objective is to provide opportunities for the couple to examine options for improving their relationship, clients set the agenda.

The importance of primary health care has been recognized by Relate and some 120 Relate counsellors now do all or part of their work in a health centre or surgery (French 1995). In addition to Relate, high proportions of GPs now employ counsellors in their surgery. Studies of counsellors in primary care all indicate that a large proportion of the clients referred have relationship difficulties of some kind (Corney & Jenkins 1993) and many of these counsellors employed by GPs were originally trained by Relate.

As counsellors working in general practice can only see a few individuals per week, it is important that clients at most risk are referred. Alternatively, counsellors can use their time by running groups or by facilitating the development of skills in other members of the team. In addition to receiving referrals from GPs, practice nurses, health visitors and others, counsellors could make themselves available at clinics where marital and sexual problems among patients may arise.

Descriptions of some of these counsellor arrangements have been published (see Corney & Jenkins 1993 for a review). All these reports are enthusiastic about the advantages to the participants concerned and give the following advantages: fewer drop-outs between referral and presentation (Watkins 1983); decrease in psychotropic drug prescriptions and consultations (Waydenfeld & Waydenfeld 1980); increase in doctors' awareness of marital disharmony as the source of many patients' somatic presenting problems; saves doctors' time and protects from the stress of consultations that they do not feel equipped for (Marsh & Barr 1975); enables patients to work at their own problems (Martin & Mitchell 1983).

Although these reports are enthusiastic, there have been few independent evaluations of the outcome of marital therapy, particularly in the primary care setting itself. One clinical trial was attempted by Stanton & Corney (1995); however, the number of subjects (47) entered into the trial and followed up after 6 months was too small to allow definitive conclusions from the data. While there was evidence that those seeing the counsellor were less depressed at 6 months than those who were treated by the GP 'as usual' (57% rated as improved using the Centre for Epidemiological Studies Depression scale, compared with 21% of the controls), there was less evidence that it had reduced the extent of marital dysfunction or marital breakup (Stanton & Corney 1995).

A number of studies in the USA have evaluated marital therapies of various kinds. Reviews of the effectiveness of marital interventions have indicated that virtually all marital therapy approaches are effective relative to non-treatment control groups. However, the statistically significant findings are often more due to the fact that the waiting-list control groups remain unchanged or deteriorate during the waiting period, rather than the active treatment groups improving markedly. In many studies, there is only a small improvement over time in the treated groups (Jacobsen & Addis 1993). No therapy consistently results in more than half the couples reliably moving from marital distress to marital satisfaction by the end of therapy. As Jacobsen & Addis indicated, 'all treatments are leaving substantial numbers of couples unchanged or still distressed by the end of therapy; all treatments appear to have about the same success rate'.

Improvement in approximately half of the couples receiving therapy would seem a relatively positive outcome and worth the investment of employing counsellors in this field (particularly if there was little evidence of harm caused by therapy). However, long-term outcome is perhaps more important in evaluating the effectiveness of a service. Studies do suggest that a fair proportion of couples treated with marital therapy are likely to experience relapse or divorce over the course of 2–4 years following therapy. One study of insight-orientated marital therapy has indicated that this type of therapy may lead to better long-term outcome, but this study does need to be repeated (Snyder, Wills & Grady-Fletcher 1991).

Early results from the pilot phase of Relate's evaluative research programme show that nine out of ten couples who manage to complete a counselling course (on average five sessions) are still living together when it ends. Information about longer-term outcome is being collected but is not yet available (French 1995).

Divorce Counselling and Mediation

Deciding on what is termed a successful outcome of therapy is not always straightforward, as keeping an unhappy marriage intact may not always be the most beneficial outcome for the health and well-being of the partners involved or their children. One study, for example, found that family break-up in a social services population of cases was related to better outcome at 12 months (Huxley et al 1989).

Referral to counsellors at the time of a divorce or separation may reduce the distress caused by these events and any subsequent adjustments that have to be made. Relate also offers counselling to those who have entered the divorce process or are at any stage in it. This service offers clients a context in which to reflect upon their relationship, move on or back, change direction if they so wish and explore all their options without prejudice (French 1995).

Family mediation is a process in which an impartial third person, the mediator, assists those involved in family breakdown to make arrangements following separation or divorce, to communicate better and to reach their own agreed joint decisions. The issues to be decided may concern the divorce, the separation, the children, finance and property. The principle that decision-making authority rests with the participants is fundamental to mediation. The mediator has no stake in the dispute, is not identified with any of the competing interests and has no power to impose a settlement on the participants.

Different models of mediation practice have emerged, ranging from strictly task-centred mediation to counselling, which includes the exploration of interpersonal conflicts and established patterns. An evaluation in five centres found that comprehensive mediation, helping couples to reach property settlements as well as arrangements for children, is even more likely to reduce acrimony on either side than mediation which focused mainly on arrangements for children (Walker, McCarthy & Timms 1994).

The recent White Paper on divorce reform advocates the use of mediators in divorce. The White Paper recommends that the law be changed so that couples have to wait for 12 months after filing a statement of marriage breakdown before they can obtain a divorce (1995). In addition, the partner seeking a divorce will have to meet a marriage panel who will give the details of the marriage guidance, counselling and mediation services available and will be encouraged to use them.

Support or Self-help Groups

It has to be recognized that there will never be enough professional support available to help all couples when they need help. It is therefore important to facilitate schemes which involve non-specialists and voluntary help from members of the community.

Support and self-help groups for individuals can have a number of functions. They can reduce the possibility of marital disharmony (by reducing external pressures on the marital relationship) and they can support individuals who are experiencing marital difficulties, thus reducing the likelihood of depression occurring as a result. Support and self-help groups can also be particularly supportive after a couple splits up or divorces.

Studies have shown that support given by others can reduce an individual's psychiatric risk. Brown and colleagues found that married women who had not received support from their husbands had a reduced risk of depression if they received help from someone else they considered close (Brown et al 1986). This support could be offered by volunteers if family or friendship networks were not available or not suitable. Parkes' (1980) review of bereavement counselling studies indicated that guidance offered to socially isolated individuals by trained professionals or volunteers backed by professionals could reduce their psychiatric risk.

A number of schemes offer a befriending service or encourage friendships using volunteers. Although some schemes such as Newpin and Homestart focus primarily on parents and parenthood, it is likely that they are providing support to individuals with relationship difficulties as well. Non-professionals may have a number of advantages over the professional. There is more chance of friendship on equal terms with the client being able to reciprocate, dependency can be discouraged and the clients can learn to develop their own coping skills (Gottlieb 1983).

Self-help groups may also have a protective function. If the group's aims are to develop the self-esteem of individuals and their sense of being in control is enhanced, this may reduce their feelings of helplessness, which has been hypothesized as contributing towards depression (Seligman 1975). Women's groups may help women to become more aware of their rights, to see themselves in a more positive light and to become more active, assertive and independent.

Support for the Individual or for the Couple

Self-help groups and supportive relationships may be particularly valuable for single mothers or for women who have recently separated or divorced. However, their effect on women currently in relationships may not be so straightforward and caution may need to be exercised. While an increase in independence and assertiveness may strengthen the individual, it may not necessarily have a beneficial effect on his/her relationships with his/her partner, particularly in the short term. The same is true for counselling. Difficulties can ensue when one individual within a troubled relationship receives some kind of therapy, counselling or outside support and the partner is not involved. The dilemma exists that what may be best for a specific individual (including their mental health) may not be best for the partner or for the family as a whole.

REFERENCES

Alexander D (1987) Intervention in marital problems in general practice. *Update* 1 July, 47–56.

Amato P & Keith B (1991) Parental divorce and the well-being of children: a meta-analysis. *Psychol Bull* **110**(1), 26–46.

Beach S & O'Leary KD (1986) The treatment of depression occurring in the context of marital discord. *Behav Ther* **17**, 43–9.

Birtchnell J & Kennard J (1983) Does marital maladjustment lead to mental illness? *Soc Psychiat* **18**, 79–88.

Bloom BL, Asher S & White S (1978) Marital disruption as a stressor: a review and analysis. *Psychol Bull* **85**, 867–94.

Briscoe C & Smith J (1975) Depression in bereavement and divorce. *Arch Gen Psychiat* **32**, 439–43.

Brown G & Harris T (1978) *Social Origins of Depression: A Study of Psychiatric Disorder in Women.* London: Tavistock.

Brown G, Andrews B, Harris T, Adler Z & Bridge L (1986) Social support, self-esteem and depression. *Psychol Med* **16**, 813–31.

Brown G, Harris T & Bifulco A (1986) Long-term effect of early loss of parent. In M Rutter, C Izard & P Read (eds) *Depression in Childhood: Developmental Perspectives.* New York: Guilford.

Burgess L (1994) *Lone Parenthood and Family Disruption: the Outcomes for Children.* Social Policy Research Findings 44. York: Family Policy Studies Centre, Joseph Rowntree Foundation.

Burnell A (1993) *Supporting Families in the Workplace. Family Policy Bulletin* (December), p 8. Social Policy Research Findings 69. York: Family Policy Studies Centre, Joseph Rowntree Foundation.

Chester R (1987) *Domestic Stress and Work Performance.* Proceedings of a seminar organized by the Marriage Research Centre, Central Middlesex Hospital, London.

Corney R, Cooper A & Clare A (1984) Seeking help for marital problems: the role of the general practitioner. *J R Coll Gen Pract* **34**, 431–3.

Corney R (1987) Marital problems and treatment outcomes in depressed women: a clinical trial of social work intervention. *Br J Psychiat* **151**, 652–9.

Corney R & Jenkins R (1993) *Counselling in General Practice.* London: Routledge.

Cowan C & Cowan P (1992) *When Partners Become Parents: The Big Life Change for Couples.* New York: Basic Books.

Dominian J (1968) *Marital breakdown.* Harmondsworth: Penguin.

Duck S (1986) *Human Relationships.* London: Sage.

Flaherty E, Marecek J, Olsen K & Wilcove G (1983) Preventing adolescent pregnancy: an interpersonal problem-solving approach. *Prevent Human Serv* **2**(3), 49–64.

French D (1995) Services addressing severe relationship difficulties in families. Paper to the JRF family and parenthood seminars. York: Joseph Rowntree Foundation.

Goode W (1971) Force and violence in the family. *J Marriage Family* **33**, 624–36.

Gottlieb B (1983) *Social Support Strategies: Guidelines for Mental Health Practice.* Beverly Hills: Sage.

Gove W (1972) Sex, marital status and suicide. *J Health Soc Behav* **13**, 204–13.

Greeley A (1991) *Faithful Attraction.* New York: Tor Books.

Haskey J & Kiernan K (1989) Cohabitation in Great Britain—characteristics and estimated numbers of cohabiting partners. *Pop Trends* **58**, 23–32. London: HMSO.

Hetherington E (1979) Divorce: a child's perspective. *Am Psychol* **34**(10), 851–8.

Holmes T & Rahe R (1967) The social readjustment rating scale. *J Psychosomat Res* **11**, 213–18.

Hunt P (1985) *Clients' Responses to Marriage Counselling.* Rugby: National Marriage Guidance Council.

Huxley P, Goldberg D, Maguire G & Kincey V (1979) The prediction of the course of minor psychiatric disorders. *Br J Psychiat* **135**, 535–43.

Huxley P, Raval H, Korer J & Jacob C (1989) Psychiatric morbidity in the clients of social workers: clinical outcome. *Psychol Med* **19**, 189–98.

Inglehart R (1990) *Culture Shift in Advanced Industrial Society.* Princeton, NJ: Princeton University Press.

Jacob A (1985) Frequent attenders, workload and optimum list size. *J R Coll Gen Pract* **35**, 585–6.

Jacobson N & Addis M (1993) Research on couple therapy. What do we know? Where are we going? Submitted.

Jenkins R, Mann A & Belsey E (1981) The background, design and use of a short interview to assess social stress and support in research and clinical settings. *Soc Sci Med* **151**, 195–203.

Keithley J (1982) Marriage counselling. An assessment of the work of marriage guidance counsellors in a general medical practice. Unpublished PhD thesis, Durham University.

Kiecolt-Glaser J, Fisher L, Ogroki P, Stout J, Speicher C & Glaser R (1987) Marital quality, marital disruption and immune function. *Psychosomat Med* **49**(1), 15–34.

Levine M (1975) Interparental violence and its effect on the children: a study of 50 families in general practice. *Med Sci Law* **15**(3), 172–6.

Lynch J (1977) *The Broken Heart.* New York: Basic Books.

Marsh G & Barr J (1975) Marriage guidance counselling in a group practice. *J Coll Gen Pract* **25**, 74–5.

Martin E & Fisher T (1986) Children and divorce. *J R Coll Gen Pract* **36**, 492–3.

Martin E & Mitchell H (1983) A counsellor in general practice: a one-year survey. *J R Coll Gen Pract* **33**, 366–7.

McMurray L (1970) Emotional stress and driving performance: the effect of divorce. *Behav Res Highway Safety* **1**, 100–14.

Mechanic D & Hansell S (1989) Divorce, family conflict and adolescents' well-being. *J Health Soc Behav* **30**, 105–16.

Murch M (1979) Evidence to the Working Party on Marriage Guidance. London: Home Office.

Newsome J & Newsome E (1976) *Seven Years Old in the Home Environment.* London: Allen & Unwin.

OPCS (Office of Population Censuses and Surveys) (1994) *1992 Marriage and Divorce Statistics: England and Wales.* London: HMSO.

Osofsky H, Osofsky J, Kendall N & Rajan R (1973) Adolescents as mothers: an interdisciplinary approach to a complex problem. *J Youth Adolesc* **2**(3), 233–49.

Paykel E, Myers J, Dienelt M, Klerman G, Lindenthal J & Pepper M (1969) Life events and depression. *Arch Gen Psychiat* **21**, 753–60.

Parkes C (1980) Bereavement counselling: does it work? *Br Med J* **281**, 3–6.

Phillips R (1988) *Putting Asunder. A History of Divorce in Western Society.* Cambridge: Cambridge University Press.

Quinton D & Rutter M (1983) Parenting behaviour of mother raised in care. In A Nicol (ed) *Practical Lessons from Longitudinal Studies.* Chichester: Wiley.

Quinton D, Rutter M & Liddle C (1984) Institutional rearing, parenting difficulties and marital support. *Psychol Med* **14**, 107–24.
Rosenblatt S, Cross M, Malenowski B, Broman M & Lewis E (1971) Marital status and multiple psychiatric admissions for alcoholism: a cross-validation. *Qu J Study Alcoholism* **32**, 1092–6.
Rounsanville B, Weissman M, Prusoff B & Herceg-Baron R (1979) Marital disputes and treatment outcomes in depressed women, *Comp Psychiat* **20**(5), 483–90.
Rust J, Golombok S & Pickard C (1987) Marital problems in general practice. *J Sex Marit Ther* **2**(2), 127–30.
Rutter M (1971) Parent–child separation: psychological effects on the children. *J Child Psychol Psychiat All Discip* **12**, 233–60.
Schneidman E & Farberow N (1961) Statistical comparisons between attempted and committed suicides. In N Farberow & E Schneidman (eds) *The Cry for Help*. New York: McGraw Hill.
Segraves R (1980) Marriage and mental health. *J Sex Marit Ther* **6**(3), 187–98.
Seligman M (1975) *Helplessness: On Depression, Development and Death*. San Francisco: Freeman.
Shepherd M, Cooper B, Brown A & Kalton G (1966) *Psychiatric Illness in General Practice*. London: Oxford University Press.
Snyder D, Wills R & Grady-Fletcher A (1991) Long-term effectiveness of behavioural versus insight-oriented marital therapy. A 4-year follow-up study. *J Consult Clin Psychol* **59**(1), 138–41.
Somers AR (1979) Marital status, health and use of health services. *J Am Med Assoc* **241**, 1818–22.
Stanton R & Corney R (1995) A clinical trial of marital therapy in general practice. Unpublished manuscript.
Steinmetz S & Straus M (eds) (1974) *Violence in the Family*. New York: Dodd, Mead & Co.
Thomas R & Corney R (1993) The role of the practice nurse in mental health: a survey. *J Ment Health* **2**, 65–72.
Utting D (1995) *Family and Parenthood*. York: Joseph Rowntree Foundation.
Walker J, McCarthy P & Timms N (1994) Mediation: the making and remaking of co-operative relationships—an evaluation of the effectiveness of comprehensive mediation. Social Policy Research Findings 48. University of Newcastle Upon Tyne: RELATE Centre for Family Studies.
Watkins J (1983) Marriage counselling in our practice. *Br Med J* **287**, 808.
Waydenfeld D & Waydenfeld S (1980) Counselling in general practice. *J R Coll Gen Pract* **30**, 671–7.
Westhead J (1985) Frequent attenders in general practice: medical, psychological and social characteristics. *J R Coll Gen Pract* **35**, 337–40.

38

Parents' Problems

J Tsiantis, Th Dragonas & A Cox
Athens University Medical School, Greece

The prevention of mental illness, with emphasis on the promotion of the psycho-social health of children, is of the greatest importance. Prevention programmes are now given top priority, particularly since the adoption by the member-states of the European office of the World Health Organization (WHO) 'Health for All by the year 2000' programme (WHO 1979) and the evaluation of its goals (WHO 1986). On the other hand, the appropriate psychosocial development of children is of decisive importance for reinforcing not only those abilities which help the individual cope with psychosocial stress originating chiefly in the social and ecological environment but also the mechanisms which permit the individual to resist health-damaging behaviours.

In one sense, we are constantly intervening in the development and growth of children. We influence their health, their abilities and their self-concept by means of our everyday behaviour. In the psychological sense, however, 'intervention' means the planned provision of care and training (both formal and informal) intended to maximize the genetic potential of each child. Recent research has provided a wealth of evidence to associate the quality of parental care with the future mental health of the child in adolescence and adulthood, and this connection seems to be particularly true of disturbances such as depression, personality disorders and delinquency. Such data emphasize the importance of preventive action in early childhood. Many studies, particularly in the USA, have indicated that early preventive intervention can improve the quality of the care children receive and promote their development, thus boosting their school and work performance, reducing crime and lowering the incidence of pregnancy in adolescence.

Similarly, recent empirical research has indicated that measures of interaction between the dominant care-givers and 1 year-old children are better predictors of psychosocial development at the age of 4 and 5 than individual measures of the children themselves (Klein, Wieder & Greenspan 1987). Sensitive and responsive interaction between care-giver and child seems to be the key element required for normal psychosocial development, both psychosocially and intellectually (Sroufe &

Preventing Mental Illness: Mental Health Promotion in Primary Care. Edited by R. Jenkins and T.B. Üstün.
© 1998 John Wiley & Sons Ltd.

Fleeson 1988; Moriset et al 1990; Speltz, Greenberg & DeKlyen 1990; Lamb et al 1991).

It is also known that programmes which sensitize caregivers to the basic principles of care and communication are much more feasible on a large scale than programmes using professionals in direct clinical work with children, and there is evidence of their efficacy (Rae Grant 1991).

In the area of prenatal/infant development programmes it was found that the programmes with greatest impact had multiple components, were of long duration (2–5 years), began prenatally and had home visits as a major component. It was concluded that there was evidence of both short-term and long-term positive effects (Rae Grant 1991). Such reinforcement programmes also indicate what can be done with high-risk populations. Successful programmes cover the family as a whole and do not focus on the child alone. I will now describe an intervention study which is based on a multi-centre interstate collaborative effort, a mainly mental health promotion project entitled 'Provision of Primary Health Care for the Promotion of Children's Early Psychosocial Development'.

AIMS

The present study has stemmed from the recognition of the importance of children's psychosocial development, the significance of the context in which it occurs and the need for primary prevention. The aims of the study are multiple:

1. To develop specific methods to be used by the personnel involved in the provision of primary health care services during their contact with families, which will inform and sensitize caregivers to issues pertaining to healthy psychosocial development during infancy and childhood and reinforce parental responsiveness to the child's emotional and social needs.
2. To develop a training programme for primary health care workers (PHCWs) which: (a) ensures that the methods to promote children's psychosocial development are implemented effectively; (b) strengthens PHCWs' ability to monitor children's psychosocial development and the factors affecting it; and (c) encourages PHCWs to engage care-givers in problem-solving strategies.
3. To evaluate the effectiveness of the programme both nationally and across a number of different countries, through the utilization of identical instruments by teams of different countries. This cross-cultural dimension of the programme permits an examination of sociocultural variations and the relevance of sociocultural factors to early psychosocial development.
4. To promote the implementation of the developed intervention techniques throughout the network of primary health care services in the participating countries, by the integration of the training programme into the educational curriculum of undergraduate students, such as health visitors, nurses and others, who are going into primary health care services.

HISTORICAL BACKGROUND OF THE PROGRAMME— SCOPE AND CONTENT OF THE PREVENTIVE APPROACH

This study was initiated under the auspices of the WHO Regional Office for Europe. It was launched in May 1990 at a meeting in Athens and the research design was finalized at a WHO meeting in Sofia in 1992. The scope and the content of the programme includes:

- The initial focus is on the period from conception to the end of the second year of the child's life.
- The programme has three main components: (a) training for the PHCWs, which has been developed by the Athens group; (b) the semi-structured interview, which has been developed by the Belgrade group; (c) the evaluation component, which has been developed by the Thomas Coram Research Unit of the Institute of Education of the University of London. The United Medical and Dental Schools of Guy's and St Thomas's Hospitals of the University of London have a consulting role in the programme.
- The training will have content and structure that is feasible within existing primary health care resources, working in collaboration with specialist mental health services.
- The approach, modified to local conditions, is being applied in six countries: Cyprus, Greece, Portugal, New Yugoslavia, Republic of Slovenia and Turkey.
- This programme has also been approached as a Biomed I programme (Biomedical and Health Research programme, 1990–1994) D.6. XII/E/4, No. PL 931161 and the centres in England, Greece and Portugal are carrying the study with funds from the European Community. The coordinator of the programme is Professor J Tsiantis.

The training will be evaluated (a) in terms of PHCWs' knowledge, attitudes, beliefs and practices; and (b) in terms of its impact on maternal well-being, parent–child relationships and the children's development (outcome evaluation).

SAMPLE

Twenty PHCWs in each participating country have been recruited from Health Care Centres taking part in the programme. The selection of the PHCWs is based on their motivation and their availability for approximately 3 years, which is the estimated duration of the programme. Ten PHCWs comprise the experimental group and the other 10 the comparison group.

Each PHCW randomly selects 10 women out of his/her routine antenatal clients. Thus, a total of 200 mothers and their infants, in each participating centre, are taking part in the study, 100 for the experimental group and another 100 for the comparison group. It follow, therefore, that the sample is drawn from the normal population attending the antenatal clinic and does not belong to a high-risk group.

TRAINING

The aim of the training was to produce a direct, specific and measurable effect on the attitudes, beliefs and practices of PHCWs. This requires the provision to PHCWs of some basic knowledge of psychosocial development and a knowledge of the functioning of the family and the changes that occur within the family with the advent of a new child.

The PHCWs' Training Programme

The training was organized by the Greek team to produce a direct, specific and memorable effect on the attitudes, beliefs and activities of PHCWs with regard to everyday practice in order to broaden the focus and later the style of practice used by the PHCW.

The training programme is organized into three phases:

- Phase 1: pregnancy to 3 months after birth.
- Phase 2: 3–12 months.
- Phase 3: 12–24 months.

Training aims at sensitizing the PHCWs in:

- Psychological issues relevant to the transition to parenthood.
- General indicators of good parenting.
- Issues on psychosocial development.
- Children's needs.

It thus enables the PHCWs to:

- Be more effective in their interventions with families.
- Identify cases for referral.
- Define their own boundaries in relation to mental health personnel.

Each training phase involves 10–12 3-hour sessions, each session including a theoretical and an experiential part. The theoretical part presents the PHCWs belonging to the experimental group with theoretical and research material relevant to the key issues of training. The experiential part is structured around carefully chosen examples amplifying the key issues, and is based on small group dynamics. About three sessions of each training phase are devoted to the introduction and application of the open-ended interview. The comparison group receives one lecture covering early psychosocial development and guidelines on how to apply the semi-structured interview, but no detailed training with respect to the content of the programme and its implementation. As the training programme is quite intensive, it is important to determine whether the resources deployed for that purpose influence the effectiveness of the implementation of the semi-structured interview.

The basic axes of the training philosophy were thus:

1. The importance of acquiring the ability to adopt an approach whose fundamental component was *empathy*. Empathy is a process whereby PHCWs become more capable of sensitive communication with the client, of understanding the real needs, and of responding in as individualized a manner as possible. This should make the PHCW more effective in intervention and, if necessary, be capable of making referral to specialized professionals without undermining the confidence with the client.

2. To encourage the *modelling* strategy. Modelling is a practice whereby positive identification can be fostered. This facilitates recognition of the PHCW as a competent, positive figure who does not criticize. Instead, the PHCW *models* how best to act, how to interact with the baby, not just at the cognitive level but socially and emotionally. As the mother identifies with the PHCW, this reinforces her positive maternal investment in the baby.

3. To ensure that an adequate and 'good enough' early parent–child relationship develops in a *climate of mutual pleasure and trust*.

4. The aim of the training generally is to teach PHCWs to use the semi-structured interview in a fashion that alerts care-givers to their children's needs and encourage them to adopt problem-solving approaches, using the parents' own resources when appropriate.

Content of the Training

The content of the theoretical part of the training is structured around the information, attitudes, beliefs and practices a 'good enough' health care professional should impart to a mother during the transition to parenthood. The different phases of the training cover the following subjects:

1. *Pregnancy to the first 3 months of life.* The basic themes of this phase are:
   - The normal anxieties of pregnancy.
   - The father's role.
   - The investment in the child on the part of the mother and her partner.
   - The preparation of siblings.

- The basic needs of newborns and infants.
- Bonding.
- Mother–infant communication.

2. *4–12 Months postnatally.* This phase of the training elaborates on the following themes:
   - Mother–child emotional coordination and communication.
   - Father–infant relationship.
   - Ego formation in the first year of life.
   - Mother–infant play.
   - Alterations inside the family connected with the arrival of the new baby.
   - Mother–infant separation and weaning.
   - Failures of early interaction.
   - Dysfunctions in infancy connected with sleep, appetite, level of activity and psychosomatic disorders.

3. *The second year of life.* The content of the training for this period focuses on the following:
   - The process by which the young child gains autonomy.
   - The difficulties characterizing the autonomy process/separations.
   - Cognitive development, communication and development of language.
   - Sociability, play with parents, siblings and peers.
   - The organization of the somatic ego, including sphincter control.

THE SEMI-STRUCTURED INTERVIEW

The interview schedule developed by the Belgrade research team aims at providing the PHCWs with an instrument which will guide and facilitate their contacts with the families. The principles underlying the construction and use of the interview are those of semi-structured interviews (Cox 1994). This means that the schedule is principally intended to pinpoint areas for the PHCWs to discuss in their inter-actions with the parents. Suggested questions are included to offer ways in which the PHCWs may bring up an area or topic in an open-ended fashion. Further questioning is chosen by a PHCW according to the individual needs of the parent or child. For each topic, the PHCW encourages the parent to talk in order to discover whether there are any particular concerns. If there are, he/she explores to see whether these concerns are having any adverse effect on the parent, the child or the relationship between the two. If there is evidence of an adverse impact, then the PHCW enquires what the parent has done about it. If this appears adequate they review the situation at a suitable time interval to determine whether there has been benefit from what the parent is already doing. If in the first place the parent has taken no action or inappropriate action, the PHCW enquires about relevant resources that may be available to the parent, starting with the parent's own family. The PHCW then encourages the parent to use those resources, and reviews the situation after a suitable interval. If there is at any point major concern at a level where the use of readily available family resources are unlikely to be effective, then the PHCW brings in appropriate professional resources. There are essentially four interview schedules that cover six to eight project contacts: (a) for pregnancy (one or two contacts); (b) for the first 3 months in the child's life (one or two contacts, preferably one before 6 weeks); (c) one between 4 and 7 months, and one between 8 and 12 months; and (d) second year of life (two contacts, of which one is before 18 months). The content of the semi-structured interviews is closely related to the content and timing of the training sessions.

EVALUATION OF THE EFFECTIVENESS OF THE PROGRAMME

The evaluation strategy was developed by the Thomas Coram Research Unit of the Institute of Education, London University. Evaluation of the effectiveness of the programme is of the very greatest importance, and for that reason two different types of control procedures have been used. Under the first type, interest will focus on the degree to which the training programme has been effective in causing a *change* in the knowledge, attitudes and beliefs of the PHCWs in terms of child development and the parental capacity. Here we are concerned to identify change over time: the type of change in which each trainee PHCW, at work, acts with his/her own personal form of control, before and after the training. Given that the training programme is very brief in duration, we can be sure that the changes which arise are the outcome of the training rather than of exogenous factors.

The second control procedure is interdepartmental in nature and involves evaluating the extent to which there are *differences* in practice between the PHCWs who have taken the training programme and those who have not had that experience. In order to identify such differences, the PHCWs who belong to the comparison group stem from the same population as the trainees, and there are no systematic differences between the experimental and comparison groups other than the factors of training.

The instruments to be used in the evaluation of the effectiveness of PHCWs' training are as follows:

- Three multiple-choice questionnaires (MCQs): the members of the experimental and comparison groups will complete a multiple-choice questionnaire before and after each phase of training. These MCQs are specially devised to assess the impact of training on PHCWs' beliefs, attitudes and knowledge concerning infant behaviour and development.
- The PHCWs complete an interview record form and an interview diary after every family contact. The purpose is to assess the impact of training on PHCWs' behaviours with mothers and infants and also to serve as an instrument for PHCW self-assessment. A neutral observer (psychologist) observes

TABLE 38.1 Provision of primary health care for the promotion of children's early psychosocial development.* Evaluation instruments—training and process

Training	Pregnancy	6 weeks	6 months	12 months		2nd year	
MCQs (PHCWs)	*			*		*	

Process	Pregnancy	6 weeks	6 months	12 months	18 months	24 months
Diary record (PHCWs)	*	*	*	*	*	*
Interview record form (PHCWs)	*	*	*	*	*	*
Interview observation (psychologist)	*	*			*	*

* Funded by the EU and WHO Regional Office for Europe

  interviews conducted by the experimental and comparison groups of PHCWs and scores the implementation of the interview by the PHCWs according to an observation schedule designed for the purposes of the study.

- Every family included in the project, both target families and their controls, is evaluated for maternal well-being, mother–infant interaction, maternal satisfaction with the caring role and infant psychosocial development. While the main outcome evaluation is the one when the child is 24 months old, several measures are systematically administered prospectively at other time points. In particular, maternal well-being is measured at the 6-week, 6-month, 12-month and second-year contacts by mothers completing the Edinburgh Postnatal Depression Scale (Cox, Holden & Sagovsky 1987). At the 12-month and second-year contacts, maternal satisfaction with the caring role is assessed by the mother completing the Daily Hassles Scale (Crnic & Booth 1991). Mother–child interaction is evaluated at the 6-week, 6-month, 12-month and second-year contacts by a psychologist who acts as an independent observer. The first three measures were developed for the purpose of the parent study, while the fourth is a modification of one of the scales of the Home Observation for Measurement of the Environment (Caldwell & Bradley 1984). At the 6- and 12-month contacts, infant psychosocial development is assessed by a psychologist using a modification of the Bayley Scale (Bayley 1969), and at the second-year contact, language development is assessed similarly by a psychologist using the Bzoch–League Receptive Expressive Emergent Language Scale (REEL) (Bzoch & League 1971). Finally, at the second-year contact, the mother completes the Bates Infant Characteristics Questionnaire (Bates 1988).

Tables 38.1 and 38.2 summarize the different time points of the evaluation of the various components.

TABLE 38.2 Provision of primary health care for the promotion of children's early psychosocial development.* Evaluation instruments—outcome

Outcome	Pregnancy	6 weeks	6 months	12 months	18 months	24 months
Edinburgh Postnatal Depression Scale (mother)		*	*	*		*
Daily Hassles Scale (mother)			*			*
Mother–child interaction (psychologist)						
(i) Specially constructed		*	*			
(ii) Specially constructed				*		
(iii) Home Scale						*
Infant Observation Bayley Scale (psychologist)			*	*		
The Bates Infant Characteristics Questionnaire (mother)						*
Reel Scale (psychologist)						*

* Funded by the EU and WHO Regional Office for Europe.

REFERENCES

Bates JE (1988) Information on the Infant Characteristics Questionnaire. The Bates Infant Characteristics Questionnaire. Unpublished manuscript, Department of Psychology, Indiana University, Bloomington.

Bayley N (1969) *Bayley Scaler of Infant Development*. New York: Psychological Corporation.

Bzoch KR & League R (1971) Administration manual for the Bzoch–League Receptive Expressive Emergent Language Scale: *REEL Scale*. Baltimore: University Park Press (2nd edn, 1994, Windson: NFER/Nelson).

Caldwell BM & Bradley RH (1984) Home Observation for Measurement of the Environment—Administration Manual, *The HOME Scale* (revised edn). Little Rock, Arkansas: University of Little Rock.

Cox A (1994) Interviews with parents. In M Rutter, E Taylor & L Hersov (eds) *Child and Adolescent Psychiatry: Modern Approaches*, pp 34–50. Oxford: Blackwell.

Cox JL, Holden JM & Sagovsky R (1987) Detection of postnatal depression: development of the 10-item Edinburgh Postnatal Depression Scale. *Br J Psychiat* **150**, 782–6.

Crnic K & Booth CL (1991) Mothers' and fathers' perceptions of daily hassles of parenting across early childhood. The Daily Hassles Scale. *J Marriage Family* **53**, 1042–50.

Klein P, Wieder S & Greenspan SI (1987) A theoretical overview and empirical study of mediated learning experiences: prediction of preschool performance from mother–infant interaction patterns. *Infant Ment Health J* **8**(2), 110–29.

Lamb ME, Nash A, Teti, DM & Bornstein MH (1991) Infancy. In M Lewis (ed) *Child and Adolescent Psychiatry: A Comprehensive Textbook*, pp 222–56. Baltimore: Williams and Wilkins.

Morisset CE, Barnard KE, Greenberg MT, Booth CL & Spieker J (1990) Environmental influences on early language development: the context of social risk. *Dev Psychopathol* **2**, 127–49.

Rae Grant NI (1991) Primary prevention. In M Lewis (ed) *Child and Adolescent Psychiatry: A Comprehensive Textbook*, pp 198–209. Baltimore: Williams and Wilkins.

Speltz ML, Greenberg MT & DeKlyen M (1990) Attachment in pre-schoolers with disruptive behaviour: a comparison of clinic referred non-problem children. *Dev Psychopathol* **2**, 31–46.

Sroufe LA & Fleeson J (1988) The coherence of family relationships. In RA Hinde & J Stevenson-Hinde (eds) *Relationships within Families: Mutual Influences*, pp 24–47. Oxford: Oxford University Press.

WHO (World Health Organization) (1979) *World Health Assembly, Resolution 32.30.* Geneva: WHO.

WHO (World Health Organization) (1986) *Evaluation of the Strategy for Health for All by the Year 2000: Seventh Report on the World Health Situation*, vol 5, European Region. Copenhagen: Regional Office for Europe.

Preventive Approaches to Alcohol and Drug Problems

John B Saunders, Katherine M Conigrave* and Michelle K Gomel**

*University of Queensland, Brisbane; *University of Sydney and Royal Prince Alfred Hospital, Sydney, Australia; and **World Health Organization, Geneva, Switzerland*

Alcohol and drug misuse cause an array of mental and physical health problems, and impose a major burden on the economies of many countries. In Australia, for example, deaths from substance use number over 26 000 per year (approximately 21% of all deaths), of which approximately 6500 are attributed to alcohol, 19 000 to tobacco, and 400 each to opiates and sedative-hypnotics (Commonwealth Department of Human Services and Health 1994). The annual economic cost amounts to $6 billion for alcohol, $7 billion for tobacco, and $1.5 billion for other drugs (Collins & Lapsley 1991). This experience is equalled or exceeded in many countries in Europe and America, where alcohol and cigarette consumption has been traditionally high, and where there are well established importation routes for illicit drugs such as cannabis, heroin and cocaine. Alcohol and tobacco misuse is increasing in the developing world, sometimes replacing indigenous substances. This has created a host of problems for which many countries have lacked societal codes, appropriate laws and the economic capacity to develop services.

THE FOCUS ON PREVENTION

The response to alcohol and drug problems in recent years has been influenced by two major policy directions. The first emphasizes prevention and early intervention rather than treatment of persons with late-stage problems. The second identifies primary care as the most important setting for intervention rather than specialist services.

There are several reasons for the emphasis on prevention. First, by the time persons with drug and alcohol problems seek treatment, dependence is usually well established. The prognosis at this stage is often poor. Studies of the natural history

Preventing Mental Illness: Mental Health Promotion in Primary Care. Edited by R. Jenkins and T.B. Üstün.

of persons with alcohol and opiate dependence have shown that 15–30% die within 10 years, and a further 30–40% continue harmful use (Vaillant 1983).

Secondly, the effectiveness of specialist treatments such as residential rehabilitation, therapeutic communities and outpatient counselling has been called into question. A comprehensive review of the evidence is beyond the scope of this chapter. Briefly, although a few controlled trials have shown that highly structured residential programs for alcohol-dependent persons result in a better outcome than loosely structured or outpatient programs, the evidence is inconsistent (Keso & Salaspuro 1990; Saunders 1994; Mattick & Jarvis 1994). The evidence for the efficacy of rehabilitation programs for illicit drug use is modest. The longer an individual remains in rehabilitation, the better the prognosis, but only a small proportion of drug-dependent individuals can be persuaded to enter such a program (Mattick & Hall 1994). Inpatient programs are expensive. In developing countries they can easily absorb the entire budget allocated to drug and alcohol services. Given the degree of efficacy and the fact that they attract only a minority of patients, they are considered by many to represent poor value for money. This has made them vulnerable to government and health insurance company policies, which are increasingly predicated on the need for cost containment. In many countries residential programs have been closed and lengths of stay considerably reduced.

The third consideration is that epidemiological studies have demonstrated that much of the harm from substance misuse occurs not in persons with established dependence, but in the far larger proportion of individuals who have hazardous or harmful use, but are not dependent. Such individuals rarely contact specialist treatment services. Given the size of the population (e.g. 20% of men and 8% of women in Australia are hazardous or harmful alcohol users), prevention or early intervention is more realistic than attempting to provide individualized treatment. This shift has reflected a more general reorientation in the provision of health care, with greater emphasis on promotion of health and achieving health outcomes at a population level. In the USA, the Surgeon General referred to this change in orientation as the second great public health revolution (Orlandi 1987). Fifteen priority areas, including alcohol abuse, were identified in which health promotion and disease prevention were expected to achieve significant gains.

'Harm reduction' is a related philosophy which has a preventive aim. Harm reduction aims at preventing adverse consequences of substance use, without necessarily affecting the level of use. As applied to alcohol, harm reduction would involve supplementation of alcoholic drinks with thiamine to prevent Wernicke–Korsakoff syndrome. In relation to injecting drug use, it aims to lessen the likelihood of acquiring infections such as hepatitis B and C and HIV. Examples include methadone maintenance, which reduces the frequency of injecting drug use, and needle-syringe exchange programs which aim to reduce HIV and hepatitis transmission caused by sharing contaminated injecting equipment.

In summary, there are cogent arguments for switching emphasis from specialist treatment and rehabilitation to a preventive, early intervention and harm reduction approach. This perspective, which focuses on the population rather than the individual, has been endorsed by many governments and advisory bodies (Institute of Medicine 1990; Commonwealth Department of Human Services and Health 1994).

INVOLVING PRIMARY CARE

There are several reasons why primary health care services, and particularly general practice, have a key role in a population-based response to substance use problems (Heather et al 1987; Roche, Saunders & Elvy 1992).

1. *Accessibility.*   In many countries general practitioners are the most numerous primary health care professionals, and represent the most accessible point of contact with the health care system. The nature of general practice varies appreciably from country to country, but in many, including Australia, at least 80% of the population visit a general practitioner annually or more frequently (Australian Bureau of Statistics 1986).
2. *Availability.*   In general practice there is usually little waiting time, compared with specialist services. Such ready availability means that patients will sometimes approach the general practitioner at times of crisis when intervention for an alcohol or drug problem may have particular potency.
3. *Expectations of patients.*   Surveys indicate that patients are comfortable with their doctor raising questions on alcohol and other substance use, and would not be prompted to change to another doctor as a result (Slama et al 1989). In one study, over two-thirds of patients considered it to be a medical responsibility for general practitioners to give advice about drinking (Murphy 1980). The majority of North American patients with substance misuse problems seek help from primary care physicians rather than specialists (Kamerow, Pincus & MacDonald 1986) and Australian surveys (Moore, Makkai & McAllister 1989) have also indicated that general practitioners are the preferred source of information and advice on alcohol and other drug-related matters.
4. *Lack of stigma.*   No stigma is attached to a general practitioner consultation. Seeing the family doctor is a routine occurrence in everyday life. It has no special significance attached to it, as visiting a specialist drug and alcohol service, for instance, may have. The general practitioner is bound to confidentiality by the code of medical ethics.
5. *A whole person perspective.*   As substance use problems are neither solely medical nor solely social concerns, the general practitioner is well placed to offer an intervention which addresses a range of influences that may be affecting an individual. General practitioners, who see their role as dealing with the whole person, can enlist the assistance of family and friends.
6. *Network of support and continuity of care.*   In many countries general practitioners can refer to a wide variety of other health workers. In some there are formally

structured primary care teams. In addition, given their residential stability, general practitioners can offer care over long periods of time, in contrast to the turnover of staff in specialist services. At the present time the potential for prevention is greater than the actuality. Although persons with alcohol and drug problems present more frequently than others for medical attention, as noted earlier, they tend not to seek help unless there are serious complications (Bucholz, Homan & Helzer 1992). Only 20–35% of problem drinkers are known to their general practitioners or clinic staff (Persson & Magnusson 1989; Reid et al 1986). General practitioners have little training in this area, and traditionally they have not offered preventive interventions.

SOME EXAMPLES OF PREVENTIVE APPROACHES

We shall now describe some preventive and early intervention approaches to alcohol and drug problems which have been developed for general practice settings. We shall concentrate on the work undertaken at the Centre for Drug and Alcohol Studies over the past 10 years in developing strategies to reduce hazardous alcohol consumption and implementing them in general practice. This work has been undertaken in three phases, and has involved three WHO collaborative studies. Two other preventive initiatives will then be described—an intervention program designed to reduce inappropriate prescribing of benzodiazepines, and the establishment of a training program for general practitioners to provide methadone maintenance.

Early Intervention for Hazardous Alcohol Use

Early intervention aims to prevent the development of dependence and other forms of harm from alcohol. It combines systematic detection of persons with hazardous or harmful alcohol consumption, and brief therapy, which typically is offered at the point of first contact. Early intervention was endorsed by a WHO Expert Committee in 1980 and three collaborative studies, with which our centre has been involved, have been undertaken since then.

Phase I—the WHO Collaborative Study on Early Detection of Harmful Alcohol Consumption

Several methods of detecting hazardous and harmful alcohol use have been developed in recent years. They include questionnaires, check-lists, physical examination rating scales and laboratory tests (Saunders & Conigrave 1990). Physical examination has the drawback of requiring a skilled and highly trained examiner and facilities to perform such an examination. Furthermore, physical changes are usually not apparent in early-stage problem drinkers. Laboratory tests, such as γ-glutamyl-transferase (GGT), may become elevated before there are physical complications of alcohol use, but it usually takes many years of regular heavy drinking to produce an abnormal result. Only 30% of heavy drinkers in a community setting show abnormal values (Conigrave, Saunders & Whitfield 1995). In addition, laboratory markers are not specific, so that up to 50% of elevated results in healthy people are caused by factors other than alcohol. Questionnaires have been available for many years: the first were developed in the 1960s and early 1970s to detect alcoholism. However, their sensitivity in detecting persons with hazardous and harmful alcohol consumption is low, of the order of 40–50% (Saunders & Conigrave 1990; Rydon et al 1992).

The aim of the collaborative study was to develop a simple screening instrument for hazardous and harmful alcohol consumption which would have the following characteristics (Saunders & Aasland 1987):

1.   It would enable the detection of persons with harmful alcohol consumption and those at risk of developing harm.
2.   It would be valid across different settings and cultures and particularly in primary care settings.
3.   It would be simple enough to encourage its use by health professionals.
4.   It would be useful for the purpose of intervention.

Nearly 2000 subjects were recruited from a variety of primary health care settings in six countries (Australia, Bulgaria, Kenya, Mexico, Norway and the USA). From 150 questions asked in a structured interview, 10 were selected for a screening instrument on the basis of: (a) their correlation with reported alcohol intake; (b) their representativeness for the major conceptual domains (e.g. dependence on alcohol, adverse psychological reactions to drinking, physical and social complications of drinking); (c) their ability to discriminate between hazardous and harmful use and non-hazardous use; and (d) the clinical importance of an individual item and its value in guiding later counselling. The screening instrument developed, the Alcohol Use Disorders Identification Test ('AUDIT'), has three questions on alcohol intake, three on features of alcohol dependence, and four on complications of drinking. Responses are scored from 0 to 4, giving a range of scores for the complete instrument of 0–40 (Saunders et al 1993). Using ROC analysis, a cut-off point of 8 was determined as the most appropriate one to identify hazardous or harmful drinkers. Using this cut-off point, AUDIT detected 92% of persons drinking at hazardous and harmful levels in this sample (specificity 94%) (Saunders et al 1993).

In a 3-year follow-up study a raised AUDIT score was found to be a significant predictor of alcohol-related harm (Conigrave, Saunders & Reznik 1995). Those who scored 8 or more had a sixfold greater risk of social problems related to their drinking, and were four times more likely to experience liver disease or gastro-intestinal bleeding, and twice as likely to experience hypertension or trauma over the next 2–3 years when compared with those scoring below this level. AUDIT was a better predictor of social problems than was alcohol intake or blood tests, and was comparable to laboratory markers in its ability to predict medical problems. Thus it provides a simple way of identifying persons with hazardous and harmful consumption, and has good capacity to predict harmful consequences.

Phase II—the WHO Collaborative Study on Early Intervention for Harmful Alcohol Consumption

The second phase of work involved the development and evaluation of brief intervention strategies (Babor et al 1987; Saunders 1987; Babor & Grant 1992). Men and women attending three different primary health care settings, namely general practice, hospital clinics and a health screening programme, were recruited on the basis of one of the following inclusion criteria: (a) average weekly alcohol consumption of 300 g or more (men) or 180 g or more (women); (b) two or more episodes of intoxication per month, intoxication being defined for men as consumption of ten standard drinks (100 g alcohol) in a single session, and for women consumption of six standard drinks (60 g alcohol); or (c) experience of alcohol-related harm in the previous 6 months and continued drinking. They were randomly assigned to one of four intervention conditions: (a) no treatment; (b) simple advice over 5 minutes; (c) advice and counselling for 20 minutes; and (d) advice and extended counselling, amounting to 40 minutes over 2–3 sessions.

Those who drew the control condition were thanked for participating, asked to complete some research questionnaires, and invited to be re-interviewed in 6 months' time. They were given no advice about alcohol consumption or any other health information. In the simple advice condition the therapist informed individuals of their average weekly alcohol consumption, compared their intake with that of the general population for their age and sex, and pointed out any physical or social problems which were related to drinking. They described a 'standard drink' (in Australia this is 10 g alcohol), and recommended that they keep below 16 standard drinks per week (men) or nine standard drinks (women). Subjects left with a simple information leaflet that covered all the main points mentioned by the therapist. In the advice and counselling conditions, the therapist gave the simple advice with an additional 15 minutes of counselling in problem-solving strategies. Subjects were asked to identify situations which would put them at high risk of heavy drinking and, with the therapist's help, to devise means by which they would deal with these situations without recourse to heavy drinking. They were asked to enlist a support person, and alternative activities to drinking were explored. Subjects were asked to record all alcoholic drinks on diary cards, together with details of where drinking took place and their mood state. Subjects who drew the extended counselling condition had the same advice and counselling, and were then asked to return for counselling on two occasions. On their return, results of biochemical tests were relayed to them, the therapist reviewed their drink diary

TABLE 39.1 Adjusted average weekly alcohol intake at recruitment and follow-up

Condition	Intake at recruitment (g)	Intake at follow-up (g)	Reduction (%)
Control	402	402	0
Simple advice	424	307	27.5
Advice and counselling	480	341	29.0
Extended counselling	460	285	38.0

Intake adjusted for age, group, sex, site of recruitment and mean alcohol intake at recruitment and follow-up

cards, reiterated the advice to keep drinking below the target levels, and encouraged them to apply the problem-solving strategies.

Among those who drew the simple advice, advice and brief counselling, and extended counselling conditions, there were statistically significant reductions in alcohol intake of 28%, 29% and 38% respectively, whereas among control subjects alcohol intake was unchanged (Table 39.1). There was also a significant effect on frequency of intoxication, with reductions of 27%, 29% and 28% in the simple advice, advice and counselling, and extended counselling groups, respectively, compared with 16% in the control group. Serum AST and ALT activities declined by 14–20% in those who received advice or extended counselling, whereas there was no change in the control group.

The finding that the simplest intervention, 5 minutes of advice, was effective in enabling subjects to reduce their consumption and frequency of intoxication, is particularly important for the implementation of early intervention techniques within general practice. An intervention which required prolonged counselling or multiple sessions, or where feedback of laboratory results was an essential component, would neither be feasible for most primary care services nor likely to be cost-effective. For example, the counselling employed by Kristenson et al (1983) entailed up to fortnightly sessions over 2 years. The intervention employed by Wallace, Cutler & Haines (1988) was equivalent to the advice and brief counselling condition used in the present study, but multiple sessions were permitted if the general practitioner considered this was indicated. Other interventions have involved feedback of biochemical results and reinforcement of behavioural strategies, equivalent to our extended counselling condition (reviewed in Bien, Miller & Tonigan 1993).

Phase III—WHO Collaborative Study on Implementation of Early Intervention in Primary Health Care

By the early 1990s the essential elements of a successful early intervention strategy were in place. A simple screening instrument was available, and a 5-minute intervention had been shown to be effective. It would, however, be excessively optimistic to assume that such interventions would be taken up immediately by primary care practitioners. The history of health care is replete with examples of interventions which have been shown to result in positive outcomes in randomized controlled trials, but which have taken 20 or more years to be incorporated into routine practice.

Barriers include lack of relevant knowledge and skills (Roche 1990; Roche, Guray & Saunders 1991; Saunders & Roche 1991; Weller et al 1992), negative attitudes towards, and beliefs about, people with alcohol problems (Clement 1986), and poor outcome expectations (Wechsler et al 1983; Anderson 1985). Others include organizational and structural factors. Time constraints (Rowland et al 1987) and lack of financial incentive (Dickinson et al 1984) are often cited as major barriers to carrying out preventive activities (Roche, Guray & Saunders 1991).

In 1992 we commenced work on developing social marketing strategies to promote early intervention within general practice, and in developing methods of training and supporting general practitioners to undertake early intervention within their own practices (Gomel et al 1994). Flay (1986) refers to this stage as 'dissemination' research and argues its importance for ensuring the successful implementation of community health programs. Our work has been adopted as the model for a WHO collaborative study, which also includes assessments of the knowledge and views of general practitioners on early intervention, and the perceived barriers and incentives to provide intervention (Saunders, Roche & Elvy 1992).

Social marketing provides a useful conceptual framework for understanding the dissemination of ideas or products. Although health professionals have been slow to adopt and systematically use marketing concepts to promote health products, these methods have been used extensively in the commercial world. Pharmaceutical companies, for example, use a variety of strategies to market products to physicians, including advertisements in professional journals, direct mail, continuing education programs and detailing (Caudill, Lurie & Rich 1992; Soumerai & Avorn 1990). An important concept in social marketing that is relevant to the dissemination of health interventions is the concept of the marketing mix. It involves the development of 'the right product backed by the right promotion and put into the right place at the right price' (Kottler & Zaltman 1971). In relation to the dissemination of an intervention to general practitioners, it is essential that: (a) the intervention is perceived to be clinically efficacious and well presented ('product'); (b) the benefits associated with the use of the package outweigh the associated costs such as time, effort and emotional energy ('price'); (c) the product is easily obtainable ('place'); and (d) the product is promoted in an acceptable manner that maximizes their interest. It is also imperative that a large number of general practitioners are reached by the promotional strategy ('promotion') (Gomel et al 1994).

We have evaluated three strategies to promote the uptake of an early intervention approach called 'Drinkless', which employs AUDIT to screen and is based on the 5-minute intervention and associated materials used in the WHO early intervention trial. The strategies are: (a) direct mail; (b) telephone marketing; and (c) personal marketing (Gomel et al 1994). Each strategy emphasizes the benefits (for general practitioners and patients) of engaging in early intervention, promotes endorsements of the program by major national and local medical authorities and addresses a range of known barriers, e.g. time constraints and opportunity costs. In the direct mail condition, a promotional brochure and personalized letter were mailed to general practitioners. In the tele-marketing condition a sales script was used to promote the intervention package to general practitioners over the telephone. In the personal marketing condition, the consultant visited the GP to demonstrate the program materials. As for the tele-marketing condition, a sales script was used to promote the program.

Six hundred and twenty-eight general practitioners were randomly assigned to one of the three marketing conditions. The major outcome measure was the uptake rate, i.e. the number of general practitioners requesting the intervention package expressed as a function of those offered the package. Preliminary results indicate very high uptake rates of approximately 80% for the tele-marketing and personal marketing conditions. Although cost-effectiveness analyses have not been completed, the tele-marketing strategy appears to be the cheapest one to implement and hence is likely to be the most cost-effective.

The initial acceptance of a product does not guarantee its continued use. In the commercial world 'augmented product features', e.g. product service and support, further influence whether it will be used (Donovan & Owen 1994). For general practitioners, a service that helps them overcome a range of attitudinal, skill and logistic barriers has the potential to influence the extent to which they offer intervention (Gomel et al 1994). We have now examined the effectiveness of various training and support strategies for enhancing the long-term use of the program with patients. One hundred and fifty-four general practitioners who requested the intervention package during the marketing phase and agreed to be involved in a 3-month evaluation of the program were matched into one of four training and support conditions—control, no support, minimal support and maximal support.

The conditions differed in terms of the intensity of support provided to general practitioners and their receptionists. General practitioners in the control condition did not receive any training in the use of the early intervention package over the 3-month period of the trial. Those in the no support condition received initial training in the use of the package but were not provided with any support thereafter. In the minimal support condition general practitioners and receptionists received initial training. Additionally, they were 'phoned 3–7 days following training to ensure data collection procedures were followed accurately. Thereafter, receptionists received data collection reminders through the 'phone once very 2 weeks. No further contact was made with the general practitioner until study completion. General practitioners and receptionists in the maximal support condition received the same assistance as those in the minimal support condition. Additionally, they received ongoing advice and support through alternate telephone contact and visits every 2 weeks. The issues covered centred around: (a) factors relating to the intervention (approaching patients to complete question- naires, dealing with negative or defensive patient reactions, and issues relating to giving the patient feedback and advice); (b) factors specific to receptionists and general practitioners (attitudes and beliefs about problem drinkers, the concept of early intervention, the importance of systematic screening, role legitimacy and self- efficacy); and (c) logistic factors (time constraints, coordinating the program with other practice staff, integrating the program into normal work routine). General practitioners also received a monthly summary letter giving feedback on their screening and counselling rates for that period (Gomel et al 1994).

Preliminary results suggest that there is a dose–response effect between the amount of support provided to general practitioners and receptionists and the proportion of patients that are screened for hazardous and harmful alcohol consumption. To date, approximately 19% (of some 24 000 patients) have had AUDIT scores in the hazardous intake range, and a further 3% have scores which indicate the likelihood of dependence. The proportion of hazardous drinkers counselled by general practitioners is higher in the maximal support condition than in the other conditions. The different levels of training and support seem to exert their effect mainly through promoting screening. Once patients are screened and identified to be at risk, they are more likely to be counselled regardless of the extent of training and support provided.

These findings demonstrate the potential of social marketing and support strategies to encourage general practitioners to take up a new preventive activity and incorporate it in their practices. Information from the WHO collaborative study will identify the incentives needed to ensure that early intervention is integrated in the routine work of general practice in the long term.

Intervention Programs to Reduce Inappropriate Benzodiazepine Prescribing

Two other approaches to prevention of substance-related harm in primary health care will be briefly described. The first is a program of training of general prac- titioners in appropriate prescribing of benzodiazepines. In Australia, approximately 7% of the adult population take prescribed sedative–hypnotic drugs in any 2-week period. Nearly all these drugs are benzodiazepines. Although they are relatively safe when used for short periods, they have significant dependence potential, with approximately 40% of persons taking therapeutic doses for 3 months or more experiencing a withdrawal syndrome when they are discontinued.

de Burgh et al (1995) have developed an educational intervention designed to reduce inappropriate prescribing of benzodiazepines by general practitioners. This consisted of a 20-minute visit to the practice by a doctor or a pharmacist, and employed the principles of pharmaceutical 'detailing' similar to those used in the 'Drinkless' project. General practitioners were invited to give their views on benzodiazepines and related topics, and were offered educational material, including management guidelines on anxiety, sleep disturbance and the treatment of benzodiazepine-dependent persons. Although there was no statistically significant difference in overall prescribing rates between general practitioners who received the intervention and the control group, there was a reduction in prescriptions for benzodiazepines issued for new diagnoses of insomnia (de Burgh et al 1995). There were substantial reductions in prescribing in both groups and an overall effect of the intervention may have been obscured by what the authors term an 'audit effect'. Doctors may have become more aware of their prescribing through a process of self-monitoring triggered by a pre-intervention survey. Although an on-site educational program on benzodiazepine prescribing could not be justified on the basis of these results, a more focused program on the management of specific clinical problems such as insomnia would be merited. An approach involving self-monitoring alone would seem to offer considerable scope for reducing inappropriate prescribing.

Training and Supporting General Practitioners in Methadone Prescribing

Methadone maintenance has been employed for many years as a means of rehabilitation of heroin-dependent persons. Typically, it has been provided in specialist units within the framework of a comprehensive rehabilitation program. Patients would be prescribed methadone for a period of 6–12 months to provide some pharmacological stability, during which time it was argued they would develop the motivation and resources to remain drug-free thereafter. Evidence has accumulated that for most heroin users this is unrealistic. There is a very high rate of relapse into heroin use when patients are removed from methadone maintenance, especially if this is initiated by the clinic rather than the patient (Caplehorn & Bell 1991; Caplehorn, Irwig & Saunders in press). Furthermore, the risk of transmission of infections such as HIV seems to be reduced only when patients are on methadone, and rises once more when they leave the program, a reflection presumably of the increase in injecting drug use and sharing of equipment.

Because of the evidence of benefit from prolonged methadone maintenance, and the public health need to make methadone available to as many injecting users as request it, a new paradigm for providing methadone has had to be developed. In Australia, methadone is being provided increasingly by general practitioners rather than specialist clinics. In New South Wales a training program for general practitioners was established under the auspices of the Australian Professional Society on Alcohol and Other Drugs (Bell 1995). It involves attending a workshop where information is provided on pharmacological and clinical aspects of methadone maintenance, the necessary legal and procedural requirements, and where attitudes and assumptions about drug use and methadone maintenance can be challenged and discussed. Participants receive a prescribers' manual and undertake a clinical placement which is designed to assess and promote clinical skills. At the end of the course there is an examination. Successful completion of the course and examination entitles the general practitioner to become an authorized prescriber. The course has had the salutary effect of shifting the emphasis from one of bureaucratic regulation of methadone prescribing to one of good clinical practice which is overseen by a professional organization. The course has attracted nearly 100 general practitioners so far.

CONCLUSIONS

Three initiatives to involve primary care practitioners in interventions to prevent harm from alcohol and drug use have been described. In many countries general practice is in a process of redefining its role, and general practitioners are expressing the desire to take on a more planned and pro-active role which emphasizes preventive approaches and which aims to reduce illness and promote health at a population level. The key requirement now is for preventive medicine to be legitimized through the policies of government and professional bodies, and for an appropriate system of remuneration to be introduced. As a general practitioner said when interviewed in the WHO collaborative study, 'Enough of the rhetoric, give us some tangible support'.

ACKNOWLEDGEMENTS

We thank our many colleagues who have played key roles in the program of early intervention research described here, including Dr Robert Reznik, Dr Harding Burns, Dr Ann Roche, Mr Steven Hanratty, Ms Jan Clarke, Dr Geoffrey Elvy, Dr Phillip Anderson and Dr Michael Adena.

The program of research on early intervention is supported by the Drug and Alcohol Directorate, New South Wales Department of Health, the Research into Drug Abuse Program of the Commonwealth Department of Health, the National Health and Medical Research Council, and the World Health Organization. We acknowledge the contributions and support of Dr Peter Anderson of the WHO Regional Office for Europe, and Dr Norman Sartorius, Mr Marcus Grant, Dr Bedirhan Üstün and Dr Andrew Ball of WHO Headquarters, Geneva, in the collaborative work described here.

REFERENCES

Anderson P (1985) Managing alcohol problems in general practice. *Br Med J* **290**, 1873–6.
Australian Bureau of Statistics (1986) *Australian Health Survey 1983*. Sydney: Australian Bureau of Statistics.
Babor TF & Grant M (1992) *Project on Identification and Management of Alcohol-related Problems. Report on Phase II: A Randomized Clinical Trial of Brief Interventions in Primary Health Care.* Geneva: World Health Organization.

Babor TF, Korner P, Wilber C & Good SP (1987) Screening and early intervention strategies for harmful drinkers: initial lessons from the Amethyst Project. *Australian Drug Alcohol Rev* **6**, 325–39.

Bell JR (1995) Lessons from a training program for methadone prescribers. *Med J Austral* **162**, 143–4.

Bien TH, Miller WR & Tonigan JS (1993) Brief interventions for alcohol problems: a review. *Addiction* **88**, 315–36.

Bucholz K, Homan SM & Helzer JE (1992) When do alcoholics first discuss drinking problems? *J Stud Alcohol* **53**, 582–9.

Caplehorn JRM & Bell J (1991) Methadone dosage and retention of patients in maintenance treatment. *Med J Austral* **154**, 195–9.

Caplehorn JRM, Irwig L & Saunders JB (1996) Physicians' attitudes and retention of patients in their methadone treatment programs. *Substance Use Misuse.*

Caudill TS, Lurie N & Rich EC (1992) The influence of pharmaceutical industry advertising on physician prescribing. *J Drug Issues* **22**, 331–8.

Clement S (1986) The identification of alcohol-related problems by general practitioners. *Br J Addict* **81**, 257–64.

Collins DJ & Lapsley HM (1991) *Estimating the Economic Costs of Drug Abuse in Australia. National Campaign Against Drug Abuse Monograph No 24.* Canberra: Australian Government Publishing Service.

Commonwealth Department of Human Sciences and Health (1994) *Statistics on Drug Abuse in Australia.* Canberra: Australian Government Publishing Service.

Conigrave KM, Saunders JB & Reznik RB (1995) Predictive capacity of the AUDIT questionnaire for alcohol-related harm. *Addiction* **90**, 1479–85.

Conigrave KM, Saunders JB & Whitfield JB (1995) Diagnostic tests for alcohol consumption. *Alcohol Alcoholism* **30**, 13–26.

de Burgh S, Mant A, Mattick RP, Donnelly N, Hall W & Bridges-Webb C (1995) A controlled trial of educational visiting to improve benzodiazepine prescribing in general practice. *Austral J Publ Health* **19**, 142–8.

Dickinson JA, Hall J, Logan J & McDonald ML (1984) An economic model of general practice. *Med J Austral*, 652–8.

Donovan R & Owen N (1994) Social marketing and mass intervention. In RK Dishman (ed) *Exercise Adherence: Implications for Public Health*, 2nd edn. Illinois: Human Kinetics.

Flay BR (1986) Efficacy and effectiveness trials (and other phases of research) in the development of health promotion programs. *Prevent Med* **15**, 451–74.

Gomel MK, Saunders JB, Burns L, Hardcastle D & Sumich M (1994) Dissemination of early intervention for harmful alcohol consumption in general practice. *Health Promotion J Austral* **4**, 65–9.

Heather N, Campion PD, Neville RG & MacCabe D (1987) Evaluation of a controlled drinking minimal intervention for problem drinkers in general practice (the DRAMS scheme). *J Coll Gen Pract* **37**, 358–63.

Institute of Medicine (1990) *Broadening the Base of Treatment for Alcohol Problems.* Washington, DC: National Academy Press.

Kamerow DB, Pincus HA & MacDonald DI (1986) Alcohol abuse, other drug use, and mental health disorders in medical practice. *J Am Med Assoc* **255**, 2054–7.

Keso L & Salaspuro M (1990) Inpatient treatment of employed alcoholics: a randomized clinical trial on Hazelden-type and traditional treatment. *Alcoholism Clin Exp Res* **14**, 584–9.

Kotler P & Zaltman G (1971) Social marketing: an approach to planned social change. *J Marketing* **35**, 3–12.

Kristenson H, Ohlin H, Hulter-Nosslin MS, Trell E & Hood B (1983) Identification and intervention of heavy drinkers in middle-aged men: results and follow up of 24–60 months of long-term study with randomized controls. *Alcoholism Clin Exp Res* **7**, 203–9.

Mattick RP & Hall W (1994) A summary of recommendations for the management of opiate dependence: the Quality Assurance in the Treatment of Drug Dependence Project. *Drug Alcohol Rev* **13**, 319–26.

Mattick RP & Jarvis T (1994) In-patient setting and long duration for the treatment of alcohol dependence? Out-patient care is as good. *Drug Alcohol Rev* **13**, 127–35.

Moore R, Makkai T & McAllister I (1989) *Perceptions and Patterns of Drug Use: Changed Since the Drug Offensive*. Canberra: Department of Community Services and Health.

Murphy HBM (1980) Hidden barriers to the diagnosis and treatment of alcoholism and other alcohol misuse. *J Stud Alcohol* **41**, 417–28.

Orlandi MA (1987) Promoting health and preventing disease in health care settings: an analysis of barriers. *Prevent Med* **16**, 119–30.

Persson J & Magnusson P-H (1989) Early intervention in patients with excessive consumption of alcohol: a controlled study. *Alcohol* **6**, 403–8.

Reid ALA, Webb GR, Hennrikus D & Sanson-Fisher RW (1986) Detection of patients with high alcohol intake by general practitioners. *Br Med J* **293**, 735–7.

Roche AM (1990) When to intervene for patients' alcohol consumption: what general practitioners say. *Med J Austral* **152**, 622–5.

Roche AM, Guray C & Saunders JB (1991) General practitioners' experiences of patients with drug and alcohol problems. *Br Addict* **86**, 263–75.

Roche AM, Saunders JB & Elvy GA (1992) *The Role of General Practice Settings in the Prevention and Management of the Harm Done by Alcohol Use*. Copenhagen: World Health Organization Regional Office for Europe.

Rowland N, Maynard A, Beveridge A, Kennedy P & Wintersgill W (1987) Doctors have no time for alcohol screening. *Br Med J* **295**, 95–6.

Rydon P, Redman S, Sanson-Fisher RW & Reid ALA (1992) Detection of alcohol-related problems in general practice. *J Stud Alcohol* **53**, 197–202.

Saunders JB (1987) The WHO project on early detection and treatment of harmful alcohol consumption. *Austral Drug Alcohol Rev* **6**, 303–8.

Saunders JB (1994) Towards quality care in drug and alcohol practice. *Drug Alcohol Rev* **13**, 115–17.

Saunders JB & Aasland OG (1987) *WHO Collaborative Project on the Identification and Treatment of Persons with Harmful or Hazardous Alcohol Consumption. Report on Phase I: The Development of a Screening Instrument*. Geneva: World Health Organization.

Saunders JB, Aasland OG, Babor TF, de la Fuente JR & Grant M (1993) Development of the Alcohol Use Disorders Identification Test (AUDIT): WHO collaborative project on early detection of persons with harmful alcohol consumption—II. *Addiction* **88**, 791–803.

Saunders JB & Conigrave KM (1990) Early identification of alcohol problems. *Can Med Assoc J* **143**, 1060–69.

Saunders JB & Roche AM (1991) Medical education in substance use disorders. *Drug Alcohol Rev* **10**, 263–75.

Saunders JB, Roche AM & Elvy GA (1992) *Implementing Early Intervention in Primary Health Care: A Proposal to Establish a WHO Collaborative Study*. Copenhagen: World Health Organization Regional Office for Europe.

Slama KJ, Redman S, Cockburn J & Sanson-Fisher RW (1989) Community views about the role of general practitioners in disease prevention. *Family Practitioner* **6**, 203–9.

Soumerai SB & Avorn J (1990) Principles of education outreach (academic detailing) to improve clinical decision making. *J Am Med Assoc* **263**, 549–56.

Vaillant G (1983) *The Natural History of Alcoholism*. Cambridge, MA: Harvard University Press.

Wallace P, Cutler S & Haines A (1988) Randomized controlled trial of general practitioner intervention in patients with excessive alcohol consumption. *Br Med J* **297**, 663–8.

Wechsler H, Levine S, Idelson RK, Rohman M & Taylor JO (1983) The physicians' role in health promotion. A survey of primary-care practitioners. *N Engl J Med* **308**, 939–55.

Weller DP, Litt JCB, Pols RG, Ali RL, Southgate DO & Harris RD (1992) Drug- and alcohol-related health problems in primary care—what do GPs think? *Med J Austral* **156**, 43–8.

40

AIDS and Drugs

H Sell

World Health Organization, New Delhi, India

Epidemiological considerations make it clear that AIDS is not a pandemic as often described, which puts 'everybody at risk' as plague did in medieval times, but a series of localized circumscribed epidemics. The dynamic of each epidemic is determined by the type of risk behaviour involved, the vulnerability of the persons engaged in the risk behaviour, and the frequency of this behaviour. On the other hand, the sequence of localized epidemics is determined by the 'social or geographical mobility' of the persons likely to be infected, and their 'transmission capability' across various groups. 'Social and geographical mobility' means risk behaviour outside a circumscribed group of persons. Sex workers, for example, may have a high social mobility because they may receive clients from a variety of social strata and localities, whereas truck drivers who have sex with women in different localities have the geographical mobility to spread the infection. 'Transmission capability' across groups means the capability to spread the infection from one group engaged in a certain risk behaviour to another, e.g. drug-injecting sex workers, or drug-injecting blood donors (where blood is not effectively tested before transfusion), or drug-injecting homosexual men or, even more so, drug-injecting male sex workers. Each localized epidemic leads to the establishment of a reservoir of virus which can spill into the general population. If general vulnerability is low (especially a low prevalence of sexually transmitted diseases and low levels of risk behaviours) such spill-overs will represent individual tragedies, but not an initiation of new small epidemics.

Injecting drug users (IDUs) are, in Europe, the USA and some other parts of the world, a very important reservoir of the HIV virus. The act of sharing injecting equipment carries the risk of transmitting the infection in a similar order of magnitude to sexual intercourse. However, where this is established practice in a group of IDUs, it tends to occur much more frequently, often three or more times per day, and female IDUs often turn to commercial sex work to fund their drug expenses (this pathway, although often quoted, does not seem to be substantiated by empirical evidence: there are many commercial sex workers who socialized into

Preventing Mental Illness: Mental Health Promotion in Primary Care. Edited by R. Jenkins and T.B. Üstün.
Published 1998 John Wiley & Sons Ltd.

drug use only after beginning commercial sex work, or were introduced to drug use either in their working environment (e.g. by drug-dealing pimps, who thereby increase the sex worker's dependency and the reliability of access to their income). On the other hand, brothel owners often want to make sure that their establishments are 'drug-free', so that sex workers are expelled from such establishments if they take drugs, e.g. this is a regular feature in Bangkok. They then end up as freelance or street sex workers, difficult to reach for preventive or empowerment workers.

In most countries the consumption of any unprescribed scheduled drug is still a criminal offence, and illicit selling of these drugs is still considered a criminal activity in all. This puts drug workers in a difficult arguing position, knowing that Governments subsidize tobacco cultivation, and levy taxes on tobacco and alcohol products, but simultaneously punish the use or sale of products which may be less harmful to health, e.g. cannabis.

This generates a difficult situation for dealers, users and drug workers alike. Drugs, licit or illicit, happen to be a commodity accessible to and consumed by many. I have no doubt that more people in the world use drugs than own cars or TV sets or refrigerators. But owners of the latter commodities tend to be proud and happy about them. Users of drugs—if they happen to have been declared illicit by the Government, often under pressure from foreign agencies— tend to be unhappy, at least from the moment when they realize that the dependence syndrome has set in. From this point of the argument onwards, we should leave out tobacco. It is a licit drug which has a record of high addictive potential and substantial health risks, but has little other impact on people's social functioning or other aspects of performance. Tobacco use can, therefore, become dysfunctional only in the very poor, for financial reasons, or for the heavily dependent smoker in smoke-free workplaces. But tobacco is probably a particularly good example of an important feature common to all drugs of addiction: its effects at initial use are strongly unpleasant (unless preconditioned by, say, the presence of an admired smoking father): giddiness, cough, a bitter taste (unbearable for 'tasters' with taste buds particularly sensitive to bitter substances; they seem to be genetically endowed with an incapability to become smokers). As a consequence, it requires probably much harder work to become a smoker than to become a heroin user.

BECOMING A DRUG USER

Since the effects of all drugs of addiction are initially unpleasant, at least if taken in effectively mind-altering amounts (giddiness is the most common 'psycho-active' effect, nausea the other), becoming a drug user is a puzzling phenomenon (Fekjaer 1993). How do people manage to label as pleasurable the process of getting drunk when it leads to loss of control over certain motor skills, vomiting, perhaps an afterwards extremely frightening blackout, and a very unpleasant hangover the next morning? Why is self-induced giddiness through, say, hyperventilation so rare compared to drug-induced giddiness? The answer probably lies in the social circumstances of the initiation into drug use; the rituals, the social meaning of drug use; or the status quality of being able to 'enjoy' what novices perceive as unpleasant and parents and teachers forbid or present as dangerous; thereby adding thrill to the experience without changing the perception of risk (Sell et al 1992). Rituals help us to reinterpret the world around us, to give meaning and order to otherwise random or uncontrollable or threatening events. The rituals helping to socialize people into alcohol use are innumerable. Initiation into beer drinking, for example, is often done as a rite of passage by the family in Southern Germany, for example on the day of the 'confirmation', the formal admission to membership in the Protestant parish, around the age of 14 years. And the boy is expected (to pretend) to like it. Different types of glasses are to be used for different alcoholic beverages (the average European of some 'culture' would consider it terribly improper to be offered champagne in a coffee mug or a plastic cup), and are to be consumed at specified times of the day. And a group of students sharing a 'joint' (of cannabis) would probably lose their ability to enjoy it if a senior faculty member tried to join in. I know of very few individuals who were alone when they first tried heroin, induced by little else than curiosity generated by the antidrug propaganda, and have still to find a regular user who worked himself into regular, non-ritualized use on his own. One more point: when first taking a mind-altering drug, especially an illicit one, the person may feel considerable anticipatory fear of the unknown. The anxiety-releasing effect of the drug may then add a relaxing 'pleasant surprise' to the otherwise unpleasant experience. This pleasant surprise will, of course, be stronger with the strength of the anticipatory fear of doing something bad and dangerous, if the adolescent believes in the usual anti-drug propaganda. It seems a bit like someone riding a fearsome roller-coaster for the first time: 'Oh, its not all that bad after all. Let me try again'.

BECOMING A DRUG INJECTOR

If the drug effect is initially unpleasant, poking a needle into one's arm must be even more so. No uninitiated person will perceive pleasure when this is done. There is, therefore, a natural protection against injecting. Yet, in drug cultures in some parts of South East Asia, e.g. Myanmar, Thailand and the north-eastern states of India, where injecting is the main route of drug administration, it takes only an average of about 1 month of regular drug use to join the 'mainstream' of injecting. Why will people undergo the pain of injecting, mostly with needles blunted from previous use, when they have the alternative of inhaling? In my experience, it is pressure to conform socially, to share behaviour which differentiates between the group and the others-than-us, and the achievement of 'having made it'. We have to admit that it is indeed an achievement to perceive pleasure from the pain of poking a needle through one's skin. This quality of achievement and perceived status is probably also the reason why injectors do not normally mix with inhalers. There seems to exist a caste-like system in places where I am somewhat familiar with the drug scene: injectors despise all other users of any drug as inferior, heroin-inhalers despise cannabis users, and these in turn have pity on those who consume only licit alcohol.

I had an interesting experience in Sri Lanka when a snowball survey was done on drug users not in prison or on treatment. Of about 1000 heroin users identified, only three had ever injected (NDDCB 1990). However, at about the same time I was introduced to a number of drug users in one locality in Colombo and was shown a shooting gallery. None of the 30 or so users I talked to knew of substantial numbers of inhaling users. I also saw an impressive example of conformity pressure some years ago in Bombay, when I was discussing reconverting to inhaling (because of the AIDS risk) with a group of heroin injectors. They ridiculed the idea, because you could get the 'flash' only from injecting, and I asked for a demonstration of this wonderful experience. One volunteered and signalled the 'aah' experience less than 3 seconds after the beginning of injecting. I explained that not a molecule of heroin could possibly have reached his brain yet, and why. One of the group said: 'Doctor, I am so happy you say this, because I never had one. I always pretended'.

I have seen much pride in early injectors, a pride which generates a feeling of invulnerability from AIDS: 'Besides, doctor, we like to play a little Russian roulette'.

BECOMING DEPENDENT

The use of illicit drugs (and tobacco) is so emotionally and politically charged that it is little wonder that definitions are hard to come by; and if they are attempted, they tend not to be accepted. WHO published a 'WHO memorandum' aiming at promoting the use of non-judgemental terminology and proposing a set of definitions (WHO 1981). One of the judgemental terms to be avoided was 'drug abuse'. Yet, the relevant division in WHO Headquarters is still called 'Program on Substance Abuse'. It appears that the ritualistic underpinnings of drug use are in some ways mimicked by the ritualistic nature of the 'war on drugs'. The social learning process attaching pleasure to a basically unpleasurable or, at best, neutral drug effect seems to be paralleled by a social learning process attaching rejection and disgust towards those who have gone the other way. One is reminded, in this context, of basic Darwinian survival advantages of fighting the other-than-us. How else can one explain why politicians who have worked themselves into enjoying alcohol are willing to imprison those who happen to do a similar thing in other ways?

With drug dependence, a slide into a particularly important aspect of the dependence syndrome occurs: 'the salience of drug-seeking behaviour relative to other important priorities' (WHO 1981).

The exception here is tobacco. It is normally easily available, and does not (at least initially) interfere with daily functioning. Smokers are therefore protected against this particular component of the dependence syndrome. Alcohol is also normally widely available. But its interference with daily functioning may be so strong that alcoholism can impose serious limitations on the 'social menu'. With illicit opiates, the root of this aspect of the dependence syndrome is their criminalization, leading to low availability, unpredictable purity and high price, marginalization of the user and consequent socialization into the 'drug subculture'. Methadone maintenance programs are normally too high-threshold to permit entry before opiate dependents have become fully-fledged 'junkies'; opiate dependents tend to have to cross the threshold into full 'junky' status, which is difficult to reverse, before they are permitted to benefit from a service which could have prevented it.

All of us have a variety of social roles, e.g. in the family, in a job, with friends, as members of a club, in addition to the roles we fantasize ourselves into. This 'social menu' is severely reduced in many alcoholics and most persons dependent on illicit drugs: in alcoholics it consists of the continuous effort to hide the amount of consumption from family, employers and others, and to appear reasonably functional during the hours of the day; in those dependent on illicit drugs it is the overriding issue of finding the money and the drugs every day, and hiding this from the family as long as possible and, after having been expelled from home, from the police; in addition to having to learn and accept the rules of the drug subculture. These are intense pressures. They force people into a very limited but emotionally intense lifestyle. A Nepali heroin addict put it very succinctly: 'Of course, I would stop stealing if I could quit heroin. But how could I make a living after that?' We are beginning to realize that the lifestyle people socialize into when becoming increasingly dependent is probably the most critical issue. The particular substance of addiction is of additional relevance only if it significantly interferes with daily functioning. The only substance to do this is alcohol. (Interestingly, opiates do so to some extent when this effect is culturally assigned to them, e.g. east of the Chittagong Hills at the Bangladesh–Myanmar border, opium is perceived as incapacitating; whereas in India it is taken to enable users to work harder; and Rajput warriors took it to be tougher in battle and, incidentally, to lose less blood when wounded.) There may therefore be good reason to include alcohol as the offending substance, in rehabilitation programs for alcoholics, as well as aiming for enrichment of the social menu, but one may ignore the substance of other dependencies, especially opiates, and work on lifestyle enrichment alone.

This narrowing down of lifestyle choices, or of the social menu of drug dependents in the process of 'junkyization', includes a pervasive feeling of helplessness, a perceived incapacity to care for others or oneself, and a 'forgetting of meaning', which explains much of the suicidal ideation and suicides amongst drug dependents. This is, of course, a clear reversal of the pride in achieving IDU status mentioned above. The transition from the glory of being able to inject with pleasure, to the abyss of 'just to disappear, to be there no more, that would be the best' (*Der Spiegel* No. 8, 1984) symbolizes this final loss of meaning. We may tentatively conclude from this that 'meaning' may, of necessity, include choices.

And by concluding this, we are approaching a value-judgement: choices as an indicator for quality of life. Perhaps drug work will be able to contribute this to the international quality of life debate.

FROM DRUGS TO AIDS

I have above outlined some of the behavioural characteristics of IDUs which, in my view, make them particularly vulnerable to the risk of HIV infection. One is the feeling of invulnerability which often comes with the pride of 'having made it' into injecting. Incidentally, this transition takes a very different form if it occurs under circumstantial pressure. In July 1991, heroin virtually disappeared from Madras in Southern India after the assassination of Rajiv Gandhi and the ensuing clamp-down on Sri Lankan Tamils. The only alternative heroin inhalers knew about was injectable buprenorphine. Even 1 month after this enforced shift to injecting, most users I met were longing for heroin to inhale, because they felt that the pain of injecting was a very high price indeed to pay for their 'high'. They still hated it.

The pressure to conform is certainly instrumental in socializing users into injecting, but I have seen little evidence that this would significantly contribute to the sharing of needles or to resistance to ending the practice if needles were easily available. A 'blood brotherhood'—feeling involved in sharing needles and some blood which is left in them—is mentioned sometimes, but I have rarely seen evidence that this is a major issue in most groups of IDUs. I have the feeling that more often than not this somewhat romantic notion was introduced through leading questions from interviewers, rather than reflecting indigenous feelings. The pressure to conform may be very strong, yet group cohesion is often quite weak and social relations in user groups may become quite chaotic over time. More important is the feeling of helplessness and loss of meaning with 'junkyization', the feeling of inability to care for oneself and others, and often an anhedonia reminding one of survivors of concentration camps or long-term inmates in refugee camps. Messages about preventing HIV/hepatitis infection may be heard and understood, but are difficult to implement. This concerns self-protection by avoiding equipment-sharing or decontamination, as well as protection of or from a sexual partner by condom use. In fact, from the literature it appears that caring for others may even be more affected by the general loss of meaning than self-protection.

OPPORTUNITIES FOR INTERVENTIONS

It has often been argued that primary prevention of drug use, i.e. prevention of initiation, is not possible. In fact, it has been shown that such efforts may, in fact, be counterproductive (see Sell 1990; for tobacco use, see Flay et al 1989). However, it has been pointed out, at least for smoking, that adolescent substance use is quite volatile, and that one should focus on the prevention of dependent use rather than on the prevention of any use (Clearly et al 1988). Whether it is possible to prevent inhalers turning to injecting is a moot point. If injecting is the 'normal' route of administration in a drug subculture, this is probably very difficult, unless it is accompanied by rigorous efforts to reconvert injectors to oral means of drug administration, especially if it can be facilitated by oral substitution maintenance.

In countries/areas with low rates of injecting but high rates of oral routes of drug administration, the rate of conversions to injecting in previous non-injectors tends to be low, because the 'caste-system' limits contacts between injectors and others. However, in order to keep the conversion rate low, a continuous 'qualitative monitoring' of the drug scene is necessary. There may be a wave of accidental conversions, as described for Madras. To prevent this wave from happening, it would have been enough to spread the message that buprenorphine also exists in sublingual form (and to ensure that it is on the market, which was not the case at that time). Such monitoring would also have discovered the rather disastrous impact of a widely shown 'health education' video on the horrors of narcotics, which showed exactly how to make #3 heroin injectable (unlike #4, it is not water-soluble), inadvertently glamourising this method of ingestion and resulting in a rapid outbreak of injecting. It would also permit the timely discovery of drug peddlers who, for a little extra income, mesmerize their clients into the superiority of injecting, as happened recently in a slum of Delhi. By the time he was expelled from the slum by a group of (ex)user-activists, a group of users had already been socialized into injecting (although most could be re-converted by an on-the-spot buprenorphine maintenance program).

The 'junkyized' and helpless are often socially chaotic but not at all chaotic in their lifestyle and daily routine. On the contrary, they tend to suffer from excessively structured daily life and lack of choice: money and drugs, a fearsome straitjacket (I have always been amazed by the logic of boot-camp type approaches to bringing order into the chaotic lives of dependents. Their chaotic social lives are due to a loss of meaning, the tenor of a meaningless daily routine of money and drugs mimicked very well by the meaningless routines of many therapeutic communities and boot camps). To promote the mental health of anhedonic, socially chaotic, helpless and hopeless long-term dependents would appear to be a precondition before even considering the special problems their drug use may imply, including a substantial risk reduction for HIV infection. We call this approach to the promotion of mental health among severely drug-dependent persons, including the establishment of a basis for effective HIV prevention in this high-risk group, the 'open community approach' whose main ingredient is rehabilitation without detoxification. Rehabilitation, i.e. mental health promotion, means the building of optimism and social cohesion or togetherness, demystification and deglamorization of drugs, and enrichment of lifestyle. This, of course, is a slow process. The changes we want to achieve may, at times, be too upsetting and frightening for the 'junkyized' dependent. He/she may, for temporary comfort, relax back into the old lifestyle, just as torture victims on the way to improvement sometimes slip back into nightmares and anhedonia. We do not use the word relapse for this. We talk about 'in-and-out-flexibility'.

Promoting the mental health of drug dependents and AIDS high-risk groups, rather than 'treating' them, has not yet been scientifically evaluated. In fact, we still lack the instruments to do this convincingly. But semi-quantitative evaluations have shown amazingly positive results.

REFERENCES

Cleary PD, Hitchcock JL, Semmer N, Flinchbaugh LJ & Pinney JM (1988) Adolescent smoking: research and health policy. *Milbank Qu* **66**, 137–71.

Fekjaer HO (1993) *Alcohol and Illicit Drugs. Myths and Realities.* Colombo: IOGT, Alcohol and Drug Information Centre.

Flay BR, Koepke D, Thomson SJ, Santi S, Best JA & Brown KS (1989) Six-year follow-up of the first Waterloo school smoking prevention trial. *Am J Publ Health* **79**, 1371–6.

NDDCB (National Dangerous Drugs Control Board) (1990) *Careers Study of Heroin Users in Sri Lanka.* Colombo: Research Unit NDDCB/UNFDAC/WHO Project.

Sell J, Mochney A & Khodakevich N (1992) Adolescent risk-taking behaviour. Paper presented at the IIIrd Asia–Pacific Conference on AIDS, New Delhi.

Sell HL (1992) Alcohol, drugs and smoking in youth. In HM Wallace & K Giri (eds) *Health Care of Women and Children in Developing Countries*, pp 476–90. Oakland, CA: Third Party Publishing Company.

WHO (World Health Organization) (1981) Nomenclature and classification of drug- and alcohol-related problems: a WHO memorandum. *Bull WHO* **59**, 225–42.

41

A Regional Effort to Reduce Corporal Punishment in Children— The Promotion of Community Programs in the Americas through Primary Care*

I Levav, R Guerrero, L Phebo, G Coe and MT Cerqueira

World Health Organization, Washington, DC, USA

A CASE FOR ACTION

Few violations of human rights awaken greater societal concern and repugnance than those perpetrated against children. Yet the number of reports of child maltreatment has not only reached overwhelming proportions but even seems to be rising (Reiss & Roth 1993). Indeed, both the scientific literature and the media often report on children being subjected to violence at home, in the community and in schools. In the USA, 2.7 million children were reported abused or neglected in 1991 (Hoekelman 1992). In Brazil, merchants reportedly ordered the murder of street children because they were perceived as a public nuisance (Cruz Neto & Minayo 1994).

For some countries in the Americas, the future does not bode well in regard to child maltreatment due to the spread of all types of violent behavior and mounting social ills, such as premature parenthood, divorce, substance abuse and the disruption of social support groups due to urban migration.

Reluctantly in some countries, less ambivalently in others, the health sector has joined other social sectors in addressing the problem of violence, recognizing that it has adverse effects on health and that the multiple determinants and expressions of

---

* This chapter was first published in *Bull PAHO* 1996, **30**(1), 70–79

Preventing Mental Illness: Mental Health Promotion in Primary Care. Edited by R. Jenkins and T.B. Üstün.
Published 1998 John Wiley & Sons Ltd.

violence (abuse, neglect, homicide) require a multifaceted approach to its control and prevention (PAHO/WHO 1994).

In reference to violence against children, the 1960s may be a temporal landmark with the description and labeling of the battered child syndrome (Kempe et al 1962); since then, the literature on the subject has escalated. Despite research efforts, much remains unknown of the epidemiology, etiology and mechanisms involved, as well as of the most effective interventions to prevent violence against children (Reiss & Roth 1993). It is our contention, however, that the knowledge accrued so far is adequate to build 'a case for action' (Kark 1974) and to develop intervention programs that are scientifically grounded.

Conceptually and operationally, program development on the subject of interpersonal violence is facilitated by the emergence of health promotion as a legitimate field of action as defined by the Ottawa Charter and similar position statements. Health promotion targets healthy lifestyles—of which eradication of violent behavior and its replacement by pacific communication is a part—as a strategy to enhance health in the communities.

This chapter will review one type of violent behavior against children—corporal punishment—and will delineate a regional initiative for its prevention and control, rooting the intervention strategies in community-orientated primary health care, social communication and health education, and in the promotion of healthy public policies.

CORPORAL PUNISHMENT

Corporal punishment is defined as the infliction of pain with the purpose of modifying behavior which is undesirable in the perception of the person in charge of disciplining a child. It includes different means, such as spanking, slapping, grabbing, shoving and hitting with objects (Straus 1991). Corporal punishment is the most frequent violent behavior against children. Straus (1991) found that over 90% of parents in the USA use it in an attempt to exert discipline. One may be tempted to dismiss findings from the USA, since statistics on violence in this country are relatively high (Reiss & Roth 1993). Yet, even countries with which violence is seldom associated are not exempt from corporal punishment at home. For instance, Tonella & Zuppinger (1994) in Switzerland, a country that for centuries has been spared war, reports that one-third of parents use corporal punishment. Krugman, Mata & Krugman (1992) found in a survey in Costa Rica, a country that abolished its national army in the late 1940s, that 82% of male university students and 77% of female students acknowledged that they had been spanked in their lives. Furthermore, 35% of male students and 25% of female students had experienced whipping or flogging. The study also showed that abuse took place mainly between the ages of 5 and 10.

The widespread frequency of the phenomenon may lead to the mistaken conclusion that it is a normal societal event and thus hardly merits intervention by the health sector. Does the fact that it is frequent imply that there are no adverse health effects? McCormick (1992), after reviewing several sources, stated:

> Corporal punishment contributes to the problem [of violence] by serving as a model of problem solving using interpersonal violence . . . [it] is ineffective and even counterproductive as a child-rearing strategy . . . .

By example, adults implicitly tell children that spanking, slapping and other violent means of discipline are acceptable and necessary. It is also implicit in this message that those who have more power can use it against those who have less, or none in the case of adult–child interaction.

Empirical evidence on the immediate and late effect of physical discipline is now available. Holmes & Robins (1988) carefully examined the role of parental disciplinary practices in the development of depression and alcoholism by checking both parental psychiatric history and SES. Their case-controlled study relied on an examination of 200 respondents chosen from the National Institutes of Mental Health (NIMH)–St Louis Epidemiologic Catchment Area site. They concluded that:

> . . . harsh and inconsistent childhood discipline appears to be an important predictor of depression and alcoholism in adulthood in families with and without sick parents and in both poor and well-to-do families . . . .

The putative role of corporal punishment on self-esteem (Oates, Forrest & Peacock 1985), aggressive behavior (Weiss & Dodge 1992) and the child's moral development (Hoffman & Saltzstein 1967) has also been pointed out. Straus & Kaufman Kantor (1994) argue that available data seem to suggest that corporal punishment in adolescents may be a risk factor for depression, suicide, alcohol abuse, physical abuse of children and physical assault on wives.

Corporal punishment is not restricted to the home but includes schools as well. The American Medical Association (AMA) defined this type of violence as the:

> . . . intentional infliction of pain or discomfort and/or use of physical force upon a student as punishment for an offense or behavior . . . (AMA/OGC 1992).

Schools in many states of the USA still use corporal punishment under the protection of the law. The American Academy of Pediatrics estimated that corporal punishment is administered between 1 and 2 million times a year (AAP/CSH 1991). In other countries of the Americas, little is known about its frequency but we know from informants that it exists, e.g. Anderson & Payne (1994) have documented its use in Barbados.

Corporal punishment at school constitutes a violation of human rights; furthermore, it is not free from adverse physical, psychological and academic effects (AAP/CSH 1991; Monyooe 1993; Lepen Cherian 1994). Following a review of its effects, the American Medical Association has advocated its abolition (AMA/OGC 1992); so have other professional organizations, but the practice has not yet been discontinued.

There are additional reasons to advocate eradication of corporal punishment at schools and also at home. The border between its use as a method of discipline and as a method of child abuse is far from clear. The harsher the disciplinary method used the more blurred is the dividing line and thus the higher the risk to the child's life and integrity. It has been said that 'societal permission to use corporal punishment is the child's ticket to victimization' (McCormick 1992). Belsky (1993) concurred by stating:

> . . . it is doubtful that maltreatment can be eliminated so long as parents rear their offspring in a society in which . . . corporal punishment is condoned . . . .

Furthermore, even though Kaufman & Ziegler (1987) and Widom (1989) have cautioned against the facile conclusion that abused children become abusive parents or that violence in childhood necessarily leads to later violent or criminal acts, there are nevertheless grounds to suspect that those who experienced violent behavior in childhood are prone to replicate it in adulthood. Buntain-Ricklefs et al (1994) showed in a cross-sectional survey carried out in several teaching pediatric clinics in two states in the USA that:

> The strongest risk factor for approving of any type of punishment [physical or emotional] was having experienced that punishment as a child . . . .

Vargas et al (1993a), in a group of parents and guardians ($n = 527$) in Chile, found an odds ratio of 4.9, indicating the high probability that parents who had been punished physically in their childhood used the same means with their own children. Hemenway, Solnick & Carter (1994) agreed with such a conclusion; these authors noted, however, that there are parents who succeed in breaking the cycle of violence. Fry (1993), using an anthropological approach, was able to ascertain the intergenerational transmission of violence at the level of the community by studying two native neighboring villages in Mexico. These were Zatopec communities of contrasting level of violence, as measured by fighting, wife-beating, assaults and homicide. The two communities differed in the patterns of child-rearing, the more pacific one advocating positive verbal strategies for disciplining while the other used corporal punishment more often. Most of the studies mentioned above are not entirely free from some methodological limitations; taken together, however, they serve to show that research evidence indicates that we need to be worried that violence begets violence.

Health promotion, in its striving to achieve well-being and a higher quality of life, advocates the replacement of all violent behavior for pacific means of communication, whether or not the current or future damage to the individual's health is marked or minimal. In doing so, the health sector will help society to respect the rights of children. It is important to note that this the only age group with the dubious privilege of being subjected to corporal punishment for the sake of discipline. Such a practice is no longer tolerated for other groups in society.

INTERVENTION STRATEGIES

The introduction of community-based programs to reduce or abolish corporal punishment is bound to meet formidable obstacles from several sources. First, resistance comes from the culture itself, inasmuch as it sanctions corporal punishment as an integral component of child-rearing practices and of school discipline: see, for instance, the case of the West Indies, where longstanding use of corporal punishment in child discipline seems to have its origin in the traumatic history of slavery of the peoples of the Caribbean (Arnold 1982). A recent study on a population in a Mexican state (Corral-Verdugo et al 1995) indicates that the practice of corporal punishment is encouraged by societal beliefs about the benefits of its corrective effects: according to the authors, this practice receives positive sanction from local state law. *It is noteworthy that in cultures in which physical punishment is rare, child abuse is quite unusual* (Belsky 1993).

It is thus not surprising, given widespread cultural approval of the use of physical discipline, that legislation against its use world-wide is more the exception than the rule. Indeed, the case of Sweden remains outstanding; this country not only legislated against corporal punishment in schools but went as far as to preclude parental punishment as well (Ziegert 1983).

The second obstacle may stem from the perpetrators themselves. As noted above, parents often use corporal punishment (90% in the USA, Straus 1991; in Chile, at least 60% of parents/guardians of schoolchildren interviewed in three grammar schools in Santiago admitted they administered corporal punishment, Vargas et al 1993b) making its use the norm, reckoned as needing no modification. To promote such a modification, it is proposed that the following three simultaneous actions should take place: to make it dissonant; to persuade parents that other means of discipline are just as, or more, effective; and to properly equip parents with these tools.

In schools, important changes have taken place to eradicate corporal punishment as a disciplinary measure. In the USA, for example, several states and a number of important cities have abolished corporal punishment in schools, although in many more it is still legally used. All teachers and school authorities have yet to become knowledgeable about the adverse effects of corporal punishment as well as of the existence of alternative means of control. The Office of the General Counsel of the AMA (AMA/OGC 1992) listed available effective means for behavioral control, e.g. praise, role modeling and student involvement in the development of disciplinary codes.

The third obstacle to the introduction of a community program may, paradoxically, stem from the former victims themselves. A study conducted in Barbados on school students' opinion on corporal punishment showed that the majority of boys and girls interviewed stated that the current level of flogging/caning experienced at the hands of the school authority was 'about right' or 'not enough'. Only a relative minority (47% of boys and 29% of girls) viewed it as applied 'too often' (Anderson & Payne 1994). Vargas et al (1994), in a sample of schools in Santiago, Chile, found that 63% of the pupils of a municipal school and 25% of those attending a private school justified the use of physical discipline by parents. A study by Rausch & Kuntson (1991) investigated the extent to which students of a USA university assessed their own and sibling punishment during childhood. The respondents were nearly twice as likely to report having a sibling who had been physically abused as they were to label themselves as physically abused. Although the study may be biased by the fact that a respondent could have selected for contrast the sibling most vulnerable to physical punishment in the family, several subtests in the study tend to show that:

> . . . persons from severely punitive backgrounds are unlikely to classify their [own] experiences as abusive (Rausch & Kuntson 1991).

Other studies agree with such findings (see Berger et al 1988). Weller, Romney & Orr (1987) showed that physically punished adolescents, going through a development stage in which corporal punishment is less frequently used by parents or guardians than with children (Straus 1991), were more likely to recommend it as a method of controling misbehavior than those who did not experience physical punishment. Socolar and Stein (1995), who studied mothers' belief in spanking in two socioeconomically contrasting USA clinics ($n = 204$), found that a history of being spanked as a child was significantly associated ($p < 0.002$) with the mothers' belief. In contrast, Carlson (1986), using a different methodology, found that 9–12 year-olds were able to choose alternative means of discipline when confronted with vignettes depicting different types of child misbehavior. Despite the latter study, the bulk of the evidence indicates that subjects seem to downplay the nature and extent of the discipline to which they themselves may have been subjected. This may impede an insightful view of these experiences and the possibility of modifying their behavior as parents.

The fourth obstacle may arise from the health agents themselves. The pediatrician's roles in violence prevention in schools and other community settings are to be 'initiator, educator, collaborator and advocate' (Wilson-Brewer & Spivak (1994), in addition to the more traditional tasks of a clinical practitioner (see below). Yet studies have found that the primary care doctor, family physician or pediatrician may be reluctant to step into territory for which the training provided was limited or affected by personal experience and values. Wissow & Roter (1994), in a study conducted in a USA inner-city pediatric clinic, found that physicians 'were relatively unaware of parental concern and distress about child behavior'. Only 27% of the 89 mothers who reported to the researchers that physically abusive levels of violence had taken place within the family had been identified by the physicians. Sugg & Inui (1992), using quantitative methods to investigate the attitudes of mostly family practitioners working in a USA health maintenance organization, noted marked reluctance to deal with issues related to domestic violence. The subtitle of their paper—'Opening a Pandora's box'—was the reason most often given by doctors for shying away from this subject. Morris, Johnson & Clasen (1985), in a study conducted in the USA affected to some extent by a high non-compliance rate, found that 90% of the 58 physicians interviewed thought that to 'spank bottom with an open hand, lightly' was not inappropriate discipline; 55% thought that 'to spank bottom with an open hand, leaving red' was not inappropriate, while 28% thought that 'to spank with belt, etc., lightly' was not inappropriate. McCormick (1992) conducted a study in Ohio, USA, on a larger sample of pediatricians and family physicians, with a response rate of 61%. The results showed that 67% of respondents would support corporal punishment, depending on the situation (e.g. child runs into the street without looking). The family physicians in the sample supported it more frequently (70%) than did the pediatricians (59%). Interestingly, younger physicians supported it more often than older practitioners.

Lastly, an organizational obstacle to the successful implementation of a program stems from the system of mental health care in some countries of the Americas. Following a traditional model of care, specialized personnel, psychiatrists, psychologists, etc. operate apart from general health services; thereby making it more difficult to train primary health care workers to identify and manage psychosocial problems in their practice. Conversely, the movement of services into the community, as initiated in this region, facilitates coordination between the specialist in human behavior and the primary health worker (Levav et al 1994).

In sum, a review of the obstacles noted by PAHO/WHO indicates the urgent need to devise appropriate intervention strategies to promote alternative strategies to reduce corporal punishment in children.

A MODEL PROGRAM

Kark (1974) drew the steps of an epidemiologically-orientated community-based program with the intention of providing a scientific basis for developing a model program (see Figure 41.1) that would limit or eradicate corporal punishment.

The development and implementation of this model program is complex and long-range, and requires different steps. It will commence with program trials (Abramson 1979) in one or two countries to develop and test the program methods, including indicators, and will investigate the feasibility, acceptability and efficacy of the interventions. This initial stage will be followed by additional tests in four or five diverse countries until a model program is submitted to the countries of the region for wider implementation after local adaptations are introduced. Agreeing with Fry (1993), initially the model program will include all or most of the components described below, since at this stage we do not possess firm knowledge regarding the relative contribution of each to the effectiveness of the intervention.

FIGURE 41.1   Steps of a community-based program to reduce/eliminate corporal punishment

Components of the Model Program

The modification of cultural beliefs, attitudes and practices that uphold corporal punishment, and their replacement with alternative means of behavioral control, will be the chief target of the model program, which will include the following components: social communication, health education, and the formulation and adoption of public policies and legislation.

In recent years, considerable advances have been made in increasing the effectiveness of health communication, utilizing both the media and interpersonal communication. Recent research findings indicate that theory-driven health communication programs based on well-defined targeting strategies have been effective forces to promote health and well-being (Fly 1987; Rice & Paisley 1990), thus making both social communication and health education suitable measures to promote beliefs and practice modifications. The communication–behavior-change framework provides an appropriate perspective on how individuals and groups acquire new knowledge, attitudes and behaviors. Several workers have contributed to this understanding, among them Cartwright (1949), on the role of interpersonal influence as a needed trigger for action, McGuire (1968) on the processing of information, Fishbein & Ajzen (1975) on the communication–persuasion model, Bandura (1977) on the social learning model, and others.

Health education constitutes a key strategy in providing participative learning opportunities and creating environments conducive to engaging people of all ages in learning processes concerning their health behavior, both individual and collective. In this initiative both social communication and health education strategies will be used in combination, since it is expected that they will complement and potentiate each other.

Collective interventions targeting attitudinal and behavioral changes will be conducted in the community with parents, parents-to-be, grandparents and key community leaders, including the clergy, for the purpose of advocacy, mutual support and assistance in the spread of information regarding alternative measures of discipline. At schools, work with groups, whether homogeneous or mixed, will include teachers, school administrators, parents and students to develop guidelines for disciplining unacceptable behavior. Needless to say, training teachers to manage student discipline is of paramount importance. The school curriculum will emphasize components related to violence, will promote pacific communication and negotiation among students, parents and school personnel so that there is less likelihood of school authorities counteracting misbehavior with violence.

The fact that there are cultures that make no or limited use of corporal punishment (see Belsky 1993; Fry 1993; and others) make these intervention strategies reasonably hopeful.

Regarding legislation, it is worth noting that the introduction of legislation abolishing corporal punishment by parents in Sweden was preceded and accompanied by additional measures since, by itself, legislation was not deemed advisable as the sole response to the problem. Among the strategies implemented concomitantly was wide dissemination of alternative strategies through the media, parent training and community-based activities by child protection organizations (Ziegert 1983). This author quotes the results of a survey by a Swedish opinion research institute which found that in 1961–81 there was a steady decline in the number of parents who believed that children should sometimes be given corporal punishment and, conversely, a steady increase in parents who thought that corporal punishment was not an appropriate way to bring up children (Gelles & Edfeldt 1986).

Legislation to banish corporal punishment in schools is more widespread than the legislation on discipline by parents or guardians. Nevertheless, legislation prohibiting corporal punishment in schools has not yet been fully adopted and/or enforced across all countries of the Americas.

Lastly, the model program will pivot around the primary health care setting. The two strategies to be used in this context are the inclusion of behavior control in children as one of the subjects dealt with by the doctor and/or nurse during the antenatal (Soumenkoff et al 1982) and postnatal (Howard 1991) clinic visits, and home visits by community health workers or trained volunteers.

Wissow & Roter (1994), in addition to appealing to 'clinicians as a group . . . [to] demonstrate a united stand against the use of violence within families', discussed different intervention strategies in the practice setting, all aimed at clarifying for parents the difference between discipline and punishment and ways of enforcing the former and reducing or abolishing the latter. In order to be able to intervene, primary health care workers will need to be sensitized to the problem and trained to focus on both ways to counsel parents and promote informed attitudes concerning non-violent ways to discipline children (Woolf et al 1988). Professionals from the behavioral sciences will be called in to collaborate with the training program.

TABLE 41.1 Matrix of interventions by priority target groups

Aims	Parents	Teachers	Health caregivers
Base line data Identify attitudes, beliefs and practices	Focus groups, surveys	Focus groups, surveys	Interview guide, registration forms
Policy Establish healthy public policies	Adopt legislation to abolish corporal punishment	Adopt school policies to abolish corporal punishment	Introduce guidelines for counseling and criteria for reporting on corporal punishment
Communication Build awareness, influence public agenda and mobilize public opinion	Radio and TV spots; time in regular programs; press releases; audio-visual materials with positive parenting skills	Training materials on positive discipline measures in the classroom and conflict resolution; newsletters and posters; audio-visual materials	Training and reference material; newsletter; pamphlets for clients
Health education Identify positive parenting skills; learn positive communication, discipline techniques, and conflict resolution skills	Community groups; grass-roots education strategy with NGOs; peer support groups	Teaching training; parent–teacher meetings; child-to-child network	Training seminars and workshops

The second measure to be implemented in the primary health care setting is home visits. This type of intervention has proved very effective in reducing violence against children. Olds et al (1986) conducted a randomized trial of home visits by nurses to mothers in high-risk situations, e.g. teenage, unmarried or of low socio-economic status. The results reported were favourable on a number of parameters, such as being seen less often in the emergency room. Of interest to us is that to a statistically significant degree:

> Within the group at highest risk . . . the nurse-visited women were observed in their homes, when their babies were 10 and 22 months of age, to punish and restrict their children less frequently than their counterparts in the comparison group.

In schools, the nurse or the psychologist, if the latter is available, are the health workers best positioned to interact with school personnel to promote newer practices. The guidelines to the pediatrician working in educational settings provided by Poole et al (1991) serve as an additional reinforcement to the activities developed by these former health workers (see Table 41.1).

CONCLUSION

This chapter has reviewed the case for action and sketched the outline of a community-based program to reduce the practice of corporal punishment at home, school and community in selected countries of Latin America and the Caribbean. This regional effort is only now beginning and, admittedly, its goals are almost as distant as the horizon. The authors are fully aware that the initiative is of Quixotic proportions; in the face of the violence crippling our communities, however, we are left with no other options.

REFERENCES

Abramson JH (1979) The four types of evaluation: clinical reviews, clinical trials, program reviews, and program trials. *Publ Health Rep* **94**, 210–15.

AAP/CSH (American Academy of Pediatrics/Committee on School Health) (1990–1991). *Pediatrics* **88**, 173.

AMA/OGC (American Medical Association/Office of the General Counsel) (1992) Corporal punishment in the schools. *J Am Med Assoc* **267**, 3205–8.

Anderson S & Payne MA (1994) Corporal punishment in elementary education: views of Barbadian schoolchildren. *Child Abuse Neglect* **18**, 377–86.

Arnold E (1982) The use of corporal punishment in child rearing in the West Indies. *Child Abuse & Neglect* **6**, 141–5.

Bandura A (1977) *Social Learning Theory*. Englewood Cliffs, NJ: Prentice Hall.

Belsky J (1993) Etiology of child maltreatment: a developmental–ecological analysis. *Psychol Bull* **114**, 413–34.

Berger AM, Knutson JF, Mehm JG & Perkins KA (1988) The self-report of punitive childhood experiences of young adults and adolescents. *Child Abuse Neglect* **12**, 251–62.

Buntain-Ricklefs JJ, Kemper KJ, Bell M & Babonis T (1994) Punishments: what predicts adult approval. *Child Abuse Neglect* **18**, 945–55.

Carlson BE (1986) Children's belief about punishment. *Am J Orthopsychiat* **56**, 308–12.

Cartwright D (1949) Some principles of mass persuasion: selected findings from research on the sale of United States war bonds. *Human Relations* **2**, 53–69.

Cruz Neto O & Minayo MC (1994) Violence and banalization of life. *Caderno de Saude Publica* **10**(suppl 1) (in Portuguese).

Corral-Verdugo V, Frias-Armenta M, Romero M & Munoz A (1995) Validity of a scale measuring beliefs regarding the 'positive' effects of punishing children: a study of Mexican mothers. *Child Abuse Neglect* **19**, 669–79.

Fishbein M & Ajzen I (1975) *Belief, Attitude, Intention and Behavior*. Reading, MA: Addison-Wesley.

Fly B (1987) Mass media and smoking cessation: a critical review. *Am J Publ Health* **77**, 153–60.

Fry DP (1993) The intergenerational transmission of disciplinary practices and approach to conflict. *Human Organization* **52** 176–85.

Gelles RJ & Edfeldt AW (1986) Violence towards children in the United States and Sweden. *Child Abuse Neglect* **10**, 501–10.

Hemenway D, Solnick S & Carter C (1994) Child-rearing violence. *Child Abuse Neglect* **18**, 1011–20.

Hoekelman RA (1992) Doom and gloom again—what we can do about it? *Pediat Ann* **21**, 471–2.

Hoffman ML & Saltzstein HD (1967) Parent discipline and the child's moral development. *J Pers Soc Psychol* **5**, 45–57.

Holmes SJ & Robins LN (1988) The role of parental disciplinary practices in the development of depression and alcoholism. *Psychiatry* **51**, 24–36.

Howard BJ (1991) Discipline in early childhood. *Pediat Clin N Am* **38**, 1351–69.

Kark SL (1974) *Epidemiology and Community Medicine*. New York: Appleton-Century Crofts.

Kaufman J & Ziegler E (1987) Do abused children become abusive parents? *Am J Orthopsychiat* **57**, 186–92.

Kempe Ch, Silverman F, Steele B, Droegemueller W & Silver H (1962) The battered child syndrome. *J Am Med Assoc* **181**, 17–24.

Krugman S, Mata L & Krugman R (1992) Sexual abuse and corporal punishment during childhood: a pilot retrospective survey of university students in Costa Rica. *Pediatrics* **90**, 157–61.

Lepen Cherian V (1994) Self-reports of corporal punishment by Xhosa children from broken and intact families and their academic achievement. *Psychol Rep* **74**, 867–74.

Levav I, Restrepo H & Guerra de Macedo C (1994) The restructuring of psychiatric care in Latin America. A new policy for mental health services. *J Publ Health Pol* **15**, 71–83.

McCormick KF (1992) Attitudes of primary care physicians toward corporal punishment. *J Am Med Assoc* **267**, 3161–5.

McGuire WJ (1968) Personality and attitude change: an information processing theory. In AG Greenwalt, TC Brock & TM Ostrom (eds) *Psychological Foundations of Attitudes*. Orlando, FL: Academic Press.

Monyooe LA (1993) Perspective reports of corporal punishment by pupils in Lesotho schools. *Psychol Rep* **73**, 515–18.

Morris JL, Johnson Ch F & Clasen M (1985) To report or not to report. Physicians' attitudes toward discipline and child abuse. *Am J Dis Child* **139**, 194–7.

Oates RK, Forrest D & Peacock A (1985) Self-esteem of abused children. *Child Abuse Neglect* **9**, 159–63.

Olds DL, Henderson CR, Chamberlin R & Tatelbaum R (1986) Preventing child abuse and neglect: a randomized trial of nurse home visitation. *Pediatrics* **78**, 65–78.

PAHO/WHO (Pan American Health Organization/World Health Organization) (1994) *Health and Violence—Regional Plan of Action*. Washington, DC: WHO.

Poole SV, Ushkow MC, Nader PR, Bradford BJ, Ashbury JR, Worthington DC, Sanabria KE & Carruth T (1991) The role of the pediatrician in abolishing corporal punishment in schools. *Pediatrics* **88**, 162–7.

Rausch K & Kuntson JF (1991) The self-report of personal punitive childhood experiences and those of siblings. *Child Abuse Neglect* **15**, 29–36.

Reiss AJ & Roth JA (eds) (1993) *Understanding and Preventing Violence*. Washington, DC: National Academy Press.

Rice RE & Paisley WJ (1990) *Public Communications Campaigns*. Beverly Hills, CA: Sage.

Socolar RRS & Stein REK (1995) Spanking infants and toddlers: maternal belief and practice. *Pediatrics* **95**, 105–11.

Soumenkoff G, Marneffe C, Gerard M, Limet R, Beeckmans M & Hubinont PO (1982) A coordinated attempt for prevention of child abuse at the antenatal care level. *Child Abuse Neglect* **6**, 87–94.

Straus MA (1991) Discipline and deviance: physical punishment of children and violence and other crime in adulthood. *Soc Probl* **38**, 133–53.

Straus MA & Kaufman Kantor G (1994) Corporal punishment of adolescents by parents: a risk factor in the epidemiology of depression, suicide, alcohol abuse, child abuse, and wife beating. *Adolescence* **29**, 543–61.

Sugg NK & Inui T (1992) Primary care physicians' response to domestic violence. Opening a Pandora's box. *J Am Med Assoc* **267**, 3157–60.

Tonella A & Zuppinger K (1994) L'enfant maltraite et negligée en Suisse. Schweiz Med Wochensch **124**, 2331–40.

Vargas CNA, Lopez SD, Perez RP, Toro VG, Zuniga CP & Ciocca BP (1993a) El castigo fisico a los niños: opinion y conducta de los adultos. *Rev Med Chile* **121**, 567–73.

Vargas CNA, Lopez SD, Perez RP, Toro VG, Zuniga CP & Ciocca BP (1993b) Caracteristicas del castigo fisico infantil administrado por padres de tres colegios de Santiago. *Rev Chile Pediat* **64**, 333–6.

Vargas CNA, Lopez SD, Ciocca BP & Lopez GC (1994) Castigo fisico infantil: opiniones de los niños de dos colegios. *Rev Med Chile* **122**, 958–63.

Weiss B & Dodge KA (1992) Some consequences of early harsh discipline: child aggression and a maladaptive social information processing style. *Child Dev* **63**, 1321–35.

Weller SC, Romney AK & Orr DP (1987) The myth of a sub-culture of corporal punishment. *Hum Organiz* **46**, 39–47.

Widom CS (1989) The cycle of violence. *Science* **244**, 160–66.

Wilson-Brewer R & Spivak H (1994) Violence prevention in schools and other community settings: the pediatrician as initiator, educator, collaborator, and advocate. *Pediatrics* **94**, 623–30 (suppl).

Wissow LS & Roter D (1994) Toward effective discussion of discipline and corporal punishment during primary care visits: findings from studies of doctor–patient interaction. *Pediatrics* **94**, 587–93.

Woolf A, Taylor L, Melnicoe L, Andolsek K, Dubowitz H, De Vos E & Newberger E (1988) What residents know about child abuse. Implications of a survey of knowledge and attitudes. *Am J Dis Child* **142**, 668–72.

Ziegert KA (1983) The Swedish prohibition of corporal punishment: a preliminary report. *J Marriage Family* **45**, 917–26.

Domestic Violence—An Issue for Primary Health Care Professionals

Michelle K Gomel

World Health Organization, Geneva, Switzerland

For years domestic violence was considered to be a private matter within the family. However, health professionals have recently reframed this issue as a public health problem. This follows extensive documentation of its prevalence within the community as well as the physical and mental health consequences for victims and any children.

This chapter addresses domestic violence as a major psychosocial issue which leads to people presenting to primary health care settings because of its effect on their mental and physical well-being. To a large degree increased physician awareness of domestic violence has centred around the physical health consequences, such as injury and the risk of mortality. However, the predominant focus on physical health has overshadowed the serious mental health sequelae of domestic violence. Where mental health problems are dealt with by physicians they are often regarded as primary and the underlying causes are not addressed.

WHAT IS DOMESTIC VIOLENCE

The meaning of the term 'domestic violence' has varied considerably in the literature. This is evident in the breadth of issues it attempts to cover, for example, the gender and age of those involved and the purported function of the violence. The types of violence experienced include physical, psychological and sexual; however, domestic violence has been associated predominantly with the physical aggression occurring within an intimate relationship. Physical aggression is an important aspect of domestic violence, and also has the most visible effect, but to focus on it exclusively may obscure: (a) the importance of the other forms of violence; and (b) the mental health effects on the person who is being victimized.

Throughout this chapter I will be limiting the discussion of domestic violence to the abuse occurring between two adults in a current or previously intimate

Preventing Mental Illness: Mental Health Promotion in Primary Care. Edited by R. Jenkins and T.B. Üstün.
Published 1998 John Wiley & Sons Ltd.

relationship and I will refer to this as spouse or partner abuse. However, the focus will be on the abuse perpetrated by men against their female partners. Because men are generally larger and stronger, women are much more likely to be physically injured and to experience fear (Margolin & Burman 1993).

The Extent of the Problem

Spouse abuse can be lethal. Statistics from a number of countries indicate that female homicide is most frequently perpetrated by family members, with spouses representing the largest percentage of offenders (Kruttschnitt 1993). In 1984, almost 25% of all homicide victims in the USA were related to their assailants. Of homicides occurring within the family, 48% involved spouses. Approximately two-thirds comprised wives who were killed by their husbands; and the remaining one-third were husbands killed by their wives. A large proportion of wives who killed their partners were 'battered women' and did so in response to frequent and severe abuse (Browne 1988).

Cases of spouse abuse leading to homicide represent only a small proportion of females who are abused by their partners. The majority experience a range of physical injuries and mental health problems which are not thoroughly documented.

Population Surveys

Our knowledge of the extent of spouse abuse is derived largely from surveys conducted in North America. Because physical abuse is more easily defined than the other forms of abuse, the majority of surveys have reported rates for physical abuse. In the Second National Family Violence Survey conducted in the USA in 1985, 16% of married couples reported at least one violent act against their partners in the 12-month period prior to the survey. One-third of these couples reported the use of severe violence such as kicking, biting, hitting with a fist, using a knife or firing a gun (Straus & Gelles 1986). Canadian rates using the same criteria for severe and all levels of violence over a 12-month period were similar (Kennedy & Dutton 1989).

Heise, Pitanguy & Germain (1994) reviewed the data from 34 studies in several countries and found that from one-quarter to more than half of women reported being physically abused by a present or previous partner. Variation in prevalence rates across countries was evident. For example, in North Korea prevalence rates for the use of severe and all levels of violence against women were more than three times higher than those reported in North America.

UTILIZATION OF PRIMARY HEALTH CARE SERVICES

The physical and mental health problems related to spouse abuse place a heavy burden on health care resources. Using data from the National Crime Survey (NCS) in 1980, it has been estimated that the annual medical care costs directly attributable to domestic violence are approximately $US44 million a year. However, because the NCS data are likely to underestimate prevalence and morbidity associated with domestic violence, it has been argued that the estimates should be multiplied by a factor ranging from 10 to 40 (McLeer & Anwar 1987).

Women who have been abused use a disproportionate share of health services (Jones 1993). The most frequently used services are in primary health care settings, in particular emergency departments and general practice. Roberts et al (1993) found that 78% of victims attending an emergency department reported treatment for injuries or health problems related to the abuse during the previous year. Approximately 51% had attended a general practitioner, 40.4% had attended a large urban hospital emergency department, 10.6% had attended other hospitals. This contrasts with the lower rates of women using specialist mental health services. The percentage of abused women who had consulted a psychiatrist or counsellor was only 6.3% and 2.1% respectively. The reluctance to seek assistance from mental health professionals has been documented by others (Rounsaville & Weissman 1978; Koss 1993; Hansen et al 1987). For example, Rounsaville & Weissman (1978) found that, of women presenting with injuries in an emergency department, only 35% attended a follow-up session with a psychiatrist, despite there being no monetary charge.

Emergency Departments

Two major findings have been generated by research in emergency departments. These relate to the high prevalence of people who have ever been abused and the finding that abused women are more likely to present for trauma-related injuries than women who are not abused.

In one emergency department study, 14% of persons presenting disclosed a history of domestic violence (Roberts et al 1993). Higher rates of 22% were found by Goldberg & Tomlanovich (1984). Appleton (1980) reported that 35% of women presenting to an emergency department reported being physically abused by their partners at some point in their relationships. It is difficult to ascertain how representative these studies are and extrapolating the higher rates to the population would probably be unwise. Nevertheless, these studies suggest that at least one-tenth, and perhaps up to one-quarter, of people attending emergency departments have been abused at some stage during an intimate relationship.

The increased risk of trauma-related injuries for women who are being abused has been documented in many studies of emergency departments. McLeer et al

(1989), in a survey of female patients, found that 30% of women with trauma-related injuries (excluding natural disasters and motor vehicle accidents) had injuries or symptoms related to physical abuse by a current or previous intimate partner. Goldberg & Tomlanovich (1984) reported that the domestic violence group had trauma-related complaints significantly more often than the domestic violence-free group.

Women who present with physical injuries at the emergency department represent only a small proportion of women who are currently experiencing domestic violence. Many others are not injured severely enough to require emergency treatment but nevertheless experience physical injuries and mental health problems from the abuse. Frequently, victims' first point of contact with the health system is through the general practitioner, either for routine health care, or more directly for the treatment of the physical and mental health effects of the abuse (Hamberger, Saunders & Hovey 1992).

General Practice

Two studies examining the prevalence of spouse abuse amongst general practice patients have been identified. Twenty-eight percent (Gin et al 1991) and 40% (Hamberger, Saunders & Hovey 1992) of persons presenting for primary health care disclosed a history of physical abuse during their lifetime. Of these, 14% (Gin et al 1991) and 23% (Hamberger, Saunders and Hovey 1992) were currently experiencing spouse abuse. As in emergency department research, variation in violence rates across studies most likely reflects differences between the clinics sampled and their patients, and the higher rates reported need to be interpreted with caution. Nevertheless, even the more conservative estimate of 14% highlights the need for physicians to be aware that a large number of their patients may be victims of spouse abuse.

Studies of the effects of criminal victimization demonstrate substantial increases in the amount of primary medical care required by abused women. Koss and her colleagues examined the effects of criminal victimization on the use of medical services amongst women enrolled in a worksite health maintenance service. In their sample, 29% of assaults and 39% of rapes were perpetrated by partners/husbands or other family members (Koss, Koss & Woodruff 1991). Medical records indicated that 93% of all crime victims visited their physician during the year following the crime and all had visited during the second year (Koss, Woodroff & Koss 1991). Severely victimized women, compared with non-victims, made visits to physicians twice as frequently in the index year and had outpatient medical expenses 2.5 times higher. During the year of the crime, visits to physicians increased by 15% and 18% from pre-crime levels for assault and rape victims, compared with less than 2% for non-victims (Koss 1993).

MENTAL HEALTH EFFECTS OF SPOUSE ABUSE

There have not been any studies in primary health care settings that examine the types and prevalence of mental health disorders experienced by spouse abuse victims. Rather, our knowledge of the effects of spouse abuse on mental health comes primarily from two areas of research; population surveys and studies of battered women. These studies, which are discussed below, have demonstrated that the mental health effects are severe and result in a number of clearly identified conditions such as depression, anxiety, post-traumatic stress disorder (PTSD), drug and alcohol abuse and a variety of vague psychological and somatic complaints.

Population Studies

Gelles & Harrop (1989), as part of the Second National Family Violence Survey, examined the relationship between spouse abuse and psychological distress (stress, depression and somatic symptoms) in a sample of 3000 female respondents. They found that the severity of abuse was positively associated with the experience of both 'moderate' and 'severe' psychological distress, and was independent of marital distress and demographic variables such as age, sex and education.

Psychiatric symptomatology using the General Health Questionnaire (GHQ) was assessed in a representative sample of 1516 women in New Zealand. An additional randomly selected sub-sample was assessed using the short-form Present State Examination (PSE). Of the sub-sample, 16% had been hit and physically abused as an adult but only 3% reported being current victims of domestic violence. Women who reported a history of abuse had significantly higher GHQ and PSE scores, and were more likely to be identified as a psychiatric case by these measures. Women who had been hit on three or more occasions had significantly higher scores on the PSE than women who had been hit on one or two occasions; suggesting a positive association between the frequency of abuse and mental health problems. Given that only a small proportion of women were currently experiencing abuse, these results point to lasting mental health problems despite cessation of the abuse (Mullen et al 1988).

Ratner (1993) examined the impact of spouse abuse on the mental health status of women in a representative community sample. Three groups of women were compared: those who were physically abused; those who were psychologically but not physically abused; and those who were not abused within the previous year. Physically abused women, most of whom were also abused psychologically, reported more somatic complaints and had higher levels of anxiety and insomnia and more symptoms of depression than the non-abused and psychologically abused group. However, the significant effect of psychological abuse on mental health was also apparent. When compared to women who were not abused, women who were abused psychologically but not physically demonstrated significantly higher scores on the somatic complaints and the anxiety and insomnia subscales of the GHQ.

Alcohol abuse, as assessed by the CAGE questionnaire, differed significantly between the three groups of wives. While only 2.4% of the non-abused wives were found to abuse alcohol, the percentages of physically and psychologically abused wives who did so were 16% and 11% respectively.

While population studies have established that female victims of spouse abuse experience mental health problems significantly more often than women who are not abused, these studies have used global measures of psychopathology and do not provide diagnoses. The next section will review studies of battered women. Although less representative of the population of abused women, they provide us with a better understanding of the types of mental health problems experienced.

Studies of Battered Women

Victims of spouse abuse are at significant risk of developing a lifetime mental disorder (Koss 1990; Gleason 1993; Mullen et al 1988). A recent study reported that 73% of women seeking assistance for battering were suffering from major depression; this compared with community norms of 7% (Gleason 1993). Other psychological disorders reported included PTSD (36% vs. 1%), generalized anxiety disorder (45% vs. 3%), various phobias (19–73% vs. 8–15%), obsessive–compulsive disorder (40% vs. 3%), alcohol abuse (34% vs. 4%) and drug abuse (34% vs. 4%) (Gleason 1993).

PTSD, which is characterized by fear/avoidance, affective constriction, disturbances of self-concept/self-efficacy and sexual dysfunction, has been identified as a key mental health problem affecting women who have been abused by their partners and also women who have been victims of other violence crimes by strangers (Koss 1990). The effects of the trauma upon spouse abuse victims may be even worse than those experienced by the victims of crime by strangers. First, they may be exacerbated by the occurrence of ongoing abuse. Second, the perpetrator is someone whom they may trust, love or depend on (American Medical Association 1992a).

Suicidal behaviour is more prevalent amongst battered women than non-battered women and appears to be a direct consequence of the abuse. In fact, Stark & Flitcraft (1988) identify battering as the single most important factor leading to suicide attempts by females. They report that battered women are 4.8 times more likely than non-battered women to attempt suicide and that the difference in relative risk emerges after the first reported episode of abuse.

Many studies report on the increased likelihood of mental health problems such as depression and PTSD as the severity of physical abuse increases (Astin, Lawrence & Foy 1993; Follingstad, Neckerman & Vormbrock 1988). Although the effects on victims' mental health are long-lasting, studies have shown that, for some women, symptoms of depression and PTSD may decrease in severity with the passage of time since the last episode of abuse (Walker 1983; Astin, Lawrence & Foy 1993).

Other factors related to the emergence and severity of mental health problems include developmental history, life events and the availability of a social support structure. The presence of social supports and the experience of positive life events are associated with lower levels of PTSD, while stressors during childhood and negative life events are associated with higher levels of PTSD (Astin, Lawrence & Foy 1993). Jaffe et al (1986) reported that somatic complaints and levels of depression and anxiety were higher in battered women who had experienced negative life events in the last 12 months. Mitchell & Hodson (1983) reported that women who were better educated, employed and had social supports were not as adversely affected by the abuse as women who lacked these resources.

The battered women described in these studies had all sought assistance for the abuse and consequently may represent the more severely affected. Not all abused women can be considered to be battered and not all women who are battered have a well-defined mental disorder. Often victims of spouse abuse present to their doctors with vague health complaints long before they acknowledge the presence of violence or otherwise seek help (Knowlden & Frith 1993). They may present with a variety of psychological and somatic symptoms that are difficult to diagnose. However, these are of sufficient severity to affect their quality of life and hence warrant intervention. Examples include the milder forms of anxiety and depression, problems with low self-esteem and complaints of headache, abdominal discomfort, palpitations, diarrhoea, insomnia and chronic pain states (Mitchell & Hodson 1983; Knowlden & Frith 1993). Recognition of these symptoms can assist the early identification and treatment of spouse abuse victims and may also prevent the development of more serious mental health problems.

PRIMARY HEALTH CARE AND THE PREVENTION OF DOMESTIC VIOLENCE

From a public health perspective, Flitcraft et al (1992, p 8) argue that:

> Domestic violence and its medical and psychiatric sequelae are sufficiently prevalent to justify 'routine screening' of all women patients in emergency, surgical, primary care, paediatric, prenatal and mental health settings.

Recently, the American Medical Association Council on Ethical and Judicial Affairs (1992b) has presented a set of ethical considerations for the recognition of, and response to, domestic violence by physicians. Two central concepts in this paper are the classic principles of beneficence and non-maleficence. The principle of beneficence is interpreted as requiring physicians to address the 'psychological, social, even spiritual dimensions' (p 3190) of abuse as well as the physical effects. The principle of non-maleficence is also brought to bear, directing physicians to identify domestic violence in order to avoid offering harmful or inappropriate treatment, such as unnecessary medication (American Medical Association 1992b).

Medical Practitioners' Response to Domestic Violence

Despite the high prevalence of victims of spouse abuse presenting to primary health care services, physicians have been slow to recognize and respond to the problem (Kurz 1987; Stark, Flitcraft & Frazier 1979; Burris & Jaffe 1984). They often fail to inquire about spouse abuse or adequately document information pertaining to the violence, even when it is evident.

Few abused women attending emergency departments in the USA may be 'recognized' as such by health care workers and offered appropriate treatment. A study by Rounsaville & Weissman (1978) in an emergency department revealed that although over half of the women had presented to the same department previously, documentation of the abuse was made in only three cases (15%). Kurz (1987) found that in 40% of cases where physicians interacted with battered women in an emergency department setting, physicians made no response to the abuse.

McLeer et al (1989) reported that the use of a spouse abuse protocol in an emergency department increased detection rates from 6% to 30%. However, these rates were not maintained at an 8-year follow-up; only 8% of victims were identified. The authors argue that it is necessary to institutionalize systems for identifying and treating battered women. It seems that adequate treatment is not ensured even when a protocol for identifying and treating victims is being used. Warshaw (1989) found that in 92% of cases the discharge diagnosis did not reflect the presenting problem of spouse abuse, despite documentation or strong indicators for abuse on the woman's chart. Also, in the majority of cases staff did not refer women for consultation to a psychiatrist or social worker or provide a list of resources and referrals, despite these being clearly specified in the protocol.

Similarly, in general practice the rate of identification and appropriate response to spouse abuse is poor. In one study (Hamberger, Saunders & Hovey 1992), physicians in a community-based practice inquired about abuse in only 4% of patients. Although 14% of patients in three community practices reported being currently abused and having seen a physician in the last year, less than 30% of these patients had discussed the abuse with that physician (Gin et al 1991).

These studies make it clear that physicians and other health care professionals do not recognize or respond to the fact that the issue underlying injuries and mental health problems of some women in primary health care is spouse abuse. The failure to acknowledge the experience of their abused patients can by itself cause psychological damage by contributing to the victims' sense of isolation and helplessness (Warshaw 1989; American Medical Association 1992b; Jones 1993).

Numerous factors have been identified as barriers to the adoption of a more proactive role by physicians in identifying and intervening with patients experiencing spouse abuse. Sugg & Inui (1992) interviewed 38 primary care physicians and asked them to describe spouse abuse cases they had managed, and their perceptions of their role in identifying and intervening in spouse abuse cases. Their main finding was that exploring domestic violence in a clinical setting was analogous to 'opening Pandora's box'. Physicians were reluctant to deal with the 'unleashing' of many issues that routine enquiry would elicit. Physicians reported feelings of powerlessness, a fear of offending patients and a concern about time constraints. They also expressed a concern about having a 'too close for comfort' relationship with the patient and were less likely to suspect abuse in those patients who came from similar backgrounds to themselves.

Additionally, there is a reluctance to interfere with family issues, which are culturally defined to be private, sacred and hidden from public view (Warshaw 1989; Jecker 1993; Kurz 1987). Training in the medical model of disease may interfere with the readiness of physicians to explore the cultural and social contexts in which health problems arise (Jecker 1993; Warshaw 1989).

Screening and Intervention for Spouse Abuse: Recommendations for Practice

The patient–doctor encounter forms a key element of a secondary approach to the prevention of spouse abuse. Ideally, all patients should be routinely screened for domestic violence to enable the identification and appropriate intervention and/or referral of victims of abuse. Such a screening program would also serve to heighten awareness in those patients who are not in a violent relationship. At a community level, it would raise the profile of domestic violence as being a serious health problem (American Medical Association 1992a; Flitcraft 1993).

The American Medical Association (1992a) has reviewed four important areas in which medical practitioners could assist women who have been abused. They propose routine screening, validation of the experience, careful record-keeping and referral. Although not specifically mentioned in the guidelines, where possible the medical practitioner should provide ongoing support and follow-up, even when referral is made to other services.

Routine Screening

The identification of victims of spouse abuse is often difficult because of the reluctance of many abused women to volunteer information about the abuse. However, a number of signs may raise the physician's index of suspicion. These include physical injury, psychological and somatic complaints.

Abused women are more likely than accident victims to have contusions or minor lacerations to the face, head, breast, chest or abdomen and they are much more likely to have multiple injuries than accident victims. Evidence of old injuries may also be present (Morrison 1988; Randall 1990; American Medical Association 1992a). However, more frequently women will present with signs of psychological distress such as depression, anxiety and sleep problems and a range of somatic complaints including headaches, muscle aches or abdominal pains; there may be no obvious physical injury (Mitchell & Hodson 1983; Knowlden & Frith 1993; Randall 1990). Because psychological and somatic complaints commonly occur with other life stressors the recognition of a woman who is in an abusive relationship is difficult without direct and empathic questioning about her relationship with her partner. The failure to identify abuse as a cause of mental health problems often leads to women being misdiagnosed as having a primary anxiety or depression disorder or being labelled as 'neurotic', 'hysterical', 'hypochondriac', 'chronic somatizer' or 'problem patient' (American Medical Association 1992b; Stark, Flitcraft & Frazier 1979). These labels impede effective diagnosis and intervention and imply that time spent with the person is not worthwhile (Fullin, Cosgrove & Kenosha 1992).

If abuse is established it is essential to obtain a detailed history of the abusive relationship and its physical and mental health impact. Of particular importance is an assessment for depression, anxiety, PTSD, drug and alcohol dependence and suicidal behaviour. Additionally, coping mechanisms and available supports need to be assessed, together with safety issues for the woman and any children (McLeer & Anwar 1987).

Intervention

A powerful intervention in its own right is the validation of the woman's experience. It is important to demonstrate an understanding of the seriousness and effects of the violence, and the difficulties and fears about disclosing abuse (American Medical Association 1992a). Acknowledging that spouse abuse is common and that the woman's emotional and behavioural responses are 'normal reactions' to a distressing and fear-provoking situation is essential to challenge her own beliefs that she is 'going mad' or that she is the cause of the problem.

Intervention should include the formulation of a safety plan, particularly for women who are currently living in an abusive situation. Having a bag packed with essential items such as important documents, money, extra set of car keys and clothes for emergencies (Holtz & Furniss 1993) and developing a signal system with children or neighbours that indicates the need to call the police (Hodges 1993) are some recommended strategies. Additionally, knowledge of the whereabouts of safe places such as the emergency room, local shelter, a trusted friend's home and police station can help protect the woman and her children from harm (Hodges 1993).

In treating mental health problems such as anxiety and depression, physicians need to be cautious about prescribing medication. Although sometimes there is a need for the short-term use of psychotropic medications in conjunction with other interventions (Rounsaville & Weissman 1978), their use has to be carefully monitored given the potential for misuse and the increased risk of drug dependency (American Medical Association 1992b). Long-term drug treatment is contraindicated and should not be substituted for other forms of intervention (Jecker 1993; American Medical Association 1992b).

It is important that a range of legal, housing and other service options be presented clearly to the woman; however, it is not advisable to force the woman into an option which she is not willing or ready to accept. The woman's decision should be supported even if the physician does not agree with it (Fullin, Cosgrove & Kenosha 1992; American Medical Association 1992b). Physicians need to be aware of the woman's low self-esteem and should challenge beliefs about self-blame and responsibility for the violence. Encouraging the women to build up social supports is also critical.

Referrals can be made to a variety of community-based programs designed to assist and support abused women. These include legal services, shelters, support groups and also individual counsellors experienced in the area of domestic violence. Referral to couples counselling is contraindicated because the woman is less able to speak freely and without intimidation (Fullin, Cosgrove & Kenosha 1992; American Medical Association 1992a). If referrals are made it is important to provide the opportunity for ongoing monitoring and support, even if the situation has improved temporarily. This provides a secure base for the woman and informs her that the problem is being taken seriously and that there is a willingness to provide long-term assistance.

Documentation of the abuse can be powerful evidence for the woman in legal proceedings. It should cover the current trauma, including photographs of injuries (where consent has been obtained), a history of the trauma, mental health sequelae linked to the victimization, and any referrals made (Holtz & Furniss 1993; McLeer & Anwar 1987). Detailed records also provide a basis for reviewing progress and monitoring treatment (American Medical Association 1992a).

ACKNOWLEDGEMENTS

I would like to thank Dr Robert Gertler and Dr James Lemon for their valuable comments in the preparation of this chapter; and Ms Christy Chan for collecting and organizing reference material.

REFERENCES

American Medical Association (Council on Scientific Affairs) (1992a) Violence against women: relevance for medical practitioners. *J Am Med Assoc* **267**(23), 3184–9.

American Medical Association (Council on Ethical and Judicial Affairs) (1992b) Physicians and domestic violence: ethical considerations. *J Am Med Assoc* **267**, 3190–93.

Appleton W (1980) The battered woman syndrome. *Ann Emerg Med* **9**, 84–91.

Astin MC, Lawrence KJ & Foy DW (1993) Post-traumatic stress disorder among battered women: risk and resiliency factors. *Violence Victims* **8**, 17–28.

Browne A (1988) Family homicide: when victimized women kill. In VB Van Hasselt, RL Morrison, AS Bellack, M Hersen (eds) *Handbook of Family Violence*, pp 271–92. New York: Plenum.

Burns CA & Jaffe P (1984) Wife battering: a well-kept secret. *Can J Criminol* **26**, 171–7.

Kennedy LW & Dutton DG (1989) The incidence of wife assault in Alberta. *Can J Behav Sci* **21**, 40–54.

Flitcraft AH et al (1992) *Diagnostic and Treatment Guidelines on Domestic Violence*, p 8. Chicago, IL: American Medical Association.

Flitcraft A (1993) Physicians and domestic violence: challenges for prevention. *Health Affairs* **12**, 154–61.

Follingstad DR, Necherman AP & Vormbrock J (1988) Reactions to victimization and coping strategies of battered women: the ties that bind. *Clin Psychol Rev* **8**, 373–90.

Fullin KJ & Cosgrove A (1992) Empowering physicians to respond to domestic violence. *Wisconsin Med J* **91**, 280–83.

Gelles RJ & Harrop JW (1989) Violence, battering, and psychological distress among women. *J Interpers Violence* **4**, 400–420.

Gin NE, Rucker L, Frayne S, Cygan R & Hubbell FA (1991) Prevalence of domestic violence among patients in three ambulatory care internal medicine clinics. *J Gen Int Med* **6**, 317–22.

Gleason WJ (1993) Mental disorders in battered women: an empirical study. *Violence Victims* **8**, 53–68.

Goldberg WG & Tomlanovich MC (1984) Domestic violence victims in the emergency department: new findings. *J Am Med Assoc* **251**, 3259–64.

Hamberger LK, Saunders DG & Hovey M (1992) Prevalence of domestic violence in community practice and rate of physician inquiry. *Family Med* **24**, 283–7.

Hansen JP, Bobula J, Meyer D, Kushner K & Pridham K (1987) Treat or refer: patients' interest in family physician involvement in their psychosocial problems. *J Family Pract* **24**, 499–503.

Heise LL, Pitanguy J & Germain A (1994) *Violence Against Women. The Hidden Health Burden.* World Bank Discussion Papers. Washington, DC: World Bank.

Hodges K (1993) Domestic violence: a health crisis. *North Carolina Med J* **54**, 213–6.

Holtz H & Furniss KK (1993) The health care provider's role in domestic violence. *Law Ethics* **8**, 47–53.

Jaffe P, Wolfe DA, Wilson S & Zak L (1986) Emotional and physical health problems of battered women. *Can J Psychiat* **31**, 625–9.

Jecker NS (1993) Privacy beliefs and the violent family. *J Am Med Assoc* **269**, 776–80.

Jones RF (1993) Domestic violence: an epidemic. *Int J Gynaecol Obstet* **41**, 131–3.

Kennedy LW & Dutton DG (1989) The incidence of wife assault in Alberta. *Can J Behav Sci* **21**, 40–54.

Knowlden SM & Frith JF (1993) Domestic violence and the general practitioner. *Med J Austral* **158**, 402–6.

Koss MP (1993) The impact of crime victimization on women's medical use. *J Women's Health* **2**, 67–72.

Koss MP, Koss PG & Woodruff WJ (1991) Deleterious effects of criminal victimization on women's health and medical utilization. *Arch Int Med* **151**, 342–7.

Koss MP, Woodruff WJ & Koss PG (1991) Criminal victimization among primary care medical patients: prevalence, incidence, and physician usage. *Behav Sci Law* **9**, 85–96.

Koss MP (1990) Violence against women. *Am Psychol* **45**, 374–80.

Kruttschnitt C (1993) Violence by and against women: a comparative and cross-national analysis. *Violence Victims* **8**, 253–70.

Kurz D (1987) Emergency department responses to battered women: resistance to medicalization. *Social Problems* **34**, 69–81.

Margolin G & Burman B (1993) Wife abuse versus marital violence: different terminologies, explanations, and solutions. *Clin Psychol Rev* **13**, 59–73.

McLeer SV & Anwar RA (1987) The role of the emergency physician in the prevention of domestic violence. *Ann Emerg Med* **16**, 1155–61.

McLeer SV, Anwar RA, Herman S & Maquiling K (1989) Education is not enough: a systems failure in protecting battered women. *Ann Emerg Med* **18**, 651–3.

Mitchell RE & Hodson CA (1983) Coping with domestic violence: social support and psychological health among battered women. *Am J Comm Psychol* **11**, 629–54.

Morrison LJ (1988) The battering syndrome: a poor record of detection in the emergency department (review). *J Emerg Med* **6**, 521–6.

Mullen PE, Roman-Clarkson SE, Walton VA & Herbison PE (1988) Impact of sexual and physical abuse on women's mental health. *Lancet* **1**, 841–5.

Randall T (1990) Domestic violence begets other problems of which physicians must be aware to be effective. *J Am Med Assoc* **264**, 940–44.

Ratner PA (1993) The incidence of wife abuse and mental health status in abused wives in Edmonton, Alberta. *Can J Publ Health* **84**, 246–9.

Roberts GL, O'Toole BI, Lawrence JM & Raphael B (1993) Domestic violence victims in a hospital emergency department. *Med J Austral* **159**, 307–10.

Rounsaville BJ & Weissman MM (1978) Battered women: a medical problem requiring detection. *Int J Psychiat Med* **8**, 1977–8.

Stark E & Flitcraft A (1988) Violence among intimates: an epidemiological review. In VB Van Hasselt, RL Morrison, AS Bellack & M Hersen (eds) *Handbook of Family Violence*, pp 293–318. New York: Plenum.

Stark E, Flitcraft A & Frazier W (1979) Medicine and patriarchal violence: the social construction of a 'private' event. *Int J Health Serv* **9**, 461–93.

Straus MA & Gelles RJ (1986) Societal change and change in family violence from 1975 to 1985 as revealed by two national surveys. *J Marriage Family* **48**, 465–79.

Sugg NK & Inui T (1992) Primary care physicians' response to domestic violence. *J Am Med Assoc* **267**, 3157–60.

Walker L (1983) Victimology and the psychological perspectives of battered women. *Victimology* **8**, 82–104.

Warshaw C (1989) Limitations of the medical model in the care of battered women. *Gender Society* **3**, 506–17.

General Practitioner Perspective

Denis Pereira Gray OBE

Postgraduate Medical School, University of Exeter, UK

THE IMPORTANCE OF MENTAL ILLNESS TO GENERAL PRACTICE

The importance of mental illness can be summarized very simply: quantity, quality, and the opportunity for effective intervention.

Quantity

Figures on the quantity of mental illness have been known for some time. Historically the first report was in a little known book by two British general practitioners, Arthur and Beatrice Watts. They noted as early as 1952 that 18% of the work in their British general practice was about emotional rather than physical problems.

Shepherd, Cooper & Brown (1966), 14 years later, in their much better known text *Psychiatric Illness in General Practice*, produced a classic text which documented precisely for general practice the huge extent of problems associated with the mind as opposed to problems primarily associated with the body.

There is interesting evidence from all the benzodiazepine prescribing that flooded the Western world in the 1970s and early 1980s. Those prescriptions were inappropriate by today's standards and are not to be recommended, but their use by the million is evidence that general practitioners were recognizing emotional distress *en masse*. Patients kept coming back for more because they acknowledged their problems were psychological in origin and thought these drugs were helping them.

The benzodiazepine story is thus a cloud with a silver lining. It shows general practitioners do recognize and respond to emotional distress in the consulting

Preventing Mental Illness: Mental Health Promotion in Primary Care. Edited by R. Jenkins and T.B. Üstün.
© 1998 John Wiley & Sons Ltd.

room. It strongly suggests that if practical, simple instruments and consulting techniques can be introduced to disentangle depression from anxiety in primary care, much more specific treatment can be expected. A second silver lining is the fact that as early as 1980, Goldberg et al noted that there were some general practitioners who could diagnose depression virtually every time and, whilst working within the time-frame of ordinary general practice consultations, could equal hour-long interviews by specialist psychiatrists. More recently, Tylee has confirmed this (personal communication, 1995) and he and I hope to explore these special skills further.

Meanwhile, there has been a series of studies, mainly community-based, showing that the quantity of mental illness in health settings is substantial and that much of it—up to 50%—is unrecognized by hospital doctors in the physical specialties (Maguire et al 1974) or by general practitioners (Freeling et al 1985).

In terms of life-time incidence, an episode of depression is now the commonest chronic disease diagnosed in some general practices (Pereira Gray 1995).

Quality

It is not easy to quantify the impact of different diseases, but measures are emerging of the quality of life. From the perspective of general practice, with its liking for the simple pragmatic measures which are easily determined in the consulting room and which apply quite broadly, it is clear that emotional problems and especially depression must rank very high, if not at the top of the causes of suffering.

First, the epidemiology of depression makes it a serious illness. There are still about 5000 deaths from suicide each year, deaths which have to be a target for prevention. How many of these are depressives, and more difficult, how many can be detected and treated are current research questions of importance.

Second, most of us would, I think, rather have any of the common chronic diseases of our time (asthma, arthritis, hypertension, diabetes) than chronic depression. Depression disables the whole person in a way that none of the others does and quality of life is reduced by definition, i.e. the central capacity of the person to enjoy life, perhaps at all, is diminished or abolished.

In my own practice, about half of all depressives answer 'Yes' to the question 'Is life sometimes not worth living?' This applies to about 60 of my own personal patients *each year* or 5% of my whole list of 1187. This is surely a quick key to identifying considerable suffering.

Effectiveness

As long ago as 1976 Johnstone & Goldberg (1976) showed that acknowledgement of emotional distress was of itself beneficial to patients.

More recently still, Wilson et al (1995) have shown clearly that acknowledgement, i.e. recognition and discussion in primary care of the patient's emotional distress, of itself and regardless of the precision or not of the psychiatric diagnosis, leads to greater satisfaction by patients.

FRAMEWORK FOR PREVENTION OF MENTAL ILLNESS IN PRIMARY CARE

There has been argument in psychiatric circles about how far the public health model of prevention is or is not applicable in primary care. Jenkins (1994), as a psychiatrist, holds that it can and should apply and she supports Caplan who, as a child psychiatrist, advocated this as early as 1964. Medical generalists (Pereira Gray et al 1994) would strongly support this view. The model of primary, secondary and tertiary prevention mainly applies in physical medicine, is simple and sensible and, for generalists applies to the remaining work as well.

There are some differences in definition. The Royal College of General Practitioners (RCGP 1982) definitions are helpful, i.e. primary prevention is the prevention of illness in the first place (e.g. immunization). Secondary prevention is the detection of the illness at a presymptomatic stage or phase (i.e. when the patient does not know that the disease exists and the doctor detects it at a presymptomatic stage, e.g. by cervical cytology). Tertiary prevention is the treatment of established disease in such a way as to prevent continuation, complications or relapse.

Primary Prevention

The first systematic attempt to identify the potential for prevention of psychiatric disorders in UK general practice came, like so many of the progressive developments in general practice/primary care, from the Royal College of General Practitioners.

In 1980 the College, led by Dr John Horder, set up a series of working parties on health and prevention. One of these was chaired by Dr Philip Graham, a child psychiatrist. Child psychiatry shares with primary care a natural interest in relationships and their long-term effects and, like Caplan, an interest in prevention. This multi-disciplinary Working Party contained both Professor Murray Parkes, as another psychiatrist, Professor George Brown, as a medical sociologist, Ms Sheila Ball, a health visitor, and two leading general practitioners, Dr Peter Tomson, who has illuminated the medical significance of the family so well, and Dr Andrew Markus from Oxford. Its report was published (RCGP 1981) and supported by the Mental Health Foundation. It put the challenge of the prevention of mental illness on the agenda for primary care. It was sent to every member of the RCGP and set the scene for this conference 14 years later.

This report offered the first approach, essentially the identification of risk factors or groups (primary prevention). Second, it suggested that primary care team workers should concentrate on 'transitions' or changes in the stages of an individual's life, e.g. pregnancy, bereavement, etc. The authors encouraged talking through emotional feelings (secondary prevention). They argued for the evaluation of counselling in primary care, especially for those at psychosocial transitions (Parkes 1971). The report identified the need for much better and more relevant education about mental illness for undergraduates, in vocational training, and during continuing education in general practice.

It is sobering that even 14 years later only a minority of general practitioners receive specialist postgraduate training in mental illness and, worse still, virtually all specialist psychiatrists are still emerging untrained in the medical discipline which detects and treats most mental illness. Even in 1995 the first reports of training psychiatric trainees in general practice were only just appearing (Burns et al 1995).

Finally, these authors pointed the way ahead with the need for much more research: 'Much of the work of this type could be carried out by general practitioners, especially if there is the possibility of advice from university departments of general practice and psychiatry'. They correctly predicted that the General Health Questionnaire (Goldberg & Blackwell 1970) 'could be considered more extensively than at present . . . for seeking prevalence or early identification'.

Primary Care

Definitions

First, it is necessary to draw a distinction between general practice and general practitioners. In the UK they are increasingly different, as general practice operates through a multi-disciplinary primary health care team.

Multi-disciplinary Primary Health Care Team in the UK

In my own practice in Exeter, which is quite typical for the West of England, we have about 6500 patients, four general practitioners (3.5 full-time equivalents (FTE)), nine nurses (practice nurses, district nurses and health visitors, 5.5 FTE), one FTE manager and four administrative staff in the core team, i.e. the group who go to work together in one building. In addition, an attached physiotherapist, an attached midwife, and an attached community psychiatric nurse come in at specified times to support specified functions. This is clearly a multi-disciplinary team and the general practitioners are a minority within it. Arrangements vary in different countries, but the trend towards a multi-disciplinary group working in the 'front line of health services' (RCGP 1987) is clear worldwide.

The arithmetic of general practice needs to be kept in mind. This year's report on the Fourth National Morbidity Study showed that in a single year as many as 78% of all the population consulted their GPs (McCormick, Fleming & Charlton 1995).

The contact rate in this national survey was 2.9 contacts per patient per year calculated for all those registered, but of those 78% who consulted, it was 3.8. All contacts with district nurses and health visitors were in addition to this, as were all telephone consultations and repeat prescriptions, when the patient was not seen (McCormick, Fleming & Charlton 1995). Other evidence from the Department of Health (1991) indicates that the duration of a consultation in general practice is now 8.8 minutes. Thus, the average general practitioner has 33.4 minutes per year for the average patient.

Patients with depression consult much more often, many twice as often and some three times as frequently. Even a contact rate of 10 consultations per year gives the doctor 88 minutes (about 1.5 hours) in the year. This is on top of the average 25.5 minutes (2.9 consultations for 8.8 minutes) each year spent with every other member of the household, as well as the average 5 hours (2.9 × 8.8 × 12 = 306 minutes) spent with the average patient during the average *12 years'* previous registration in the NHS.

The conclusion is that general practice, contrary to widespread belief, has the time but fails to use it. Why this is so is a major research question. Two reasons can be identified: (a) lack of a systematic approach to history-taking in emotional illness; (b) a failure to adopt personal lists (Pereira Gray 1979), so that many of these consultations occur with different doctors who cannot so easily summate the patient's total experience. All these statistics exclude contacts with health visitors, although the Fourth National Morbidity Survey did include consultations with practice nurses.

All this leads to the conclusion that education is the key. And the immediate need is for practical working examples of techniques of diagnosis and care developed by working generalists within the setting in which they will be used. Thus, the initiative of the Mental Health Research Fellow, Dr André Tylee, supported by the Department of Health, a major charity, the Mental Health Foundation, and the leading national academic body in the field, the Royal College of General Practitioners, is timely and exciting.

PREVENTION

Prevention of illness remains better than cure. General practitioners operate at nine levels of care (Pereira Gray 1978), ranging from counselling the bereaved to health promotion. The highest and optimum level is the work the primary health care team does to prevent illness. However, interventions must be effective, researched and cost-efficient, so much research is needed to clarify the options. In

1995, the state-of-the-art of practice suggests that a limited number of possibilities for prevention likely to be worthwhile do exist.

Primary Prevention

Before examining the individual possibilities for primary prevention, it is worth noting the clear association between depression, social vulnerability and social deprivation. Although this topic is not fashionable, it is clear that the conditions in which the most socially vulnerable live are one important factor in the genesis of depression. In so far that members of primary healthcare teams are often influential in calling for more national and local services and resources, there is a broad social role which, if it could improve social conditions, could be expected to reduce the prevalence of depression.

Primary prevention of depression can be justified by advice on alcohol consumption, contraceptive care, and counselling in transitional stages, especially after pregnancy and bereavement.

Alcohol Consumption

Recording the drinking histories of all adults is already good practice and many practices now have figures for 90% or more of their patients. Advising patients about sensible drinking is logical and general practitioner interventions have been shown to be effective (Wallace, Cutler & Haines 1988).

As far as depression is concerned, much will now depend on the identification of risk factors, a topic of interest to the Exeter Institute of General Practice. If these can be clarified, then prevention seems possible. Certainly in the elderly, loneliness appears to be one social factor which can be countered through contact with day centres, societies or CRUSE. This is important in a population like mine, in which every sixth household is a pensioner living alone.

Contraception and Preconceptual Care

General practice is the main source of contraceptive care. Department of Health statistics for England (1993) show that over the last 10 years a bigger proportion of general practitioners have been offering the service and a bigger proportion of patients have been accepting family planning in general practice. Unwanted pregnancies can provoke depression either through abortion or continuation, and remain a high challenge to the whole practice. Similarly, I see about half of all patients registered with me for preconceptual counselling before they start a pregnancy. This can be another opportunity for prevention.

Counselling after Loss

Sensitive counselling after major loss such as bereavement has been shown to reduce subsequent depression (Parkes 1981). This is a traditional role of both district nurses and general practitioners and needs to be built into practice protocols.

Relationships

Being a family doctor, district nurse or health visitor brings one face to face with the all-pervasive influence in homes of human relationships in relation to health and illness. Of all the associated factors for depression among my patients, unsatisfactory personal relationships seem to be among the most important factors, at least in women, who are the principal sufferers. Similarly, many of the child healthcare problems seen in primary care are to do with parent–child relationships in one form or another.

Primary health care teams may well have to call for and lead a new emphasis on the importance of human relationships in the home. Unrealistic expectations of young people, a disastrous failure rate for marriages among teenagers and lack of personal negotiating skills all make more of the present generation vulnerable to personal upheavals.

Marriage is also currently relatively unfashionable, yet in relationship terms it may still be a better structure for a couple, especially when having children, than current alternatives. When more couples are *not* marrying than ever before, we might anticipate a blurring of the difference in outcomes for children born in or out of wedlock.

Yet the infant mortality rate remains twice as high for those children whose parents have not married compared with those who have. If mortality differences are so great, how much more are the morbidity rates, especially for emotional problems? Perhaps schools and practices should teach human relationships as one of the key living skills now needed in our society?

Secondary Prevention

The promotion of mental health through secondary prevention is much more practical and there is potential for a whole range of possibilities in general practice.

Education

Advising patients about risk factors, including a positive family history, and encouraging early consultations for those with a history of previous depression or attempted suicide is quick and logical. Sharp (1992) has shown that about 15% of all mothers develop postnatal depression, so good teamwork with health visitors, midwives and GPs in the practice should pick these up and depression should be sought in all.

Risk Factors

As risk factors for depression are identified they are found to fall into two categories: genetic, which are unalterable; and environmental, which are in theory open to change. It may well be that depression is like ischaemic heart disease, a condition which also has several risk factors, and it may be the accumulation of factors which in some way yet to be determined (perhaps in a combination of genetic susceptibility) triggers the condition we call depression. If so, then the next step is to identify, document and then seek to alter, one by one, those factors which can be changed in the environment. Here the new computer systems are bound to be a great advantage and British primary care has adopted computers more than the hospital service and more than general practice in other countries.

Practice Organization—Personal Lists

Practice organization can do much to help GPs be better informed and more sensitive to their patients' lives. Most recent research has supported the three-pronged approach to patients as people, first described in general practice a quarter of a century ago. This was later adopted by the Royal College of General Practitioners in 1972 in its classic text, *The Future General Practitioner—Learning and Teaching*, and much more recently taken up by psychiatrists as 'multi-axial classification'.

The original description (Pereira Gray 1969) spoke of 'three-dimensional care', a term used to describe the three domains of physical, psychological and social factors, and also used in 1969 to indicate that such care for patients when provided was more solid and systematic.

There is, however, a paradox, that of all kinds of doctors the family doctor knows most about the family and the home, which they have usually visited; and they have continuity of care for about 12 years (Difford 1990, personal communication). Yet general practice is characteristically non-systematic in recording this uniquely valuable information.

Family household charts described by Zander (1978) are a first step and personal lists, a term coined in Exeter, seem to be a key step in encouraging patients and doctors to get to know each other over time. In that way the social background can be built up and real mutual understanding achieved. More particularly, risk factors for depression become known, get recorded, and start to sink into medical thinking.

Those outside general practice underestimate this process. It can, and has, taken me 33 years of continuous care before some women have entrusted me with the information that they have been sexually abused in the past, a major risk factor for depression.

Personal lists are likely to improve both doctor and patient satisfaction, and may actually be cheaper to operate as more advice can be given to doctors on the telephone and better advice returned when patients and doctors know each other well.

Sensitive Doctor–Patient Relationships

One major principle in secondary prevention is that patients should be able to access the practice without hassle and then, when alone with their doctors, be able to talk freely about whatever concerns them. Ever since Balint's (1957) work, the doctor has been seen as the principal 'drug' used in general practice.

In this way, whenever good relationships are established, psychosocial material will emerge and will contribute properly to diagnosis. Wilson et al (1995) show that some GPs are simply more skilled than others in this work and their patients are correspondingly more satisfied.

It has been shown that training is important, as is the possession of higher professional qualifications, so encouraging new GPs to take and value the MRCGP is likely to lead to more competent generalists.

General Practitioners as Lead Professionals

Finally, there is currently discussion as to which profession in the primary health care team should receive priority for education on depression. The answer may change over the years, but now it seems clear that it should be the GPs, for four reasons:

- First, GPs see more individual patients than any other member of the primary health care team, e.g. about four times as many people as practice nurses, and about 20 times as many as district nurses (although those that do receive district nursing are a highly vulnerable group).
- Second, the diagnostic problems of somatization (Wright 1990) are essentially a medical, not a nursing, issue. Somatization is among the most difficult intellectual and emotional problems seen in primary care. Nurses are excellent at following protocols, but doing so for a physical problem can actually impede the sensitive discussion needed to convince a somatizer that not all the symptoms and problems are necessarily to do with physical disease, even when present. Professor Grol's (1988) book, *To Heal or to Harm?* is virtually required reading in this respect.

- Third, work on depression is extra work at extra cost for practices in relation to practice nurse time. However, good early diagnoses of depression and care can be expected to reduce the general practitioner's workload. Depressives are high *doctor* consulters and good care reduces the number and time spent on relatively unproductive consultations.
- Finally, there is a morale problem at present in primary care, worst among the doctors. Helping them make sense of a large part of their daily work (e.g. as suggested by Tylee & Freeling 1987) and gaining job satisfaction from managing it well can be expected to improve morale. Personally, I find diagnosing and treating depression to be among the most satisfying parts of my job as a GP.

About twice as many consultations are spent with depressives as with other patients, often in the guise of allegedly physical problems. GPs thus often have 10 consultations a year of, say, 9 minutes each, with depressives. This is plenty of time if it is really professionally used. Systematic enquiry and recording are the keys, along the lines suggested by Goldberg et al (1988).

Tertiary Prevention

This is the area in which British primary care currently has the most to offer. Depression is a serious condition with a high chance of relapse. Mann, Jenkins & Beasley (1981) showed that as many as one-third of patients with depression had substantial problems a year after diagnosis. Thus, immediate diagnosis, with treatment being started at the first consultation, and skilful follow-up and support, will reduce the time of the illness, vastly reduce the suffering by the patient and improve patient satisfaction (Wilson et al 1995). Research on general practice consultations using video recording will lead to new skills in the consultation which are likely to lead to earlier diagnoses (Tylee & Freeling 1987). Recent evidence strongly suggests that prolonging the duration of treatment of depression in both adults and the elderly reduces the likelihood of recurrence, which is by definition tertiary prevention.

SUMMARY

Starting with tertiary care, it is the traditional role of GPs in the Western world to detect and treat over 80% of those with mental illness known to the health services. This great tradition is likely to continue. Recent work, some in progress, strongly suggests that, with education and support, detection rates can be greatly increased without significant loss of specificity. Treating disease when it presents is the traditional, still valuable, but essentially the old role of primary care.

Secondary preventive techniques are moving out of the conceptual and research settings into clinical general practice. It is becoming possible to help patients with risk factors to present earlier, to follow up those at risk, and to make diagnoses when the patients are not primarily seeking help.

The future is now in sight. Clarification of risk factors will inevitably move the challenge on towards reducing at least some of them. To this extent, the serious possibility of prevention of at least some forms of mental illness can now be seen on the horizon.

REFERENCES

Balint M (1957) *The Doctor, His Patient and the Illness*. London: Tavistock.

Burns L, Macdonald L, Sibbald B, Gask L & Roberts G (1995) Educational assessment of general practice experience for psychiatric trainees. *Med Ed* **29**(2), 159–64.

Caplan G (1964) *Principles of Preventive Psychiatry*. London: Tavistock.

Department of Health (1991) *Workload Survey in General Practice*. London: Department of Health.

Department of Health (1993) *Health and Personal Social Services Statistics for England*, Table 5.31. London: HMSO.

Freeling P, Rao BM, Paykel ES et al (1985) Unrecognized depression in general practice. *Br Med J* **290**, 1880–83.

Goldberg D & Blackwell B (1970) Psychiatric illness in general practice. *Br Med J* **2**, 439–43.

Goldberg DP et al (1980) Training family doctors to recognise psychiatric illness with increased accuracy. *Lancet* **2**, 521–3.

Goldberg D, Bridges K, Duncan Jones P et al (1988) Detecting anxiety and depression in medical settings. *Br Med J* **297**, 897–9.

Grol R (1988) *To Heal or to Harm?* Exeter: Royal College of General Practitioners.

Johnstone A & Goldberg D (1976) Psychiatric screening in general practice. *Lancet* **1**, 605–8.

Mann AH, Jenkins R & Beasley E (1981) The 12-month outcome of patients with neurotic illness in general practice. *Psychol Med* **11**, 535–50.

Maguire GP, Julier DL, Hawton KE et al (1974) Psychiatric morbidity and referral on two general medical wards. *Br Med J* **1**, 268–70.

McCormick A, Fleming D & Charlton J (1995) *Morbidity Statistics from General Practice. Fourth National Study 1991–1992*, Table 2a, p xiv. London: HMSO.

Parkes CM (1971) Psychosocial transitions: a field for study. *Soc Sci Med* **5**, 101–15.

Parkes CM (1981) Evaluation of a bereavement service. *J Prevent Psychiat* **1**, 179–88.

Pereira Gray DJ (1969) The care of the handicapped child (Gold Medal Essay). *Trans Hunterian Soc* **28**, 3–47.

Pereira Gray DJ (1978) Feeling at home (James MacKenzie Lecture, 1978). *J R Coll Gen Pract* **28**, 6–17.

Pereira Gray DJ (1979) The key to personal care. *J R Coll Gen Pract* **29**, 666–78.

Pereira Gray DJ, Steele R, Sweeney K & Evans P (1994) Generalists in medicine. Editorial. *Br Med J* **308**, 406–7.

Pereira Gray DJ (1995) Primary care and the public health. Harben Lecture 1994. *Health Hyg* **16**, 49–62.

RCGP (Royal College of General Practitioners) (1972) *The Future General Practitioner—Learning and Teaching*. London: RCGP.

RCGP (Royal College of General Practitioners) (1981) *Prevention of Psychiatric Disorders in General Practice*. Report from General Practice 20. London: RCGP.

RCGP (Royal College of General Practitioners) (1982) *Healthier Children—Thinking Prevention.* Report from General Practice 22. London: RCGP.

RCGP (Royal College of General Practitioners) (1987) *The Front Line of the Health Service.* Report from General Practice 25. London: RCGP.

Sharp D (1992) Predicting postnatal depression. In R Jenkins, J Newton & P Young (eds) *The Prevention of Depression and Anxiety.* London: HMSO.

Shepherd M, Cooper M, Brown AC et al (1966) *Psychiatric Illness in General Practice.* Oxford: Oxford University Press.

Tylee A & Freeling P (1987) Consultation analysis by triggers and symptoms (CATS). *Family Pract* **4**, 260–65.

Wallace P, Cutler S & Haines A (1988) Randomized controlled trial of general practitioner intervention in patients with excessive alcohol consumption. *Br Med J* **297**, 663–8.

Watts CAH & Watts BM (1952/1994) *Psychiatry in General Practice* (republished 1994). London: RCGP.

Wilson PMJ, Sullivan F, Hussein S et al (1995) Examination of the effects of emotional disturbance and its detection on general practice patients' satisfaction with the consultation. *Br J Gen Pract* **45**, 304–9.

Wright A (1990) A study of the presentation of somatic symptoms in general practice by patients with psychiatric disturbance. *Br J Gen Pract* **40**, 459–63.

Zander L, Beresford AS & Thomas P (1978) *Medical Records in General Practice.* Occasional Paper 5. Exeter: Royal College of General Practitioners.

44

Application of Promotion Principles

J Orley
World Health Organization, Geneva, Switzerland

In discussing the application of mental health promotion principles in primary health care, we need to be clear as to what we mean by the two terms 'mental health promotion' on the one hand and 'primary health care' on the other.

There is frequently some confusion between the prevention of mental disorders and the promotion of mental health. The two need to be kept conceptually distinct, and there are dangers in not maintaining the distinction. Unfortunately the term 'mental health' is now used loosely to mean mental illness, possibly because it is used as a shorthand for mental health problems. Prevention in the mental health field is about the prevention of mental disorders, and is a worthy activity, but prevention of disease should not be confused with promotion of health.

According to the WHO definition (and we do not seem to have a better one), health is a state of complete physical, mental and social well-being and not merely the absence of disease or infirmity. Obtaining health, or maintaining it, is therefore about two things. It is about preventing and treating diseases, but not merely that. The definition implies that health cannot be obtained merely by preventing and treating diseases and neither, we should assume, can mental health be obtained by merely preventing and treating mental disorders. If we accept the WHO definition, then a service whose objective is to maintain the health of a nation must contain provisions for fostering mental health and well-being and not merely for preventing and treating mental disorders. Furthermore, mental health promotion should not be confused with issues around mental disorders. Stigma, for instance, is a mental health issue, but the stigma attached to, say, AIDS or epilepsy is as much a mental health issue as the stigma attached to mental illness. A psychiatrist will be concerned particularly about the stigma attached to those with mental illness, just as a neurologist should be concerned about the stigma attached to his/her patients with epilepsy. A 'mental health' professional should be concerned about stigma, whatever the cause, even racial stigma! To many who work within a health service, this may sound unrealistic. If, however, we have institutions such as the National Health Service or the World Health Organization, then these must concern

Preventing Mental Illness: Mental Health Promotion in Primary Care. Edited by R. Jenkins and T.B. Üstün.
Published 1998 John Wiley & Sons Ltd.

themselves with other issues besides merely preventing or treating diseases. If they do not, then they need to change their definition of health or change their name (e.g. The British National Illness Service or The World Centre for Disease Control). Both the NHS and WHO put the vast majority of their resources into disease control. There can, however, be realistic activities undertaken for health besides controlling disease.

Besides being clear about what is mental health promotion, we need to define what we mean by the term 'primary health care'. It should not be confused with primary medical care, exemplified, for instance, by general practitioners (GPs) in the UK, although a system for providing efficient first-contact medical care, with support from higher levels of care, can be considered as a part of primary health care. As conceived of by WHO, primary health care involves the mobilization of resources at community level in favour of actions that will improve health and control disease. The agents of such change, primary health workers or community health workers, need not be physicians. Such an approach is not just necessary for countries which are too poor to afford anything else, although the concept did arise in part as a reaction to the horrific inequalities that exist in medical care, in which a large proportion of the health budget goes towards a few specialist hospitals, usually teaching hospitals, and very few resources remain to go to the grass-roots level, where in fact small investments can bring rich dividends in terms of indicators of health for a nation.

One principle underlying primary health care is the identification of simple technologies that can be used by people with relatively little training, emphasizing self-help so that people (or communities) take responsibility for their own health. The emphasis is on prevention and promotion and the agents need not be from within the health sector. The health sector's role may not be one of implementation of interventions, but one of advocacy and monitoring. A supply of clean water is good for health. The health sector can identify whether water is clean, whether it contains pollutants and bacteria, it can suggest ways of removing them and how best to monitor quality. The health sector, however, will not be responsible for digging wells, building reservoirs, laying pipes, waste disposal or operating purification plants. Health professionals have a role in advocating and promoting good environmental health, and this should include promoting a mentally healthy environment.

Primary health care is about ensuring that health is on the agenda of each local community. Local physicians, where they exist, should be part of this process, but much primary health care can happen without physicians, and in fact not all local physicians concern themselves with this more broadly conceived primary health care.

What then can be done for mental health promotion in primary health care? This is not the same as asking what can be done for mental health promotion by GPs, or others involved in disease control at first-contact level. It is more of a matter of what can be done for mental health at community level by local agents, whoever they might be.

A description of some of the activities of the WHO Mental Health Promotion Unit can illustrate what can be done. WHO's activities concerning mental health promotion at primary care level are not primarily activities that are carried out by GPs, although a good GP should take on the function of advocating for such activities in his/her practice area. One group of activities of the WHO program, however, is more directly related to general practice and that is the teaching of communication skills. As a contribution to mental health and well-being, the GP should be able to manage his/her consultation and communicate with patients in ways that are both efficient and humane, and the evidence is that the two go together. The WHO efforts in this field, however, are really directed at medical students learning in hospitals, rather than at GPs in their practice. Besides the general area of doctor–patient communication, WHO has looked at particular situations which require good communication skills, such as giving bad news to patients or preparing patients for surgery, and WHO has prepared learning modules for these. Such skills are advocated not just to prevent mental illness, but because a mentally healthy environment within a hospital or practice is a sufficient end in itself.

Another two areas in which WHO carries out mental health promotion activities are on quality of life measures and on the mental health and well-being of special groups. The development of a measure of quality of life in health care settings focuses attention on this as a possible outcome measure, with mental well-being an important component of quality of life. This takes us beyond symptoms and disablements as the sole preoccupation of health care. The indicators that are chosen for monitoring health can have an important influence on the shaping of the services provided. An emphasis on infant mortality rates, for instance, can push a service in one direction, such as intensive care units for newborns, sometimes at the expense of other possible provision. Similarly, the use of morbidity rates may confirm disease control as the only worthwhile intervention. The use, therefore, of quality of life and well-being measures can have the effect of encouraging interventions that are aimed at improving well-being, and hence the interest within WHO in developing such indicators.

As for special or vulnerable groups, there is often talk of the adverse mental health consequences of rapid urbanization, migration, disasters or belonging to minority or even majority groups (e.g. women and mental health). Whilst it is often true that rates of mental disorder are higher in such groups, this is not usually what people are referring to when they talk of adverse mental health consequences. For refugees, therefore, WHO has produced a mental health manual for use by community workers which does not concentrate on mental disorder but on improving mental health. It is perhaps one of the few internationally directed manuals which has a strong element of mental health promotion.

There are two WHO activities that concern the promotion of good mental health and psychosocial development in children, one in preschool and the other in school-age children. In the first years of children's lives, the health sector typically concerns itself with their physical health, ensuring a safe birth, preventing tetanus, encouraging breastfeeding, ensuring adequate nutrition, including vitamins and other essential nutrients. Mothers are targeted as being in need of help to make sure they understand the importance of all these, and are helped to put them into effect. It is, however, assumed that mothers can take care of their infant's *psychosocial* needs, almost by instinct; that they will provide an adequate psychosocial environment for their child without any help. Of course, some mothers do not need help with this, just as some mothers do not need help to provide the right physical environment for their child. Why, however, is the psychosocial side neglected? This is presumably due to an undervaluing of this mental and psychosocial side of life and an attitude that sees babies only as small animals or plants that need to be fed, watered and physically protected in order to develop. We know, however, that what might be called the 'psychosocial nutrition' of children is important, comparable to their physical nutrition, and that certain families are at particular risk. This latter includes those without a 'grandmother' who can pass on culturally appropriate child-rearing information to her daughter or daughter-in-law; or a single parent; or those having a large number of closely-spaced children; or where the parents work long hours or are under other pressures. Children with intellectual or sensory impairments may need extra psychosocial nutrition, just as a child with some malabsorption syndrome may need physical nutrition supplements.

The WHO approach to improving the psychosocial environment of the child involves using the child's existing caretakers, usually its mother, and using or adapting the local ways of bringing up the child, rather than introducing practices alien to the existing culture. It is, therefore, a matter of identifying the best of existing practices and positively reinforcing these. In order to help pick out what might be the best, WHO has identified a set of eight guidelines for psychosocial interactions between mothers and children. The emphasis is on the interaction between the mother and child. This must not be seen as a one-way process in which the mother stimulates her infant. What has to be emphasized is the communications that come from the child to which the mother has to be sensitive and respond. Through understanding the importance of this interaction, the mother should develop a greater sense of her own efficacy as the person who will be responsible for her child's psychosocial development. Through understanding the simple guidelines that have been prepared by WHO, she comes to know more about what she is doing and can begin to mark or label those activities that are beneficial to her child's development. Knowledge alone, however, is not enough, and the emphasis in the program is in getting the mother to learn the necessary skills to interact better with the baby and introduce it to the wider society and world. The WHO approach emphasizes both the emotional communication that is necessary between mother and child as well as the mediational learning experience that the mother can provide as she guides her child into the world and culture around it.

The program's emphasis is one of reinforcing existing good practices and not one of correcting what seems to be wrong. It is, however, sometimes difficult for those working in the health sector to take on this role of identifying positive aspects of existing interactions and reinforcing them. Too often, health professionals are taught to make a diagnosis; that is, to find out what is wrong, and then to point this out and try to correct it. It requires a considerable reorientation in attitude by doctors, nurses or clinical psychologists, to look for more positive attributes in their clients which they can reinforce, rather than to look for faults which they can correct.

How could such a programme be put in place? Certainly the health sector is the one typically involved in the care of children 0–3 years old. It would, however, require considerable resources to provide training courses for mothers and it will be a rare country, health service, or health worker who would commit resources to such an activity. One way forward would be to use a more 'pyramidal selling' method, whereby selected mothers who have good skills and have been involved in the program, would be used as trainers of others, either as volunteers or for some kind of small honorarium. Such a system, however, requires resources to set it up in the first place, and must have a good system for maintaining quality control thereafter.

It is important to focus health promotion activities on children and young people in attempting to affect long-term behaviour change, since this is the time of life when patterns of behaviour and attitudes are established. Mental health promotion, however, is not just a matter of preventing behaviours which have adverse health consequences, and there are cogent reasons for promoting mental health in all sections of the population as an end in itself. Nevertheless, one can argue that in promoting good mental health, one will at the same time be preventing many behaviours which can lead to poor health.

There is a place for mental health professionals to work with the education sector by pooling the expertise from those two sectors in order to improve the mental health and psychosocial development of the children passing through the education system. To this end, the WHO Program on Mental Health has examined a series of programs called 'Life Skills Education', which provide inputs into the education system, and noted how these can be used not just to improve the psychosocial competencies of the children but, at the same time, provide more effective health education messages to the children which are more likely to be responded to. Health education messages on their own, i.e. just providing knowledge concerning health and informing young people about the dangers of certain behaviours, appear to have very little influence upon their activities. Knowing about the danger of smoking does not usually deter young people from starting to smoke. Neither does it seem sufficient to exhort them to change their behaviour with such messages as 'Just say no'. What does seem to be more effective is providing programs which encourage children to take more responsibility for their lives and their health, which enable them to feel more effective in being able to control their own lives, and this can be achieved through life skills education programs. Health education messages concerning drugs and unprotected sex, when imbedded into such programs, seem to lead to more change than programs which are not so arranged, in which health education messages stand alone.

The term 'life skills' in this context refers to a particular general set of skills for the promotion of psychosocial competence amongst young people. It is, however, sometimes used to refer to livelihood or practical skills which might be required by young people in some contexts, particularly as they leave school. These might be the kinds of skills needed to set up a small business, to obtain a job, to operate a computer or plan healthy meals. These, however, are not what is referred to in the kinds of programs which will be discussed here. Other skills which can be called life skills refer to those associated with the reduction of specific risk situations or events. Included here would be the skills of being able to refuse an offered cigarette or to negotiate condom use within a sexual encounter. Although these are related to life skills, they are again not what is specifically being discussed within the term 'life skills education'. This latter refers specifically to more generic life skills which can be learnt at any stage and applied in a general way to many areas of life, such as:

- Problem solving.
- Critical thinking.
- Communication.
- Self-awareness.
- Coping with stress.
- Decision-making.
- Creative thinking.
- Interpersonal skills.
- Empathy.
- Coping with emotions.

Learning these skills should help young people become more mentally mature and able to deal with life and, in doing so, able to take more control of their lives and avoid influences which would be likely to damage their health. The skills can be learnt at any stage at an increasing degree of complexity and with a greater ability to perform the skill effectively, as the child passes through childhood. If we take the example of communication skills, these are important to children and can be learnt at a young age where, from a health perspective, they may be relevant to the prevention of, for instance, child abuse. Communication skills may enable the child to be more effective in getting away from a situation where they may be abused, or to talk more effectively to another adult about what is happening to them. At a slightly older age, improved communication and other interactional skills can help the child to avoid, or not be persuaded to accept, cigarettes. At an even later stage these same skills should be useful in avoiding drug use or the misuse of alcohol. These same communication skills in the later teens can be applied to yet other situations which are important for health, such as the negotiations that might be necessary in terms of sexual behaviour and condom use. The same skill, therefore, can be learnt for use in increasingly complex situations, and the child's proficiency in that skill can grow over the years.

This same logic that would guide the teaching of communication skills in progressively complex ways as the child gets older, can also be applied to other skills. By following such a logic, we can develop a program by which the underlying skill can be taught at any age, provided they are made appropriate to that age. If we wish to develop an AIDS prevention program, for instance, we cannot teach the more 'advanced' skills of AIDS prevention to children of 8 years old. They can, however, be taught the underlying skills so that when the time comes, at the age of say 16+, to learn about matters related to sexual behaviour, the educational ground will have been prepared for the relevant messages. If we take the parallel of learning calculus, we do not start at the age of 8 with this subject, but we teach simple arithmetic and set the basis for being able to learn more advanced mathematical skills in the future.

It should be said that life skills programs are not a new and untried strategy. There are a number of programs which have existed in this field for many years. Many of the programs began as focused prevention initiatives, e.g. to prevent teenage pregnancy or drug abuse. At the start, such programs concentrated on matters very directly related to the problem behaviour. However, it rapidly became clear to those working in the programs that they would not succeed without providing a broader framework aimed at the overall development of the child, both physical and mental. There are, therefore, a number of existing education programs, providing the opportunities for children to learn a broad range of life skills, even though some of them may have a particular underlying focus for prevention incorporated within them.

- Lions Quest Skills for Adolescence (drugs/alcohol).
- Skills for the Primary School Child TACADE (child abuse/safety).
- Life Planning Education—CPO (adolescent pregnancy).
- The CoRT Thinking Program—de Bono (improving intelligence).
- Life Skills Training—Botvin (smoking and other substance use).

Although the focus of these programs is on the teaching of life skills, there is an underlying agenda for increasing the *sense* of competence and self-efficacy of the pupils. Obviously one way of increasing a sense of competence is to increase the competence itself and this is the aim of the life skills education programs. To increase competencies, it is necessary to move beyond traditional classroom teaching methods, involving the teacher providing a one-way flow of information to the pupils. The learning of life skills requires much more participation by the students in the process, with discussion, role-plays and giving practical exercises to be undertaken outside school. This should involve more cooperation and inter-action between the pupils. Most programs also include the participation of parents in one way or another. As can be appreciated, it is not possible to improve life skills to any appreciable extent by just hearing about them and having them explained; it is necessary for the pupils to be able to practise the skills in the classroom, at least in a role-play situation, and then to be encouraged to continue this practice outside the classroom.

Experience with these programs indicates that teachers and students enjoy the experience of a more interactional form of learning, and that once any fear of this has been overcome, some teachers at least begin applying the methods to the teaching of other subjects. Students begin to find that their sense of competence begins to extend to other types of skills, beyond those in the life skills program, such as mathematical skills. So it is that students' self-esteem and feelings of self-efficacy can be enhanced by their schooling, which can become a positive mental health experience, instead of a negative one, as it so often is. A greater awareness of the importance of life skills, and a greater sensitivity that is encouraged in both the pupils and the teachers through such programs, can lead to a better atmosphere in the school. Where this is associated with particular policies, e.g. related to the elimination of bullying from a school, then these latter programs can be enhanced. A greater sensitivity, too, can help teachers become more aware, for instance, of the negative effects of competition in addition to its positive effects. They can begin to see that for every winner in the class in a situation of competition, there will be a great number of losers, and the likelihood is that without careful attention, the self-esteem of the losers is likely to suffer.

The role of the health sector in all of this may not be immediately clear. In the first instance, the psychological expertise available in the health sector can be added to that already available in the educational sector to refine, develop and apply such programs in schools. It is true that in many educational systems, the role of the psychologist is primarily that of assessment of children with possible problems. Psychologists in the health sector can work with those in the educational sector for the development and implementation of programs for the improvement of the mental well-being of the pupils. In addition, there may be within schools a place in the curriculum for 'health education', into which such life skills education teaching can be inserted. Mental health professionals can indeed play a role in effecting such changes, both as advocates for change and as a resource within any development process.

The WHO, through its Mental Health Promotion Unit, has developed a number of documents which provide information concerning these sorts of approaches. There is a broad description of mental health programs in schools, as well as a document which focuses more specifically on life skills education programs. In addition to this, WHO has reviewed and provided annotations for a number of programs which are in place around the world, which could be used as models for adaptation or development of new programs in countries.

CONCLUSION

Mental health promotion is not just about preventing mental disorders or indeed any disease, important though that is. Activities to promote mental health should not have to be justified as a way of reducing the costs of mental illness, since positive mental health and well-being can be aspired to and are desirable ends in themselves. Mental health promotion does, however, have a cost, and a return on investment is unlikely to be seen in the short term. The return may not be a reduction in disease, either, so that the health sector (if it is primarily a 'disease control sector') may not see it as a reasonable economic investment if investing in health really means investing in the absence of disease. The role of the health sector in mental health promotion may not involve the investment of large amounts of resources. The health sector, however, can help by pointing to actions that are needed, it can help with their initiation and it can be involved in subsequent monitoring and quality control.

Mental health promotion is therefore about putting mental health and well-being on the agenda of local authorities, in schools, in workplaces and elsewhere. 'Mental health' cannot be dealt with only by health authorities and it is too important to be left just to health professionals.

WHO RESOURCE DOCUMENTS

1. *Mental Health Programmes in Schools* (WHO/MNH/PSF/93.3.Rev.1). Geneva: WHO.
2. *Life Skills Education in Schools—Introduction and Guidelines to Facilitate the Development and Implementation of Life Skills Programmes*, Parts 1 & 2 (WHO/MNH/PSF/93.7A.Rev.1). Geneva: WHO.
3. *Training Workshops for the Development and Implementation of Life Skills Programmes.* Part 3 of the Document on Life Skills Education in Schools (WHO/MNH/PSF/93.7B.Rev.1). Geneva: WHO.
4. *The Development and Dissemination of Life Skills Education: An Overview* (MNH/PSF/94.7). Geneva: WHO.
5. *Skills for Life Newsletter.* Geneva: WHO.
6. *Quality of Life Assessment: International Perspectives.* Orley J & Kuyken W (eds) (1994) New York: Springer-Verlag.
7. The WHOQOL Group (1995). The World Health Organization Quality of Life Assessment (WHOQOL): position paper from the World Health Organization. *Soc Sci Med* **41**(10), 1403–9.
8. *Improving the Psychosocial Development of Children—Programmes for Enriching their Human Environment* (MNH/PSF/93.6). Geneva: WHO.
9. *Improving the Psychosocial Development of Children—A Programme for the Enrichment of Interactions between Mothers and Children* (MNH/PSF/95.4). Geneva: WHO.
10. *Doctor–Patient Interaction and Communication* (WHO/MNH/PSF/93.11). Geneva: WHO.

Conclusion

45

Epilogue: The Way Forward— Proposals for Action*

T Bedirhan Üstün and Rachel Jenkins**

*World Health Organization, Geneva, Switzerland, and **Institute of Psychiatry, London, UK*

A decade or two ago prevention and promotion in psychiatry and particularly primary mental health care was mainly of academic interest. The collection of contributions presented in this book is proof that the topic is having a grass-roots effect and is becoming a movement.

There are many conceptual issues regarding prevention of mental illness and promotion of mental health that need to be considered in order to root these activities in primary care settings and make them an integral part of the primary health care approach.

PRIMARY HEALTH CARE SETTING—ADVANTAGES AND DISADVANTAGES

Primary care facilities have a great organizational relevance to basic prevention and promotion activities. There is a great need for a systematic effort to implement structured programs for prevention of mental disorders and mental health promotion.

Enlarging the Definition of Primary Care

Although primary care is usually seen as general practice, it is much larger than general medical practice. Primary care is organized to optimize the resources of the

---

* This chapter summarizes the views expressed in the overall discussion session which took place at the end of the Conference. The participants were: Drs Armstrong, Bertolote, Bosanquet, Buda, Corney, Costa e Silva, D'Arrigo Busnello, Deva, Eisenberg, Sampaio Faria, Gögüs, Goldberg, Gomel, Hosman, Huxley, Jenkins, Levav, Magruder, Mann, Miller, Mohit, Mrazek, Mubbashar, Murthy, Odejide, Orley, Price, Raphael, Regier, Sartorius, Saunders, Sell, Sharpe, Sutherland, Styles, Tsiantis, Tylee, Walker, Wilkinson & Üstün.

Preventing Mental Illness: Mental Health Promotion in Primary Care. Edited by R. Jenkins and T.B. Üstün.
Published 1998 John Wiley & Sons Ltd.

community to serve best the wide range of health problems: it should be continuous, integrated, multi-sectoral and coordinated. To be more effective in helping people at the primary care level, individuals should be seen as members of a family and a community. It is therefore important to include family and community members in prevention and promotion activities. Within primary care there are schools, workplaces and other community settings. There is recognition that mental health promotion should take place within all settings. In order to promote mental health and for all to have a role, whether in the workplace or other community settings including voluntary groups, we all need to work together and learn together.

Many methods of delivery of health information, e.g. media (newspapers, radio, television), computers and Internet or telephone advisory services, may be useful for counselling and advisory services for the general public. In terms of mental health promotion, these tools may have a role in public education and awareness.

Health and above all perhaps mental health is too important to leave to the health sector. Our priority must be to put mental health on to the agenda of other sectors and other services. It can not be just left to the local health service. We want to get mental health onto the agenda of schools and into the workplace, not just by having an occupational physician stationed there, but by having occupational health policies that address mental health.

Effective interagency working is crucial for primary care team programs in the field of mental health. A clear understanding should be established of the roles and responsibilities of other sectors (schools, media and environmental agencies). For example, schools could educate children in parenting skills, mothering, coping. Environmental agencies could give children a consistent caring environment, and improve the buildings in which people live. Politicians could be persuaded that the disparity in income between rich and poor people is exceedingly bad for the health of the population (poverty is a risk factor for illness), so that more egalitarian policies could be developed.

It is possible to improve mental health through actions in the wider community. Good role models are needed. One example is taking mental health into the schools. It is necessary to look at some concrete examples and try to develop specific programs and evaluate them. In the field of early childhood, a whole range of programs exists and they need to be looked at carefully and the implications of how they can be encouraged in the community thought out. Early childhood is of course a concern for the health sector but nonetheless some actions cannot be carried out totally within the health sector. To move out into the wider community it is important to think about how to involve more people. What the health sector needs to do is not so much to implement programs but to start them up and to ensure quality control. Other people must be involved. Self-empowerment and people taking responsibility must become real aims.

Mental health is too important to leave just to the professionals. One of the barriers to effectiveness of prevention and health promotion programs is the focus on professionals only. If the prevention programs are not planned together with the users as 'partners', they won't be as effective as they could be. Therefore, it is important to extend primary care into the community.

Integration of Mental Health into Primary Health Care

There still appears to be a division/dichotomy between so-called 'physical' and 'mental' health. Consequently, this reflects on the primary care practice as though the primary care providers were responsible for physical health matters that seem to be more 'concrete', while the mental health matters which are 'abstract' and poorly defined lie more in the realm of specialist services such as psychiatry, psychology, counselling or social work. This leads to fragmentation and results in a poor link between primary care workers and specialist services. This is unfortunate because a large majority of people with mental health problems are seen within primary care facilities and, for most parts of the world, this is the only possible health care that is practically available.

There are often barriers to patients getting the care they need, particularly those with mental health problems, learning disabilities or substance abuse problems. These barriers may relate to knowledge and attitudes of the public, e.g. stigma associated with mental problems; organization of care, e.g. separation of mental health from the realm of general health; and education of health care personnel, e.g. lack of appropriate knowledge and skills to identify and manage mental health problems. These barriers should be identified and effective ways found to remove them.

TRAINING PRIMARY HEALTH CARE WORKERS

There is a difficulty in understanding the complexity of presentation of mental health problems in primary care. Most primary care providers—and also their trainers—have not been trained to conceive and analyse the mixture of psychological and social factors in that setting. Additionally, most problems coexist with physical disease and/or are presented in the context of a physical disease.

In primary care systems, we should think not only about doctors but also about other primary care providers (e.g. nurses and all the other staff: midwives, counsellors, medical assistants) patients come into contact with. Much could be done to promote mental health by training ancillary staff as much as health professionals.

The objectives of training in primary care can be summarized as follows: it should be relevant to everyday work; it should be skill-orientated; it should affect attitudes; it should have an impact on services in terms of outcomes; it should be compatible with the level of performance expected.

Primary care providers are not really trained to detect and manage the majority of mental health problems that occur in the community. The training of primary care workers needs to be addressed from their initial undergraduate education and be made a constant part of their education. Undergraduate and postgraduate training for primary care providers contain extremely little about health promotion or prevention. These are the foundations of primary care providers of tomorrow. Tomorrow's primary care providers should be given the knowledge and skills to deal with mental health problems during their training and thereafter during their practice as hands-on in-job training.

There is a need for professionals to learn about behaviour change. Too much time is spent telling people what they should be doing and not how they should be doing it, i.e. disseminating knowledge rather than skills. This implies that communications skills are necessary in order to persuade people to change their ideas. Professionals are also beginning to learn a lot of the skills about how to motivate people to change. The skills need to be spread much more widely across the curriculum and the training programs.

There is immense variation between primary care physicians. It is customary to look at means: e.g. mean detection of illness. There are primary care physicians who are good and there are those who haven't the first idea about how to handle mental health matters. The discrepancy between abilities in care providers must be addressed.

How can training be changed? One method might be to decide that certain curricula, focusing on knowledge only and described as inappropriate, ought to be changed. That is the stick approach. There is also the carrot approach: to help people to obtain training in mental health skills for which they should get paid.

Training in Awareness of Mental Health Problems

What needs to be emphasized at all levels is a concern for populations, so that the patient before the health care professional is not the only person of concern. We have to enlarge the vision of the practitioners to the total population they are taking care of—that larger group of 2000 or so people. As a result, significant opportunities to implement mental health interventions arise in primary care practice. There are remarkable opportunities in the primary care encounter to conduct preventive mental health care, e.g. asking, 'Do you want another baby? How soon? What are you doing about family planning?' could be integrated into any pregnancy or baby visit to induce awareness: this type of family planning strategy could have positive mental health consequences.

To look at populations, professionals require a much broader training in social change. The primary care providers could then formulate better policies with community participation, e.g. how can change be brought about effectively together with the politicians?

PRIMARY CARE: MODEL OF ORGANIZATION

Primary Health Care as a System

Little is known conceptually about primary health care as a 'system' and its organization. The image that comes to mind is a single practitioner operating alone with perhaps some additional staff. More needs to be learned with a particular conceptual lens that thinks of this as a whole system, thinking of primary care as an organizational system of social actors who respond to incentives and are competing for scarce resources. What do we know about the structure of primary care in terms of structure, process and outcomes? How can prevention and promotion activities be put into that structure?

In the analysis of the organization of the primary care system it is important to understand the barriers and incentives to implementing preventive practices today. The system needs to be defined broadly, including funders, practitioners, patients, family members, the medical education system, employers and policy-makers. One should focus on each of these sets of actors, assumptions, beliefs, practices, the incentives that drive them, the actual knowledge they have about prevention and promotion and the barriers that they see to change. The intended outcome would be a plan to attack the barriers and rearrange the incentives in the primary care system to achieve that shift in orientation toward prevention and promotion.

The focus needs to be on creating a broad intervention orientation. In the primary health care system, one should not focus narrowly on mental health but look at a whole range of outcomes, disability, mental health and health. It's the emphasis on the preventive orientation that should be the main concern.

Primary Health Care: Structural Limitations

There are many possibilities and tasks for primary care providers but there are also limitations in terms of their time, resources and finances, expertise and skills, and intersectoral cooperation.

If the workforce is to implement prevention initiatives they need to be supported. It is very difficult, particularly in hard-pressed primary care teams, to expect them to do mental health promotion if they feel on their knees themselves. For prevention to work, the health care professionals must be given support for themselves. In addition, the program must be nicely packaged for the primary care team so that it is possible to introduce it into the normal working practice.

Primary Health Care: International Variations

Prime care is organized differently in different countries: there are very different systems and the barriers are different for each of the systems. We need to look into problems at the community level and how local practices can be improved. There are different hierarchies of needs, different pointers which will lead to different solutions, different priorities. Different systems will have to come up with very different incentives to give the kind of prevention programs we want in place.

There is no single statement one could make about the structure of primary care. It is different in each country. Primary care in the USA is very unsystematic and the changes under way currently are considerable, starting with the new driving concept of managed care. It is extremely difficult to get the message about prevention and health promotion across within a managed care environment. Preparing all parties concerned to be aware of the impact of social factors on health, and the broader context of the patient, it is necessary to shift the focus to include prevention and promotion.

On the other hand, the UK health care system is privileged because, although it has undergone many changes, the whole population (98%) is registered with the health service. Access to the front line which can be called general practice (or family medicine) is free of charge. The patient doesn't have to pay anything for the doctor, nurse, health visitor or referral to the hospital or to see a specialist. That means that GPs are uniquely well placed to look after the most disadvantaged members of society. In the UK, people with problems are probably seen earlier because there are no financial barriers. The concepts of primary health care and its wider social implications keep coming up. Of the British population, 15% see a GP face-to-face every fortnight. The contact rate for under 5s and over 75s, nationally on random samples, is seven face-to-face contacts a year. Half those contacts are in the home. That is an enormous contact rate and in that setting there are opportunities for practising and preventing problems which are unequalled in any other setting. The challenge is to find practical things for the primary team to do in which they have faith and which work. The challenge is to package the care so that it makes sense to the people who have this huge contact—free access and tremendous volume plus a registration period of 10 years' continuous care for the average patient within the same practice. We do not yet exploit this opportunity.

No country, however rich, has enough resources for specialist care to be available to everyone with a mental disorder. In developing countries there are two psychiatrists for 2 million people. The only way to improve the situation for mental health prevention and promotion and secondary prevention is by making knowledge available to everyone. In the example of first aid, when somebody falls on the street, a non-medical layman can often deal with the basic treatment. But if a patient becomes depressed or suicidal, nobody knows what to do. This is the sad truth about the level to which knowledge and understanding of mental health has spread around, despite all the training. The knowledge gathered in books has not adequately filtered down to the ordinary human being or to the average GP. How can packages be constructed so that mental health interventions become an essential part of regular use by doctors and health personnel, in fact as ordinary people? Everybody should know that mental disorders are ordinary medical illnesses, they are not magic; they are treatable and there is no reason for unnecessary suffering. The curriculum of the medical and nursing schools and for all health professionals must include a general practice level of knowledge about mental health.

INTERVENTIONS: CONVERTING EXISTING SCIENTIFIC KNOWLEDGE INTO PRACTICE

Interventions in the area of prevention and promotion have to be based on successful scientific examples. One of the major contributions of psychiatry to understanding has been the delineation, classification and treatment of major depression. This piece of information has yet to be fully put into practice in primary care.

There is too much emphasis on diagnosis and not enough on preventing disability and suffering in the way goals are now thought about. Disability takes a huge toll on human productivity. It creates a care burden for others and affects their well-being. The correlation between diagnosis and disability is modest except at the extreme end of the distribution, and disability and suffering are some of the bottom lines that should fundamentally concern us.

It is most important to remember that most prevention and promotion applications are trying to improve the health of the population. They may not necessarily seem to work for each individual case. The attributable risk that you can hope to do something about in morbidity is actually quite small. But the most efficient thing to do to the health of the population should be done for the health of the whole population.

With a little thought one could be much more proactive with individuals regarding prevention in certain situations. Thinking about potential situations or life events one may develop prevention strategies for those who may be experiencing a mental health problem. Very often one knows when somebody is going to be bereaved, when somebody is going to have a baby. Marriage breakdown or job losses can be anticipated. Opportunities are often missed to help people to prepare for what are going to be stressful life events which may precipitate some sort of mental health problem.

Regarding possibilities, one should remain focused and should not oversell intervention, which should remain limited to the little knowledge base available and be cautious.

Which Programs?

A potential danger of bringing *prevention* and *promotion* together is that disease prevention will be more powerful at the cost of mental health promotion. On the other hand, mental health promotion is directing itself at common or global factors, non-specific factors that play a role in many diseases. There have been focused, albeit fragmented, approaches to developing prevention programs for single diseases. There may also be prevention programs that address groups of diseases, such as reduction of stress.

Mental health promotion is relatively underdeveloped compared to physical health promotion. When considering the effectiveness of physical health interventions, the determinants for physical diseases are known and therefore professionals know what to do and what outcomes to expect. The problem with mental health promotion is that there are many unknowns. Effective interventions cannot be expected until what is being intervened in and what is expected as an outcome is known. It may be dangerous to apply the same language to mental health that is used in terms of physical health. For example, if someone goes to a GP saying they are unwell, the GP may diagnose a heart problem and suggest cutting out smoking, being more active and getting the blood pressure down, and may also consider some genetic issues involved. If the person presents some sort of mental health problem, the GP may be able to diagnose depression, but less confident to identify the issues causing the depression or what can be done in the same way as for physical issues.

There is generally a lag period between the prevention and promotion and its positive impact. An intervention at age 3 at nursery school could lead to an enduring effect 30 years later, but the vicissitudes of life in between are uncontrolled and uncontrollable. In this respect, the immunization model is misleading. The elimination of smallpox was possible because the virus came in only one form; immunity is life-long; the patient is infectious only while the scars and scabs are evident. So there is a set of conditions that made it possible with a life-long effect to prevent the disease with one intervention.

Targets

Talking about promotion and prevention implies talking about enhancement of human potential and treatment of disease. One each of those four activities should be selected, which is going to be pushed for 5 years. Examples of successes are needed to demonstrate that something works and that example can then be used as an incentive for the next: select a very small number of interventions and push them for a number of years until they have results which can be shown to everybody, as with WHO's success with smallpox eradication. This field of promotion needs some examples of success.

It is possible to create a limited number of persuasive, powerful and scientifically validated examples of programmatic interventions for prevention and promotion in primary care. No new paradigm is a serious candidate for adoption without a convincing example. A package will be convincing if it is based on successful intervention packages. It should be addressed not only to policy-makers but also to practitioners to adopt and in effect reinvent these programs in their own settings.

However, there is still some way to go. Currently there are no five programs that could be confidently implemented around the world at this time. However, there exists many effective programs in the UK, Australia, the USA and The Netherlands that are ready for large-scale field trials. Programs are ready to be tested on a much larger scale and those could then be tailored to the specific community needs.

Most prevention services have no evaluation at all in the sense of randomized trials, just in the sense of a fairly high standard of baseline and outcome data. Communities are increasingly being asked to do this by their own people and policy-makers. They need help. That is an area where a more standardized approach could be a productive contribution: i.e. how to go about gathering baseline and outcome data.

Selecting the Right Interventions

Selecting some of the best programs available now would be a good starting point. Although they may have been evaluated only a few times, it is important to remember that they have been developed on the basis of scientific knowledge about risk factors and on their effectiveness in very well-designed experience. Some could be very simple, e.g. telling pregnant women not to smoke, a simple straightforward intervention for which evidence is available. A small number of interventions could be selected and evaluated.

Choosing the Target Groups

An interesting example is a program for preventing marital distress, shown to be effective 4 years after the intervention. A training course with eight meetings resulted in the experimental group having a lower rate of divorce, higher marital happiness and lower marital distress. This US experiment was repeated in The Netherlands with one change: it was offered to a high-risk group where the chance of its effectiveness was even larger. However, the randomized control trial proved not to be effective. The difference between the American intervention and the Dutch intervention turned out to be that of age. The Dutch offered this program in developing communication skills to an age group averaging 25–27 years. In the American situation it was offered to a much younger group, and that could have had a significant influence. This example proves how important the time of intervention is.

Impact of Primary Care Interventions—Outcomes Research

We have to look at procedures in terms of their ultimate impact on the health of the population. Making a right diagnosis and giving the presumed right treatment is certainly good, but is not enough. We should always look at the impact of intervention on outcome: are the patients better off? More research is needed in primary care, by primary care providers, into 'What is practical and what works?' Primary care workers are eager to seize new ideas and techniques once they are convinced that they are useful and practical.

The evaluation of effectiveness is neglected and it is crucial that we look in future towards investing in effectiveness, at the same time disinvesting in things which we know are not effective or which could be harmful. It is dangerous to base programs solely on the benefits of investments.

It is very important to do studies with controlled trials and obtain strong evidence whether a prevention program is effective or not. The reason this kind of research appears attractive is because researchers like to have very strong proof of the effectiveness of a certain program or intervention. But what also needs to be compared are different kinds of programs within an experimental situation to compare different sub-groups—who will profit the most from an intervention? It is also important to use qualitative studies. The consumers should be asked what they have learned and why, what was most intriguing, most helpful, in a certain course or in their contact with a GP. This type of approach would allow us, step-by-step, to build an idea of what are the main determinants of effectiveness in intervention. Some information is already available about the different factors connected to the program, or to the target group, or to the social conditions offered, or to the process of the development of a new intervention program. All those sectors contain factors that have a determining influence on effectiveness and it is possible to make a list of them and to translate them into a kind of quality list—what should practitioners do to guarantee more effectiveness? The WHO could be helpful by bringing together all the experiences from different fields.

The Cost of Research—Need for Evidence and Action

It is important to remain realistic in terms of research. The cost of doing really good prevention research is high. Implementing a self-esteem program in new nursery schools in a randomized control trial and testing whether it affects self-esteem, reduction in rates of depression, reduction in rates of marital abuse, involves conducting follow-up studies for 30 or 40 years. At some point, logic and common sense must enter the equation as well as research evidence. Smoking is an example. It is still not solidly established that cigarettes cause lung cancer—it is simply highly likely, and that, of course, is enough to decide to take action immediately because of the extremely heavy consequences of not taking action.

Before setting up research studies, it is necessary to have some good developmental projects up and running, so that the research is well rather than badly directed. Evidence cannot always come first, which is why money has to be put where the heart is—if prevention is likely to be helpful, then it can be implemented, and once implemented then results can begin to be evaluated.

Research results will be noted in the long run as we fine-tune our programs, but in the early stage of knowledge we have to make a start somewhere, otherwise we would not have anything to evaluate and we would never gather significant evidence.

INTERNATIONAL COORDINATION AND COOPERATION

There are still very grey areas of knowledge and a lack of understanding about mental health promotion. Many people are doing small, qualitative pieces of work on mental health promotion. There are large organizations trying hard to get in quickly with randomized control trials, and we need to bring these groups of people together so that we can understand the basis under which we can then do good quantitative work.

Connections among several people and groups must be kept and work should be done internationally in this field. It is easier to convince people in different countries if their neighbour has already done it. An enormous amount is learned from what other countries are doing and it would be unfortunate not to continue to build up those networks and links. It will also be an incentive to learn that other people have similar problems and similar disappointments and difficulties. This should be a joint effort. Other sectors should put mental health on their agenda. Everybody should be doing something. The consumers (or rather 'partners') should join in combating disease, as it was originally envisioned in the primary health care approach for 'Health for All' and 'All for Health'.

46

Summing Up

Hastings EA Carson

Royal Institute of Public Health and Hygiene, London, UK

OVERVIEW

This collection of chapters resulted from a fine conference during which a galaxy of distinguished contributors fulfilled admirably the tasks of authoritatively reviewing the primary care of mental health and of stimulating fresh thinking about the way ahead.

From the concluding panel discussion, firm proposals for future action emerged which will maintain the momentum. The publication of the proceedings of the conference is most welcome in the context of spreading current knowledge globally so that the best use can be made of finite resources. Re-inventing the wheel is an expensive exercise in both human and financial terms.

It is clearly not possible in summing up to do justice to all the individual contributions, but a few general comments may not be out of place.

First, the Royal Institute of Public Health and Hygiene was especially glad and privileged to have been associated with such an impressive international gathering, since it regards the primary care scene as a key setting for the promotion of health and the prevention of illness.

MULTIDISCIPLINARY COLLABORATION AND TEAMWORK

The most recent initiative of the Royal Institute in the field of primary care (with the key help of Dr Rachel Jenkins, a member of its Council) is in the form of a collaborative venture with the Department of Health to develop a multidisciplinary distance learning course to equip all members of the primary care team concerned with the necessary knowledge, skills and attitudes to detect and respond appropriately to mental health problems encountered in the practice setting. A third pilot course has been completed, proving hearteningly successful, and a national launch took place in the autumn of 1995.

Preventing Mental Illness: Mental Health Promotion in Primary Care. Edited by R. Jenkins and T.B. Üstün.
© 1998 John Wiley & Sons Ltd.

This educational initiative reflects the importance rightly attached to teamwork in promoting and preserving mental health in the primary care setting. A mutual appreciation of individual roles and competences is the prerequisite for successful multidisciplinary collaboration; this necessarily rests upon appropriate basic in-service training. Success in a common endeavour also requires a sense of direction and achievement. Evaluation of progress is of the essence.

A RECIPE FOR SUCCESS IN THE FIELD

Against a background of widely varying circumstances in different parts of the globe, all concerned with the mental health scene share a common desire to make the best use of the resources available. In this regard, a few years ago a leading industrialist, closely associated with policy-shaping at a national level for the National Health Service as a whole, defined the following ingredients in his recipe for success in any business or service venture.

1. *A clear-cut strategy* set out on paper indicating the overall objectives and how it is proposed to achieve them. The 'Health of the Nation' strategy, with the formulation of targets in relation to five key areas including mental illness, and the subsequent circulation of guidelines to shape local action, are a good illustration of the firm overall guidance required. It was good to hear the Parliamentary Under-Secretary for Health emphasize in his opening address the need to develop a *coherent preventive strategy* in the field of mental illness and of the *crucial contribution of research* in this context. Even more heartening was the announcement by Mr Bowis of a new mental health research initiative on the part of the Department of Health which would enjoy 'ring-fenced' funding. Both this development and the recent introduction of a national psychiatric morbidity survey to provide sorely needed information reflect a most welcome recognition of the importance of establishing *a sound epidemiological and research base* as the foundation for the shaping of a sensible public policy in relation to the mental health field as a whole. Clearly, an element of flexibility in applying national guidelines is desirable to take account of varying circumstances locally.
2. *Communication of the broad features of the strategy throughout the organization to obtain the commitment of all concerned.* Individuals should be left in no doubt as to the significance of their particular contribution to the overall effort. Adequate *training* should be provided to meet the objectives described by Dr Ahmad Mohit in his chapter. *Skills* (e.g. those of the psychiatric community nurse) should be kept finely honed, implying full and appropriate use and the opportunity for refresher training to keep fully abreast of new knowledge; this implies in turn the availability of the necessary time to undertake the task properly—thus building quality as well as quantity into the service equation. From a mental health standpoint, achieving these goals entails agreement within the primary care team, at the interface between primary and secondary

care, and between the health and social (and other statutory and voluntary) services; such co-operation is vital in meeting effectively the multifactorial multisectoral challenge posed by mental illness and its prevention. Thus, roles and necessary supporting facilities have to be clearly defined and agreed to ensure the necessary commitment to active and effective collaboration. Prior consultation with all concerned is implicit in implementing any strategy successfully; active encouragement in the field also helps! Again, circulation of information regarding best practice is a healthy stimulant and a valuable educational tool, well illustrated by Dr Bedirhan Üstün in his presentation.

3. *Funding the strategy adequately*, since failure to do so destroys credibility. In the context of obtaining value for money it seems eminently sensible from a financial as well as a human standpoint—given the identification of specific roles and skills—to provide at the very least a minimum viable service presence, viz. that level of activity which enables a positive impact to be made. This premise underlies the concept of performance budgeting, designed to give satisfaction to both providers and users of services by enabling appropriate standards to be maintained within the overall finance available.

   Failure to ensure an effective presence devalues the very cause being promoted. Inability to undertake a clearly relevant task efficiently through case overload leads to physical or emotional 'burn-out', to the very considerable detriment of the service. Here it is pertinent to note that the subject of staff burn-out has been of sufficient concern on an international scale to cause the WHO Division of Mental Health to issue guidelines for its primary prevention, as mentioned by Dr Jose Bertolote in his chapter. Poor morale is inimical to progress.

4. *Reviewing the strategy regularly* in the light of the progress achieved. Implicit in measuring quality is the outcome of the service intervention. Continuing evaluation on the basis of outcome (and adjusting the service input accordingly) is of the essence in ensuring value for money in terms of cost-effectiveness, as well as of efficiency in the use of the resources to hand, giving satisfaction to the public and the service alike.

Raising standards of performance entails more than imparting the essential facts to those affected. Beyond doubt, increasing knowledge and acquiring skills are vital if higher levels of achievement are to be attained; just as crucial to lasting success is the development of a caring attitude. An informed caring approach is the hallmark of quality in any human endeavour, and none more so than in the broad field of mental health.

Here it is pertinent to highlight the need for a greater awareness generally of the nuances of human relationships—witness the lessons to be learned from the excellent CBI/DoH publication *Prevention of Mental Ill-health at Work*. Good health, good communications, productivity and profitability in an endeavour go hand in hand. The perceived relevance of the task and the quality of performance loom large in this context.

THE ULTIMATE GOAL

In essence, the modern public health message portrays a healthy lifestyle allied to a healthy environment as a feasible and sensible goal if both the individual and the community play an active part in fulfilling a shared responsibility overall. This is as true of mental health as it is of physical health. The home, the school and the workplace loom large in shaping that well-rounded, well-informed individual with a well-founded sense of confidence and appropriate self-esteem which connotes good mental health. A healthy mind in a healthy body must be the ultimate goal.

Man cannot live by bread alone. A vision of the ideal provides galvanizing inspiration. For myself—and I suspect this to be true of many fellow delegates—the refreshing realism, enthusiasm and wisdom of Professor Norman Sartorius, so evident throughout the conference, was epitomized in his picturesque comment, 'Mental health is a cloudless sky'.

Similar inspiration can be gained from the vision of perfect health conjured up in the words of the nineteenth-century industrialist, social reformer and poet, William Morris:

> First of all I claim good health; to feel mere life is a pleasure; to enjoy the moving of one's limbs and exercising one's bodily powers; to play, as it were, with sun and wind and rain; yes, the wherewithal to be well-formed, straight-limbed, straightly knit and expressive of countenance.

CONCLUSION

In conclusion, I would like to think that this notable conference will contribute positively to the furthering of that majestic goal in the years ahead. I wish, therefore, to express the warmest thanks of all participants to the sponsors and organizers of a memorable event illumined by distinguished contributions from the platform and the floor. All of us were indebted to the chairmen of individual sessions, the presenters of papers, and the members of the concluding discussion panel on the way ahead; the additional information provided by the statutory and voluntary agencies taking part in the exhibition associated with the conference was also greatly appreciated. Finally, and in particular, I am very conscious of the special debt of gratitude which we owe to Dr Rachel Jenkins and Dr Bedirhan Üstün as the co-architects of a truly excellent international program wholly worthy of its theme.

Index

Index compiled by Annette Musker